Drug Abuse Bibliography

for 1990

Drug Abuse Bibliography

for 1990

Compiled by

Bonnie L. Clements

The Whitston Publishing Company
Troy, New York
1993

Copyright 1993
The Whitston Publishing Company

Library of Congress Catalog Card Number 79-116588

ISBN 0-87875-439-3

Printed in the United States of America

016.362293
D 794
1990

CONTENTS

Periodical Literature (continued)

PREFACE

This bibliography is the twentieth annual supplement to DRUGS OF ADDIC-TION AND NON-ADDICTION, THEIR USE AND ABUSE: A COMPREHENSIVE BIBLIOGRAPHY, 1960-1969, compiled by Joseph Menditto (Whitston, 1970). It is a near complete bibliography of world literature surrounding drug and alcohol abuse for the year 1989. Entries earlier than 1989 coming to our attention after the 1988 volume are included here.

Periodical literature is listed under the most appropriate subject headings. Because of the vast amount of material dealing specifically with alcohol abuse, all entries pertaining to alcohol have been grouped under ALCOHOL and then under the appropriate sub-heading (see **Alcohol** in the Subject Index on p. 5XX).

A list of journals cited, a subject index and an author index all enhance the usefulness of this bibliography.

The following bibliographies, indexes and abstracts have been searched in compiling this volume:

Abstracts of Popular Culture
Access
Air University Library Index to Military Periodicals
Alternative Press Index
America: History and Life
American Humanities Index
American Reference Books Annual
Applied Science and Technology Index
Bibliography Index
Biological Abstracts
Biological and Agricultural Index
Book Review Digest
Books in Print
British Humanities Index
Business Periodicals Index
Canadian Education Index
Canadian Periodical Index
Catholic Periodical and Literature Index
College Student Personnel Abstracts
Communication Abstracts
Criminal Justice Abstracts
Criminal Justice Periodical Index
Criminology and Penology Abstracts
Cumulative Book Index
Cumulative Index to Nursing & Allied Health Literature
Current Index to Journals in Education

Dissertation Abstracts International A: Social Sciences & Humanities
Dissertation Abstracts International B: Science & Engineering
Education Index
Environment Index
Essay and General Literature Index
Family Studies Abstracts
General Science Index
Hospital Literature Index
Human Resources Abstracts
Humanities Index
Index Medicus
Index to Jewish Periodicals
Index to Legal Periodicals
International Nursing Index
Media Review Digest
Music Index
PAIS
PAIS Foreign Language Index
Philosophers Index
Police Science Abstracts
Popular Periodical Index
Psychological Abstracts
Readers Guide to Periodical Literature
Religion Index One: Periodicals, Religious & Theological Abstracts
Sage Urban Studies Abstracts
Social Sciences Index
Social Work Research & Abstracts
Sociological Abstracts
Women's Studies Abstracts

Bonnie Clements
Troy, New York

LIST OF JOURNALS CITED

ABA Journal: American Bar Association
  Journal
Academe
Academic Medicine
Acadiensis
Accident Analysis and Prevention
Acta Chirurgica Belgica
Acta Cytologica
Acta Dermato-Venereologica
Acta Diabetologica Latina
Acta Endocrinologica
Acta Geneticae Medicae e Gemellologiae
Acta Geneticae Medicae e Gemellologiae:
  Twin Research
Acta Medica Hungarica
Acta Medica Portuguesa
Acta Neurologica Scandinavica
Acta Neuropathologica
Acta Ophthalmologica
Acta Paediatrica Scandinavica
Acta Physiologica Hungaricae
Acta Physiologica Scandinavica
Acta Psychiatrica Scandinavica
Acta Psychiatrica y Psicologica de America
  Latina
Actas Luso-Espanolas de Neurologia,
  Psiquiatria y Ciencias Afines
Activitas Nervosa Superior
Activities, Adaptation and Aging
Actualite
Adapted Physical Activity Quarterly
Addictive Behaviors
Adolescence
Adolescent Psychiatry
Advances
Advances in Alcohol and Substance
  Abuse
Advances in Behavior Research and
  Therapy

Advances in Experimental Medicine and
  Biology
Advertising Age
Advocate
AELE Liability Reporter: Law Enforce-
  ment Legal Liability Reporter
Affilia
African Journal of Medicine and Medical
  Sciences
Against the Current
Agents Action
Aging
AIDS
AIDS and Public Policy Journal
AIDS Care
AIDS Education and Prevention
AIDS Research: Human Retroviruses
Air Force Times
Air Progress
Airman
AJR: American Journal of Roentgenology
Akusherstvo i Ginekologiia
Alberta (Western) Report
Alcohol
Alcohol and Alcoholism
Alcohol, Drugs and Driving
Alcoholism
Alcoholism: Clinical and Experimental
  Research
Alcoholism Treatment Quarterly
Algemeen Politieblad
Alkoholipolitiikka
Allergologia et Immunopathologia
Ambulance World
American Atheist
American Behavioral Scientist
American City and County
American Criminal Law Review
American Demographics
American Economic Review

American Family Physician
American Film
American Health
American Indian and Alaska Native Mental Health Research
American Industrial Hygiene Association Journal
American Journal of Cardiology
American Journal of Clinical Nutrition
American Journal of Clinical Pathology
American Journal of Community Psychology
American Journal of Criminal Law
American Journal of Diseases of Children
American Journal of Drug and Alcohol Abuse
American Journal of Emergency Medicine
American Journal of Epidemiology
American Journal of Family Therapy
American Journal of Forensic Medicine and Pathology
American Journal of Gastroenterology
American Journal of Health Promotion
American Journal of Hematology
American Journal of Hospital Pharmacy
American Journal of Human Genetics
American Journal of Hypertension
American Journal of Industrial Medicine
American Journal of Infection Control
American Journal of Medical Sciences
American Journal of Medicine
American Journal of Mental Retardation
American Journal of Nursing
American Journal of Obstetrics and Gynecology
American Journal of Occupational Therapy
American Journal of Ophthalmology
American Journal of Orthopsychiatry
American Journal of Perinatology
American Journal of Pharmaceutical Education
American Journal of Physiology
American Journal of Police
American Journal of Preventive Medicine
American Journal of Psychiatry
American Journal of Psychology
American Journal of Psychotherapy
American Journal of Public Health
American Journal of Sociology
American Journal of Sports Medicine
American Mining Congress Journal
American Nurseryman
American Pharmacy
American Printer
American Psychologist
American Review of Respiratory Disease

American Scholar
American School Board Journal
American Secondary Education
American Spectator
American Speech
American Teacher
American University Law Review
Anaesthesia
Anales Espanoles de Pediatria
Analyst
Analytical Biochemistry
Analytical Chemistry
Anarchy
Anatomischer Anzeiger
Anesthesiology
Anglican Journal
Annales de Dermatologie et de Venerologie
Annales de Medecine Interne
Annales de Pathologie
Annales d'Otolaryngologie et de Chirurgie Cervico-Faciale
Annales Medico-Psychologiques
Annali dell'Istituto Superiore di Sanita
Annali di Igiene
Annals of the Academy of Medicine, Singapore
Annals of Clinical and Laboratory Science
Annals of Clinical Biochemistry
Annals of Clinical Psychiatry
Annals of Emergency Medicine
Annals of Human Biology
Annals of Internal Medicine
Annals of Neurology
Annals of Pathology
Annals of Plastic Surgery
Annals of Surgery
Annee Therapeutique e Clinique en Ophthalmologie
Annual Review of Genetics
Annual Review of Medicine
Annual Review of Sociology
Anthropology Today
Antimicrobial Agents and Chemotherapy
Archaeology
Archiv fur Kriminologie
Archiv fur Wissenschaft und Praxis der Sozialen Arbeit
Archives Belges
Archives Francaise de Pediatrie
Archives of Clinical Neuropsychology
Archives of Disease in Childhood
Archives of Emergency Medicine
Archives of Environmental Health
Archives of General Psychiatry
Archives of Gynecology and Obstetrics
Archives of Internal Medicine

Archives of Neurology
Archives of Ophthalmology
Archives of Pathology and Laboratory
  Medicine
Archives of Psychiatric Nursing
Archives of Surgery
Archivio Monaldi per le Malattie del Torace
Archivos de Neurobiologia
Archivos del Instituto de Cardiologia de
  Mexico
Archivos Espanoles de Urologia
Archiwum Kryminologii
Arctic Medical Research
Arhiv za Higijenu Rada i Toksikologija
Army
Arquivos de Neuro-Psiquiatria
Arrest Law Bulletin
Artery
Arukoru Kenkyuto Yakubutsu Ison
Arzneimittel-Forschung
Arztliche Jugendkunde
Atherosclerosis
Athletics
Atlantic
Atlantic Advocate
Australian and New Zealand Journal of
  Criminology
Australian and New Zealand Journal of
  Medicine
Australian and New Zealand Journal of
  Obstetrics and Gynaecology
Australian and New Zealand Journal of
  Psychiatry
Australian Family Physician
Australian Journal of Hospital Pharmacy
Australian Journal of Psychology
Australian Police Journal
Australian Social Work
Aviation, Space and Environmental Medi-
  cine
Aviation Week and Space Technology
Bangladesh Medical Research Council
  Bulletin
Bank Marketing
Banker
Barrons
Basic and Applied Social Psychology
Baylor Law Review
BC Report
Behavior Analyst
Behavior Genetics
Behavior Research and Therapy
Behavioral and Neural Biology
Behavioral Assessment
Behavioral Brain Research
Behavioral Neuroscience

Behaviour Change
Behavioural Psychotherapy
Behavioural Residential Treatment
Behavioural Therapeutics
Beijing Review
Beitrage zur Gerichtlichen Medizin
Better Homes and Gardens
Bicycling
Biochemical Journal
Biochemical Medicine and Metabolic
  Biology
Biochemical Pharmacology
Biochemical Society Transactions
Biochemistry International
Biochimica et Biophysica Acta
Biofeedback and Self Regulation
Biological Psychiatry
Biology of the Neonate
Biomedicine and Pharmacotherapy
Bioscience
Biotechniques
Biulleten Eksperimentalnoi Biologii i
  Meditsiny
Black Enterprise
Black Issues in Higher Education
Blood
Blut
Blutalkohol
BMJ: British Medical Journal
Boletin-Asociacion Medica de Puerto Rico
Boletin de la Oficina Sanitaria Panameri-
  cana
Bollettino dell Istituto Sieroterapico Mila-
  nese
Brain Injury
Brain Research
Brain Research Bulletin
Bratislavske Lekarske Listy
Brazilian Journal of Medical and Biological
  Reearch
Bristol Medico-Chirurgical Journal
British Dental Journal
British Heart Journal
British Journal of Addiction
British Journal of Anaesthesia
British Journal of Cancer
British Journal of Clinical Psychology
British Journal of Criminology
British Journal of Educational Psychology
British Journal of Experimental Pathology
British Journal of General Practice
British Journal of Hospital Medicine
British Journal of Neurosurgery
British Journal of Obstetrics and Gynae-
  cology
British Journal of Occupational Therapy

British Journal of Ophthalmology
British Journal of Oral and Maxillofacial
Surgery
British Journal of Pharmacology
British Journal of Psychiatry
British Journal of Sociology
British Journal of Sports Medicine
British Journal of Surgery
British Journal of Urology
Brooklyn Law Review
Broomstick
Bulletin de l'Academie Nationale de
Medicine
Bulletin du Cancer
Bulletin et Memoirs de L'Academie Royale
de Medecine de Belgique
Bulletin of the American Academy of
Psychiatry and the Law
Bulletin of the New York Academy of
Medicine
Bulletin of the Pan American Health
Organization
Bulletin of the Psychonomic Society
Bulletin on Narcotics
Business and Health
Business and Society Review
Business/Commercial Aviation
Business Horizons
Business Insurance
Business Month
Business Quarterly
Business Week
Cahiers des Ameriques Latines
Calcified Tissue International
California Prisoner
Campus Law Enforcement Journal
Canada's Mental Health
Canadian Art
Canadian Association of Radiologists
Journal
Canadian Business
Canadian Dental Association Journal
Canadian Journal of Aging
Canadian Journal of Anaesthesiology
Canadian Journal of Community Mental
Health
Canadian Journal of Criminology
Canadian Journal of Education
Canadian Journal of Geriatrics
Canadian Journal of Physiology and
Pharmacology
Canadian Journal of Psychiatry
Canadian Journal of Public Health
Canadian Lawyer
Canadian Police College Journal
Canadian Social Trends

Canadian Society of Forensic Science
Journal
Canadian Speeches
Cancer Detection and Prevention
Cancer
Cancer Letters
Cancer Nursing
Cancer Research
Car and Driver
Carcinogenesis
Cardiologia
Cardiovascular Clinics
Cardiovascular Research
Casopis Lekaru Ceskych
Cell Biology and Toxicology
Cell Biology International Reports
Central African Journal of Medicine
Cephalalgia
Cerebrovascular and Brain Metabolism
Reviews
Ceskoslovenska Farmacie
Ceskoslovenska Gynekologie
Ceskoslovenska Neurologie a Neuro-
chirurgie
Ceskoslovenska Psychiatrie
Ceskoslovenska Zdravotnictvi
Ceylon Medical Journal
Chain Reaction
Champion
Changing Men
Channels
Chatelaine
Chemical and Pharmaceutical Bulletin
Chemical Engineering News
Chemical Industry
Chemical Marketing Report
Chemical Week
Chemico-Biological Interactions
Chest
Child Abuse and Neglect
Child: Care, Health and Development
Child Development
Child Psychiatry and Human Development
Childhood Education
Children Today
Chinese Journal of Physiology
Chinese Medical Journal
Chirurg
Chirurgia e Patologia Sperimentale
Christian Century
Christianity and Crisis
Christianity Today
Chronicle of Higher Education
Chung Hua Chung Liu Tsa Chih
Chung Hua Shen Ching Ching Shen Ko
Tsa Chih

Chung Hua Yu Fang I Hsueh Tsa Chih
City Magazine
Civil War Times Illustrated
Clearing House
Cleveland Clinic Journal of Medicine
Clinica Terapeutica
Clinical and Experimental Allergy
Clinical and Experimental Hypertension.
    Part A: Theory and Practice
Clinical and Experimental Immunology
Clinical and Experimental Neurology
Clinical and Experimental Pharmacology
    and Physiology
Clinical and Laboratory Medicine
Clinical Cardiology
Clinical Chemistry
Clinical Gerontologist
Clinical Nephrology
Clinical Neuropharmacology
Clinical Nuclear Medicine
Clinical Pediatrics
Clinical Pharmacology and Therapeutics
Clinical Pharmacy
Clinical Physiology and Biochemistry
Clinical Radiology
Clinical Rheumatology
Clinical Sociology Review
Clinics in Chest Medicine
CMAJ: Canadian Medical Association
    Journal
Cognitive Therapy and Research
College Student Affairs Journal
College Student Journal
College Teaching
Colorado Medicine
Commentary
Commerce
Common Cause Magazine
Commonweal
Communication Research
Community Dentistry and Oral Epidemi-
    ology
Community Health Studies
Community Mental Health Journal
Comprehensive Psychiatry
Computers in Human Services
Congressional Research Service Review
Connecticut Medicine
Contact Dermatitis
Contemporary Crises
Contemporary Drug Problems
Contemporary Longterm Care
Contributions to Nephrology
Convulsive Therapy
Cornell Law Review
Corporate Security
Corporate Security Digest

Corrections Digest
Corrections Today
Counseling and Values
Counselling Psychology Quarterly
Covert Action Information Bulletin
Crime and Delinquency
Crime and Social Justice
Crime Control Digest
Crime Victims Digest
Criminal Justice
Criminal Justice and Behavior
Criminal Justice Ethics
Criminal Justice Newsletter
Criminal Justice Review
Criminal Law Quarterly
Criminal Law Reporter
Criminal Law Reporter: Court Decisions
Criminal Law Reporter: Opinion of the
    United States Supreme Court
Criminal Law Reporter: Supreme Court
    Proceedings
Criminal Law Review
Criminologist
Criminology
Critical Care Medicine
Critical Reviews in Oncology/Hematology
Critique of Anthropology
Cultural Survival Quarterly
Culture, Medicine and Psychiatry
CUPA Journal
Current
Current Health 2
Current Medical Research and Opinion
Current Problems in Pediatrics
Cutis
Daedalus
DAI A: Dissertation Abstracts International
    A: Humanities and Social Sciences
DAI C: Dissertation Abstracts International
    C: European Abstracts
Defense
Defense and Diplomacy
Defense Science
Delaware Medical Journal
Department of State Bulletin
Deutsche Medizinische Wochenschrift
Development
Development and Psychopathology
Developmental Medicine and Child Neu-
    rology
Developmental Psychology
Deviant Behavior
Diabetic Medicine
Diagnostic Microbiology and Infectious
    Disease
DICP: Drug Intelligence and Clinical
    Pharmacy

Die Neue Polizei
Digestion
Digestive Diseases and Sciences
Dimensions in Health Service
Diplomatic History
Discover
Diseases of the Colon and Rectum
Diseases of the Nervous System
Dissent
Documenta Ophthalmologica
Doklady Akadamii Nauk SSSR
Dollars and Sense
Drug and Alcohol Dependence
Drug Metabolism and Disposition
Drug Safety
Drug Topics
Drugs and Society
Duke Law Journal
Early Child Development and Care
Economist
Editorial Research Reports
Educacion Medica y Salud
Education
Education Digest
Educational Digest
Educational Record
Electrical World
Electroencephalography and Clinical
    Neurophysiology
Electronic Learning
Electrophoresis
Emergency Medicine Clinics of North
    America
Employee Assistance Quarterly
Employee Benefits Journal
Employee Relations Law Journal
Employee Relations Today
Employee Responsibilities and Rights
    Journal
Encephale
Encounter
Enforcement Journal
ENR: Engineering News-Record
Environment and Behavior
Environmental and Molecular Mutagene-
    sis
Enzyme
Epidemiologia e Prevenzione
Epidemiological Bulletin
Esquire
Essence
ETC: A Review of General Semantics
Ethos
EURO Reports and Studies
European Archives of Psychiatry and
    Neurological Sciences

European Journal of Applied Physiology
    and Occupational Physiology
European Journal of Cancer and Clinical
    Oncology
European Journal of Cardio-Thoracic
    Surgery
European Journal of Clinical Investigation
European Journal of Clinical Nutrition
European Journal of Clinical Pharma-
    cology
European Journal of Epidemiology
European Journal of Haematology
European Journal of Pharmacology
European Journal of Radiology
European Respiratory Journal
Evaluation Review
Exceptional Children
Executive Educator
Exercise and Sport Sciences Reviews
Experimental Neurology
Experimental Pathology
Extra
Families in Society
Family and Community Health
Family Law Reporter: Court Opinions
Family Medicine
Family Practice
Family Practice Research Journal
Family Process
Family Relations
Family Systems Medicine
Family Therapy
Family Therapy Networker
Far Eastern Economic Review
Farmakologiya i Toksikologiya
FASEB Journal: Federation of American
    Societies for Experimental Biology
    Journal
FBI Law Enforcement Bulletin
FDA Consumer
Federal Probation
Federal Register
Fertility and Sterility
Financial Post
Fire Engineering
Fiziologicheskii Zhurnal
Fiziologicheskii Zhurnal SSSR
Fiziologiia Cheloveka
Flying
Flying Safety
Focus
Folio
Food Additives and Contaminants
Food and Chemical Toxicology
Forbes
Foreign Policy

Forensic Science International
Forensic Science Review
Foresight
Forest Industries
Fortschritte der Medizin
Fortschritte der Neurologie-Psychiatrie
Fortune
Free Inquiry in Creative Sociology
Free Radical Biology and Medicine
Functional Neurology ·
Fundamental and Applied Toxicology
Future Choices
Futurist
Gaceta Sanitaria
Gallup Pole Monthly
Gallup Report
Gan No Rinsho
Gan To Kagaku Ryoho
Gastroenterologie Clinique et Biologique
Gastroenterologisches Journal
Gastroenterology
Gastrointestinal Endoscopy
Gematologiia i Transfuziologiia
Gender and Society
General Hospital Psychiatry
Genetic, Social, and General Psychology
    Monographs
Genetika
Genitourinary Medicine
Gentlemen's Quarterly
Geographical Magazine
Georgia Journal of International and Com-
    parative Law
Gigiyena i Sanitariya
Gigiyena Truda i Profession'nyve Zabole-
    vaniya
Giornale di Clinica Medica
Giornale Italiano di Cardiologia
Glamour
Good Housekeeping
Good Times
Governing
Government Executive
Growth, Development, and Aging
Guardian
Gut
Gynecologic and Obstetric Investigation
Hand Clinics
Harefuah
Harper's
Harvard Law Review
Harvard Women's Law Journal
Hastings Center Report
Hawaii Medical Journal
Head and Neck Surgery
Health
Health Affairs

Health and Social Work
Health Bulletin
Health Care Management Review
Health Care Supervisor
Health Education
Health Education Quarterly
Health Education Research
Health Marketing Quarterly
Health News
Health Pac Bulletin
Health Policy
Health Progress
Health Promotion
Health Psychology
Health Trends
Healthcare Forum Journal
Healthright
Healthspan
Hepatology
High School Journal
High Technology Business
Hillside Journal of Clinical Psychiatry
Hispanic Journal of Behavioral Sciences
Histopathology
Hockey News
Home Office Research and Statistics
    Department Research Bulletin
Homemaker's Magazine
Hospital and Community Psychiatry
Hospital Pharmacy
Hospital Practice
Hospital Security and Safety Management
Hospitals
Houston Law Review
Howard Journal of Criminal Justice
Howard Law Journal
Human and Experimental Toxicology
Human Events
Human Organization
Human Pathology
Human Rights
Human Psychopharmacology Clinical and
    Experimental
Human Services in the Rural Environment
Human Toxicology
Humanist
Hygie
Hypatia
IARC Monographs on the Evaluation of
    the Carcinogenic Risk of Chemicals to
    Humans
Igiene Moderna
Illinois Historical Journal
Illustrierte Rundschau der Osterreichi-
    schen Gendarmie
Immunopharmacology and Immunotoxi-
    cology

Journal of the American Dental Association

Journal of the American Dietitic Association

Journal of the American Geriatrics Society

Journal of American Indian Education

Journal of the American Medical Women's Association

Journal of the American Osteopathic Association

Journal of the American Podiatric Medical Association

Journal of the American Veterinary Medical Association

Journal of Analytical Toxicology

Journal of Applied Behavior Analysts

Journal of Applied Behavioral Science

Journal of Applied Gerontology

Journal of Applied Physiology

Journal of Applied Psychology

Journal of Applied Rehabilitation Counseling

Journal of Applied Social Psychology

Journal of Applied Social Sciences

Journal of the Arkansas Medical Society

Journal of the Association of Official Analytical Chemists

Journal of the Association of Physicians of India

Journal of Behavioral Medicine

Journal of Biological Chemistry

Journal of Biosocial Science

Journal of Bone and Joint Surgery. British Volume

Journal of Business Ethics

Journal of California Law Enforcement

Journal of Cancer Education

Journal of Cardiology

Journal of Career Development

Journal of Chemical Dependency Treatment

Journal of Chemical Education

Journal of Child Neurology

Journal of Child Psychology and Psychiatry and Allied Disciplines

Journal of Chromatography

Journal of Church and State

Journal of Clinical and Laboratory Immunology

Journal of Clinical Chemistry and Clinical Biochemistry

Journal of Clinical Endocrinology and Metabolism

Journal of Clinical Epidemiology

Journal of Clinical Gastroenterology

Journal of Clinical Investigation

Journal of Clinical Microbiology

Journal of Clinical Neuro-Ophthalmology

Journal of Clinical Pharmacy and Therapeutics

Journal of Clinical Psychiatry

Journal of Clinical Psychology

Journal of Clinical Psychopharmacology

Journal of Collective Negotiations in the Public Sector

Journal of College and University Law

Journal of College Student Development

Journal of College Student Psychotherapy

Journal of Communication Disorders

Journal of Community Health

Journal of Computor Assisted Tomography

Journal of Consulting and Clinical Psychology

Journal of Consumer Policy

Journal of Contemporary Criminal Justice

Journal of Contemporary Ethnography

Journal of Continuing Education in the Health Professions

Journal of Counseling and Development

Journal of Counseling Psychology

Journal of Criminal Justice

Journal of Criminal Law

Journal of Criminal Law and Criminology

Journal of Cutaneous Pathology

Journal of Dental Education

Journal of Dentistry

Journal of Developmental and Behavioral Pediatrics

Journal of Developmental Education

Journal of Divorce

Journal of Drug Education

Journal of Drug Issues

Journal of Early Adolescence

Journal of Emergency Medicine

Journal of Employment Counseling

Journal of Endocrinology

Journal of Epidemiology and Community Health

Journal of the Experimental Analysis of Behavior

Journal of Family Issues

Journal of Family Practice

Journal of Family Psychology

Journal of Family Psychotherapy

Journal of the Florida Medical Association

Journal of Forensic Identification

Journal of the Forensic Science Society

Journal of Forensic Sciences

Journal of Gambling Behavior

Journal of Gay and Lesbian Psychotherapy

Journal of General Internal Medicine

Journal of General Psychology
Journal of Genetic Psychology
Journal of Gerontological Nursing
Journal of Health and Social Behavior
Journal of Health Politics, Policy and Law
Journal of Higher Education
Journal of Histochemistry and Cyto-
chemistry
Journal of Homosexuality
Journal of Human Hypertension
Journal of Hygiene, Epidemiology, Micro-
biology and Immunology
Journal of Hypertension
Journal of Immunology
Journal of Infection
Journal of Infectious Diseases
Journal of Instructional Psychology
Journal of Interamerican Studies and
World Affairs
Journal of Internal Medicine
Journal of Interpersonal Violence
Journal of the Kentucky Medical
Association
Journal of Laboratory and Clinical Medi-
cine
Journal of Law and Education
Journal of Learning Disabilities
Journal of the Louisiana State Medical
Society
Journal of Marriage and the Family
Journal of the Medical Association of
Georgia
Journal of Medical Virology
Journal of Medicinal Chemistry
Journal of Medicine
Journal of the Melanie Klein Society
Journal of Mental Health Administration
Journal of Mental Health Counseling
Journal of the Mississippi State Medical
Association
Journal of Molecular Recognition
Journal of the National Cancer Institute
Journal of the National Medical Associa-
tion
Journal of Nervous and Mental Disease
Journal of Neurochemistry
Journal of the Neurological Sciences
Journal of Neurology
Journal of Neurology, Neurosurgery and
Psychiatry
Journal of Neuropsychiatry and Clinical
Neurosciences
Journal of Neuroscience
Journal of the New York State School
Boards Association
Journal of Nurse-Midwifery
Journal of Nursing Education

Journal of Nutrition
Journal of Obstetric, Gynecologic, and
Neonatal Nursing
Journal of Occupational Medicine
Journal of Offender Counseling, Services
and Rehabilitation
Journal of Offender Monitoring
Journal of the Oklahoma State Medical
Association
Journal of Oral and Maxillofacial Surgery
Journal of Oral Pathology and Medicine
Journal of Pain and Symptom Manage-
ment
Journal of Pediatric Gastroenterology and
Nutrition
Journal of Pediatric Psychology
Journal of Pediatrics
Journal of Perinatal Medicine
Journal of Perinatology
Journal of Periodontology
Journal of Personality and Social
Psychology
Journal of Personality Assessment
Journal of Personality Disorders
Journal of Pharmacology and Experi-
mental Therapeutics
Journal of Police Science and Administra-
tion
Journal of Policy Analysis and Manage-
ment
Journal of Political Economy
Journal of Postgraduate Medicine
Journal of Primary Prevention
Journal of Property Management
Journal of Psychiatric Research
Journal of Psychoactive Drugs
Journal of Psychology
Journal of Psychology and Theology
Journal of Psychophysiology
Journal of Psychosocial Nursing and
Mental Health Services
Journal of Psychoteraphy and the Family
Journal of Public Health Dentistry
Journal of Public Health Policy
Journal of Quantitative Criminology
Journal of Reality Therapy
Journal of Reproductive Medicine
Journal of Research in Crime and
Delinquency
Journal of Rheumatology
Journal of the Royal College of General
Practitioners
Journal of the Royal Society of Medicine
Journal of School Health
Journal of Sex and Marital Therapy
Journal of Sex Education and Therapy
Journal of Sex Research

Journal of Social and Clinical Psychology
Journal of Social Behavior and Personality
Journal of Social History
Journal of Social, Political and Economic
    Studies
Journal of Social Psychology
Journal of Social Service Research
Journal of Social Work Education
Journal of the Society of Occupational
    Medicine
Journal of the South African Veterinary
    Association
Journal of the South Carolina Medical
    Association
Journal of Strategic and Systematic Thera-
    pies
Journal of Studies on Alcohol
Journal of Submicroscopic Cytology and
    Pathology
Journal of Substance Abuse Treatment
Journal of Surgical Research
Journal of the Tennessee Medical Asso-
    ciation
Journal of Toxicology: Clinical Toxicology
Journal of Traffic Safety Education
Journal of Training and Practice in Profes-
    sional Psychology
Journal of Trauma
Journal of Traumatic Stress
Journal of Ultrasound in Medicine
Journal of the University of Ottawa
Journal of Urology
Journal of Youth and Adolescence
JPEN: Journal of Parenteral and Enteral
    Nutrition
Judicature
Jurimetrics
Justice Quarterly
Justitiele Verkenningen
Juvenile and Family Court Journal
Juvenile and Family Law Digest
Juvenile Justice Digest
Kansas Medicine
Kardiologia Polska
Kardiologiia
Kardiologiya
Khirurgiia
Kidney International
Klinicheskaia Meditsina
Klinische Wochenschrift
Kokyu To Junkan
Kriminalist
Kriminalistik
Labor Law Journal
Laboratornoe Dela
Laboratory Animals

Laboratory Investigation
Ladies Home Journal
Lakartidningen
Lambda Rising Book Reports
Lancet
Laryngoscope
Latin American Perspectives
Law and Human Behavior
Law and Order
Law and Policy
Law and Society Review
Law Enforcement News
Law Officer's Bulletin
Learning
Learning 89
Legal Medicine
Leisure Studies
Lesbian Contradiction
Liaisons
Life
Life Sciences
Lijecnicki Vjesnik
Liver
Los Angeles
Lucha
Lung
Lutheran Education
Maclean's
Mademoiselle
Management Today
Management World
Marine Corps Gazette
Marketing
Maryland Medical Journal
Mass Transit
Masui
Mayo Clinic Proceedings
McCalls
MCN: American Journal of Maternal-Child
    Nursing
Medecine Interne
Medical Care
Medical Hypotheses
Medical Journal of Australia
Medical Journal of Malaysia
Medical Science Research
Medicina
Medicina Clinica
Medicine and Law
Medicine and Science in Sports and Exer-
    cise
Medicine, Science and the Law
Medicinski Arhiv
Medicinski Pregled
Medico-Legal Bulletin
Meditsinskaia Parazitologiia i Parazitarnye
    Bolezni

Medizinische Monatsschrift fur Pharma-
zeuten
Mental Retardation
Metabolism
Methods and Findings in Experimental
and Clinical Pharmacology
Michigan Medicine
Microwaves and RF
Mid-American Review of Sociology
Midwest Quarterly
Milbank Quarterly
Military Intelligence
Military Medicine
Military Review
Military Technology
Minerva Ginecologia
Minerva Medica
Minerva Psichiatrica
Minnesota Medicine
Minority Trendsletter
Missouri Medicine
MMWR: Morbidity and Mortality Weekly
Report
Modern Asian Studies
Modern Healthcare
Modern Law Review
Modern Maturity
Modern Pharmacology
Momentum
Monatsschrift fur Kriminologie und
Strafrechtsieform
Monthly Labor Review
Monthly Review
Morphologiai es Igazsagugyi Orvosi
Szemle
Morphologie et Embryologie
Mother Jones
Motor Boating and Sailing
Movement Disorders
Ms
Multivariate Behavioral Research
Multivariate Experimental Clinical Re-
search
Mutation Research
NACLA's Report on the Americas
Narcotics Control Digest
Narcotics Demand Reduction Digest
Narcotics Law Bulletin
NASPA Journal
NASSP Bulletin
Nation
National Geographic
National Guard
National Journal
National Review
National Security
National Sheriff

National Underwriter. Life and Health/
Financial Services Edition
Nation's Business
NATO's Sixteen Nations
Natural History
Nature
Naunyn-Schmiedeberg's Archives of
Pharmacology
Nebraska Medical Journal
Nederlands Tijdschrift voor Geneeskunde
Neighborhood Works
Nephrology, Dialysis, Transplantation
Nephron
Nervenarzt
Neue Praxis
Neurochemical Research
Neurologia
Neurologia et Psychiatrie
Neurologia i Neurochirurgia Polska
Neurology
Neuropediatrics
Neuropeptides
Neuropharmacology
Neurophysiologie Clinique
Neuropsychiatrie de l'Enfance et de
l'Adolescence
Neuropsychobiology
Neuropsychologia
Neuropsychopharmacology
Neuroscience and Biobehavioral Reviews
Neuroscience Letters
Neurosurgical Review
Neurotoxicology
Neurotoxicology and Teratology
Neuva Antropologia
New Age
New Directions for Student Services
New Directions for Women
New England Journal of Medicine
New Jersey Medicine
New Law Journal
New Leader
New Maritimes
New Republic
New Scientist
New Statesman and Society
New York
New York Review of Books
New York State Bar Journal
New York State Journal of Medicine
New York Times Magazine
New Yorker
New Zealand Medical Journal
Newsweek
NIDA Research Monograph Series:
National Institute on Drug Abuse
Research Monograph Series

Nippon Eiseigaku Zasshi
Nippon Kyobu Shikkan Gakkai Zasshi
Nippon Naika Gakkai Zasshi
Nippon Rinsho
Nippon Shokakibyo Gakkai Zasshi
Nordisk Medicin
Nordisk Psykiatrisk Tidsskrift
North Carolina Medical Journal
Notre Dame Law Review
Nuclear Medicine Communications
Nurse Practitioner
Nursing
Nursing 89
Nursing 90
Nursing Economics
Nursing Management
Nutrition and Cancer
Nutrition Reviews
Observer Magazine
Obstetrical and Gynecological Survey
Obstetrics and Gynecology
Occupational Health and Safety
Occupational Health and Safety Canada
Off Our Backs
Offentliche Gesundheitswesen
Officier de Police
Oftalmologicheskii Zhurnal
Ohio Medicine
Omni
Oral Surgery, Oral Medicine, Oral Patholo-
gy
Organized Crime Digest
ORL: Journal of Oto-Rhino-Laryngology
and its Related Specialties
Ortopediia Travmatologiia i Protezirovanie
Orvosi Hetilap
Otolaryngology—Head and Neck Surgery
Our Times
Padagogik Heute
Paediatric and Perinatal Epidemiology
Pancreas
Panminerva Medica
Papua New Guinea Medical Journal
Parents
Pastoral Psychology
Patologia Polska
Patologichesaia Fiziologiia i Eksperi-
mentalnaia Terapiia
Pavlovian Journal of Biological Science
Pediatric Clinics of North America
Pediatric Emergency Care
Pediatric Neuroscience
Pediatrician
Pediatrics
Pennsylvania Medicine
Pension World

People Weekly
Peptides
Perceptual and Motor Skills
Person-Centered Review
Personality and Individual Differences
Personality and Social Psychology Bulle-
tin
Personnel
Personnel Psychology
Pharmacological Research
Pharmacological Reviews
Pharmacology and Toxicology
Pharmacology, Biochemistry and Be-
havior
Pharmacopsychiatry
Pharmacotherapy
Pharmazie in Unserer Zeit
Phi Delta Kappan
Philadelphia Magazine
Physical Education
Physician and Sportsmedicine
Physiology and Behavior
PIMA Magazine
Plastic and Reconstructive Surgery
Playboy
Pneumologie
Police Chief
Police Journal
Police Officer Grievances Bulletin
Police Review
Police Stress
Police Studies
Policia
Policing
Policy Review
Polish Journal of Pharmacology and Phar-
macy
Political Affairs
Political Quarterly
Polski Archivum Medycyny Wewnetrznej
Polski Tygodnik Lekarski
Polygraph
Popular Mechanics
Postgraduate Medical Journal
Postgraduate Medicine
Practitioner
Praxis der Kinderpsychologie und
Kinderpsychiatrie
Presbyterian Record
Presse Medicale
Preventing School Failure
Prevention in Human Services
Preventive Medicine
Principal
Prison Service Journal
Problemy Endokrinologii

Problemy Tuberkulloza
Proceedings of the National Academy of Sciences USA
Professional Psychology: Research and Practice
Professional Safety
Profiles in Healthcare Marketing
Progress in Brain Research
Progress in Clinical and Biological Research
Progress in Drug Research
Progress in Neuropsychopharmacology and Biological Psychiatry
Progressive
Prostaglandins
Provider
Przeglad Dermatologiczny
Przeglad Epidemiologiczny
Przeglad Lekarski
Psychiatria et Neurologia Japonica
Psychiatria Polska
Psychiatric Annals
Psychiatric Clinics of North America
Psychiatric Forum
Psychiatric Hospital
Psychiatric Journal of the University of Ottawa
Psychiatric Quarterly
Psychiatrie de l'Enfant
Psychiatrie, Neurologie und Medizinische Psychologie
Psychiatrische Praxis
Psychiatry
Psychiatry in Medicine
Psychiatry Research
Psychoanalytic Quarterly
Psychobiology
Psychological Bulletin
Psychological Medicine
Psychological Medicine. Monograph (Suppl)
Psychological Reports
Psychological Review
Psychology and Aging
Psychology of Addictive Behaviors
Psychoneuroendocrinology
Psychopharmacology
Psychopharmacology Bulletin
Psychosocial Rehabilitation Journal
Psychosomatics
Psychotherapie, Psychosomatik, Medizinische Psychologie
Psychotherapy
Psychotherapy in Private Practice
Psychotherapy Patient
PTA Today
Public Administration Review

Public Citizen
Public Health
Public Health Reports
Public Interest
Public Management
Public Opinion Quarterly
Public Personnel Management
Public Welfare
Purchasing
QRB: Quality Review Bulletin
Quarterly Journal of Experimental Psychology. A
Quill and Quire
Radiography Today
Radiologia Diagnostica
Radiology
Railway Age
RCMP Gazette
Reader's Digest
Reader's Digest (Canada)
Real Estate Today
Recent Developments in Alcoholism
Recenti Progressi in Medicina
Redbook
Reports from the Department of Psychology, University of Stockholm
Research Communications in Substance Abuse
Review of Contemporary Fiction
Reviews of Infectious Diseases
Revista Clinica Espanola
Revista de Investigacion Clinica
Revista de Sanidad e Higiene Publica
Revista de Saude Publica
Revista do Hospital das Clinicas; Faculdade de Medicina da Universidade de Sao Paulo
Revista Espanola de Cardiologia
Revista Espanola de Fisiologia
Revista Espanola de las Enfermedades del Aparato Digestivo
Revista Europea per le Scienze Mediche e Farmacologiche
Revista Medica de Chile
Revista Medico-Chirurgicala a Societatii de Medici si Naturalista Din Iasi
Revista Mexicana de Sociologia
Revista Portuguesa de Cardiologia
Revue de Droit Penal et de Criminologie
Revue d'Epidemiologie et de Sante Publique
Revue de Science Criminelle et de Droit Penal Compare
Revue Medicale de la Suisse Romande
Revue Neurologique
RFD
Rhode Island Medical Journal

Rinsho Shinkeigaku
Risk Analysis
RN
Roczniki Akademii Medycznej Imeni Juli-
ana Marchlewskiego W Bialymstoku
Rolling Stone
Runner's World
Safety and Health
Salud Publica de Mexico
Saturday Evening Post
Saturday Night
Scandinavian Journal of Dental Research
Scandinavian Journal of Gastroenterology
Scandinavian Journal of Primary Health
Care
Scandinavian Journal of Psychology
Scandinavian Journal of Social Medicine
Scandinavian Journal of Urology and
Nephrology
Schizophrenia Bulletin
Scholastic Coach
Scholastic Update
School Administrator
School Counselor
School Law Bulletin
School Psychology Review
School Science and Mathematics
Schweizer Archiv fur Neurologie und Psy-
chiatrie
Schweizerische Medizinische Wochen-
schrift
Schweizerische Rundschau fur Medizin
Praxis
Science
Science News
Sciences
Scientific American
Scottish Medical Journal
Sea Power
Sea Technology
Search and Seizure Bulletin
Security
Security Letter. Part I
Security Management
Seishin Shinkeigaku Zasshi
Seminars in Arthritis and Rheumatism
Seventeen
Sewanee Review
Sex Roles
Signal
Singapore Medical Journal
Ski Canada
Small Group Behavior
Small Group Research
Smith College Studies in Social Work
Social Behavior and Personality
Social Casework

Social Cognition
Social Education
Social Justice
Social Policy
Social Problems
Social Psychiatry and Psychiatric Epi-
demiology
Social Science and Medicine
Social Science Quarterly
Social Service Review
Social Work
Social Work in Education
Social Work Research and Abstracts
Social Work in Health Care
Socialism and Democracy
Societes
Society
Socijalna Psihijatrija
Sociological Analysis
Sociological Perspectives
Sociological Quarterly
Sociological Review
Sociology and Social Research
Soldiers
Somatosensory and Motor Research
Sotsiologicheskie Issledovaniya
South African Medical Journal
Southern Communication Journal
Southern Economic Journal
Southern Medical Journal
Sovetskoe Zdravookhronenie
Soviet Education
Soviet Journal of Psychology
Soviet Medicine
Soviet Neurology and Psychiatry
Soviet Studies
Sozial -und Praventivmedizin
Spectator
Sport
Sport Psychology
Sports Illustrated
Sports Medicine
St. Louis Journalism Review
Stanford Law and Policy Review
Stanford Law Review
State Court Journal
State of Black America
Stomatologiia
Stores
Stroke
Sudebno-Meditsinskaia Ekspertiza
Sunday Times Magazine
Supervision
Supervisory Management
Surgical Neurology
Technology Review
Teen

Terapevticheskii Arkhiv
Teratology
Texas Medicine
Texas Monthly
Therapeutische Umschau
Therapie
Thorax
Thrombosis and Haemostasis
Thrust
Tidsskrift for den Norske Laegeforening
Tijdschrift voor Criminologie
Tijdschrift voor Kindergeneeskunde
Time
Times
Times Educational Supplement
Times Higher Education Supplement
Times Literary Supplement
Today's Health
Toxicology
Toxicology and Applied Pharmacology
Toxicology Letters
Tradeswoman
Traffic Safety
Traffic World
Training
Training Aids Digest
Transplantation
Transportation and Distribution
Trends in Pharmacological Sciences
Trial
Trustee
Tsitologiya i Genetika
Tumori
Tunisie Medicale
TV Guide
Ugeskrift for Laeger
Ukraineskii Biokhimicheskii Zhurnal
Ulster Medical Journal
UN Chronicle
Union Medicale du Canada
Update on Law-Related Education
Upsala Journal of Medical Sciences
Urologila i Nefrologila
US Army Aviation Digest
US Banker
US Catholic
US Naval Institute. Proceedings
US News and World Report
USA Today
Utne Reader
Vaccine
Vanguard
Vasa
Versicherungsmedizen
Vestnik Dermatologii i Venerologii
Vestnik Khirurgii Imeni I. I. Grekova
Vestnik Oto-Rino-Laringologii

Veterinary and Human Toxicology
Veterinary Clinics of North America. Small
    Animal Practice
Veterinary Record
Violence, Aggression and Terrorism
Violence and Victims
Virginia Medicine
Vital Health Statistics
Vital Speeches of the Day
Vocational Education Journal
Voenno-Meditsinskii Zhurnal
Vogue
Voprosy Meditsinskai Khimii
Voprosy Pitaniia
Vrachebnoe Delo
Vutreshni Bolesti
Wall Street Journal
Washington Monthly
Weekly Compilation of Presidential Docu-
    ments
West Indian Medical Journal
Western Journal of Black Studies
Western Journal of Medicine
Western Political Quarterly
WHO Regional Publications European
    Series
WHO Technical Report Series
Wiadomscl Lekarskie
Wiener Klinische Wochenschrift
Windspeaker
Wisconsin Medical Journal
Women and Criminal Justice
Women and Health
Women and Therapy
Women's Review of Books
Women's Studies International Forum
Working Woman
World and I
World Health Forum
World Journal of Surgery
World Marxist Review
World Policy Journal
World Press Review
World Review of Nutrition and Dietetics
Yakubutsu Seishin Kodo
Young Children
Youth and Society
Zdravotnicke Aktuality
Zeitschrift fur Arztliche Fortbildung
Zeitschrift fur die Gesamte Innere Medizin
    und Ihre Grenzgebiete
Zeitschrift fur die Gesamte Strafrechtswis-
    senschaft
Zeitschrift fur Erknankungen der
    Atmungsorgane
Zeitschrift fur Gastroenterologie
Zeitschrift fur Hautkrankheiten

BOOKS, MONOGRAPHS AND PAMPHLETS

Adrian, M., P. Jull, and R. Williams, comps. STATISTICS ON ALCOHOL AND DRUG ABUSE IN CANADA AND OTHER COUNTRIES. Toronto: Addiction Research Foundation, 1989. 2 v. $60.00/set (looseleaf with binder). ISBN 0-88868-168-2.

Albrecht, H.-J and A. Van Kalmthout, eds. DRUG POLICIES IN WESTERN EUROPE. Freiburg: Max Planck Institute, 1989. 479 pp. ISBN 3-922498-46-9.

ALCOHOL, DRUG, AND NARCOTIC ABUSE AMONG JUVENILES. Rockville: NIJ/NCJRS, 1989. $17.50. Topical Bibliography No. 45.

Australia. Parliamentary Joint Committee on the National Crime Authority. DRUGS, CRIME AND SOCIETY. Canberra: Australian Government Publishing Service, 1989. 136 pp.

Baggott, Rob. ALCOHOL, POLITICS AND SOCIAL POLICY. Brookfield: Gower, 1990. 176 pp. $49.95. ISBN 0-566-07075-8.

Bailor, Bernard S. A PRACTITIONER'S GUIDE TO THE ANTI-DRUG ABUSE ACT OF 1988. Washington: ABA, 1989. 64 pp.

Balfour, D. J. K., ed. PSYCHOTROPIC DRUGS OF ABUSE (International Encyclopedia of Pharmacology and Therapeutics, section 130). Elmsford: Pergamon Press, 1990.

Beattie, Melody. BEYOND CODEPENDENCY; AND GETTING BETTER ALL THE TIME. New York: Harper & Row, 1989. 252 pp. $9.95 (paper). ISBN 0-06-255418-2.

Berg, Steven L., et al. THE NALGAP ANNOTATED BIBLIOGRAPHY: RESOURCES ON ALCOHOLISM, SUBSTANCE ABUSE, AND LESBIANS/GAY MEN. National Association of Lesbian & Gay Alcoholism Professionals, 1987. 259 pp.

Berger, Gilda. DRUG ABUSE: THE IMPACT ON SOCIETY. New York: Watts, 1988. 144 pp. $12.90. ISBN 0-531-10579-2.

—. MAKING UP YOUR MIND ABOUT DRUGS. Lodestar Books, 1988. 89 pp. $10.95 (cloth), ISBN 0-525-67251-6; $3.95 (paper), ISBN 0-525-67256-7.

—. VIOLENCE AND DRUGS. New York: Watts, 1989. 112 pp. $12.90. ISBN 0-531-10818-X.

Berridge, Virginia, ed. DRUGS RESEARCH AND POLICY IN BRITAIN: A REVIEW OF THE 1980S. Hampshire: Gower, 1990. 298 pp. $57.75. ISBN 0-566-07045-6.

Boaz, David, ed. THE CRISIS IN DRUG PROHIBITION. Washington: Cato Institute, 1990. 148 pp. $8.00.

Botero, Cecilia. DRUGS AND LATIN AMERICA: A BIBLIOGRAPHY. Monticello: Vance Bibls, 1990. 21 pp.

Brounstein, Paul J., et al. PATTERNS OF SUBSTANCE USE AND DELINQUENCY AMONG INNER CITY ADOLESCENTS. Washington: Urban Institute, 1989. 194 pp.

California. Department of Alcohol and Drug Programs. CALIFORNIA MASTER PLAN TO REDUCE DRUG AND ALCOHOL ABUSE: YEAR TWO; A PLANNED RE-SPONSE TO MEET THE GOALS OF SENATE BILL 2599. Sacramento: DOADP, 1990.

Carpenter, Ted Galen and R. Channing Rouse. PERILOUS PANACEA: THE MILITARY IN THE DRUG WAR. Washington: Cato Institute, 1990. 34 pp.

Chaiken, Marcia R. IN-PRISON PROGRAMS FOR DRUG-INVOLVED OFFENDERS. Washington: NIJ, 1989. 87 pp.

—, ed. STREET-LEVEL DRUG ENFORCEMENT: EXAMINING THE ISSUES. Washington: NIJ/OJP, 1989. 55 pp.

Coldren, James R., Jr., Kenneth R. Coyle, and Sophia D. Carr. CRIME LABORATORIES 1988: A KEY PROGRAM OF STATE DRUG CONTROL STRATEGIES. Washington: US Bureau of Justice Assistance, 1990. 44 pp.

—. MULTI-JURISDICTIONAL DRUG CONTROL TASK FORCES 1988: CRITICAL COM-PONENTS OF STATE DRUG CONTROL STRATEGIES. Washington: U.S. Bu-reau of Justice Assistance, 1990. 69 pp.

Cole, Lewis. NEVER TOO YOUNG TO DIE: THE DEATH OF LEN BIAS. New York: Pan-theon Books, 1989. 252 pp. $18.95. ISBN 0-394-56440-5.

Collett, Merrill. THE COCAINE CONNECTION: DRUG TRAFFICKING AND INTER-AMERI-CAN RELATIONS. Foreign Policy Association, 1989. 71 pp. $4.00 (paper). ISBN 0-87124-128-5.

Connors, Edward F., III and Hugh Nugent. STREET-LEVEL NARCOTICS ENFORCE-MENT. Washington: U.S. Bureau of Justice Assistance, 1990. 64 pp.

Cooper, Mary H. THE BUSINESS OF DRUGS. Washington: Congressional Quarterly, 1990. 165 pp.

Council of Europe. ANTI-DOPING CONVENTION. Council of Europe, 1989. 19pp. ISBN 92-871-1782-9.

Criminal Justice Statistics Association. DRUG CONTROL AND USE SURVEYS: A PO-TENTIAL TOOL FOR DEVELOPING STATE DRUG CONTROL STRATEGIES. Washington: Bureau of Justice Assistance, 1990. 49 pp.

De Loor, A. ECSTASY IS NOT A SINGLE DRUG: AN INVESTIGATION. Amsterdam: Ad-viesburo Drugs, 1989. 47 pp.

Derivan, William J. PREVENTION EDUCATION: A GUIDE TO RESEARCH. New York: Garland, 1990. 282 pp. $34.00. ISBN 0-8240-3716-2.

Ditton, J. and A. Taylor. SCOTLAND'S DRUG MISUSE AGENCIES: 1987 SURVEY. Edinburgh: University of Glasgow, 1990. 132 pp. ISSN 0950-2254.

Dobinson, Ian and Patrizia Poletti. BUYING AND SELLING HEROIN: A STUDY OF HEROIN USERS/DEALERS. New South Wales: NSW Bureau of Crime Statistics and Research, 1989. 121 pp.

DRUG LAW ENFORCEMENT. Rockville: NIJ/NCJRS, 1989. $17.50. Topical Bibliography No. 44.

DRUGS AND CRIME. Rockville: NIJ/NCJRS, 1989. $17.50. Topical Bibliography No. 43.

Eck, J. E. POLICE AND DRUG CONTROL: A HOME FIELD ADVANTAGE. Washington: Police Executive Research Forum, 1989. 32 pp.

Fahlman, R. C. RCMP NATIONAL DRUG INTELLIGENCE ESTIMATE 1987/88. WITH TREND INDICATORS THROUGH 1990. Ottawa: RCMP Headquarters, 1988. 110 pp. ISBN 0-662-56131-7.

Fisher, G. L. and S. J. Jenkins. SUBSTANCE USE AND ATTITUDES OF PROSPECTIVE COUNSELORS. Reno: University of Nevada Press, 1989. 4 pp.

Friedman, David. FOCUS ON DRUGS AND THE BRAIN. New York: 21st Century Books, 1989. 64 pp. $14.95. ISBN 0-941477-95-9.

Glick, Ronald and Joan Moore, ed. DRUGS IN HISPANIC COMMUNITIES. New Brunswick: Rutgers University Press, 1990. 275 pp. $37.00 (cloth), ISBN 0-8135-1568-8); $14.00 (paper), ISBN 0-8135-1569-6).

Goldkamp, John S., et al. VOLUME 1: ASSESSING THE IMPACT OF DRUG-RELATED CRIMINAL CASES ON THE JUDICIAL PROCESSING OF CRIMINAL CASES, CROWDING AND PUBLIC SAFETY. Philadelphia: Temple University Press, 1989. 169 pp.

Gonzalez, Guadalupe and Marta Tienda, eds. THE DRUG CONNECTION IN U.S.-MEXICAN RELATIONS (V. 4 of DIMENSIONS OF UNITED STATES-MEXICAN RELATIONS). San Diego: University of California Press, 1989. 137 pp.

Goodwin, Donald W. ALCOHOL AND THE WRITER. Andrews & McMeel, 1988. 210 pp. $16.95. ISBN 0-8362-5925-4.

Groenhuijsen, M. S. and A. M. Van Kalmthout, eds. DUTCH DRUGS POLICY FROM A WESTERN EUROPEAN PERSPECTIVE. Arnhem: Gouda Quint, 1989. 178pp. ISBN 90-6000-614-3.

Hammersley, R. HEROIN USE AND CRIME. A COMPARISON OF HEROIN USERS AND NON-USERS IN AND OUT OF PRISON. Edinburgh: Scottish Office Central Research Paper, 1990. 27 pp. ISBN 0-7480-0293-6.

Hester, R. K. and W. R. Miller, eds. HANDBOOK OF ALCOHOLISM TREATMENT APPROACHES: EFFECTIVE ALTERNATIVES (PERGAMON GENERAL PSYCHOLOGY SERIES, V. 157). New York: Pergamon Press, 1989. 297 pp. $35.00.

Hubbard, R. L. DRUG ABUSE TREATMENT: A NATIONAL STUDY OF EFFECTIVE-NESS. Chapel Hill: University of North Carolina Press, 1989. 213 pp. $29.95.

Huyghe-Braeckmans, B. REPORT OF THE INTERNATIONAL NARCOTICS CONTROL BOARD FOR 1989. Vienna: INCB/United Nations, 1990. 40 pp.

Hyde, Margaret Oldroyd. ALCOHOL: USES AND ABUSES. Enslow Pubs., 1988. 96 pp. $13.95. ISBN 0-89490-155-9.

Inciardi, James A., ed. HANDBOOK OF DRUG CONTROL IN THE UNITED STATES. Westport: Greenwood Press, 1990. 440 pp. $65.00.

INTERNATIONAL CRIMINAL POLICE ORGANIZATION INTERNATIONAL CRIME STATISTICS 1985-1986. Lyons: ICPO-INTERPOL General Secretariot, 1987. 208 pp.

Kleiman, Mark A. R., et al. STREET-LEVEL DRUG ENFORCEMENT: EXAMINING THE ISSUES. Washington: USNIJ, 1988. 55 pp.

Koslowski, Lynn T., et al. RESEARCH ADVANCES IN ALCOHOL AND DRUG PROB-LEMS. New York: Plenum Publishing Corp, 1990. 409 pp. $79.50. ISBN 0-306-43295-1.

Lee, Essie E. BREAKING THE CONNECTION: HOW YOUNG PEOPLE ACHIEVE DRUG-FREE LIVES. New York: Messner, 1988. 191 pp. $10.29 (cloth), ISBN 0-671-63637-5; $5.95 (paper), ISBN 0-671-67059-X.

Lenck, William. TRACKING DRUG PROCEEDS: BANK SECRECY ACT REPORT #11. Washington: Police Executive Research Forum, 1989. 28 pp.

Levine, Michael. DEEP COVER: THE INSIDE STORY OF HOW DEA INFIGHTING, IN-COMPETENCE AND SUBTERFUGE LOST US THE BIGGEST BATTLE OF THE DRUG WAR. New York: Delacorte Press, 1990. 319 pp. $19.95.

Lobb, Michael L. and T. D. Watts. NATIVE AMERICAN YOUTH AND ALCOHOL: AN AN-NOTATED BIBLIOGRAPHY. Westport: Greenwood Press, 1989. 165 pp. $39.95. ISBN 0-313-25618-7.

Lyman, Michael D. PRACTICAL DRUG ENFORCEMENT: PROCEDURES AND ADMIN-ISTRATION. New York & Amsterdam: Elsevier, 1989. 390 pp.

Mabry, Donald J., ed. THE LATIN AMERICAN NARCOTICS TRADE AND U.S. NATIONAL SECURITY. Westport: Greenwood Press, 1989. 206 pp.

May, Gerald G. ADDICTION AND GRACE. New York: Harper & Row, 1988. 200 pp. $16.95. ISBN 0-06-065536-4.

Meyer, J., ed. CRIMINAL DRUG LAWS IN WESTERN EUROPE: A COMPARATIVE LE-GAL STUDY COMMISSIONED BY THE FEDERAL CRIMINAL POLICE OFFICE. Freiburg: Max-Planck Institut, 1987. 835 pp. ISBN 3-992498-95-7.

Meyer, J., A. Dessecker, and J. R. Smettan, eds. CONFISCATION OF PROFITS DERIVED FROM DRUG OFFENSES. COMPARATIVE LEGAL AND CRIMINO-LOGICAL STUDY. Wiesbaden: Bundeskriminalamt, 1989. 681 pp. ISSN 0174-5433.

Minnesota. Department of Human Services. Chemical Dependency Program Division. DRUG EDUCATION PROGRAM OF MINOR OFFENDERS: 1990 EVALUATION. St. Paul: The Department, 1990. 87 pp.

Moser, Leslie E. CRACK, COCAINE, METHAMPHETAMINE AND ICE. Multi-Media Productions, 1990.

Nahas, Gabriel G. COCAINE: THE GREAT WHITE PLAGUE. Middlebury: P. S. Ericksson, 1989. 300 pp. $19.95.

National Governors' Association. Committee on Justice and Public Safety. DRUG ABUSE AND TRAFFICKING: STATES MEETING THE CHALLENGE. Washington: The Committee, 1990. 27 pp.

National Research Council. Committee on Aids Research and the Behavioral, Social, and Statistical Sciences. AIDS: SEXUAL BEHAVIOR AND INTRAVENOUS DRUG USE. National Academic Press, 1989. 589 pp. $34.95 (cloth), ISBN 0-309-03976-2; $24.95 (paper), ISBN 0-309-03948-7.

O'Neill, Catherine. FOCUS ON ALCOHOL. New York: 21st Century Books, 1990. 56 pp. $14.95. ISBN 0-941477-96-7.

Parry, O. THE NEWPORT ALCOHOL ABUSE AND SOCIAL DISORDER DEMONSTRATION PROJECT. A MULTI-AGENCY APPROACH TO LOCAL PROBLEM SOLVING. FINAL REPORT: BACKGROUND, SUMMARY AND RECOMMENDATIONS. Cardiff: University of Wales College of Cardiff, 1990. 9 pp.

Peele, Stanton. DISEASING OF AMERICA: ADDICTION TREATMENT OUT OF CONTROL. Lexington: Lexington Books, 1989. 321 pp. $19.95. ISBN 0-669-20015-8.

Plant, Martin, ed. AIDS, DRUGS, AND PROSTITUTION. London: Routledge, 1990. 213 pp. $36.00. ISBN 0-415-04108-2.

Polish Academy of Sciences. Institute of State and Law. Department of Criminology. PROBLEMS OF SOCIAL MALADJUSTMENT AND CRIME IN POLAND. Wroclaw: Zaklad Norodowy im Ossolinskich, 1989. 294 pp. ISBN 83-04-01802-0.

Potter-Efron, Ronald T. and Patricia S. Potter-Efron, eds. AGGRESSION, FAMILY VIOLENCE AND CHEMICAL DEPENDENCY. New York: Haworth Press, 1990.

Prestwich, Patricia E. DRINK AND THE POLITICS OF SOCIAL REFORM: ANTIALCOHOLISM IN FRANCE SINCE 1870. Society for the Promotion of Science & Scholarship, 1988, 365 pp. $36.00. ISBN 0-930664-08-6.

Rayner, Claire. THE DON'T SPOIL YOUR BODY BOOK. Barron's Educ. Ser., 1989. 48 pp. $6.95 (paper). ISBN 0-8120-6098-9.

Read, Edward M. and Dennis C. Daley. GETTING HIGH AND DOING TIME: WHAT'S THE CONNECTION? Laurel, MD: American Correctional Association, 1990. 80 pp.

Reuter, Peter, Robert MacCoun and Patrick Murphy. MONEY FROM CRIME: A STUDY OF THE ECONOMICS OF DRUG DEALING IN WASHINGTON, D.C. Santa Monica: Rand Corp, 1990. 172 pp. $15.00 (paper). ISBN 0-8330-1069-7.

Rice, Berkeley. TRAFFICKING: THE BOOM AND BUST OF THE AIR AMERICA COCAINE RING. New York: Scribner, 1990. 303 pp. $22.95. ISBN 0-684-19024-9.

Ridlon, Florence V. A FALLEN ANGEL: THE STATUS INSULARITY OF THE FEMALE ALCOHOLIC. Louisberg: Bucknell University Press, 1988. 180 pp. $27.50. ISBN 0-8387-5115-6.

Robertson, K. G. 1992: THE SECURITY IMPLICATIONS. London: Institute for European Defence & Strategic Studies, 1989. 42 pp. ISBN 0-907967-11-6.

Roman, Paul M., ed. ALCOHOL PROBLEM INTERVENTION IN THE WORKPLACE: EMPLOYEE ASSISTANCE PROGRAMS AND STRATEGIC ALTERNATIVES. Westport: Quorum Books, 1990. 413 pp. $65.00. ISBN 0-89930-459-1.

Roorda, P. A. DRUGS BEHIND THE REVOLVING DOOR: INFORMATION ABOUT AD-DICTION AND ADDICTS FOR POLICE AND JUSTICE. Haarlem: De Toorts, 1989. 192 pp. ISBN 90-6020-583-9.

Rosenbaum, Marsha. JUST SAY WHAT? AN ALTERNATIVE VIEW ON SOLVING AMERICA'S DRUG PROBLEM. San Francisco: National Council on Crime and Delinquency, 1990. 24 pp.

Sarre, Rick, Adam Sutton, and Tim Pulsford. CANNABIS: THE EXPIATION NOTICE AP-PROACH. Adelaide: South Australian Attorney-General's Department, 1989. 52 pp.

Schneider, J. C. and B. Porter-Shirley, eds. PETERSON'S DRUG AND ALCOHOL PRO-GRAMS AND POLICIES AT FOUR-YEAR COLLEGES. Princeton: Peterson's Guides, 1989. 445 pp. $19.95 (paper). ISBN 0-87866-731-8.

Seixas, Judith S. LIVING WITH A PARENT WHO TAKES DRUGS. Greenwillow Books, 1989. 102 pp. $11.95. ISBN 0-688-08627-6.

Shuker, Nancy. EVERYTHING YOU NEED TO KNOW ABOUT AN ALCOHOLIC PAR-ENT. New York: Rosen Publishing Group, 1989. 64 pp. $12.95. ISBN 0-8239-1011-3.

Shulman, Jeffrey. FOCUS ON COCAINE AND CRACK. New York: 21st Century Books, 1990. 56 pp. $14.95. ISBN 0-941477-98-3.

Siegel, Ronald K. INTOXICATION: LIFE IN PURSUIT OF ARTIFICIAL PARADISE. New York: Dutton, 1989. 390 pp. $19.95. ISBN 0-525-24764-5.

Smith, H. E., ed. TRANSNATIONAL CRIME: INVESTIGATIVE RESPONSES. Chicago: University of Illinois Press, 1989. 136 pp. ISBN 0-942511-22-0.

Snyder, Solomon, H. BRAINSTORMING: THE SCIENCE AND POLITICS OF OPIATE RESEARCH. Cambridge: Harvard University Press, 1989. 208 pp. $22.50. ISBN 0-674-080480-3.

Sonnenstuhl, William J. and Harrison M. Trice. STRATEGIES FOR EMPLOYEE ASSIS-TANCE PROGRAMS: THE CRUCIAL BALANCE. ILR Press, 1990. 81 pp. $10.00 (paper). ISBN 0-87546-167-0.

Speller, J. S. EXECUTIVES IN CRISIS: RECOGNIZING AND MANAGING THE ALCO-HOLIC, DRUG-ADDICTED, OR MENTALLY ILL EXECUTIVE. San Francisco: Jossey-Bass, 1989. 164 pp. $19.95.

Spence, Annette. SUBSTANCE ABUSE. New York: Facts on File, 1989. 128 pp. $18.95. ISBN 0-8160-1668-2.

Sterling, Claire. OCTOPUS: THE LONG REACH OF THE INTERNATIONAL SICILIAN MAFIA. New York: W. W. Norton, 1990. 384 pp.

Strong, A. C. CORRIDO DE COCAINE: INSIDE STORIES OF HARD DRUGS, BIG MONEY AND SHORT LIVES. Tucson: Harbinger House, Inc., 1990. 211 pp. ISBN 0-943173-57-4.

SUBSTANCE ABUSE & KIDS: A DIRECTORY OF EDUCATION, INFORMATION, PRE-VENTION, AND EARLY INTERVENTION PROGRAMS. Phoenix: Oryx Press, 1989. 466 pp. $65.00 (paper). ISBN 0-89774-583-3.

Tarazona-Sevillano, Gabriela. SENDERO LUMINOSO AND THE THREAT OF NAR-COTERRORISM. New York: Praeger Publishing, 1990. 168 pp. $35.00 (cloth), ISBN 0-275-93642-2; $12.95 (paper), ISBN 0-275-93643-0.

Texas. Criminal Justice Policy Council. DRUG USE AND RECIDIVISM: ANALYSIS OF DRUG OFFENDERS ADMITTED TO TEXAS PRISONS. Austin: The Council, 1989. 20 pp.

Tonry, M. and J. Q. Wilson. DRUGS AND CRIME. Chicago: University of Chicago Press, 1990. 574 pp. $39.95. ISBN 0-226-80810-6.

Treback, Arnold S. and Kevin B. Zeese, eds. DRUG POLICY 1989-1990: A RE-FORMER'S CATALOGUE. Washington: Drug Policy Foundation, 1990. 451 pp.

Tresz, P. L. INSTRUCTORS' AND INVESTIGATORS' GUIDE TO THE WAR ON DRUGS. Wiesbaden: Bundeskriminalamt, 1988. 174 pp.

United Nations. International Narcotics Control Board. REPORT OF THE INTERNA-TIONAL NARCOTICS CONTROL BOARD FOR 1989. Vienna: United Nations, 1990. 40 pp.

United States. Alcohol, Drug Abuse, and Mental Health Administration. THE ECO-NOMICS COSTS OF ALCOHOL AND DRUG ABUSE AND MENTAL ILLNESS: 1985. Rockville: DHHS, 1990. 296 pp. $15.00 (paper).

United States. Alcohol, Drug Abuse, and Mental Health Administration. PROCEEDINGS OF A NATIONAL CONFERENCE ON PREVENTING ALCOHOL AND DRUG ABUSE IN BLACK COMMUNITIES, MAY 22-24, 1987, WASHINGTON, DC. Rockville: DHHS, 1990. 257 pp.

United States. Alcohol, Drug Abuse, and Mental Health Administration. Office for Sub-stance Abuse Prevention. CITIZEN'S ALCOHOL AND OTHER DRUG PREVEN-TION DIRECTORY: RESOURCES FOR GETTING INVOLVED. Washington: GPO, 1990. 261 pp. $13.00 (paper).

United States. Alcohol, Drug Abuse, and Mental Health Administration. Office for Treat-ment Improvement. SELF-RUN, SELF-SUPPORTED HOUSES FOR MORE EF-FECTIVE RECOVERY FROM ALCOHOL AND DRUG ADDICTION: RECOVERY, RESPONSIBILITY, REPLICATION; A TECHNICAL ASSISTANCE MANUAL FOR IMPLEMENTATION OF THE GROUP RECOVERY HOMES PROVISION OF THE ANTI-DRUG ABUSE ACT OF 1988. Rockville: DOH, 1990.

United States. Congress. Office of Technical Assessment. THE EFFECTIVENESS OF DRUG ABUSE TREATMENT: IMPLICATIONS FOR CONTROLLING AIDS/HIV IN-FECTION. Washington: GPO, 1990. 152 pp. $7.50 (paper).

United States. Department of Education. Office of Education Research and Improvement. Programs for the Improvement of Practice. PROFILES OF SUCCESSFUL DRUG PREVENTION PROGRAMS, 1988-89: DRUG FREE SCHOOL RECOGNITION PROGRAM. Washington: DOE, 1990. 64 pp.

United States. Department of Justice. Office of Justice Programs. DRUG USE FORECASTING (DUF) RESEARCH UPDATE. Washington: DOJ, 1989. 8 pp.

United States. Department of Justice. Office of Justice Programs. IMPLEMENTING PROJECT DARE: DRUG ABUSE RESISTANCE EDUCATION. INFORMATION AND OPERATION GUIDE FOR LAW ENFORCEMENT PERSONNEL, EDUCATION PERSONNEL, AND FEDERAL, STATE AND LOCAL AGENCIES REPLICATING THE DARE PROGRAM. Washington: DOJ, 1988. 134 pp.

United States. Department of Justice. Office of Justice Programs. AN INVITATION TO PROJECT DARE: DRUG ABUSE RESISTANCE EDUCATION. INFORMATION YOU NEED TO DECIDE WHETHER YOUR COMMUNITY IS PREPARED TO COMMIT THE TIME, ENERGY AND RESOURCES REQUIRED TO IMPLEMENT THIS PROGRAM. Washington: DOJ, 1988. 10 pp.

United States. Department of Justice. Office of Justice Programs. Bureau of Justice Statistics. STATE DRUG RESOURCES: A NATIONAL DIRECTORY. Rockville: Drugs & Crime Data Center & Clearinghouse, 1990. 117 pp.

United States. Department of Justice. Office of the Attorney General. DRUG TRAFFICKING: A REPORT TO THE PRESIDENT OF THE UNITED STATES. Washington: GPO, 1989. 60 pp.

United States. Department of Justice. PRISON PROGRAMS FOR DRUG-INVOLVED OFFENDERS. Washington: NCJ, 1989. 6 pp.

United States. Executive Branch. Office of the President. Office of National Drug Control Policy. LEADING DRUG INDICATORS: WHITE PAPER. Washington: GPO, 1990. 36 pp.

United States. Executive Branch. Office of the President. Office of National Drug Control Policy. NATIONAL DRUG CONTROL STRATEGY: BUDGET SUMMARY. Washington: GPO, 1990. 159 pp.

United States. Executive Branch. Office of the President. Office of National Drug Control Policy. NATIONAL DRUG CONTROL STRATEGY: JANUARY 1990. Washington: GPO, 1990. 142 pp.

United States. Executive Branch. Office of the President. Office of National Drug Control Policy. UNDERSTANDING DRUG TREATMENT: WHITE PAPER, JUNE 1990. Washington: GPO, 1990. 31 pp. $3.00.

United States. General Accounting Office. COORDINATION BETWEEN DEA AND THE FBI. Washington: GPO, 1990. 17 pp.

United States. General Accounting Office. DRUG CONTROL: ANTI-DRUG EFFORTS IN THE BAHAMAS. Washington: GAO, 1990. 74 pp.

United States. General Accounting Office. DRUG CONTROL: ENFORCEMENT EFFORTS IN BURMA ARE NOT EFFECTIVE. Washington: GAO, 1989. 38 pp.

United States. House. Committee on Armed Services. THE ANDEAN DRUG STRATEGY AND THE ROLE OF THE U.S. MILITARY: PROCEEDINGS OF A SEMINAR

HELD BY THE CONGRESSIONAL RESEARCH SERVICE, NOVEMBER 9, 1989; REPORT OF THE DEFENSE POLICY PANEL AND INVESTIGATIONS SUB-COMMITTEE. Washington: GPO, 1990. 41 pp.

United States. House. Committee on Banking, Finance, and Urban Affairs. MONEY LAUNDERING: HEARINGS, DECEMBER 6-7, 1989. Washington: GPO, 1990. 355 pp.

United States. House. Committee on Banking, Finance, and Urban Affairs. Subcommittee on Financial Institutions' Supervision, Regulation, and Insurance. MONEY LAUNDERING: HEARINGS, NOVEMBER 14-15, 1989. Washington: GPO, 1990. 209 pp.

United States. House. Committee on Energy and Commerce. Subcommittee on Health and the Environment. AIDS ISSUES: HEARINGS: PTS. 1-2, APRIL 4-SEPTEM-BER 18, 1989. Washington: GPO, 1989/90.

United States. House. Committee on Foreign Affairs. CONNECTION BETWEEN ARMS AND NARCOTICS TRAFFICKING: HEARING, OCOTOBER 31, 1989. Washington: GPO, 1990. 142 pp.

United States. House. Committee on Foreign Affairs. EUROPEAN INTEGRATION, THE UNITED STATES, AND NARCOTICS CONTROL: RHETORIC AND REALITY; REPORT, MARCH 1990, OF A STAFF STUDY MISSION TO GREAT BRITAIN, ITALY, PORTUGAL, SPAIN, AND KENYA, JANUARY 8-26, 1990. Washington: GPO, 1990. 27 pp.

United States. House. Committee on Government Operations. Government Information, Justice, and Agriculture Subcommittee. FEDERAL WITNESS SECURITY PRO-GRAM AND PROTECTION OF FOREIGN NATIONALS: HEARING, MARCH 1, 1990. Washington: GPO, 1990. 71 pp.

United States. House. Committee on the Judiciary. Subcommittee on Crime. AN-ABOLIC STEROID RESTRICTION ACT OF 1989: HEARING, MARCH 23, 1989, ON H.R. 995. Washington: GPO, 1989. 90 pp.

United States. House. Committee on the Judiciary. Subcommittee on Crime. EFFORTS OF THE U.S. GOVERNMENT TO REDUCE THE FLOW OF ILLEGAL DRUGS INTO THE UNITED STATES FROM FOREIGN COUNTRIES: HEARING, APRIL 12, 1989. Washington: GPO, 1990. 280 pp.

United States. House. Committee on the Judiciary. Subcommittee on Crime. FEDERAL DRUG AFTERCARE AND DRUG TESTING PROGRAMS: HEARING, JULY 27, 1989, ON H. R. 3007, DRUG AND ALCOHOL DEPENDENT OFFENDERS TREATMENT ACT OF 1989. Washington: GPO, 1990. 182 pp.

United States. House. Committee on the Judiciary. Subcommittee on Crime. FEDERAL DRUG FORFEITURE ACTIVITIES: HEARING, APRIL 24, 1989. Washington: GPO, 1990. 316 pp.

United States. House. Committee on the Judiciary. Subcommittee on Crime. USE OF MINORS IN DRUG CRIMES: HEARING, JULY 13, 1989, ON H.R. 1305, TO AMEND THE CONTROLLED SUBSTANCES ACT TO STRENGTHEN MINIMUM IMPRISONMENT PROVISIONS FOR EMPLOYING PERSONS UNDER 18 YEARS OF AGE IN DRUG OPERATIONS. Washington: GPO, 1990. 40 pp.

United States. House. Committee on Post Office and Civil Service. Subcommittee on Postal Personnel and Modernization. PRE-EMPLOYMENT DRUG TESTING

PROGRAM OF THE U.S. POSTAL SERVICE: HEARING, APRIL 12, 1989. Washington: GPO, 1989. 114 pp.

United States. House. Committee on Ways and Means. Subcommittee on Human Resources. THE ENEMY WITHIN: CRACK-COCAINE AND AMERICA'S FAMILIES, JUNE 12, 1990. Washington: GPO, 1990. 93 pp.

United States. House. Select Committee on Narcotics Abuse and Control. ASIAN HEROIN PRODUCTION AND TRAFFICKING: HEARING, AUGUST 1, 1989. 124 pp. Washington: GPO, 1990.

United States. House. Select Committee on Narcotics Abuse and Control. DRUG CRISIS IN HAWAII: HEARING, JANUARY 13, 1990. Washington: GPO, 1990. 241 pp.

United States. House. Select Committee on Narcotics Abuse and Control. THE FEDERAL DRUG STRATEGY: HEARING, SEPTEMBER 25, 1989. Washington: GPO, 1990. 199 pp.

United States. House. Select Committee on Narcotics Abuse and Control. THE FEDERAL DRUG STRATEGY UPDATE: HEARING, FEBRUARY 7, 1990. Washington: GPO, 1990. 107 pp.

United States. House. Select Committee on Narcotics Abuse and Control. THE FEDERAL DRUG STRATEGY: WHAT DOES IT MEAN FOR BLACK AMERICA? HEARING, SEPTEMBER 15, 1989. Washington: GPO, 1990. 190 pp.

United States. House. Select Committee on Narcotics Abuse and Control. THE FLOW OF PRECURSOR CHEMICALS AND ASSAULT WEAPONS FROM THE UNITED STATES INTO THE ANDEAN NATIONS: HEARING, NOVEMBER 1, 1989. Washington: GPO, 1990. 285 pp.

United States. House. Select Committee on Narcotics Abuse and Control. NARCOTIC AND DANGEROUS DRUG CONTROL: PENALTIES UNDER THE CONTROLLED SUBSTANCES ACT AND OTHER FEDERAL STATUTES. Washington: GPO, 1990. 18 pp.

United States. House. Select Committee on Narcotics Abuse and Control. NATIONAL DRUG CONTROL STRATEGY: HEARING, SEPTEMBER 13, 1989. Washington: GPO, 1990. 65 pp.

United States. House. Select Committee on Narcotics Abuse and Control. NATIONAL DRUG STRATEGY GOALS AND THE ROOT CAUSES OF DRUG ADDICTION AND DRUG CRIME: HEARING, NOVEMBER 15, 1989. Washington: GPO, 1990. 160 pp.

United States. House. Select Committee on Narcotics Abuse and Control. THE REEMERGENCE OF METHAMPHETAMINE: HEARING, OCTOBER 24, 1989. Washington: GPO, 1990. 158 pp.

United States. National Institute of Justice. DRUGS AND CRIME IN AMERICA. Washington: NIJ, 1990. 27 pp.

United States. National Institute on Alcohol Abuse and Alcoholism. ALCOHOL AND HEALTH: SEVENTH SPECIAL REPORT TO THE CONGRESS FROM THE SECRETARY OF HEALTH AND HUMAN SERVICES. Rockville: HHS, 1990. 440 pp.

United States. National Institute on Drug Abuse. NATIONAL DIRECTORY OF DRUG ABUSE AND ALCOHOLISM TREATMENT AND PREVENTION PROGRAMS, 1989 SURVEY. Rockville: DHHS, 1990. 408 pp.

United States. National Institute on Drug Abuse. Division of Epidemiology and Prevention Research. NATIONAL HOUSEHOLD SURVEY ON DRUG ABUSE: HIGHLIGHTS 1988. Rockville: DHHS, 1990. 73 pp.

United States. National Institute on Drug Abuse. Division of Epidemiology and Prevention Research.· NATIONAL HOUSEHOLD SURVEY ON DRUG ABUSE: MAIN FINDINGS 1988. Rockville: DHHS, 1990. 135 pp.

United States. Senate. Committee on Commerce, Science, and Transportation. Subcommittee on Foreign Commerce and Tourism. U.S. CHEMICAL EXPORTS TO LATIN AMERICA: HEARING, FEBRUARY 6, 1990. Washington: GPO, 1990. 87 pp.

United States. Senate. Committee on Environment and Public Works. Subcommittee on Water Resources, Transportation, and Infrastructure. DRUG OFFENDER'S DRIVING PRIVILEGES SUSPENSION ACT OF 1989: HEARING, NOVEMBER 15, 1989, ON S. 1804, A BILL TO AMEND TITLE 23. Washington: GPO, 1990. 121pp.

United States. Senate. Committee on Foreign Relations. DRUGS IN MASSACHUSETTS: THE DOMESTIC IMPACT OF A FOREIGN INVASION; A REPORT, JANUARY 1990. Washington: GPO, 1990. 35 pp.

United States. Senate. Committee on Governmental Affairs. AVERTING ALCOHOL ABUSE: NEW DIRECTIONS IN PREVENTION POLICY; HEARINGS, JUNE 15 21, 1989. Washington: GPO, 1990. 596 pp. Paper.

United States. Senate. Committee on Governmental Affairs. MISSING LINKS: COORDINATING FEDERAL DRUG POLICY FOR WOMEN, INFANTS, AND CHILDREN; HEARING, JULY 31, 1989. Washington: GPO, 1990. 154 pp.

United States. Senate. Committee on Governmental Affairs. Permanent Subcommittee on Investigations. COCAINE PRODUCTION, ERADICATION, AND THE ENVIRONMENT: POLICY, IMPACT AND OPTIONS; PROCEEDINGS OF A SEMINAR HELD BY THE CONGRESSIONAL RESEARCH SERVICE, FEBRUARY 14, 1990. Washington: GPO, 1990. 192 pp.

United States. Senate. Committee on Governmental Affairs. Permanent Subcommittee on Investigations. DRUGS AND VIOLENCE: THE CRIMINAL JUSTICE SYSTEM IN CRISIS; HEARINGS, PTS. 1-2, JUNE 26, 1989-MARCH 19, 1990. Washington: GPO, 1989/90. 2 pts.

United States. Senate. Committee on Governmental Affairs. Subcommittee on Federal Services, Post Office, and Civil Service. DRUG PROBLEMS IN ARKANSAS: THE STATE AND LOCAL RESPONSE; HEARING, JANUARY 17, 1990. Washington: GPO, 1990. 125 pp.

United States. Senate. Committee on Governmental Affairs. Subcommittee on General Services, Federalism, and the District of Columbia. FEDERAL, STATE, AND LOCAL SOLUTIONS TO DRUG ABUSE AND DRUG-RELATED CRIME: EDUCATION AND PREVENTION PROGRAMS FOR CHILDREN AND YOUTH; HEARING, SEPTEMBER 1, 1989. Washington: GPO, 1990. 91 pp.

United States. Senate. Committee on the Judiciary. HARD-CORE COCAINE ADDICTS: MEASURING—AND FIGHTING— THE EPIDEMIC: A STAFF REPORT, MAY 10, 1990. Washington: GPO, 1990. 37 pp.

United States. Senate. Committee on the Judiciary. INCARCERATION AND ALTER-NATIVE SANCTIONS FOR DRUG OFFENDERS: HEARING, JULY 25, 1989. Washington: GPO, 1990. 117 pp.

United States. Senate. Committee on the Judiciary. PHARMACOTHERAPY: A STRAT-EGY FOR THE 1990S: A STAFF REPORT, DECEMBER 13, 1989. Washington: GPO, 1989. 38 pp.

United States. Senate. Committee on Labor and Human Resources. DRUG CRISIS: TREATMENT AND PREVENTION; HEARING, AUGUST 3 AND OCTOBER 25, 1989. Washington: GPO, 1990. 208 pp.

United States. Senate. Committee on Labor and Human Resources. DRUG PREVEN-TION AND EDUCATION: HEARING, SEPTEMBER 26, 1989, ON EXAMINING THE ISSUES OF WHAT WORKS, WHAT FAILS AND WHAT THE FEDERAL GOVERNMENT SHOULD BE DOING TO COMBAT THIS NATIONAL SCOURGE. Washington: GPO, 1990. 83 pp.

United States. Senate. Committee on Labor and Human Resources. Subcommittee on Children, Family, Drugs, and Alcoholism. ADOLESCENT SUBSTANCE ABUSE: BARRIERS TO TREATMENT; HEARING, MAY 2, 1989, ON EXAMINING ALCO-HOL AND OTHER DRUG ABUSE TREATMENT OF ADOLESCENTS. Washing-ton: GPO, 1990. 117 pp.

Wadler, Gary I. DRUGS AND THE ATHLETE. F. A. Davis, 1989. 353 pp. $45.00. ISBN 0-8036-9008-8.

Wallace, LeAnn. COURT CASES INVOLVING DRUGS: OBSERVATIONS CONCERNING FUTURE VOLUME OF COURT CASES IN NORTH CAROLINA. Raleigh: Admin-istrative Office of the North Carolina Courts, 1989. 13 pp.

Webster, B. and J. G. Brown. MANDATORY AND RANDOM DRUG TESTING IN THE HONOLULU POLICE DEPARTMENT. Washington: NIJ, 1989. 8 pp.

Weisel, Deborah Lamm. TACKLING DRUG PROBLEMS IN PUBLIC HOUSING: A GUIDE FOR POLICE. Washington: Police Executive Research Forum, 1990. 138 pp.

Weisheit, R., ed. DRUGS, CRIME AND THE CRIMINAL JUSTICE SYSTEM. Cincinnati: Anderson Publishing Co., 1990. 405 pp. ISBN 0-87084-225-0.

Williams, Terry M. THE COCAINE KIDS: THE INSIDE STORY OF A TEENAGE DRUG RING. New York: Addison-Wesley, 1989. 140 pp. $16.95. ISBN 0-201-09360-X.

WOMEN'S RECOVERY PROGRAMS: A DIRECTORY OF RESIDENTIAL ADDICTION TREATMENT CENTERS. Phoenix: Oryx Press, 1990. 339 pp. $55.00 (paper). ISBN 0-89774-584-1.

Yoder, Barbara. THE RECOVERY RESOURCE BOOK. New York: Simon & Shuster, 1990. 314 pp. $12.95 (paper). ISBN 0-671-66873-0.

Zander, M. CONFISCATION AND FORFEITURE: ENGLISH AND AMERICAN COMPAR-ISONS. London: The Police Foundation, 1989. 61 pp. ISBN 0-947692-18-5.

DISSERTATIONS

Baker, Elizabeth Anne. THE CALVERT COUNTY STUDY: A PROGRAM EVALUATION OF DWI PROBATIONERS USE OF AN IN-CAR ALCOHOL BREATH ANALYZER IGNITION INTERLOCK SYSTEM. Ph.D. Dissertation, University of Maryland College Park, 1989. 147 pp.

Bartlett, Kerry Thomas. IMPERSISTENCE: PROBLEM-SOLVING DEFICITS IN AN ALCOHOLIC POPULATION. Ph.D. Dissertation, University of Iowa, 1988. 229 pp.

Berg, Steven Lorain. AA, SPIRITUAL ISSUES, AND THE TREATMENT OF LESBIAN AND GAY ALCOHOLICS. Ph.D. Dissertation, Michigan State University, 1989. 220 pp.

Caracci, O. Kathleen. AN ANALYSIS OF THE RELATIONSHIP AMONG SELECTED DEMOGRAPHIC VARIABLES, ALCOHOL KNOWLEDGE, ASSERTIVENESS, SELF-ESTEEM, FAMILY ALCOHOL BACKGROUND, GENERAL WELL-BEING, AND SELF-REPORTED ALCOHOL-RELATED BEHAVIOR OF PENNSYLVANIA NURSES. Ph.D. Dissertation, Pennsylvania State University, 1989. 186 pp.

Combs, Donald S. AN OCCUPATIONAL DRUG ABUSE STUDY. Ph.D. Dissertation, Union for Experimental Colleges and Universities, 1988. 401 pp.

Davidge, Anne M. THE RELATIONSHIP BETWEEN STRESS, COPING AND ADOLESCENT SUBSTANCE USE. Ph.D. Dissertation, University of South Carolina, 1989. 209 pp.

Gordon, A. N. THE EFFECTS OF DRUG USE AND PSYCHIATRIC STATUS ON INHOSPITAL AND POSTHOSPITAL ADJUSTMENT. DSW Dissertation, Columbia University, June 1990.

Graybeal, C. T. CHILDREN OF ALCOHOLICS: A CRITICAL ANALYSIS OF DEVELOPING THEORY. Ph.D. Dissertation, Rutgers University, May 1990.

Griffiths, Lynda May. PERSONALITY STYLES AND COPING STRATEGIES OF ALCOHOLIC MEN. Ph.D. Dissertation, University of Alberta, 1989.

Hall, John Mark. CHANGES IN ALCOHOLIC'S VERBAL AND FACIAL RECOGNITION DURING THE FIRST MONTH OF ABSTINENCE. Ph.D. Dissertation, Emory University, 1988. 81 pp.

Howard, M. O. AVERSION TREATMENT OF ALCOHOL DEPENDENCE WITH EMETINE HYDROCHLORIDE: STRENGTH OF CONDITIONING AND ITS RELATION TO FOLLOW-UP STATUS. Ph.D. Dissertation, University of Washington, June 1990.

LaBlance, Shaun Patrick. THE PSYCHOSOCIAL DEVELOPMENT OF PREFERENTIAL ABUSERS OF HEROIN OR COCAINE BASED ON ERIKSON'S DEVELOPMEN-TAL THEORY. Ph.D. Dissertation, Michigan State University, 1989. 181 pp.

Langley, Mervin John. DEVELOPMENT OF A COPING SKILL TREATMENT PRO-GRAMME FOR RELAPSE PREVENTION WITH ALCOHOLICS. D.Phil. Dissera-tion, University of South Africa, 1987.

Leonelli, Bernard Thomas. THE RELATIONSHIP BETWEEN ALCOHOLISM AND ALIENATION FROM FAMILY, RELIGION, AND ETHNIC GROUP. Ph.D. Disserta-tion, Hofstra University, 1989. 85 pp.

Maracle, Marilyn Frances. BEYOND ABSTINENCE: A STUDY OF RECOVERY AMONG WOMEN IN ALCOHOLICS ANONYMOUS. Ph.D. Dissertation, Washington Uni-versity, 1989. 286 pp.

Nofz, M. P. PERSONAL AND SOCIAL PERCEPTIONS OF COLLEGE DRINKING: IMPLI-CATIONS FOR ABUSE PREVENTION. Ph.D. Dissertation, University of Illinois at Urbana-Champaign, January 1990.

Rhodes, Jean Edit. AN EMPIRICAL ANALYSIS OF ADOLESCENT SUBSTANCE ABUSE: A FURTHER INVESTIGATION OF THE RETROSPECTIVE PRETEST AND AN EXAMINATION OF THE SOCIAL STRESS MODEL USING STRUC-TURAL EQUATION MODELLING. Ph.D. Dissertation, DePaul University, 1988. 176 pp.

Robertson, Bozena-Eva. LIFE EXPERIENCES OF ADULT DAUGHTERS OF ALCO-HOLICS: A QUALITATIVE STUDY. Ph.D. Dissertation, Syracuse University, 1989. 212 pp.

Rohrbach, Louise Ann. DISSEMINATION OF SCHOOL-BASED SUBSTANCE ABUSE PREVENTION PROGRAMS: PREDICTORS OF PROGRAM IMPLEMENTATION. Ph.D. Dissertation, University of Southern California, 1989.

Segars, L. B. SOCIAL SUPPORT AND STRESSORS AS PREDICTORS OF ALCOHOL PROBLEM RECOVERY. Ph.D. Dissertation, University of Pittsburgh, 1989.

Thomas, Tania N. A CROSS-CULTURAL ANALYSIS OF ALCOHOLISM AND SOCIAL ALIENATION IN PANAMA AND THE UNITED STATES. Ph.D. Dissertation, Hofs-tra University, 1989. 179 pp.

PERIODICAL LITERATURE

ACETAMINOPHEN
see also: Paracetamol

Acetaminophen hepatotoxicity in the alcoholic, by F. T. Wootton, et al. SOCIAL SCIENCE AND MEDICINE 83(9):1047-1049, September 1990

Effect of posture on intracranial pressure and cerebral perfusion pressure in patients with fulinant hepatic and renal failure after acetaminophen self-poisoning, by A. Davenport, et al. CRITICAL CARE MEDICINE 18(3):286-289, March 1990

Epidemiological studies of the frequency of the abuse of analgesics, by T. Mohr, et al. DEUTSCHE MEDIZINISCHE WOCHENSCHRIFT 115(4):129-132, Janaury 26, 1990

Identifying the acetaminophen overdose, by W. A. Watson. ANNALS OF EMERGENCY MEDICINE 18(10):1126-1127, October 1989

Research
Hepatoxicity evaluation in rats given a single overdose of acetaminophen (paracetamol), by E. O. Udosen, et al. CENTRAL AFRICAN JOURNAL OF MEDICINE 35(10):495-496, October 1989

ADDICTION RESEARCH FOUNDATION *see*: ARF

ADVERTISING
Antidrug ads for dope fiends, by C. Holden. SCIENCE 250:1202, November 30, 1990

Tele-direct publications to give $3M in anti-drug advertising space in *Yellow Pages* directories. MARKETING 95(27):2, July 2, 1990

United States TV addicted to drug commericals, by T. Wood. MARKETING 95:20, April 30, 1990

AGING AND THE AGED

Abuse of alcohol and drugs in homes for the aged, by H. J. Luderer, et al. FORT-SCHRITTE DER MEDIZIN 108(9):176-177, March 30, 1990

Are you an unwitting addict: you may be if you are not careful when using prescription and over-the-counter medication, by S. Curson. GOOD TIMES 1(9):32-34, October 1990

Can overuse of psychotropic drugs by the elderly be prevented?, by R. W. Lyndon, et al. AUSTRALIAN AND NEW ZEALAND JOURNAL OF PSYCHIATRY 24(1):77-81, March 1990

How to diagnosis and treat chemical dependency in the elderly, by L. K. Johnson. JOURNAL OF GERONTOLOGICAL NURSING 15(12):22-26, December 1989

Interdisciplinary treatment of drug misuse among older people of color: ethnic considerations for social work practice, by P. R. Raffoul, et al. JOURNAL OF DRUG ISSUES 19(2):297-313, Spring 1989

Nutritional implications of medication use and misuse in elderly, by M. C. Cook, et al. JOURNAL OF THE FLORIDA MEDICAL ASSOCIATION 77(6):606-613, June 1990

Patient age as a factor in drug prescribing practices, by J. A. Ferguson. CANADIAN JOURNAL OF AGING 9(3):278-295, Autumn 1990

Patient-phyician communications as a determination of medication misuse in older, minority women, by T. F. Garrity, et al. JOURNAL OF DRUG ISSUES 19(2):245-259, Spring 1989

Portrayal of the elderly in drug advertisements: a factor in inappropriate prescribing, by J. Lexchin. CANADIAN JOURNAL OF AGING 9(3):296-303, Autumn 1990

Social emergencies in the elderly, by A. J. McDonald, et al. EMERGENCY MEDICINE CLINICS OF NORTH AMERICA 8(2):443-459, May 1990

Testing drugs in older people, by J. Folkenberg. FDA CONSUMER 24:24-27, November 1990

AIDS (ACQUIRED IMMUNE DEFICIENCY SYNDROME)

Abdominal and anorectal surgery and the acquired immune deficiency syndrome in heterosexual intravenous drug users, by A. F. Wolkomir, et al. DISEASES OF THE COLON AND RECTUM 33(4):267-270, April 1990

Addicted with AIDS: seeing beyond the label, by P. Scherer. NONVIOLENT ACTIVIST 7(5):9, July 1990

Administrative challenges to working with HIV-positive clients: experiences in Florida, by M. G. Dow, et al. JOURNAL OF MENTAL HEALTH ADMINISTRATION 16(2):80-90, Fall 1989

After the epidemic: follow up study of HIV seroprevalence and changing patterns of drug use, by C. A. Skidmore, et al. BMJ 300(6719):219-233, January 27, 1990

AIDS and chemical dependency: special issues and treatment barriers for gay and bi-sexual men, by R. P. Cabaj. JOURNAL OF PSYCHOACTIVE DRUGS 21(4):387-393, October/December 1989

AIDS and cocaine: a deadly combination facing the primary care physician, by S. P. Weinstein, et al. JOURNAL OF FAMILY PRACTICE 31(3):253-254, September 1990

AIDS and drug abuse: some aspects of psychiatric consultation, by A. Musacchio de Zan, et al. MEDICINE AND LAW 8(2):119-123, 1989

AIDS and the future, by J. Palca. SCIENCE 248(4962):1484, June 22, 1990

AIDS and intravenous drug abuse, by C. Schuster, et al. NIDA RESEARCH MONO-GRAPH SERIES 90:1-13, 1988

AIDS and intravenous drug use, by J. A. Inciardi. AMERICAN BEHAVIORAL SCIEN-TIST 33:397-502, March/April 1990; also in JOURNAL OF DRUG ISSUES 20(2):179-347, Spring 1990

AIDS and the IV drug users in the criminal justice system, by D. C. McBride, et al. JOURNAL OF DRUG ISSUES 20(2):267-280, Spring 1990

AIDS and the social relations of intravenous drug users, by S. R. Friedman, et al. MIL-BANK QUARTERLY 68(Suppl)1:85-100, 1990

AIDS in New York City: the role of intravenous drug users, by A. Ron, et al. BULLETIN OF THE NEW YORK ACADEMY OF MEDICINE 65(7):787-800, September 1989

AIDS-related illness and AIDS risk in male homo-bisexual substance abusers: case reports and clinical issues, by J. Westermeyer, et al. AMERICAN JOURNAL OF DRUG AND ALCOHOL ABUSE 15(4):443-461, December 1989

AIDS-related risk behaviors among substance abusers, by G. Ottomanelli, et al. IN-TERNATIONAL JOURNAL OF THE ADDICTIONS 25(3):291-300, 1990

Anti-cardiolipin antibodies and HIV infection, by C. Maclean, et al. CLINICAL AND EX-PERIMENTAL IMMUNOLOGY 81(2):263-266, 1990

Anti-HIV and anti-HBc antibodies and HBsAg in postmortem blood of drug addicts: the picture for 1988, by P. Tappero, et al. PANMINERVA MEDICA 31(3):137-139, July/September 1989

Are injectors' HIV rates stabilizing?, by H. McConnell. JOURNAL OF THE ADDICTION RESEARCH FOUNDATION 19(11):2, January 1, 1990

Are "sex-for-drugs" exchanges accelerating the risk of AIDS? OHIO MEDICINE 86(5):346, May 1990

Bacteriological findings in patients affected by HIV, by M. T. Mascellino, et al. BOL-LETTINO DELL ISTITUTO SIEROTERAPICO MILANESE 68(3):271-276, 1989

Being positive: drug injectors' experiences of HIV infection, by N. McKeganey. BRI-TISH JOURNAL OF ADDICTION 85(9):1113-1124, 1990

Beliefs about AIDS, use of alcohol and drugs, and unprotected sex among Massachusetts adolescents, by R. W. Hingson, et al. AMERICAN JOURNAL OF PUBLIC HEALTH 80(3):295-299, March 1990

Buspirone in drug users with AIDS or AIDS-related complex, by S. L. Batki. JOURNAL OF CLINICAL PSYCHOPHARMACOLOGY 10(Suppl)3:111-15, June 1990

Cardiac surgery in human immunodeficiency virus (HIV) carriers, by R. W. Frater, et al. EUROPEAN JOURNAL OF CARDIO-THORACIC SURGERY 3(2):146-150, 1989

Characterization of AIDS-associated tumors in Italy: report of 435 cases of an IVDA-based series, by S. Monfardini, et al. CANCER DETECTION AND PREVENTION 14(3):391-393, 1990

Chondrocostal and chondrosternal tuberculosis in 2 heroin addicts infected with the human immunodeficiency virus, by J. A. Martos, et al. MEDICINA CLINICA 93(12):467-470, October 21, 1989

Cocaine abuse and acquired immunodeficiency syndrome: a tale of two epidemics, by W. D. Lerner. AMERICAN JOURNAL OF MEDICINE 87(6):661-663, December 1989

Cocaine-HIV alert is raised in study, by K. Fournis. JOURNAL OF THE ADDICTION RESEARCH FOUNDATION 19(12):1, December 1, 1990

Cofactors of progression to acquired immunodeficiency syndrome in a cohort of male sexual contacts of men with human immunodeficiency virus disease, by R. A. Coates, et al. AMERICAN JOURNAL OF EPIDEMIOLOGY 132(4):717-722, October 1990

Comment on Stimson's "AIDS and HIV": AIDS and HIV— the way forward, by D. Black. BRITISH JOURNAL OF ADDICTION 85(3):350-351, March 1990

Comment on Stimson's "AIDS and HIV": British drug services re-opening under new paradigm, by D. C. Drummond. BRITISH JOURNAL OF ADDICTION 85(3):341-342, March 1990

Comment on Stimson's "AIDS and HIV": HIV and AIDS—a clinician's response, by J. Strang. BRITISH JOURNAL OF ADDICTION 85(3):344-348, March 1990

Comment on Stimson's "AIDS and HIV": the public health paradigm for AIDS and drug use—shifting the time frame, by D. C. des Jarlais, et al. BRITISH JOURNAL OF ADDICTION 85(3):348-350, March 1990

Contrasting prevalence of delta hepatitis markers in parenteral drug abusers with and without AIDS, by M. J. Kreek, et al. JOURNAL OF INFECTIOUS DISEASES 162(2):538-541, August 1990

Coping with AIDS: strategies for patients and staff in drug abuse treatment programs, by J. L. Sorensen, et al. JOURNAL OF PSYCHOACTIVE DRUGS 21(4):435-440, October/December 1989

Crack users: the new AIDS risk group, by R. E. Fullilove, et al. CANCER DETECTION AND PREVENTION 14(3):363-368, 1990

Current epidemiology of AIDS among i.v. drug users in New York City, by D. Des Jar lais. NIDA RESEARCH MONOGRAPH SERIES 90:311-313, 1988

Demographic, behavioral and clinical features of HIV infection in New York City intra- venous drug abusers, by L. S. Brown, Jr., et al. NIDA RESEARCH MONOGRAPH SERIES 95:413-414, 1989

Does fear of AIDS affect behavior of addicts?, by R. S. Schottenfield, et al. NIDA RE- SEARCH MONOGRAPH SERIES 95:411-412, 1989

Drug injecting and syringe sharing in custody and in the community: an exploratory survey of HIV risk behaviour, by K. A. Dolan, et al. HOWARD JOURNAL 29:177- 186, August 1990

Drug use and the risk of AIDS, by C. B. McCoy, et al. AMERICAN BEHAVIORAL SCI- ENTIST 33(4):419-431, March/April 1990

Drugs, sex, and AIDS risk: cocaine users versus opiate users, by D. D. Chitwood, et al. AMERICAN BEHAVIOR SCIENTIST 33:465-477, March/April 1990

Dual HIV-1-HIV-2 reactivity in Italian i.v. drug abusers re-evaluated by synthetic pep- tide spot-test, by P. Ferroni, et al. EUROPEAN JOURNAL OF EPIDEMIOLOGY 5(4):534-535, December 1989

Edinburgh cohort of HIV-positive drug users: current intellectual function is impaired, but not due to early AIDS dementia complex, by V. G. Egan, et al. AIDS 4(7):651- 656, July 1990

Effect of the revised AIDS case definition on AIDS reporting in San Francisco: evi- dence of increased reporting in intravenous drug users, by S. F. Payne, et al. AIDS 4(4):335-339, April 1990

Elevated levels of CD4 antigen in sera of human immunodeficiency virus-infected populations, by M. M. Reddy, et al. JOURNAL OF CLINICAL MICROBIOLOGY 28(8):1744-1746, 1990

Epidemiology of reported cases of AIDS in lesbians: United States, 1980-1989, by S. Y. Chu, et al. AMERICAN JOURNAL OF PUBLIC HEALTH 80:1380-1381, November 1990

Ethnopharmacology: an interdisciplinary approach to the study of intravenous drug use and HIV, by J. Johnson. JOURNAL OF CONTEMPORARY ETHNOGRAPHY 19:3249-369, October 1990

European patterns of alcohol use on AIDS and drug abuse, Stockholm 25-28 Sep- tember 1989, by E. Segest. UGESKRIFT FOR LAEGER 152(6):406, February 5, 1990

Evaluation of a hospital based substance abuse intervention and referral service for HIV affected patients, by J. Guydish, et al. GENERAL HOSPITAL PSYCHIATRY 12(1):1-7, January 1990

Evidence of HIV-2 infection in parenteral drug addicts in the province of Malaga, by F. M. Gomez Trujillo, et al. MINERVA MEDICA 94(13):517-518, April 7, 1990

Evidence of infection by type 2 (HIV-2) human immunodeficiency virus in heroin addicts in Barcelona, by V. Soriano, et al. MEDICINA CLINICA 93(6):204-206, September 9, 1989

Examination of drug addicts on methadone treatment: HIV antibodies in the county of Frederiksborg, by P. P. Ege. UGESKRIFT FOR LAEGER 151(51):3484-3486, December 18, 1989

Fourth Okey Memorial Lecture: AIDS and HIV—the challenge for British drug services, by G. V. Stimson. BRITISH JOURNAL OF ADDICTION 85(3):329-339, March 1990

Generational differences in HIV risk and AIDS, by D. C. McBride. AMERICAN BEHAVIORAL SCIENTIST 33(4):491-502, March/April 1990

Government approves report on AIDS and drug misuse. RADIOGRAPHY TODAY 55(631):7, December 1989

Heterosexual behaviour of intravenous drug users in Amsterdam: implications for the AIDS epidemic, by A. van den Hoek, et al. AIDS 4(5):449-453, May 1990

Heterosexual HIV-infection in Denmark: observations from a department for infectious diseases, by E. Smith, et al. UGESKRIFT FOR LAEGER 152(23):1668-1670, 1990

High *staphylococcus aureus* nasal carriage rate in patients with acquired immunodeficiency syndrome or AIDS-related complex, by M. C. Raviglione, et al. AMERICAN JOURNAL OF INFECTION CONTROL 18(2):64-69, 1990

HIV, AIDS and intravenous drug use: some considerations, by J. A. Inciardi. JOURNAL OF DRUG ISSUES 20(2):181-194, Spring 1990

HIV-AIDS in prisons, by P. A. Thomas. HOWARD JOURNAL OF CRIMINAL JUSTICE 29(1):1-13, February 1990

HIV, drugs, and ecology, by S. Blower, et al. SCIENCE 246(4935):1236, December 8, 1989

HIV in intravenous drug users. NEW ENGLAND JOURNAL OF MEDICINE 322(9): 632-633, March 1, 1990

HIV infected hospital patients in New York State, USA: the development of longitudinal information from a hospital discharge data system, by G. I. Kaufman, et al. NEW YORK STATE JOURNAL OF MEDICINE 90(5):238-242, 1990

HIV-infected i.v. drug users in methadone treatment: outcome and psychological correlates: a preliminary report, by S. L. Batki, et al. NIDA RESEARCH MONOGRAPH SERIES 95:405-406, 1989

HIV infection and drug users: setting up support groups, by G. Mulleady, et al. COUNSELLING PSYCHOLOGY QUARTERLY 2(1):53-57, 1989

HIV infection and intravenous drug users: implications for emergency services, by G. D. Kelen, et al. EMERGENCY MEDICINE CLINICS OF NORTH AMERICA 8(3): 653-664, August 1990

HIV infection in the general population from various areas of the Veneto Region, Italy, by L. Majori, et al. IGIENE MODERNA 94(1):90-98, 1990

HIV infection in intravenous drug abusers in Berlin, West Germany: risk factors and time trends, by K. Stark, et al. KLINISCHE WOCHENSCHRIFT 68(8):415-420, April 17, 1990

HIV infection in patients attending clinics for sexually transmitted diseases in England and Wales: United Kingdom, 1988, by S. Polakoff. GENITOURINARY MEDICINE 66(2):57-61, 1990

HIV infection, race, and drug-treatment history, by J. K. Watters, et al. AIDS 4(7):697, July 1990

HIV-positive intravenous drug abuser, by G. C. O'Rourke. AMERICAN JOURNAL OF OCCUPATIONAL THERAPY 44(3):280-283, March 1990

HIV prevalence in blood donors in urban and in rural areas of West Germany, by D. Glueck, et al. BLUT 60(5):304-307, 1990

HIV-related behaviour among a non-clinic sample of injecting drug users, by N. McKeganey, et al. BRITISH JOURNAL OF ADDICTION 84(12):1481-1490, December 1989

HIV-related risk-taking behavior, knowledge and serostatus of intravenous drug users in Sydney, Australia, by J. Wolk, et al. MEDICAL JOURNAL OF AUSTRALIA 152(9):453-458, May 7, 1990

HIV seropositivity in a Yugoslav prison population, by Z. Radovanovic, et al. JOURNAL OF HYGIENE, EPIDEMIOLOGY, MICROBIOLOGY AND IMMUNOLOGY 34(1):7-29, 1990

HIV seropositivity of needles from shooting galleries in south Forida, by D. D. Chitwood, et al. AMERICAN JOURNAL OF PUBLIC HEALTH 80(2):150-152, February 1990

HIV seroprevalence among male IVDUs in Houston, Texas, by M. L. Williams. AMERICAN JOURNAL OF PUBLIC HEALTH 80:1507-1509, December 1990

HIV spread among drug addicts in the Federal Republic of Germany, by W. Kindermann. BRITISH JOURNAL OF ADDICTION 84(11):1372-1373, November 1989

HIV transmission and risk behavior among drug addicts at a treatment institution in Copenhagen: Klub 47, by P. P. Ege. UGESKRIFT FOR LAEGER 151(51):3482-3484, December 18, 1989

HIV-1 and AIDS in Belle Glade, Florida: a reexamination of the issues, by E. J. Trapido, et al. AMERICAN BEHAVIORAL SCIENTIST 33(4):451-464, March/April 1990

HIV-1 primo-infection and cytomegalovirus reactivation in two intravenous drug users: prognostic significance, by J. P. Routy, et al. ANNALES DE MEDECINE INTERNE 141(2):194-195, 1990

HIV-1-related and nonrelated diseases among IV drug users and sexual partners, by E. J. Trapido, et al. JOURNAL OF DRUG ISSUES 20(2):245-266, Spring 1990

HIV-2 and AIDS in Belle Glade, Florida: a reexamination of the issues, by E. J. Trapido, et al. AMERICAN BEHAVIORAL SCIENTIST 33(4):451-464, 1990

Homeless intravenous drug abuser and the AIDS epidemic, by H. Joseph, et al. NIDA RESEARCH MONOGRAPH SERIES 93:210-253, 1990

HTLV-I-II seropositivity and death from AIDS among HIV-1 seropositive intravenous drug users, by J. B. Page, et al. LANCET 355(8703):1439-1441, June 16, 1990

Human immunodeficiency virus and viral hepatitis seroepidemiology in New York City intravenous drug abusers, by L. S. Brown, Jr., et al. NIDA RESEARCH MONO-GRAPH SERIES 95:443-444, 1989

Human immunodeficiency virus in drug misusers and increased consultation in general practice, by J. J. Roberts, et al. JOURNAL OF THE ROYAL COLLEGE OF GENERAL PRACTITIONERS 39(326):373-374, September 1989

Human immunodeficiency virus infection in a Dublin general practice, by G. Bury, et al. JOURNAL OF THE ROYAL COLLEGE OF GENERAL PRACTITIONERS 39(320):101-103, March 1989

Human immunodeficiency virus infection in tuberculosis patients, by C. P. Theuer, et al. JOURNAL OF INFECTIOUS DISEASES 162(1):8-12, 1990

If I have sex with a duck does that make me a drake: the Albion Street AIDS Centre, intravenous drug use and prostitution, by B. Donovan, et al. MEDICAL JOURNAL OF AUSTRALIA 152(9):498-499, May 7, 1990

Impact of AIDS on Puerto Rican intravenous drug users, by M. Sufian, et al. HISPANIC JOURNAL OF BEHAVIORAL SCIENCES 12(2):122-134, May 1990

Injecting drug use, HIV and AIDS, by G. J. Hart. AIDS CARE 1(3):237-245, 1989

Intra-arterial injection of oral medication of HIV positive drug addicts, by P. A. Stonebridge, et al. BRITISH JOURNAL OF SURGERY 77(3):333-334, March 1990

Intravenous drug abuse and the HIV epidemic in two midwestern cities: a preliminary report—Dayton and Columbus, by H. A. Siegal. JOURNAL OF DRUG ISSUES 20(2):281-290, Spring 1990

Intravenous drug use and AIDS, by J. K. Watters, et al. JOURNAL OF DRUG ISSUES 19:1-162, Winter 1989

Intravenous drug users who present to the Albion Street AIDS Centre for diagnosis and management of human immunodeficiency virus infection, by A. Morlet, et al. MEDICAL JOURNAL OF AUSTRALIA 152(2):78-80, January 15, 1990

Introduction of HIV infection among intravenous drug abusers in low prevalence areas, by R. J. Battjes, et al. JOURNAL OF THE ACQUIRED IMMUNE DEFICIENCY SYNDROME 2(6):533-539, 1989

Investigation into support for restrictions on HIV carriers in the Chicago, Illinois, USA, metropolitan area, by R. L. Goldsteen, et al. REVISTA DE SAUDE PUBLICA 24(1):28-38, 1990

Issues in the clinical management of intravenous drug users with HIV infection, by P. A. Selwyn. AIDS 3(Suppl)1:201-208, 1989

Iv drug use and HIV infection: perspective from a small city, by P. M. Ford, et al. CMAJ 142(5):469-471, March 1, 1990

Let the debate begin: status of IVDA's with AIDS, by R. Aquila. AMERICAN JOURNAL OF PSYCHOTHERAPY 44(1):155-156, January 1990

Liver biopsies in the acquired immune deficiency syndrome: influence of endemic disease and drug abuse, by G. M. Comer, et al. AMERICAN JOURNAL OF GASTROENTEROLOGY 84(12):1525-1531, December 1989

Low incidence of bleeding from HIV-related thrombocytopenia in drug addicts and hemophiliacs: implications for therapeutic strategies, by G. Finazzi, et al. EUROPEAN JOURNAL OF HAEMATOLOGY 45(2):82-85, 1990

Low prevalence in Apulia, southern Italy, of HTLV 1 infection in drug addicts during 1986-1988, by M. Quarto, et al. EUROPEAN JOURNAL OF EPIDEMIOLOGY 5(3):405-406, September 1989

Methadone maintenance programmes and AIDS, by D. Serraino, et al. LANCET 2(8678-8679):1522-1523, December 23-30, 1989

Misinformation and manipulation: politics of AIDS, by J. Peacott. ANARCHY (24):14, March 1990

Mode of HIV transmission among seroconverted intravenous drug users (IVDUs): 1987 and 1988 cohort study, by T. Nemoto, et al. NIDA RESEARCH MONOGRAPH SERIES 95:407-408, 1989

Neurologic complications of HIV infection and drug abuse. ARCHIVOS DE NEUROBIOLOGIA 52(Suppl)1:1-194, 1989

Neurologic disease in human immunodeficiency virus-infected drug abusers, by R. Malouf, et al. ARCHIVES OF NEUROLOGY 47(9):1002-1007, September 1990

New York and AIDS: the politics of disease, by D. Lazare. IN THESE TIMES 14(23):3, May 2, 1990

Nutritional status assessment of HIV-positive drug addicts, by P. Varela, et al. EUROPEAN JOURNAL OF CLINICAL NUTRITION 44(5):415-418, May 1990

On the structure of the epidemic spread of AIDS: the influence of an infectious coagent, by J. Weyer, et al. INTERNATIONAL JOURNAL OF MEDICAL MICROBIOLOGY 273(1):52-67, May 1990

Perinatal outcome in HIV-infected pregnant women, by A. E. Semprini, et al. GYNECOLOGIC AND OBSTETRIC INVESTIGATION 30(1):15-18, 1990

Prevalence of hepatitis B virus, delta agent and human immunodeficiency virus infections in drug addicts, by D. Bailly, et al. BIOMEDICINE AND PHARMACOTHERAPY 43(6):431-437, 1989

Prevalence of HIV in normal and at risk population: seroepidemiological investigation during two years, by G. Barbarini, et al. BOLLETTINO DELL INSTITUTO SIERO-TERAPICO MILANESE 68(1):51-56, 1989

Prevalence of HIV-1 among deaths connected with drug abuse in various West German cities and in West Berlin between 1985 and 1988, by K. Pueschel, et al. ZEITSCHRIFT FUR RECHTSMEDIZIN 103(6):407-414, 1990

Prevalence of HIV-1 infection in intravenous drug dependent patients 1986 to 1989 in Vienna, by N. Loimer, et al. WIENER KLINISCHE WOCHENSCHRIFT 102(4): 106-110, February 16, 1990

Re: an autopsy of epidemiologic methods—the case of "poppers" in the early epidemic of the acquired immunodeficiency syndrome (AIDS). AMERICAN JOURNAL OF EPIDEMIOLOGY 131(1):195-200, January 1990

Regional variations in HIV seroprevalence among injecting drug users in Italy, by G. Rezza. REVUE D'EPIDEMIOLOGIE ET DE SANTE PUBLIQUE 38(3):263-264, 1990

Relationship of cocaine use to syphilis and human immunodeficiency virus infections among inner city parturient women, by H. L. Minkoff, et al. AMERICAN JOURNAL OF OBSTETRICS AND GYNECOLOGY 163(2):521-526, August 1990

Renal involvement in patients infected with HIV: experience at San Francisco, California, USA, general hospital, by S. A. Mazbar, et al. KIDNEY INTERNATIONAL 37(5):1325-1332, 1990

Risk behaviors and perceptions of AIDS among street injection drug users, by F. Rhodes, et al. JOURNAL OF DRUG EDUCATION 20(4):271-288, 1990

Risk behaviors for HIV transmission among intravenous-drug users not in drug treatment: United States, 1987-1989. MMWR 39(16):273-276, April 27, 1990

Risk behaviour and HTLV-1 seropositivity in injecting drug user, by G. Rezza, et al. BRITISH JOURNAL OF ADDICTION 85(5):686-687, May 1990

Risk behaviours of HIV infection among drug users in prison, by A. L. Carvell, et al. BMJ 300(6736):1383-1384, May 26, 1990

Risk factors for human immunodeficiency virus infection among parenteral drug abusers in a low-prevalence area, by P. H. Chandrasekar, et al. SOUTHERN MEDICAL JOURNAL 83(9):996-1001, September 1990

Risk of AIDS in HIV seroconverters: a comparison between intravenous drug users and homosexual males, by G. Rezza, et al. EUROPEAN JOURNAL OF EPIDEMIOLOGY 6(1):99-101, March 1990

Role of intravenous drug use in cases of AIDS in adolescents and young adults, by H. Gayle. NIDA RESEARCH MONOGRAPH SERIES 90:314-315, 1988

Routine human immunodeficiency virus infection screening of woman requesting induced first-trimester abortion in an inner-city population, by M. K. Lindsay, et al. OBSTETRICS AND GYNECOLOGY 76(3 Pt 1):347-350, 1990

Sex, drugs, and HIV infection in a New York City hospital outpatient population, by M. Marmor, et al. JOURNAL OF THE ACQUIRED IMMUNE DEFICIENCY SYNDRME 3(4):307-318, 1990

Sexual behavior and the risk of HIV infection, by H. V. McCoy. AMERICAN BEHAV- IORAL SCIENTIST 33(4):432-450, March/April 1990

Sexual behavior of intravenous drug users: assessing the risk of sexual transmission of HIV, by T. E. Feucht, et al. JOURNAL OF DRUG EDUCATION 20:195-213, Spring 1990

Sexual behaviour of injecting drug users and associated risks of HIV infection for non- injecting sexual partners, by M. C. Donoghoe, et al. AIDS CARE 1(1):51-58, 1989

Sexual partners of injecting drug users: the risk of HIV infection, by H. Klee, et al. BRITISH JOURNAL OF ADDICTION 85(3):413-418, March 1990

Shooting galleries and AIDS: infection probabilities and "tough" policies, by D. C. Des Jarlais, et al. AMERICAN JOURNAL OF PUBLIC HEALTH 80:142-144, February 1990

Shooting scenarios and risk of HIV-1 infection, by J. B. Page. AMERICAN BEHAV- IORAL SCIENTIST 33(4):478-490, March/April 1990

Silent HIV infection in heterosexual partners of seropositive drug abusers in Spain, by V. Soriano, et al. LANCET 335(8693):860, April 7, 1990

Stress and emotional distress as possible co-factors in the development of AIDS in a sample intravenous drug users, by V. Catan. NIDA RESEACH MONOGRAPH SERIES 95:445-446, 1989

Tuberculin skin reactivity in HIV-seropositive intravenous drug addicts, by C. F. Robert, et al. NEW ENGLAND JOURNAL OF MEDICINE 321(18):1268, Novem- ber 2, 1989

Tuberculosis, AIDS and i.v. drug abuse, by R. J. Lamb, et al. NEW JERSEY MEDI- CINE 87(56):413-415, May 1990

When IV drug abuse complicates AIDS, by D. Schmitz. RN 53:60-67, January 1990

Education
AIDS and drug use: breaking the link: Citizens Commission on AIDS for New York City and northern New Jersey, by C. Levin. AIDS EDUCATION AND PREVENTION 1(3):231-246, Fall 1989

AIDS education and prevention programs for intravenous drug users: the California experience, by M. Jang, et al. JOURNAL OF DRUG EDUCATION 20(1):1-13, 1990

AIDS education for the IV drug abusers: the challenge for the nineties, by M. B. Ayres, et al. NATIONAL SHERIFF 41(4):54+, August/September 1989

AIDS education in the therapeutic community: implementation and results among high-risk clients and staff, by R. P. Galea, et al. INTERNATIONAL JOURNAL OF THERAPEUTIC COMMUNITIES 9(1):9-16, 1988

AIDS intervention design for program evaluation: the Miami Community Outreach Project, by H. V. McCoy, et al. JOURNAL OF DRUG ISSUES 20(2):223-243, Spring 1990

AIDS-related knowledge, attitudes and behaviour in injection drug users attending a Toronto treatment facility, by M. Millson, et al. CANADIAN JOURNAL OF PUBLIC HEALTH 81(1):46-49, January/February 1990

Behavioural changes in intravenous drug users in Geneva: rise and fall of HIV infection: 1980-1989, by C. F. Robert, et al. AIDS 4(7):657-660, July 1990

Changes in AIDS risk behavior among intravenous drug abusers in New York City, by R. E. Harris, et al. NEW YORK STATE JOURNAL OF MEDICINE 90(3):123-126, March 1990

Drug and AIDS education for Australian youth: the Get Real Project, by A. Wodak, et al. HYGIE 9(2):8-11, June 1990

Drug users' AIDS-related knowledge, attitudes, and behaviors before and after AIDS education sessions, by L. Dengelegi, et al. PUBLIC HEALTH REPORTS 105: 504-510, September/October 1990

Dynamics of black mobilization against AIDS in New York City, by E. Quimby, et al. SOCIAL PROBLEMS 36:413-415, October 1989

Fear of AIDS and risk reduction among heroin-addicted female street prostitutes: personal interviews with 72 southern California subjects, by D. J. Bellis. JOURNAL OF ALCOHOL AND DRUG EDUCATION 35:26-37, Spring 1990

Sexual behavior and knowledge about AIDS in a group of young adolescent girls in Leeds, England, United Kingdom, by J. Clarke, et al. GENITOURINARY MEDICINE 66(3):189-192, 1990

Prevention

African-American youth and AIDS high-risk behavior: the social context and barriers to prevention, by B. P. Bowser, et al. YOUTH AND SOCIETY 22:54-66, September 1990

AIDS, addiction and condom use: sources of sexual risk for heterosexual women, by S. Kane. JOURNAL OF SEX RESEARCH 27:427-444, August 1990

AIDS and chemical dependency: prevention needs of adolescents, by M. Hochhauser. JOURNAL OF PSYCHOACTIVE DRUGS 21(4):381-385, October/ December 1989

AIDS and HIV: the challenge for British drug services—paper delivered as *The Fourth Thomas James Okey Memorial Lecture* at the Institute of Psychiatry, London, May 25, 1989, by G. V. Stimson. BRITISH JOURNAL OF ADDICTION 85(3):329-339, 1990

AIDS and intravenous drug use: future directions for community-based prevention research. NIDA RESEARCH MONOGRAPH SERIES 1-299, 1990

AIDS prevention and chemical dependence treatment needs of women and their children, by L. D. Karan. JOURNAL OF PSYCHOACTIVE DRUGS 21(4):395-399, October/December 1989

AIDS prevention for intravenous drug users in the community: street-based education and risk behavior, by J. K. Watters, et al. AMERICAN JOURNAL OF COMMUNITY PSYCHOLOGY 18(4):587-596, August 1990

AIDS prevention for i.v. drug users and their sexual partners in Philadelphia, by J. Liebman, et al. AMERICAN JOURNAL OF PUBLIC HEALTH 80(5):615-616, May 1990

AIDS prevention programs for intravenous drug users: diversity and evolution, by D. C. des Jarlais, et al. INTERNATIONAL REVIEW OF PSYCHIATRY 1(1-2):101-108, March 1989

AIDS prevention: the role of the pharmacist. JOURNAL OF ADVANCED NURSING 15(7):761, July 1990

AIDS watch: offering alternatives to drugs, by N. Freudenberg. HEALTH PAC BULLETIN 20(1):35, Spring 1990

Behavioral risk factors of human immunodeficiency virus infection among intravenous drug users and implications for preventive interventions, by T. Nemoto, et al. AIDS EDUCATION AND PREVENTION 2(2):116-126, Summer 1990

Black intravenous drug users: prospects for intervening in the transmission of human immunodeficiency virus infection, by L. S. Brown, Jr. NIDA RESEARCH MONOGRAPH SERIES 93:53-67, 1990

Brief counseling to reduce AIDS risk in intravenous drug users and their sexual partners: preliminary results, by D. R. Gibson, et al. COUNSELLING PSYCHOLOGY QUARTERLY 2(1):15-19, 1989

Changing behaviour to prevent the spread of the human immunodeficiency virus, by R. Borland, et al. MEDICAL JOURNAL OF AUSTRALIA 151(6):305-306, September 18, 1989

Community-based AIDS prevention interventions: special issues of women intravenous drug users, by J. Mondanaro. NIDA RESEARCH MONOGRAPH SERIES 93:68-82, 1990

Community pharmacies and prevention of AIDS among injecting drug users, by D. S. Sloan. BMJ 299(6714):1525-1526, December 16, 1989

Community prevention efforts to reduce the spread of AIDS associated with intravenous drug abuse, by R. J. Battjes, et al. NIDA RESEARCH MONOGRAPH SERIES 93:288-299, 1990

Coupon program: drug treatment and AIDS education, by J. F. Jackson, et al. INTERNATIONAL JOURNAL OF THE ADDICTIONS 24(11):1035-1051, November 1989

Designing interventions to prevent HIV-1 infection by promoting use of condoms and spermicides among intravenous drug abusers and their sexual partners, by A. J. Stone, et al. AIDS EDUCATION AND PREVENTION 1(3):171-183, Fall 1989

DMI-measured defenses and HIV-related risk behaviors in i.v. compared to non-i.v. substances abusers, by G. Ottomanelli, et al. JOURNAL OF SUBSTANCE ABUSE TREATMENT 6(4):251-256, 1989

Epidemiology and prevention of AIDS among intravenous drug users, by R. A. Coutinho. JOURNAL OF THE ACQUIRED IMMUNE DEFICIENCY SYNDROME 3(4):413-416, 1990

Experiences from two HIV prevention projects among drug abusers in Olso: is methadone maintenance treatment useful?, by M. Skogstad. TIDSSKRIFT FOR DEN NORSKE LAEGEFORENING 110(15):1978-1980, June 10, 1990

Federal efforts to control the spread of HIV and AIDS among IV drug users, by J. A. Inciardi. AMERICAN BEHAVIORAL SCIENTIST 33(4):408-418, March/April 1990

Fighting AIDS on the streets, by R. Mason. AIDS EDUCATION AND PREVENTION 2(1):84-85, Spring 1990

HIV seroprevalence surveys in drug treatment centers, by T. S. Jones, et al. PUBLIC HEALTH REPORTS 105(2):125-130, March/April 1990

HIV status and changes in risk behaviour among intravenous drug users in Stockholm 1987-1988, by K. I. Kall, et al. AIDS 4(2):153-157, February 1990

Implementation of an experimental research design in the evaluation of an intervention to prevent AIDS among IV drug users, by C. B. McCoy, et al. JOURNAL OF DRUG ISSUES 20(2):215-222, Spring 1990

Integrating AIDS prevention and chemical dependency treatment. JOURNAL OF PSYCHOACTIVE DRUGS 21(4):361-442, October/December 1989

Lost opportunity to combat AIDS: drug abusers in the criminal justice system, by E. D. Wish, et al. NIDA RESEARCH MONOGRAPH SERIES 93:187-209, 1990

Methadone maintenance programs should be considered in HIV-prevention, by M. Skogstad. TIDSSKRIFT FOR DEN NORSKE LAEGEFORENING 110(15):1978-1980, 1990

New AIDS groups organize to save lives. MINORITY TRENDSLETTER 3(4):9, Fall 1990

New York City AIDS needle policy draws activists' fire, by B. Day. GUARDIAN 42(30):9, May 23, 1990

Patients successfully maintained with methadone escaped human immunodeficiency virus infection, by A. Barthwell, et al. ARCHIVES OF GENERAL PSYCHIATRY 46(10):957-958, October 1989

Pediatric AIDS: adolescence, delinquency, drug abuse, and AIDS, by J. A. Mangos, et al. TEXAS MEDICINE 86(7):100-103, July 1990

Preventing AIDS: prospects for change in white male intravenous drug users, by J. L. Sorensen. NIDA RESEARCH MONOGRAPH SERIES 93:83-107, 1990

Preventing the spread of HIV injecting drug users: the experience of syringe-exchange schemes in England and Scotland, by G. Stimson, et al. NIDA RESEARCH MONOGRAPH SERIES 90:302-310, 1988

Prevention of AIDS transmission by syringes and needles in France and Africa, by J. C. Petithory, et al. BULLETIN DE l'ACADEMIE NATIONALE DE MEDICINE 173(4):415-419, April 1989

Prevention of HIV infection among drug addicts, by A. Stapinski, et al. PREZEGLAD LEKARSKI 76(4):326-333, July/August 1989

Providing HIV counseling and testing services in methadone maintenance programs, by M. L. Cartter, et al. AIDS 4(5):463-465, May 1990

Reducing HIV transmission in intravenous-drug users not in drug treatment: United States. MMWR 39(31):529+, August 10, 1990

Role of drug abuse treatment programs in AIDS prevention and education programs for intravenous drug users: the New Jersey experience, by J. F. Jackson, et al. NIDA RESEARCH MONOGRAPH SERIES 93:167-186, 1990

Self-instruction to prevent HIV infection among African-American and Hispanic-American adolescents, by S. P. Schinke, et al. JOURNAL OF CONSULTING AND CLINICAL PSYCHOLOGY 58(4):432-436, 1990

Softly softy on new HIV funding initiative. BRITISH JOURNAL OF ADDICTION 84(9):1101, September 1989

Stages in the response of the drug abuse treatment system to the AIDS epidemic in New York City, by D. C. des Jarlais. JOURNAL OF DRUG ISSUES 20(2):335-347, Spring 1990

Substance abuse treatment modalities in the age of HIV spectrum disease, by J. A. Nathan, et al. JOURNAL OF PSYCHOACTIVE DRUGS 21(4):423-429, October/December 1989

Target groups for preventing AIDS among intravenous drug users: II—the "hard" data studies, by D. C. des Jarlais, et al. JOURNAL OF CONSULTING AND CLINICAL PSYCHOLOGY 58(1):50-56, February 1990

Treatment, care and prevention for HIV-positive intravenous drug addicts, by S. Henriksson. NORDISK MEDICIN 105(3):95-96, 1990

What is bleach: used to fight drugs and AIDS, by H. W. Carlhoff. ZENTRALBLATT FUR JUGENDRECHT 76(1):35-36, 1989

Working with drug users to prevent the spread of HIV: the application of an analytical framework to a range of programmes, by L. D. Jones. HEALTH EDUCATION RESEARCH 5(1):5-16, March 1990

Addict beliefs about access to HIV test results, by D. A. Calsyn, et al. NIDA RESEARCH MONOGRAPH SERIES 95:417, 1989

Argument against HIV-antibody testing in chemical dependence treatment programs, by S. J. Sorrell, et al. JOURNAL OF PSYCHOACTIVE DRUGS 12(4):419-421, October/December 1989

Arguments for HIV-antibody testing in chemical dependence treatment programs, by E. F. Howell, et al. JOURNAL OF PSYCHOACTIVE DRUGS 21(4):415-417, October/December 1989

HIV seroprevalence and the acceptance of voluntary HIV testing among newly incarcerated male prison inmates in Wisonsin, USA, by N. J. Hoxie, et al. AMERICAN JOURNAL OF PUBLIC HEALTH 80(9):1129-1131, 1990

HIV testing and risk-prone behavior among drug abusers in Oslo, by G. K. Welle-Strand. TIDSSKRIFT FOR DEN NORSKE LAEGEFORENING 110(12):1551-1554, May 10, 1990

Psychiatric diagnosis before serological testing for the human immunodeficiency virus, by S. W. Perry, et al. AMERICAN JOURNAL OF PSYCHIATRY 147:89-93, January 1990

Psychiatric symptoms in HIV test consenters and refusers, by G. Woody, et al. NIDA RESEARCH MONOGRAPH SERIES 95:415-416, 1989

Reactions of methadone patients to HIV antibody testing, by S. Magura, et al. ADVANCES IN ALCOHOL AND SUBSTANCE ABUSE 8(3-4):97-111, 1990

Serological inquiry for the detection of antibodies against the human immunodeficiency virus (HIV) in children in a general ward, by A. A. Osmo, et al. REVISTA DE SAUDE PUBLICA 24(2):113-118, 1990

System for screening and epidemiologic monitoring of HIV infection in drug addicts: a working model and analysis of data related to 1517 subjects from the Veronese area, by G. Serpelloni, et al. EPIDEMIOLOGIA E PREVENZIONE 10(37):38-48, December 1988

Testing for human immunodeficiency virus in chemical dependence treatment programs, by S. A. Mersky. JOURNAL OF PSYCHOACTIVE DRUGS 21(4):407-413, October/December 1989

Use of paper-absorbed fingerstick blood samples for studies of antibody to human immunodeficiency virus type 1 in intravenous drug users, by K. A. Steger, et al. JOURNAL OF INFECTIOUS DISEASES 162(4):964-967, October 1990

Therapy

Primary care for AIDS and chemical dependence, by L. D. Karan. WESTERN JOURNAL OF MEDICINE 152(5):538-542, May 1990

Primary care for patients with human immunodeficiency virus (HIV) infection in a methadone maintenance treatment program, by P. A. Selwyn, et al. ANNALS OF INTERNAL MEDICINE 111(9):761-763, November 1, 1989

Treatment, care and prevention for HIV-positive intravenous drug addicts, by S. Henriksson. NORDISK MEDICIN 105(3):95-96, 1990

ALCOHOL (ALCOHOLICS AND ALCOHOLISM)
Acoustically evoked brain stem potentials in acute alcoholic intoxication, by B. Klemm, et al. PSYCHIATRIE, NEUROLOGIE UND MEDIZINISCHE PSYCHOLOGIE 42(2): 102-106, February 1990

Acoustically evoked brain stem potentials in chronic alcoholism and withdrawal, by U. Fichtel, et al. PSYCHIATRIE, NEUROLOGIE UND MEDIZINISCHE PSYCHOLOGIE 41(11):660-663, November 1989

Activity of tyrosine hydroxylase and monoamine oxidase in human platelets during alcoholism, by A. Z. Drozdov, et al. VOPROSY MEDITSINSKAI KHIMII 36(1):54-57, January/February 1990

Alcohol: America's no. 1 addiction. SCHOLASTIC UPDATE 123:2-4+, November 16, 1990

Alcohol and thiamine of the brain, by G. Rindi. ALCOHOL AND ALCOHOLISM 24(6): 493-495, 1989

Alcohol and you: danger, by H. Shubin, et al. PENNSYLVANIA MEDICINE 92(10):8, October 1989

Alcohol consumption and plasma lipoproteins, by S. Moorjani, et al. CMAJ 142(10): 1089, May 15, 1990

Alcohol has been taken its toll, by N. J. Blyan. WINDSPEAKER 8(4):4, May 11, 1990

Alcohol, iron and oxidative stress, by R. Nordmann, et al. BULLETIN DE l'ACADEMIE NATIONALE DE MEDICINE 174(1):95-102, January 1990

Alcohol remains worst problem among natives, by J. Hollobon. JOURNAL OF THE ADDICTION RESEARCH FOUNDATION 19(7-8):4, July/August 1990

Alcohol use and aquatic activities: Massachusetts, 1988. MMWR 39(20):332-334, May 25, 1990

Alcoholics dying from smoking ills. JOURNAL OF THE ADDICTION RESEARCH FOUNDATION 19(11):1, January 1, 1990

Alcoholism, by D. D. Collins. AMERICAN FAMILY PHYSICIAN 41(1):74+, January 1990

Alcoholism and cardiac graft, by L. Singer, et al. ANNALES MEDICO-PSYCHOLOGIQUES 148(1):124-126, January 1990

Alcoholism, freedom, and moral responsibility, by W. Lehman. INTERNATIONAL JOURNAL OF LAW AND PSYCHIATRY 13(1-2):103-121, 1990

Alcoholism: the time factor. HEALTH 22:11, March 1990

ALCOHOL

Anomie, alcohol abuse and alcohol consumption: a prospective analysis, by D. J. Lee, et al. JOURNAL OF STUDIES ON ALCOHOL 51(5):415-421, 1990

AST:ALT ratios, by P. M. George, et al. NEW ZEALAND MEDICAL JOURNAL 103 (897):433, September 12, 1990

Asymmetric distribution of a fluorescent sterol in synaptic plasma membranes: effects of chronic ethanol consumption, by W. G. Wood, et al. BIOCHIMICA ET BIO-PHYSICA ACTA 1025(2):243-246, June 27, 1990

Basal activities of adenylate and guanylate cyclase in lymphocytes and platelets of alcohoholics, by I. P. Anokina, et al. BIOMEDICA, BIOCHIMICA ACTA 48(8):593-596, 1989

Basal ganglia-limbic striatal and thalamocortical involvement in craving and loss of control in alcoholism, by J. G. Modell, et al. JOURNAL OF NEUROPSYCHIATRY AND CLINICAL NEUROSCIENCES 2(2):123-144, Spring 1990

Behind the label "alcoholic," by D. M. Wright. JOURNAL OF COUNSELING AND DEVELOPMENT 67(8):482-483, April 1989

Biophysical membrane correlates of tolerance and dependence on alcohol, by F. Beauge, et al. DRUG AND ALCOHOL DEPENDENCE 25(1):57-65, February 1990

Calling time on takeaway terror, by B. Knox. POLICE REVIEW 98(5081):1860-1861, 1990

Canned ashes, by D. A. Curran. MEDICAL JOURNAL OF AUSTRALIA 151(11-12): 728, December 4-18, 1989

Cerebrospinal fluid levels of somatostatin, corticotropin-releasing hormone and corti-cotropin in alcoholism, by A. Roy, et al. ACTA PSYCHIATRICA SCANDINAVICA 82(1):44-48, July 1990

Changes in blood acetaldehyde levels after ethanol administration in alcoholics, by S. Takase, et al. ALCOHOL 7(1):37-41, January/February 1990

Characteristics of lipid peroxidation in alcoholic intoxication, by L. N. Ovchinnikova, et al. VOPROSY MEDITSINSKAI KHIMII 35(5):86-90, September/October 1989

Characterization of the increased binding of acetaldehyde to red blood cells in alcoholics, by R. Hernandez-Munoz, et al. ALCOHOLISM 13(5):654-659, October 1989

Cheers? SECURITY MANAGEMENT 34(6):109, June 1990

Chemical dependency, by E. G. Onet. JOURNAL OF THE AMERICAN VETERINARY MEDICAL ASSOCIATION 196(2):184-185, January 15, 1990

Chronic alcohol intake does not change thiopental anesthetic requirement, pharma-cokinetics, or pharmacodynamics, by B. N. Swerdlow, et al. ANESTHESIOLOGY 72(3):455-461, March 1990

Chronic alcoholic intoxication and the trace element composition of the hair, by A. V. Skal'nyi, et al. SUDEBNO-MEDITSINSKAIA EKSPERTIZA 33(1):42-43, January/March 1990

Comments on Gorman's "is the 'new' problem drinking concept of Heather and Robertson more helpful in advancing our scientific knowledge than the 'old' disease concept," by N. Heather. BRITISH JOURNAL OF ADDICTION 84(8):847-848, August 1989

Comments on a paper by M. L. Plant and M. A. Plant, by I. Murray-Lyon, et al. ALCOHOL AND ALCOHOLISM 24(4):355-357, 1989

Concurrent use of cigarettes, alcohol, and coffee, by K. J. Zavela, et al. JOURNAL OF APPLIED SOCIAL PSYCHOLOGY 20(pt 1):835-845, June 1990

Danish tolerance, by J. Partanen. ALKOHOLIPOLITIIKA 54(1):11-22, 1989

Determinants of plasma retinol, beta-carotene, and alpha-tocopherol, by B. Herbeth, et al. AMERICAN JOURNAL OF EPIDEMIOLOGY 132(2):394-396, August 1990

Don't drink and dive, by E. Alexander, Jr. SURGICAL NEUROLOGY 34(3):159, September 1990

Drug self-administration procedures: alcohol and marijuana, by N. K. Mello, et al. NIDA RESEARCH MONOGRAPH SERIES 92:147-170, 1989

Dynamics of ethanol metabolism in patients with chronic alcoholism, by F. Teodorescu, et al. REVISTA MEDICO-CHIRURGICALA A SOCIETATII DE MEDICI SI NATURALISTA DIN IASI 93(4):699-703, October/December 1989

Effect of alcohol dose on plasma lipoproten subfractions and lipolytic enzyme activity in active and inactive men, by G. H. Hartung, et al. METABOLISM 39(1):81-86, January 1990

Effect of alcohol on blood doplichol concentration, by R. P. Roine, et al. ALCOHOLISM 13(4):519-522, August 1989

Effects of various levels of alcohol consumption on plasma lipoproteins and apoproteins, by R. J. Andrade Bellido, et al. MEDICINA CLINICA 93(5):169-172, July 1, 1989

Ethanol and isopropanol consumption, by R. Iffland, et al. BEITRAGE ZUR GERICHTLICHEN MEDIZIN 47:369-378, 1989

Ethanol: a chemical cocktail, by W. Glenn. OCCUPATIONAL HEALTH AND SAFETY CANADA 6(3):42+, March/April 1990

Ethanol: an enhancer of transplantation antigen expression, by D. S. Singer, et al. ALCOHOLISM 13(4):480-484, August 1989

Ethanol-induced lipid peroxidation and oxidative stress in extrahepatic tissues, by R. Nordmann, et al. ALCOHOL AND ALCOHOLISM 25(2-3):231-237, 1990

Ethanol tolerance and alcoholism. AMERICAN FAMILY PHYSICIAN 42:1124, October 1990

ALCOHOL

Facing up to alcohol over-use: alcohol is one of our society's most destructive drugs. HEALTH NEWS 8(4):1-7, August 1990

Fatty acid and lipid levels in the blood platelets of patients with alcoholism, by I. U. Iusupova, et al. GEMATOLOGIIA I TRANSFUZIOLOGIIA 34(6):31-37, June 1989

Flavor and alcohol-use, by R. Gilbert. JOURNAL OF THE ADDICTION RESEARCH FOUNDATION 19(7-8):5, July/August 1990

Free carnitine and acylacarnitine levels in sera of alcoholics, by C. Alonso de la Pena, et al. BIOCHEMICAL MEDICINE AND METABOLIC BIOLOGY 44(1):77-83, August 1990

Free fatty acids in the serum of patients with alcoholism, by M. Rosnowska, et al. POLSKI TYGODNIK 44(24):575-578, June 12, 1989

From drinking to disease, by C. Gloeckner. CURRENT HEALTH 2 17:23-25, October 1990

Human aldehyde dehydrogenases: their role in alcoholism, by D. P. Agarwal, et al. ALCOHOL 6(6):517-523, November/December 1989

Human leukocyte beta-adrenergic stimulated cyclic AMP in ethanol intoxication and withdrawal, by R. M. Swift, et al. ALCOHOLISM 14(1):58-62, February 1990

Human neutrophilis are not severely injured in conditions mimicking social drinking, by J. X. Corberand, et al. ALCOHOLISM 13(4):542-546, August 1989

Hyperuricemia-hyperlipemia association in the absence of obesity and alcohol abuse, by E. Collantes Estevez, et al. CLINICAL RHEUMATOLOGY 9(1):28-31, March 1990

Hypophyseal-adrenal system in chronic alcoholism, by S. Abrikosova, et al. SOVIET MEDICINE (2):12-14, 1990

Increase in the brain homocarosine level during alcohol intoxication, by R. I. Kukharenko, et al. UKRAINESKII BIOKHIMICHESKII ZHURNAL 62(1):92-94, January/February 1990

Individual sociomedical problems of alcoholism, by R. Scarzella, et al. MINERVA MEDICA 81(5):415-425, May 1990

Intracellular peroxidation processes in chronic alcohol intoxication, by S. V. Pirozhkov, et al. UKRAINESKII BIOKHIMICHESKII ZHURNAL 61(4):3-16, July/August 1989

Just what does Weber mean?, by B. J. Crigger. HASTINGS CENTER REPORT 20(1):2-3, January/February 1990

Light to moderate drinkers cause most woes, by H. McConnell. JOURNAL OF THE ADDICTION RESEARCH FOUNDATION 19(3):1-2, March 1, 1990

Medicalization and regulation of alcohol and alcoholism: the professions and disciplinary measures, by B. E. Burtch, et al. INTERNATIONAL JOURNAL OF LAW AND PSYCHIATRY 13(1-2):127-147, 1990

Models of problem drinking and the place for causality: a reply to Gorman, by I. Robertson. BRITISH JOURNAL OF ADDICTION 84(8):8484-849, August 1989

Multiple alcohol-related problems in the United States on the rise, by D. S. Hasin, et al. JOURNAL OF STUDIES ON ALCOHOL 51:485-493, November 1990

Narrow battling drug-alcohol problems, by J. Morrow. WINDSPEAKER 8(3):3, April 27, 1990

Nation under the influence, by S. Nelson. SEVENTEEN 49:183-184, March 1990

Nature of inebriety: more than one way of seeing things, by G. Edwards. BRITISH JOURNAL OF ADDICTION 84(8):850-859, August 1989

New definition of alcoholism. AMERICAN FAMILY PHYSICIAN 42:238, July 1990

New disease model of alcoholism, by J. Wallace. WESTERN JOURNAL OF MEDICINE 152(5):502-505, May 1990

Nonmatching-oddity, and delayed nonmatching-to-sample performance in aging, alcoholic, and alcoholic Korsakoff individuals, by M. Oscar-Berman, et al. PSYCHO-BIOLOGY 17(4):424-430, December 1989

On the rebound: alcohol and sleep, by L. Dotto. JOURNAL OF THE ADDICTION RESEARCH FOUNDATION 19(4):12, April 1, 1990

Other drug problem, by D. W. Kinnaird. JOURNAL OF THE KENTUCKY MEDICAL ASSOCIATION 88(6):307-308, June 1990

Pharmacokinetics of epirubicin in alcoholic patients, by H. Swirsky, et al. BULLETIN DU CANCER 76(8):897-901, 1989

Pharmacology of acute alcoholic intoxication, by R. Fernandez del Moral, et al. REVISTA ESPANOLA DE FISIOLOGIA 45(Suppl):337-346, 1989

Plasma B-endorphin levels in chronic alcoholics, by J. C. Aguirre, et al. ALCOHOL 7(5):409-412, 1990

Platelet serotonin decrease in alcoholic patients, by D. Bailly, et al. ACTA PHYSIOLOGICA SCANDINAVICA 81(1):68-72, January 1990

Prevalence of lifestyle risk factors in a family practice, by J. Chao, et al. PREVENTIVE MEDICINE 19(5):533-540, 1990

Problem drinker, by R. Hunt. PRACTITIONER 233(1471):895, June 22, 1989

Problems of ethanol "absorption deficiency," by H. D. Wehner, et al. BLUTALKOHOL 25(5):299-309, 1988

Promille limits and health policy, by J. Steensberg. UGESKRIFT FOR LAEGER 152(6):404-406, February 5, 1990

Proposal for considering intoxication at sentencing hearings: part II, by C. J. Felker. FEDERAL PROBATION 54(1):3-14, 1990

Protein-acetaldehyde adducts in serum of alcoholic pateints, by R. C. Lin, et al. ALCOHOLISM: CLINICAL AND EXPERIMENTAL RESEARCH 14(3):438-443, June 1990

Retention of orienting reaction habituation in chronic alcoholics, by R. Rogozea, et al. PAVLOVIAN JOURNAL OF BIOLOGICAL SCIENCE 25(1):1-13, January/March 1990

Role of the gastric and hepatic vagus in voluntary alcohol intake, by P. Toth, et al. PHARMACOLOGY, BIOCHEMISTRY AND BEHAVIOR 36(1):69-76, May 1990

Salsolinol, an endogenous molecule: possible implications in alcoholism, Parkinson's disease and pain, by D. Vernay, et al. ENCEPHALE 15(6):511-516, November/December 1989

Senseless! Senseless! Senseless, by W. H. Havener. OHIO MEDICINE 85(12):930-931, December 1989

Sexes just aren't equal when it comes to booze, by C. DeMarco. TODAY'S HEALTH 8(1):13-18, February/March 1990

Shifting boundaries of alcohol policy, by D. C. Walsh. HEALTH AFFAIRS 9(2):47-62, Summer 1990

Short- and middle-latency auditory evoked potentials in abstinent chronic alcoholics: preliminary findings, by F. Diaz, et al. ELECTROENCEPHALOGRAPHY AND CLINICAL NEUROPHYSIOLOGY 77(2):145-150, March/April 1990

Smokescreen of addiction, by E. Van den Haag. NATIONAL REVIEW 42:84-85, November 5, 1990

Superoxide dismutase in the errthrocytes of acute alcoholics during detoxification, by H. K. Rooprai, et al. ALCOHOL AND ALCOHOLISM 24(6):503-507, 1989

Swift increase in alcohol metabolism in humans, by R. G. Thurman, et al. ALCOHOLISM 13(4):572-576, August 1989

Sympathetic innervation and functioning of the heart conduction system in alcoholism, by V. V. Anikin, et al. TERAPEVTICHESKII ARKHIV 62(4):43-45, 1990

Trouble with alcohol, by P. E. Forge. FLYING SAFETY 45(12):8-11, December 1989

Type 1 and type 2 alcoholics: Schuckit and Irwin reply, by M. A. Schuckit, et al. BRITISH JOURNAL OF ADDICTION 85(5):684-685, May 1990

Type 1 and type 2 alcoholics: Schuckit and Irwin's negative findings, by F. M. Vanclay, et al. BRITISH JOURNAL OF ADDICTION 85(5):683-685, May 1990

Unresolved questions about alcoholism: the debate (war?) goes on: is a resolution possible?, by B. Goodyear. ALCOHOLISM TREATMENT QUARTERLY 6(2):1-27, 1989

Untimely acts: extending the interactionist conception of deviance, by W. A. Reese, II, et al. SOCIOLOGICAL QUARTERLY 30:159-184, Summer 1989

Urinary sodium and potassium excretion, body mass index, alcohol intake and blood pressure in three Japanese populations, by T. Hashimoto, et al. JOURNAL OF HUMAN HYPERTENSION 3(5):315-321, October 1989

Visual evoked potentials in chronic alcoholics, by P. Urban, et al. CESKOSLOVEN-SKA NEUROLOGIE A NEUROCHIRURGIE 52(4):271-276, July 1989

We should be concerned, by M. L. Christianson. CANADIAN DENTAL ASSOCIA-TION JOURNAL 55(11):866, November 1989

Why forget the false positives?, by P. Tyler, et al. BRITISH JOURNAL OF ADDICTION 28(4):377-378, November 1989

Adult Children of Alcoholics (ACOAS)
Adult children of alcoholics: characteristics and problems, by C. Rategan. SAFETY AND HEALTH 141:68-71, April 1990

Adult children of alcoholics: is it really a separate field for study?, by R. J. Beidler. DRUGS AND SOCIETY 3(3-4):133-141, March/April 1989

Adult children of alcoholics: self-help or self-pity, by R. Simon. FAMILY THERAPY NETWORKER 14(1):22-43, January/February 1990

Adult children of alcoholics: a valid diagnostic group, by A. I. Fulton, et al. JOURNAL OF NERVOUS AND MENTAL DISEASE 178(8):505-509, August 1990

Adult children of problem drinkers in an urban community, by N. A. El-Guebaly, et al. BRITISH JOURNAL OF PSYCHIATRY 156:249-255, February 1990

Adult survivors of parental alcoholism: implications for primary care, by B. P. Starling, et al. NURSE PRACTITIONER 15(7):16+, July 1990

Brief treatment for adult children of alcoholics: accessing resources for self-care, by J. S. Crandell. PSYCHOTHERAPY 26(4):510-513, Winter 1989

Collaborative investigation of adult children of alcoholics with anxiety, by M. R. Haack. ARCHIVES OF PSYCHIATRIC NURSING 4(1):62-66, February 1990

Leading an Adlerian group for adult children of alcoholics, by E. S. Delaney, et al. IN-DIVIDUAL PSYCHOLOGY: JOURNAL OF ADLERIAN THEORY, RESEARCH AND PRACTICE 45(4):490-499, December 1989

Life experiences of adult daughters of alcoholics: a qualitative study, by B. E. Robert-son. DAI A 50(7):2258, January 1990

Locus of control and self-esteem of adult children of alcoholics, by J. C. Churchill, et al. JOURNAL OF STUDIES ON ALCOHOL 51(4):373-376, July 1990

Psychological profiles of adult children of alcoholics in search of therapy, by J. D. Baker, et al. COUNSELLING PSYCHOLOGY QUARTERLY 2(4):451-457, 1989

Psychotherapeutic approach to treatment of a population at high risk for alcoholism: adult children of alcoholics, by S. I. Eve. MEDICINE AND LAW 8(4):357-363, 1989

Therapeutic conceptualization of adult children of alcoholics, by D. L. Klonblauch, et al. JOURNAL OF COLLEGE STUDENT PSYCHOTHERAPY 4(1):37-52, 1989

Advertising

Advertising popular drugs, by R. Gilbert. JOURNAL OF THE ADDICTION RESEARCH FOUNDATION 19(6):9, June 1, 1990

Alcohol advertising and sport: a role for preventive medicine, by G. W. Sivyer. MEDICAL JOURNAL OF AUSTRALIA 153(4):230-231, August 20, 1990

Alcohol advertising in college newspapers: a 7-year follow-up, by W. Breed, et al. JOURNAL OF AMERICAN COLLEGE HEALTH 38(6):255-262, May 1990

Alcohol advertising in developing countries, by P. P. Aitken. BRITISH JOURNAL OF ADDICTION 84(12):1443-1445, December 1989

Andrettis drive home Molson's new message. MARKETING 95(22):2, May 28, 1990

ARF recommends ban on all drink ads. JOURNAL OF THE ADDICTION RESEARCH FOUNDATION 19(12):11-12, December 1, 1990

Brought to you by: in the world of advertising unreality can become reality, by W. Howell. JOURNAL OF THE ADDICTION RESEARCH FOUNDATION 19(12):13, December 1, 1990

Does advertising have any effects on the consumption of alcoholic beverages, by M. Salo. ALKOHOLIPOLITIIKKA 54(2):77-82, 1989

EC (European Commission) bans all ads for alcohol, beer. JOURNAL OF THE ADDICTION RESEARCH FOUNDATION 19(11):1, November 1, 1990

EC (European Commission) moving on alcohol, tobacco advertising, by S. Milmo. JOURNAL OF THE ADDICTION RESEARCH FOUNDATION 19(7-8):1+, July/August 1990

Europe cuts alcohol-tobacco ads on kids' TV, by K. Birchard. JOURNAL OF THE ADDICTION RESEARCH FOUNDATION 19(11):9, November 1, 1990

Fighting ads in the inner city: alcohol and tobacco ads targeted to blacks, by M. Mabry. NEWSWEEK 115:46, February 5, 1990

French move to ban tobacco, drink ads. JOURNAL OF THE ADDICTION RESEARCH FOUNDATION 19(6):9, June 1, 1990

Study group report on the impact of televised drinking and alcohol advertising on youth, by M. D. Resnick. JOURNAL OF ADOLESCENT HEALTH CARE 11(1):25-30, January 1990

Tilting at billboards: opposition to alcohol and tobacco ads targeted to blacks, by B. Wildavsky. NEW REPUBLIC 203:19-20, August 20-27, 1990

Alcohol abuse: contamination by western influences of the rural African village, by T. Ntusi. MEDICINE AND LAW 8(1):53-57, 1989

Alcohol in Botswana: a historical overview, by L. Molamu. CONTEMPORARY DRUG PROBLEMS 16(1):3-42, Spring 1989

Alcoholics Anonymous

AA spiritual issues, and the treatment of lesbian and gay alcoholics, Michigan State University, by S. L. Berg. DAI A 50(7):2121, 1990

AA story "a guide on how to think," by H. McConnell. JOURNAL OF THE ADDICTION RESEARCH FOUNDATION 19(2):2, February 1, 1990

Al-Anon: a resource for families and friends of alcoholics, by A. Kverme. TIDSSKRIFT FOR DEN NORSKE LAEGEFORENING 110(5):608-609, February 20, 1990

Alcoholics Anonymous: the heart of treatment for alcoholism, by J. J. Hinrichsen. AGING (361):12-17, 1990

Alcoholics Anonymous: a society which greatly helps alcoholics, by A. Kverme. TIDSSKRIFT FOR DEN NORSKE LAEGEFORENING 110(5):606-607, February 20, 1990

Bibliotherapy and gay American men of Alcoholics Anonymous, by R. J. Kus. JOURNAL OF GAY AND LESBIAN PSYCHOTHERAPY 1(2):73-86, 1989

Combined Alcoholics Anonymous and professional care for addicted physicians, by M. Galanter, et al. AMERICAN JOURNAL OF PSYCHIATRY 147(1):64-68, January 1990

Jewish experiences of Alcoholics Anonymous, by L. Master. SMITH COLLEGE STUDIES IN SOCIAL WORK 59(2):183-199, March 1989

Patriarchy and recovery in AA: discussion of December 6, 1989 article, "Twelve Steps for Women Alcoholics," by G. Unterberger. CHRISTIANITY TODAY 107:338-340, April 4, 1990

Relationship between alcohol expectancies and length of abstinence among Alcoholics Anonymous members, by B. C. Rather, et al. ADDICTIVE BEHAVIORS 14(5):531-536, 1989

Spirituality and recovery: relationships between levels of spirituality, contentment and stress during recovery from alcoholism in AA, by J. E. Corrington. ALCOHOL AND ALCOHOLISM 6(3-4):151-165, 1989

Success of alcoholics anonymous, by G. K. Hoffman. AMERICAN JOURNAL OF PSYCHIATRY 147(8):1104, August 1990

Twelve steps to sobriety: probation officers "working the program," by E. M. Read. FEDERAL PROBATION 54(4):34-42, 1990

What practicing physicians need to know about self-help for chemical dependents, by B. E. Donovan. RHODE ISLAND MEDICAL JOURNAL 72(12):443-449, December 1989

Asia

Alcoholism: North America and Asia—a comparison of population surveys with the diagnostic interview schedule, by J. E. Helzer, et al. ARCHIVES OF GENERAL PSYCHIATRY 47(4):313-319, April 1990

Attitudes

Alcohol consumption and the perceived situational appropriateness of consuming different types of alcoholic beverages, by H. Klein, et al. ALCOHOL AND ALCOHOLISM 24(5):479-490, 1989

Attitudes and expectancies as predictors of drinking habits: a comparison of three scales, by B. C. Leigh. JOURNAL OF STUDIES ON ALCOHOL 50:432-440, September 1989

Attitudes changing toward underage drinking. JUVENILE JUSTICE DIGEST 17(19): 6-7, October 4, 1989

Attitudes of chronic inebriates toward alcoholism treatment modalities, by T. A. Buhr, et al. FREE INQUIRY IN CREATIVE SOCIOLOGY 18(1):77-85, May 1990

Attitudes of students and house staff toward alcoholism. JAMA 263(9):1198-1199, March 2, 1990

Does endorsement of the disease concept of alcoholism predict humanitarian attitudes to alcoholics, by J. R. Crawford, et al. INTERNATIONAL JOURNAL OF THE ADDICTIONS 24(1):71-77, January 1989

Irish "ambivalence" to alcohol criticized, by K. Birchard. JOURNAL OF THE ADDICTION RESEARCH FOUNDATION 19(12):13, December 1, 1990

Message mixes distort: alcohol could be sent the way of high-fat diets, by H. McConnell. JOURNAL OF THE ADDICTION RESEARCH FOUNDATION 19(11):2, November 1, 1990

New temperance movement: through the looking glass, by D. B. Heath. DRUGS AND SOCIETY 3(3-4):143-168, March/April 1989

Opinions on alcoholic beverage consumption and alcoholism among university students, by G. L. Guimaraes Borges. EDUCACION MEDICA Y SALUD 23(4):406-410, October/December 1989

Prevention messages heard but not heeled: lying adults change attitudes about drinking but not behavior, by D. Haynes. JOURNAL OF THE ADDICTION RESEARCH FOUNDATION 19(4):3, April 1, 1990

Public opinion on alcohol policies, by A. C. Wagenaar, et al. JOURNAL OF PUBLIC HEALTH POLICY 11(2):189-205, Summer 1990

Public opinion on alcohol policies, by L. L. Pendleton, et al. BRITISH JOURNAL OF ADDICTION 85(1):125-130, January 1990

Public policy on alcohol and illicit drugs, by D. Cahalan. DRUGS AND SOCIETY 3(3-4):169-186, March/April 1989

R. v Tandy and the concept of alcoholism as a disease, by J. Goodlyfe. MODERN LAW REVIEW 53(6):809-814, 1990

Status quo on alcohol "obscene," by B. L. Lee. JOURNAL OF THE ADDICTION RESEARCH FOUNDATION 19(2):1-2, February 1, 1990

Two procedures to reduce response bias in reports of alcohol consumption, by C. E. Werch. JOURNAL OF STUDIES ON ALCOHOL 51(4):327-330, July 1990

What's the harm in just a drink?, by H. G. Tittmar. ALCOHOL AND ALCOHOLISM 25(2-3):287-291, 1990

Women and alcohol: mother's ruin: society's attitude to female drinkers, by M.C. Mason. GUARDIAN May 1, 1990, p. 21

Australia
Alcohol consumption across the lifecycle in Australia: 1985-1988, by T. Makkai, et al. DRUG AND ALCOHOL DEPENDENCE 25(3):305-313, June 1990

Dusty town drowning in drink: Australian Aborigines combat a pernicious alcohol problem, by B. Rodolph. TIME 136(13):55, September 24, 1990

Canada
Bottle of the best: Alberta's alcohol habits take a turn to the abstemious—and sophisticated, by G. Heaton. ALBERTA (WESTERN) REPORT 17(31):23, July 16, 1990

Care—Hospitals
Alcohol histories in hospital: does the age and sex of the patient make a difference?, by I. Awad, et al. BRITISH JOURNAL OF ADDICTION 85(1):149-150, January 1990

Alcohol-related problems and public hospitals: defining a new role in prevention, by D. H. Jernigan, et al. JOURNAL OF PUBLIC HEALTH POLICY 10(3):324-352, Autumn 1989

Comparative analysis of a hospitalized population because of alcohol "dependence" or "abuse" and other similar alcoholic populations: a study of 1300 patients, by V. Lopez, et al. ACTAS LUSO-ESPANOLAS DE NEUROLOGIA, PSIQUIATRIA Y CIENCIAS AFINES 18(2):81-99, March/April 1990

Compulsory admission to hospital, by N. J. O'Connell. JOURNAL OF THE ROYAL COLLEGE OF GENERAL PRACTITIONERS 39(327):434, October 1989

Compulsory admission to hospital of an alcoholic patient under mental health act, by M. F. McGhee. JOURNAL OF THE ROYAL COLLEGE OF GENERAL PRACTITIONERS 39(324):301, July 1989

Compulsory hospitalization of psychiatric patients today: a part of emergency management, by E. Kormendy. OFFENTLICHE GESUNDHEITSWESEN 52(6):273-276, June 1990

Deviants in a deviant institution: a case study of a Polish alcohol treatment hospital, by J. Moskalewicz, et al. CONTEMPORARY DRUG PROBLEMS 16(2):157-176, Summer 1989

Impact of alcohol on the acute hospital service: patient presentation, admission and the perception of alcohol use in such groups, by C. E. Robertson, et al. ALCOHOL AND ALCOHOLISM 24(5):405-408, 1989

New York Hospital, Westchester Division, Cornell University Medical College: a tradition in the treatment of alcoholism, by N. S. Miller, et al. JOURNAL OF SUBSTANCE ABUSE TREATMENT 6(3):201-204, 1989

New York launches alcohol intervention demonstration in 11 hospitals statewide, by J. N. Heckler. PUBLIC HEALTH REPORTS 105:211-212, March/April 1990

Care—Nurses

Alcoholic patient: rude and abusive. NURSING 90 20:91, June 1990

Consumption of alcohol and tobacco during pregnancy by health advisors: an investigation of nurses, nurses' aides, physicians and school teachers, by J. G. Frische, et al. UGESKRIFT FOR LAEGER 152(9):2101-2104, July 16, 1990

Learning to care for Junior, by P. Carr. NURSING 90 20:160, April 1990

Nursing attitudes toward geriatric alcoholism, by H. P. Parette, et al. JOURNAL OF GERONTOLOGICAL NURSING 16(1):26-31, January 1990

Role of the psychiatric nurse in the prevention and treatment of alcoholism at the Avalon Treatment Centre, Cape Town, by R. Wentzel. MEDICINE AND LAW 98(5):439-444, 1989

Care—Physicians

Alcohol and health: attitudes, habits and knowledge of a group of young physicians, by N. Comodo, et al. ANNALI DI IGIENE 1(3-4):679-691, May/August 1989

Alcohol: a public health problem—is there a role for the general practitioner, by C. Robertson. JOURNAL OF THE ROYAL SOCIETY OF MEDICINE 83(4):232-236, April 1990

Alcoholism: a challenging physician-patient encounter, by B. Johnson, et al. JOURNAL OF GENERAL INTERNAL MEDICINE 4(5):445-452, September/October 1989

Bright lights in dark places: physician recognition of alcoholism, by G. L. Phelps, et al. JOURNAL OF THE SOUTH CAROLINA MEDICAL ASSOCIATION 86(1):17-18, January 1990

Consumption of alcohol and tobacco during pregnancy by health advisors: an investigation of nurses, nurses' aides, physicians and school teachers, by J. G. Frische, et al. UGESKRIFT FOR LAEGER 152(9):2101-2104, July 16, 1990

Cooperation between the general practitioner and social medicine service, by W. Ringli, et al. THERAPEUTISCHE UMSCHAU 47(5):374-378, May 1990

GPs "uncomfortable" with alcohol treatment: cigs, drugs, exercise rated more important, by P. Szabo. JOURNAL OF THE ADDICTION RESEARCH FOUNDATION 19(12):3, December 1, 1990

Larger role for GPs (general practitioners): brief interventions work. JOURNAL OF THE ADDICTION RESEARCH FOUNDATION 19(9):4, September 1, 1990

Majority of physicians: alcohol drinking anamnesis contributes significant and relevant information, by M. Montin, et al. LAKARTIDNINGEN 86(37):3057-3058, September 13, 1989

MDs urge 25% cut in drinking. JOURNAL OF THE ADDICTION RESEARCH FOUNDATION 19(12):5, December 1, 1990

Physicians can help the addicted, by D. C. Lewis. RHODE ISLAND MEDICAL JOURNAL 72(12):435-436, December 1989

Physician's role: in society's response to alcohol problems, by R. E. Kendell. CMAJ 143(10):1042-1047, November 15, 1990

Preventing alcohol problems: preparing physicians for their roles and responsibilities, by J. G. Rankin, et al. CMAJ 143(10):1005-1006, November 15, 1990

Role of the physician in expert testimony leading to an arrest, by Z. Marek, et al. PREZEGLAD LEKARSKI 46(10):732-735, 1989

When to intervene for male and female patients' alcohol consumption: what general practitioners say, by A. M. Roche. MEDICAL JOURNAL OF AUSTRALIA 152(12):622-625, June 18, 1990

Why this time: a family physician's role in the rehabilitation of a young man, by R. G. Justin. AMERICAN FAMILY PHYSICIAN 42:1197, November 1990

Case Studies

Beast was me, by L. Hudson. BROOMSTICK 12(5):13, September 1990

Case history of an East Indian Trinidadian alcoholic, by M.V. Angrosino. ETHOS 17(2):202-225, 1989

Severe alcohol intoxication: a study of 204 consecutive patients, by G. E Minion, et al. JOURNAL OF TOXICOLOGY: CLINICAL TOXICOLOGY 27(6):375-384, 1989

Trouble with David. READER'S DIGEST (CANADA) 137(823):55-59, November 1990

Alcoholism and abuse of other drugs: prevention programs in Santiago, Chile, by R. Florenzano. BOLETIN DE LA OFICINA SANITARIA PANAMERICANA 107(6):577-589, December 1989

Alcoholism and other substance abuse: preventive programs in Santiago, Chile, by R. Florenzano. BULLETIN OF THE PAN AMERICAN HEALTH ORGANIZATION 24(1):86-96, 1990

Clinics
Edinburgh Alcohol Problems Clinic, by B. Ritson. BRITISH JOURNAL OF ADDICTION 85(1):25-29, January 1990

Colombia
Alcoholism and substance abuse, Colombia 1987. EPIDEMIOLOGICAL BULLETIN 9(4):11-15, 1988

Complications
see also: Alcohol and Diabetes
            Alcohol and Pregnancy
            Alcohol and Transplants
            Fetal Alcohol Syndrome

Acetaminophen hepatotoxicity in the alcoholic, by F. T. Wootton, et al. SOCIAL SCIENCE AND MEDICINE 83(9):1047-1049, September 1990

Acute alcohol intoxication and cognitive functioning, by J. B. Peterson, et al. JOURNAL OF STUDIES ON ALCOHOL 51(2):114-122, March 1990

Acute or subacute alcoholic neuropathy mimicking Guillain-Barre syndrome, by F. Tabaraud, et al. JOURNAL OF NEUROLOGICAL SCIENCES 97(2-3):195-205, July 1990

Acute renal failure during alcohol-induced rhabdomyolysis, by J. Starzyk, et al. WIADOMSCI LEKARSKIE 42(10):662-665, May 15, 1989

Acute rhabdomyolysis, myoglobinuria and renal insufficiency caused by ethanol: review of the literature and description of a clinical case with fatal outcome, by I. Piazza, et al. GIORNALE DI CLINICA MEDICA 70(11):661-669, November 1989

Additional psychiatric illness by diagnostic interview schedule in male alcoholics, by L. R. Herz, et al. COMPREHENSIVE PSYCHIATRY 31(1):72-79, January/February 1990

Afferent information processing in patients with chronic alcoholism: an evoked potential study, by H. M. Meinck, et al. ALCOHOL 7(4):311-313, July/August 1990

Alcohol, by O. G. Aasland. TIDSSKRIFT FOR DEN NORSKE LAEGEFORENING 110(3):325, January 30, 1990

Alcohol abuse and osteoporosis, by D. Schapir. SEMINARS IN ARTHRITIS AND RHEUMATISM 19(6):371-376, June 1990

Alcohol abuse as the cause of admission to a medical department, by G. Stene-Larsen, et al. TIDSSKRIFT FOR DEN NORSKE LAEGEFORENING 110(14): 1838-1840, May 30, 1990

Alcohol abuse in patients with dilated cardiomyopathy: laboratory vs clinical detection, by R. Y. Wang, et al. ARCHIVES OF INTERNAL MEDICINE 150(5):1079-1082, May 1990

Alcohol abuse-related mesangial glomerulonephritis: immunoelectron microscopy, by S. M. Smith, et al. JOURNAL OF HISTOCHEMISTRY AND CYTOCHEMISTRY 8(5):699-702, May 1990

Alcohol and arterial blood pressure: the role of alcohol as a risk factor of arterial hypertension, by K. Kawecka-Jaszcz, et al. PRZEGLAD LEKARSKI 46(12):811-815, 1989

Alcohol and breast cancer, by A. B. Lowenfels. LANCET 335(8699):1216, May 19, 1990

Alcohol and breast cancer: update from an Italian case-control study, by C. La Vecchia, et al. EUROPEAN JOURNAL OF CANCER AND CLINICAL ONCOLOGY 25(12):1711-1717, December 1989

Alcohol and cancer. LANCET 335(8690):634-635, March 17, 1990

Alcohol and cancer of the sigmoid colon. LANCET 2(8674):1270, November 25, 1989

Alcohol and the cardiovascular system, by T. J. Regan. WESTERN JOURNAL OF MEDICINE 151(4):454-456, October 1989; also in JAMA 264(3):377-381, July 18, 1990

Alcohol and cerebrovascular and cardiac pathology: review of the literature, by P. V. Voloshin, et al. ZHURNAL NEVROPATOLOGII I PSIKHIATRII IMENI S. S. KORSAKOVA 89(9):122-126, 1989

Alcohol and diseases of the internal organs, by S. Alt. ZEITSCHRIFT FUR ARZTLICHE FORBILDUNG 83(16):815-818, 1989

Alcohol and drug abuse in treated alcoholics: a comparison of men and women, by H. E. Ross. ALCOHOLISM: CLINICAL AND EXPERIMENTAL RESEARCH 13(6): 810-816, December 1989

Alcohol and the heart, by M. M. Lopes. REVISTA PORTUGUESA DE CARDIOLOGIE 8(6):435-439, June 1989

Alcohol and hypertension, by F. Hesse. HOSPITAL PRACTICE 25(3):13, March 15, 1990

Alcohol and infections, by B. Morland, et al. TIDSSKRIFT FOR DEN NORSKE LAEGEFORENING 110(4):490-493, February 10, 1990

Alcohol and membrane-associated signal transduction, by J. B. Hoek, et al. ALCOHOL AND ALCOHOLISM 25(2-3):143-156, 1990

Alcohol and neoplasms of the brain, by E. D. Krasik, et al. ZHURNAL NEVROPA-TOLOGII I PSIKHIATRII IMENI S. S. KORSAKOVA 89(7):38-40, 1989

Alcohol and relative polycythemia, by T. Singh, et al. JOURNAL OF THE ASSOCIA-TION OF PHYSICIANS OF INDIA 37(6):416, June 1989

Alcohol and skeletal muscle disease, by V. R. Preedy, et al. ALCOHOL AND ALCO-HOLISM 25(2-3):177-187, 1990

Alcohol, beer and cancer of the pancreas, by C. Bouchardy, et al. INTERNATIONAL JOURNAL OF CANCER 45(5):842-846, May 15, 1990

Alcohol, cancer, and immunomodulation, by S. I. Mufti, et al. CRITICAL REVIEWS IN ONCOLOGY/HEMATOLOGY 9(3):243-261, 1989

Alcohol consumption aggravates copper deficiency, by M. Fields, et al. METABO-LISM 39(6):610-613, June 1990

Alcohol consumption alters the pharmacodynamics of alfentanil, by H. J. Lemmens, et al. ANESTHESIOLOGY 71(5):669-674, November 1989

Alcohol consumption and blood pressure in the 1982 Maryland Hypertension Sur-vey, by R. D. Moore, et al. AMERICAN JOURNAL OF HYPERTENSION 3(1):1-7, January 1990

Alcohol consumption and cancers of hormone-related organs in females, by I. Kato, et al. JAPANESE JOURNAL OF CLINICAL ONCOLOGY 19(3):202-207, Septem-ber 1989

Alcohol consumption and carotid atherosclerosis in the Lausanne Stroke Registry, by J. Bogousslavsky, et al. STROKE 21(5):715-720, May 1990

Alcohol consumption and casualities: a comparison of emergency room populations in the United States and Mexico, by C. J. Cherpitel, et al. JOURNAL OF STUDIES ON ALCOHOL 51(4):319-326, July 1990

Alcohol consumption and the risk of breast cancer, by S. Y. Chu, et al. AMERICAN JOURNAL OF EPIDEMIOLOGY 130(5):867-877, November 1989

Alcohol consumption, serum lipids and severity of angiographically determined coro-nary artery disease, by K. Handa, et al. AMERICAN JOURNAL OF CARDIOLOGY 65(5):287-289, February 1, 1990

Alcohol dependence in ICD-9 and DSM-III-R: a comparative polydiagnostic study, by W. Hiller. EUROPEAN ARCHIVES OF PSYCHIATRY AND NEUROLOGICAL SCIENCES 239(2):101-108, 1989

Alcohol dose, frequency and age at first exposure in relation to the risk of breast cancer, by P. van 't Veer, et al. INTERNATIONAL JOURNAL OF EPIDEMIOLOGY 18(3):511-517, September 1989

Alcohol drinking: biological data relevant to the evaluation of carcinogenic risk to hu-mans. IARC MONOGRAPH ON THE EVALUATION OF THE CARCINOGENIC RISK OF CHEMICALS TO HUMANS 44:101-152, 1988

Alcohol drinking: epidemiological studies of cancer in humans. IARC MONOGRAPH ON THE EVALUATION OF THE CARCINOGENIC RISK OF CHEMICALS TO HUMANS 44:153-250, 1988

Alcohol histories in hospital: does the age and sex of the patient make a difference?, by I. Awad, et al. BRITISH JOURNAL OF ADDICTION 85(1):149-150, January 1990

Alcohol-induced bone marrow damage: status before and after a 4-week period of abstinence from alcohol with or without disulfirm: a randomized bone marrow study in alcohol-dependent individuals, by G. Casagrande, et al. BLUT 59(3):231-236, September 1989

Alcohol-induced coronary spastic angina associated with myocardial bridge: a case report, by K. Nishitani, et al. JOURNAL OF CARDIOLOGY 22(Suppl):90-93, 1989

Alcohol-induced damage of the liver, by T. Laskus, et al. POLSKI ARCHIVUM MEDYCYNY WEWNETRZNEJ 82(2-3):105-113, August/September 1989

Alcohol-induced hypertension, by J. Papke, et al. ZEITSCHRIFT FUR DIE GESAMTE INNERE MEDIZIN UND IHRE GRENZGEBIETE 45(1):22-23, January 1, 1990

Alcohol-induced ischemia may contribute to pancreatitis, by J. E. Valenzuela. AMERICAN FAMILY PHYSICIAN 41:1550, May 1990

Alcohol intake and acute duodenal ulcer healing, by B. Battaglia, et al. AMERICAN JOURNAL OF GASTROENTEROLOGY 85(9):1198-1199, September 1990

Alcohol intake and blood pressure in young adults: the CARDIA study, by A. R. Dyer, et al. JOURNAL OF CLINICAL EPIDEMIOLOGY 43(1):1-13, 1990

Alcohol intake: a risk factor for psoriasis in young and middle aged men, by K. Poilolainen, et al. BMJ 300(6727):780-783, March 24, 1990

Alcohol intakes and deficiencies in thiamine and vitamin B6 in black patients with cardiac failure, by S. L. Tobias, et al. SOUTH AFRICAN MEDICAL JOURNAL 76(7): 299-302, October 7, 1989

Alcohol intoxication blunts sympatho-adrenal activation following brain injury, by P. D. Woolf, et al. ALCOHOLISM 14(2):205-209, April 1990

Alcohol-related admissions in a community hospital, by J. Birnbaum, et al. HAREFAUH 118(2):85-88, January 15, 1990

Alcohol-related admissions to a district hospital, by G. Bovim, et al. TIDSSKRIFT FOR DEN NORSKE LAEGEFORENING 110(3):376-379, January 30, 1990

Alcohol-related cancers in Mediterranean countries, by A. J. Tuyns. TUMORI 76(4): 315-320, August 31, 1990

Alcohol use and later hospitalization experience, by M. A. Armstrong, et al. MEDICAL CARE 27(12):1099-1108, December 1989

Alcohol use and reninal vessels: insights into the mechanism of alcohol-induced stroke, by M. J. Klag, et al. INTERNATIONAL JOURNAL OF EPIDEMIOLOGY 18(3):619-625, September 1989. Erratum. 19(1):225, March 1990

Alcohol versus mnemosyne: blackouts, by D. F. Sweeney. JOURNAL OF SUB-STANCE ABUSE TREATMENT 6(3):159-162, 1989

Alcohol withdrawal concealing symptoms of subdural hematoma: a caveat, by E. K. Koranyi, et al. PSYCHIATRIC JOURNAL OF THE UNIVERSITY OF OTTAWA 15(1):15-17, March 1990

Alcoholic beverage consumption and the risk of endometrial cancer: cancer and steroid hormone study group, by L. A. Webster, et al. INTERNATIONAL JOUR-NAL OF EPIDEMIOLOGY 18(4):786-791, December 1989

Alcoholic cardiomyodystrophy, by K. Schmidt. ZEITSCHRIFT FUR ARZTLICHE FORTBILDUNG 83(15):751-757, 1989

Alcoholic lesions of the digestive system, by K. Brailski. VUTRESHNI BOLESTI 28(4):12-18, 1989

Alcoholic myopathy, by T. Shimpo. NIPPON RINSHO 48(7):1547-1551, July 1990

Alcoholic pancreatitis, by Z. Laszik, et al. ORVOSI HETILAP 130(47):2527-2531, November 19, 1989

Alcoholic polyneuropathy and myopathy: a contribution to clinico-neurologic diagno-sis of alcoholic patients, by H. Grosse Aldenhovel. BLUTALKOHOL 27(4):272-278, July 1990

Alcoholism and associated malnutrition in the elderly, by F. L. Iber. PROGRESS IN CLINICAL AND BIOLOGICAL RESEARCH 326:157-173, 1990

Alcoholism and drug addiction among patients with active tuberculosis, by G. T. Khauadamova, et al. PROBLEMY TUBERKULIOZA (10):7-10, 1989

Alcoholism and panic disorder: is the comorbidity more than coincidence, by D. T. George, et al. ACTA PSYCHIATRICA SCANDINAVICA 81(2):97-107, February 1990

Alcoholism and psychiatric disorder in patients who present to different services in Wellington, by K. Peace, et al. NEW ZEALAND MEDICAL JOURNAL 102(879): 577-580, November 8, 1989

Alcoholism: a disease of internal medicine, by C. S. Lieber. JOURNAL OF STUDIES ON ALCOHOL 51:101-103, March 1990

Alcoholism in patients with pharyngeal cancer, by I. Rzewnicki, et al. POLISKI TY-GODNIK LEKARSKI 44(24):581-583, June 12, 1989

Alcoholism-induced zinc deficiency in mother and fetus, by A. Jendryczko, et al. WIADOMSCI LEKARSKIE 42(19-21):1052-1054, October 1-November 1, 1989

Alcoholism-mental ills jibe: New Zealand studies shows 95% correlation, by P. Mc-Carthy. JOURNAL OF THE ADDICTION RESEARCH FOUNDATION 19(2):4, February 1, 1990

Analysis of the deterioration rates of liver function in cirrhosis, based on galactose elimination capacity, by G. Marchesini, et al. LIVER 10(2):65-71, 1990

Analysis of the MCMI-I at the item level, by M. Lorr, et al. JOURNAL OF CLINICAL PSYCHOLOGY 45(6):884-890, November 1989

Antemortem diagnosis of Marchiafava-Bignami disease, by J. Shiota, et al. RINSHO SHINKEIGAKU 29(6):701-706, June 1989

Anxiety and alcoholism, by M. I. Linnoila. JOURNAL OF CLINICAL PSYCHIATRY 50(Suppl):26-29, November 1989

AST-ALT ration and alcohol abuse, by I. Kawachi, et al. NEW ZEALAND MEDICAL JOURNAL 103(895):382, August 8, 1990

AST-ALT ration and alcohol abuse, by T. H. Evans. NEW ZEALAND MEDICAL JOUR-NAL 103(894):356, July 25, 1990

"Ball's sign" or "Bell's sign," by J. Harvey. BRISTOL MEDICO-CHIRURGICAL JOUR-NAL 104(4):108, November 1989

Basic principles of the prevention of cardiovascular diseases in light of knowledge and opinions of the Polish community: II—knowledge of coronary disease risk factors, by H. Wagrowska, et al. KARDIOLOGIA POLSKA 32(Suppl):47-55, 1989

Benign symmetrical lipomatosis: a complication of excessive alcohol consumption—a case report, by R. Wood. SOUTH AFRICAN MEDICAL JOURNAL 77(7):369-370, April 7, 1990

Biological changes caused by ethanol: their sequelae and importance in the diagnosis of alcoholism, by L. Cap, et al. THERAPEUTISCHE UMSCHAU 47(5):350-357, May 1990

Biological markers in the accurate diagnosis of chronic alcohol intoxication: the significance of gamma-glutamyl transpeptidase, by P. Boisteanu, et al. REVISTA MEDICO-CHIRURGICALA A SOCIETATII DE MEDICI SI NATURALISTA DIN IASI 93(3):491-496, July/September 1989

Biological markers of alcoholism, by L. G. Schmidt, et al. NERVENARZT 61(3):140-147, March 1990

Blood coagulation and fibrinolysis in patients with pulmonary tuberculosis suffering from chronic alcoholism, by V. G. Larionov, et al. VRACHEBNOE DELO (8):46-47, August 1989

Both ethanol consumption and protein deficiency increase the fragility of pancreatic lysosomes, by J. S. Wilson, et al. JOURNAL OF LABORATORY AND CLINICAL MEDICINE 115(6):749-755, June 1990

Brain injured patients: comorbidities and ancillary medical requirements, by J. B. Parkerson, Jr., et al. MARYLAND MEDICAL JOURNAL 39(3):259-262, March 1990

Cancer incidence among Swedish brewery workers, by J. M. Carstensen, et al. INTERNATIONAL JOURNAL OF CANCER 45(3):393-396, March 15, 1990

Carbohydrate deficient transferrin: a marker for alcohol abuse, by A. Kapur, et al. BMJ 299(6696):427-431, August 12, 1989

Cardiac rhythm and conduction disturbances in patients with chronic alcoholism, by A. I. Lukoshyavichyute, et al. KARDIOLOGIYA 29(11):111-113, 1989

Cardiomyopathy. JOURNAL OF THE NATIONAL MEDICAL ASSOCIATION 82(8): 554, August 1990

Cardiovascular effects of alcohol, by D. M. Davidson. WESTERN JOURNAL OF MEDICINE 151(4):430-439, October 1989

Case-control study of alcohol beverage consumption and breast cancer, by L. Rosenberg, et al. AMERICAN JOURNAL OF EPIDEMIOLOGY 13(1):6-14, January 1990

Case-control study of male colorectal cancer in Aichi Prefecture, Japan: with special reference to occupational activity level, drinking habits and family history, by I. Kato, et al. JAPANESE JOURNAL OF CANCER RESEARCH 81(2):115-121, February 1990

Case of alcoholic liver injury associated with acute alcoholic myopathy, by N. Yoshida, et al. NIPPON SHOKAKIBYO GAKKAI ZASSHI 86(8):1701-1704, August 1989

Case of wet beriberi, by E. Borghi, et al. RECENTI PROGRESSI IN MEDICINA 80(11): 588-590, November 1989

Central pontine myelinolysis associated with low potassium levels in alcoholism, by M. Bahr, et al. JOURNAL OF NEUROLOGY 237(4):275-276, July 1990

Cerebral hemodynamic and metabolic effects of chronic alcoholism, by J. Lotfi, et al. CEREBROVASCULAR AND BRAIN METABOLISM REVIEWS 1(1):2-25, Spring 1989

Cerebrospinal fluid study of the pathophysiology of panic disorder associated with alcoholism, by D. T. George, et al. ACTA PSYCHIATRICA SCANDINAVICA 82(1):1-7, July 1990

Changes in the peripheral nerve trunks of the extremities in patients with peptic ulcer and chronic alcoholism, by V. G. Panikarskii, et al. VRACHEBNOE DELO (3):78-80, March 1990

Characteristics of clients in alcohol- and drug-treatment centers: South Carolina, 1989. MMWR 39(30):519-520, August 3, 1990

Characteristics of the clinical course of peptic ulcer in patients with chronic alcoholism, by V. G. Panikarskii, et al. VRACHEBNOE DELO (1):25-27, January 1990

Characteristics of the course of sluggish psychopathoid schizophrenia complicated by alcoholism, by B. V. Shostakovich, et al. SOVIET NEUROLOGY AND PSY-CHIATRY 22(4):87-95, Winter 1989/1990

Characteristics of laboratory markers in alcohol-related organ damage, by M. Salaspuro. SCANDINAVIAN JOURNAL OF GASTROENTEROLOGY 24(7):769-780, September 1989

Characteristics of tuberculosis risk factors in new cases, by B. U. Abdaev. PROBLEMY TUBERKULIOZA (11):44-46, 1989

Characterization of alcohol use, misuse and dependence and the clinical relations, by G. Richter. ZEITSCHRIFT FUR ARZTLICHE FORTBILDUNG 83(16):803-809, 1989

Chronic alcoholic intoxication at an internal disease clinic, by V. S. Moiseev, et al. SOVIET MEDICINE (9):68-71, 1989

Chronic alcoholism and low testosterone levels, by D. M. Gallant. ALCOHOLISM 13(5):721, October 1989

Chronic alcoholism and male sexual dysfunction, by R. C. Schiavi. JOURNAL OF SEX AND MARITAL THERAPY 16(1):23-33, Spring 1990

Chronic pancreatitis in Mexico City, Mexico, by G. Robles-Diaz, et al. PANCREAS 5(4):479-483, 1990

Cigarette smoking and alcohol consumption in the aetiology of uterine cervical cancer, by J. C. Licciardone, et al. INTERNATIONAL JOURNAL OF EPIDEMIOLOGY 18(3):533-537, September 1989

Clinical and experimental study of the contribution of lipid metabolism disorders to development of eczema and psoriasis in chronic alcoholism, by A. P. Lashmanova, et al. VESTNIK DERMATOLOGII I VENEROLOGII (3):54-57, 1990

Clinical and prognostic value of serum procollagen levels in chronic alcoholic liver disease, by E. Gonzalez-Reimers, et al. DRUG AND ALCOHOL DEPENDENCE 25(1):91-95, February 1990

Clinical and ultrasonic diagnosis of diseases of the hepatobiliary system in chronic alcoholics, by P. S. Fedishin, et al. VRACHEBNOE DELO (9):65-67, September 1989

Clinical course of peptic ulcer in patients with chronic alcoholism, by V. G. Panikarskii, et al. VRACHEBNOE DELO (1):25-27, 1990

Clinical importance of age at onset in Type 1 and Type 2 primary alcoholics, by M. Irwin, et al. ARCHIVES OF GENERAL PSYCHIATRY 47(4):320-324, April 1990

Clinico-nosographic considerations on the relation of depression and alcoholism in a population of 450 hospitalized alcoholics, by G. Angelini, et al. MINERVA PSICHIATRICA 31(1):41-45, January/March 1990

Co-existence of hepatocyte ground-glass inclusions from several causes, by C. Alonso-Marti, et al. HISTOPATHOLOGY 16(3):304-307, March 1990

Cognitive effects of alcohol abuse: a controlled study, by C. M. Williams, et al. BRITISH JOURNAL OF ADDICTION 85(7):911-917, July 1990

Cognitive impairment in alcoholics, by A. S. Tamkin, et al. PERCEPTUAL AND MOTOR SKILLS 70(3 Pt 1):816-818, June 1990

Cognitive impairments in abstinent alcoholics, by G. Fein, et al. WESTERN JOURNAL OF MEDICINE 152(5):531-537, May 1990

Comatose patients smelling of alcohol, by G. Quaghebeur, et al. BMJ 299(6696):410, August 12, 1989+

Comment on prevalence of hepatitis B virus markers among Polish urban alcoholics: infection 16—1988, by F. Raheman. INFECTION 17(5):331-332, September/October 1989

Comparison of CAGE questionnaire and computer-assisted laboratory profiles in screening for covert alcoholism, by T. P. Beresford, et al. LANCET 336(8713): 482-485, August 25, 1990

Complex forms of higher nervous activity in patients with chronic alcoholism, by V. N. Kuznetsov, et al. ZHURNAL VYSSHEI NERVNOI DELATEL-NOSTI IMENI I P PAVLOVA 39(6):1142-1145, November/December 1989

Computer assisted screening for alcohol-related problems in a general hospital setting, by R. Hecker, et al. MEDICAL JOURNAL OF AUSTRALIA 152(10):556, May 21, 1990

Conference at the Salpetriere, October 1987: chronic meningitis in a young alcoholic woman, by J. Bille, et al. REVUE NEUROLOGIQUE 145(6-7):485-491, 1989

Consequences of alcohol addiction, by N. S. Miller. KANSAS MEDICINE 90(12):339-343, December 1989

Consistency of reported levels of alcohol-related problems in the community, by E. B. Ritson, et al. BRITISH JOURNAL OF ADDICTION 84(8):901-905, August 1989

Consumption of tobacco, alcohol and the risk of adenocarcinoma in Barrett's oesophagus, by F. Levi, et al. INTERNATIONAL JOURNAL OF CANCER 45(5):852-854, May 15, 1990

Contemporary alcoholic, by N. S. Miller, et al. NEW JERSEY MEDICINE 87(1):35-39, January 1990

Content of somatotropic hormone and prolactin in men with chronic alcoholism in a state of abstinence, by S. Y. Abrikosova. TERAPEVTICHESKII ARKHIV 62(4):45-47, 1990

Copper and zinc status in moderate alcohol intake, by N. A. Frimpong, et al. ADVANCES IN EXPERIMENTAL MEDICINE AND BIOLOGY 258:145-154, 1989

Correction with formate of metabolic disorders in alcoholic intoxication, by M. F. Gulyi, et al. UKRAINESKII BIOKHIMICHESKII ZHURNAL 62(3):107-111, May/June 1990

ALCOHOL—Complications

Correlation of etiology and severity in a series of 506 cases of acute pancreatitis, by B. Oller, et al. REVISTA ESPANOLA DE LAS ENFERMEDADES DEL APARATO DIGESTIVO 76(6 Pt 2):640-644, December 1989

Correlations between changes in hearing and cerebral hemodynamics in patients with chronic alcoholism, by V. Khlystov, et al. VESTNIK OTO-RINO-LARINGOLOGII (5):5-8, September/October 1989

Course of acute hepatitis B in alcoholism, by T. Laskus, et al. POLSKI TYGODNIK LEKARSKI 44(24):571-572, June 12, 1989

Cross-model functions in alcoholism and aging, by M. Oscar-Berman, et al. NEU-ROPSYCHOLOGIA 28(8):851-870, 1990

Current bone mass and body weight changes in alcoholic males, by R. G. Crilly, et al. CALCIFIED TISSUE INTERNATIONAL 46(3):169-172, March 1990

Cytosolic NAD[P]: [quinone-acceptor]oxidoreductase in human normal and tumor tissue: effects of cigarette smoking and alcohol, by J. J. Schlager, et al. INTERNATIONAL JOURNAL OF CANCER 45(3):403-409, March 15, 1990

Dementia syndrome of dependency, by R. Howells, et al. BRITISH JOURNAL OF PSYCHIATRY 154:872-876, June 1989; Erratum. 155:566-567, October 1989

Denfenestration of hepatic sinusoids in the pathogenesis of alcoholic hyperliproteinemia, by R. Scheig. HEPATOLOGY 11(1):148-149, January 1990

Dental erosion in patients with chronic alcoholism, by B. G. Smith, et al. JOURNAL OF DENTISTRY 17(5):291-221, October 1989

Dental pathology and alcohol-related indicators in an outpatient clinic sample, by H. R. Kranzler, et al. COMMUNITY DENTISTRY AND ORAL EPIDEMIOLOGY 18(4):204-207, August 1990

Deranged vitamin D metabolism but normal bone mineral density in Finnish noncirrhotic male alcoholics, by K. Laitinen, et al. ALCOHOLISM: CLINICAL AND EXPERIMENTAL RESEARCH 14(4):551-556, 1990

Derivation and validation of a prediction rule for identifying heavy consumers of alcohol, by M. J. Lichtenstein, et al. ALCOHOLISM 13(5):626-630, October 1989

Dermal vascular IgA deposits in IgA nephropathy secondary to alcohol abuse, by S. M. Smith, et al. JOURNAL OF CUTANEOUS PATHOLOGY 17(4):193-196, August 1990

Dermatologic pathology in chronic alcoholics, by V. V. Evstaf'ev, et al. VESTNIK DERMATOLOGII I VENEROLOGII (8):72-74, 1989

Diagnosis and treatment of alcoholism: psychiatric aspects, by J. Raisin, et al. THERAPEUTISCHE UMSCHAU 47(5):358-363, May 1990

Diagnosis and treatment of patients with preclinical forms of alcoholism under ambulatory conditions, by N. N. Ivanets, et al. SOVIET MEDICINE (8):106-110, 1989

Diagnosis of alcohol use disorders in schizophrenia, by R. E. Drake, et al. SCHIZO-PHRENIA BULLETIN 16(1):57-67, 1990

Diagnosis of depression in alcoholics, by L. E. Domino, et al. BIOLOGICAL PSYCHI-ATRY 28(1):84-85, July 1990

Diagnostic value of immunologic indicators in patients with alcoholism, by V. A. Iakovchenko, et al. LABORATORNOE DELA (9):54-55, 1989

Diagnostic value of serum gamma-glutamyl-transferase activity and mean corpuscular volume in alcoholic patients with or without cirrhosis, by S. Pol, et al. ALCO-HOLISM 14(2):250-254, April 1990

Diaplacental poisoning with narcotics and alcohol in newborn infants, by A. Kloppel, et al. BEITRAGE ZUR GERICHTLICHEN MEDIZIN 47:77-79, 1989

Diet, alcohol and hypertensin, by L. J. Beillin. CLINICAL AND EXPERIMENTAL HY-PERTENSION. PART A: THEORY AND PRACTICE 11(5-6):991-1010, 1989

Digital amputations in neuropathic feet, by B. Greteman, et al. JOURNAL OF THE AMERICAN PODIATRIC MEDICAL ASSOCIATION 80(3):120-126, March 1990

Diminished ACTH response to insulin induced hypoglycemia in nondepressed, actively drinking male alcoholics, by J. D. Berman, et al. JOURNAL OF CLINICAL ENDOCRINOLOGY AND METABOLISM 71(3):712-717, 1990

Discrimination on the grounds of diagnosis, by M. Farrell, et al. BRITISH JOURNAL OF ADDICTION 85(7):883-890, July 1990

Disorders in basic brain biological function in patients with chronic alcoholism and those under conditions of exposure to carbon disulfide, by E. Dzialek, et al. MEDICINSKI PREGLED 41(2):119-124, 1990

Disorders of the cerebellar development in alcoholic embryopathy, by N. S. Kovetskii. ZHURNAL NEVROPATOLOGII I PSIKHIATRII IMENI S. S. KORSAKOVA 89(7): 45-49, 1989

Disorders of heart rhythm and conduction in patients with chronic alcoholism, by A. Lukoshiaviciute, et al. KARDIOLOGIIA 29(11):111-113, November 1989

Disseminated nocardiosis in a patient with chronic alcoholism, by M. E. Valencia, et al. REVISTA CLINICA ESPANOLA 186(3):146-147, February 1990

Does acute consumption of large alcohol amounts lead to pancreatic injury: a prospective study of serum pancreatic enzyme in 300 drunken drivers, by N. Niederau, et al. DIGESTION 45(2):115-120, 1990

Dry look for brain cells: effects of ethanol. DISCOVER 11:15, August 1990

DSM-III-R and ICD 10 classifications of alcohol use disorders and associated disabilities: a structural analysis, by B. F. Grant. INTERNATIONAL REVIEW OF PSYCHI-ATRY 1(1-2):21-39, March 1989

Dynamics of activity of creatine kinase and its isoenzymes in the serum of patients with alcoholism, by I. V. Chuvaev, et al. VOPROSY MEDITSINSKAI KHIMII 36(3):39-41, May/June 1990

EEG, CAT and alcoholism, by V. Conde Lopez, et al. ACTAS LUSO-ESPANOLAS DE NEUROLOGIA, PSIQUIATRIA Y CIENCIAS AFINES 18(1):7-25, January/February 1990

Effect of acute alcohol intake on certain cardiovascular functions in healthy young males, by V. Movai, et al. ORVOSI HETILAP 130(52):2785-2789, December 24, 1989

Effect of alcohol consumption on recency discrimination ability: an early screening test for alcohol-induced cognitive impairment, by F. A. Alderdice, et al. BRITISH JOURNAL OF ADDICTION 85(4):531-534, April 1990

Effect of alcohol on the stomach, by G. Wolff. GASTROENTEROLOGISCHES JOURNAL 49(2):45-49, 1989

Effect of combined substance use on laboratory markers of alcoholism, by M. M. Chang, et al. JOURNAL OF STUDIES ON ALCOHOL 51(4):61-65, July 1990

Effect of ethanol on exercise-induced muscle damage, by P. M. Clarkson, et al. JOURNAL OF STUDIES ON ALCOHOL 51(1):19-23, January 1990

Effect of smoking and drinking habit on the process from liver cirrhosis to liver cancer, by Y. Inaba, et al. GAN NO RINSHO February 1990, pp. 299-304

Effect of steroid therapy in experimental head trauma, by C. R. Spillert, et al. BRAIN INJURY 4(2):199-201, April/June 1990

Effects of alcohol on the acoustic-phonetic properties of speech: perceptual and acoustic analyses, by D. B. Pisoni, et al. ALCOHOLISM 13(4):577-587, August 1989

Effects of chronic alcohol intake on placental transport of IgG, by W. P. Jollie, et al. PROGRESS IN CLINICAL AND BIOLOGICAL RESEARCH 325:201-209, 1990

Effects of sex, race and year in college on self-reported drinking-related problem behaviors, by K. Curtis, et al. PSYCHOLOGICAL BULLETIN 66(3 Pt 1):871-874, June 1990

Efficacy of multimodality therapy of chronic alcoholism in patients with pulmonary tuberculosis revealed for the first time, by V. S. Krutko, et al. VRACHEBNOE DELO (4):70-71, 1990

Efficacy of x-ray skeletal diagnosis in chronic alcoholics, by H. J. Reumuth, et al. RADIOLOGIA DIAGNOSTICA 30(3):281-289, 1989

Electroneuromyographic study of alcoholic polyneuropathies and the possibilities of using anticholinesterase drugs, by G. N. Avakian, et al. ZHURNAL NEVROPATOLOGII I PSIKHIATRII IMENI S. S. KORSAKOVA 90(3):44-49, 1990

Endogenous toxemia in pancreatic necrosis of alcoholic etiology, by I. Belokurvo, et al. KHIRURGIIA (1):52-56, January 1990

Endoscopic detection of dysplasia and subclinical cancer of the esophagus: results of a prospective study using toluidine blue vital staining in 100 patients with alcoholism and smoking, by J. F. Seitz, et al. GASTROENTEROLOGIE CLINIQUE ET BIOLOGIQUE 14(1):15-21, 1990

Enhanced prevalence of red blood cell macrocytosis in psoriatic patients: a sign of ethanol abuse, by G. Zanetti, et al. ACTA DERMATO-VENEREOLOGICA 146: 196-198, 1989

Enhancement of chronic viral hepatitic changes by alcohol intake in patients with persistent HVs-antigenemia, by T. Murata, et al. AMERICAN JOURNAL OF CLINICAL PATHOLOGY 94(3):270-273, September 1990

Enzyme activity and thymol test of the blood serum in chronic alcoholics, by N. K. Kharchenko, et al. VRACHEBNOE DELO (9):67-69, September 1989

Epidemiological analysis of alcohol and drug use as risk factors for psychotic experiences, by A. Y. Tien, et al. JOURNAL OF NERVOUS AND MENTAL DISEASE 178(8):473-480, August 1990

Epidemiology and etiology of chronic pancreatitis in Brazil: a tale of two cities, by R. Dani, et al. PANCREAS 5(4):474-478, 1990

Epidemiology and etiopathogenesis of colorectal cancer: the role of a western diet, by A. Amato, et al. CHIRURGIA E PATOLOGIA SPERIMENTALE 36(2):69-77, April 1988

Epidemiology of alcoholism and liver cancer, by A. Oshima, et al. GAN NO RINSHO May 1989, pp. 62-68

Esophageal motor disorder in alcoholics: result of alcoholism or withdrawal, by A. Keshavarzian, et al. ALCOHOLISM: CLINICAL AND EXPERIMENTAL RESEARCH 14(4):561-567, 1990

Ethanol and the pancreas: current status, by M. Singh, et al. GASTROENTEROLOGY 98(4):1051-1062, April 1990

Ethanol-associated metabolic disorders, by R. S. Hoffman, et al. EMERGENCY MEDICINE CLINICS OF NORTH AMERICA 7(4):943-961, November 1989

Ethanol intoxication and cholesterosis, by G. Bozhko, et al. KARDIOLOGIIA 29(8): 114-118, August 1989

Etiology of chronic pancreatitis in Sao Paulo: a study of 407 cases, by C. de B Mott, et al. REVISTA DO HOSPITAL DAS CLINICAS; FACULDADE MEDICINA DA UNIVERSIDADE DE SAO PAULO 44(5):214-220, September/October 1989

Etiopathogenic study of digestive cancer in Viscaya, with special emphasis on the role of diet and alcohol and tobacco use, by F. J. Goiriena de Gandarias, et al. REVISTA DE SANIDAD E HIGIENE PUBLICA 62(1-4):1411-1430, January/April 1988

Evaluation of carbohydrate-deficient transferrin compared with Tf index and other markers of alcohol abuse, by F. Schellenberg, et al. ALCOHOLISM 13(5):605-610, October 1989

Evaluation of MAST-LAST ratio as a marker of alcohol misuse in a non-selected population, by B. Nalpas, et al. ALCOHOL AND ALCOHOLISM 24(5):415-419, 1989

Evidence of limited repair of brain damage in a patient with alcohol-tobacco amblyopia, by G. Sivyer. MEDICAL JOURNAL OF AUSTRALIA 151(9):541, November 6, 1989

Excitatory and inhibitory processes in the spinal cord in alcoholic intoxication, by D. N. Khudaverdian, et al. FIZIOLOGICHESKII ZHURNAL SSSR 75(7):911-916, July 1989

Extinction of orienting reaction in chronic alcoholic, by R. Rogozea, et al. NEUROLOGIA ET PSYCHIATRIE 27(4):287-304, October/December 1989

Factor structure of the DSM-III-R and ICD-10 concepts of alcohol dependence, by R. Caetano. ALCOHOL AND ALCOHOLISM 25(2-3):303-318, 1990

Female alcohol abuser: vulnerability to multiple organ damage, by D. M. Gallant. ALCOHOLISM 14(2):260, April 1990

Four cases found at screening in general practice, by P. Ellis. PRACTITIONER 233 (1469):758-759, May 22, 1989

Functional status of the heart in patients with chronic alcoholism and disorders of intraventricular conduction, by A. S. Smetnev, et al. VRACHEBNOE DELO (1):69-72, January 1990

Gastroesophageal reflux in chronic alcoholics: endoesophageal pH determinations using Heidelberg telemetring capsule, by T. Banciu, et al. MEDECINE INTERNE 27(4):279-282, October/December 1989

Gender differences in retrieval from long-term memory following acute intoxication with ethanol, by J. S. Haut, et al. PHYSIOLOGY AND BEHAVIOR 45(6):1161-1165, June 1989

Genesis of alcoholic brain tissue injury, by O. E. Pratt, et al. ALCOHOL AND ALCOHOLISM 25(2-3):217-230, 1990

Gonadal function in chronic alcohol abuse with or without cirrhosis: state of the art, by G. Tarantino, et al. REVISTA EUROPEA PER IE SCIENZE MEDICHE E FARMACOLOGICHE 11(1):3-5, February 1989

Half of all severe neurotrauma is related to alcohol, by P. Mellergard, et al. LAKARDNINGEN 87(16):1348-1351, April 18, 1990

Heart diseases in alcoholics, by V. A. Jakovcenko, et al. BRATISLAVSKE LEKARSKE LISTY 91(2):100-105, February 1990

Hematological complications of alcoholism, by H. S. Ballard. ALCOHOLISM 13(5): 706-720, October 1989

Hemostasis system and immune reactivity in patients with acute pneumonia and chronic alcoholism, by Z. M. Sulelmanov. KLINICHESKAIA MEDITSINA 68(4): 115-117, April 1990

Hepatic alcohol dehydrogenase activity in alcoholic subjects with and without liver disease, by F. Vidal, et al. GUT 31(6):707-711, June 1990

High alcohol consumption, liver toxic drugs and brain damage: a population study, by S. Mutzell, et al. UPSALA JOURNAL OF MEDICAL SCIENCES 94(3):305-315, 1989

High versus low-dose piracetam in alcohol organic mental disorder: a placebo controlled study, by C. Barnas, et al. PSYCHOPHARMACOLOGY 100(3):361-365, March 1990

Holiday heart syndrome: spontaneous reversibility of the electrocardiographic and echocardiographic alterations, by S. Morelli, et al. CARDIOLOGIA 34(8):721-724, August 1989

Hospital admissions for somatic care among young men: the role of alcohol, by S. Andreasson, et al. BRITISH JOURNAL OF ADDICTION 85(7):935-941, July 1990

Human immunodeficiency virus and hepatitis B virus infections in alcoholics, by J. M. Jacobson, et al. PROGRESS IN CLINICAL AND BIOLOGICAL RESEARCH 325:67-73, 1990

Hyperprolinemia and lactatemia in alcoholic liver disease: relationships to abstinence and histological findings, by M. Rojkind. HEPATOLOGY 11(3):511-512, March 1990

Hypogonadism in men with alcoholic liver disease, by H. Bell, et al. TIDSSKRIFT FOR DEN NORSKE LAEGEFORENING 110(11):1361-1365, 1990

Hypokalaemia in alcoholics, by A. F. Dominiczak, et al. SCOTTISH MEDICAL JOURNAL 34(4):489-494, August 1989

Hypothalamic-pituitary-adrenal axis functioning and cerebrospinal fluid corticotropin releasing hormone and corticotropin levels in alcoholics after recent and long-term abstinence, by B. Adinoff, et al. ARCHIVES OF GENERAL PSYCHIATRY 47(4):325-330, April 1990

Hypothalamic-pituitary and thyroid function in chronic alcoholics with neurological complications, by G. M. Knudsen, et al. ALCOHOLISM: CLINICAL AND EXPERIMENTAL RESEARCH 14(3):363-367, May/June 1990

Hysterical psychosis: its clinical and etiopathogenic aspects, by K. Fujiya, et al. PSYCHIATRIA ET NEUROLOGIA JAPONICA 92(2):89-116, 1990

Identification of health damage due to alcohol abuse: importance of alterations in cardiac function and blood chemistries, by V. Morvai, et al. ACTA MEDICA HUNGARICA 46(4):263-273, 1989

Identification of patients at risk of alcohol related damage, by O. G. Aasland, et al. TIDSSKRIFT FOR DEN NORSKE LAEGEFORENING 110(12):1523-1527, May 10, 1990

Importance of abstention from alcohol in alcoholic heart disease, by H. Molgaard, et al. INTERNATIONAL JOURNAL OF CARDIOLOGY 26(3):373-375, March 1990

Impulsive violence, by M. Virkkunen. ALKOHOLIPOLITIIKKA 54(5):228-233, 1989

Incidence of alcoholism and drug addiction among patients with active tuberculosis, by G. T. Khauadamova, et al. PROBLEMY TUBERKULIOZA (10):7-10, 1989

Incidence of diphtheria in alcoholic adults. AMERICAN FAMILY PHYSICIAN 41:1278, April 1990

Incidence of pulmonary tuberculosis associated with chronic alcoholism and a complex treatment of those diseases, by N. M. Rudoi, et al. PROBLEMY TUBERKULIOZA (10):3-7, 1989

Increased incidence of hepatocellular carcinoma in abstinent patients with alcoholic cirrhosis, by M. Nishiuchi, et al. GAN TO KAGAKU RYOHO 17(1):1-6, January 1990

Increased osmolal gap in alcoholic ketoacidosis and lactic acidosis, by J. R. Schelling, et al. ANNALS OF INTERNAL MEDICINE 113(8):580-582, October 15, 1990

Influence of bouts of acute pancreatitis on the course of chronic alcoholic pancreatitis in man, by P. Levy, et al. GASTROENTEROLOGIE CLINIQUE ET BIOLOGIQUE 13(12):1050-1054, December 1989

Interactions of alcohol, malnutrition and ill health, by I. Darnton-Hill. WORLD REVIEW OF NUTRITION AND DIETETICS 59:95-125, 1989

Intercurrent relationship of alcoholism and panic attack disorder, by A. Masi, et al. MINERVA PSICHIATRICA 30(3):173-174, July/September 1989

Interrelation between alcohol and accidents, by N. A. Jacobs, et al. JOURNAL OF THE ROYAL SOCIETY OF MEDICINE 82(7):447, July 1989

Intervention in early alcohol problems is a significant effect, by G. Dahl, et al. LAKARTIDNINGEN 86(36):2947-2950, September 6, 1989

Intracranial CSF volumetry in alcoholics: study with MRI and CT, by K. Mann, et al. PSYCHIATRY RESEARCH 29(3):277-279, September 1989

Ischemic cerebral stroke and alcohol, by W. Zawadzka-Tolloczko, et al. POLSKI TYGODNIK LEKARSKI 44(24):579-580, June 12, 1989

Laboratory diagnosis of visceral disorders in alcoholism, by A. T. Staroverov, et al. KLINICHESKAIA MEDITSINA 68(1):26-35, January 1990

Lasting nutritional imbalance following abstinence in patients with alcoholic cirrhosis, by A. Watanabe, et al. JOURNAL OF MEDICINE 20(5-6):331-336, 1989

Lead exposure: assessment of the risk for the general Italian population, by G. Morisi, et al. ANNALI DELL'INSTITUTO SUPERIORE DI SANITA 25(3):423-435, 1989

Learning disabilities in alcohol-dependent adults: a preliminary study, by S. S. Rhodes, et al. JOURNAL OF LEARNING DISABILITIES 23:551-556, November 1990

Left ventricular volumes in moderate alcohol users: a study from the workplace, by J. S. Sillberberg, et al. AUSTRALIAN AND NEW ZEALAND JOURNAL OF MEDICINE 19(5):449-353, October 1989

Lifetime alcohol intake and risk of rectal cancer in western New York, by J. L. Freudenheim, et al. NUTRITION AND CANCER 13(102):101-109, 1990

Liver cancer and life style: drinking habits and smoking habits, by T. Hiyama, et al. GAN NO RINSHO February 1990, pp. 249-256

Liver damage in alcoholics, by T. Laskus, et al. POLSKI ARCHIVUM MEDYCYNY WEWNETRZNEJ 8195):275-282, May 1989

Liver disease among Polish alcoholics: contribution of chronic active hepatitis to liver pathology, by T. Laskus, et al. LIVER 10(4):221-228, 1990

Liver function, plasma dexamethasone, and DST results in detoxified alcoholics, by S. W. Carson, et al. PSYCHIATRY RESEARCH 30(2):217-221, November 1989

Liver plasma membrane proteins in chronic ethanol intoxication, by P. P. Babu, et al. BIOCHEMISTRY INTERNATIONAL 20(3):573-577, 1990

Low frequency of associated liver cirrhosis in chronic alcohol pancreatitis, by T. Tanaka. AMERICAN JOURNAL OF GASTROENTEROLOGY 85(2):213, February 1990

Majority of physicians: alcohol drinking anamnesis contributes significant and relevant information, by M. Montin, et al. LAKARTIDNINGEN 86(37):3057-3058, September 13, 1989

Marchiafava-Bignami disease: consecutive observation at acute stage by magnetic resonance imaging and computerized tomography, by A. Ikeda, et al. JAPANESE JOURNAL OF MEDICINE 28(6):740-743, November/December 1989

Marchiafava-Bignami disease with recovery diagnosed by CT and MRI: demyelination affects several CNS structures, by R. Baron, et al. JOURNAL OF NEUROLOGY 236(6):364-366, September 1989

Marked spontaneous improvement in ejection fraction in patients with congestive heart failure, by G. S. Francis, et al. AMERICAN JOURNAL OF MEDICINE 89(3): 303-307, 1990

Markers of fibrogenesis and basement membrane formation in alcoholic liver disease: relation to severity, presence of hepatitis, and alcohol intake, by O. Niemela, et al. GASTROENTEROLOGY 98(6):1612-1619, June 1990

Markers of infection with hepatitis B virus in alcoholics, by T. Laskus, et al. POLSKI ARCHIVUM MEDYCYNY WEWNETRZNEJ 80(1):23-27, July 1988

Massive pancreatic pleural effusion: pathogenesis of pancreatic duct disruption, by D. Semba, et al. GASTROENTEROLOGY 99(2):528-532, August 1990

Mechanisms of regulation of tyrosine metabolism in ethanol poisoning, by K. Kurbanov, et al. VOPROSY MEDITSINSKAI KHIMII 35(4):102-105, July/August 1989

Memory retraining with adult male alcoholics, by R. Hannon, et al. ARCHIVES OF CLINICAL NEUROPSYCHOLOGY 4(3):227-232, 1989

Methods of statistical analysis in the complex evaluation of disorders of the blood levels of free amino acids in alcoholic abstinence syndrome, by A. V. Kozlovskii, et al. ZHRUNAL NEVROPATOLOGII I PSIKHIATRII IMENI S. S. KORSAKOVA 90(2):74-77, 1990

Michigan Alcoholism Screening Test (MAST): its possibilities and shortcomings as a screening device in a pre-selected non-clinical population, by I. G. Tulevski. DRUG AND ALCOHOL DEPENDENCE 24(3):255-260, December 1989; Erratum in DRUG AND ALCOHOL DEPENDENCE 25(3):327, June 1990

Microanalysis of ethanol-induced disruption of body sway and psychomotor performance in women, by B. W. Lex, et al. NIDA RESEARCH MONOGRAPH SERIES 95:463, 1989

Microcirculation in patients with delirium tremens as determined by conjunctival biomicroscopy, by E. D. Maiburd, et al. SOVIET NEUROLOGY AND PSYCHIATRY 22(4):48-59, Winter 1989-1990

Mini-mental state examination and brain age quotient: short form—relationship and demographic correlates, by A. M. Horton, Jr., et al. PERCEPTUAL AND MOTOR SKILLS 69(3 Pt 2):1177-1178, December 1989

Moderate alcohol consumption and stroke: the epidemiologic evidence, by C. A. Camargo, Jr. STROKE 20(12):1611-1626, December 1989

Morphologic changes in the small intestine after chronic alcohol consumption, by J. Persson, et al. SCANDINAVIAN JOURNAL OF GASTROENTEROLOGY 25(2): 173-184, February 1990

Movement disorders in alcoholism: a review, by J. Neiman, et al. NEUROLOGY 40(5): 741-746, May 1990

MR tomography and computer tomograpy of alcohol-induced brain tissue changes, by B. Ostertun, et al. ROFO 152(1):87-90, January 1990

Multiple withdrawals from chronic ethanol "kindles" inferior collicular seizure activity: evidence for kindling of seizures associated with alcoholism, by T. J. McCown, et al. ALCOHOLISM: CLINICAL AND EXPERIMENTAL RESEARCH 14(3):394-399, 1990

Myocardiopathy, alcoholism and systemic embolism, by R. Estruch, et al. REVISTA CLINICA ESPANOLA 186(7):358, April 1990

Natural killer cell activity in alcoholic cirrhosis: influence of nutrition, by F. Ledesma, et al. EUROPEAN JOURNAL OF CLINICAL NUTRITION 44:733-740, October 1990

Nature of changes in central hemodynamics and myocardial contractile capacity of the left ventricle during volumetric loading in patients with chronic alcoholism in relation to the duration of alcohol abuse, by A. S. Smetnev, et al. TERAPEVTICHESKII ARKHIV 61(9):69-71, 1989

Nervous and mental disorders in patients with chronic alcoholic pancreatitis, by V. B. Gel'land, et al. KLINICHESKAIA MEDITSINA 68(4):111-114, April 1990

Neurologic effects of alcoholism, by P. Barreiro Tella. ARCHIVES DE NEUROBIOLO-GIA 52(Suppl)1:183-194, 1989

Neutrophil elastase activity and superoxide production are diminished in neutrophils of alcoholics, by C. W. Sachs, et al. AMERICAN REVIEW OF RESPIRATORY DISEASE 141(5 Pt 1):1249-1255, May 1990

New measuring design for autonomic dysfunction of skin in neuropathies: hyper-thermal laser-Doppler flowmetry, by P. Koltringer, et al. ACTA NEUROLOGICA SCANDINAVICA 80(6):589-592, December 1989

Nighttime hypoxemia is increased in abstaining chronic alcoholic men, by M. V. Vi-tiello, et al. ALCOHOLISM 14(1):38-41, February 1990

Obstructive ileus and acute pancreatitis, by T. W. Frick, et al. ZEITSCHRIFT FUR GASTROENTEROLOGIE 28(4):206-207, April 1990

On the role of alcohol in nonvehicular unintentional injuries among adolescents, by I. R. Rockett, et al. JOURNAL OF THE TENNESSEE MEDICAL ASSOCIATION 83(4):169-173, April 1990

One hundred impotent men, by L. Forsberg, et al. SCANDINAVIAN JOURNAL OF UROLOGY AND NEPHROLOGY 24(2):83-88, 1990

Operationalization of alcohol and drug dependence criteria by means of a structured interview, by L. B. Cottler, et al. RECENT DEVELOPMENTS IN ALCOHOLISM 8:69-83, 1990

Osteomyelitis of the mandible: a complication of routine dental extractions in alco-holics, by H. T. Davies, et al. BRITISH JOURNAL OF ORAL AND MAXILLOFA-CIAL SURGERY 28(3):185-188, 1990

Pancreatic denervation for pain relief in chronic alcohol associated pancreatitis, by H. H. Stone, et al. BRITISH JOURNAL OF SURGERY 77(3):303-305, March 1990

Pancreatic lesions in alcoholism: a review of the literature, by A. P. Peleshcuk, et al. VRACHEBNOE DELO (7):37-41, July 1989

Pancreatic pseudoaneurysm monitoring the success of transcatheter embolization with duplex sonography, by G. M. Lim, et al. JOURNAL OF ULTRASOUND IN MEDICINE 8(11):643-646, November 1989

Panic attacks and related disorders in alcohol-dependent, depressed, and nonclinical samples, by C. A. Pollard, et al. JOURNAL OF NERVOUS AND MENTAL DIS-EASE 178(3):180-185, March 1990

Parkinsonism in alcohol withdrawal: a follow-up study, by M. Shandling, et al. MOVE-MENT DISORDERS 5(1):36-39, 1990

Paroxysmal disorders: the clinical course of alcoholism—review of the literature, by V. M. Karpiak. ZHURNAL NEVROPATOLOGII I PSIKHIATRII IMENI S. S. KORSAKO-VA 89(7):132-140, 1989

Pathogenesis of acute alcoholic pancreatitis, by J. M. Gronroos. LANCET 335(8696): 1046, April 28, 1990

Pathomechanism of Zieve's syndrome: observation of patients treated at the Infectious Disease Clinic, Medical Academy, in Bydogszcz, by W. Halota, et al. PRZEGLAD EPIDEMIOLOGICZNY 43(3):325-330, 1989

Pathomorphosis of acute alcoholic hallucinosis, by M. G. Gulyamov, et al. SOVIET NEUROLOGY AND PSYCHIATRY 22(4):28-37, Winter 1989/1990

Pathomorphosis of delirium tremens, by M. G. Gulyamov, et al. SOVIET NEUROLOGY AND PSYCHIATRY 22(4):38-47, Winter 1989/1990

Patterns of neuropsychological deficit in alcoholic Korsakoff's syndrome, by R. R. Jacobson, et al. PSYCHOLOGICAL MEDICINE 20(2):321-334, May 1990

Perils of perservance: crash of Simmons Airlines Banedirante on second ILS approach to Alpena Airport, Michigan, by N. Moll. FLYING 117:84+, August 1990

Peripheral bone mineral content in patients with fatty liver and hepatic cirrhosis, by H. P. Resch, et al. SCANDINAVIAN JOURNAL OF GASTROENTEROLOGY 25(4):412-416, 1990

Persistent immune deficiency in patients with alcoholic hepatitis, by M. G. Mutchnick, et al. AMERICAN JOURNAL OF GASTROENTEROLOGY 85(4):428-434, 1990

Perspectives on the validity for self-reported alcohol use, by L. T. Midanik. BRITISH JOURNAL OF ADDICTION 84(12):1419-1423, December 1989

Pneumonia in patients with pulmonary tuberculosis and alcoholism, by V. S. Krut'ko. PROBLEMY TUBERKULIOZA (1):64-66, 1990

Polymorphism of aldehyde dehydrogenase and its application to alcoholism, by S. Harada. ELECTROPHORESIS 10(8-9):652-655, August/September 1989

Possible involvement of kininis in cardiovascular changes after alcohol intake, by K. Hatake, et al. PHARMACOLOGY, BIOCHEMISTRY AND BEHAVIOR 35(2):437-442, February 1990

Post-arrest memory disorders: results of a retrospective study, by I. Barbey. BLUTALKOHOL 27(4):241-259, July 1990

Prediction of alcohol-related casualities among emergency room admissions, by C. J. Cherpitel. INTERNATIONAL JOURNAL OF THE ADDICTIONS 24(8):725-737, August 1989

Prevalence of depression among Israeli alcoholics, by J. Backon. JOURNAL OF CLINICAL PSYCHOLOGY 46(1):96-102, January 1990

Prevalence of pulmonary tuberculosis associated with chronic alcoholism and combined treatment of the diseases, by N. M. Rudoi, et al. PROBLEMY TUBERKOLIOZA (10):3-7, 1989

Prevention of acute renal failure in rhabdomyolysis caused by alcohol and drug intoxication, by I. Karpati, et al. ORVOSI HETILAP 131(21):1147-1150, May 27, 1990

Primary liver and esophageal neoplasms in an alcoholic patient, by M. Olm, et al. AMERICAN JOURNAL OF GASTROENTEROLOGY 85(1):108, January 1990

Prostacyclin-thromboxane balance and risk factors of ischemic heart disease, by K. Markov. KARDIOLOGIIA 29(9):5-12, September 1989

Psoriasis in persons suffering from chronic alcoholism, by P. T. Zoirov, et al. VESTNIK DERMATOLOGII I VENEROLOGII (10):26-28, 1989

Psychopathological characteristics in alcohol hallucinosis and paranoid schizophrenia, by M. Soyka. ACTA PSYCHIATRICA SCANDINAVICA 81(3):255-259, March 1990

Quinidine disposition in relation to antipyrine elimination and debrisoquine phenotype in alcoholic patients with and without cirrhosis, by D. Debruyne, et al. INTERNATIONAL JOURNAL OF CLINICAL AND PHARMACOLOGICAL RESEARCH 9(5):319-325, 1989

Rarity of EEF photo-paroxysmal and photo-myogenic responses following treated alcohol-related seizures, by D. G. Vossler, et al. NEUROLOGY 40(4):723-724, April 1990

Rational approach to liver transplantation for the alcoholic patient, by T. P. Beresford, et al. PSYCHOSOMATICS 31(3):241-254, Summer 1990

Re: "the relations of alcoholic beverage use to colon and rectal cancer," by A. Paganini-Hill, et al. AMERICAN JOURNAL OF EPIDEMIOLOGY 132(2):394, August 1990

Red cell folate concentrations in psychiatric patients, by M. W. P. Carney, et al. JOURNAL OF AFFECTIVE DISORDERS 19(3):207-214, 1990

Reduced benzo-a-pyrene activation potential in lymphocytes from chronic alcoholics, by M. Schmitt, et al. ALCOHOL 7(2):137-143, March/April 1990

Regression of autonomic symptoms in alcoholic polyneuropathy, by W. Wetzel, et al. PSYCHIATRIE, NEUROLOGIE UND MEDIZINISCHE PSYCHOLOGIE 41(9):553-555, September 1989

Relation between alcohol problems and the anxiety disorders, by M. G. Kushner, et al. AMERICAN JOURNAL OF PSYCHIATRY 147(6):685-695, June 1990

Relationship between alcohol dependence and alcohol-related problems in a clinical population, by D. C. Drummond. BRITISH JOURNAL OF ADDICTION 85(3):357-366, March 1990

Relationship between alcohol use and attempts and success at smoking cessation, by R. S. Zimmerman, et al. ADDICTIVE BEHAVIORS 15(3):197-207, 1990

Relationship between neuropsychological impairment in alcoholics and treatment outcome at one year, by S. N. Macciocchi, et al. ARCHIVES OF CLINICAL NEUROPSYCHOLOGY 4(4):365-370, 1989

Relationship of alcohol abuse history to nightime hypoxemia in abstaining chronic alcohol men, by M. V. Vitiello, et al. JOURNAL OF STUDIES ON ALCOHOL 51(1): 29-33, January 1990

Renal sodium retention complicating alcoholic liver disease: relation to portosystemic shunting and liver function, by W. G. Rector, Jr., et al. HEPATOLOGY 12(3 Pt 1): 455-459, 1990

Response of alcoholic and nonalcoholic panic patients to lactate infusion, by M. R. Liebowitz, et al. AMERICAN JOURNAL OF PSYCHIATRY 147(6):819-820, June 1990

Results of combined treatment of patients with pulmonary tuberculosis and chronic alcoholism, by V. V. Kolesnikov, et al. PROBLEMY TUBERKULIOZA (2):61-64, 1990

Results of the multimodality treatment of patients with pulmonary tuberculosis combined with chronic alcoholism, by V. Kolesnikov, et al. PROBLEMY TUBERKU-LIOZA (2):61-64, 1990

Rhabdomyolysis in a depressed patient following overdose with combined drug therapy and alcohol, by A. Lazarus. JOURNAL OF CLINICAL PSYCHOPHARMA-COLOGY 10(2):154-155, April 1990

Risk factors for simultaneous carcinoma of the head and neck, by M. Hsairi, et al. HEAD AND NECK SURGERY 11(5):426-430, September/October 1989

Risk of vocal chord dysplasia in relation to smoking, alcohol intake and occupation, by M. C. Grasl, et al. EUROPEAN JOURNAL OF EPIDEMIOLOGY 6(1):45-48, March 1990

Role of acetyl-L-carnitine in the treatment of cognitive deficit in chronic alcoholism, by E. Tempesta, et al. INTERNATIONAL JOURNAL OF CLINICAL PHARMACOLOG-ICAL RESEARCH 10(1-2):101-107, 1990

Role of alcohol in nonfatal bicycle injuries, by S. Olkkonen, et al. ACCIDENT ANALY-SIS AND PREVENTION 22(1):89-96, February 1990

Role of alcohol in oral and pharyngeal cancer in non-smokers, and of tobacco in non-drinkers, by R. Talamini, et al. INTERNATIONAL JOURNAL OF CANCER 46(3): 391-393, September 15, 1990

Role of lipid metabolic disorders in the development of eczema and psoriasis in chronic alcoholism: clinical and experimental research, by A. P. Lashmanova, et al. VESTNIK DERMATOLOGII I VENEROLOGII (3):54-57, 1990

Routines, lifestyles and predatory victimization: a causal analysis, by J. R. Lasley. JUSTICE QUARTERLY 6(4):529-542, 1989

Sarcoidosis presenting as recurrent alcohol-induced pancreatitis, by M. J. Peters, et al. MEDICAL JOURNAL OF AUSTRALIA 153(2):104-105, July 16, 1990

Schizoid personality disorder: a rare type in alcoholic populations, by R. M. Costello. JOURNAL OF PERSONALITY DISORDERS 3(4):321-328, Winter 1989

Screening elderly veterans for alcoholism, by M. B. Moran, et al. JOURNAL OF GENERAL INTERNAL MEDICINE 5(4):361-364, July/August 1990

Seizure induction by alcohol in patients with epilepsy experience in two hospital clinics by J. Heckmatt, et al. JOURNAL OF THE ROYAL SOCIETY OF MEDICINE 83(1):6-9, January 1990

Separating cognitive impairment in neurologically asymptomatic alcoholism from Wernicke-Korsakoff syndrome: is the neuropsychological distinction justified?, by S. C. Bowden. PSYCHOLOGICAL BULLETIN 107(3):355-366, May 1990

Sequelae of alcoholism: neurologic diseases caused by chronic alcohol consumption, by H. C. Diener. MEDIZINISCHE MONATSSCHRIFT FUR PHARMAZEUTEN 13(2):38-40, February 1990

Serum beta-hexosaminidase as a marker of heavy drinking, by P. Karkkainen, et al. ALCOHOLISM 14(2):187-190, April 1990

Severe frostbite of the upper extremities: a psychosocial problem mostly associated with alcohol abuse, by I. Antti-poika, et al. SCANDINAVIAN JOURNAL OF SOCIAL MEDICINE 18(1):59-61, 1990

Short REM latency in primary alcohol patients with secondary depression, by J. C. Gillin, et al. AMERICAN JOURNAL OF PSYCHIATRY 147:106-109, January 1990

Sickness, absenteeism and mortality in patients with excessive drinking in somatic out-patient care, by J. Persson, et al. SCANDINAVIAN JOURNAL OF PRIMARY HEALTH CARE 7(4):211-217, December 1989

Smoking, consumption of alcoholic beverages and coffee as factors associated with the development of cancer of the pancreas, by F. Pfeffer, et al. REVISTA DE INVESTIGACION CLINICA 41(3):205-208, July/September 1989

Social diseases, by K. Palmer. PRACTITIONER 234(1483):164-165, February 22, 1990

Spectrum and natural history of common bile duct stenosis in chronic alcohol-induced pancreatitis, I. Kalvaria, et al. ANNALS OF SURGERY 210(5):608-613, November 1989

Spontaneous rupture of the bladder, by N. A. Shor, et al. VESTNIK KHIRURIGII IMENI I. I. GREKOVA 144(12):78-79, December 1989

Standardized scale instruments for evaluating the relational meansing of motivation, pathogenesis and care in alcoholism, by T. Pirozynski, et al. REVISTA MEDICO-CHIRURGICALA A SOCIETATII DE MEDICI SI NATURALISTA DIN IASI (3(3):485-489, July/September 1989

Stasis pigmentation and chronic alcoholism, by C. E. Gonzalez-Reimers, et al. DRUG AND ALCOHOL DEPENDENCE 25(1):49, February 1990

State of the equilibrium function in patients with chronic alcoholism, by L. A. Luchikhin, et al. VESTNIK OTO-RINO-LARINGOLOGII (4):19-22, July/August 1989

Status of alcohol as a risk factor for stroke, by P. B. Gorelick. STROKE 20(12):1607-1610, December 1989

Stroke from alcohol and drug abuse: a current social peril, by P. B. Goerlick. POST-GRADUATE MEDICINE 88(2):171-174+, August 1990

Study of cardiac vagal function in chronic alcoholics, by H. T. Sorensen, et al. UGESKRIFT FOR LAEGER 151(42):2727-2728, October 16, 1989

Study of some complex forms of higher nervous activity in patients with chronic alcoholism, by V. N. Kuznetsov, et al. ZHURNAL VYSSHEI NERVNOI DEIATEL-NOSTI IMENI I P PAVLOVA 39(6):1142-1145, 1989

Substance abuse, by Y. Kaminer. JOURNAL OF THE AMERICAN ACADEMY OF CHILD AND ADOLESCENT PSYCHIATRY 28(5):798, September 1989

Suppurative pulmonary diseases in chronic alcoholics, by V. A. Barkov, et al. KLINICHESKAIA MEDITSINA 68(2):107-111, February 1990

Survey of muscle function in detoxified alcoholics, by D. R. Pendergast, et al. ALCO-HOL 7(4):361-366, July/August 1990

Tardive dyskinesia in psychiatric patients with substance use disorders, by A. A. Olivera, et al. AMERICAN JOURNAL OF DRUG AND ALCOHOL ABUSE 16(1-2):57-66, 1990

Thyrotropin and prolactin response to thyrotropin-releasing hormone in depressed and nondepressed alcoholic men, by M. L. Willenbring, et al. BIOLOGICAL PSY-CHIATRY 27(1):31-38, January 1, 1990

To err is human: estimating alcohol content and its effects, by D. J. Giacopassi, et al. JOURNAL OF CONTEMPORARY CRIMINAL JUSTICE 5(2):102-113, 1989

Tobacco and alcohol as risk factors in cancer of the larynx in Kerala, India, by R. Sankaranarayanan, et al. INTERNATIONAL JOURNAL OF CANCER 45(5):879-882, May 15, 1990

Tobacco chewing, alcohol and nasal snuff in cancer of the gingiva in Kerala, India, by R. Sankaranarayanan, et al. BRITISH JOURNAL OF CANCER 60(4):638-643, October 1989

Transcerebral effect of ultrahigh frequency-electric field on endocrine function in chronic alcoholics, by A. S. Bobkova, et al. PROBLEMY ENDOKRINOLOGII 36(2):49-51, 1990

Traumatic rupture of the anterior communicating artery, by H. Bratzke, et al. BEITRAGE ZUR GERICHTLICHEN MEDIZIN 47:437-440, 1989

Treatment of alcoholic pancreatic ascites by intravenous infusion of ascitic fluid, by M. H. Giaffar, et al. JOURNAL OF CLINICAL GASTROENTEROLOGY 11(5):568-570, October 1989

Trends in alcohol-related damages in Norway, by O. J. Skog. TIDSSKRIFT FOR DEN NORSKE LAEGEFORENING 110(3):372-375, January 30, 1990

Two faces of alcohol myopia: attentional mediation of psychological stress, by R. A. Josephs, et al. JOURNAL OF ABNORMAL PSYCHOLOGY 9(2):115-126, May 1990

Unusual medical consequences of seismic activity, by N. Porter, et al. MEDICAL JOURNAL OF AUSTRALIA 152(11):616, June 4, 1990

Use of the ethanol test in the diagnosis of occupational diseases and alcoholism, by S. A.Veimer, et al. GIGIYENA TRUDA I PROFESSION'NYVE ZABOLEVANIYA (8):19-21, 1989

Using the Millon Clinical Multiaxial Inventory's Scale B and the MacAndrew Alcoholism Scale to identity alcoholics with concurrent psychiatric diagnoses, by H. R. Miller, et al. JOURNAL OF PERSONALITY ASSESSMENT 54(3-4):736-746, Summer 1990

Vagal neuropathy in chronic alcoholics: relation to ethanol consumption, by J. Villalta, et al. ALCOHOL AND ALCOHOLISM 24(5):421-425, 1989

Various biochemical mechanisms of alcoholic liver cirrhoisis, by C. Skarbek-Galamon, et al. PRZEGLAD EPIDEMIOLOGICZNY 43(3):263-271, 1989

Visual hemineglect and hemihallucinations in a patient with a subcortical infarction, by A. Chamorro, et al. NEUROLOGY 40(9):1463-1464, 1990

Vitamin and trace metal disturbances in alcoholism: potential effects on the immune system, by N. W. Alcock. PROGRESS IN CLINICAL AND BIOLOGICAL RESEARCH 325:419-432, 1990

Why bother: reasons for action, by G. L. Phelps, et al. JOURNAL OF THE SOUTH CAROLINA MEDICAL ASSOCIATION 86(1):66, January 1990

Conferences

International trends in alcohol consumption: a report on a symposium, by M. E. Hilton, et al. CONTEMPORARY DRUG PROBLEMS 15(4):685-716, Winter 1988

ISBRA-RSA congress 1990 June 17-22, 1990, Toronto, Canada: abstracts. ALCOHOLISM 14(2):262-362, April 1990

Preventing alcohol problems: the challenge for medical education—proceedings of a national conference, Niagara-on-the-Lake, October 16-17, 1989. CMAJ 143(10): 1041-1098, November 15, 1990

Counseling

Alcohol and drug abuse: a needs assessment of rural counselors, by D. J. Hawes, et al. SCHOOL COUNSELOR 38:40-45, September 1990

Driving-impaired patients leaving the emergency department: the problem of inadequate instructions, by D. L. Simel, et al. ANNALS OF INTERNAL MEDICINE 112(5):365-370, March 1, 1990

Effects of counselor gender and drinking status on the perceptions of the counselor, by M. E. Johnson, et al. JOURNAL OF ALCOHOL AND DRUG EDUCATION 35(3):38-44, Spring 1990

Native American alcoholism: a transcultural counseling perspective, by L. French. COUNSELLING PSYCHOLOGY QUARTERLY 2(2):153-166, 1989

Working through denial in alcoholism, by M. Amodeo, et al. FAMILIES IN SOCIETY 71(3):131-135, March 1990

Czechoslovakia

Alcohol abuse and its psychosocial correlates in sons of alcoholics as young men and in the general population of young men in Prague, by L. Kubicka, et al. JOURNAL OF STUDIES ON ALCOHOL 51(1):49-58, January 1990

Denmark

Drinking, everyday life situations and cultural norms in Denmark, Finland, and Western Germany: an experiment with nonactive role-playing, by J. Simpura, et al. JOURNAL OF DRUG ISSUES 20(3):403-416, Summer 1990

Developing Countries

Alcohol advertising in developing countries, by P. P. Aitken. BRITISH JOURNAL OF ADDICTION 84(12):1443-1445, December 1989

Alcohol in developing countries (book review), by J. Maula, et al. JOURNAL OF THE ADDICTION RESEARCH FOUNDATION 19(9):10, September 1, 1990

Diagnosis

Ability of physicians to predict electrolyte deficiency from the ECG, by K. D. Wrenn, et al. ANNALS OF EMERGENCY MEDICINE 19(5):580-583, May 1990. Erratum 19(8):905, August 1990

Abnormal gangliosides in the plasma of alcoholics, by S. Westphal, et al. DRUG AND ALCOHOL DEPENDENCE 24(3):251-253, December 1989

Alcohol use and dependency in youth: examining DSM-III diagnostic criteria, by W. F. Filstead, et al. DRUGS AND SOCIETY 3(1-2):145-170, 1988

Alcoholic polyneuropathy and myopathy: a contribution to clinico-neurologic diagnosis of alcoholic patients, by H. Grosse Aldenhovel. BLUTALKOHOL 27(4):272-278, July 1990

Application of the Tridimensional Personality Questionaire to a population of alcoholics and other substance abusers, by S. J. Nixon, et al. ALCOHOLISM: CLINICAL AND EXPERIMENTAL RESEARCH 14(4):513-517, 1990

Are you an alcoholic: quiz prepared by John Braggio. USA TODAY 119:51, December 1990

Biological factors in alcohol use and abuse: implications for recognizing and preventing alcohol problems in adolescence, by D. W. Goodwin. INTERNATIONAL REVIEW OF PSYCHIATRY 1(1-2):41-49, March 1989

Biological markers in the accurate diagnosis of chronic alcohol intoxication: the significance of gamma-glutamyl transpeptidase, by P. Boisteanu, et al. REVISTA MEDICO-CHIRURGICALA A SOCIETATII DE MEDICI SI NATURALISTA DIN IASI 93(3):491-496, July/September 1989

Biological markers of alcoholism, by L. G. Schmidt, et al. NERVENARZT 61(3):140-147, March 1990

Blood alcohol concentration measurement using a salivary reagent stick: a reliable tool for emergency departments, by I. C. Phair, et al. ARCHIVES OF EMERGENCY MEDICINE 7(2):69-72, June 1990

Bright lights in dark places: physician recognition of alcoholism, by G. L. Phelps, et al. JOURNAL OF THE SOUTH CAROLINA MEDICAL ASSOCIATION 86(1):17-18, January 1990

Comprehensive analysis of the data of clinicopsychologic examination of patients with alcoholism to predict early disease relapses, by Y. Tyul'pin, et al. ZHURNAL NEVROPATOLOGII I PSIKHIATRII IMENI S. S. KORSAKOVA 90(2):62-66, 1990

Computer-assisted evaluation of the status of the peripheral nervous system in alcoholics, by M. Niewiadomska, et al. NEUROLOGIA I NEUROCHIRURGIA POLSKA 23(3):220-226, May/June 1989

Computerized administration of alcoholism screening tests in a primary care setting, by K. L. Barry, et al. JOURNAL OF THE AMERICAN BOARD OF FAMILY PRACTICE 3(2):93-98, April/June 1990

Concanavalin A crossed affinity immunoelectrophoresis and image analysis for semiquantitative evaluation of microheterogeneity profiles of human serum transferrin from alcoholics and normal individuals, by N. H. Heegaard, et al. ELECTROPHORESIS 10(12):836-840, December 1989

Concept of pathologic drunkenness and diagnosis, by Z. Zheng. CHUNG HUA SHEN CHING CHING SHEN KO TSA CHIH 23(2):114-116, April 1990

Correlation of self-administered alcoholism screening test with hemoglobin-associated acetaldehyde, by C. M. Peterson, et al. ALCOHOL 7(4):289-293, July/August 1990

Derivation and validation of a prediction rule for identifying heavy consumers of alcohol, by M. J. Lichtenstein, et al. ALCOHOLISM 13(5):626-630, October 1989

Desialyted transferrin and mitochondrial aspartate aminotransferase compared as laboratory markers of excessive alcohol consumption, by I. Kwoh-Gain, et al. CLINICAL CHEMISTRY 36(6):841-845, June 1990

Detection of alcoholic patients using the systematic CAGE autoquestionnaire in out patients, by B. Rueff, et al. PRESSE MEDICALE 18(33):1654-1656, October 14, 1989

Detection of alcoholism in hospitalized schizophrenics: a comparison of the MAST and the MAC, by J. S. Searles, et al. ALCOHOLISM: CLINICAL AND EXPERIMENTAL RESEARCH 14(4):557-560, 1990

Diagnostic value of the MMPI alcoholism scales in assessing the risk of alcohol dependence among students, by J. B. Slawinska, et al. PSYCHIATRIA POLSKA 23(3):194-199, May/June 1989

Early identification of alcohol problems by J. B. Saunders, et al. CMAJ 143(10):1060-1069, November 15, 1990

Effect of acute alcoholic intoxication on the body's immunologic and biochemical indices, by O. F. Mel'nikov, et al. VRACHEBNOE DELO (8):85-87, August 1989

Ethanol distribution in body fluids in the human from a forensic medicine viewpoint: prepared as an initial study, by F. M. Trela. BLUTALKOHOL 26(5):305-318, September 1989

Evaluation of the diagnostic usefulness of inventory scales of the symptoms of alcohol dependence, by S. Kruszynski, et al. PSYCHIATRIA POLSKA 22(6):463-468, November/December 1988

Examination of Cloninger's type I and II alcoholism with a sample of men alcoholics in treatment, by E. C. Penick, et al. ALCOHOLISM: CLINICAL AND EXPERIMENTAL RESEARCH 14(4):623-629, 1990

General practice trial with breath alcohol analysis, by G. Schoknecht. BLUTALKOHOL 27(3):145-153, May 1990

Hair levels of lead, antimony, chromium, cadmium, titanium, nickel and strontium in alcoholism, by A. V. Skal'nyi, et al. GIGIYENA I SANITARIYA (5):80-82, May 1990

Health profiles of problem drinkers. AMERICAN FAMILY PHYSICIAN 42:1364, November 1990

Identification and intervention for alcohol abuse, by S. Holt. JOURNAL OF THE SOUTH CAROLINA MEDICAL ASSOCIATION 85(12):554-559, December 1989

Influence of psychiatric service resources on the identification of mental patients in the populations of Siberia and the Far East: Russian SPSR, USSR, by A. I. Potapov, et al. ZHURNAL NEVROPATOLOGII I PSIKHIATRII IMENI S. S. KORSAKOVA 90(3):103-107, 1990

Is the health profile of problem drinkers different from that of other patients?, by B. Rush, et al. JOURNAL OF FAMILY PRACTICE 31(1):42-46, July 1990

Knowledge, attitudes, and reported practices of medical students and house staff regarding the diagnosis and treatment of alcoholism, by G. Geller, et al. JAMA 261:3115-3120, June 2, 1989

Laboratory marker for alcohol abuse. AMERICAN FAMILY PHYSICIAN 41:1598, May 1990

Macrocytosis as an indicator of human disease, by W. F. Keenan, Jr. JOURNAL OF THE AMERICAN BOARD OF FAMILY PRACTICE 2(4):252-256, October/December 1989

Methanol intoxication: clinical features and differential diagnosis, by P. F. Suit, et al. CLEVELAND CLINIC JOURNAL MEDICINE 57(5):464-471, July/August 1990

Methodological variations in the use of the MMPI for diagnosis of borderline personality disorder among alcoholics, by P. Horvath, et al. JOURNAL OF CLINICAL PSYCHOLOGY 46(2):238-243, March 1990

Modulation of cytochrome P450 isozymes in human liver, by ethanol and drug intake, by N. Perrot, et al. EUROPEAN JOURNAL OF CLINICAL INVESTIGATION 19(6):549-555, December 1989

Molecular analysis of HDL particles: clinical applications, by G. Luc, et al. PRZEGLAD LEKARSKI 46(7):563-565, 1989

Natural history of alcohol abuse: implications for definitions of alcohol use disorders, by D. S. Hasin, et al. AMERICAN JOURNAL OF PSYCHIATRY 147:1537-1541, November 1990

New methods of pharmacokinetics evaluation of alcohol and its metabolites in female and male probands, by K. Kohlenberg-Muller, et al. BLUTALKOHOL 27(1):40-48, January 1990

NIAAA issues report on screening for alcoholism. AMERICAN FAMILY PHYSICIAN 42:1664+, December 1990

Obvious markers for alcohol dependency do not yet exist, by B. Sternebring. LAKARTIDNINGEN 86(39):3271-3273, September 27, 1989

Periodic health examination: update 1989—early diagnosis of latent alcoholism, by R. Goldbloom, et al. UNION MEDICALE DU CANADA 119(1):16-17+, January/February 1990

Programming and structure of a relation-oriented data bank system for registration, blood alcohol values and documentation of findings at the Forensic Medicine Institute of the Heidelberg University, by R. Kuntz, et al. BEITRAGE ZUR GERICHTLICHEN MEDIZIN 47:301-307, 1989

Recognition and evaluation of red blood cell macrocytosis in the primary care setting, by A. Wymer, et al. JOURNAL OF GENERAL INTERNAL MEDICINE 5(3):192-197, May/June 1990

Reduction of the threshold value for absolute driving incapacity due to improved measuring quality in forensic blood alcohol determination, by O. Gruner, et al. BLUTALKOHOL 27(3):175-181, May 1990

Replicated factor structure of the Beck Depression Inventory, by J. Louks, et al. JOURNAL OF NERVOUS AND MENTAL DISEASE 177(8):473-479, August 1989

Role of the physician in expert testimony leading to an arrest, by Z. Marek, et al. PREZEGLAD LEKARSKI 46(10):732-735, 1989

Screening for alcoholism, by M. G. Cyr, et al. JOURNAL OF GENERAL INTERNAL MEDICINE 5(4):379-380, July/August 1990

Screening for alcoholism among alcohol users in a traditional Arab Muslim society, by E. A. al-Ansari, et al. ACTA PSYCHIATRICA SCANDINAVICA 81(3):284-288, March 1990

Screening for alcoholism in family medicine: pilot study combining the Michigan Alcoholism Screening Test and measurement of serum y-glutamyltransferase, by P. J. Leouffre, et al. CMAJ 143(6):504-506, 1990

Screening tests identify the prevalence of alcohol use among freshman medical students and among students' family of origin, by N. P. Johnson, et al. JOURNAL OF THE SOUTH CAROLINA MEDICAL ASSOCIATION 86(1):13-14, January 1990

Significance of the photostress test for assessing the function of the macular area in chronic alcoholics, by I. V. Val'kova, et al. OFTALMOLOGICHESKII ZHURNAL (3):175-177, 1989

Some clinical associations of the Michigan Alcoholism Screening Test and diagnostic implications, by A. Blankfield, et al. ACTA PSYCHIATRICA SCANDINAVICA 81(5): 483-487, May 1990

Syndrome analysis: chronic alcoholism in adults, by J. E. Pendorf. JOURNAL OF ALCOHOL AND DRUG EDUCATION 36:115-126, Fall 1990

Use of the MacAndrew Alcoholism Scale in detecting substance abuse and antisocial personality, by A. W. Wolf, et al. JOURNAL OF PERSONALITY ASSESSMENT 54(3-4):747-755, Summer 1990

Use of the T-ACE questions to detect risk-drinking, by D. L. Elliot, et al. AMERICAN JOURNAL OF OBSTETRICS AND GYNECOLOGY 163(2):684-685, August 1990

Using the Millon Clinical Multiaxial Inventory's Scale B and the MacAndrew Alcoholism Scale to identity alcoholics with concurrent psychiatric diagnoses, by H. R. Miller, et al. JOURNAL OF PERSONALITY ASSESSMENT 54(3-4):736-746, Summer 1990

Validity of the CAGE in screening for problem drinking in college students, by E. J. Heck, et al. JOURNAL OF COLLEGE STUDENT DEVELOPMENT 31:359-364, July 1990

Value and justification of screening for alcoholism, by B. Yersin. SCHWEIZERISCHE MEDIZINISCHE WOCHENSHCRIFT 120(27-28):1014-1024, July 10, 1990

Value of alcohol tests, by R. Andersen, et al. UGESKRIFT FOR LAEGER 152(21): 1541-1542, May 21, 1990

Value of the CAGE questionnaire in the screening of alcoholism, by M. C. Dombret, et al. PRESSE MEDICALE 19(7):334, February 24, 1990

Alcohol and street traffic: critical comments from the legal and traffic medicine viewpoint, by U. Heifer. BLUTALKOHOL 27(1):50-63, January 1990

Alcohol consumption awareness in young male drivers, by S. Myers, et al. MEDICAL JOURNAL OF AUSTRALIA 152(9):503, May 7, 1990

Alcohol: crash involvement drops in 80s. TRAFFIC SAFETY 90(2):7, March/April 1990

Alcohol related to trucker accidents. LAW AND ORDER 38(5):5, May 1990

Alcohol-related traffic fatalities during holidays: United States, 1988. MMWR 38(50): 861-863, December 1989

Alcohol-related vehicle deaths. TRAFFIC SAFETY 90(2):18, March/April 1990

Alcohol use and the appearance of alcohol problems among first offender drunk drivers, by P. J. Gruenewald, et al. BRITISH JOURNAL OF ADDICTION 85(1):107-117, January 1990

All-too-usual: alcohol-server intervention, by A. Lauersdorf. TRAFFIC SAFETY 90(3): 8-11, May/June 1990

Altruism in drunk driving situations: personal and situational factors in intervention, by J. Rabow, et al. SOCIAL PSYCHOLOGY QUARTERLY 53:199-213, September 1990

Attribution theory perspective on alcohol-impaired driving, by D. M. DeJoy. HEALTH EDUCATION QUARTERLY 6(3):359-372, Fall 1989

Behavioral scientific model of the drunk driver, by J. Ehret. BLUTALKOHOL 26(6): 381-395, November 1989

California's ongoing battle against DUI: part of a special focus on highway safety, by M. J. Hannigan. POLICE CHIEF 57:51-53, July 1990

Cars can reverse drunk drivers. TRAFFIC SAFETY 90(3):24-27, May/June 1990

Characteristics of 167 consecutive traffic accident victims with special reference to alcohol intoxication: a prospective emergency room study, by D. Wyss, et al. SOZIAL -UND PRAVENTIVMEDIZIN 35(3):108-116, 1990

Characteristics of alcoholics in treatment arrested for driving while impaired, by S. MacDonald, et al. BRITISH JOURNAL OF ADDICTION 85(1):97-105, January 1990

Community pride answers basic DUI questions, by B. G. Crouch. POLICE CHIEF 56(7):49, July 1989

Comparative viewpoint of expert assessment by the federal health office in relation to "on the question of alcohol in traffic infractions," 1966, and "on safety values in blood values in blood alcohol determination," 1989, by O. Gruner, et al. BLUTALKOHOL 27(3):222-226, May 1990

Comparison of the psychosocial characteristics of alcoholics responsible for impaired and nonimpaired collisions, by S. MacDonald. ACCIDENTAL ANALYSIS AND PREVENTION 21(5):493-508, October 1989

Death takes a ride: alcohol-associated single vehicle fatalities revisited, by M. J. Hyland, et al. NEW YORK STATE JOURNAL OF MEDICINE 90(7):349-351, July 1990

Detect drivers under influence of alcohol or drugs: New Jersey. SEARCH AND SEIZURE BULLETIN April 1989, p. 3

Developments in street traffic from 1975 to 1988 from a statistical viewpoint, by W. Barth. BLUTALKOHOL 27(2):73-82, March 1990

Drinking and driving, by C. J. Hospedales. WEST INDIAN MEDICAL JOURNAL 39(2): 132, June 1990

Drinking and driving among youth: a study of situational risk factors, by M. E. Vegega, et al. HEALTH EDUCATION QUARTERLY 16(3):373-388, Fall 1989

Drinking, driving, and health promotion, by D. A. Sleet, et al. HEALTH EDUCATION QUARTERLY 16(3):329-333, Fall 1989

Drinking, drug use, and driving among rural midwestern youth, by P. D. Sarvela, et al. JOURNAL OF SCHOOL HEALTH 60(5):215-219, May 1990

Drunk driving: analysis of statistics from the city of Sherbrooke, by S. Brochu, et al. CANADIAN JOURNAL OF CRIMINOLOGY 32(2):279-290, 1990

Drunk driving: consumption of medications containing alcohol. CRIMINAL LAW REPORTER: COURT DECISIONS 47(1):1016, April 4, 1990

Drunk driving: mens rea—involuntary intoxication. CRIMINAL LAW REPORTER: COURT DECISIONS 46(25):1543, March 28, 1990

Drunk-driving penalties: a state-by-state report, by S. Nielson. GOOD HOUSEKEEPING 211:186-187, July 1990

Drunk driving, sensation seeking, and egocentrism among adolescents, by J. Arnett. PERSONALITY AND INDIVIDUAL DIFFERENCES 11(6):541-546, 1990

Drunk driving: trends and statistics, by O. P. Burden. NATIONAL SHERIFF 41(4):20-21, August/September 1989

Drunk while off duty: fatal auto accident—Los Angeles. POLICE OFFICER GRIEVANCES BULLETIN April 1990, pp. 5-6

DUI statistics often don't add up, by T. E. Wade. CRIMINAL JUSTICE 5(1):18-20+, Spring 1990

Ecological approach to the prevention of injuries due to drinking and driving, by B. G. Simons-Morton, et al. HEALTH EDUCATION QUARTERLY 16(3):397-411, Fall 1989

Effect of alcohol on visual constancy values and possible relation to driving performance, by T. Farrimond. PERCEPTUAL AND MOTOR SKILLS 70(1):291-295, February 1990

Effect on casualty traffic accidents of changing Sunday alcohol sales legislation in Victoria, Australia, by D. I. Smith. JOURNAL OF DRUG ISSUES 20:417-426, Summer 1990

Effects of alcohol drinking and cigarette smoking on serum alpha- and beta-carotene concentrations in healthy adults, by Y. Ito, et al. NIPPON EISEIGAKU ZASSHI 44(2):607-614, June 1989

Effects of paroxetine and other antidepressants in combination with alcohol on psychomotor activity related to care driving, by I. Hindmarch, et al. ACTA PSYCHIATRICA SCANDINAVICA 350(Suppl):45, 1989

Effects of terfenadine with and without alcohol on an aspect of car driving performance, by J. Z. Bhatti, et al. CLINICAL AND EXPERIMENTAL ALLERGY 19(6): 609-611, November 1989

Epidemiology of drinking and driving: results from the Behavioral Risk Factor Surveillance System, 1986; Behavioral Risk Factor Surveillance Group, by P. F. Smith, et al. HEALTH EDUCATION QUARTERLY 16(3):345-358, Fall 1989

Focus group study on decision processes of young drivers: reasons that may support a decision to drink and drive, by C. E. Basch, et al. HEALTH EDUCATION QUARTERLY 16(3):389-396, Fall 1989

From the scene to the crime: the effect of alcohol and social context on moral judgment, by K. Denton, et al. JOURNAL OF PERSONALITY AND SOCIAL PSYCHOLOGY 59(2):242-248, August 1990

Head injuries due to motorcycle accidents: crash helmets and alcoholism, by H. E. Diemath. NEUROSURGICAL REVIEW 12(Suppl)1:458-464, 1989

Impairment cited in trucker fatalities. JOURNAL OF THE ADDICTION RESEARCH FOUNDATION 19(3):2, March 1, 1990

Injury report. TRAFFIC SAFETY 90(2):18, March/April 1990

Introduction: drinking, driving, and health promotion, by D. A. Sleet, et al. HEALTH EDUCATION QUARTERLY 16(3):329-333, Fall 1989

Irish senator avoids charge of driving drunk, by K. Birchard. JOURNAL OF THE ADDICTION RESEARCH FOUNDATION 19(7-8):9, July/August 1990

Isn't it rude to drive like THAT? TRAFFIC SAFETY 90(3):28, May/June 1990

Israel tackles DWI teens. JOURNAL OF THE ADDICTION RESEARCH FOUNDATION 19(6):9, June 1, 1990

Kevin Tunell is paying $1 week for a death he caused and finding the price unexpectedly high: death of S. Herzog in drunk driving accident, by B. Hewitt. PEOPLE WEEKLY 33:118-119, April 16, 1990

Measuring self-reported deviance: cross-sectional or panel data, by D. E. Green. SOCIAL SCIENCE RESEARCH 19:301-321, December 1990

Nature of the alcohol problem in United States fatal crashes, by J. C. Fell, et al. HEALTH EDUCATION QUARTERLY 16(3):335-343, Fall 1989

Next big one, by P. Bedard. CAR AND DRIVER 35:14, May 1990

Note on drinking, driving and enforcement costs, by P. E. Graves, et al. SOUTHERN ECONOMIC JOURNAL 56:793-796, January 1990

Past behavior as a measure of actual future behavior: an unresolved issue in perceptual deterrence research, by D. E. Green. JOURNAL OF CRIMINAL LAW AND CRIMINOLOGY 80:781-804, Fall 1989

Patty's legacy: school bus crash in Kentucky, by K. Nunnallee. LADIES HOME JOURNAL 107:28+, April 1990

Policy alternatives and traffic safety: mandatory seat belts and drunk driving reform in California, by J. S. Legge. WESTERN POLITICAL QUARTERLY 43:613-630, September 1990

Policy alternatives for alcohol-impaired driving, by S. Farrell. HEALTH EDUCATION QUARTERLY 16(3):413-427, Fall 1989

Pretrial diversion: drunk driving—prosecutorial discretion. CRIMINAL LAW REPORTER: COURT DECISIONS 46(9):1195-1196, November 29, 1989

Problem drinking and depression among DWI offenders: a three-wave longitudinal study, by M. Windle, et al. JOURNAL OF CONSULTING AND CLINICAL PSYCHOLOGY 58(2):166-174, April 1990

Relative influence of alcohol and seatbelt usage on severity of injury from motor vehicle crashes, by J. A. Andersen, et al. JOURNAL OF TRAUMA 30(4):415-417, April 1990

Risk for DWI: a new look at gender differences in drinking and driving influences, experiences, and attitudes among new adolescent drivers, by J. A. Farrow, et al. HEALTH EDUCATION QUARTERLY 17(2):213-221, Summer 1990

Search and seizure: drunk-driving roadblocks. CRIMINAL LAW REPORTER: COURT DECISIONS 46(2):1038, October 11, 1989

Search and seizure: sobriety checkpoints. CRIMINAL LAW REPORTER: SUPREME COURT PROCEEDINGS 46(23):3177-3179, March 14, 1990

Servers: at licensed establishments, take responsibility. HEALTH PROMOTION 28(3):20-21, Winter 1989-1990

Situational riskiness of alcoholic beverages, by M. Hennessy, et al. JOURNAL OF STUDIES ON ALCOHOL 51(5):422-427, 1990

Social psychological and sociocultural aspects of alcohol drinking and alcoholic intoxication behind the wheel, by W. Bocher. BLUTALKOHOL 27(2):95-105, March 1990

Some focal points for penalty apportionment and penalty suspension in the assessment of alcohol-related road traffic accidents, by G. Zabel, et al. BLUTALKOHOL 27(4):260-271, July 1990

States' experience with inexperienced drivers, by J. Tannahill, et al. TRAFFIC SAFETY 90(1):81-21, January/February 1990

States of intoxication, by J. Castelli. TRAFFIC SAFETY 90(1):11, January/February 1990

Status of alcohol absorption among drinking dirvers, by A. W. Jones, et al. JOURNAL OF ANALYTICAL TOXICOLOGY 14(3):198-200, May/June 1990

Surgeon General's final target: drunk driving, by C. Marwick. JAMA 262:181, July 14, 1989

Ten myths about drunk driving, by A. S. Tamshen. JOURNAL OF TRAFFIC SAFETY EDUCATION 37:10+, July 1990

Weekends, rural roads, alcohol among risk factors gleaned from traffic death data, by P. Gunby. JAMA 262(16):2196, October 27, 1989

Young driver fatalities: the roles of drinking age and drinking experience, by P. Asch, et al. SOUTHERN ECONOMIC JOURNAL 57(2):512-520, 1990

Drunk Driving—Education

Drunk-driving enforcement training, by J. P. Foley, et al. POLICE CHIEF 57:39-41, November 1990

Irrefutable benefits of courses for alcohol intoxicated drivers, by H. D. Utzelmann. BLUTAKOHOL 27(2):106-109, March 1990

Once upon a stretcher: docu-drama, by P. A. Donahue. TRAFFIC SAFETY 90:19-22, March/April 1990

Remedial courses for alcohol apprehended drivers are effective, by M. Jensch. BLUTALKOHOL 27(4):285-288, July 1990

Should courses for alcohol intoxicated automobile drivers be legally introduced: an answer based on public economics, by G. Hundhausen. BLUTALKOHOL 26(5): 329-346, September 1989

Students experience driving drunk. TRAFFIC SAFETY 90(3):7, May/June 1990

Students write their own scripts: for drinking and driving prevention videos, by K. Vincent. JOURNAL OF THE ADDICTION RESEARCH FOUNDATION 19(5):8, May 1, 1990

Traffic psychology comment on "a cost-benefit analysis of courses for repeatedly intoxicated automobile drivers," by E. Stephan, et al. BLUTALKOHOL 26(5):347-351, September 1989

Alone at six o'clock. TRAFFIC SAFETY 89(6):18, November/December 1989

Blood alcohol in fatally injured drivers and the minimum legal drinking age, by L. S. Robertson. JOURNAL OF HEALTH POLITICS, POLICY AND LAW 14(4):817-825, Winter 1989

Can mandatory jail-laws deter drunk driving: the Arizona case, by H. L. Ross, et al. JOURNAL OF CRIMINAL LAW AND CRIMINOLOGY 81:156-170, Spring 1990

Case and comment: road traffic. CRIMINAL LAW REVIEW November 1989, pp. 832-833

Case and comment: road traffic, by L. Knapman, et al. CRIMINAL LAW REVIEW October 1989, pp. 741-742

Case and comment: road traffic, by T. Rees, et al. CRIMINAL LAW REVIEW April 1990, pp. 269-271

City aims to rid itself of drinking-driving, by J. Middleton, et al. WORLD HEALTH FORUM 10(2):219-221, 1989

Common-law forfeiture supports forfeiture of auto operated by drunk driver. CRIMINAL LAW REPORTER: COURT DECISONS 46(17):1362-1363, January 31, 1990

Concept on the decision by the Federal Court of Appeals of 27 October 1988: blood alcohol 26, 61-63: 1989, by M. T. Sunder. BLUTALKOHOL 26(5):297-304, September 1989

Court upholds brief stops of cars at sobriety checkpoints. LAW OFFICER'S BULLETIN 14(24):139, June 21, 1990

Destruction of confidence in established jurisprudence: 1.1 promille as the new limit value of absolute inability to drive, by H. Salger. BLUTALKOHOL 27(Suppl):1-8, January 1990

Drinking-driving compliance in Great Britain: the role of law as a "threat" and as a "moral eye-opener," by J. R. Snortum. JOURNAL OF CRIMINAL JUSTICE 18(6):479-499, 1990

Drunk-drivers' PACE rights: a cause for concern, by D. Tucker. CRIMINAL LAW REVIEW 177-180, March 1990

Drunk driving: are random checkpoints constitutional, by M. Granzotto. ABA JOURNAL 76:45, April 1990

Drunk driving: arrestee's request to contact relative—exclusion of evidence. CRIMINAL LAW REPORTER: COURT DECISIONS 47(4):1075, April 25, 1990

Drunk driving plus fatal accident make out vehicular homicide offense. CRIMINAL LAW REPORTER: COURT DECISIONS 46(6):1118, November 8, 1989

DUI arrestee needn't be mirandized before booking: sobriety testing. LAW OFFICER'S BULLETIN 14(24):139-140, June 21, 1990

DWI: police and the criminal justice system, by J. Hoffmann. LAW AND ORDER 38(5):56-59, May 1990

Evidentiary use of refusal to perform sobriety tests: offenders; Virginia constitution. CRIMINAL LAW REPORTER: COURT DECISIONS 47(5):1088-1089, May 2, 1990

Fatal crash involvement and laws against alcohol-impaired driving, by P. L. Zador, et al. JOURNAL OF PUBLIC HEALTH POLICY 10(4):467-485, Winter 1989

"Funny" drunks on the rocks, by M. J. Hannigan. TRAFFIC SAFETY 90(3):20-22, May/June 1990

Homicide: vehicular homicide—causal connection between drinking and fatal accident. CRIMINAL LAW REPORTER: COURT DECISIONS 46(1):1021, October 4, 1989

Incorrect procedures in drunk-driving cases, by M. Hirst. CRIMINAL LAW REVIEW March 1990, pp. 143-152

International news: Canada—drunk driving laws yield big results, by A. Harman. LAW AND ORDER 38(4):8, April 1990

Intoxicated driver: reasonable suspicion/sufficient facts—highway open to public; Vermont. ARREST LAW BULLETIN May 1990, p. 3

Justices weigh legality of "sobriety checkpoints." LAW OFFICER'S BULLETIN 14(17):101, March 14, 1990

Minnesota appeals court upholds use of drunk drivers checkpoints. CRIME CONTROL DIGEST 24(23):8, August 20, 1990

North Carolina governor wants tougher DUI level. TRAFFIC SAFETY 90(3):7, May/June 1990

Perspective. LAW OFFICER'S BULLETIN 14(24):144, June 21, 1990

Reckless driving: vehicular homicide arrest for public intoxication. ARREST LAW BULLETIN September 1989, p. 6

Sobriety checkpoints: threat to freedom—state senator, by J. Wellborn. HUMAN EVENTS 50:10+, May 26, 1990

Sobriety roadblock need not be publicized in advance. LAW OFFICER'S BULLETIN 14(15):85-86, February 15, 1990

Sobriety roadblock needn't be justified with statistics. LAW OFFICER'S BULLETIN 14(6):31-32, October 12, 1989

Social control of drinking and driving: the effectiveness of Pennsylvania Act 289-1982, by B. A. Woodruff. DAI A 50(10):3368, April 1990

Supreme Court reviews constitutionality of sobriety checkpoints. CRIME CONTROL DIGEST 23(41):9, October 16, 1989

Supreme Court upholds sobriety checkpoints. CRIME CONTROL DIGEST 24(24):9-10, June 18, 1990

Texas Court of Criminal Appeals divides over constitutionality of DWI checkpoints. CRIMINAL LAW REPORTER: COURT DECISIONS 46(7):1145-1146, November 15, 1989

Drunk Driving—Legal Issues

Adjudication of alcohol-related criminal driving cases in Ontario: a survey of Crown attorneys, by E. Vingilis, et al. CANADIAN JOURNAL OF CRIMINOLOGY 32(4):639-649, October 1990

Breathalyzer accuracy challenged, by G. Sargeant. TRIAL 25(1):22, December 1989

California's drunk drivers lose licenses immediately. CRIME CONTROL DIGEST 24(29):10, July 23, 1990

Court agrees to hear Miranda case. CRIME CONTROL DIGEST 23(42):8, October 23, 1989

Court hears arguments on sobriety checkpoints. CRIME CONTROL DIGEST 24(10): 10, March 12, 1990

Court rules against double jeopardy in New York case. CRIME CONTROL DIGEST 24(23):8-9, June 11, 1990

Crackdown on suspended drivers. LAW AND ORDER 37(12):4, December 1989

Criminality and driving while intoxicated: a comparison of DWI's and a random sample of licensed drivers, by L. A. Gould, et al. JOURNAL OF CONTEMPORARY CRIMINAL JUSTICE 5(2):114-126, 1989

Double jeopardy: automobile accidents—prosecution for homicide after guilty plea to lesser offenses. CRIMINAL LAW REPORTER: SUPREME COURT PROCEEDINGS 47(1):3004-3006, April 4, 1990

Driver's breath-to-blood alcohol ratio is irrelevant to per se breath-alcohol offense. CRIMINAL LAW REPORTER: COURT DECISIONS 46(10):1212-1213, December 6, 1989

Driving under the influence: arrest outside of city limits proper—Wisconsin. ARREST LAW BULLETIN October 1989, pp. 6-7

Driving while intoxicated: linking test results to last known operation. SEARCH AND SEIZURE BULLETIN July 1989, p. 8

Drunk driver Larry Mahoney gets 16 years for the Kentucky bus crash that claimed 27 lives, by J. S. Kunen. PEOPLE WEEKLY 33:51-53, January 8, 1990

Drunk driving: collateral estoppel—effect of findings made at prior summary license suspension proceeding. CRIMINAL LAW REPORTER: COURT DECISIONS 47(6):1117, May 9, 1990

Drunk driving: per se offense— relation-back evidence. CRIMINAL LAW REPORTER: COURT DECISIONS 47(16):1323-1324, July 25, 1990

Drunk driving: presentation of case to grand jury—prior convictions. CRIMINAL LAW REPORTER: COURT DECISIONS 46(2):1036-1037, October 11, 1989

Drunk driving: repeat offenders—due process. CRIMINAL LAW REPORTER: COURT DECISIONS 47(4):1075-1076, April 25, 1990

Drunk driving: roadblocks—need for proof of effectiveness. CRIMINAL LAW REPORTER: COURT DECISIONS 46(9):1195, November 29, 1989

DUI roadblock can be upheld without proof of its effectiveness. LAW OFFICER'S BULLETIN 14(10):55-56, December 7, 1989

DUI roadblock stop may include demand for documents. LAW OFFICER'S BULLETIN 14(11):62, December 21, 1989

DWI enforcement lowers alcohol-related accident rate. LAW OFFICER'S BULLETIN 38(5):57+, May 1990

How judges sentence DUI offenders: an experimental study, by T. J. Lange, et al. AMERICAN JOURNAL OF DRUG AND ALCOHOL ABUSE 16(1-2):125-133, March/June 1990

Interrogation. CRIMINAL LAW REPORTER: SUPREME COURT PROCEEDINGS 47(12):2165-2176, June 20, 1990

Liability for drunk driving. CORPORATE SECURITY February 1990, p. 4

License suspension. TRAFFIC SAFETY 90(2):17-18, March/April 1990

Minnesota court declines to exceed federal protections in implied-consent context. CRIMINAL LAW REPORTER: COURT DECISIONS 47(10):1187-1188, June 6, 1990

Motorists boil and civil libertarians burn as New Jersey police set a broad net to discourage drunk drivers: sobriety check point on Route 202, by K. S. Schneider. PEOPLE WEEKLY 33:69-70+, June 11, 1990

New Philadelphia story: the effects of severe punishment for drunk driving, by H. L. Ross, et al. LAW AND POLICY 12(1):51-79, 1990

New rules for road. JOURNAL OF THE ADDICTION RESEARCH FOUNDATION 19(7-8):2, July/August 1990

Officer injured: bar owner neglient—Los Angeles. POLICE OFFICER GRIEVANCES BULLETIN December 1989, p. 3

Party guest and hosts beware. ENFORCEMENT JOURNAL 28(3):39, July/August 1989

Police civil liability for failure to arrest intoxicated drivers, by V. E. Kappeler, et al. JOURNAL OF CRIMINAL JUSTICE 18(2):117-131, March 1990

Police documentation of drunk-driving arrests: jury verdicts and guilty pleas as a function of quantity and quality of evidence, by J. R. Snortum, et al. JOURNAL OF CRIMINAL JUSTICE 18(2):99-116, March 1990

Police to seize vehicles used by drunken drivers. CRIME CONTROL DIGEST 23(51): 2, December 25, 1989

Probable cause: driving while under the influence— Idaho. ARREST LAW BULLETIN June 1990, p. 5

Sentencing: drunk driving—credit for time in treatment program. CRIMINAL LAW REPORTER: COURT DECISIONS 46(9):1197-1198, November 29, 1989

Six-month jail term: 15-year mandatory license revocation trigger jury trial right. CRIMINAL LAW REPORTER: COURT DECISIONS 47(11):1209-1210, June 13, 1990

Some surprise twists on DWI. TRAFFIC SAFETY 89(6):5, November/December 1989

Standard blood-alcohol level sought. LAW AND ORDER 38(8):4, August 1990

Streamlining the DUI process, by S. Toland. POLICE CHIEF 56(7):46-48, July 1989

Sun sets on the sundowner: states crack down on happy hour promotions, by G. R. McCarthy. TRAFFIC SAFETY 89(6):17-18, November/December 1989

Supreme Court preview: by J. H. Reske. ABA JOURNAL 76:40, March 1990

Survey of 700 cases of blood alcohol when driving: medicolegal considerations and legal aspects, by H. Richou, et al. ANNALES MEDICO-PSYCHOLOGIQUES 147(10):1019-1036, December 1989

Termination: driving under the influence—Kentucky. POLICE OFFICER GRIEVANCES BULLETIN April 1990, p. 6

Termination: officer fired for lying—Nebraska. POLICE OFFICER GRIEVANCES BULLETIN April 1990, pp. 7-8

Traffic stop: suspicion of criminal conduct required—Virginia. ARREST LAW BULLETIN May 1990, p. 4

Drunk Driving—Prevention

222-MUCH: a ride you can live with, by N. Caputo. PROFESSIONAL SAFETY 35:34-37, May 1990

Are legal sanctions for improving traffic safety adequate?, by K. Geppert. BLUTALKOHOL 27(1):23-39, January 1990

ATA announces policy opposing alcohol sales at truck stops. CORPORATE SECURITY DIGEST 4(6):3, February 12, 1990; also in CRIME CONTROL DIGEST 24(6):3-4, February 12, 1990

Bad drivers: identification of a target group for alcohol-related prevention and early intervention, by D. M. Donovan, et al. JOURNAL OF STUDIES ON ALCOHOL 51(2):136-141, March 1990

Bartender tips. TRAFFIC SAFETY 90(3):11, May/June 1990

Cause celeb: work of E. J. Olmos, by E. Dutka. MCCALLS 118:70+, November 1990

Drunk driving: official's standing to challenge issuance of restricted driver's license. CRIMINAL LAW REPORTER: COURT DECISIONS 45(20):2368, August 23, 1989

Effects of televised alcohol messages on teenage drinking patterns, by C. K. Atkin. JOURNAL OF ADOLESCENT HEALTH CARE 11(1):10-24, January 1990

Examination of the effects of an interlock device on the First Offense Drinking Driver, by A. B. Crowe. DAI A 50(10):3375, April 1990

Expanded DWI education program planned in Texas. CRIME CONTROL DIGEST 23(34):6, August 28, 1989

Ignition interlocks help deter drunk drivers: Texas, by C. S. Kent. POLICE CHIEF 57(4):54-55, April 1990

Impact of support resources on local chapter operations in the antidrunk-driving movement, by F. J. Wee. SOCIOLOGICAL QUARTERLY 30(1):77-91, March 1989

Jail less effective than license suspension to prevent repeat drunk driving. CORRECTIONS DIGEST 21(18):8-9, September 5, 1990

Long-term effect of courses for repeat alcohol intoxication in automobile drivers: studies after 60 months probation, by W. Winkler, et al. BLUTALKOHOL 27(3):154-174, May 1990

MADD, insurance company give police agencies DUI cameras. CRIME CONTROL DIGEST 24(15):10, April 16, 1990

Modern posses lasso bad drivers: drunk busters, by T. Frisbie. TRAFFIC SAFETY 90(2):8-10, March/April 1990

Neurodynamics of relapse prevention: a neuronutrient approach to outpatient DUI offenders, by R. J. Brown, et al. JOURNAL OF PSYCHOACTIVE DRUGS 22(2):173-187, April/June 1990

Nissan, Canada, helps out with contribution against drinking and driving, by K. Riddell. MARKETING 95(13):26, March 26, 1990

None for the road, by C. Purdy. CURRENT HEALTH 2 17:14-16, October 1990

Not all drinkers are drunks: antabuse drug-based treatment for alcoholism, by C. Brewer. GUARDIAN January 5, 1990, p. 32

OMA (Ontario Medical Association) tackles drunk drivers. JOURNAL OF THE ADDICTION RESEARCH FOUNDATION 19(7-8):2, July/August 1990

President proclaims national drive for life weekend, by G. Bush. CRIME VICTIMS DIGEST 6(8):6, August 1989

Reforming highway safety in New York State: an evaluation of alternative policy interventions, by J. S. Legge. SOCIAL SCIENCE QUARTERLY 71:373-382, June 1990

Resource guide to alcohol-impaired driving programs and materials, by D. A. Sleet, et al. HEALTH EDUCATION QUARTERLY 16(3):439-447, Fall 1989

SADD announces initiatives for the nineties. JUVENILE JUSTICE DIGEST 18(8):1+, April 18, 1990

Vehicle stops. CRIMINAL LAW REPORTER: SUPREME COURT PROCEEDINGS 47(11):2153-2163, June 13, 1990

Vehicle stops: drunk-driving roadblocks—advance publicity. CRIMINAL LAW REPORTER: COURT DECISIONS 46(18):1388, February 7, 1990

Victim-activist role in the anti-drunk driving movement, by F. J. Weed. SOCIOLOGICAL QUARTERLY 31(3):459-473, 1990

War on drunk driving: the P.E.I. crackdown is a major success, by A. Prodanou. MACLEAN'S 103(15):66, April 9, 1990

Drunk Driving—Testing

Absolute driving incapacity at 1.0 promille: an erroneous limit, by H. P. Kruger. BLUTALKOHOL 27(3):182-201, May 1990

Application of learning theory to driving confidence: the effect of age and the impact of random breath testing, by R. F. Job. ACCIDENT ANALYSIS AND PREVENTION 22(2):97-107, April 1990

Breath-taking decision: an ex-Miss Calgary beats an impaired rap, by G. Heaton. ALBERTA (WESTERN) REPORT 17(50):37-38, November 26, 1990

Disappearance rate of alcohol from the blood of drunk drivers calculated from two consecutive samples: what do the results really mean?, by W. Neuteboom, et al. FORENSIC SCIENCE INTERNATIONAL 45(1-2):107-115, March 1990

Expert assessment of the blood alcohol value in traffic accidents, by J. Missliwetz. BEITRAGE ZUR GERICHTLICHEN MEDIZIN 47:615-618, 1989

Get out of my car: police roadblocks and sobriety screening, by R. Ceppos. CAR AND DRIVER 36:24, December 1990

International news: Australia tests to warn bad drivers, by A. Harman. LAW AND ORDER 38(3):5, March 1990

"Random breath tests," by J. Harvard. MEDICAL JOURNAL OF AUSTRALIA 152(6): 282, March 19, 1990

Screening for drug use among Norwegian drivers suspected of driving under the influence of alcohol or drugs, by A. S. Christophersen, et al. FORENSIC SCIENCE INTERNATIONAL 45(1-2):5-14, March 1990

Sobriety test results need not be related back to time of driving. CRIMINAL LAW RE-
PORTER: COURT DECISIONS 47(11):1216-1217, June 13, 1990

Statistical evaluation of 60,000 blood alcohol values form 1964 to 1983: III—multiple
convictions, by M. D. Cubric, et al. BLUTALKOHOL 27(4):289-298, July 1990

Tests positive for high tech drunk driving safeguard. CRIME CONTROL DIGEST
23(18):7-8, May 7, 1990

Use of breathalyzers in Austria, by W. Soural. ILLUSTRIERTE RUNDSCHAU DER
OSTERREICHISCHEN GENDARMIE 41(6):13-15, 1988

Will NTSB proposal mean stone sober truck drivers?, by M. E. MacDonald. TRAFFIC
SAFETY 29:20-21, May 1990

Drunk Driving—Testing—Laws

Alcohol in drunk driving swabs: does it make any difference, by P. G. Carter, et al.
MEDICINE, SCIENCE AND THE LAW 30(1):90, January 1990

Drunk driving: blood tests—use of criminal prosecution. CRIMINAL LAW RE-
PORTER: COURT DECISIONS 45(20):2368, August 23, 1989

Drunk driving: breath-test results—"relation-back" evidence. CRIMINAL LAW RE-
PORTER: COURT DECISIONS 47(13):1256-1257, June 27, 1990

Drunk driving: breath-test results— relation back to time of driving. CRIMINAL LAW
REPORTER: COURT DECISIONS 46(11):1236, December 13, 1989

Drunk driving: breath-test results—standards for administration of gas chromatography. CRIMINAL LAW REPORTER: COURT DECISIONS 47(8):1155, May 23,
1990

Drunk driving: breath tests— failure to comply with rule governing administration of
test. CRIMINAL LAW REPORTER: COURT DECISIONS 46(7):1150, November
15, 1989

Drunk driving: evidence—breath and blood samples. CRIMINAL LAW REPORTER:
COURT DECISIONS 47(4):1075, April 25, 1990

Drunk driving: evidence—horizontal-gaze test. CRIMINAL LAW REPORTER: COURT
DECISIONS 47(13):1257, June 28, 1990

Drunk driving: evidence—refusal to submit to testing. CRIMINAL LAW REPORTER:
COURT DECISIONS 46(8):1173, November 22, 1989

Drunk driving: evidence—results of field sobriety test. CRIMINAL LAW REPORTER:
COURT DECISIONS 47(14):1277, July 4, 1990

Drunk driving: failure of breath test to yield result—retesting.CRIMINAL LAW RE-
PORTER: COURT DECISIONS 47(2):1035, April 11, 1990

Drunk driving: field sobriety tests— level of suspicion required to conduct test.
CRIMINAL LAW REPORTER: COURT DECISIONS 46(1):1020, October 4, 1989

Drunk driving: forcible extraction of blood sample in jail. CRIMINAL LAW REPORTER 46(24):1520, March 21, 1990

Drunk driving: "horizontal gaze nystagmus" test—permissible use at trial. CRIMINAL LAW REPORTER: COURT DECISIONS 46(3):1059, October 18, 1989

Drunk driving: implied-consent law—officer's violation of department policy as to test offered. CRIMINAL LAW REPORTER: COURT DECISIONS 46(4):1081, October 25, 1989

Drunk driving: implied consent law—silence as refusal to take breath test. CRIMINAL LAW REPOTER: COURT DECISIONS 46(12):1259, December 20, 1989

Drunk driving: per se urine offense—collection procedure. CRIMINAL LAW REPORTER: COURT DECISIONS 46(25):1543-1544, March 28, 1990

Drunk driving: post-arrest breath-test results beneath prima facie intoxication level. CRIMINAL LAW REPORTER: COURT DECISIONS 46(24):1520, March 21, 1990

Drunk driving: preliminary breath test—reference to fact of administration. CRIMINAL LAW REPORTER: COURT DECISIONS 47(10):1199-1200, June 6, 1990

Drunk driving: refusal to submit to breath test—admissibility of refusal evidence; state law. CRIMINAL LAW REPOTER: COURT DECISIONS 46(1):1020, October 4, 1989

Drunk driving: search and seizure—withdrawal of blood from unconscious motorist. CRIMINAL LAW REPORTER: COURT DECISIONS 47(14):1277, July 4, 1990

Drunk driving: statutory right to independent blood-alcohol test—police conduct; remedy. CRIMINAL LAW REPORTER: COURT DECISIONS 47(11):1220, June 13, 1990

Drunk driving: subpoena for blood-test results. CRIMINAL LAW REPORTER: COURT DECISIONS 47(1):1016-1017, April 4, 1990

Drunk driving: violation of rules governing administration of breath tests. CRIMINAL LAW REPORTER: COURT DECISIONS 46(8):1173, November 22, 1989

Due process doesn't give DWI suspect right to consult counsel prior to breath test. CRIMINAL LAW REPORTER: COURT DECISIONS 46(10):1011-1012, October 4, 1989

Due process permits instruction that high BAC is enough for DUI convictions. CRIMINAL LAW REPORTER: COURT DECISIONS 46(25):1540-1541, March 28, 1990

DUI arrestee may be physically restrained so blood can be drawn. LAW OFFICER'S BULLETIN 14(5):25, September 28, 1989

Evidence: drunk driving—blood-alcohol test procured by defendant. CRIMINAL LAW REPORTER: COURT DECISIONS 46(7):1151, November 15, 1989

Evidence: drunk driving—relation-back of breath-test result to time of driving. CRIMINAL LAW REPORTER: COURT DECISIONS 46(10):1216-1217, December 6, 1989

Field tests admissable. LAW AND ORDER 38(6):5, June 1990

Law authorizing blood testing after serious auto accident violates fourth amendment. CRIMINAL LAW REPORTER: COURT DECISIONS 47(14):1265-1266, July 4, 1990

New Hampshire Supreme Court upholds drunken driving test. CRIME CONTROL DIGEST 23(47):6, November 27, 1989

Probable cause: intoxicated driver/experienced officer—refusal to take blood test; Illinois. ARREST LAW BULLETIN June 1990, p. 4

Probable cause: refusal to take test admissible—videotape admissible; Montana. ARREST LAW BULLETIN October 1989, pp. 4-5

Restraining DUI suspect for blood test held reasonable under fourth amendment. CRIMINAL LAW REPORTER: COURT DECISIONS 45(24):2437-2438, September 20, 1989

Search and seizure: taking of blood from motorist without formal arrest: state consitutional law. CRIMINAL LAW REPORTER: COURT DECISIONS 46(3):1061, October 18, 1989

Drunk Driving—Testing—Legal Issues

New Jersey rejects challenge to routine admissibility of breath-test results. CRIMINAL LAW REPORTER: COURT DECISIONS 46(21):1449-1450, February 28, 1990

Officer may testify on "horizontal gaze" test results without expert support. CRIMINAL LAW REPORTER: COURT DECISIONS 46(20):1427-1428, February 21, 1990

Privilege communications: physician and patient—blood-alcohol test results. CRIMINAL LAW REPORTER: COURT DECISIONS 46(9):1196, November 29, 1989

Remark made during videotaped sobriety test is admissible despite request for counsel. CRIMINAL LAW REPORTER: COURT DECISIONS 47(7):1132-1133, May 16, 1990

Right to independent sobriety test doesn't require saving breath sample. CRIMINAL LAW REPORTER: COURT DECISIONS 47(16):1312-1313, July 25, 1990

Economics

15 communities get grants to fight drugs and alcohol. PUBLIC HEALTH REPORTS 105:323-324, May/June 1990

ADAMHA awards record total of alcohol and drug grants. PUBLIC HEALTH REPORTS 105:213-214, March/April 1990

Alcohol beverages in Ireland: market forces and government policy, by B. M. Walsh. BRITISH JOURNAL OF ADDICTION 84(10):1163-1171, October 1989

Alcohol, tobacco and public policy: the contribution of economics, by K. Hartley. BRITISH JOURNAL OF ADDICTION 84(10):1113-1121, October 1989

Economist in alcohol policy country, by M. J. van Iwaarden. BRITISH JOURNAL OF ADDICTION 84(10):1205-1216, October 1989

Factors influencing the consumption of alcohol and tobacco: the use and abuse of economic models, by C. Godfrey. BRITISH JOURNAL OF ADDICTION 84(10): 1123-1138, October 1989

Per drink prevention tax urged, by J. Hollobon. JOURNAL OF THE ADDICTION RE-SEARCH FOUNDATION 19(9):8, September 1, 1990

Relation of rural alcoholism to farm economy, by H. H. Hsieh, et al. COMMUNITY MENTAL HEALTH JOURNAL 25(4):341-347, Winter 1989

Tax on alcohol: boozers' budget—Great Britain. ECONOMIST 310:60, March 11, 1989

Ecuador

Prevalence of the improper use of alcohol, tobacco and drugs in the Ecuadorian population, by E. Aguilar. BOLETIN DE LA OFICINA SANITARIA PANAMERI-CANA 107(6):510-513, December 1989

Education

see also: Prevention

Alcohol education for 13 year olds: does it work?—results from a controlled evaluation, by G. Bagnall. BRITISH JOURNAL OF ADDICTION 85(1):89-96, January 1990

Alcoholism and substance abuse teaching in child psychiatry residency programs, by J. A. Steg, et al. JOURNAL OF THE AMERICAN ACADEMY OF CHILD AND ADOLESCENT PSYCHIATRY 29(5):813-816, September 1990

Chemistry, law, and alcohol abuse: an elective for the nonscience major, by D. A. Labianca. COLLEGE TEACHING 38:93-95, Summer 1990

College drinking attitude scale: a tool for alcohol education program assessment, by G. M. Gonzalez. INTERNATIONAL JOURNAL OF THE ADDICTIONS 25(2):121-132, 1990

Comments regarding alcohol knowledge, drug use and drinking practices: implications for programming on a college campus, by J. W. Lammers, et al. HEALTH EDUCATION 21:27-31, July/August 1990

Consumption of alcohol and tobacco during pregnancy by health advisors: an investigation of nurses, nurses' aides, physicians and school teachers, by J. G. Frische, et al. UGESKRIFT FOR LAEGER 152(9):2101-2104, July 16, 1990

Development of medical education on alcohol- and drug-related problems at the University of Toronto, by J. G. Rankin. CMAJ 143(10):1083-1091, November 15, 1990

Drinking, driving, and health promotion, by D. A. Sleet, et al. HEALTH EDUCATION QUARTERLY 16(3):329-333, Fall 1989

Drug and alcohol medical education in Australia: on the map at last, by A. M. Roche. MEDICAL JOURNAL OF AUSTRALIA 152(9):503, May 7, 1990

Evaluation of an alcohol education package for non-specialist health care and social workers, by D. M. Gorman, et al. BRITISH JOURNAL OF ADDICTION 85(2):223-233, February 1990

Evaluation of the effects of college alcohol education on the prevention of negative consequences, by W. G. Meacci. JOURNAL OF ALCOHOL AND DRUG EDUCATION 35:66-72, Spring 1990

Failure of a 2-hour motivational intervention to alter recurrent drinking behavior in alcoholics with gastrointestinal disease, by V. Kuchipudi, et al. JOURNAL OF STUDIES ON ALCOHOL 51(4):356-360, July 1990

Group role reversal between students and inpatient alcoholics, by W. M. London, et al. HEALTH EDUCATION 21:54-55, September/October 1990

Knowledge about alcohol is important to health, by A. L. Reid. MEDICAL JOURNAL OF AUSTRALIA 152(12):620-621, June 18, 1990

Multimedia program on problem drinking in later life. AGING (361):43-45, 1990

New resource for communities. HEALTH PROMOTION 28(2):15, Fall 1989

Patient education: alcohol abuse, by J. Murtagh. AUSTRALIAN FAMILY PHYSICIAN 18(12):1548, December 1989

Prevention of alcoholism among forestry workers, by T. V. Chizhova. GIGIYENA I SANITARIYA (8):32-34, August 1989

Problem of preventing alcohol traumatism, by D. O. Alks, et al. ORTOPEDIIA TRAVMATOLOGIIA I PROTEZIROVANIE (1):38-42, January 1990

Rural independent movie theaters as a channel for disseminating alcohol information, by K. Moffatt, et al. HUMAN SERVICES IN THE RURAL ENVIRONMENT 13(2):36-39, Fall 1989

Science aid to policy dilemmas: implications of alcohol research to policy formulation in U.S.A, by E. Gordis. DRUG AND ALCOHOL DEPENDENCE 25(2):183-186, April 1990

Supporting students who choose not to use, by R. Soulis. INDEPENDENT SCHOOL 49:37-38+, Spring 1990

Teaching medical students about alcohol, by E. B. Ritson. BMJ 301(6744):134-135, July 21, 1990

Use of professional journals in internship alcoholism treatment training, by G. J. Connors, et al. PSYCHOLOGY OF ADDICTIVE BEHAVIORS 3(1):1-7, 1989

WHO collaborative study on alcohol education and young people: outcomes of a four-country pilot study, by C. L. Perry, et al. INTERNATIONAL JOURNAL OF THE ADDICTIONS 24(12):1145-1171, December 1989

Drinking in England and Wales: the latest news from OPCS, by J. B. Davies. BRITISH JOURNAL OF ADDICTION 84(9):957-959, September 1989

Drinking in England and Wales: reply to John Booth Davies, by E. Goddard. BRITISH JOURNAL OF ADDICTION 84(9):967-968, September 1989

Epidemiology

Addiction to drugs and alcohol among physicians and nurses, by A. S. Sorensen, et al. UGESKRIFT FOR LAEGER 151(41):2660-2664, October 9, 1989

Alcohol abuse: contamination by western influences of the rural African village, by T. Ntusi. MEDICINE AND LAW 8(1):53-57, 1989

Alcohol problem in universities and the professions, by A. W. Clare. ALCOHOL AND ALCOHOLISM 25(2-3):277-285, 1990

Alcohol problem increase while physician attention declines 1967 to 1984, by D. S. Hasin, et al. ARCHIVES OF INTERNAL MEDICINE 150(2):397-400, February 1990

Alcohol-related problems in high-risk groups: report on a WHO study. EURO REPORTS AND STUDIES (109):1-114, 1989

Alcoholism and other substance abuse: preventive programs in Santiago, Chile, by R. Florenzano. BULLETIN OF THE PAN AMERICAN HEALTH ORGANIZATION 24(1):86-96, 1990

Alcoholism in an industrial population: diagnosis, prevalence and conditioning factors, by P. Fidalgo, et al. ACTA MEDICA PORTUGUESA 2(2):77-82, March/April 1989

Alcoholism: North America and Asia—a comparison of population surveys with the diagnostic interview schedule, by J. E. Helzer, et al. ARCHIVES OF GENERAL PSYCHIATRY 47(4):313-319, April 1990

Are women drinking more like men: an empirical examination of the convergence hypothesis, by P. W. Mercer, et al. ALCOHOLISM: CLINICAL AND EXPERIMENTAL RESEARCH 14(3):461-466, June 1990

Association between alcohol intake and adiposity in the general population, by W. L. Hellerstedt, et al. AMERICAN JOURNAL OF EPIDEMIOLOGY 132(4):594-611, October 1990

Biological study of alcohol dependence syndrome with reference to ethnic difference: report of a WHO collaborative study, by I. Yamashita, et al. JAPANESE JOURNAL OF PSYCHIATRY AND NEUROLOGY 44(1):79-84, March 1990

Comorbidity of mental disorder with alcohol and other drug abuse: results from the Epidemiologic Catchment Area (ECA) study, by D. A. Regier, et al. JAMA 264:2511-2518, November 21, 1990

Comparing distributions of alcohol consumption: empirical probability plots, by P. H. Lemmens, et al. BRITISH JOURNAL OF ADDICTION 85(6):751-758, June 1990

Comparison of 7-day retrospective and prospective alcohol consumption diaries in a female population in Perth, Western Australia: methodological issues, by B. Corti, et al. BRITISH JOURNAL OF ADDICTION 85(3):379-388, March 1990

Comparison of the abuse of alcohol, tobacco and drugs between students and delinquents in the Bahamas, by R. G. Smart, et al. BOLETIN DE LA OFICINA SANITARIA PANAMERICANA 107(6):514-522, December 1989

Drinking in England and Wales: the latest news from OPCS, by J. B. Davies. BRITISH JOURNAL OF ADDICTION 84(9):957-959, September 1989

Drinking in England and Wales: reply to John Booth Davies, by E. Goddard. BRITISH JOURNAL OF ADDICTION 84(9):967-968, September 1989

Drinking problems, by E. H. Kua, et al. SINGAPORE MEDICAL JOURNAL 31(3):247-249, June 1990

Epidemiologic aspects of alcoholism, by M. Spinatsch. SCHWEIZER ARCHIV FUR NEUROLOGIE UND PSYCHIATRIE 140(6):539-553, 1989

Epidemiologic investigation of alcohol-dependent schizophrenics, by A. E. Pulver, et al. ACTA PSYCHIATRICA SCANDINAVICA 79(6):603-612, June 1989

Epidemiologic study of alcohol and tobacco among adolescents of the Autonomous Basque Community, by F. J. Goiriena de Gandarias, et al. REVISTA DE SANIDAD E HIGIENE PUBLICA 62(9-12):1749-1764, September/December 1988

Epidemiologic study of alcohol use as a predictor of psychiatric distress over time, by A. Dryman, et al. ACTA PSYCHIATRICA SCANDINAVICA 80(4):315-321, October 1989

Epidemiology, advocacy and ideology in alcohol studies, by T. F. Barbor. JOURNAL OF STUDIES ON ALCOHOL 51(4):293-295, July 1990

Epidemiology of alcohol and its sequelae in Switzerland, by T. Abelin. THERAPEUTISCHE UMSCHAU 47(5):379-383, May 1990

Epidemiology of alcoholism and liver cancer, by A. Oshima, et al. GAN NO RINSHO May 1989, pp. 62-68

Five-year reliability of self-reported alcohol consumption, by D. M. Czarnecki, et al. JOURNAL OF STUDIES ON ALCOHOL 51(1):68-76, January 1990

Incidence of alcohol drinking and the structure of causes of death in men 40-54 years of age, by K.V. Markov, et al. SOVETSKOE ZDRAVOOKHRONENIE (4):15-18, 1990

Medicosocial characteristics of hospitalized alcoholic patients in 2 internal medicine departments of hospitals in French-speaking Switzerland, by Y. Trisconi, et al. SCHWEIZERISCHE MEDIZINISCHE WOCHENSCHRIFT 119(52):1907-1912, December 30, 1989

Methodological issues in the epidemiological study of alcohol-drug problems: sources of confusion and misunderstanding, by J. Westermeyer. AMERICAN JOURNAL OF DRUG AND ALCOHOL ABUSE 16(1-2):47-55, March/June 1990

Nicotine dependence and alcoholism epidemiology and treatment, by J. K. Bobo. JOURNAL OF PSYCHOACTIVE DRUGS 21(3):323-329, July/September 1989

Opisthorchiasis and alcoholism: a clinico-epidemiological and social psychology study, by A. M. Bronshtein, et al. MEDITSINSKAIA PARAZITOLOGIIA I PARAZI-TARNYE BOLEZNI (1):44-46, January/February 1990

Patterns of alcohol abuse among black and white alcoholics, by J. E. Robyak, et al. INTERNATIONAL JOURNAL OF THE ADDICTIONS 24(7):715-724, July 1989

Prevalence of alcohol dependence and cocaine dependence in an inpatient population, by N. S. Miller, et al. ANNALS OF CLINICAL PSYCHIATRY 1(2):93-97, June 1989

Prevalence of alcohol related admissions to general medical units, by D. E. Lange, et al. INTERNATIONAL JOURNAL OF PSYCHIATRY IN MEDICINE 19(4):371-384, 1989

Prevalence of chronic drinkers in Mexico: an ecologic analysis, by G. Borges. SALUD PUBLICA DE MEXICO 31(4):503-518, July/August 1989

Proposal to study sociocultural influences leading to alcoholism, by J. J. Lindethal, et al. MEDICINE AND LAW 8(1):37-44, 1989

Regularity in alcohol distributions: implications for the collective nature of drinking behaviour, by E. S. Tan, et al. BRITISH JOURNAL OF ADDICTION 85(6):745-750, June 1990

Scheme for determining the prevalence of alcoholism in hospitalized patients, by M. A. Baird, et al. ALCOHOLISM: CLINICAL AND EXPERIMENTAL RESEARCH 13(6):782-785, December 1989

Several aspects of alcohol use among students, by T. Z. Seisembekov, et al. SOVETSKOE ZDRAVOOKHRONENIE (12):36-40, 1989

Shetland: psychiatric symptoms and alcohol consumption in a community undergoing socioeconomic development, by D. J. Voorhees, et al. ACTA PSYCHIATRICA SCANDINAVICA 348(Suppl):141-155, 1989

Trends in drinking habits among Finnish youth from 1973 to 1987, by O. Rahkonen, et al. BRITISH JOURNAL OF ADDICTION 84(9):1075-1083, September 1989

Tromso study: distribution and population determinants of gamma-glutamyltrans-ferase, by O. Nilssen, et al. AMERICAN JOURNAL OF EPIDEMIOLOGY 132(2): 318-326, August 1990

Etiology

Addictive independent factors that predict risk for alcoholism, by J. R. Stabenau. JOURNAL OF STUDIES ON ALCOHOL 51(2):164-174, March 1990

Alcohol and the central nervous system: fundamental neurochemical aspects of alcohol dependence, by N. Filipovic, et al. MEDICINSKI ARHIV 42(3):143-147, 1988

Alcohol: mechanisms of addiction and reinforcement, by M. J. Lewis. ADVANCES IN ALCOHOL AND SUBSTANCE ABUSE 9(1-2):47-66, Spring 1990

Alcoholism: etiologies proposed and therapeutic approaches tried, by J. B. Murray. GENETIC, SOCIAL, AND GENERAL PSYCHOLOGY MONOGRAPHS 115(1):81-121, February 1989

Biological markers for increased risk of alcoholism and for quantitation of alcohol consumption, by D. W. Crabb. JOURNAL OF CLINICAL INVESTIGATION 85(2):311-315, February 1990

Central dopaminergic mechanisms and the effect of ethyl alcohol, by W. Kostowski, et al. PSYCHIATRIA POLSKA 23(3):200-208, May/June 1989

Experimental models of alcoholism, by G. L. Gessa, et al. RECENTI PROGRESSI I MEDICINA 81(3):162-165, March 1990

Is "disease model" an appropriate term to describe the alcohol dependence syndrome?, by D. M. Gorman. ALCOHOL AND ALCOHOLISM 24(6):509-512, 1989

Neurohormones and alcoholism, by N. A. Aliev. PATOLOGICHESAIA FIZIOLOGIIA I EKSPERIMENTALNAIA TERAPIIA (5):85-90, September/October 1989

Neurophysiological and pathomorphological characteristics of alcoholism formation: an experimental study, by T. M. Vorobe'eva, et al. ZHURNAL NEVROPATOLOGII I PSIKHIATRII IMENI S. S. KORSAKOVA 90(2):77-84, 1990

Pendulum swings the other way: the role of environment obscured by genes, by G. E. Vaillant. ARCHIVES OF GENERAL PSYCHIATRY 46(12):1151-1152, December 1989

Psychosocial factors in the origin and prognosis of alcoholism, by M. De Vanna, et al. MINERVA PSICHIATRICA 30(3):175-177, July/September 1989

Europe
Alcohol warnings for new Europe, by A. MacLennan. JOURNAL OF THE ADDICTION RESEARCH FOUNDATION 19(7-8):1-2, July/August 1990

European patterns of alcohol use on AIDS and drug abuse, Stockholm 25-28 September 1989, by E. Segest. UGESKRIFT FOR LAEGER 152(6):406, February 5, 1990

Fetal Alcohol Syndrome
Children in peril: A. Kayitah, Apache child with fetal alcohol syndrome, by M. Brower. PEOPLE WEEKLY 33:86-89, April 16, 1990

Desperate crack legacy: fetal alcohol syndrome and crack babies, by M. Dorris. NEWSWEEK 114(26):8, June 25, 1990

Fetal Alcohol Syndrome: a description of oral motor articulatory, short-term memory, grammatical, and semantic abilities, by M. Becker, et al. JOURNAL OF COMMUNICATION DISORDERS 23(2):97-124, April 1990

Fetal Alcohol Syndrome: diagnosis and syndromal variability, by L. Burd, et al. PHYSIOLOGY AND BEHAVIOR 46(1):39-43, July 1989

Fetal Alcohol Syndrome: liability for failure to warn—should liquor manufacturers pick up the tab?, by R. Goble. JOURNAL OF FAMILY LAW 28(1):71-85, 1989-1990

Fetal Alcohol Syndrome prevention in American Indian communities of Michigan's Upper Peninsula, by K. J. Plaisier. AMERICAN INDIAN AND ALASKA NATIVE MENTAL HEALTH RESEARCH 3(1):16-33, Summer 1989

Indian health threat: fetal alcohol syndrome, by L. Plunkett. UTNE READER (37):62, January 1990

Teratologists: the fetal alcohol syndrome, and alcohol addiction: are we doing enough?, by R. L. Brent. TERATOLOGY 41(4):491-493, April 1990

Finland
Drinking, everyday life situations and cultural norms in Denmark, Finland, and Western Germany: an experiment with nonactive role-playing, by J. Simpura, et al. JOURNAL OF DRUG ISSUES 20(3):403-416, Summer 1990

Genetics
Adult children of alcoholics: a valid diagnostic group, by A. I. Fulton, et al. JOURNAL OF NERVOUS AND MENTAL DISEASE 178(8):505-509, August 1990

Alcohol abuse and its psychosocial correlates in sons of alcoholics as young men and in the general population of young men in Prague, by L. Kubicka, et al. JOURNAL OF STUDIES ON ALCOHOL 51(1):49-58, January 1990

Alcohol and aldehyde dehydrogenase, by T. Ehrig, et al. ALCOHOL AND ALCOHOLISM 25(2-3):105-116, 1990

Alcohol and drug use by college males as a function of family alcoholism history, by M. E. McCaul, et al. ALCOHOLISM: CLINICAL AND EXPERIMENTAL RESEARCH 14(3):467-471, June 1990

Alcohol consumption and menstrual distress in women at higher and lower risk for alcoholism, by L. Charette, et al. ALCOHOLISM 14(2):152-157, April 1990

Alcohol cue reactivity and ad lib drinking in young men at risk for alcoholism, by K. S. Walitzer, et al. ADDICTIVE BEHAVIORS 15(1):29-46, 1990

Alcoholism and the "new genetics," by M. Mullan. BRITISH JOURNAL OF ADDICTION 84(12):1433-1440, December 1989

Aldehyde dehydrogenases and alcoholism, by D. M. Gallant. ALCOHOLISM 14(2):260-261, April 1990

Allelic association of human dopamine D2 receptor gene in alcoholism, by K. Blum, et al. JAMA 263(15):2055-2060, April 18, 1990

Are children with alcohol embryopathy latent alcoholics: a study of the risk for developing dependence, by H. Loser, et al. PRAXIS DER KINDERPSYCHOLOGIE UND KINDERPSYCHIATRIE 39(5):157-162, May/June 1990

Childhood antecedents of antisocial behavior: parental alcoholism and physical abusiveness, by V. E. Pollock, et al. AMERICAN JOURNAL OF PSYCHIATRY 147 (10):1290-1293, October 1989

Children of alcoholic patients, by A. von Gontard. ZEITSCHRFIT FUR KINDER- UND JUGENDPSYCHIATRIE 18(2):87-98, June 1990

Children of psychiatrically ill parents: a prevention perspective, by M. M. Silverman. HOSPTIAL AND COMMUNITY PSYCHIATRY 40(12):1257-1265, December 1989

Concurrent validity of the MacAndrew Alcoholism Scale: mixed-group validation, by E. E. Knowles, et al. JOURNAL OF STUDIES ON ALCOHOL 51(3):257-262, May 1990

Controlled family history study of Tourette's syndrome: II—alcoholism, drug abuse and obesity, by D. E. Comings, et al. JOURNAL OF CLINICAL PSYCHIATRY 51(7):281-287, July 1990

Diagnosis of alcohol and cannabis dependence in their families, by N. S. Miller, et al. BRITISH JOURNAL OF ADDICTION 84(12):1491-1498, December 1989

DNA and the desire to drink: researchers discover a gene at the root of alcoholism, by A. Purvis. TIME 135(18):54, April 30, 1990

DNA and the desire to drink: role of dopamine receptors, by A. Purvis. TIME 135(18):88, April 30, 1990

Drink link: questions concerning alcohol gene findings of Kenneth Blum and Ernest Noble, by R. Bazell. NEW REPUBLIC 202:13-14, May 7, 1990

Drinking habits may be all in the family: research by Kenneth Blum and Ernest Noble, by S. Diamond. MADEMOISELLE 96:136, August 1990

EEG fast frequency activity in the sons of alcoholics, by C. L. Ehlers, et al. BIOLOGICAL PSYCHIATRY 27(6):631-641, March 15, 1990

Effect of being reared with an alcoholic half-sibling: a classic study reanalyzed, by W. L. Cook, et al. FAMILY PROCESS 29(1):87-93, March 1990

Effects of alcohol on psychophysiological hyperreactivity to nonaversive and aversive stimuli in men at high risk for alcoholism, by P. R. Finn, et al. JOURNAL OF ABNORMAL PSYCHOLOGY 99(1):79-85, February 1990

Effects of social drinking and familial alcoholism risk on cognitive functioning: null findings, by A. I. Alterman, et al. ALCOHOLISM: CLINICAL AND EXPERIMENTAL RESEARCH 13(6):799-803, December 1989

Ending the gene(s) for alcoholism, by E. Gordis, et al. JAMA 263(15):2094-2095, April 18, 1990

Ethanol self-administration in males with and without an alcoholic first-degree relative, by H. de Wit, et al. ALCOHOLISM: CLINICAL AND EXPERIMENTAL RESEARCH 14(1):63-70, February 1990

Familial and personality correlates of alcohol-related problems, by E. E. Knowles, et al. ADDICTIVE BEHAVIORS 14(5):537-543, 1989

Familial transmission of alcohol use norms and expectancies and reported alcohol use, by R. C. Johnson, et al. ALCOHOLISM 14(2):216-220, April 1990

Families of drug addicts, by A. F. Radchenko, et al. ZHURNAL NEVROPATOLOGII I PSIKHIATRII IMENI S. S. KORSAKOVA 90(2):38-42, 1990

Finding the gene(s) for alcoholism, by E. Gordis, et al. JAMA 263:2094-2095, April 18, 1990

From the Alcohol, Drug Abuse, and Mental Health Administration: alcoholism genetics research, by F. K. Goodwin, et al. JAMA 263(3):352, January 19, 1990

Gene and the bottle: dopamine receptor gene research by Kenneth Blum, by G. Cowley. NEWSWEEK 115:59, April 30, 1990

Gene linked with excessive drinking, by C. Joyce. NEW SCIENTIST 126:20, April 21, 1990

Gene may be tied to "virulent" alcoholism: dopamine D2 receptor gene: research by Kenneth Blum, by B. Bower. SCIENCE 137(16):246, April 21, 1990

Genes with a don't drink label: dopamine receptor may be linked to alcoholism—research by Ernest Noble and Kenneth Blum. US NEWS AND WORLD REPORT 108:15, April 30, 1990

Genetic aspects of alcoholism, by M. Zawadzka-Kos. POLSKI TYGODNIK LEKARSKI 44(24):563-566, June 12, 1989

Genetic epidemiology of alcoholism, by K. R. Merikangas. PSYCHOLOGICAL MEDICINE 20(1):11-22, February 1990

Genetic epidemiology of ethanol metabolic enzymes: a role for selection, by D. Goldman, et al. WORLD REVIEW OF NUTRITION AND DIETETICS 63:143-160, 1990

Genetic polymorphism of aldehyde dehydrogenase and its physiological significance to alcohol metabolism, by S. Harada. PROGRESS IN CLINICAL AND BIOLOGICAL RESEARCH 344:289-294, 1990

Genetic regulation of dihydropyridine-sensitive calcium channels in brain may determine susceptibility to physical dependence on alcohol, by C. H. Brennan, et al. NEUROPHARMACOLOGY 29(5):429-432, May 1990

Genetic up-regulation of calcium channels in cellular model of ethanol dependence, by J. C. Harper, et al. NEUROPHARMACOLOGY 28(12):1299-1302, December 1989

Genetically determined alcohol preference and cyclic AMP binding proteins in mouse brain, by K. R. Beeker, et al. ALCOHOLISM 14(2):158-164, April 1990

Genetically-induced variability of alcohol metabolism and its effect on drinking behavior and predisposition to alcoholism, by R. Eckey, et al. ZEITSCHRIFT FUR RECHTSMEDIZIN 103(3):169-190, 1990

Genetics of alcoholism, by C. C. Cook. BRITISH JOURNAL OF PSYCHIATRY 156: 284, February 1990

Heritability of alcoholism: science and social policy, by D. Lester. DRUGS AND SOCIETY 3(3-4):29-68, March/April 1989

HLA and alcoholism, by C. Baldauf, et al. PSYCHIATRIE, NEUROLOGIE UND MEDIZINISCHE PSYCHOLOGIE 42(5):305-307, May 1990

Inherited predisposition to alcoholism: characteristics of sons of male alcoholics, by R. O. Pihl, et al. JOURNAL OF ABNORMAL PSYCHOLOGY 99:291-301, August 1990

Interviewing adolescents by telephone: is it a useful methodological strategy?, by W. Riech, et al. COMPREHENSIVE PSYCHIATRY 31(3):211-215, May/June 1990

Lifetime prevalence of psychopathology in men with multigenerational family histories of alcoholism, by P. R. Finn, et al. JOURNAL OF NERVOUS AND MENTAL DISEASE 178(8):500-504, August 1990

Linkage of c-Harvey-ras-1 and INS DNA markers to unipolar depression and alcoholism is ruled out in 18 families, by R. B. Wesner, et al. EUROPEAN ARCHIVES OF PSYCHIATRY AND NEUROLOGICAL SCIENCES 239(6):356-360, 1990

Molecular genetics of alcoholism. BRITISH JOURNAL OF PSYCHIATRY 155:564-565, October 1989

Neuroelectric processes in individuals at risk for alcoholism, by H. Begleiter, et al. ALCOHOL AND ALCOHOLISM 25(2-3):251-256, 1990

Personality resemblance in relatives of male alcoholics: a comparison with families of male control cases, by S. Y. Hill, et al. BIOLOGICAL PSYCHIATRY 27(12):1305-1322, June 15, 1990

Platelet MAO in subtypes of alcoholism, by J. L. Sullivan, et al. BIOLOGICAL PSYCHIATRY 27(8):911-922, April 15, 1990

Platelet monoamines oxidase, plasma dopamine beta-hydroxylase activity, dementia and family history of alcoholism in chronic alcoholics, by E. Lykouras, et al. ACTA PSYCHIATRICA SCANDINAVICA 80(5):487-491, November 1989

Population and pedigree studies reveal a lack of association between the dopamine D2 receptor gene and alcoholism, by A. M. Bolos, et al. JAMA 264:3156-3160, December 26, 1990

Preference for ethanol in males with or without an alcoholic first degree relative, by H. de Wit, et al. NIDA RESEARCH MONOGRAPH SERIES 95:374-375, 1989

Psychopathy, aggression, and family history in male veteran substance abuse patients: a factor analytic study, by H. B. Moss. ADDICTIVE BEHAVIORS 14(5):565-570, 1989

Second thoughts about a gene for alcoholism: research by Kenneth Blum and Ernest Noble, by S. Peele. ATLANTIC 266(2):52-58, August 1990

Segregation analysis of alcoholism in families ascertained through a pair of male alcoholics, by C. E. Aston, et al. AMERICAN JOURNAL OF HUMAN GENETICS 46(5): 879-887, May 1990

Serious alcohol and drug problems among adolescents with a family history of alcoholism, by R. J. Pandina, et al. JOURNAL OF STUDIES ON ALCOHOL 51(3):278-282, May 1990

Social complications of chronic alcohol abuse: relative influence of family history and severity of alcohol dependence, by D. C. Schachter, et al. CANADIAN JOURNAL OF PSYCHIATRY 35(4):320-323, May 1990

Specific cognitive impairment in sons of early onset alcoholics, by R. E. Tarter, et al. ALCOHOLISM 13(6):786-789, December 1989

Structure of marriages and human resistance to the disease of alcoholism, by L. A. Atramentova, et al. TISITOLOGIYA I GENETIKA 23(6):18-21, November/December 1989

Subtyping male alcoholics by family history of alcohol abuse and co-occuring psychiatric disorder: a bi-dimensional model, by M. R. Read, et al. BRITISH JOURNAL OF ADDICTION 85(3):367-378, March 1990

Temperament deviation and risk for alcoholism, by R. E. Tarter, et al. ALCOHOLISM: CLINICAL AND EXPERIMENTAL RESEARCH 14(3):380-382, May/June 1990

This and that: genetics, statistics and common sense, by B. Max. TRENDS IN PHARMACOLOGICAL SCIENCES 11(8):311-314, August 1990

TSH response to TRH and family history of alcoholism, by M. G. Monteiro, et al. BIOLOGICAL PSYCHIATRY 27(8):905-910, April 15, 1990

When dad drinks: can his liquor intake impair his future offspring?, by J. Horgan. SCIENTIFIC AMERICAN 262(2):23, February 1990

Germany
Blood pressure and relative body weight, alcohol consumption and electrolyte excretion in West Germany and East Germany: the Intersalt study group from the FRG and the GDR. KLINISCHE WOCHENSCHRIFT 68(13):655-663, July 5, 1990

Drinking, everyday life situations and cultural norms in Denmark, Finland, and Western Germany: an experiment with nonactive role-playing, by J. Simpura, et al. JOURNAL OF DRUG ISSUES 20(3):403-416, Summer 1990

Governing images of alcoholism in Germany: 1870-1920, by I. Vogt. INTERNATIONAL JOURNAL OF LAW AND PSYCHIATRY 13(1-2):149-154, 1990

Great Britain
British keep drinking heavily. JOURNAL OF THE ADDICTION RESEARCH FOUNDATION 19(10):3, October 1, 1990

Drink, the muse and me: painter and writer Molly Parkin describes her years of alcoholism during which she was unable to paint, by M. Parkin. GUARDIAN (Suppl): 14-15, February 3, 1990

Greenland
Alcohol related deaths in Greenland, by P. Bjerregaard. ARCTIC MEDICAL RESEARCH 47(Suppl)1:596-597, 1988

History
Abuse of drugs other than alcohol and tobacco in the Soviet Union, by M. S. Conroy. SOVIET STUDIES 42:447-480, July 1990

Alcohol: historical aspects, by A. Stettler. THERAPEUTISCHE UMSCHAU 47(5):344-349, May 1990

Alcohol in Botswana: a historical overview, by L. Molamu. CONTEMPORARY DRUG PROBLEMS 16(1):3-42, Spring 1989

Alcoholism as a disease, by F. W. Kielhorn. NERVENARZT 61(7):431-434, July 1990

Disease and death of Olaf Bull: thoughts about alcohol, disease and creativity, by P. Hjort. TIDSSKRIFT FOR DE NORSKE LAEGEFORENING 109(3-4):3557-3561, December 10, 1989

"Do not drink wine or strong drink": alcohol and responsibility in ancient Jewish sources, by S. S. Kottek. MEDICINE AND LAW 8(3):255-259, 1989

Governing images of alcoholism in Germany: 1870-1920, by I. Vogt. INTERNATIONAL JOURNAL OF LAW AND PSYCHIATRY 13(1-2):149-154, 1990

Historical archaeology and the demand for alcohol in 17th century Newfoundland, by P. Pope. ACADIENSIS 19(1):72-90, Fall 1989

Historical studies and strategies against alcohol and drug abuse, by T. Baasher. DRUG AND ALCOHOL DEPENDENCE 25(2):215-219, April 1990

Prevalence of alcoholism during 3 decades in Chile: 1952-1982, by P. Naveillan, et al. REVISTA DE SAUDE PUBLICA 23(2):128-135, April 1989

Psychiatric nosology and taxonomy in ancient India, by C. V. Haldipur. ACTA PSYCHIATRICA SCANDINAVICA 80(2):148-150, August 1989

Towards the cultural history of alcohol in France, by T. Brennan. JOURNAL OF SOCIAL HISTORY 23:71-92, 1989

Trends in alcohol consumption in Spain, Portugal, France and Italy from the 1950s until 1980, by E. Pyorala. BRITISH JOURNAL OF ADDICTION 85(4):469-477, April 1990

Hotlines
222-MUCH: a ride you can live with, by N. Caputo. PROFESSIONAL SAFETY 35:34-37, May 1990

Clinico-immunological efficacy of dioxidine in the combined treatment of acute abscessing pneumonias in persons who abuse alcohol, by A. V. Nikitin, et al. TERAPEVTICHESKII ARKHIV 62(1):78-81, 1990

Ethanol and soluble mediators of host response, by G. A. Roselle, et al. ALCOHOLISM 13(4):494-498, August 1989

Ethyl alcohol and alcoholism and the macrophage-monocyte system, by W. Michalczak. WIADOMSCI LEKARSKIE 43(1-2):85-87, January 1-15, 1990

Evaluation of interferon system among chronic alcoholics, by K. C. Chadha, et al. PROGRESS IN CLINICAL AND BIOLOGICAL RESEARCH 325:123-133, 1990

Mechanisms of suppression of cellular immunity induced by ethanol, by T. R. Jerrells, et al. ALCOHOLISM 13(4):490-493, August 1989

Receptor modulation as a primary target of the immunological effects of alcohol and other drugs of abuse, by R. M. Donahoe. PROGRESS IN CLINICAL AND BIOLOGICAL RESEARCH 325:305-312, 1990

Response to hepatitis B vaccine in Alaska natives with chronic alcoholism compared with non-alcoholic control subject, by B. J. McMohon, et al. AMERICAN JOURNAL OF MEDICINE 88(5):460-464, May 1990

Kenya
Alcoholism among outpatients of a rural district general hospital in Kenya, by M. F. Nielsen, et al. BRITISH JOURNAL OF ADDICTION 84(11):1343-1351, November 1989

Labrador
Labrador coast has problems: alcohol abuse. JOURNAL OF THE ADDICTION RESEARCH FOUNDATION 19(6):2, June 1, 1990

Laws
Alcohol: a bigger drug problem, by J. Rosengren. MINNESOTA MEDICINE 73(4):33-34, April 1990

Alcohol use among college students: responses to raising the purchase age, by J. E. Davis, et al. JOURNAL OF AMERICAN COLLEGE HEALTH 38(6):263-269, May 1990

Coast Guard begins enforcing boating-while-intoxicated law. CRIME CONTROL DIGEST 23(31):3-4, August 7, 1989

Deputy was justified in shooting drunken man who took his night stick and was advancing on him with night stick upraised. AELE LIABILITY REPORTER 200:118-119, August 1989

Drunk with freedom: a Lethbridge judge strikes down the public drunkenness law, by D. Burns. ALBERTA (WESTERN) REPORT 17(5):23, January 15, 1990

Gallup fights status as drunkest city in United States. LAW ENFORCEMENT NEWS 15(291):7+, April 30, 1989

Insanity: voluntary intoxication: CORPORATE SECURITY July 1990, p. 4

Insanity: voluntary intoxication. CRIMINAL LAW REPORTER: COURT DECISIONS 46(19):1412, February 14, 1990

International news: Britain—underage drinking prevention. LAW AND ORDER 38(8): 6, August 1990

Knoxville ponders what to do with drunks. CRIME CONTROL DIGEST 24(17):5, April 30, 1990; also in CORRECTIONS DIGEST 21(11):3, May 30, 1990

Labyrinth of laws, by K. Monagle. SCHOLASTIC UPDATE 123:12-13, November 16, 1990

Letting drunks be: civil libertarians argue that being soused isn't a crime, by S. Vana-gas. BC REPORT 1(50):2, August 20, 1990

Negligence: marijuana and alcohol—sufficiency of evidence; Oregon. NARCOTICS LAW BULLETIN June 1990, p. 7

New York State's 21 alcohol purchase age: anticipated consequences in the college community, by K. M. Hayes-Sugarman. DAI A 49(9):2612, 1989

Raising the minimum drinking age: some unintended consequences of good intentions, by L. Lanza-Kaduce, et al. JUSTICE QUARTERLY 6(2):247-262, March 1989

Voluntary intoxication cannot negate specific intent—Arkansas court rules. CRIMINAL LAW REPORTER: COURT DECISIONS 46(20):1423-1424, February 21, 1990

Legal Issues

Against all odds: casino wins suit raising issue of duty to drunken gambler, by K. Klages. ABA JOURNAL 75:30+, September 1989

"Alcohol intoxication" or "drunkenness": is there a difference?, by K. J. B. Rix. MEDICINE, SCIENCE AND THE LAW 29(2):100-106, 1989

Alcohol must be labeled. TRIAL 26(5):100, May 1990

Alcoholic wife's refusal of treatment should be factored into maintenance award. FAMILY LAW REPORTER: COURT OPINIONS 15(45):1540-1541, September 19, 1989

Alimony and maintenance: diminished earning capacity—obligor's alcoholism. FAMILY LAW REPORTER: COURT DECISIONS 16(5):1058, December 5, 1989

Double jeopardy: confinement in residential alcohol treatment facility—improper delegation. CRIMINAL LAW REPORTER: COURT DECISIONS 45(20):2367, August 23,1989

Intoxication as a defense against criminal charges in Florida, by R. F. Massey. CRIMINAL JUSTICE AND BEHAVIOR 16(3):325-344, September 1989

It's a slap in the face of AA, by R. Pulliam. SATURDAY EVENING POST 262:57, March 1990

Legal limitations on alcohol control by the police, by S. Legat. BLUTALKOHOL 25(6): 374-379, 1988

Settling the score: a $20-million accident settlement ends a family's long ordeal, by G. Heaton. ALBERTA (WESTERN) REPORT 17(17):34, April 9, 1990

Literature
Addiction and Emma Bovary, by P. H. Schmidt. MIDWEST 31:153-170, Winter 1990

Care and feeding of scientists: excerpt from *The Addiction Research Foundation: A Voyage of Discovery*, by H. David. JOURNAL OF THE ADDICTION RESEARCH FOUNDATION 19(6):7, June 1, 1990

Effectiveness of restrictions on availability as a means of preventing alcohol-related problems: review of the literature, by D. I. Smith. CONTEMPORARY DRUG PROBLEMS 15:627-684, Winter 1988

Impact of alcoholism: the writer, the story, the student, by R. Starling. COLLEGE TEACHING 38:88-92, Summer 1990

Joyce Cary's first trilogy, by B. Reid. SEWANEE REVIEW 98:50-74, Winter 1990

Kitty Dukakis: the true story (excerpt from *Now You Know*, by K. Dukakis). GOOD HOUSEKEEPING 211:202+, September 1990

Over a few drinks: a history of alcoholism, by J. C. Sournia, et al. TIMES LITERARY SUPPLEMENT June 29, 1990, p. 701

Literature—Book Reviews
7th Special Report to the United States Congress on Alcohol and Health (book review). JOURNAL OF THE ADDICTION RESEARCH FOUNDATION 19(11):8, November 1, 1990

Alcohol in developing countries (book review), by J. Maula, et al. JOURNAL OF THE ADDICTION RESEARCH FOUNDATION 19(9):10, September 1, 1990

Alcohol, politics and social policy (book review), by R. Baggott. JOURNAL OF THE ADDICTION RESEARCH FOUNDATION 19(12):13, December 1, 1990

Alcoholism in minority populations (book review), by T. D. Watts, et al. JOURNAL OF THE ADDICTION RESEARCH FOUNDATION 19(4):10, April 1, 1990

Politics in/of research: surrounding alcohol-related casualities (excerpt from the book *Drinking and Casualties*, by R. A. Draper). JOURNAL OF THE ADDICTION RESEARCH FOUNDATION 19(7-8):7-8, July/August 1990

State monopolies and alcohol prevention (book review), by T. Kortteinen. JOURNAL OF THE ADDICTION RESEARCH FOUNDATION 19(10):10, October 1, 1990

Statistics on alcohol and drug use in Canada and other countries (book review), by M. Adrian, et al. JOURNAL OF THE ADDICTION RESEARCH FOUNDATION 19(3):8, March 1, 1990

You are what you drink (book review), by A. Luks, et al. JOURNAL OF THE ADDICTION RESEARCH FOUNDATION 19(11):10, January 1, 1990

MADD (Mothers Against Drunk Drivers)
MADD endorses mandatory random drug testing bill. CORPORATE SECURITY DIGEST 4(9):8-9, March 5, 1990

MADD, insurance company give police agencies DUI cameras. CRIME CONTROL DIGEST 24(15):10, April 16, 1990

Mortality
Acute rhabdomyolysis, myoglobinuria and renal insufficiency caused by ethanol: review of the literature and description of a clinical case with fatal outcome, by I. Piazza, et al. GIORNALE DI CLINICA MEDICA 70(11):661-669, November 1989

Alcohol and death certification: influencing current practice and atittudes, by G. Bell, et al. BRITISH JOURNAL OF ADDICTION 84(12):1523-1525, December 1989

Alcohol and drowning: an analysis of contributing factors and a discussion of criteria for case selection, by G. J. Wintemute, et al. ACCIDENT ANALYSIS AND PREVENTION 22(3):291-296, June 1990

Alcohol and fatal injuries: temporal patterns, by S. M. Smith, et al. AMERICAN JOURNAL OF PREVENTIVE MEDICINE 5(5):296-302, September/October 1989

Alcohol and mortality: a review of prospective studies, by A. G. Shaper. BRITISH JOURNAL OF ADDICTION 85(7):837-847, July 1990

Alcohol and statistics of causes of death in middle-aged men in Oslo: a forensic study, by K. Skullerud, et al. TIDSSKRIFT FOR DEN NORSKE LAEGEFORENING 110 (11):1366-1371, April 30, 1990

Alcohol and street traffic: critical comments from the legal and traffic medicine viewpoint, by U. Heifer. BLUTALKOHOL 27(1):50-63, January 1990

Alcohol consumption, cigarette sales and mortality in the United Kingdom: an analysis of the period 1970-1985, by J. Sales, et al. DRUG AND ALCOHOL DEPENDENCE 24(2):155-160, October 1989

Alcohol consumption in males with sudden unexpected death in Helsinki, by A. Pentdtila, et al. BEITRAGE ZUR GERICHTLICHEN MEDIZIN 47:361-368, 1989

Alcohol-induced accidents within the scope of official statistics, by K. Handel. BLUTALKOHOL 26(5):319-329, September 1989

Alcohol related deaths in Greenland, by P. Bjerregaard. ARCTIC MEDICAL RESEARCH 47(Suppl)1:596-597, 1988

Alcohol-related disease impact: Wisconsin, 1988. MMWR 39(11):178+, March 23, 1990; also in WISCONSIN MEDICAL JOURNAL 89(5):232-236, May 1990

Alcohol-related mortality and years of potential life lost: United States, 1987. MMWR 39(11):173-178, March 23, 1990

Alcohol-related traffic fatalities during holidays: United States, 1988. MMWR 38(50): 861-863, December 1989

Alcohol-related vehicle deaths. TRAFFIC SAFETY 90(2):18, March/April 1990

Blood alcohol in fatally injured drivers and the minimum legal drinking age, by L. S. Robertson. JOURNAL OF HEALTH POLITICS, POLICY AND LAW 14(4):817-825, Winter 1989

Fatal anguilluliasis in an alcoholic patient, by J. M. Guerin, et al. PRESSE MEDICALE 18(33):1666-1667, October 14, 1989

Fatal ethanol poisoning in 1984-1986, by A. F. Rubtsov. SUDEBNO-MEDITSIN-SKAIA EKSERTIZA 32(4):50-51, October/December 1989

Fatal thrombosis of the basilar artery due to a minor head injury, by S. Sprogoe-Jakobsen, et al. FORENSIC SCIENCE INTERNATIONAL 45(3):239-245, April 1990

Five-year-old Texas boy dies after drinking liquor: case of R. Griffin. JET 77:33, March 19, 1990

Impairment cited in trucker fatalities. JOURNAL OF THE ADDICTION RESEARCH FOUNDATION 19(3):2, March 1, 1990

Mortality caused by cirrhosis and alcohol consumption, by G. Pequignot. GAS-TROENTEROLOGIE CLINIQUE ET BIOLOGIQUE 13(8-9):687-689, August/September 1989

Mortality in dilated cardiomyopathies as a function of the pursuing of alcohol drinking habit, by R. N. Sachs, et al. PRESSE MEDICALE 18(30):1483, September 30, 1989

Mortality in a follow up study of 616 alcoholics admitted to an inpatient alcoholism clinic 1972-1976, by J. E. Wells, et al. NEW ZEALAND MEDICAL JOURNAL 103(882):1-3, June 24, 1990

Re: medical-examiner-reported fatal occupational injuries, North Carolina: 1978-1984, by F. E. Mirer. AMERICAN JOURNAL OF INDUSTRIAL MEDICINE 17(4):531+, 1990

Relationship between morbidity and mortality due to alcoholic cardiomyopathy and alcohol consumption in Australia, by D. I. Smith. ADVANCES IN ALCOHOL AND SUBSTANCE ABUSE 8(3-4):57-65, Spring 1990

Role of alcohol in mortality and morbidity from interpersonal violence, by M. Y. Morgan, et al. ALCOHOL AND ALCOHOLISM 24(6):565-576, 1989

Statistical control in research on alcohol and tobacco: an example from research on alcohol and mortality, by L. T. Kozlowski, et al. BRITISH JOURNAL OF ADDICTION 85(2):271-278, February 1990

Use of aggregate data in alcohol epidemiology, by T. Norstrom. BRITISH JOURNAL OF ADDICTION 84(9):969-977, September 1989; Erratum. 84(12):1554, December 1989·

Mortality—Autopsy

Alcoholism and morphologic findings of the nervous system in autopsy cases, by K. H. Pollak. PSYCHIATRIE, NEUROLOGIE UND MEDIZINISCHE PSYCHOLOGIE 41(11):664-679, November 1989

Blood alcohol concentration at post-mortem in 175 fatal cases of alcohol intoxication, by M. K. Heatley, et al. MEDICINE, SCIENCE AND THE LAW 30(2):101-105, April 1990

Statistical study on the rate of participation of alcohol ingestion with autopsies at our department, by A. Ito, et al. ARUKORU KENKYUTO YAKUBUTSU ISON 25(1): 37-47, February 1990

The Netherlands

Alcohol control policy in The Nederlands, by S. van Ginneken, et al. HEALTH POLICY 13(2):109-113, November 1989

New Zealand

Alcoholism-mental ills jibe: New Zealand studies shows 95% correlation, by P. McCarthy. JOURNAL OF THE ADDICTION RESEARCH FOUNDATION 19(2):4, February 1, 1990

Norway

Alcohol and statistics of causes of death in middle-aged men in Oslo: a forensic study, by K. Skullerud, et al. TIDSSKRIFT FOR DEN NORSKE LAEGEFORENING 110 (11):1366-1371, April 30, 1990

Papua New Guinea

Prevention and management of problems related to alcohol abuse in Papua New Guinea through primary health care, by F. Y. Johnson. MEDICINE AND LAW 98(2):175-189, 1989

Pathology

Alcohol-induced bone marrow damage: status before and after a 4-week period of abstinence from alcohol with or without disulfirm: a randomized bone marrow study in alcohol-dependent individuals, by G. Casagrande, et al. BLUT 59(3):231-236, September 1989

Alteration in the function of cerebral neurotransmitter receptors during the establishment of alcohol dependence: neurochemical aspects, by K. Kuriyama, et al. ALCOHOL AND ALCOHOLISM 25(2-3):239-245, 1990

Analysis of postmortem brain samples from 32 alcoholic and nonalcoholic individuals for protein III, a neuronal phosphoprotein, by J. A. Grebb, et al. ALCOHOLISM 13(5):673-679, October 1989. Erratum. 14(1):126, February 1990

Do alcoholics have abnormal benzodiazepine receptors, by S. S. Missak. MEDICAL HYPOTHESES 32(1):59-60, May 1990

Effects of chronic ethanol consumption beginning at adolescence: increased numbers of dendritic spines on cortical pyramidal cells in the adulthood, by I. Ferrer, et al. ACTA NEUROPATHOLOGICA 78(5):528-532, 1989

Histochemical study of the skeletal muscle in chronic alcoholism, by M. L. Ferraz, et al. ARQUIVOS DE NEURO-PSIQUIATRIA 47(2):139-149, June 1989

Neuronal counts from four cortical regions of alcoholic brains, by J. J. Kril, et al. ACTA NEUROPATHOLOGICA 79(2):200-204, 1989

Neuropathology of alcoholism, by C. G. Harper, et al. ALCOHOL AND ALCOHOLISM 25(2-3):207-216, 1990

Ultrastructural detection of cholesterol in the liver in chronic alcoholic intoxication, by A. S. Loginov, et al. BIULLETEN EKSPERIMENTALNOI BIOLOGII I MEDITSINY 109(6):619-621, June 1990

Validity of post-mortem alcohol reports, by P. J. Karhunen, et al. ALCOHOL AND ALCOHOLISM 25(1):25-32, 1990

Poland

Alcohol consumption and alcohol-induced psychoses in Poland in the years 1956-1986, by Z. Jaroszewski, et al. PSYCHIATRIA POLASKA 23(2):97-103, March/April 1989

Alcohol consumption in males with sudden unexpected death in Helsinki, by A. Pentdtila, et al. BEITRAGE ZUR GERICHTLICHEN MEDIZIN 47:361-368, 1989

Prevention
see also: Education

1989 Senator Lothar Danner Gold Medal for Professor Dr. Phil Werner Winkler, by W. Winkler. BLUTALKOHOL 27(1):64-68, January 1990

Agenda for action: on the prevention of alcohol problems, by M. J. Ashley, et al. CMAJ 143(10):1097-1098, November 15, 1990

Alcohol abuse, by C. S. Wurm. AUSTRALIAN FAMILY PHYSICIAN 19(5):782-873, May 1990

Alcohol abuse: opportunities for prevention. NEW YORK STATE JOURNAL OF MEDICINE 89(10):588-589, October 1989

Alcohol advertising and sport: a role for preventive medicine, by G. W. Sivyer. MEDICAL JOURNAL OF AUSTRALIA 153(4):230-231, August 20, 1990

Alcohol and the effects of control measures, by H. Bostrom, et al. LAKARTIDNINGEN 86(40):3389-3391, October 4, 1989

Alcohol and health: do we know enough, by M. Myszor, et al. HEALTH TRENDS 22(1):23-27, 1990

Alcohol and the moderate drinker. FUTURIST 24:47, November/December 1990

Alcohol as a field of legal study, by R. J. Bonnie. JOURNAL OF STUDIES ON ALCO-HOL 51(3):197-200, May 1990

Alcohol control policy in The Nederlands, by S. van Ginneken, et al. HEALTH POLICY 13(2):109-113, November 1989

Alcohol-related problems and public hospitals: defining a new role in prevention, by D. H. Jernigan, et al. JOURNAL OF PUBLIC HEALTH POLICY 10(3):324-352, Autumn 1989

Alcoholism and abuse of other drugs: prevention programs in Santiago, Chile, by R. Florenzano. BOLETIN DE LA OFICINA SANITARIA PANAMERICANA 107(6):577-589, December 1989

Alcoholism: prevention beginning at primary care, by J. Auba Llambrich, et al. MEDICINA CLINICA 94(6):230-233, February 17, 1990

Antabuse implants: a useful surgical procedure, by M. Welch, et al. BRITISH JOUR-NAL OF SURGERY 77(7):821, July 1990

Assessment of parent-led prevention programs: a national descriptive study, by M. Klitzner, et al. JOURNAL OF DRUG EDUCATION 20(2):111-125 1990

Assessment of parent-led prevention programs: a preliminary assessment of impact, by M. Klitzner, et al. JOURNAL OF DRUG EDUCATION 20(1):77-94, 1990

Banning alcohol in a major college stadium: impact on the incidence and patterns of injury and illness, by D. W. Spaite, et al. JOURNAL OF AMERICAN COLLEGE HEALTH 39:125-128, November 1990

Behavioral self-control strategies for deliberately limiting drinking among college students, by C. E. Werch. ADDICTIVE BEHAVIORS 15(2):118-128, 1990

Behavioral strategies for alcohol abuse prevention with high-risk college males, by R. B. Garvin, et al. JOURNAL OF ALCOHOL AND DRUG EDUCATION 36:23-34, Fall 1990

Being tested, by D. G. Sessions. MISSOURI MEDICINE 86(11):735-736, November 1989

Beverage alcohol spending in Singapore: a potential development constraint, by R. L. Curry, Jr. INTERNATIONAL JOURNAL OF THE ADDICTIONS 24(8):821-828, August 1989

Bold stand against alcohol and drugs, by R. Maher, et al. NASSP BULLETIN 74:126-127, September 1990

British perspective on alcohol problems in relation to European community policy, by B. Braine. BRITISH JOURNAL OF ADDICTION 85(5):677-681, May 1990

Case report: negligent treatment with drugs, by H. F. Laufenburg. WISCONSIN MEDICAL JOURNAL 89(4):166-168+, April 1990

Catchers in the rye, by J. E. Schowalter. JOURNAL OF THE AMERICAN ACADEMY OF CHILD AND ADOLESCENT PSYCHIATRY 29(1):10-16, January 1990

Changes in the control of alcohol misuse, by R. Bunton. BRITISH JOURNAL OF ADDICTION 85(5):605-615, May 1990

Children's self-selection into prevention programs: evaluation of an innovative recruitment strategy for children of alcoholics, by L. K. Gensheimer, et al. AMERICAN JOURNAL OF COMMUNITY PSYCHIATRY 18:707-723, October 1990

College student's recommendations to combat abusive drinking habits, by L. F. Burrell. JOURNAL OF COLLEGE STUDENT DEVELOPMENT 31:562-563, November 1990

Community gatekeeper training model for reducing alcohol abuse and alcohol-related injury, by C. R. Harrington, et al. RHODE ISLAND MEDICAL JOURNAL 72(12): 459-463, December 1989

Conversation with Ignacy Wald. BRITISH JOURNAL OF ADDICTION 84(9):961-965, September 1989

Cooperative agreements for communications programs for the prevention of illegal drug use or the illegal use or abuse of alcohol: ADAMHA. FEDERAL REGISTER 55(59):11258-11263, March 27, 1990

Dealing with drinking: how to quit or cut down. JOURNAL OF THE ADDICTION RESEARCH FOUNDATION 19(12):16, December 1, 1990

Evaluated community action projects in alcohol problems prevention, by R. Saltz, et al. CONTEMPORARY DRUG PROBLEMS 17:323-459, Fall 1990

Evaluating and improving the functioning of a peer-based alcohol abuse prevention organization, by R. F. Massey, et al. JOURNAL OF ALCOHOL AND DRUG EDUCATION 235(2):24-35, Winter 1990

Fetal Alcohol Syndrome prevention in American Indian communities of Michigan's Upper Peninsula, by K. J. Plaisier. AMERICAN INDIAN AND ALASKA NATIVE MENTAL HEALTH RESEARCH 3(1):16-33, Summer 1989

Glasgow's temperature story: changing approaches towards the control of alcohol abuse, by K. Mullen. HEALTH BULLETIN 47(6):304-310, November 1989

Improvement of narcotic dependence care and prevention of alcoholism in seamen, by P. I. Sidorov, et al. SOVETSKOE ZDRAVOOKHRONENIE (9):41-45, 1989

Leadership experience of oral antialcohol propangada among the troops of a military district, by V. F. Vlasenko, et al. VOENNO-MEDITSINSKII ZHURNAL (9):64-66, September 1989

Main trends of antialcoholism campaign and its role in reduction of injuries in fishermen, by P. I. Sidorov, et al. GIGIYENA I SANITARIYA (4):26-28, April 1990

Methodologic aspects of the propaganda on a sober life style, by V. V. Boiko, et al. SOVETSKOE ZDRAVOOKHRONENIE (7):21-24, 1989

Minimal and self-help methods in the secondary prevention of alcohol misuse, by J. Barber. AUSTRALIAN SOCIAL WORK 42(2):13-19, June 1989

New legislative modification regarding the prevention of alcoholism and other drug addictions, by A. Homolacova. CESKOSLOVENSKA ZDRAVOTNICTVI 37(12): 542-548, December 1989

On the construction of drinking norms in work organizations, by H. M. Trice, et al. JOURNAL OF STUDIES ON ALCOHOL 51(3):201-220, May 1990

Ounce of prevention: productive remedies for alcoholism, by J. Mullahy, et al. JOURNAL OF POLICY ANALYSIS AND MANAGEMENT 9:249-253, Spring 1990

Per drink prevention tax urged, by J. Hollobon. JOURNAL OF THE ADDICTION RESEARCH FOUNDATION 19(9):8, September 1, 1990

Preventing alcohol problems: local action and licensing law—a case study, by A. Lockwood. COMMUNITY HEALTH STUDIES 13(4):456-462, 1989

Preventing alcohol problems: survey of Canadian medical schools, by J. M. Brewster, et al. CMAJ 143(10):1076-1082, November 15, 1990

Preventive intervention with children of alcoholics, by J. G. Emshoff. PREVENTIVE AND HUMAN SERVICES 7(1):225-253, 1989

Production of an anti-tobacco television public service announcement by middle school students, by G. Sedlacek, et al. JOURNAL OF SCHOOL HEALTH 59(9): 401-403, November 1989

Professional responses to alcohol related problems: a study of a health centre, by J. D. Sanderson. HEALTH BULLETIN 47(6):315-319, November 1989

Reducing adolescent drug abuse: sociological strategies for community practice, by W. D. Watts. CLINICAL SOCIOLOGY REVIEW 7:152-171, 1989

Reducing alcohol consumption through television advertising, by J. G. Barber, et al. JOURNAL OF CONSULTING AND CLINICAL PSYCHOLOGY 57(5):613-618, October 1989

Role of medical personnel of therapeutic-preventive establishments in antialcoholic campaign, by E. A. Purina, et al. SOVETSKOE ZDRAVOOKHRONENIE (9):38-41, 1989

Role of medical schools in the prevention of alcohol-related problems, by J. C. Negrete. CMAJ 143(10):1048-1053, November 15, 1990

Rural community organizing and development strategies in Alaska native villages, by L. Marum. ARCTIC MEDICAL RESEARCH 47(Suppl)1:354-356, 1988

Shifting boundaries of alcohol policy, by D. C. Walsh. HEALTH AFFAIRS 9(2):47-62, Summer 1990

Soviet alcoholism, by E. P. Dunn. SCIENCE 247(4942):515-516, February 2, 1989

Spectrum of drinkers and intervention opportunities, by H. A. Skinner. CMAJ 143 (10):1054-1059, November 15, 1990

State monopolies and alcohol prevention (book review), by T. Kortteinen. JOURNAL OF THE ADDICTION RESEARCH FOUNDATION 19(10):10, October 1, 1990

Tackling the alcohol problem: the case for secondary prevention, by S. Holt. JOURNAL OF THE SOUTH CAROLINA MEDICAL ASSOCIATION 85(12):582-584, December 1989

Tighter United States laws fail to dent liquor's appeal. TIMES HIGHER EDUCATION SUPPLEMENT 909:10, April 6, 1990

Psychiatry and Psychology

Actions and interactions of hypnotics on human performance: single doses of zopiclone, triazolam and alcohol, by T. Kuitunen, et al. INTERNATIONAL CLINICAL PSYCHOPHARMACOLOGY 5(Suppl)2:115-130, April 1990

Acute effects of ethanol on regional brain glucose metabolism and transport, by N. D. Volkow, et al. PSYCHIATRY IN MEDICINE 35(1):39-48, April 1990

Alcohol abuse on skid row: in sight, out of mind, by F. J. Dunne. ALCOHOL AND ALCOHOLISM 25(1):13-15, 1990

Alcohol and the brain, by W. A. Lishman. BRITISH JOURNAL OF PSYCHIATRY 156: 635-644, May 1990

Alcohol and masculinity, by R. Lemle, et al. JOURNAL OF SUBSTANCE ABUSE TREATMENT 6(4):213-222, 1989

Alcohol and self-evaluation: is a social cognition approach beneficial?, by M. R. Banaji, et al. SOCIAL COGNITION 7(2):137-151, Summer 1989

Alcohol consumption and alcohol-induced psychoses in Poland in the years 1956-1986, by Z. Jaroszewski, et al. PSYCHIATRIA POLASKA 23(2):97-103, March/April 1989

Alcohol consumption and rates of personal violence, suicide and homicide, by D. Lester. ACTIVITAS NERVOSA SUPERIOR 31(4):248-251, December 1989

Alcohol input and creative output, by A. M. Ludwig. BRITISH JOURNAL OF ADDICTION 85(7):953-963, July 1990

Alcohol intoxication and psychosocial problems among children, by A. Lamminpaa, et al. ACTA PSYCHIATRICA SCANDINAVICA 81(5):468-471, May 1990

Alcohol problems in conditions of the North, by C. P. Korolenko. ARCTIC MEDICAL RESEARCH 47(Suppl)1:593-595, 1988

Alcohol-related cognitions: do they predict treatment outcome?, by J. Guydish, et al. ADDICTIVE BEHAVIORS 15(5):423-430, 1990

Alcohol, subliminal stimulation, and disinhibitory processes, by R. Gustafson, et al. PERCEPTUAL AND MOTOR SKILLS 70(2):495-502, April 1990

Alcohol themes within country-western songs, by G. J. Connors, et al. INTERNA-TIONAL JOURNAL OF THE ADDICTIONS 24(5):445-451, May 1989

Alcohol, tobacco and cannabis: 12-year longitudinal associations with antecedent social context and personality, by M. F. Sieber, et al. DRUG AND ALCOHOL DE-PENDENCE 25(3):281-292, June 1990

Alcohol use and psychological distress: a comparison of Americans and West Germans, by W. C. Cockerham, et al. INTERNATIONAL JOURNAL OF THE ADDIC-TIONS 24(10):951-961, October 1989

Alcoholic delusion of jealousy: psychopathologic characteristics of 2 types of disease course, by M. Soyka, et al. PSYCHIATRISCHE PRAXIS 16(5):189-193, September 1989

Alcoholic housewives and role satisfaction, by B. Farid, et al. ALCOHOL AND ALCO-HOLISM 24(4):331-337, 1989

Alcoholic patient in general practice: problems without solutions, by T. Schweizer. THERAPEUTISCHE UMSCHAU 47(5):370-373, May 1990

Alcoholism and depressive disorders: is cholinergic sensitivity a biological marker?, by D. H. Overstreet, et al. ALCOHOL AND ALCOHOLISM 24(3):253-255, 1989

Alcoholism: can honest mistake about one's capacity for self control be an excuse, by H. Fingarette. INTERNATIONAL JOURNAL OF LAW AND PSYCHIATRY 13(1-2):77-93, 1990

Analysis of screening questionnaires for differences in alcoholism between men and women, by A. Nociar. BRATISLAVSKE LEKARSKE LISTY 91(1):44-51, January 1990

Antecedents of personality disorders in a community sample of men, by R. E. Drake, et al. JOURNAL OF PERSONALITY DISORDERS 2(1):60-68, Spring 1988

Approach and avoidance coping responses among older problem and nonproblem drinkers, by R. H. Moos, et al. PSYCHOLOGY AND AGING 5(1):31-40, March 1990

Attribution theory perspective on alcohol-impaired driving, by D. M. DeJoy. HEALTH EDUCATION QUARTERLY 6(3):359-372, Fall 1989

Autonomic and subjective responses to alcohol stimuli with appropriate control stim-uli, by D. B. Newlin, et al. ADDICTIVE BEHAVIORS 14(6):625-630, 1989

Behavioral factors in the choice of drugs, by D. B. Heath. RECENT DEVELOPMENTS IN ALCOHOLISM 9:245-254, 1990

Behavioral hyporeactivity to physostigmine in detoxified primary alcoholics, by D. S. Janowsky, et al. AMERICAN JOURNAL OF PSYCHIATRY 146:538-539, April 1989

Behavioral pharmacology of alcohol and other drugs: emerging issues, by M. E. Carroll, et al. RECENT DEVELOPMENTS IN ALCOHOLISM 8:5-46, 1990

Behavioral scientific model of the drunk driver, by J. Ehret. BLUTALKOHOL 26(6): 381-395, November 1989

Bellman's poetry touch the vital nerve of alcohol drinking, by L. Sjostrand. LAKARTIDNINGEN 87(26-27):2269-2272, June 27, 1990

Block constructions of chronic alcoholic and unilateral brain-damaged patients: a test of the right hemisphere vulnerability hypothesis of alcoholism, by N. Akshoomoff, et al. ARCHIVES OF CLINICAL NEUROPSYCHOLOGY 4(3):275-281, 1989

Changes in the psychological defence system as a function of alcohol intoxication in men, by R. Gustafson, et al. BRITISH JOURNAL OF ADDICTION 84(12):1515-1521, December 1989

Characteristics of alcoholics in treatment arrested for driving while impaired, by S. MacDonald, et al. BRITISH JOURNAL OF ADDICTION 85(1):97-105, January 1990

Characteristics of psychiatric emergency room patients with alcohol- or drug-induced disorders, by R. R. Szuster, et al. HOSPITAL AND COMMUNITY PSYCHIATRY 41(12):1342-1345, 1990

Cheating following success and failure in heavy and moderate social drinkers, by K. J. Corcoran, et al. JOURNAL OF GENERAL PSYCHOLOGY 116(3):311-316, July 1989

Clinical neuropsychological investigation and personality assessment in alcohol abuse, by T. Loberg. TIDSSKRIFT FOR DEN NORSKE LAEGEFORENING 110(6):721-724, February 28, 1990

Clinico-pathogenetic aspects of pathologic premorbid conditions in alcoholic psychoses, by A. Imamov. ZHRUNAL NEVROPATOLOGII I PSIKHIATRII IMENI S. S. KORSAKOVA 90(2):47-51, 1990

Clinico-pathologenetic aspects of hypochondriac conditions of exogenous-organic nature and their treatment, by R. G. Golodets, et al. ZHURNAL NEVROPA-TOLOGII I PSIKHIATRII IMENI S. S. KORSAKOVA 90(2):84-89, 1990

Cognitive function in alcoholics in a double-blind study of piracetam, by I. Buranji, et al. LIJECNICKI VJESNIK 112(3-4):111-114, March/April 1990

Cognitive model of drug urges and drug-use behavior: role of automatic and nonautomatic processes, by S. T. Tiffany. PSYCHOLOGICAL REVIEW 97(2):147-168, April 1990

Cognitive moderators of alcohol's effects on anxiety, by M. A. Sayette, et al. BEHAVIOR RESEARCH AND THERAPY 27(6):685-690, 1989

Cognitive style and alcoholics: a comment on Robertson, et al, by M. Kirton. PSYCHOLOGICAL REPORTS 65(2):456-468, October 1989

Comparison of methods for assessing sociopathy in male and female alcoholics, by N. L. Cooney, et al. JOURNAL OF STUDIES ON ALCOHOL 51(1):42-48, January 1990

Comparison of primary alcoholics, secondary alcoholics, and nonalcoholic psychiatric patients on the MacAndrew Alcoholism scale, by L. C. Ward, et al. JOURNAL OF PERSONALITY ASSESSMENT 54(3-4):729-735, Summer 1990

Comparison of a prospective diary and two summary recall techniques for recording alcohol consumption, by M. E. Hilton. BRITISH JOURNAL OF ADDICTION 84(9): 1085-1092, September 1989

Comparison of a quantity-frequency method and a diary method of measuring alcohol consumption, by G. R. Webb, et al. JOURNAL OF STUDIES ON ALCOHOL 51(3):271-277, May 1990

Complex analysis of the data of clinico-psychological examination of patients with alcoholism for predicting early recurrences, by I. Tiul'pin. ZHURNAL NEVROPATOLOGII I PSIKHIATRII IMENI S. S. KORSAKOVA 90(2):62-66, 1990

Conditioned learning in alcohol dependence: implications for cue exposure treatment, by D. C. Drummond, et al. BRITISH JOURNAL OF ADDICTION 85(6):725-743, June 1990

Conditioned opponent responses: effects of placebo challenge in alcoholic subjects, by M. E. McCaul, et al. ALCOHOLISM 13(5):631-635, October 1989

Connection between the psychological characteristics of alcoholic patients and the parameters of discrete omegametry, by A. Y. Grinenko, et al. ZHURNAL VYSSHEI NERVNOI DEIATEL-NOSTI IMENI I P PAVLOVA 39(6):1014-1017, 1989

Considering the psychotropic effect of alcohol, by J. P. von Wartburg. THERAPEUTISCHE UMSCHAU 47(5):399-404, May 1990

Construct validity of an altereffect-based subtyping system for alcoholics, by C. G. Watson, et al. JOURNAL OF CLINICAL PSYCHOLOGY 46(4):507-517, 1990

Contextual cueing effects in the remote memory of alcoholic Korsakoff patient and normal subjects, by A. J. Parkin, et al. QUARTERLY JOURNAL OF EXPERIMENTAL PSYCHOLOGY. A 42(3):585-596, 1990

Contribution of problem drinking to the level of psychiatric morbidity in the general hospital, by M. A. Schofield. BRITISH JOURNAL OF PSYCHIATRY 155:229-232, August 1989

Coping with drinking: how do females and males relate to their alcoholic partners, by E. Stumm, et al. PSYCHOTHERAPIE, PSYCHOSOMATIK, MEDIZINISCHE PSYCHOLOGIE 40(6):223-229, June 1990

Cross-cultural and cross-temporal explanations of drinking behavior: contributions from epidemiology, life-span developmental psychology and the sociology of aging, by E. Hartka, et al. BRITISH JOURNAL OF ADDICTION 84(12):1409-1417, December 1989

CSF diazepam-binding inhibitor in alcoholics and normal controls, by A. Roy, et al. PSYCHIATRY RESEARCH 31(3):261-266, March 1990

CSF galanin in alcoholics, pathological gamblers, and normal controls: a negative report, by A. Roy, et al. BIOLOGICAL PSYCHIATRY 27(8):923-926, April 15, 1990

CSF gamma-aminobutyric acid in alcoholics and control subjects, by A. Roy, et al. AMERICAN JOURNAL OF PSYCHIATRY 147(10):1294-1296, October 1990

Dependence syndrome concept as applied to alcohol and other substances of abuse, by T. A. Kosten, et al. RECENT DEVELOPMENTS IN ALCOHOLISM 8:47-68, 1990

Differential anxiety symptoms in cocaine vs. alcoholic patients, by H. Pettinati, et al. NIDA RESEARCH MONOGRAPH SERIES 95:471-472, 1989

Dimensions of alcoholism: a multivariate analysis, by R. K. Brooner, et al. JOURNAL OF STUDIES ON ALCOHOL 51(1):77-81, January 1990

Does neuropsychological test performance predict resumption of drinking in post-treatment alcoholics?, by O. A. Parsons, et al. ADDICTIVE BEHAVIORS 15(3): 297-307, 1990

Drinking and the perpetuation of social inequality in Australia, by M. Sargent. MEDICINE AND LAW 8(5):507-516, 1989

Drinking routines: lifestyles and predatory victimization—a causal analysis, by J. R. Lasley. JUSTICE QUARTERLY 6(4):529-542, December 1989

Drug and alcohol problems and the developing world, by T. Baasher. INTERNA-TIONAL REVIEW OF PSYCHIATRY 1(1-2):13-16, March 1989

Drug use and its social covariates from the period of adolescence to young adult-hood: some implications from longitudinal studies, by K. Yamaguchi. RECENT DEVELOPMENTS IN ALCOHOLISM 8:125-143, 1990

Dynamics of alcoholic psychoses in recent years under conditions of an intensified struggle against drunkenness and alcoholism, by M. I. Vorob'ev, et al. SOVIET NEUROLOGY AND PSYCHIATRY 22(4):22-27, Winter 1989-1990

Effect of alcohol intoxication on primary and secondary processes in male social drinkers, by R. Gustafson, et al. BRITISH JOURNAL OF ADDICTION 84(12):1507-1513, December 1989

Effect of the benzodiazepine antagonist, flumazenil, on psychometric performance in acute ethanol intoxication in man, by T. G. Clausen, et al. EUROPEAN JOURNAL OF CLINICAL PHARMACOLOGY 38(3):233-236, 1990

Effect of co-occurring disorders on criminal careers: interaction of antisocial personal-ity, alcoholism, and drug disorders, by K. M. Abram. INTERNATIONAL JOURNAL OF LAW AND PSYCHIATRY 12(2-3):133-148, 1989

Effect of thyrotropin releasing hormone on the verbal forms of mental activity in patients with alcoholism, by V. V. Beliaeva. ZHURNAL NEVROPATOLOGII I PSIKHIATRII IMENI S. S. KORSAKOVA 90(2):104-106, 1990

Effect of TRH on the verbal forms of mental activity of patients with alcoholism, by V. V. Belyaeva. ZHURNAL NEVROPATOLOGII I PSIKHIATRII IMENI S. S. KORSAKOVA 90(2):104-106, 1990

Effects of alcohol on human aggression: an integrative research review, by B. J. Bushman, et al. PSYCHOLOGICAL BULLETIN 107(3):341-354, May 1990

Effects of infant cries on alcohol consumption in college males at risk for child abuse, by P. R. Stasiewicz, et al. CHILD ABUSE AND NEGLECT 13(4):463-470, 1989

Effects of sex, race and year in college on self-reported drinking-related problem behaviors, by K. Curtis, et al. PSYCHOLOGICAL BULLETIN 66(3 Pt 1):871-874, June 1990

Effects of social drinking and familial alcoholism risk on cognitive functioning: null findings, by A. I. Alterman, et al. ALCOHOLISM: CLINICAL AND EXPERIMENTAL RESEARCH 13(6):799-803, December 1989

Efficacy expectations among alcohol-dependent patients: a Swedish version of the Situational Confidence Questionnaire, by C. Sandahl, et al. ALCOHOL AND ALCOHOLISM 25(1):67-73, 1990

Efficacy of treatment for drinking problems, by J. B. Saunders. INTERNATIONAL REVIEW OF PSYCHIATRY 1(1-2):121-137, March 1989

Emergence of alcohol expectancies in childhood: a possible critical period, by P. M. Miller, et al. JOURNAL OF STUDIES ON ALCOHOL 51(4):343-349, July 1990

Emotional perception and memory in alcoholism and aging, by M. Oscar-Berman, et al. ALCOHOLISM: CLINICAL AND EXPERIMENTAL RESEARCH 14(3):383-393, May/June 1990

Endorsement and strength of alcohol expectancies, by R. L. Collins, et al. JOURNAL OF STUDIES ON ALCOHOL 51(4):336-342, July 1990

Ethanol beverage anticipation: effects on plasma testosterone and luteinizing hormone levels: a pilot study, by R. E. Meyer, et al. JOURNAL OF STUDIES ON ALCOHOL 51(4):350-355, July 1990

Ethnicity and psychosocial factors in alcohol and tobacco use in adolescence, by B. A. Bettes, et al. CHILD ABUSE AND NEGLECT 61(2):557-565, April 1990

Evoked cortical activity to the varying probability of significant stimuli in healthy subjects and alcoholics, by O. A. Genkina, et al. FIZIOLOGII CHELOVEKA 16(1):33-39, January/February 1990

Expectancy and drinking, by R. Gilber. JOURNAL OF THE ADDICTION RESEARCH FOUNDATION 19(5):9, May 1, 1990

Expectancy models of alcohol use, by A. W. Stacy, et al. JOURNAL OF PERSONALITY AND SOCIAL PSYCHOLOGY 58(5):918-928, May 1990

Expectancy set, self-reported expectancies and predispositional traits: predicting interest in violence and erotica, by W. H. George, et al. JOURNAL OF STUDIES ON ALCOHOL 50(6):541-551, November 1989

Failure of a 2-hour motivational intervention to alter recurrent drinking behavior in alcoholics with gastrointestinal disease, by V. Kuchipudi, et al. JOURNAL OF STUDIES ON ALCOHOL 51(4):356-360, July 1990

Family history of alcoholism in depressed patients: DST and REM latency findings, by G. Zammit, et al. AMERICAN JOURNAL OF PSYCHIATRY 146(8):1077, August 1989

Family history of depression and alcoholism in Alzheimer patients and age-matched controls, by B. A. Lawlor, et al. INTERNATIONAL JOURNAL OF GERIATRIC PSYCHOLOGY 4(6):321-326, November/December 1989

Fire and ice: natives, alcohol and spirituality—a northern health paradigm, by P. Colorado. ARCTIC MEDICAL RESEARCH 47(Suppl)1:598-603, 1988

Frequent repeaters in a psychiatric emergency service, by J. M. Ellison, et al. HOSPITAL AND COMMUNITY PSYCHIATRY 40(9):958-960, September 1989

From the Alcohol, Drug Abuse, and Mental Health Administration: comorbidity of mental disorders and substance abuse, by F. K. Goodwin. JAMA 261:3517, June 23-30, 1989

Heavy drinking and its correlates in young men, by A. I. Alterman, et al. ADDICTIVE BEHAVIORS 15(1):95-103, 1990

Help-seeking behaviour in problem drinkers: a review, by C. Majella Jordan, et al. BRITISH JOURNAL OF ADDICTION 84(9):979-988, September 1989

History of anxiety symptoms among 171 primary alcoholics, by M. A. Schuckit, et al. JOURNAL OF STUDIES ON ALCOHOL 51(1):34-41, January 1990

HK-MBD questionnaire: factor structure and discriminant validity with an adolescent sample, by M. Windle. ALCOHOLISM 14(2):232-237, April 1990

Homo-erotomania, by S. F. Signer. BRITISH JOURNAL OF PSYCHIATRY 154:729, May 1989

Hot-headed or impulsive, by H. G. Kennedy, et al. BRITISH JOURNAL OF ADDICTION 85(5):639-643, May 1990

How I learned to cope with stress, by P. Cove. CORRECTIONS TODAY 51(7):48-50, December 1989

Humor and the alcoholic patient: a beginning study, by E. M. Scott. ALCOHOLISM TREATMENT QUARTERLY 6(2):29-39, 1989

Identifications in several young alcoholics, by H. Menke. PSYCHIATRIE DE l'ENFANT 32(1):209-248, 1989

Immediate and overnight effects of zopiclone 7.5 mg and nitrazepam 5 mg with ethanol on psychomotor performance and memory in healthy volunteers, by I.

Hindmarch. INTERNATIONAL CLINICAL PSYCHOPHARMACOLOGY 5(Suppl)2: 105-113, April 1990

Importance of personality and sociopsychological factors in the development of chronic alcoholism, by A. V. Oleinik, et al. VRACHEBNOE DELO (8):101-103, August 1989

Incest and the development of alcoholism in adult female survivors, by D. L. Hurley. ALCOHOLISM 7(2):41-56, 1990

Initial acceptance of ethanol: gustatory factors and patterns of alcohol drinking, by A. B. Kampov-Polevoy, et al. ALCOHOL 7(2):83-85, March/April 1990

Interpersonal types among alcohol abusers: a comparison with drug abusers, J. A. Turner, et al. JOURNAL OF CLINICAL PSYCHOLOGY 46(4):500-506, July 1990

Is pregnancy a time of changing drinking and smoking patterns for fathers as well as mothers: an initial investigation, by E. J. Waterson, et al. BRITISH JOURNAL OF ADDICTION 85(3):389-396, March 1990

Lateralization of visuo-spatial function during masking in healthy subjects and in patients with chronic alcoholism, by O. A. Genkina, et al. ZHURNAL VYSSHEI NERVNOI DELATEL-NOSTI IMENI I P PAVLOVA 39(3):431-439, May/June 1989

Learned tolerance to alcohol: mental rehearsal with imagined consequences, by M. Zinatelli, et al. ALCOHOLISM: CLINICAL AND EXPERIMENTAL RESEARCH 14(4):518-521, 1990

Locus of control and perceived alcohol ingestion in performance of a fine motor skill, by R. L. Breckenridge, et al. PSYCHOLOGICAL BULLETIN 66(1):179-185, February 1990

Long-term predictors of outcome in abstinent alcoholic men, by P. T. Loosen, et al. AMERICAN JOURNAL OF PSYCHIATRY 147:1662-1666, December 1990

Low basal levels of cortisol distinguish detoxified alcoholics with major depressive disorder from non-MDDs, by U. Halbreich, et al. ALCOHOLISM: CLINICAL AND EXPERIMENTAL RESEARCH 13(6):834-836, December 1989

Low score on California psychological inventory as predictors of psychopathology in alcoholic patients, by C. Higgins-Lee. PSYCHOLOGICAL REPORTS 67:227-232, August 1990

Major depressive disorder, alcoholism, and reduced natural killer cell cytotoxicity: role of severity of depressive symptoms and alcohol consumption, by M. Irwin, et al. ARCHIVES OF GENERAL PSYCHIATRY 47(8):713-719, August 1990

MMPI comparisons of Hispanic- and white-American veterans seeking treatment for alcoholism, by R. J. Velasquez, et al. PSYCHOLOGICAL REPORTS 67(1):95-98, 1990

Models for student drinking and smoking: parents or peers, by L. Standing, et al. SOCIAL BEHAVIOR AND PERSONALITY 17(2):223-229, 1989

Neural mechanism of subconscious attraction to alcohol in chronic alcoholics, by G. S. Shostakovich. SOVIET NEUROLOGY AND PSYCHIATRY 22(4):3-12, Winter 1989/1990

Neurocognitive deficits of alcoholism: an intervention, by D. L. Wetzig, et al. JOURNAL OF CLINICAL PSYCHOLOGY 46(2):219-229, March 1990

Neuropsychodynamics of alcoholism and addiction: personality, psychopathology, and cognitive style, by L. Miller. JOURNAL OF SUBSTANCE ABUSE TREATMENT 7(1):31-49, 1990

Offspring of parents with drinking problems: drinking and drug-taking as young adults, by J. Orford, et al. BRITISH JOURNAL OF ADDICTION 85(6):770-784, June 1990

On the importance of the psychotropic effects of alcohol, by J. P. von Wartburg. DRUG AND ALCOHOL DEPENDENCE 25(2):135-139, April 1990

Oral ethanol self-administration: a behavioral pharmacological approach to CNS control mechanisms, by H. H. Samson, et al. ALCOHOL 7(3):187-191, May/June 1990

Outcome and efficacy expectancy in the prediction of post-treatment drinking behaviour, by K. E. Solomon, et al. BRITISH JOURNAL OF ADDICTION 85(5):659-665, May 1990

Patterns of adjustment problems and alcohol abuse in early adulthood: a prospective longitudinal study, by T. Andersson, et al. DEVELOPMENT AND PSYCHOPATHOLOGY 1(2):119-131, 1989

Peculiarities of alcoholism in the north, by C. P. Korolenko. ARCTIC MEDICAL RESEARCH 47(Suppl)1:36-37, 1988

Peer attitudes, sex, and the effects of alcohol on simulated driving performance, by T. P. Oei, et al. AMERICAN JOURNAL OF DRUG AND ALCOHOL ABUSE 16(1-2):135-146, 1990

Personality and situation as determiners of desire to drink among problem drinkers, by J. D. Hundleby, et al. INTERNATIONAL JOURNAL OF THE ADDICTIONS 24(8):755-763, August 1989

Personality charcteristics of sons of alcohol abusers, by E. E. Knowles, et al. JOURNAL OF STUDIES ON ALCOHOL 51(2):142-147, March 1990

Personality differences associated with MacAndrew scores, by J. P. Allen, et al. PSYCHOLOGICAL REPORTS 66(2):691-698, 1990

Personality factors in holistic living: improvement among inpatient alcoholics, by J. Stoudenmire, et al. JOURNAL OF SOCIAL BEHAVIOR AND PERSONALITY 4(4):457-462, 1989

Personality factors in transient versus endurin depression among inpatient alcoholic women: a preliminary analysis, by R. C. McMahon, et al. JOURNAL OF PERSONALITY DISORDERS 4(2):150-160, Summer 1990

Personality profiles of children of alcoholics, by P. Calder, et al. PROFESSIONAL PSYCHOLOGY: RESEARCH AND PRACTICE 20(6):417-418, December 1989

Personality risk and alcohol consumption: a latent variable analysis, by M. Earleywine, et al. ADDICTIVE BEHAVIORS 15(2):183-187, 1990

Personality variables as mediators and moderators of family history risk for alcoholism: conceptual and methodological issues, by F. Rogosch, et al. JOURNAL OF STUDIES ON ALCOHOL 51(4):310-318, July 1990

Pimozide in pathological jealousy, by S. I. Cohen. BRITISH JOURNAL OF PSYCHIATRY 155:714, November 1989

Predicting the drinking behavior of older adults from questionnaire measures of alcohol consumption, by J. A. Tucker, et al. ADDICTIVE BEHAVIORS 14(6):655-658, 1989

Pretest expectancies and cognitive impairment in alcoholics, by A. M. Sander, et al. JOURNAL OF CONSULTING AND CLINICAL PSYCHOLOGY 57(6):705-709, December 1989

Principal components analysis of the inventory of drinking situations: empirical categories of drinking by alcoholics, by D. S. Cannon, et al. ADDICTIVE BEHAVIORS 15(3):265-269, 1990

Problem drinking and alcohol problems: widening the circle of covariations, by S. W. Sadava. RECENT DEVELOPMENTS IN ALCOHOLISM 8:173-201, 1990

Problem drinking as a form of learned behaviour: a final rejoinder to Gorman and Edwards, by N. Heather. BRITISH JOURNAL OF ADDICTION 85(5):617-620, May 1990

Psycholinguistic study of a special vocabulary used by alcoholics, by A. P. Vasilevich, et al. ZHURNAL NEVROPATHOLOGII I PSIKHIATRII IMENI S. S. KOSAKOVA 90(2):66-71, 1990

Psychological characteristics of the motivation for alcohol use in adolescents, by K. V. Mosketi, et al. ZHURNAL NEVROPATOLOGII I PSIKHIATRII IMENI S. S. KORSAKOVA 90(2):51-55, 1990

Psychological profile of social drinkers, by P. Robson. BRITISH JOURNAL OF ADDICTION 84(11):1329-1336, November 1989

Reactivity to alcohol cues and induced moods in alcoholics, by M. D. Litt, et al. ADDICTIVE BEHAVIORS 15(2):137-146, 1990

Relation of alcohol expectancies to drinking patterns among alcoholics: generalization across gender and race, by R. B. Kline. JOURNAL OF STUDIES ON ALCOHOL 51(2):175-182, March 1990

Relation of psychological characteristics of alcoholics and indices of discrete omega measurement, by A. Grinenko, et al. ZHURNAL VYSSHEI NERVNOI DELATELNOSTI IMENI P PAVLOVA 39(6):1014-1017, November/December 1989

Relationship between neuropsychological and late component evoked potential measures in chronic alcoholics, by B. W. Patterson, et al. INTERNATIONAL JOURNAL OF NEUROSCIENCE 49(3-4):319-327, December 1989

Relationship between psychiatric distress and alcohol use: findings from the Eastern Baltimore Mental Health Survey, by A. Dryman, et al. ACTA PSYCHIATRICA SCANDINAVICA 80(4):310-314, October 1989

Relationship of DUI recidivism to moral reasoning, sensation seeking, and MacAndrew alcoholism scores, by G. L. Little, et al. PSYCHOLOGICAL REPORTS 65(3 Pt 2):1171-1174, December 1989

Reliability and validity of the Inventory to Diagnose Depression (IDD) with an inpatient alcoholic population, by A. M. Horton, et al. PSYCHOTHERAPY IN PRIVATE PRACTICE 7(3):55-60, 1989

Resistance to alcohol impairment of visual-motor performance: II—effects for attentional set and self-reported concentration, by W. H. George, et al. PHARMACOLOGY, BIOCHEMISTRY AND BEHAVIOR 36(2):261-266, June 1990

Response to adults' angry behavior in children of alcoholic and nonalcoholic parents, by M. Ballard, et al. JOURNAL OF GENERAL PSYCHOLOGY 151(2):195-209, June 1990

Response to Kirton, by E. Robertson, et al. PERCEPTUAL AND MOTOR SKILLS 69(3 Pt 1):1037-1038, December 1989

Role of some personality mechanisms in alcohol dependency syndrome, by E. Motak. PSYCHIATRIA POLSKA 23(2):140-145, March/April 1989

Roles of intoxicated practice in the development of ethanol tolerance, by A. D. Le, et al. PSYCHOPHARMACOLOGY 99(3):366-370, 1989

Schedule-induced oral self-administration of cocaine and ethanol solutions: lack of effect of chronic desipramine, by M. Tang, et al. DRUG AND ALCOHOL DEPENDENCE 25(1):21-25, February 1990

Self-esteem, depression, and alcohol dependency among high school students, by M. Workman, et al. PSYCHOLOGICAL REPORTS 65(2):451-455, October 1989

Self-focused attention in clinical disorders: review and a conceptual model, by R. E. Ingram. PSYCHOLOGICAL BULLETIN 107:156-176, March 1990

Self-regulation and self-medication factors in alcoholism and the addictions: similarities and differences, by E. J. Khantzian. RECENT DEVELOPMENTS IN ALCOHOLISM 8:255-271, 1990

Self-report issues in alcohol abuse: state of the art and future directions, by L. C. Sobell, et al. BEHAVIORAL ASSESSMENT 12(1):77-90, 1990

Self-reported illnesses in family members of alcoholics, by K. P. McGann. FAMILY MEDICINE 22(2):103-106, March/April 1990

Severity of alcohol dependence and social functioning of male patients with alcoholism: I—functioning in the sharing of marital roles, by M. Datkowski, et al. PSYCHIATRIA POLSKA 23(4):287-293, July/August 1989

Severity of alcohol dependence and social functioning of male patients with alcoholism: II—functioning in parenteral, employee's and automous roles, by M. Dabkowski, et-al. PSYCHIATRIA POLSKA 23(4):294-299, July/August 1989

Sexual differences among alcoholics at a psychiatric department, by K. Garde. UGESKRIFT FOR LAEGER 152(4):246-247, January 22, 1990

Short REM latency in primary alcoholic patients with secondary depression, by J. C. Gillin, et al. AMERICAN JOURNAL OF PSYCHIATRY 147(1):106-109, January 1990

Skin resistance reaction to alcohol-related verbal stimuli in alcoholic adolescents, by A. V. Nemtsov. ZHURNAL NEVROPATOLOGII I PSIKHIATRII IMENI S. S. KORSAKOVA 89(8):112-117, 1989

Social occasions and the perceived appropriateness of consuming different alcoholic beverages, by H. Klein, et al. JOURNAL OF STUDIES ON ALCOHOL 51(1):59-67, January 1990

Somatopathological or psychopathological determination of diminished responsibility, by H. Witter. MONATSSCHRIFT FUR KRIMINOLOGIE UND STRAFRECHSEIFORM 71(6):410-415, 1988

Some considerations on the reliability and validity of the Alcohol Expectancy Questionnaire for Adolescents, by K. J. Corcoran, et al. PSYCHOLOGY OF ADDICTIVE BEHAVIORS 3(2):43-52, 1989

Some effects of alcohol on eyewitness memory, by J. C. Yuille, et al. JOURNAL OF APPLIED PSYCHOLOGY 75(3):268-273, 1990

Stability and change in feelings of loneliness: a two-year prospective longitudinal study of advanced alcohol abusers, by I. Akerlind, et al. SCANDINAVIAN JOURNAL OF PSYCHOLOGY 30(2):102-112, 1989

Stability of coexisting psychiatric syndromes in alcoholic men after one year: commentary, by P. J. Frawley. JOURNAL OF STUDIES ON ALCOHOL 50(5):491, September 1989

Strategies of self-control in male young offenders who have reduced their alcohol consumption without formal intervention, by M. McMurran, et al. JOURNAL OF ADOLESCENCE 13(2):115-128, June 1990

Structure of depression in alcoholic women, by J. E. Turnbull, et al. JOURNAL OF STUIDES ON ALCOHOL 51(2):148-155, March 1990

Study of drinking habits of rural middle and old aged residents in Ibaraki Prefecture: relationship between problem drinking, depression and personality, part 1—on male subjects, by S. Satoh, et al. ARUKORU KENKYUTO YAKUBUTSU ISON 25(1):48-58, February 1990

Study of drinking habits of rural middle and old aged residents in Ibaraki Prefecture: relationship between problem drinking, depression and personality, part 2—on female subjects, by S. Satoh, et al. ARUKORU KENKYUTO YAKUBUTSU ISON 25(1):59-67, February 1990

Substance abuse in women: relationship between chemical dependency of women and past reports of physical and-or sexual abuse, by G. B. Ladwig, et al. INTER-NATIONAL JOURNAL OF THE ADDICTIONS 24(8):739-754, August 1989

Subtypes of substance abusers: personality differences associated with MacAndrew scores, by J. P. Allen, et al. PSYCHOLOGICAL REPORTS 66(2):691-698, April 1990

Tavern patrons and the MacAndrew alcoholism scale: self-reported drinking behavior in relation to the MMPI L and K scales, by C. Ciancio, et al. JOURNAL OF CLINI-CAL PSYCHOLOGY 46:687-691, September 1990

Tension reduction hypothesis revisited: an alcohol expectancy perspective, by R. M. Young, et al. BRITISH JOURNAL OF ADDICTION 85(1):31-40, January 1990

Test-retest reliability of the Children of Alcoholics Test, by B. E. Robinson, et al. PERCEPTUAL AND MOTOR SKILLS 70(3 Pt 1):858, June 1990

To your health: a toast to you, colleague, by B. Horn. THERAPEUTISCHE UMSCHAU 47(5):395-398, May 1990

Tridimensional personality and questionnaire scores of sons of alcoholic and nonal-coholic fathers, by M. A. Schuckit, et al. AMERICAN JOURNAL OF PSYCHIATRY 147(4):481-487, April 1990

Types of life events and the onset of alcohol dependence, by D. M. Gorman, et al. BRITISH JOURNAL OF ADDICTION 85(1):71-79, January 1990

Use of the Western Personality Test in the identification of potential alcohol abusers, by N. W. Brown, et al. ALCOHOLISM TREATMENT QUARTERLY 6(3-4):189-198, 1989

Validity of the Addiction Severity Index: adapted version, in a Costa Rican population group, by L. E. Sandi Esquivel, et al. BULLETIN OF THE PAN AMERICAN HEALTH ORGANIZATION 24(1):70-76, 1990

Verbal and nonverbal right hemisphere processing by chronic alcoholics, by L. S. Cermak, et al. ALCOHOLISM: CLINICAL AND EXPERIMENTAL RESEARCH 13(5):611-616, September/October 1989

What does the legacy of Hans Selye and Franz Alexander mean today: the psy-chophysiological approach in medical practice, by M. Kopp, et al. INTERNA-TIONAL JOURNAL OF PSYCHOPHYSIOLOGY 8(2):99-105, November 1989

Public Response To Alcohol
see also: MADD

On the front lines: women of color and war on drugs, by J. Anner. MINORITY TRENDSLETTER 3(3):10, Summer 1990

Rural community organizing and development strategies in Alaska native villages, by L. Marum. ARCTIC MEDICAL RESEARCH 47(Suppl)1:354-356, 1988

SADD announces initiatives for the nineties. JUVENILE JUSTICE DIGEST 18(8):1+, April 18, 1990

Victim-activist role in the anti-drunk driving movement, by F. J. Weed. SOCIOLOGICAL QUARTERLY 31(3):459-473, 1990

Rehabilitation

see also: Alcoholics Anonymous
Therapy

Abstinence versus nonabstinence: the objectives of alcoholism rehabilitation programs in Quebec, by S. Brochu. JOURNAL OF PSYCHOACTIVE DRUGS 22(1):15-21, January/March 1990

Action North gives alcoholics new lease on life, by J. Auger. WINDSPEAKER 7(38): 16, November 24, 1989

Alcohol education courses for offenders: an update of United Kingdom services, by S. Gamba, et al. ALCOHOL AND ALCOHOLISM 24(5):473-478, 1989

Alcohol-free living centers: hope for homeless alcoholics, by N. M. Koroloff, et al. SOCIAL WORK 34(6):497-504, November 1989

Alcohol use by heroin addicts 12 years after drug abuse treatment, by W. E. Lehman, et al. JOURNAL OF STUDIES ON ALCOHOL 51(3):233-244, May 1990

Alcoholic patient in general practice: problems without solutions, by T. Schweizer. THERAPEUTISCHE UMSCHAU 47(5):370-373, May 1990

Alcoholic patient in rehabilitation, by H. U. Niederhauser, et al. THERAPEUTISCHE UMSCHAU 47(5):405-411, May 1990

Analytically oriented group psychotherapy of patients with alcohol problems, by J. Johnsen. TIDSSKRIFT FOR DEN NORSKE LAEGEFORENING 110(7):844-846, March 10, 1990

Applications of relapse prevention with moderation goals, by M. E. Larimer, et al. JOURNAL OF PSYCHOACTIVE DRUGS 22(2):189-195, April/June 1990

Are drinkers interested in inexpensive approaches to reduce their alcohol use?, by C. E. Werch. JOURNAL OF DRUG EDUCATION 20(1):67-75, 1990

Audiotaped versus written administration of the Situation Competency Test, by D. Steiner, et al. ADDICTIVE BEHAVIORS 15(2):175-178, 1990

Autonomic withdrawal syndrome and a protracted course of the abstinence syndrome: ambulatory diagnosis and therapy, by G. Assmann. ZEITSCHRIFT FUR ARZTLICHE FORTBILDUNG 83(16):819-821, 1989

Aversive therapy revisited, by D. W. Goodwin. JOURNAL OF SUBSTANCE ABUSE TREATMENT 7(2):75-76, 1990

Barriers to the care of persons with dual diagnoses: organizational and financing issues, by M. S. Ridgely, et al. SCHIZOPHRENIA BULLETIN 16(1):123-132, 1990

Biases in relapse attributions made by alcoholics and their wives, by J. R. McKay, et al. ADDICTIVE BEHAVIORS 14(5):513-522, 1989

Body composition in detoxified alcoholics, by J. L. York, et al. ALCOHOLISM: CLINICAL AND EXPERIMENT RESEARCH 14(2):180-183, April 1990

Brief didactic treatment for alcohol and drug-related problems: an approach based on client choice, by M. Sanchez-Craig. BRITISH JOURNAL OF ADDICTION 85(2): 169-177, February 1990

Care systems for alcohol-related problems in 90 years: from psalm singing and compulsory work to ambulatory treatment and the Minnesota model, by H. Kjolstad. TISSKRIFT FOR DEN NORSKE LAEGEFORENING 110(14):1845-1847, May 30, 1990

Changes in blood Zn, Se, Cd, Pb during therapeutic abstinence from alcohol in 101 cases of alcoholism, by P. Pujatti, et al. GIORNALE DI CLINICA MEDICA 70(11): 653-654+, November 1989

Characteristics of a rural area community mental health programme; County Caroni, by K. Maharaj, et al. INTERNATIONAL JOURNAL OF SOCIAL PSYCHIATRY 35(3): 280-284, Autumn 1989

Characteristics of women receiving mandated treatment for alcohol and polysubstance dependence in Massachusetts, by B. W. Lex, et al. DRUG AND ALCOHOL DEPENDENCE 25(1):13-20, February 1990

Cognitive deficits, vitamin status and controlled thiamine substitution in alcohol dependent patients in withdrawal treatment, by A. Vischer, et al. NERVENARZT 60(10):633-640, October 1989

Cognitive functioning and treatment outcome in alcoholics, by A. I. Alterman, et al. JOURNAL OF NERVOUS AND MENTAL DISEASE 178(8):494-499, August 1990

Commitment to abstinence and acute stress in relapse to alcohol, opiates, and nicotine, by S. M. Hall, et al. JOURNAL OF CONSULTING AND CLINICAL PSYCHOLOGY 58(2):175-181, April 1990

Comparative value of self-report and blood tests in assessing outcome amongst alcoholics, by L. Keso, et al. BRITISH JOURNAL OF ADDICTION 85(2):209-215, February 1990

Cooperation between the general practitioner and social medicine service, by W. Ringli, et al. THERAPEUTISCHE UMSCHAU 47(5):374-378, May 1990

Coping with patients' problem drinking, by C. Brewer, et al. PRACTITIONER 233 (1466):475-480, April 8, 1989. Erratum 233(1470):815, June 8, 1989

Course of restitution of learning and concentrating ability in chronic alcoholics in the 1st year of abstinence, by H. Amlacher, et al. PSYCHIATRIE, NEUROLOGIE UND MEDIZINISCHE PSYCHOLOGIE 41(9):521-530, September 1989

Current problems in the rehabilitation of alcoholics, by B. I. Karon. VOENNO-MED-ITSINSKII ZHURNAL (8):57-58, August 1989

Determining alcoholism treatment outcomes: cost-effectiveness perspective, by D. M. Wing, et al. NURSING ECONOMICS 8(4):248-255, July/August 1990

Detoxification of alcoholics: improving care by symptom-triggered sedation, by A. A. Wartengberg, et al. ALCOHOLISM: CLINICAL AND EXPERIMENTAL RE-SEARCH 14(1):71-75, February 1990

Drink to the devil: former alcoholic describes his recovery, by P. Nicholson. SUNDAY TIMES MAGAZINE September 23, 1990, p. 85+

EEG sleep studies in "pure" primary alcoholism during subacute withdrawal: relation-ships to normal control, age, and other clinical variables, by J. C. Gillin, et al. BIO-LOGICAL PSYCHIATRY 27(5):477-488, March 1, 1990

Effect of the transcerebral action of an ultrahigh-frequency electrical field on en-docrine gland function in chronic alcoholics, by A. S. Bobkova, et al. PROBLEMY ENDOKRINOLOGII 36(2):49-51, March/April 1990

Effectiveness of an alcohol countermeasure program in rural Tennessee, by H. N. Mookherjee. JOURNAL OF ALCOHOL AND DRUG EDUCATION 35(2):13-19, Winter 1990

Event-related potentials in chronic alcoholics during withdrawal and abstinence, by A. Romani, et al. NEUROPHYSIOLOGIE CLINIQUE 19(5):373-384, November 1989

Factors affecting the use of mental health services in people with alcohol disorders, by M. F. Strack, et al. NEW ZEALAND MEDICAL JOURNAL 102(880):601-603, November 22, 1989

Follow-up of alcoholics: inpatients at the Solhaugen Rehabilitation Center in 1985 and 1986, by S. Bjornelv, et al. TIDSSKRIFT FOR DEN NORSKE LAEGEFOREN-ING 110(7):847-849, March 10, 1990

Forel Clinic: a specialized treatment center for alcohol dependent females and males, by G. Sondheimer. THERAPEUTISCHE UMSCHAU 47(5):420-422, May 1990

Frank, open and humane: rehabilitation program for pilots. AVIATION WEEK AND SPACE TECHNOLOGY 132:9, April 23, 1990

Home detoxification for problem drinkers: acceptability to clients, relative, general practitioners and outcome after 60 days, by T. Stockwell, et al. BRITISH JOUR-NAL OF ADDICTION 85(1):61-70, January 1990

Hospitalized with a double stigma, by C. A. de Jong. NEDERLANDS TIJDSCHRIFT VOOR GENEESKUNDE 134(27):1289-1291, July 7, 1990

Human CRH stimulation response during acute withdrawal and after medium-term ab-stention from alcohol abuse, by U. von Bardeleben, et al. PSYCHONEUROEN-DOCRINOLOGY 14(6):441-449, 1989

Inpatient alcohol rehabilitation: emergency intervention as a program, by D. Hell. THERAPEUTISCHE UMSCHAU 47(5):414-415, May 1990

Intervention: raising the bottom, by E. G. Runge, Jr. JOURNAL OF THE SOUTH CAROLINA MEDICAL ASSOCIATION 86(1):19-21, January 1990

Life-long abstainers live longer, suffer less, by A. Massam. JOURNAL OF THE AD-DICTION RESEARCH FOUNDATION 19(9):2, September 1, 1990

Long-term recovery in alcoholics, by C. B. De Soto, et al. ALCOHOLISM: CLINICAL AND EXPERIMENTAL RESEARCH 13(5):693-697, October 1989

Longitudinal characteristics of hospital use before and after alcoholism treatment, by B. M. Booth, et al. AMERICAN JOURNAL OF DRUG AND ALCOHOL ABUSE 16(1-2):161-170, 1990

Maintained controlled drinking following severe alcohol dependence: a case study, by P. G. Booth. BRITISH JOURNAL OF ADDICTION 85(3):315-322, March 1990

Major methodologic shortcomings in the article on the treatment of alcoholism, by D. Waller. LAKARTIDNINGEN 87(22):1938+, May 30, 1990

Matching alcoholics to coping skills or interactional therapies: posttreatment results, by R. M. Kadden, et al. JOURNAL OF CONSULTING AND CLINICAL PSYCHOL-OGY 57(6):698-704, 1989

Medical response to drinking, by S. M. Aronson. RHODE ISLAND MEDICAL JOUR-NAL 72(12):433, December 1989

Minimal interventions with problem drinkers: a pilot study of the effect of two interview styles on perceived self-efficacy, by I. G. Galbraith. HEALTH BULLETIN 47(6):311-314, November 1989

Minnesota Model, by R. Maggs. BRITISH JOURNAL OF ADDICTION 84(11):1367-1369, November 1989

MRI study of brain changes with short-term abstinence from alcohol, by R. B. Zipursky, et al. ALCOHOLISM 13(5):664-666, October 1989

Munchenbuchsee as a private clinic, by M. Lanz. THERAPEUTICHE UMSCHAU 47(5):416-418, May 1990

Neurodynamics of relapse prevention: a neuronutrient approach to outpatient DUI of-fenders, by R. J. Brown, et al. JOURNAL OF PSYCHOACTIVE DRUGS 22(2):173-187, April/June 1990

Never try to carry a drunk by yourself: effective use of self-help groups, by N. P. Johnson, et al. JOURNAL OF THE SOUTH CAROLINA MEDICAL ASSOCIATION 86(1):27-31, January 1990

On the wagon, by R. Doar. WASHINGTON MONTHLY 20(5):50-53, 1988

Past and future of the combined approach, by M. M. Glatt. BRITISH JOURNAL OF ADDICTION 84(9):1093-1094, September 1989

Peripheral nerve functions in chronic alcoholic patients on disulfiram: a six month fol-low up, by S. K. Palliyath, et al. JOURNAL OF NEUROLOGY, NEUROSURGERY AND PSYCHIATRY 53(3):227-230, March 1990

Plasma MHPG and age in detoxified alcoholics, by U. Halbreich, et al. BIOLOGICAL PSYCHIATRY 27(6):626-630, March 15, 1990

Practical business of treatment: 8—the Edinburgh alcohol problems clinic, by B. Ritson. BRITISH JOURNAL OF ADDICTION 85(1):25-29, January 1990

Primary health care and social services cooperate at an outpatient clinic for alcoholics in Lund, by S. Olofsson, et al. LAKARTIDNINGEN 87(3):130-131, January 17, 1990

Principles and experiences with comprehensive management strategies of patients with alcohol abuse and dependence, by H. von Keyserlingk. ZEITSCHRIFT FUR ARZTLICHE FORTBILDUNG 83(16):811-813, 1989

Private practice in psychiatry: which abusers can be treated in private ambulatory care?, by H. Kristenson. LAKARTIDNINGEN 86(49):4357-4360, December 6, 1989

Privatization of treatment services for alcohol abusers: effect on the black community, by W. Jones, Jr., et al. JOURNAL OF THE NATIONAL MEDICAL ASSOCIATION 82(5):337-342, May 1990

Process of change: a therapeutic model in alcohol abuse, by S. Fauske, et al. TIDSSKRIFT FOR DEN NORSKE LAEGEFORENING 110(14):1841-1844, May 30, 1990

Prognosis and relapse in alcoholism, by D. M. Gallant. ALCOHOLISM: CLINICAL AND EXPERIMENTAL RESEARCH 13(3):465, June 1989

Prospective multicentre study of in-patient treatment for alcoholics: 18- and 48-month follow-up—Munich Evaluation for Alcoholism Treatment (MEAT), by W. Feuerlein, et al. EUROPEAN ARCHIVES OF PSYCHIATRY AND NEUROLOGICAL SCIENCES 239(3):144-157, 1989

Randomized study of secondary prevention of early stage problem drinkers in primary health care, by A. Romelsjo, et al. BRITISH JOURNAL OF ADDICTION 84(11): 1319-1327, November 1989; Erratum 85(3):431, March 1990

Recent developments in inpatient treatment of alcoholic patients, by D. Athen. OF-FENTLICHE GENSUNDHEITSWESEN 52(2):65-68, February 1990

Rehabilitation outcomes for alcohol impaired drivers referred for assessment in two Wisconsin counties, by A. M. Gurnack. JOURNAL OF ALCOHOL AND DRUG EDUCATION 35(1):45-59, Fall 1989

Resisting temptation: a psychological analysis, by C. Brewer. BRITISH JOURNAL OF ADDICTION 84(11):1371-1372, November 1989

Role of drinking restraint success in subsequent consumption, by L. Bensley, et al. ADDICTIVE BEHAVIORS 15(5):491-496, 1990

Self-efficacy and relapse among inpatient drug and alcohol abusers: a predictor of outcome, by T. A. Burling, et al. JOURNAL OF STUDIES ON ALCOHOL 50(4): 354-360, July 1989

Should courses for alcohol intoxicated automobile drivers be legally introduced: an answer based on public economics, by G. Hundhausen. BLUTALKOHOL 26(5): 329-346, September 1989

Sladen and Mozdzierz AMA Scale: a failed replication attempt, by H. E. Doweiko. INTERNATIONAL JOURNAL OF THE ADDICTIONS 24(5):397-404, May 1989

Some factors relating to satisfactory post-discharge community maintenance of chronic psychotic patients, by M. L. Fernando, et al. CANADIAN JOURNAL OF PSYCHIATRY 35(1):71-73, February 1990

Some objective parameters of the degree of social and work decompensation and rehabilitation of chronic alcoholics, by Y. L. Gurevich, et al. SOVIET NEUROLOGY AND PSYCHIATRY 22(4):13-21, Winter 1989/1990

Story of Alkali Lake: anomaly of community recovery or national trend in Indian country, by E. Willie. ALCOHOLISM TREATMENT QUARTERLY 6(3-4):167-174, 1989

Strict abstinence, by D. Uhl. MEDIZINISCHE MONATSSCHRIFT FUR PHARMA-ZEUTEN 12(11):329, November 1989

Study of women's recovery from alcoholism, by C. Hunt, et al. PERSON-CENTERED REVIEW 5(2):233-248, May 1990

Substance dependence unit in tuberculosis care facilities, by V. I. Serdechnyi. PROBLEMY TUBERKULIOZA (2):64-65, 1990

Systems approach to estimating the required capacity of alcohol treatment services, by B. Rush. BRITISH JOURNAL OF ADDICTION 85(1):49-59, January 1990

Treating alcohol problems in Sri Lanka, by D. Samarasinghe. BRITISH JOURNAL OF ADDICTION 84(4):865-867, August 1989

Treating drunk drivers with moral reconation therapy: a two-year recidivism study, by G. L. Little, et al. PSYCHOLOGICAL REPORTS 66(pt 2):1379-1387, June 1990

Treatment for GPs with a drink probem. PRACTITIONER 233(1477):1353, October 22, 1989

Turning point, by P. Riley. HEALTH PROGRESS 71(1):118+, January/February 1990

Two-week prognosis in problem drinkers, by S. Thomas-Dobson, et al. PSYCHO-LOGICAL REPORTS 66(2):529-530, April 1990

United States general population's experiences of responding to alcohol problems, by R. Room. BRITISH JOURNAL OF ADDICTION 84(11):1291-1304, November 1989

Use of the preparation essential and hemosorption in the complex treatment of chronic alcoholism, by N. I. Khodzhaeva. ZHURNAL NEVROPATOLOGII PSIKHI-ATRII IMENI S. S. KORSAKOVA 90(2):59-62, 1990

Use of visualization as a means of integrating the spiritual dimension into treatment: part II: working with emotions, by S. Krystal, et al. JOURNAL OF SUBSTANCE ABUSE TREATMENT 6(4):223-228, 1989

Vocational rehabilitation of alcoholics: a research note on the bureaucratization of deviance, by D. H. Shamblin. DEVIANT BEHAVIOR 11(1):45-60, January/March 1990

Women in treatment: changing over time, by P. A. Harrison. INTERNATIONAL JOURNAL OF THE ADDICTIONS 24(7):655-673, July 1989

Working ability of mentally ill people in times of social crisis, by D. Kecmanovic, et al. ACTA PSYCHIATRICA SCANDINAVICA 80(4):340-345, October 1989

Research

Acute alcohol infusion does not alter plasma gonadotropins or prolactin in ovariectomized rats, by M. G. Subramanian, et al. ALCOHOLISM 14(2):191-194, April 1990

Acute and chronic ethanol on hepatic oxygen ethanol and lactate metabolism in cats, by C. V. Greenway, et al. AMERICAN JOURNAL OF PHYSIOLOGY 258(3 Pt 1):411-418, March 1990

Ad libitum alcohol ingestion does not induce renal IgA deposition in mice, by S. M. Smith, et al. ALCOHOLISM 14(2):184-186, April 1990

Adult children of alcoholics: is it really a separate field for study?, by R. J. Beidler. DRUGS AND SOCIETY 3(3-4):133-141, March/April 1989

Age dependent alterations of host immune response in the ethanol-fed rat, by G. A. Roselle, et al. JOURNAL OF CLINICAL AND LABORATORY IMMUNOLOGY 29(2):99-103, June 1989

Alcohol addiction in the offspring of white rats receiving pyrogenal and prodigiozan during pregnancy, by I. Bandazhevskii, et al. FARMAKOLOGIYA I TOKSIKOLOGIYA 52(3):86-87, May/June 1989

Alcohol and crime: issues and directions for future research, by S. Walfish, et al. CRIMINAL JUSTICE AND BEHAVIOR 16(3):370-386, September 1989

Alcohol consumption and pain phobia: toward a unifying theory of alcoholism, by A. I. Hammer, et al. ADVANCES IN ALCOHOL AND SUBSTANCE ABUSE 8(3-4):43-55, 1990

Alcohol consumption, blood alcohol level and the relevance of body weight in experimental design and analysis, by M. S. Devgun, et al. JOURNAL OF STUDIES ON ALCOHOL 51(1):24-28, January 1990

Alcohol drinking, food and fluid intakes and body weight grain in rats, by C. Larue-Achagoitis, et al. PHYSIOLOGY AND BEHAVIOR 47(3):545-548, March 1990

Alcohol or tobacco research versus alcohol and tobacco research, by L. C. Sobell, et al. BRITISH JOURNAL OF ADDICTION 85(2):263-269, February 1990

Alcohol-preferring rats: genetic sensitivity to alcohol-induced stimulation of dopamine metabolism, by F. Fadda, et al. PHYSIOLOGY AND BEHAVIOR 47(4):727-729, April 1990

Alcohol research at the Hjellestad Clinic, by J. C. Laberg, et al. BRITISH JOURNAL OF ADDICTION 84(9):999-1009, September 1989

Alcohol research in different countries: subsidiaries and projects, by H. Topel. FUNCTIONAL NEUROLOGY 4(4):411-414, October/December 1989

Alterations in the nuclear volume of neurons from the hypothalamic magnocellular nuclei of fetuses born to rats subject to chronic alcoholism, by M. Fresnillo, et al. REVISTA ESPANOLA DE FISIOLOGIA 45(Suppl):43-48, 1989

Alterations in the regulatory properties of hepatic fatty acid oxidation and carnitine palmitoyltransferase I activity after ethanol feeding and withdrawal, by M. Guzman, et al. ALCOHOLISM: CLINICAL AND EXPERIMENTAL RESEARCH 14(3):472-477, June 1990

Analysis of spontaneous alcohol drinking in rhesus monkeys, by M. Kornet, et al. PHYSIOLOGY AND BEHAVIOR 47(4):679-684, April 1990

Animal model of immune response associated with alcohol-related cancers, by S. I. Mufti, et al. PROGRESS IN CLINICAL AND BIOLOGICAL RESEARCH 325:359-371, 1990

Antagonism of ethanol intoxication in rats by inhibitors of phenylethanolamine N-methyltransferase, by I. N. Mefford, et al. ALCOHOLISM 14(1):53-57, February 1990

Application of electrophysiology to research in alcoholism, by S. O'Connor, et al. JOURNAL OF NEUROPSYCHIATRY AND CLINICAL NEUROSCIENCES 2(2):149-158, Spring 1990

Are the effects of chronic ethanol administration on erythrocyte membrane mediated by changes in plasma lipids?, by M. H. Branchey, et al. DRUG AND ALCOHOL DEPENDENCE 25(1):67-71, February 1990

Baboon alcohol dehydrogenase isozymes: purification and properties of liver class I ADH: moderate alcohol consumption reduces liver class I and class II ADH activities, by R. S. Holmes, et al. PROGRESS IN CLINICAL AND BIOLOGICAL RESEARCH 344:819-841, 1990

Behavior of alcohol-preferring AA and alcohol-avoiding ANA rat lines in test of anxiety and aggression, by K. Tuominen, et al. ALCOHOL 7(4):349-353, July/August 1990

Behavioral and subjective effects of ethanol: relationship to cerebral metabolism using PET, by H. de Wit, et al. ALCOHOLISM: CLINICAL AND EXPERIMENTAL RESEARCH 14(3):482-489, June 1990

Behavioral effects in the mouse during and following withdrawal from ethanol ingestion and/or nicotine administration, by E. S. Onaivi, et al. DRUG AND ALCOHOL DEPENDENCE 24(3):205-211, December 1989

Beta adrenergic agonist isopreterenol suppress voluntary alcohol intake in rats, by L. A. Grupp, et al. PHARMACOLOGY, BIOCHEMISTRY AND BEHAVIOR 33(2):493-495, June 1989

Beverage preference, beverage type and subject gender as determinants of alcohol consumption in the laboratory, by M. Kidorf, et al. JOURNAL OF STUDIES ON ALCOHOL 51(4):331-335, July 1990

Boozy rats take protein to stop drinking. NEW SCIENTIST 127:27, September 29, 1990

Brain and liver dolichol in chronic alcoholism: a necropsy study, by J. J. Kril, et al. ALCOHOLISM: CLINICAL AND EXPERIMENTAL RESEARCH 14(4):528-530, 1990

Broader perspective of expectancy research: comment on Corcoran and Parker, by S. A. Brown, et al. PSYCHOLOGY OF ADDICTIVE BEHAVIORS 3(2):80-84, 1989

Buthionine sulfoximine inhibition of glutathione biosynthesis enhances hepatic lipid peroxidation in rats during acute ethanol intoxication, by Y. Kera, et al. ALCOHOL AND ALCOHOLISM 24(6):519-524, 1989

Central action of an inhibitor of brain dopa-decarboxylase, NSD-1015, on cyanamide-induced alcohol drinking in rats, by F. J. Minano, et al. PHARMACOLOGY, BIO-CHEMISTRY AND BEHAVIOR 35(2):465-468, February 1990

Cerebellar white matter after long-term ethanol consumption in mice, by S. C. Phillips. JOURNAL OF STUDIES ON ALCOHOL 51(1):14-18, January 1990

Cerebellular GABAA receptor binding and function in vitro in two rat lines developed for high and low alcohol sensivity, by M. Uusi-Oukari, et al. NEUROCHEMICAL RESEARCH 14(8):733-739, August 1989

Change in cohabitation and intrapair similarity of monozygotic (MZ) cotwins for alcohol use, extraversion, and neuroticism, by J. Kaprio, et al. BEHAVIOR GENETICS 20(2):265-276, March 1990

Changes in surface activity of surfactant and ultrastructure of the air-blood barrier in alcoholic intoxication in experimental animals, by A. K. Zagorul'ko, et al. BIULLE-TEN EKSPERIMENTALNOI BIOLOGII I MEDITSINY 109(5):489-493, May 1990

Characteristics of final stages of glycolysis in the myocardium of rats with various alcohol motivation, by I. Kiselevskii, et al. VOPROSY MEDITSINKAI KHIMII 36(3):78-79, May/June 1990

Characteristics of the neurobiological mechanisms in a predisposition of the development of alcoholism in the progeny of rats hereditarily at risk for alcoholism, by T. M. Vorob'eva, et al. ZHURNAL VYSSHEI NERVNOI DEIATEL-NOSTI MENI I P PAVLOVA 40(2):389-392, March/April 1990

Characteristics of the status of autonomic innervation and of the functioning of the heart conduction system in alcoholism, by V. V. Anikin, et al. TERAPEVTICH-ESKII ARKHIV 62(4):43-45, 1990

Charting direction of alcohol studies: Academy of Sciences report. JOURNAL OF THE ADDICTION RESEARCH FOUNDATION 19(4):7, April 1, 1990

Cholecystokinin and satiation with alcohol, by P. J. Kulkosky, et al. ALCOHOL 6(5): 395-402, September/October 1989

Cholecystokinin octapeptide reduces ethanol intake in food-and water-sated rats, by P. Toth, et al. PHARMACOLOGY, BIOCHEMISTRY AND BEHAVIOR 35(2):493-495, February 1990

Chromosome aberrations and dominant lethals in rat oocytes during acute and chronic alcoholic intoxication, by N. M. Slozina, et al. GENETIKA 26(1):154-157, January 1990

Chronic alcohol consumption prevents the sepsis-induced increases in gluceogensis and metabolic clearance rate, by C. H. Lang, et al. PROGRESS IN CLINICAL AND BIOLOGICAL RESEARCH 325:373-382, 1990

Chronic ethanol and chlordiazepoxide: contrasting effects on reward learning, by S. E. File, et al. ALCOHOL 7(4):307-310, July/August 1990

Chronic ethanol and pentobarbital administration in the rat: effects on GABA receptor function and expression in brain, by A. L. Morrow, et al. ALCOHOL 7(3):237-244, May/June 1990

Chronic ethanol exposure before injury produces greater immune dysfunction after thermal injury in rats, by M. Kawakami, et al. JOURNAL OF TRAUMA 30(1):27-31, January 1990

Chronic ethanol feeding and acute ethanol exposure to vitro-effect on intestinal transport of biotin, by H. M. Said, et al. AMERICAN JOURNAL OF CLINICAL NUTRITION 52:1083-1086, December 1990

Chronic ethanol treatment selectively increases the binding of inverse agonists for benzodiazepine binding sites in cultured spinal cord neurons, by M. Mhatre, et al. JOURNAL OF PHARMACOLOGY AND EXPERIMENTAL THERAPEUTICS 251(1):164-168, October 1989

Clinical, CT and electrophysiologic studies of alcoholics with special reference to the cerebellum, by T. Domzal, et al. NEUROLOGIA I NEUROCHIRURUGIA POLSKA 23(1):17-20, January 1989

Comment on Booth's "maintained controlled drinking following severe alcohol dependence—a case study": exemplary clinical research, by M. Sanchez-Craig, et al. BRITISH JOURNAL OF ADDICTION 85(3):325-327, March 1990

Comparative study on ethanol elimination and blood acetaldehyde between alcoholics and control subjects, by J. Adachi, et al. ALCOHOLISM 13(5):601-604, October 1989

Conditioning in chronic ethanol rats, by Z. Chaloupka, et al. ACTIVITAS NERVOSA SUPERIOR 31(2):136, June 1989

Controlled comparison of effects of exercise and alcohol on blood pressure and serum high density lipoprotein cholesterol in sedentary males, by K. L. Cox, et al. CLINICAL AND EXPERIMENTAL PHARMACOLOGY AND PHYSIOLOGY 17(4):251-255, April 1990

Correlation of the behavior characteristics of animals with varying levels of alcohol motivation: motor activity, taste and electrical pain sensitivities, by V. V. Surmak, et al. ZHURNAL VYSSHEI NERVNOI DEIATEL-NOSTI IMENI I P PAVLOVA 40(1):79-84, January/February 1990

Cortical dihydropyridine binding sites are unaltered in human alcoholic brain, by J. J. Krill, et al. ANNALS OF NEUROLOGY 26(3):395-397, September 1989

Cortical microvascular changes in chronological aging, cortical insults and chronic alcohol intoxication in rats: effects of antihypoxic drugs on these phenomena, by P. De Witte, et al. ALCOHOL 6(6):423-430, November/December 1989

Corticotropin-releasing factor is altered in brains of animals with high preference for ethanol, by S. R. George, et al. ALCOHOLISM: CLINICAL AND EXPERIMENTAL RESEARCH 14(3):425-429, June 1990

Craniofacial and limb development in early rat embryos following in utero exposure to ethanol and caffeine, by C. P. Ross, et al. ANATOMISCHER ANZEIGER 170(1):9-14, 1990

Current status of alcoholism treatment outcome research, by R. Fuller. NIDA RESEARCH MONOGRAPH SERIES 95:85-91, 1989

Dietary regulation of voluntary alcohol consumption in rats: influence of a high protein diet and a methylene blue diet, by A. R. Poso, et al. BIOMEDICINE AND PHARMACOLOGY 40(6):1295-1298, September 15, 1990

Differential reinforcement and diurnal rhythms of lever pressing for ethanol in AA and Wistar rats, by P. Hyytia, et al. ALCOHOLISM: CLINICAL AND EXPERIMENTAL RESEARCH 14(3):375-379, June 1990

Discriminative stimulus properties of ethanol and acute ethanol withdrawal states in rats, by D. V. Gauvin, et al. DRUG AND ALCOHOL DEPENDENCE 24(2):103-113, October 1989

Disorders of myocardial morphology in rats after 20-week alcoholization and 6-week abstention, by D. M. Shol'ts, et al. BIULLETEN EKSPERIMENTALNOI BIOLOGII I MEDITSINY 108(8):244-247, August 1989

Diurnal difference in alcohol absorption, by J. Lotterle, et al. BLUTALKOHOL 26(6): 369-375, November 1989

Does alcohol promote reactive hypoglycemia in the rat?, by C. Larue-Achagiotis, et al. PHYSIOLOGY AND BEHAVIOR 47(5):819-823, May 1990

Does ethanol intake interfere with the evaluation of glycated hemoglobins?, by G. Ben, et al. ACTA DIABETOLOGICA LATINA 26(4):337-343, October/December 1989

Duration of paternal alcohol consumption does not influence offspring growth and development, by E. L. Abel. GROWTH, DEVELOPMENT, AND AGING 53(4): 195-199, Winter 1989

Dynamics of the activity of creatine kinase and its isoenzymes in the blood serum of patients with alcoholism, by I. V. Chuvaev, et al. VOPROSY MEDITSINSKAI KHIMII 36(3):39-41, 1990

Dynamics of methionine-enkephalin content in rat adrenal glands and blood plasma in acute alcohol intoxication, by N. A. Belyaev, et al. VOPROSY MEDITSINSKAI KHIMII 36(3):86-87, May/June 1990

Early experience and the consumption of alcohol by adult C57BL-6J mice, by A. Ho, et al. ALCOHOL 6(6):511-515, November/December 1989

Effect of acute and chronic ethanol administration on rat liver alpha 2,6-sialyltransferase activity responsible for sialylation of serum transferrin, by N. Malagolini, et al. ALCOHOLISM 13(5):649-653, October 1989

Effect of acute ethanol on beta-endorphin secretion from rat fetal hypothalamic neurons in primary cultures, by D. K. Sarkar, et al. LIFE SCIENCES 47(9):31-36, 1990

Effect of adenosine and beta-endorphin on the contractions of the vas deferens in rats with various durations of ethanol narcosis, by R. Iukhananov, et al. BIULLETEN EKSPERIMENTALNOI BIOLOGII I MEDITSINY 108(12):700-702, December 1989

Effect of alcohol on lipoprotein metabolism: II—lipolytic activities and mixed function oxidases, by J. G. Parkes, et al. ENZYME 43(1):47-55, 1990

Effect of alcohol on urinary glycosaminoglycan and protein excretion in normal and diabetic mice, by R. Ramamurthi, et al. ALCOHOL AND ALCOHOLISM 25(1):45-50, 1990

Effect of the animals' emotional state of ethanol consumption under free-choice conditions, by N. N. Kudriavtseva, et al. ZHURNAL VYSSHEI NERVNOI DEIATEL-NOSTI IMENI I P PAVLOVA 40(3):502-507, May/June 1990

Effect of carbidine on parameters of ethanol oxidation in experimental alcohol intoxication, by V. M. Gurtovenko, et al. FARMAKOLOGIYA IN TOKSIKOLOGIYA 52(3):83-86, May/June 1989

Effect of chronic alcohol feeding with a low-fat diet on acetyl CoA carboxylase and fatty acid synthase activities in rat liver, by K. J. Simpson, et al. BIOCHEMICAL SOCIETY TRANSACTIONS 17(6):1116, December 1989

Effect of chronic alcohol ingestion on free radical defense in the miniature pig, by S. Zidenberg-Cherr, et al. JOURNAL OF NUTRITION 120(2):213-217, February 1990

Effect of chronic alcoholic intoxication on the bioelectrical activity of the human brain, by P. Duplenko. FIZIOLOGICHESKII ZHURNAL 35(4):74-80, July/August 1989

Effect of chronic ethanol administration on total asialoglycoprotein receptor content and intracellular processing of asialoorosomucoid in isolated rat hepatocytes, by C. A. Casey, et al. BIOCHIMICA ET BIOPHYSICA ACTA 1052(1):1-8, April 9, 1990

Effect of chronic ethanol consumption and retroviral infection on carcinogenesis and its possible inhibition by an immunostimulant, canthaxanthin: definition of a murine model, by S. I. Mufti, et al. PROGRESS IN CLINICAL AND BIOLOGICAL RESEARCH 325:283-304, 1990

Effect of chronic intake on leucin absorption from the rat small intestine, by D. Martines, et al. ALCOHOL AND ALCOHOLISM 24(6):525-531, 1989

Effect of cigarette smoking and coffee consumption on apolipoprotein B levels, by M. Periti, et al. EUROPEAN JOURNAL OF EPIDEMIOLOGY 6(1):76-79, March 1990

Effect of clonidine and related substances on voluntary ethanol consumption in rats, by K. Opitz. DRUG AND ALCOHOL DEPENDENCE 25(1):43-48, February 1990

Effect of differing probabilities of meaningful stimuli on evoked cortical activity in healthy persons and in alcoholics, by O. A. Genkina, et al. FIZIOLOGIIA CHE-LOVEKA 16(1):33-39, 1990

Effect of ethanol upon early development in mice and rats: XIV—the effect of acute intoxication with beer and wine upon preimplantation development in rats, by I. Fazakas-Todea. MORPHOLOGIE ET EMBRYOLOGIE 35(4):241-243, October/December 1989

Effect of gender and subtypes on platelet MAO in alcoholism, by W. R. Yates, et al. JOURNAL OF STUDIES ON ALCOHOL 51(5):463-467, 1990

Effect of genetic diabetes and alcohol on tissue carnitine and inositol concentrations in mice, by A. S. Reddi, et al. ALCOHOL AND ALCOHOLISM 25(2-3):137-141, 1990

Effect of induction of antibodies to serotonin on alcohol consumption and the status of the brain mediator system in rats with various degress of alcohol motivation, by N. B. Bobkova, et al. PATOLOGICHESAIA FIZIOLOGIIA I EKSPERIMENTAL-NALA TERAPILA (3):31-36, May/June 1989

Effect of ingestion-contingent hypothermia on ethanol self-administration, by C. L. Cunningham, et al. ALCOHOL 6(5):377-380, September/October 1989

Effect of insulin on lethality in mice with acute ethanol poisoning, by E. V. Saviskaia, et al. PATOLOGICHESAIA FIZIOLOGIIA I EKSPERIMENTALNAIA TERAPIIA (1):47-48, January/February 1990

Effect of monoaminergic drugs on behavior and memory of rats chronically consuming ethanol, by S. Kalishevich, et al. ACTIVITAS NERVOSA SUPERIOR 32(1):44-47, March 1990

Effect of prolonged ethanol intake on pancreatic lipids in the rat pancreas, by H. Simsek, et al. PANCREAS 5(4):401-407, July 1990

Effect of valproic acid on sleep structure and ethanol consumption in rats with various types of individual reactivity before and after stress exposure, by A. L. Mdzinar-ishvili, et al. BIULLETEN EKSPERIMENTALNOI BIOLOGII I MEDITSINY 108(9):294-296, September 1989

Effects of 0.8 g.kg ethanol on cerebral metabolism and mood in normal volunteers, by H. de Wit, et al. NIDA RESEARCH MONOGRAPH SERIES 95:450, 1989

Effects of acute alcohol ingestion on the left ventricular performance of normal subjects before and after incomplete autonomic blockade, by J. V. Nixon, et al. AMERICAN JOURNAL OF MEDICAL SCIENCES 298(3):161-166, September 1989

Effects of acute barbiturate administration, tolerance and dependence on brain GABA system: comparison to alcohol and benzodiazepines, by S. Yu, et al. ALCOHOL 7(3):261-272, May/June 1990

Effects of acute ethanol administration on stimulated parotid secretion in the rat, by J. Scott, et al. ALCOHOLISM 13(4):560-563, August 1989

Effects of acute ethanol intoxication on aldehyde dehydrogenase in mouse liver, by Y. Tomita, et al. ARUKORU KENKYUTO YAKUBUTSU ISON 25(2):116-128, April 1990

Effects of alcohol ingestion on in vitro susceptibility of peripheral blood mononuclear cells to infection wih HIV and of selected T-cell functions, by O. Bagasra, et al. ALCOHOLISM 13(5):636-643, October 1989

Effects of alcohol ingestion on in vitro susceptibility of peripheral blood mononuclear cells to infection with HIV-1 and on CD4 and CD8 lymphocytes, by O. Bagasra, et al. PROGRESS IN CLINICAL AND BIOLOGICAL RESEARCH 325:351-358, 1990

Effects of alcohol intake on blood pressure and sympathetic nerve activity in normotensive humans: a preliminary report, by G. M. Grassi, et al. JOURNAL OF HYPERTENSION 7(Suppl)6:20-21, December 1989

Effects of alpha 2-adrenergic drugs on the alcohol consumption of alcohol-preferring rats, by E. R. Korpi. PHARMACOLOGY AND TOXICOLOGY 66(4):283-286, April 1990

Effects of alpha-methyl-p-tyrosine pretreatment on ethanol-induced narcosis and hypothermia, as well as in the development of tolerance to these effects in UChA and UChB rats, by L. Tampier, et al. ALCOHOL 7(4):327-330, July/August 1990

Effects of capsaicin [C] and dihydrocapsaicin [DC] on serum ethanol [ET] concentration of ET and CF-1 mice, by J. A. Negulesco, et al. ARTERY 17(3):144-158, 1990

Effects of chronic alcohol consumption on the steady-state kinetic properties of cytochrome oxidase in rat liver, by W. S. Thayer, et al. BIOCHIMICA ET BIOPHYSICA ACTA 101(6):333-338, April 26, 1990

Effects of chronic ethanol administration on plasma-membrane-bound glycosyltransferase activities, by A. Fernandez-Briera, et al. PHARMACOLOGY, BIOCHEMISTRY AND BEHAVIOR 35(1):75-84, January 1990

Effects of combined administration of alcohol and tobacco on the ultrastructure of ventricular cardiomyocytes in rats, by A. Zak, et al. PATOLOGIA POLSKA 40(3): 343-351, 1989

Effects of dopaminergic agents on alcohol consumption by rats in a limited access paradigm, by M. A. Linseman. PSYCHOPHARMACOLOGY 100(2):195-200, 1990

Effects of drugs on blood-brain barrier permeability in rats chronically intoxicated by ethanol, by S. A. Borisenko. ANNALI DELL'ISTITUTO SUPERIORE DI SANITÀ 26(1):39-42, 1990

Effects of environmental enrichment on voluntary ethanol intake in rats, by G. E. Rockman, et al. PHARMACOLOGY, BIOCHEMISTRY AND BEHAVIOR 34(3): 487-490, November 1989

Effects of ethanol and propylthiouracil on hepatic iron and copper contents in the male albino mouse, by E. Gonzalex-Reimers, et al. DRUG AND ALCOHOL DE-PENDENCE 24(3):261-263, December 1989

Effects of ethanol on the development of experimental atherosclerosis and car-dionecrosis in rats, by T. Wrzolkowa, et al. ALCOHOL 7(4):299-306, July/August 1990

Effects of ethanol on hepatic protein trafficking: impairment of receptor-mediated en-docytosis, by D. J. Tuma, et al. ALCOHOL AND ALCOHOLISM 25(2-3):117-125, 1990

Effects of ethanol on the NMR characteristics of rat brain: acute administration, de-pendency, and long-term effects, by J. A. Besson, et al. BRITISH JOURNAL OF PSYCHIATRY 155:818-821, December 1989

Effects of the kappa opioid receptor antagonist MR-2266-BS on the acquisition of ethanol preference, by C. Sandi, et al. LIFE SCIENCES 46(16):1119-1129, 1990

Effects of regular alcohol consumption on 24 hour ambulatory blood pressure recordings, by L. G. Howes, et al. CLINICAL AND EXPERIMENTAL PHARMA-COLOGY AND PHYSIOLOGY 17(4):247-250, April 1990

Effects of serotonin uptake blockers and of 5-hydroxytryptophan on the voluntary consumption of ethanol, water and solid food by UChA and UChB rats, by R. Al-varado, et al. ALCOHOL 7(4):315-319, July/August 1990

Effects of serum lipid concentrations and smoking and drinking habits on serum vita-min A and E levels, by H. Toyoshima, et al. NIPPON EISEIGAKU ZASSHI 44(2): 659-666, June 1989

Effects of smoking and alcohol drinking in cerebral vascular disease etiology: cooper-ative researching group on cerebrovasular diseases; PLA of Lanzhou Region. CHUNG HUA Y FANG I HSUEH TSA CHIH 23(6):338-341, November 1989

Effects of spot treatment on performance in a driving simulator under sober and alco-hol-dosed conditions, by V. J. Gawron, et al. ACCIDENT ANALYSIS AND PRE-VENTION 22(3):263-279, July 1990

Effects of thirst-inducing stimuli on consumption of ethanol solutions by golden ham-sters, by D. DiBattista. PHYSIOLOGY AND BEHAVIOR 47(6):1061-1066, June 1990

Enkephalins, their constituents and voluntary drinking of ethanol by the rat, by F. S. Messiha. PHYSIOLOGY AND BEHAVIOR 46(1):29-33, July 1989

Estimation of genetic correlation: interpretation of experiments using selectively bred and inbred animals, by J. C. Crabbe, et al. ALCOHOLISM 14(2):141-151, April 1990

Ethanol consumption during pregnancy in mice: effects on hormone concentrations, by P. J. Fielder, et al. AMERICAN JOURNAL OF PHYSIOLOGY 257(4 Pt 1):561-566, October 1989

Ethanol-induced skeletal muscle myopathy: biochemical and histochemical measurements on type 1 and type II fibre-rich muscles in the young rat, by V. R. Preedy, et al. ALCOHOL AND ALCOHOLISM 24(6):533-539, 1989

Ethanol-nicotine interactions in long-sleep and short-sleep mice, by C. M. de Fiebre, et al. ALCOHOL 7(3):249-257, May/June 1990

Evaluation of accelerated development of stable alcoholic motivation in rats for studying potential alcohol deterrents, by R. M. Salimov, et al. BIULLETEN EKSPERIMENTALNOI BIOLOGII I MEDITSINY 109(4):364-366, April 1990

Eyes have it: device that tracks eye movements can evaluate the effects on the brain of using alcohol and nicotine, by L. Dotto. JOURNAL OF THE ADDICTION RESEARCH FOUNDATION 19(7-8):12, July/August 1990

Fatty liver and plasma corticosterone levels in chronically alcohol- and pair-fed rats, by S. Venkatesan, et al. BIOCHEMICAL SOCIETY TRANSACTIONS 17(6):1114-1115, December 1989

Foetal and lactational exposure to alcohol increases oxidative capacity of brown adipose tissue in the rat: a possible relationship to cot death, by P. Huttunen, et al. BRITISH JOURNAL OF EXPERIMENTAL PATHOLOGY 70(6):691-695, December 1989

Free brain amino acids in rats variously tolerant to alcohol, by Slu Ostrovskii, et al. BIULLETEN EKSPERIMENTALNOI BIOLOGII I MEDITSINY 109(3):264-266, March 1990

Free choice ethanol intake of laboratory rats under different social conditions, by J. Wolffgramm. PSYCHOPHARMACOLOGY 101(2):233-239, 1990

Free-choice responding for ethanol versus water in alcohol preferring [P] and unselected Wistar rats in differentially modified by naloxone, bromocriptine, and methysergide, by G. Weiss, et al. PSYCHOPHARMACOLOGY 101(2):178-186, 1990

Frequency-specific auditory brainstem response analysis of young normal, aged normal and aged alcohol-addicted rats, by M. Anniko, et al. ORL 51(5):285-289, 1989

Further characterization of LSxSS recombinant inbred strains of mice: activating and hypothermic effects of ethanol, by V. G. Erwin, et al. ALCOHOLISM 14(2):200-204, April 1990

Future of biochemistry in alcohol research, by R. A. Deitrich. JOURNAL OF STUDIES ON ALCOHOL 51(1):5, January 1990

Gamma-glutamyl transferase ectoactivity in the intact rat liver: effect of chronic alcohol consumption, by H. Speisky, et al. ALCOHOL 7(4):339-347, July/August 1990

Gestational alcoholism and fetal zinc accretion in Long-Evans rats, by S. Greeley, et al. JOURNAL OF THE AMERICAN COLLEGE OF NUTRITION 9(3):265-271, June 1990

Growth and liver morphology after long-term ethanol consumption of rats, by J. A. van de Wiel, et al. LABORATORY ANIMALS 24(3):265-272, July 1990

Guidelines for use of terminology describing the impact of prenatal alcohol on the off-spring, by R. J. Sokol, et al. ALCOHOLISM: CLINICAL AND EXPERIMENTAL RESEARCH 13(4):597-598, August 1989

Hepatic phosphatidate phosphohydrolase activity in acute and chronic alcohol-fed rats, by K. J. Simpson, et al. BIOCHEMICAL SOCIETY TRANSACTIONS 17(6): 1115-1116, December 1989

Hepatic synthesis of apoproteins of very low density and high density lipoproteins in perfused rat liver: influence of chronic heavy and moderate doses of ethanol, by M. R. Lakshman, et al. ALCOHOLISM 13(4):554-559, August 1989

Higher density of serotonin-1A receptors in the hippocampus and cerebral cortex of alcohol-preferring P rats, by D. T. Wong, et al. LIFE SCIENCES 46(3):231-235, 1990

Homeostasis changes induced by the action of ethanol on the materno-fetal complex in rats: IV: late maternal effects of following acute intoxication during the preim-plantation period, by Z. Garban, et al. MORPHOLOGIE ET EMBRYOLOGIE 35(4): 289-295, October/December 1989

IgA nephropathy in alcohol abuse: an animal model, by S. M. Smith, et al. LABORA-TORY INVESTIGATION 62(2):179-184, February 1990

Immunization of white rats with a covalent conjugate of sidnofen and serum albumin suppresses chronic ethanol consumption, by I. P. Ashmarin, et al. BIULLETEN EKSPERIMENTALNOI BIOLOGII I MEDITSINY 108(12):695-697, December 1989

Immunologic consequences of acute ethanol ingestion in rats, by M. Kawakami, et al. JOURNAL OF SURGICAL RESEARCH 47(5):412-417, November 1989

Impact of research on designing strategies for preventing and treating dependence on drugs and alcohol, by W. Feuerlein. DRUG AND ALCOHOL DEPENDENCE 25(2):199-202, April 1990

Increases in Na+,K+-ATPase activity of erythrocytes and skeletal muscle after chronic ethanol consumption: evidence for reduced efficiency of the enzyme, by J. H. Johnson, et al. PROCEEDINGS OF THE NATIONAL ACADEMY OF SCIENCES USA 86(20):7857-7860, October 1989

Individual differences in the sedating effects of ethanol, by A. Zwyghuizen-Doorenbos, et al. ALCOHOLISM: CLINICAL AND EXPERIMENTAL RESEARCH 14(3): 400-404, June 1990

Influence of control over appetitive and aversive events on alcohol preference in rats, by J. R. Volpicelli, et al. ALCOHOL 7(2):133-136, March/April 1990

Influence of ethanol consumption on natural killer cell activity in mice, by G. G. Meadows, et al. ALCOHOLISM 13(4):476-479, August 1989

Initial sensitivity, acute tolerance and alcohol consumption in four inbred strains of rats, by J. M. Khanna, et al. PSYCHOPHARMACOLOGY 101(3):390-395, 1990

Integration of biological and psychosocial research on alcoholism, by P. E. Nathan. ALCOHOLISM: CLINICAL AND EXPERIMENTAL RESEARCH 14(3):368-374, May/June 1990

Interaction of ethanol and stress: research with experimental animals—an update, by L. A. Pohorecky. ALCOHOL AND ALCOHOLISM 25(2-3):263-276, 1990

Interactions of ethanol and nicotine at the receptor level, by A. C. Collins, et al. RECENT DEVELOPMENTS IN ALCOHOLISM 8:221-231, 1990

Intracerebroventricular morphine enhances alcohol consumption by rats, by M. A. Linesman, et al. PHARMACOLOGY, BIOCHEMISTRY AND BEHAVIOR 36(2):405-408, June 1990

Is risk for alcoholism predictable: a probabilistic approach to a developmental problem, by R. A. Zucker, et al. DRUGS AND SOCIETY 3(3-4):69-93, March/April 1989

Kidneys of chronic alcoholic rats are more vulnerable to ischemic insult, by M. Ishigami, et al. NEPHRON 53(2):152-156, 1989

Liver tryptophan pyrrolase: major determinant of the lower brain 5-hydroxytryptamine concentration in alcohol-preferring C57BL mice, by A. A. Badawy, et al. BIOCHEMICAL JOURNAL 264(2):597-599, December 1, 1989

Long and short alcohol deprivation: effects on AA and P alcohol-preferring rats, by J. D. Sinclair, et al. ALCOHOL 6(6):505-509, November/December 1989

Long-term alcohol consumption and brown adipose tissue in man, by P. Huttunen, et al. EUROPEAN JOURNAL OF APPLIED PHYSIOLOGY AND OCCUPATIONAL PHYSIOLOGY 60(6):418-424, 1990

Major initiatives in alcoholism research: current questions, future answers, by E. Gordis. NIDA RESEARCH MONOGRAPH SERIES 95:23-33, 1989

Mechanisms of alcohol-induced suppression of B-cell response, by M. Aldo-Benson. ALCOHOLISM 13(4):469-475, August 1989

Metabolism of glycolipids in the rat brain during acute and chronic ethanol administration, by M. I. Selevich. VOPROSY MEDITSINSKAI KHIMII 35(5):75-78, September/October 1989

Metric analysis of hippocampal granule cell dendritic trees after alcohol withdrawal in rats, by A. Cadete-Leite, et al. ALCOHOLISM 13(6):837-840, December 1989

Middle-latency auditory evoked potentials and chronic alcoholism: a pilot study, by F. Diaz Fernandez. MEDICAL SCIENCE RESEARCH 17(17):721-722, September 1989

Modifications in number and morphology of dendritic spines resulting from chronic ethanol consumption and withdrawal: a Golgi study in the mouse anterior and posterior hippocampus, by L. Lescaudron, et al. EXPERIMENTAL NEUROLOGY 106(2):156-163, November 1989

Morphometric and biochemical evidence for inhibited very-low-density-lipoprotein secretion in chronic low-fat alcohol-fed rats, by S. Venkatesan, et al. BIOCHEMICAL SOCIETY TRANSACTIONS 17(6):1117, December 1989

Naloxone attenuates voluntary ethanol intake in rats selectively bred for high ethanol preference, by J. C. Froehlich, et al. PHARMACOLOGY, BIOCHEMISTRY AND BEHAVIOR 35(2):385-390, February 1990

Nature-nurture interactions in alcoholism: twin, adoption, and high-risk studies, by J. Knop. NORDISK PSYKIATRISK TIDSSKRIFT 43(4):285-289, 1989

Necropsy study of GABA-benzodiazepine receptor binding sites in brain tissue from chronic alcoholic patients, by J. J. Kril, et al. CLINICAL AND EXPERIMENTAL NEUROLOGY 25:135-141, 1988

Neither chronic exposure to ethanol nor aging affects type I or type II corticosteroid receptors in rat hippocampus, by G. Rachamin, et al. EXPERIMENTAL NEUROLOGY 106(2):164-171, November 1989

Neurobehavioral effects of prenatal alcohol: I—research strategy, by A. P. Streissguth, et al. NEUROTOXICOLOGY AND TERATOLOGY 11(5):461-476, September/October 1989

Neurobehavioral effects of prenatal alcohol: II—partial least squares analysis, by P. D. Sampson, et al. NEUROTOXICOLOGY AND TERATOLOGY 11(5):477-491, September/October 1989

New aspects of acetaldehyde metabolism in human tissues and erythrocytes, by R. Eckey, et al. BEITRAGE ZUR GERICHTLICHEN MEDIZIN 47:397-402, 1989

Noradrenergic system: effect of DSP4 and FLA-57 on ethanol intake in ethanol preferring rats, by M. Daoust, et al. PHARMACOLOGY, BIOCHEMISTRY AND BEHAVIOR 36(1):133-137, May 1990

On terms used and abused: the concept of "codependency," by E. S. L. Gomberg. DRUGS AND SOCIETY 3(3-4):113-132, March/April 1989

Opposite changes in turnover of noradrenaline and dopamine in the DNS of ethanol-dependent mice, by G. Eisenhofer, et al. NEUROPHARMACOLOGY 29(1):37-45, January 1990

Oral ethanol self-administration in a continuous access situation: relation to food response requirements, by G. A. Tolliver, et al. ALCOHOL 6(5):381-387, September/October 1989

Oral self-administration of ethanol and not experimenter-administered ethanol facilitates rewarding electrical brain stimulation, by M. Moolten, et al. ALCOHOL 7(3): 221-225, May/June 1990

Oxygen radicals from acetaldehyde, by I. Fridovich. FREE RADICAL BIOLOGY AND MEDICINE 7(5):557-558, 1989

Parameters Vm' and Km for elimination of alcohol in young male subjects following low dose of alcohol, by J. G. Wagner, et al. ALCOHOL AND ALCOHOLISM 24(6): 555-564, 1989

Partial cross-dependence on ethanol in mice dependent on chlordiazepoxide, by A. W. Chan, et al. PHARMACOLOGY, BIOCHEMISTRY AND BEHAVIOR 35(2):379-384, February 1990

Paternal alcohol consumption: effects of age of testing and duration of paternal drinking in mice, by E. L. Abel. TERATOLOGY 40(5):467-474, November 1989

Paternal alcohol consumption: effects on ocular response and serum antibody response to pseudomonas aeruginosa infection in offspring, by R. S. Berk, et al. ALCOHOLISM 13(6):795-798, December 1989

Patterns of changes in field potentials in the isolated hippocampal slice on withdrawal from chronic ethanol treatment of mice in vivo, by M. A. Whittington, et al. BRAIN RESEARCH 523(2):237-244, July 23, 1990

Perils of Powell: in search of a factual foundation for the "disease concept of alcoholism," by H. Fingarette. DRUGS AND SOCIETY 3(3-4):1-27, March/April 1989

Perinatal undernutrition reduced ethanol intake preference in adult recovered rats, by N. E. Cordoba, et al. PHYSIOLOGY AND BEHAVIOR 47(6):111-116, June 1990

Persistence of tolerance in the P line of alcohol-preferring rats does not require performance while intoxicated, by J. M. Murphy, et al. ALCOHOL 7(4):367-379, July/August 1990

Prevention, treatment and research on alcohol, by H. McConnell. JOURNAL OF THE ADDICTION RESEARCH FOUNDATION 19(11):12, January 1, 1990

Problem drinkers confound experts: solo recovery surprise, by J. Hollobon. JOURNAL OF THE ADDICTION RESEARCH FOUNDATION 19(10):4, October 1, 1990

Problems of nosology in alcoholism treatment and research, by T. P. Beresford, et al. DRUGS AND SOCIETY 3(3-4):95-111, March/April 1989

Prostaglandin E2 reduces voluntary ethanol consumption in the rat, by A. D. Ross, et al. PHARMACOLOGY, BIOCHEMISTRY AND BEHAVIOR 36(3):527-530, July 1990

Psychological perspectives on alcohol consumption and interpersonal aggression, by A. R. Lang, et al. CRIMINAL JUSTICE AND BEHAVIOR 16(3):299-324, September 1989

Rat liver microcirculation in alcohol-induced hepatomegaly, by R. Mastai, et al. HEPATOLOGY 10(6):941-945, December 1989

Recent advances in alcoholism diagnosis and treatment research: implications for practice, by C. Cocozzelli, et al. SOCIAL SERVICE REVIEW 63(4):533-552, December 1989

Reduction in ethanol preference following injection of centrally and peripherally acting antimuscarinic agents, by A. H. Rezvani, et al. ALCOHOL AND ALCOHOLISM 25(1):3-7, 1990

Reduction of lymphocytic beta-adrenoceptor level in chronic alcoholics and rapid reversal after ethanol withdrawal, by T. Maki, et al. EUROPEAN JOURNAL OF CLINICAL INVESTIGATION 20(3):313-316, June 1990

Regulation of pancreatic amylase by dietary carbohydrate in chronic alcoholic rats, by H. Sandaran, et al. PANCREAS 4(6):733-738, 1989

Relationship between chronic ethanol exposure and cigarette smoking in the laboratory and the natural environment, by R. M. Keenan, et al. PSYCHOPHARMACOLOGY 100(1):77-83, January 1990

Relationship between flushing response and drinking behavior, by T. Mori, et al. ARUKORU KENKYUTO YAKUBUTSU ISON 24(5):439-447, October 1989

Relationship between serum gamma-glutamyl transpeptidase activity blood pressure and alcohol consumption, by Y. Yamada, et al. JOURNAL OF HUMAN HYPERTENSION 3(6):409-417, December 1989

Reports from research centres: 20—alcohol research at the Hjellestad Clinic, by J. C. Laberg, et al. BRITISH JOURNAL OF ADDICTION 84(9):999-1009, September 1989

Research examining impacts of attempts to change patterns of alcohol consumption and related behaviors, by R. A. Dodder, et al. MID-AMERICAN REVIEW OF SOCIOLOGY 14(1-2):145-150, Winter 1990

Rodent models of alcoholism: a review, by B. Keane, et al. ALCOHOL AND ALCOHOLISM 24(4):299-309, 1989

Role of central monoamine neurons in regulating voluntary ethanol consumption, by K. Kiianmaa. FARMAKOLOGIYA I TOKSIKOLOGIYA 52(5):4-10, September/October 1989

Role of excitatory amino acids and intraneuronal calcium in the acute intoxicational effects of ethanol, by S. I. Deutsch, et al. CLINICAL NEUROPHARMACOLOGY 12(6):483-489, December 1989

Safe drinking limits still unknown, by B. L. Lee. JOURNAL OF THE ADDICTION RESEARCH FOUNDATION 19(9):1, September 1, 1990

Self-reinforcement score of alcoholics, by Z. Z. Cernovsky. ADVANCES IN ALCO-
HOL AND SUBSTANCE ABUSE 8(1):67-73, Spring 1989

Serotonin, dopamine and GABA involvement in alcohol drinking of selectively bred
rats, by W. J. McBride, et al. ALCOHOL 7(3):199-205, May/June 1990

Serum gamma glutamyl transferase alkaline phosphatase as indicators of excess
chronic alcohol consumption in the rat, by G. J. Graham, et al. BIOCHEMICAL
PHARMACOLOGY 39(10):1615-1617, May 15, 1990

Short- and long-latency auditory evoked potentials and chronic alcoholism: a pilot
study, by F. Diaz. MEDICAL SCIENCE RESEARCH 17(19):817-818, October
1989

Single dose pharmacokinetics of calcium antagonist nifedipine in ethanol dependent
rats, by D. Siembab, et al. POLISH JOURNAL OF PHARMACOLOGY AND
PHARMACY 41(3):219-221, May/June 1989

Sociological research on alcohol use, problems, and policy, by K. K. Bucholz, et al.
ANNUAL REVIEW OF SOCIOLOGY 15:163-186, 1989

Some implications of animal alcohol self-administration studies for human alcohol
problems, by H. H. Samson, et al. DRUG AND ALCOHOL DEPENDENCE 25(2):
141-144, April 1990

Spiroxatrine augments fluoxetine-induced reduction of ethanol intake by the P line of
rats, by W. J. McBride, et al. PHARMACOLOGY, BIOCHEMISTRY AND BEHAV-
IOR 34(2):381-386, October 1989

Statistical control in research on alcohol and tobacco: an example from research on alcohol and mortality, by L. T. Kozlowski, et al. BRITISH JOURNAL OF ADDICTION
85(2):271-278, February 1990

Studies of whole blood associated acetaldehyde as a marker for alcohol intake in
mice, by C. M. Peterson, et al. ALCOHOLISM 13(6):845-848, December 1989

Study of the restoration and balance of thiamine in the tissues of albino mice in alcoholic intoxication, by A. Rozanov, et al. FIZIOLOGICHESKII ZHURNAL 36(1):66-
70, January/February 1990

Surface activity of pulmonary surfactant in experimental acute and chronic ethanol
poisoning, by A. K. Zagorul'ko, et al. VRACHEBNOE DELO (9):48-49, September 1989

Synthesis of subcellular protein fractions in the rat heart in vivo in response to chronic
ethanol feeding, by V. R. Preedy, et al. CARDIOVASCULAR RESEARCH
23(8):730-736, August 1989

Taste reactivity to alcohol in rats, by S. W. Kiefer, et al. BEHAVIORAL NEUROSCI-
ENCE 103(6):1318-1326, December 1989

Treatment- and task-induced changes in interhemispheric EEG, by E. Schwarz-Ot-
tersbach, et al. INTERNATIONAL JOURNAL OF NEUROSCIENCE 47(1-2):141-
148, July 1989

Ultrastructural changes in the mouse fetal choroid plexuses following chronic maternal alcoholization, by C. Craciun, et al. MORPHOLOGIE ET EMBRYOLOGIE 35(3):221-225, July/September 1989

Ultrastructural characteristics of the myocardium of newborn minipigs in long-term parental alcohol intake, by G. V. Mardanova, et al. BIULLETEN EKSPERIMENTALNOI BIOLOGII I MEDITSINY 109(4):398-400, April 1990

Ultrastructural detection of cholesterol in the liver of rats with alcoholic intoxication, by V. V. Ul'lanova, et al. BIULLETEN EKSPERIMENTALNOI BIOLOGII I MEDITSINY 109(5):510-512, May 1990

Ultrastructure of ventral hippocampus of rat with chronic ethanol intoxication, by A. Jedrzejewska, et al. ZENTRALBLATT FUR ALLEMEINE PATHOLOGIE UND PATHOLOGISCHE ANATOMIE 136(4):359-366, 1990

Vagal mediation of the effect of alcohol on heart rate, by D. B. Newlin, et al. ALCOHOLISM: CLINICAL AND EXPERIMENTAL RESEARCH 14(3):421-424, June 1990

Variabilities of kinetics of alcohol catabolism, by L. Buris, et al. MORPHOLOGIAI ES IGAZSAGUGYI ORVOSI SZEMLE 30(1):76-80, January 1990

Verapamil effects on physiological and behavioral responses to ethanol in the rat, by A. H. Rezvani, et al. ALCOHOL AND ALCOHOLISM 25(1):51-58, 1990

Voluntary alcohol drinking increases brain dopamine metabolism in rats, by G. Colombo, et al. ANNALI DELL'ISTITUTO SUPERIORE DI SANITA 26(1):95-98, 1990

Voluntary consumption of beverage alcohol by vervet monkeys: population screening, descriptive behavior and biochemical measures, by F. R. Ervin, et al. PHARMACOLOGY, BIOCHEMISTRY AND BEHAVIOR 36(2):367-373, June 1990

Voluntary ethanol consumption during pregnancy and lactation in the golden hamster, by D. DiBattista. PHYSIOLOGY AND BEHAVIOR 46(4):771-773, October 1989

Voluntary ethanol intake of individually-or pair-housed rats: effects of ACTH or dexamethasone treatment, by R. S. Weisinger, et al. PHARMACOLOGY, BIOCHEMISTRY AND BEHAVIOR 33(2):335-341, June 1989

What does research on nicotine and tobacco use have to offer alcohol researchers?, by O. F. Pomerleau. BRITISH JOURNAL OF ADDICTION 85(2):247-250, February 1990

Xanthine oxidase status in ethanol-intoxicated rat liver, by A. Abbonadanza, et al. ALCOHOLISM 13(6):841-844, December 1989

Singapore

Alcohol consumption in Chinese, Malays and Indians in Singapore, by K. Hughes, et al. ANNALS OF THE ACADEMY OF MEDICINE, SINGAPORE 19(3):330-332, May 1990

Beverage alcohol spending in Singapore: a potential development constraint, by R. L. Curry, Jr. INTERNATIONAL JOURNAL OF THE ADDICTIONS 24(8):821-828, August 1989

Sociology

Alcohol self and its social circles: review assay, by D. R. Maines. AMERICAN JOURNAL OF SOCIOLOGY 94:864-873, January 1989

Alcoholism in social fringe groups: a critical, historical examination, by J. Petry. NEUE PRAXIS 19(6):462-470, 1989

Borderline traits among community alcoholics and problem-drinkers: rural-urban differences, by M. Tousignant, et al. CANADIAN JOURNAL OF PSYCHIATRY 34(8):796-799, November 1989

Environmental determinants of party drinking: bartenders vs self-service, by E. S. Geller, et al. ENVIRONMENT AND BEHAVIOR 22(1):74-90, January 1990

Influence of sociodemographic characteristics on familial alcohol problems: data from a community sample, by M. Russell, et al. ALCOHOLISM: CLINICAL AND EXPERIMENTAL RESEARCH 14(2):221-226, April 1990

Lifestyle and alcohol, by R. Gilbert. JOURNAL OF THE ADDICTION RESEARCH FOUNDATION 19(3):5, March 1, 1990

Lifestyle: the last word, by R. Gilberg. JOURNAL OF THE ADDICTION RESEARCH FOUNDATION 19(4):5, April 1, 1990

Methods of influencing life style and risk factors, by M. Mancini, et al. GIORNALE ITALIANO DI CARDIOLOGIA 19(9):787-799, September 1989

Problem drinkers and the welfare bureaucracy, by L. A. Schmidt. SOCIAL SERVICE REVIEW 64:390-406, September 1990

Relationship between alcohol consumption and social status in Stockholm: has the social pattern of alcohol consumption changed?, by A. Romelsjo. INTERNATIONAL JOURNAL OF EPIDEMIOLOGY 18(4):842-851, December 1989

Socioeconomic significance of alcohol, by R. E. Leu. THERAPEUTISCHE UMSCHAU 47(5):384-389, May 1990

Sociological factors associated with substance abuse among new chronic patients, by L. L. Bachrach. ADOLESCENT PSYCHIATRY 16:189-201, 1989

South Africa

Alcohol in Southern Africa, by L. Molamu. CONTEMPORARY DRUG PROBLEMS 16: 1-115, Spring 1989

Shebeens and alcoholism in southern Africa with special reference to Bophuthatswana, by G. Mothibe. MEDICINE AND LAW 8(3):249-253, 1989

Psychiatric epidemiology in South Korea: part II—urban and rural differences, by C. K. Lee, et al. JOURNAL OF NERVOUS AND MENTAL DISEASE 178(4):247-252, 1990

Soviet Union
Soviet hangover, by P. Sudo, et al. SCHOLASTIC UPDATE 123:14, November 16, 1990

Watch your step: excerpts—Soviet Union, by B. M. Levin, et al. SOVIET EDUCATION 32:1-92, January 1990

Spain
Alcohol consumption of the juvenile population of Cadiz, by M. A. Ruiz Jimenez, et al. ANALES ESPANOLES DE PEDIATRIA 32(5):438-440, May 1990

Statistics
Expression of alcoholism in relation to gender and age, by A. Blankfield. ACTA PSYCHIATRICA SCANDINAVICA 81(5):448-452, 1990

Federal study finds drinking down; cocaine use up. CRIME CONTROL DIGEST 24 (20):6, May 21, 1990

From the Centers for Disease Control: apparent per capita ethanol consumption—United States, 1977-1986. JAMA 263(3):354-355, January 19, 1990

Genealogical and genetical African admixture estimations, blood pressure and hypertension in a Caribbean community, by P. Darlu, et al. ANNALS OF HUMAN BIOLOGY 17(5):387-398, 1990

Relationship between male pancreatitis morbidity and alcohol consumption in Western Australia, 1971-1984, by D. I. Smith, et al. BRITISH JOURNAL OF ADDICTION 85(5):655-658, May 1990

Sex differences in alcoholics at a psychiatric emergency clinic, by G. Krarup, et al. UGESKRIFT FOR LAEGER 151(4):2647-2650, October 9, 1989

Statistics on alcohol and drug use in Canada and other countries (book review), by M. Adrian, et al. JOURNAL OF THE ADDICTION RESEARCH FOUNDATION 19(3):8, March 1, 1990

Surveys
Comparison of alcohol sales data with survey data on self-reported alcohol use in 21 states, by P. F. Smith, et al. AMERICAN JOURNAL OF PUBLIC HEALTH 80(3): 309-312, March 1990

Drinking habits of Sikh, Hindu, Muslim and white men in the West Midlands: a community survey, by R. Cochrane, et al. BRITISH JOURNAL OF ADDICTION 85(6): 759-769, June 1990

Drinking patterns among black and white men: results from a national survey, by D. Herd. JOURNAL OF STUDIES ON ALCOHOL 51(3):221-223, May 1990

Level of agreement behavior questionnaire measures of alcohol dependence, alcoholism and problem drinking in a sample presenting at a specialist alcohol treatment service, by D. M. Gorman, et al. DRUG AND ALCOHOL DEPENDENCE 24(3):227-232, December 1989

Monitoring parent concerns about teenage drinking and driving: a random digit dial telephone survey, by K. H. Beck. AMERICAN JOURNAL OF DRUG AND ALCOHOL ABUSE 16(1-2):109-124, 1990

Prevalence in various social groups of eight different drinking patterns, from abstaining to frequent drunkenness: analysis of 10 United States surveys combined, by G. Knupfer. BRITISH JOURNAL OF ADDICTION 84(11):1305-1318, November 1989

Subgroup differences in drinking patterns among black and white men: results from a national survey, by D. Herd. JOURNAL OF STUDIES ON ALCOHOL 51(3):221-232, May 1990

Three national surveys on nonhabitual alcohol drinking practices of the Israeli Jewish adult population in the 80s: what are the trends, by H. Bar, et al. ISRAEL JOURNAL OF PSYCHIATRY AND RELATED SCIENCES 27(1):57-63, 1990

Switzerland
Epidemiology of alcohol and its sequelae in Switzerland, by T. Abelin. THERAPEUTISCHE UMSCHAU 47(5):379-383, May 1990

Testing
Action North gives alcoholics new lease on life, by J. Auger. WINDSPEAKER 7(38): 16, November 24, 1989

Agreement between two dietary methods in the measurement of alcohol consumption, by K. M. Flegal. JOURNAL OF STUDIES ON ALCOHOL 51(5):408-414, 1990

Blood alcohol concentration at post-mortem in 175 fatal cases of alcohol intoxication, by M. K. Heatley, et al. MEDICINE, SCIENCE AND THE LAW 30(2):101-105, April 1990

Comparative value of self-report and blood tests in assessing outcome amongst alcoholics, by L. Keso, et al. BRITISH JOURNAL OF ADDICTION 85(2):209-215, February 1990

Drug and alcohol rehabilitation a win-win solution, by J. P. Kinnan. SAFETY AND HEALTH 142:26-29, December 1990

Effect of hyperthermia on breath-alcohol analysis, by G. R. Fox, et al. JOURNAL OF FORENSIC SCIENCES 34(4):836-841, 1989

ALCOHOL—Testing

Effect of respiratory aerosol inhalers and nasal sprays on breath alcohol testing devices used in Great Britain, by P. J. Gomm, et al. MEDICINE, SCIENCE AND THE LAW 30(3):203-206, 1990

Expert assessment by the federal health office of accuracy of blood alcohol determination, by G. Schoknecht. BLUTALKOHOL 27(3):202-214, May 1990

Gender differences show up in detection, by B. L. Lee. JOURNAL OF THE ADDICTION RESEARCH FOUNDATION 19(7-8):3, July/August 1990

Influence of breath volume on alcohol analysis, by G. Schoknecht, et al. BLUTALKOHOL 27(2):83-94, March 1990

Laboratory tests in the follow-up of treated alcoholics: how often should testing be repeated, by L. Keso, et al. ALCOHOL AND ALCOHOLISM 25(4):359-364, 1990

MAC scale in a normal population: the meaning of "false positives," by M. R. Levenson, et al. JOURNAL OF STUDIES ON ALCOHOL 51(5):457-462, September 1990

Measurement of ethanol consumed in distilled spirits, by W. Kling. JOURNAL OF STUDIES ON ALCOHOL 50:456-460, September 1989

Publicity, police resources and the effectiveness of random breath testing, by K. A. McCaul, et al. MEDICAL JOURNAL OF AUSTRALIA 152(6):284-286, March 19, 1990

Use of breath alcohol analysis in France, by K. Fleck, et al. BLUTALKOHOL 26(6): 376-380, November 1989

Testing—Employment
Alcohol is still the worst drug: and top workplace problem. JOURNAL OF THE ADDICTION RESEARCH FOUNDATION 19(6):5, June 1, 1990

Drug and alcohol testing in the workplace: objectives, pitfalls, and guidelines, by R. S. Schottenfeld. AMERICAN JOURNAL OF DRUG AND ALCOHOL ABUSE 15(4): 413-427, 1989

Drugs and booze: how should employers deal with abuse—forest products industry, by T. Blackman. FOREST INDUSTRIES 117:12-13, May 1990

Testing—Legal Issues
International news: breath tests for Italy. LAW AND ORDER 38(8):6+, August 1990

Is blood alcohol concentration of 1.1g% the new limit value of "absolute driving fitness": forensic medicine discussion contribution on the new reduced safety value to 0.1%, by U. Heifer, et al. BLUTALKOHOL 27(3):215-221, May 1990

Legal requirement of medical-psychological examination of drunk driving offenders: should other than blood alcohol concentration and "particular circumstances" of the individual case be considered?, by A. Muller. BLUTALKOHOL 27(2):116-118, March 1990

Value of blood alcohol concentration in the assessment of legal responsibility, by E. Miltner, et al. BLUTALKOHOL 27(4):279-284, July 1990

Testing—Methods

Accuracy of blood alcohol analysis using headspace gas chromatography when performed on clotted samples, by C. M. Senkowski, et al. JOURNAL OF FORENSIC SCIENCES 35(1):176-180, January 1990

Accurate measurement of blood alcohol concentration with isothermal rebreathing, by J. Ohlsson, et al. JOURNAL OF STUDIES ON ALCOHOL 51(1):6-13, January 1990

Alcohol screening with the Alcoscan test strip in forensic praxis, by A. Penttila, et al. FORENSIC SCIENCE INTERNATIONAL 44(1):43-48, January 1990

Applying a data acquisition system to the analysis of breath alcohol profiles, by R. G. Gullberg. JOURNAL OF THE FORENSIC SCIENCE SOCIETY 29(6):397-405, November/December 1989

Blood alcohol concentration measurement using a salivary reagent stick: a reliable tool for emergency departments, by I. C. Phair, et al. ARCHIVES OF EMERGENCY MEDICINE 7(2):69-72, June 1990

Blood alcohol tests, prevalence of involvement, and outcomes following brain injury, by J. F. Kraus, et al. AMERICAN JOURNAL OF PUBLIC HEALTH 79:294-299, March 1989

Breath alcohol test precision: an in vivo vs. in vitro evaluation, by R. G. Gullberg. FORENSIC SCIENCE INTERNATIONAL 43(3):247-255, December 1989

Chemical basis of the breathalyzer: a critical analysis, by D. A. Labianca. JOURNAL OF CHEMICAL EDUCATION 67:259-261, March 1990

Computer-aided headspace gas chromatography applied to blood-alcohol analysis: importance of online process control, by A. W. Jones, et al. JOURNAL OF FORENSIC SCIENCES 34(5):1116-1127, September 1989

Effect of chronic alcohol drinking and liver cirrhosis on oro-cecal transit time: H2 breath test, by D. Huppe, et al. ZEITSCHRIFT FUR GASTROENTEROLOGIE 27(10):624-628, October 1989

Evaluation of the Alco-Sur: alco-sensor, screening device, by B.T. Hodgson, et al. CANADIAN SOCIETY OF FORENSIC SCIENCE JOURNAL 21(3):106-113, 1988

Excretion of alcohol in urine and diuresis in healthy men in relation to their age, the dose administered and the time after drinking, by A. W. Jones. FORENSIC SCIENCE INTERNATIONAL 45(3):217-224, April 1990

Factors influencing ethanol determination in urine using the TDx system, by M. Graw, et al. BEITRAGE ZUR GERICHTLICHEN MEDIZIN 47:391-396, 1989

Measurement of ethanol in the human brain using NMR spectroscopy, by C. C. Hanstock, et al. JOURNAL OF STUDIES ON ALCOHOL 51(2):104-107, March 1990

Modification of Alcomat breath alcohol measurements by various substances of routine use: mouthwash, perfume, after-shave lotion, etc., by O. Gruner, et al. BLUTALKOHOL 27(2):119-130, March 1990

Observations on the specificity of breath-alcohol analyzers used for clinical and medicolegal purposes, by A. W. Jones. JOURNAL OF FORENSIC SCIENCES 34(4): 842-847, 1989

Oxidation-reduction in blood analysis: demonstrating the reaction in a breathalyzer, by J. M. Anderson, et al. JOURNAL OF CHEMICAL EDUCATION 67:263-264, March 1990

Response of the Intoxilyzer 4011AS-A to number of possible interfering substances, by J. M. Cowan, Jr., et al. JOURNAL OF FORENSIC SCIENCES 35(4):797-812, July 1990

Superabsorbent polymers: media for the enzymatic detection of ethyl alcohol in urine, by D. A. Kidwell. ANALYTICAL BIOCHEMISTRY 182(2):257-261, November 1, 1989

Therapy
see also: Alcoholics Anonymous
Rehabilitation

$100 billion hangover, by B. Stephens. PROFILES IN HEALTHCARE MARKETING (37):83-85, January 1990

Addiction medicine. WESTERN JOURNAL OF MEDICINE 152(5):499-621, May 1990

Administration of leu-enkephalin impairs the acquisition of preference for ethanol, by C. Sandi, et al. PSYCHOPHARMACOLOGY 100(3):350-354, 1990

Alameda County Department of Alcohol and Drug Programs Comprehensive Homeless Alcohol Recovery Services: CHARS, by R. W. Bennett, et al. ALCOHOLISM TREATMENT QUARTERLY 7(1):111-128, 1990

Alcohol treatment-seeking process from a problems perspective: responses to events, by C. Weisner. BRITISH JOURNAL OF ADDICTION 85(4):561-569, April 1990

Alcohol treatment systems in Nigeria, by O. A. Odejide, et al. ALCOHOL AND ALCOHOLISM 24(4):347-353, 1989

Alcoholics' attitudes toward and experiences with disulfiram, by B. Liskow, et al. AMERICAN JOURNAL OF DRUG AND ALCOHOL ABUSE 16(1-2):147-160, March/June 1990

Alcoholism and ideology: approaches to treatment, by S. Diwan. JOURNAL OF APPLIED SOCIAL SCIENCES 14(2):221-248, Spring/Summer 1990

Alcoholism day treatment: rationale, research, and resistance, by R. Schneider, et al. JOURNAL OF DRUG ISSUES 19(4):437-449, Fall 1989

Alcoholism: a follow-up study of participants in an alcohol treatment program, by G. K. Shaw, et al. BRITISH JOURNAL OF PSYCHIATRY 157:190-196, August 1990

Alcoholism screening and intervention: 1—interviewing in a general hospital, by D. L. Weinstein, et al. SOCIAL CASEWORK 70(7):436-441, September 1989

Alcoholism screening and intervention: 3—an intake interview at a mental health clinic, by D. L. Weinstein, et al. SOCIAL CASEWORK 70(9):564-570, November 1989

Alcoholism treatment: a ten-year follow-up study, by G. M. Cross, et al. ALCOHOLISM: CLINICAL AND EXPERIMENTAL RESEARCH14(2):169-173, April 1990

Alcoholism treatment under scrutiny: disulfiram/serotonin-rich foods, by R. Cowen. SCIENCE NEWS 137:254, April 21, 1990

Alcoholism treatment: who needs it?, by H. McConnell. JOURNAL OF THE ADDICTION RESEARCH FOUNDATION 19(5):7, May 1, 1990

Ambulatory, disulfiram-antabuse-assisted management of the alcoholic patient, by F. Wicht, et al. THERAPEUTISCHE UMSCHAU 47(5):364-369, May 1990

Angiotensin converting enzyme inhibitors reduce alcohol consumption: some possible mechanisms and important conditions for its therapeutic use, by T. Lingham, et al. ALCOHOLISM 14(1):92-99, February 1990

ARF to move on liver drug: propylithiouracil (PTU), by J. Hollobon. JOURNAL OF THE ADDICTION RESEARCH FOUNDATION 19(4):1-2, April 1, 1990

Behavioral treatment of alcohol and drug abuse: what do we know and where shall we go, by R. K. Hester, et al. RECENT DEVELOPMENTS IN ALCOHOLISM 8:305-327, 1990

Brief intervention strategies for harmful drinkers: new directions for medical education, by T. F. Babor. CMAJ 143(10):1070-1076, November 15, 1990

Brief treatment for adult children of alcoholics: accessing resources for self-care, by J. S. Crandell. PSYCHOTHERAPY 26(4):510-513, Winter 1989

Co-dependency: implications for women and therapy, by K. vanWomer. WOMEN AND THERAPY 8(4):51-63, 1989

Comment on Booth's "maintained controlled drinking following severe alcohol dependence—a case study": maintained controlled drinking, by R. E. Meyer. BRITISH JOURNAL OF ADDICTION 85(3):327-328, March 1990

Comment on Booth's "maintained controlled drinking following severe alcohol dependence—a case study": an old chestnut well cracked, by T. Stockwell. BRITISH JOURNAL OF ADDICTION 85(3):323-325, March 1990

Comment on the contribution "legal aspects and experiences in reimbursement of costs and charges for medical treatment of alcohol misuse," by K. Siermann, et al. ZEITSCHRIFT FUR ARZTLICHE FORTBILDUNG 83(20):1035-1036, 1989

Communication skills training: communication skills training with family and cognitive behavioral mood management training for alcoholics, by P. M. Monti, et al. JOURNAL OF STUDIES ON ALCOHOL 51(3):263-270, May 1990

Comparison of outcome with group-marital and standard-individual therapies with alcoholics, by T. G. Bowers, et al. JOURNAL OF STUDIES ON ALCOHOL 51(4):301-309, July 1990

Comprehensive alcohol abuse treatment programme for persons with traumatic brain injury, by M. J. Langley, et al. BRAIN INJURY 4(1):77-86, January/March 1990

Compulsory admission to hospital of an alcoholic patient under mental health act, by M. F. McGhee. JOURNAL OF THE ROYAL COLLEGE OF GENERAL PRACTITIONERS 39(324):301, July 1989

Cortisol and beta-endorphin response in alcoholics and alcohol abusers following a high naloxone dosage, by A. Kemper, et al. DRUG AND ALCOHOL DEPENDENCE 25(3):319-326, June 1990

Costs and availability of alcoholism therapy and liver transplantation, by R. J. Crawsford. NEW ZEALAND MEDICAL JOURNAL 103(886):137, March 28, 1990

Covert sensitization: alternative treatment procedures for alcoholism, by W. R. Miller, et al. BEHAVIOURAL PSYCHOTHERAPY 17(3):203-220, July 1989

Differing requirements of collateral clients and primary alcohol users in outpatient treatment, by M. E. Hanna, et al. INTERNATIONAL JOURNAL OF THE ADDICTIONS 23(5):509-516, 1988

Double jeopardy: confinement in residential alcohol treatment facility—improper delegation. CRIMINAL LAW REPORTER: COURT DECISIONS 45(20):2367, August 23,1989

Early intervention in patients with excessive consumption of alcohol: a controlled study, by J. Persson, et al. ALCOHOL 6(5):403-408, September/October 1989

Effect of the antioxidant potassium fenozan on the course of acute alcoholic intoxication, by R. D. Zolotaia, et al. IZVESTIIA AKADEMII NAUK SSSR (2):303-305, March/April 1990

Effects of paced respiration on anxiety reduction in a clinical population, by M. E. Clark, et al. BIOFEEDBACK AND SELF REGULATION 15(3):273-284, 1990

Efficacy of multimodality therapy of chronic alcoholism in patients with pulmonary tuberculosis revealed for the first time, by V. S. Krutko, et al. VRACHEBNOE DELO (4):70-71, 1990

Enhancing the natural control of drinking behavior: catching up with common sense, by H. Mulford. CONTEMPORARY DRUG PROBLEMS 15:321-334, Fall 1988

Evaluation of a self-help manual for young offenders who drink: a pilot study, by M. McMurran, et al. BRITISH JOURNAL OF CLINICAL PSYCHOLOGY 29(Pt 1):117-119, February 1990

Examination of an intensive probation for alcohol offenders: five-year follow-up, by G. S. Green, et al. INTERNATIONAL JOURNAL OF OFFENDER THERAPY AND COMPARATIVE CRIMINOLOGY 34(1):31-42, April 1990

Experience in treating alcoholism in pulmonary tuberculosis patients, by E. A. Gerasimov. PROBLEMY TUBERKUIOZA (12):59-61, 1989

Factors affecting the use of medical, mental health, alcohol, and drug treatment services by homeless adults, by D. Padgett, et al. MEDICAL CARE 28(9):805-821, September 1990

Gamma-hydroxybutyric acid for alcohol withdrawal. AMERICAN FAMILY PHYSICIAN 41:1556, May 1990

Getting with the program, by D. Gates. NEWSWEEK 116(16):75, October 15, 1990

Grandiosity within alcoholism: implications for treatment, by M. S. Levy. PSYCHOTHERAPY PATIENT 5(3-4):173-180, 1989

Health belief model and entry into alcoholism treatment, by P. E. Bardsley, et al. INTERNATIONAL JOURNAL OF THE ADDICTIONS 23(1):19-28, 1988

Health locus of control beliefs and alcohol-related factors that may influence treatment outcomes, by P. R. Dean, et al. JOURNAL OF SUBSTANCE ABUSE TREATMENT 7(3):167-172, 1990

Help is available. CANADIAN LAWYER 14(2):17, March 1990

Housing models for alcohol programs serving homeless people, by F. D. Wittman. CONTEMPORARY DRUG PROBLEMS 16(3):483-504, Fall 1989

Hypochondriac conditions of exogenous organic nature: clinicopathogenetic aspects and treatment, by R. G. Golodets, et al. ZHURNAL NEVROPATOLOGII I PSIKHIATRII IMENI S. S. KORSAKOVA 90(2):84-89, 1990

Identification and intervention for alcohol abuse, by S. Holt. JOURNAL OF THE SOUTH CAROLINA MEDICAL ASSOCIATION 85(12):554-559, December 1989

Identifying and helping alcohol abusers attending general health care services, by A. C. Ogborne, et al. CANADIAN JOURNAL OF PUBLIC HEALTH 81(4):307-309, July/August 1990

Influence of neuroleptic therapy on the structure of episodes of acute alcohol psychoses, by G. F. Kolotilin, et al. SOVIET NEUROLOGY AND PSYCHIATRY 22(4): 72-78, Winter 1989-1990

Inpatient treatment of alcoholism: a necessary part of the therapeutic armanmentarium, by E. P. Nace. PSYCHIATRIC HOSPTIAL 21(1):9-12, Winter 1990

Integrating traditional alcoholic treatment programs and family-systems therapy, by R. de Maio. FAMILY SYSTEMS MEDICINE 7(3):274-291, Fall 1989

Kirchlindach Therapy Center: a treatment facility for the rehabilitation of alcohol and drug dependent males, by L. S. Liem. THERAPEUTISCHE UMSCHAU 47(5): 418-419, May 1990

Knowledge, attitudes, and reported practices of medical students and house staff regarding the diagnosis and treatment of alcoholism, by G. Geller, et al. JAMA 261: 3115-3120, June 2, 1989

Long-term abstinence from alcohol in patients receiving aversion therapy as part of a multimodal inpatient program, by J. W. Smith, et al. JOURNAL OF SUBSTANCE ABUSE TREATMENT 7(2):77-82, 1990

Male-specific group in alcoholism treatment, by K. Van Wormer. SMALL GROUP BEHAVIOR 20(2):228-242, May 1989

Medical cooperation in cases of detention: 1 year's experience in the Odense police district, by M. Hardt-Madsen, et al. UGESKRIFT FOR LAEGER 152(6):396-400, February 5, 1990

Mental health values and response to alcoholism treatment, by J. D. Tyler, et al. COUNSELING AND VALUES 33(3):204-216, April 1989

Model systems of treatment for alcohol abuse following traumatic brain injury, by J. S. Kreutzer, et al. BRAIN INJURY 4(1):1-5, January/March 1990

Multi-stage treatment concept for alcoholics: utilization and results of treatment, by D. R. Schwoon, et al. PSYCHIATRISCHE PRAXIS16(5):161-170, September 1989

National Association of Private Psychiatric Hospitals Task Force on Alcoholism, Washington, DC (NAPPH) white paper on inpatient treatment for alcoholism. PSYCHIATRIC HOSPITAL 20(3):129-133, Summer 1989

New York Hospital, Westchester Division, Cornell University Medical College: a tradition in the treatment of alcoholism, by N. S. Miller, et al. JOURNAL OF SUBSTANCE ABUSE TREATMENT 6(3):201-204, 1989

"No, thank you, I've been to Dwight": reflections on the Keeley cure for alcoholism, by H. W. Morgan. ILLINOIS HISTORICAL JOURNAL 82(3):147-166, 1989

Occupational outcome after military treatment for alcoholism, by C. Wright, et al. JOURNAL OF OCCUPATIONAL MEDICINE 32(1):24-32, January 1990

Overview of alcoholism treatment: settings and approaches, by J. Allen. JOURNAL OF MENTAL HEALTH ADMINISTRATION 16(2):55-62, Fall 1989

Patient characteristics and outcome of inpatient treatment for alcoholism, by J. L. Waisberg. ADVANCES IN ALCOHOL AND SUBSTANCE ABUSE 8(3-4):9-32, Spring 1990

Patient-treatment matching in the management of alcoholism, by H. Annis. NIDA RESEARCH MONOGRAPH SERIES 90:152-161, 1988

Pilot study of treatment of alcohol abuse: marked improvement of alcohol drinking habits of both treated and untreated persons, by S. Andreasson, et al. LAKARTIDNINGEN 87(9):627-630, February 28, 1990

Predicting new effective treatments of alcohol addiction on the basis of their properties of inhibition of noradrenergic activitiy and-or thromboxane or on the activation of the dopamine reward system and-or beta-enforphin, by J. Backon. MEDICAL HYPOTHESES 29(4):237-239, August 1989

Relaxation and imagery groups for alcoholics, by G. Kutner, et al. ADVANCES 6(3): 57-64, Fall 1989

Research issues in assessing addiction treatment efficacy: how cost effective are Alcoholics Anonymous and private treatment centers?, by S. Peele. DRUG AND ALCOHOL DEPENDENCE 25(2):179-182, April 1990

Selecting substance abusers for long-term treatment, by C. Clemens, et al. INTERNATIONAL JOURNAL OF THE ADDICTIONS 25(1):33-42, January 1990

Sentencing: alternative to punishment—disparate treatment of alcoholics and drug addicts. CRIMINAL LAW REPORTER: COURT DECISIONS 46(3):1061-1062, October 18, 1989

Serving hearing-impaired alcoholics, by J. E. Dick. SOCIAL WORK 34(6):555-556, November 1989

Treating the addicted person: beyond methodology, by M. Trachtenburg. ALCOHOLISM TREATMENT QUARTERLY 6(3-4):175-188, 1989

Treating late-life onset alcohol abusers: demonstration through a case study, by L. W. Dupree, et al. CLINICAL GERONTOLOGIST 9(2):65-68, 1989

Treatment for alcoholics in German speaking countries, by W. Feuerlein. BRITISH JOURNAL OF ADDICTION 85(3):353-356, March 1990

Treatment of alcoholics based on the control principle: a prospective study of therapeutic results, by P. B. Vendsborg, et al. UGESKRIFT FOR LAEGER 152(11): 743-747, March 12, 1990

Treatment of alcoholism at a university psychiatric clinic, by K. M. Bachmann. THERAPEUTISCHE UMSCHAU 47(5):412-413, May 1990

Treatment of homosexual alcoholics in government-funded agencies: provider training and attitudes, by R. E. Hellman, et al. HOSPITAL AND COMMUNITY PSYCHIATRY 40(11):1163-1168, November 1989

Treatment of the mentally ill chemical abuser: description of the Hutchings Day Treatment Program, by K. B. Carey. PSYCHIATRIC QUARTERLY 60(4):303-316, Winter 1989

Treatment outcome evaluation methodology with alcohol abusers: strengths and key issues, by L. C. Sobell, et al. ADVANCES IN BEHAVIOR RESEARCH AND THERAPY 11(3):151-160, 1989

Treatment program for alcoholic patients at the Basel University Psychiatric Clinic, by D. Ladewig. THERAPEUTISCHE UMSCHAU 47(5):415-416, May 1990

Treatment program suffers because of apathy: Calling Lake, Altanta, by J. Holman. WINDSPEAKER 8(5):27, May 25, 1990

Use of essentiale and hemoperfusion in multimodality treatment of chronic alcoholism, by N. I. Khodzhaeva. ZHURNAL NEVROPATOLOGII I PSIKHIATRII IMENI S. S. KORSAKOVA 90(2):59-62, 1990

Why and by whom the American alcoholism treatment industry is under seige, by S. Peele. JOURNAL OF PSYCHOACTIVE DRUGS 22(1):1-13, January/March 1990

Therapy—Acupuncture
Acupuncture may offer hope for alcoholics. RN 53:113, June 1990

Dynamics of psycho-autonomic disorders in electroacupuncture of patients with alcoholism, by D. M. Tabeeva. SOVIET MEDICINE (8):80-83, 1989

Therapy—Drug
Case report: negligent treatment with drugs, by H. F. Laufenburg. WISCONSIN MEDICAL JOURNAL 89(4):166-168+, April 1990

Dangers of antabuse therapy, by R. S. Yapa. PRACTITIONER 233(1461):13-14, January 1989

From the Alcohol, Drug Abuse, and Mental Health Administration: developing new medications for compulsive behavior, by F. K. Goodwin, et al. JAMA 263:2029, April 18, 1990

Guidelines for the drug therapy of alcoholism, by G. L. Gessa. RECENTI PROGRESSI IN MEDICINA 81(3):171-175, March 1990

Prospects for a rational pharmacotherapy of alcoholism, by R. E. Meyer. JOURNAL OF CLINICAL PSYCHIATRY 50(11):403-412, November 1989

Therapy—Drug—2-hydroxyimipramine
Intravenous pharmacokinetics of 2-hydroxyimipramine in alcoholics and normal controls, by D. A. Ciraulo, et al. JOURNAL OF STUDIES ON ALCOHOL 51(4):366-372, July 1990

Therapy—Drug—Acamprosate
Acamprosate: from pharmacology to therapeutics, by B. Nalpas, et al. ENCEPHALE 16(3):175-179, May/June 1990

Therapy—Drug—Alprazolam
Lack of interaction between disulfiram and alprazolam in alcoholic patients, by B. Diquet, et al. EUROPEAN JOURNAL OF CLINICAL PHARMACOLOGY 38(2):157-160, 1990

Therapy—Drug—Benzodiazepines
Use of benzodiazepines by alcoholics, by R. B. Lydiard. AMERICAN JOURNAL OF PSYCHIATRY 147(1):128-129, January 1990

Open trial of buspirone in alcoholics, by H. R. Kranzler, et al. JOURNAL OF CLINICAL PSYCHOPHARMACOLOGY 9(5):379-380, October 1989

Therapy—Drug—Calcium Carbimide
Calcium carbimide in alcoholism treatment: II—medical findings of a short-term, placebo-controlled, double-blind clinical trial, by J. E. Peachey, et al. BRITISH JOURNAL OF ADDICTION 84(11):1359-1366, November 1989

Therapy—Drug—Carbamazepine
Oxazepam and carbamazepine for alcohol withdrawal, by D. Ames. AMERICAN JOURNAL OF PSYCHIATRY 147(3):375-376, March 1990

Therapy—Drug—Diazepam
Diazepam loading for alcohol withdrawal: seizure risk in epileptics, by B. van Sweden. BIOLOGICAL PSYCHIATRY 26(8):853-854, December 1989

Therapy—Drug—Disulfiram
Alcoholism treatment under scrutiny: disulfiram—research by U. D. Register, by R. Cowen. SCIENCE NEWS 137:254, April 21, 1990

Assessment of intramuscular emulsified disulfiram in alcoholics by estimation of urinary diethylamine, by K. A. Carey-Smith, et al. JOURNAL OF STUDIES ON ALCOHOL 9:571-575, November 1988

Disulfiram and calcium carbimide: mode of action, adverse effects and clinical use, by J. Johnsen. TIDSSKRIFT FOR DEN NORSKE LAEGEFORENING 110(10):1224-1228, April 10, 1990

Disulfiram implants: lack of pharmacological and clinical effects, by J. Johnsen, et al. TIDSSKRIFT FOR DEN NORSKE LAEGEFORENING 110(10):1229-1230, April 10, 1990

Disulfiram in the treatment of alcoholic patients with schizophrenia, by S. J. Kingsbury, et al. HOSPITAL AND COMMUNITY PSYCHIATRY 41(2):133-134, February 1990

Disulfiram therapy in alcoholism. AMERICAN FAMILY PHYSICIAN 42:1396, November 1990

Disulfiram treatment of alcoholism, by C. Wright, et al. AMERICAN JOURNAL OF MEDICINE 88(6):647-655, June 1990

Disulfiram treatment of alcoholism, by N. Heather. BMJ 299(6697):471-472, August 19, 1989

Disulfiram treatment of alcoholism: American College of Physicians. ANNALS OF INTERNAL MEDICINE 111(11):943-945, December 1, 1989

Giving ethanol to alcoholics in a research setting: its effect on compliance with disulfiram treatment, by H. R. Kranzler, et al. BRITISH JOURNAL OF ADDICTION 85(1):119-123, Janauary 1990

Lack of interaction between disulfiram and alprazolam in alcoholic patients, by B. Diquet, et al. EUROPEAN JOURNAL OF CLINICAL PHARMACOLOGY 38(2):157-160, 1990

Peripheral nerve functions in chronic alcoholic patients on disulfiram: a six month follow up, by S. K. Palliyath, et al. JOURNAL OF NEUROLOGY, NEUROSURGERY AND PSYCHIATRY 53(3):227-230, March 1990

Pharmacokinetics study of subcutaneous disulfiram implants, by E. Cid, et al. REVISTA MEDICA DE CHILE 116(11):1119-1123, November 1988

Trace element status in alcoholism before and during disulfiram treatment, by P. Grandjean, et al. ANNALS OF CLINICAL AND LABORATORY SCIENCE 20(1): 28-35, January/February 1990

Use of leukocyte aldehyde dehydrogenase activity to monitor inhibitory effect of disulfiram treatment, by A. Helander, et al. ALCOHOLISM 14(1):48-52, February 1990

Therapy—Drug—Fluoxetine

Fluoxetine differently alters alcohol intake and other consummatory behaviors in problem drinkers, by C. A. Naranjo, et al. CLINICAL PHARMACOLOGY AND THERAPEUTICS 47(4):490-498, April 1990

Fluoxetine overdose: a case report, by T. P. Rohrig, et al. JOURNAL OF ANALYTICAL TOXICOLOGY 13(5):305-307, September/October 1989. Erratum. 14(1): 63, January/February 1990

Therapy—Drug—Glycerin

Use of medicinal glycerin in treating alcoholics, by I. K. Sosin. VRACHEBNOE DELO (5):83-85, May 1990

Therapy—Drug—Ketoconazole

Hypersensitivity to alcoholic beverages during treatment with ketoconazole, by R. H. Meyboom, et al. NEDERLANDS TIJDSCHRIFT VOOR GENEESKUNDE 133(29): 1463-1464, July 22, 1989

Therapy—Drug—Lithium

Lithium effects on adjunctive alcohol consumption: III—FT-shock as the inducing schedule, by G. Hines. PHARMACOLOGY, BIOCHEMISTRY AND BEHAVIOR 34(3):591-593, November 1989

Lithium therapy for alcoholism: further study assistance, by J. R. de la Fuente. MAYO CLINIC PROCEEDINGS 64(8):1034, August 1989

New applications of lithium therapy, by J. B. Murray. JOURNAL OF PSYCHOLOGY 124(1):55-73, January 1990

On the treatment of the alcoholic organic brain syndrome with an alpha-adrenergic agonist modafinil: double-blind, neurophysiological studies, by B. Saletu, et al. PROGRESS IN NEUROPSYCHOPHARMACOLOGY AND BIOLOGICAL PSYCHIATRY 14(2):195-214, 1990

Therapy—Drug—Oxazepam
Oxazepam and carbamazepine for alcohol withdrawal, by D. Ames. AMERICAN JOURNAL OF PSYCHIATRY 147(3):375-376, March 1990

Therapy—Drug—Phenytoin
Use of intravenous phenytoin in alcohol withdrawal seizures. AMERICAN FAMILY PHYSICIAN 42:459-460, August 1990

Therapy—Drug—Potassium Chlorazepate
Potassium chlorazepate administered orally in alcoholic detoxication, by J. P. Roussaux, et al. JOURNAL DE PHARMACIE DE BELGIQUE 44(3):192-196, May/June 1989

Therapy—Drug—Sodium Oxybutyrate
Effects of sodium oxybutyrate on the level of catecholamines and serontin and monamine oxidase activity in patients with alcoholism, by V. G. Treskov, et al. BIULLETEN EKSPERIMENTALNOI BIOLOGII I MEDITSINY 108(7):62-64, July 1989

Therapy—Drug—Teturam
Characteristics of the urinary sediment and proteinuria in chronic alcoholics before and during treatment with teturam, by T. Stanevskaia, et al. UROLOGIIA I NEFROLOGIIA (2):20-23, March/April 1990

Therapy—Employee Assistance Programs
Attitude toward and experience of industry-based alcohol recovery programmes: a survey of 161 Scottish organizations, by P. J. O'Donnell, et al. PSYCHOLOGICAL REPORTS 65(3 Pt 2):1175-1184, December 1989

Corporate responsibilities to the addicted employee: a look at practical legal, and ethical issues, by J. L. Goff. LABOR LAW JOURNAL 41:214-221, April 1990

Inpatient treatment of employed alcoholics: a randomized clinical trial on Hazelden-type and traditional treatment, by L. Keso, et al. ALCOHOLISM: CLINICAL AND EXPERIMENTAL RESEARCH 14(4):584-589, 1990

Lethality of the corporate image to the recovering corporate executive alcoholic, by D. F. Machell. JOURNAL OF ALCOHOL AND DRUG EDUCATION 36:1-5, Fall 1990

Therapy—Family
Addicted to the addict: treating addiction's other victims—Al-Anon, by L. Cohen. CMAJ 142(4):372-373+, February 15, 1990

Al-Anon: a resource for families and friends of alcoholics, by A. Kverme. TIDSSKRIFT FOR DEN NORSKE LAEGEFORENING 110(5):608-609, February 20, 1990

Behavioural marital therapy for alcoholics: effects on communication skills and marital satisfaction, by M. P. Baker, et al. BEHAVIOUR CHANGE 6(3-4):178-186, 1989

Behavioural marital therapy in the treatment of psychological disorders, by W. K. Halford, et al. BEHAVIOUR CHANGE 6(3-4):165-177, 1989

Children of parents of drug-alcohol programs: are they underserved?, by N. Van den Bergh, et al. ALCOHOLISM TREATMENT QUARTERLY 6(3-4):1-25, 1989

Family involvement and outcome in treatment of alcoholism, by J. McNabb, et al. PSYCHOLOGICAL REPORTS 65(pt 2):1327-1330, December 1989

Family treatment for homeless alcohol/drug-addicted women and their preschool children, by M. Comfort, et al. ALCOHOLISM TREATMENT QUARTERLY 7(1): 129-147, 1990

Treatment of families with alcohol dependence in Poland, by M. Zwolinski. PSYCHIATRIA POLSKA 22(6):457-462, November/December 1988

Therapy—Hemodialysis
Severe alcoholic poisoning treated by hemodialysis, by J. Y. Breurec, et al. JOURNAL DE TOXICOLOGIE CLINIQUE ET EXPERIMENTALE 9(5):351-354, September/October 1989

United States
Alcohol: America's no. 1 addiction. SCHOLASTIC UPDATE 123:2-4+, November 16, 1990

Alcohol-related mortality and years of potential life lost: United States, 1987. MMWR 39(11):173-178, March 23, 1990

Alcohol-related traffic fatalities during holidays: United States, 1988. MMWR 38(50): 861-863, December 1989

Alcoholism and other drug abuse: the South Carolina story—introduction, by G. L. Phelps, et al. JOURNAL OF THE SOUTH CAROLINA MEDICAL ASSOCIATION 86(1):6-7, January 1990

Apparent per capita ethanol consumption: United States, 1977-1986. MMWR 38(46): 800-803, November 24 1989

Wales
Drinking in England and Wales: the latest news from OPCS, by J. B. Davies. BRITISH JOURNAL OF ADDICTION 84(9):957-959, September 1989

Drinking in England and Wales: reply to John Booth Davies, by E. Goddard. BRITISH JOURNAL OF ADDICTION 84(9):967-968, September 1989

ALCOHOL

Withdrawal

Alcohol withdrawal and mood, by K. Bokstrom, et al. ACTA PSYCHIATRICA SCANDI-NAVICA 80(5):505-513, November 1989

Alcohol withdrawal and prolactin, by A. Bezzegh, et al. ACTA PHYSIOLOGICA HUN-GARICAE 75(Suppl):33-34, 1990

Alcohol withdrawal concealing symptoms of subdural hematoma: a caveat, by E. K. Koranyi, et al. PSYCHIATRIC JOURNAL OF THE UNIVERSITY OF OTTAWA 15(1):15-17, March 1990

Alcohol withdrawal delirium and hypokalemia, by J. Beckmann. NERVENARZT 61(7): 444-446, July 1990

Alcohol withdrawal in the elderly, by B. I. Liskow, et al. JOURNAL OF STUDIES ON ALCOHOL 50:414-421, September 1989

Alcohol withdrawal syndromes. AMERICAN FAMILY PHYSICIAN 42:191, July 1990

Assessment of alcohol withdrawal: the Revised Clinical Institute Withdrawal Assess-ment for Alcohol Scale (CIWA-AS), by J. T. Sullivan, et al. BRITISH JOURNAL OF ADDICTION 84(11):1353-1357, November 1989

Diazepam loading for alcohol withdrawal: seizure risk in epileptics, by B. van Sweden. BIOLOGICAL PSYCHIATRY 26(8):853-854, December 1989

Effect of hyperbaric oxygenation on the dynamics of the alcohol withdrawal syn-drome, by N. M. Epifanova, et al. SOVIET NEUROLOGY AND PSYCHIATRY 22(4):79-86, Winter 1989-1990

Effects of alcohol withdrawal on responses of platelets from alcoholics: a study using platelet-rich plasma from blood anticoagulated with D-phenylalanyl-L-prolyl-L-arginyl chloromethyl ketone: FPRCH2C1, by M. L. Rand, et al. THROMBOSIS AND HAEMASTASIS 63(2):178-182, April 12, 1990

Fluid balance, vasopressin and withdrawal symptoms during detoxification from alco-hol, by A. J. Mander, et al. DRUG AND ALCOHOL DEPENDENCE 24(3):233-237, December 1989

Insulin sensitivity in alcoholics in a withdrawal state, by N. Adner, et al. JOURNAL OF INTERNAL MEDICINE 228(1):59-64, July 1990

Observations on the management of alcohol withdrawal syndrome, by R. Vasudeva, et al. JOURNAL OF THE SOUTH CAROLINA MEDICAL ASSOCIATION 86(1):24-26, January 1990

Somatropic hormone and prolactin levels in men with chronic alcoholism in a state of abstinence, by S. Abrikosova. TERAPEVTICHESKII ARKHIV 62(4):45-47, 1990

Withdrawal symptoms and alcohol dependence: fruitful mysteries, by G. Edwards. BRITISH JOURNAL OF ADDICTION 85(4):447-461, April 1990

ALCOHOL AND AGING (AND THE AGED)

Abuse of alcohol and drugs in homes for the aged, by H. J. Luderer, et al. FORT-SCHRITTE DER MEDIZIN 108(9):176-177, March 30, 1990

Alcohol and the elderly, by S. Ticehurst. AUSTRALIAN AND NEW ZEALAND JOURNAL OF PSYCHIATRY 24(2):252-260, June 1990

Alcohol linked to falls that incapacitate elderly, by E. Hauschildt. JOURNAL OF THE ADDICTION RESEARCH FOUNDATION 19(5):4, May 1, 1990

Alcohol use by aging men, by J. Tourunen. ALKOHOLIPOLITIIKKA 54(2):64-69, 1989

Alcohol withdrawal in the elderly, by B. I. Liskow, et al. JOURNAL OF STUDIES ON ALCOHOL 50:414-421, September 1989

Alcoholic elderly subset of homeless, by E. Hauschildt. JOURNAL OF THE ADDICTION RESEARCH FOUNDATION 19(7-8):10, July/August 1990

Alcoholism and associated malnutrition in the elderly, by F. L. Iber. PROGRESS IN CLINICAL AND BIOLOGICAL RESEARCH 326:157-173, 1990

Alcoholism and the elderly: review of theories, treatment and prevention, by D. E. Maypole. ACTIVITIES, ADAPTATION AND AGING 13(4):43-54, 1989

Alcoholism in elderly native Americans, focus of AOA grants. AGING (361):53-54, 1990

Alcoholism request for financial aid at a senior citizens crisis center, by D. L. Weinstein, et al. SOCIAL CASEWORK 70(8):510-515, October 1989

Approach and avoidance coping responses among older problem and nonproblem drinkers, by R. H. Moos, et al. PSYCHOLOGY AND AGING 5(1):31-40, March 1990

Are elderly alcoholics discriminated against?, by K. Haldeman, et al. JOURNAL OF PSYCHOSOCIAL NURSING AND MENTAL HEALTH SERVICES 28(5):6-8+, May 1990

Behavioral factors related to elderly alcohol abuse: research and policy issues, by A. M. Gurnack, et al. INTERNATIONAL JOURNAL OF THE ADDICTIONS 24(7):641-654, July 1989

Comparison of three case-finding strategies relative to elderly alcohol abusers, by L. W. Dupree. JOURNAL OF APPLIED GERONTOLOGY 8(4):502-511, December 1989

Discriminant analysis of severe alcohol consumption among older persons, by C. M. Nakamura, et al. ALCOHOL AND ALCOHOLISM 25(1):75-80, 1990

Drinking habits of elderly Chinese, by E. H. Kua. BRITISH JOURNAL OF ADDICTION 85(4):571-573, April 1990

How to treat the geriatric alcoholic, by A. Wilson. CANADIAN JOURNAL OF GERIATRICS 6(7):35-40, October 1990

ALCOHOL AND AGING

Late versus early onset problem drinking in older men, by R. M. Atkinson, et al. AL-COHOLISM: CLINICAL AND EXPRIMENTAL RESEARCH 14(4):574-579, 1990

Problem drinking. AGING (361):2-64, 1990

Quantity-frequency and diary measures of alcohol consumption for elderly drinkers, by C. E. Werch. INTERNATIONAL JOURNAL OF THE ADDICTIONS 24(9):859-865, September 1989

Recognition of alcohol dependence in the elderly, by V. S. Rains, et al. JOURNAL OF THE AMERICAN GERIATRICS SOCIETY 37(12):1204, December 1989

Screening elderly veterans for alcoholism, by M. B. Moran, et al. JOURNAL OF GENERAL INTERNAL MEDICINE 5(4):361-364, July/August 1990

Social learning theory and alcohol behavior among the elderly, by R. L. Akers, et al. SOCIOLOGICAL QUARTERLY 30(4):625-638, 1989

Social, psychological and physical factors affecting the nutritional status of elderly subjects: separating cause and effect, by J. S. Goodwin. AMERICAN JOURNAL OF CLINICAL NUTRITION 50(Suppl)5:1201-1209, November 1989

Why don't we take adequate drinking histories from elderly admissions?, by R. Howard, et al. BRITISH JOURNAL OF ADDICTION 84(11):1374-1375, November 1989

ALCOHOL AND AIDS

Alcohol, AIDS risk and commercial sex: some preliminary results from a Scottish study, by M. L. Plant, et al. DRUG AND ALCOHOL DEPENDENCE 25(1):51-55, February 1990

Alcohol and immune function in HIV-1 seronegative, HTLV-I-II seronegative and positive men on methadone, by N. G. Klimas, et al. PROGRESS IN CLINICAL AND BIOLOGICAL RESEARCH 325:103-111, 1990

Alcohol, immunomodulation, and AIDS: proceedings of the Alcohol-Immunology AIDS Conference, Tucson, Arizona, April 27-29, 1989. PROGRESS IN CLINICAL AND BIOLOGICAL RESEARCH 325:1-444, 1990

Alcohol, sex and AIDS, by M. A. Plant. ALCOHOL AND ALCOHOLISM 25(2-3):293-301, 1990

Beliefs about AIDS, use of alcohol and drugs, and unprotected sex among Massachusetts adolescents, by R. W. Hingson, et al. AMERICAN JOURNAL OF PUBLIC HEALTH 80(3):295-299, March 1990

Comparison of AIDS and STD knowledge between sexually active alcohol consumers and abstainers, by S. Nagy, et al. JOURNAL OF SCHOOL HEALTH 60:276-279, August 1990

European patterns of alcohol use on AIDS and drug abuse, Stockholm 25-28 September 1989, by E. Segest. UGESKRIFT FOR LAEGER 152(6):406, February 5, 1990

ALCOHOL AND AIDS

High-risk behaviors for AIDS among heterosexual alcoholics: a pilot study, by M. Windle. JOURNAL OF STUDIES ON ALCOHOL 50(6):503-507, November 1989

HIV seropositivity in inner-city alcoholcs, by S. J. Schleifer, et al. HOSPITAL AND COMMUNITY PSYCHIATRY 41(3):248-249+, March 1990

Human immunodeficiency virus and hepatitis B virus infections in alcoholics, by J. M. Jacobson, et al. PROGRESS IN CLINICAL AND BIOLOGICAL RESEARCH 325: 67-73, 1990

Methodological issues concerning the sensitive query in AIDS-alcohol research: sample size estimates for randomized response procedures, by A. L. Golbeck, et al. PROGRESS IN CLINICAL AND BIOLOGICAL RESEARCH 325:1-10, 1990

ALCOHOL AND CELEBRITIES
Child star, child addict: D. Barrymore, by J. Kaufman. LADIES HOME JOURNAL 107: 116+, March 1990

Still struggling to save her marriage, by C. Dreifus. REDBOOK 174:38+, April 1990

ALCOHOL AND CHILDREN
see also: Alcohol—Adult Children of Alcoholics

36- and 48-month neurobehavioral follow-ups of children prenatally exposed to marijuana, cigarettes, and alcohol, by P. A. Fried, et al. JOURNAL OF DEVELOPMENTAL AND BEHAVIORAL PEDIATRICS 11(2):49-58, April 1990

Acute alcoholic intoxication in children in Vojvodina, by N. Roncevic, et al. ARHIV ZA HIGIJENU RADA I TOKSIKOLOGIJA 40(1):47-55, March 1989

Alcohol intoxication and psychosocial problems among children, by A. Lamminpaa, et al. ACTA PSYCHIATRICA SCANDINAVICA 81(5):468-471, May 1990

Baby bottles and family rattles: children and substance abuse, by N. P. Johnson, et al. JOURNAL OF THE SOUTH CAROLINA MEDICAL ASSOCIATION 86(1):32-37, January 1990

Five-year-old Texas boy dies after drinking liquor: case of R. Griffin. JET 77:33, March 19, 1990

Tobacco and alcohol use among Australian secondary schoolchildren in 1987, by D. J. Hill, et al. MEDICAL JOURNAL OF AUSTRALIA 152(3):124-130, February 5, 1990

ALCOHOL AND COLLEGE STUDENTS
Alcohol and drug experiences in criminal justice higher education, by N. R. Montgomery, Jr., et al. JOURNAL OF ALCOHOL AND DRUG EDUCATION 36:35-38, Fall 1990

Alcohol and drug use by college males as a function of family alcoholism history, by M. E. McCaul, et al. ALCOHOLISM: CLINICAL AND EXPERIMENTAL RESEARCH 14(3):467-471, June 1990

ALCOHOL AND COLLEGE STUDENTS

Alcohol and fraternities: the lessons of modern care law, by P. A. Zirkel, et al. JOURNAL OF COLLEGE STUDENT DEVELOPMENT 31:141-146, March 1990

Alcohol behavior, risk perception, and fraternity and sorority membership, by D. R. Tampke. NASPA JOURNAL 28:71-77, Fall 1990

Alcohol consumption, problem drinking and anti-social behaviour in a sample of college students, by R. West, et al. BRITISH JOURNAL OF ADDICTION 85(4):479-486, April 1990

Alcohol drinking patterns of college students, by T. Fukuda, et al. ARUKORU KENKYUTO YAKUBUTSU ISON 25(2):93-1021, April 1990

Alcohol, drug, and mental health problems among Jewish and Christian men at a university, by M. G. Monteiro, et al. AMERICAN JOURNAL OF DRUG AND ALCOHOL ABUSE 15(4):403-412, December 1989

Alcohol use among college students: responses to raising the purchase age, by J. E. Davis, et al. JOURNAL OF AMERICAN COLLEGE HEALTH 38(6):263-269, May 1990

Bad times at Hangover University: college parties lead to the ER or the drunk tank, by R. Rosenberg. NEWSWEEK 116(21):81, November 19, 1990

Banning alcohol in a major college stadium: impact on the incidence and patterns of injury and illness, by D. W. Spaite, et al. JOURNAL OF AMERICAN COLLEGE HEALTH 39:125-128, November 1990

Behavioral self-control strategies for deliberately limiting drinking among college students, by C. E. Werch. ADDICTIVE BEHAVIORS 15(2):118-128, 1990

Behavioral strategies for alcohol abuse prevention with high-risk college males, by R. B. Garvin, et al. JOURNAL OF ALCOHOL AND DRUG EDUCATION 36:23-34, Fall 1990

Campus crime linked to students' use of drugs and alcohol, by S. Dodge. CHRONICLE OF HIGHER EDUCATION 36:33+, January 17, 1990

College drinking attitude scale: a tool for alcohol education program assessment, by G. M. Gonzalez. INTERNATIONAL JOURNAL OF THE ADDICTIONS 25(2):121-132, 1990

College officials are split on alcohol policies: some seek to end underage drinking; others try to encourage "responsible" use, by C. Leatherman. CHRONICLE OF HIGHER EDUCATION 36:33+, January 31, 1990

College student drinking behaviors before and after changes in state policy, by F. G. Williams, et al. JOURNAL OF ALCOHOL AND DRUG EDUCATION 35:12-25, Spring 1990

College students' definitions of social and problem drinking, by D. B. Engwall, et al. JOURNAL OF DRUG EDUCATION 20(3):227-234, 1990

College student's recommendations to combat abusive drinking habits, by L. F. Burrell. JOURNAL OF COLLEGE STUDENT DEVELOPMENT 31:562-563, November 1990

Comparison of alcohol and illicit drug use between pharmacy students and the general college population, by C. J. Miller, et al. AMERICAN JOURNAL OF PHARMACEUTICAL EDUCATION 54(1):27-30, Spring 1990

Comparison of alcohol use and alcohol-related problems among Caucasian, Black, and Hispanic college students, by G. M. Gonzalez. NASPA JOURNAL 17:330-335, Summer 1990

Cross-cultural comparison of attitudes toward alcohol among French and United States college students, by R. D. McAnulty, et al. INTERNATIONAL JOURNAL OF THE ADDICTIONS 24(12):1229-1236, December 1989

Dancing through the wall: a UBC student shares blame for a frat house accident, by S. Hardy. BC REPORT 2(6):33, October 8, 1990

Drinking among medical students, by M. K. Duncan, et al. BMJ 299(6697):517-518, August 19, 1989

Effects of raising the drinking age and related campus initiatives on student alcohol consumption and alcohol-related problems, by G. M. Gonzalez. JOURNAL OF COLLEGE STUDENT DEVELOPMENT 31:181-183, March 1990

Environmental and behavioral factors affecting fraternity drinking, by J. E. Creeden. JOURNAL OF COLLEGE STUDENT DEVELOPMENT 31:465-477, September 1990

Examination of the tension reduction hypthesis: the relationship between anxiety and alcohol in college students, by C. R. Kalodner, et al. ADDICTIVE BEHAVIORS 14(6):649-654, 1989

Exceptions to the rule: why nondrinking college students do not drink, by H. Klein. COLLEGE STUDENT JOURNAL 24:57-71, Spring 1990

Gender differences in drinking patterns and problems among college students: a review of the literature, by R. C. Engs, et al. JOURNAL OF ALCOHOL AND DRUG EDUCATION 35:36-47, Winter 1990

Knowledge about and attitudes towards drinking among university students in Spain, by C. Del Rio, et al. REVUE D'EPIDEMIOLOGIE ET DE SANTE PUBLICIQUE 37(4):245-252, 1989

Many colleges move to restrict alcohol-related ads in student papers, vendors' sponsorship of events, by S. Dodge. CHRONICLE OF HIGHER EDUCATION 36:39-40, February 21, 1990

New York State's 21 alcohol purchase age: anticipated consequences in the college community, by K. M. Hayes-Sugarman. DAI A 49(9):2612, 1989

Opinions on alcoholic beverage consumption and alcoholism among university students, by G. L. Guimaraes Borges. EDUCACION MEDICA Y SALUD 23(4):406-410, October/December 1989

ALCOHOL AND COLLEGE STUDENTS

Patterns of alcohol use among university students in Spain, by C. Del Rio, et al. ALCOHOL AND ALCOHOLISM 24(5):465-471, 1989

Perceived problem-solving skills and drinking patterns among college students, by J. G. Williams, et al. PSYCHOLOGICAL REPORTS 65(3 Pt 2):1235-1244, December 1989

Planning and programming server intervention initiatives for fraternities and sororities: experiences at a large university, by F. D. Wittman, et al. JOURNAL OF PRIMARY PREVENTION 9(4):247-269, Summer 1989

Predicting university students' use of alcoholic beverages, by D. W. Maney. JOURNAL OF COLLEGE STUDENT DEVELOPMENT 31:23-32, January 1990

Psychosocial correlates of alcohol consumption among black college students, by D.S. Ford, et al. JOURNAL OF ALCOHOL AND DRUG EDUCATION 36:45-51, Fall 1990

Quantity and frequency of drinking among undergraduates at a southern university, by S. Haworth-Hoeppner, et al. INTERNATIONAL JOURNAL OF THE ADDICTIONS 24(9):829-857, September 1989

Reactions, expectancies, and college students' drinking, by P. B. Johnson. PSYCHOLOGICAL REPORTS 65(3 Pt 2):1245-1246, December 1989

Risk of alcohol abuse among college students, by J.B. Slawinska. PSYCHIATRIA POLSKA 23(2):111-116, March/April 1989

Social-hygienic aspects of alcoholism among students of professional technical schools located in rural areas, by V. V. Drobyshev. GIGIYENA I SANITARIYA (4): 24-26, April 1990

Social psychological bases for college alcohol consumption, by L. Goodwin. JOURNAL OF ALCOHOL AND DRUG EDUCATION 36:83-95, Fall 1990

Survey of the social context of drinking among college women, by G. C. Hunter. JOURNAL OF ALCOHOL AND DRUG EDUCATION 35:73-80, Spring 1990

Validity of the CAGE in screening for problem drinking in college students, by E. J. Heck, et al. JOURNAL OF COLLEGE STUDENT DEVELOPMENT 31:359-364, July 1990

ALCOHOL AND CRIME

Agony without ecstasy: alcohol and violence, by S. Goodman. CURRENT HEALTH 2 17:28-29, October 1990

Alcohol abuse and the young offender: alcohol education as an alternative to custodial sentencing, by C. Greer, et al. JOURNAL OF OFFENDER COUNSELING, SERVICES AND REHABILITATION 15(1):131-145, January 1990

Alcohol and crime: aggression and violence demand attention, by J. C. Van Der Stel. JUSTITIELE VERKENNINGEN 15(5):87-115, 1989

ALCOHOL AND CRIME

Alcohol and crime: issues and directions for future research, by S. Walfish, et al. CRIMINAL JUSTICE AND BEHAVIOR 16(3):370-386, September 1989

Alcohol and criminal behavior, by G. Arzt. THERAPEUTISCHE UMSCHAU 47(5):390-394, May 1990

Alcohol and the criminal justice system. CRIMINAL JUSTICE AND BEHAVIOR 16: 268-386, September 1989

Alcohol and drug use by college males as a function of family alcoholism history, by M. E. McCaul, et al. ALCOHOLISM: CLINICAL AND EXPERIMENTAL RESEARCH 14(3):467-471, June 1990

Alcohol and drug use by rapists and their victims, by J. M. Rodenas, et al. MEDICINE AND LAW 8(2):157-164, 1989

Alcohol consumption and rates of personal violence, suicide and homicide, by D. Lester. ACTIVITAS NERVOSA SUPERIOR 31(4):248-251, December 1989

Alcohol, drugs and murder: a study of convicted homicide offenders, by W. F. Wieczorek, et al. JOURNAL OF CRIMINAL JUSTICE 18(3):217-227, 1990

Alcoholism and sex abuse in the family: incest and marital rape, by C. P. Barnard. JOURNAL OF CHEMICAL DEPENDENCY TREATMENT 3(1):131-144, 1989

Campus crime linked to students' use of drugs and alcohol, by S. Dodge. CHRONICLE OF HIGHER EDUCATION 36:33+, January 17, 1990

Children of alcoholism: implications for juvenile justice, by J. E. McGaha, et al. JUVENILE AND FAMILY COURT JOURNAL 41(2):19-24, Summer 1990

Delinquency and drug use: temporal and developmental patterns, by D. H. Huiziga, et al. JUSTICE QUARTERLY 6(3):419-455, September 1989

Drugs, alcohol and crime: abstracts of the Society for the Study of Addiction to Alcohol and Other Drugs annual symposium, 16th and 17th November 1989, Leicester. BRITISH JOURNAL OF ADDICTION 84(11):1387-1392, November 1989

Effect of alcohol on life- and health-threatening punishable offenses and their prevention, by M. Mitlohner. CESKSLOVENSKA ZDRAVOTNICTVI 37(6-7):293-298, July 1989

Follow-up study of psychiatrically examined arsonists, by K. Noreik, et al. TIDSSKRIFT FOR DEN NORSKE LAEGEFORNING 110(14):1820-1822, 1990

Homicide: defenses—voluntary intoxication; malice. CRIMINAL LAW REPORTER: COURT DECISIONS 47(13):1257, June 27, 1990

Improving information on the role of alcohol in interpersonal violence in Great Britain, by R. N. Norton, et al. ALCOHOL AND ALCOHOLISM 24(6):577-589, 1989

Young people, alcohol and crime, by J. Mott. HOME OFFICE RESEARCH AND STATISTICS DEPARTMENT RESEARCH BULLETIN 28:24-28, 1990

ALCOHOL AND DENTISTS

Alcoholism and the dentist, by N. D. Robb. BRITISH JOURNAL OF ADDICTION 85(4): 437-439, April 1990

ALCOHOL AND DIABETES

Polyneuropathy in alcoholism and diabetes mellitus, by D. Uhl. MEDIZINISCHE MONATSSCHRIFT FUR PHARMAZEUTEN 13(3):82-83, March 1990

ALCOHOL AND DRUGS

Alcohol use by heroin addicts 12 years after drug abuse treatment, by W. E. Lehman, et al. JOURNAL OF STUDIES ON ALCOHOL 51(3):233-244, May 1990

Behavioral aspects of alcohol-tobacco interactions, by I. F. Zacny. RECENT DEVELOPMENTS IN ALCOHOLISM 8:205-209, 1990

Combined alcohol and other drug dependence. RECENT DEVELOPMENTS IN ALCOHOLISM 8:1-327, 1990

Comparison of the behavioral effects and abuse liability of ethanol and pentobarbital in recreational sedative abusers, by J. J. Guarino, et al. NIDA RESEARCH MONOGRAPH SERIES 85:453-454, 1989

Concurrent and simultaneous use of alcohol with cocaine: results of national survey, by B. F. Grant, et al. DRUG AND ALCOHOL DEPENDENCE 25(1):97-104, February 1990

Divided attention performance in cannabis users and non-users following alcohol and cannabis separately and in combination, by D. F. Marks, et al. PSYCHOPHARMACOLOGY 99(3):397-401, November 1989

Double whammy of alcohol and drugs, by L. Stanwood. CURRENT HEALTH 2 17:26-27, October 1990

Drug preferences of alcoholic polydrug abusers with and without panic, by C. F. Jensen, et al. JOURNAL OF CLINICAL PSYCHIATRY 51(5):189-191, May 1990

Fatal interaction of methocarbamol and ethanol in an accidental poisoning, by K. E. Ferslew, et al. JOURNAL OF FORENSIC SCIENCES 35(2):477-482, March 1990

Inhalant and alcohol use go hand in hand: beer doesn't hurt you, is the common belief. JOURNAL OF THE ADDICTION RESEARCH FOUNDATION 19(6):5, June 1, 1990

Interactions between alcohol and benzodiazepines, by L. E. Hollister. RECENT DEVELOPMENTS IN ALCOHOLISM 8:233-239, 1990

Interactions between alcohol and drugs, by J. Marland. TIDSSKRIFT FOR DEN NORSKE LAEGEFORENING 110(9):1106-1109, March 30, 1990

Levels of alcohol dependence in cocaine addicts: some clinical implications, by S. Walfish, et al. PSYCHOLOGY OF ADDICTIVE BEHAVIORS 3(2):65-68, 1989

Longitudinal patterns of alcohol use by narcotics addicts, by Y. I. Hser, et al. RECENT DEVELOPMENTS IN ALCOHOLISM 8:145-171, 1990

ALCOHOL AND DRUGS

Management of paracetamol poisoning complicated by enzyme induction due to alcohol or drugs, by B. M. McClements, et al. LANCET 335(8704):1526, June 23, 1990

Mealtime aspirin may boost alcohol high, by R. Cowen. SCIENCE NEWS 138(21): 327, November 24, 1990

Multiple addictions: co-synchronous use of alcohol and drugs, by N. S. Miller, et al. NEW YORK STATE JOURNAL OF MEDICINE 90(12):596-600, 1990

Nifedipine overdose accompanied by ethanol intoxication in a patient with congenital heart disease, by R. D. Welch, et al. JOURNAL OF EMERGENCY MEDICINE 8(2): 169-172, March/April 1990

Role of ethanol abuse in the etiology of heroin-related death, by A. J. Ruttenber, et al. JOURNAL OF FORENSIC SCIENCES 35(4):891-900, July 1990

Sedative-tranquilizer use and abuse in alcoholics currently in outpatient treatment: incidence, pattern and preference, by B. Wolf, et al. NIDA RESEARCH MONOGRAPH SERIES 95:376-377, 1989

Vascular lesions in intestinal ischemia induced by cocaine-alcohol abuse: report of a fatal case due to overdose, by A. Garfia, et al. JOURNAL OF FORENSIC SCIENCES 35(3):740-745, May 1990

ALCOHOL AND EATING DISORDERS
Bulimia nervosa and associated alcohol abuse among secondary school students, by M. G. Timmerman, et al. JOURNAL OF THE AMERICAN ACADEMY OF CHILD AND ADOLESCENT PSYCHIATRY 29(1):118-122, January 1990

Food and drug abuse: the contrasts and comparisons of eating disorders and alcoholism, by T. P. Beresford, et al. PSYCHIATRY IN MEDICINE 7(3):37-46, 1989

Influence of prior alcohol and drug abuse problems on bulimia nervosa treatment outcome, by J. E. Mitchell, et al. ADDICTIVE BEHAVIORS 15(2):169-173, 1990

ALCOHOL AND EMPLOYMENT
see also:　Alcohol: Therapy—Employee Assistance Programs
　　　　　　Alcohol: Testing—Employment

AA charges pilots with alcohol abuse, revamps inspectors' response procedures: Northwest Airlines pilots. AVIATION WEEK AND SPACE TECHNOLOGY 132: 220, March 19, 1990

Alcohol abuse and performance appraisal ratings, by J. L. Jordan, et al. PSYCHOLOGICAL REPORTS 65(pt 2):1219-1224, December 1989

Alcohol and drug abuse among the homeless population: a national response, by B. Lubran. ALCOHOLISM TREATMENT QUARTERLY 7(1):11-23, 1990

Alcohol and drugs in the workplace: major problem or myth, by B. A. Campbell, et al. BUSINESS QUARTERLY 55(2):60-63, Autumn 1990

ALCOHOL AND EMPLOYMENT

Alcohol and work, by M. A. Heimgard. TIDSSKRIFT FOR DEN NORSKE LAEGE-FORENING 110(17):2275, June 30, 1990

Alcohol and work, by O. G. Aasland, et al. TIDSSKRIFT FOR DEN NORSKE LAEGE-FORENING 110(13):1697-1699, May 20, 1990

Analyses of flushing response to alcohol and drinking behavior among shipyard workers and their family members in Hiroshima Prefecture, Japan, by T. Mori, et al. ARUKORU KENKYUTO YAKUBUTSU ISON 25(1):24-36, February 1990

Approaches to the alcohol problem in the workplace, by O. E. Pratt, et al. ALCOHOL AND ALCOHOLISM 24(5):453-464, 1989

Civil service interview: question about alcoholism—no right to arbitration, California. POLICE OFFICER GRIEVANCES BULLETIN June 1989, p. 7

Colleague with a drinking problem, by F. Keaney, et al. PRACTITIONER 233(1473): 1059-1060+, August 8, 1989

Corporate testing for drug, alcohol abuse on the increase, by M. S. Reisch. CHEMICAL ENGINEERING NEWS 68:17-18, July 16, 1990

DOT seeks comment on need for more action on alcohol abuse in transport industry. CORPORATE SECURITY DIGEST 3(47):7-8, November 27, 1989

Drinking and flying don't mix: FAA rule requiring pilots to report alcohol-related traffic violations, by J. M. McClellan. FLYING 117:42-43, December 1990

Drinking and flying: the problem of alcohol use by pilots, by J. G. Modell, et al. NEW ENGLAND JOURNAL OF MEDICINE 323(7):455-461, August 16, 1990

Drug and alcohol policies, by R. A. Marinucci. FIRE ENGINEERING 142:9-10, October 1989

Drunken pilot incident may force FAA changes. CORPORATE SECURITY DIGEST 4(15):9, April 16, 1990

Employment and drinking in early adulthood: a longitudinal perspective, by C. Power, et al. BRITISH JOURNAL OF ADDICTION 85(4):487-494, April 1990

Epidemiology of depression and alcohol abuse-dependence in a managerial and professional work force, by E. J. Bromet, et al. JOURNAL OF OCCUPATIONAL MEDICINE 32(10):989-995, 1990

Ex-Northwest pilots guilty of flying under influence, by C. Fotos. AVIATION WEEK AND SPACE TECHNOLOGY 133:7+, August 27, 1990

FAA charges pilots with alcohol abuse, revamps inspectors' response procedures: Northwest Airlines pilots. AVIATION WEEK AND SPACE TECHNOLOGY 132: 220, March 19, 1990

Flying and alcohol do not mix: Northwest Airlines crew censured. NEWSWEEK 115: 27, March 19, 1990

ALCOHOL AND EMPLOYMENT

Government failed to prove charges in prosecution of Northwest crew, by W. J. Piszczek. AVIATION WEEK AND SPACE TECHNOLOGY 135:75, October 8, 1990

Influence of alcohol and aging on radio communication during flight, by D. Morrow, et al. AVIATION, SPACE AND ENVIRONMENTAL MEDICINE 61(1):12-20, January 1990

Is workplace drinking cause for dismissal? CORPORATE SECUIRTY June 1990, p. 8

Lawyer impairment: more common than you might think; Denver survey suggests, by S. B. Goldberg. ABA JOURNAL 76:32, February 1990

Lost at sea and on land: J. Hazelwood, by P. Brock. LIFE 13:78-80+, February 1990

Motivating alcoholic workers to seek help, by D. A. Rumpel. SECURITY MANAGEMENT 33(9):80-83, October 1989

Northwest crew to contest revocation of pilots' licenses. AVIATION WEEK AND SPACE TECHNOLOGY 132:83, March 26, 1990

Perceptual acuity and the risk of industrial accidents, by A. W. Moll van Charante, et al. AMERICAN JOURNAL OF EPIDEMIOLOGY 131(4):652-663, April 1990

Perils of perservance: crash of Simmons Airlines Banedirante on second ILS approach to Alpena Airport, Michigan, by N. Moll. FLYING 117:84+, August 1990

Pilots' knowledge of blood alcohol levels and the 0.04% blood alcohol concentration rule, by S. M. Ross, et al. AVIATION, SPACE AND ENVIRONMENTAL MEDICINE 61(5):412-417, May 1990

Prevalence and sociodemographic correlates of high-risk and problem drinking at an industrial worksite, by G. R. Webb, et al. BRITISH JOURNAL OF ADDICTION 85(4):495-507, April 1990

Relationship between perceived workplace problems and alcohol consumption among single men in new resource communities: Australia, by C. C. Neil. CONTEMPORARY DRUG PROBLEMS 16:227-264, Summer 1989

Significance of unemployment for admissions to a psychiatric department, by K. Solstad, et al. UGESKRIFT FOR LAEGER 152(34):2428-2430, 1990

Staying on track: women railroad wokers, by W. Chapkis. WOMEN'S REVIEW OF BOOKS 7(7):6, April 1990

Termination: officer fired for lying—Nebraska. POLICE OFFICER GRIEVANCES BULLETIN April 1990, pp. 7-8

What shall we do with the drunken worker: screening for drug and alcohol abuse at work, by L. Gill. TIMES June 21, 1990, p. 16

When alcohol and gasoline mix, by J. Shaver. AIR FORCE TIMES 50(50):41+, January 23, 1990

ALCOHOL AND EMPLOYMENT

Work stress and alcohol effects: a test of stress-induced drinking, by M. L. Cooper, et al. JOURNAL OF HEALTH AND SOCIAL BEHAVIOR 31:260-376, September 1990

Worksite community processes and the prevention of alcohol abuse: theory to action, by M. Shain. CONTEMPORARY DRUG PROBLEMS 17:369-389, Fall 1990

Legal Issues

Alcoholic worker wins suit. CORPORATE SECURITY DIGEST 3(36):2, September 1, 1989; also in CORRECTIONS DIGEST 20(18):3, September 6, 1989 and CRIME CONTROL DIGEST 23(36):5, September 11, 1989

Alcoholism and drug abuse: some legal issues for employers, by G. Howard. BRITISH JOURNAL OF ADDICTION 85(5):593-603, May 1990

FAA adopts rule grounding pilots who drive drunk. CORPORATE SECURITY DIGEST 4(31):9, August 6, 1990

Flying too high in the sky: drinking trial of three Northwest pilots, by J. Greenwald. TIME 136:48, August 27, 1990

ALCOHOL AND EPILEPSY

Alcohol and epileptic seizures, by G. Bovim, et al. TIDSSKRIFT FOR DEN NORSKE LAEGEFORENING 110(4):493-496, February 10, 1990

Diazepam loading for alcohol withdrawal: seizure risk in epileptics, by B. van Sweden. BIOLOGICAL PSYCHIATRY 26(8):853-854, December 1989

HDL cholesterol level in patients treated with antiepileptic drugs, by K. Niedzielska, et al. NEUROLOGIA I NEUROCHIRURGIA POLSKA 23(3):193-197, May/June 1989

ALCOHOL AND THE FAMILY (AND MARRIAGE)

see also: Alcohol: Therapy—Family

Alcohol and family violence: then and now—who owns the problem, by J. P. Flanzer. JOURNAL OF CHEMICAL DEPENDENCY TREATMENT 3(1):61-79, 1989

Alcohol consumption and divorce: which causes which, by M. Magura, et al. JOURNAL OF DIVORCE 12(1):127-136, 1988

Alcohol use and its control in Finnish and Soviet marriages, by M. Holmila, et al. BRITISH JOURNAL OF ADDICTION 85(4):509-520, April 1990

Alcoholic family systems: a legacy of dysfunction, by C. Mann. ARCTIC MEDICAL RESEARCH 47(Suppl)1:611-614, 1988

Alcoholism and family structure, by R. P. Preli, et al. FAMILY THERAPY 17(1):1-8, 1990

Alcoholism and sex abuse in the family: incest and marital rape, by C. P. Barnard. JOURNAL OF CHEMICAL DEPENDENCY TREATMENT 3(1):131-144, 1989

ALCOHOL AND THE FAMILY

Analyses of flushing response to alcohol and drinking behavior among shipyard workers and their family members in Hiroshima Prefecture, Japan, by T. Mori, et al. ARUKORU KENKYUTO YAKUBUTSU ISON 25(1):24-36, February 1990

Are alcoholic homes always toxic?, by P. Jaret. HEALTH 22:12, April 1990

Assessment of parent-led prevention programs: a national descriptive study, by M. Klitzner, et al. JOURNAL OF DRUG EDUCATION 20(2):111-125 1990

Assessment of parent-led prevention programs: a preliminary assessment of impact, by M. Klitzner, et al. JOURNAL OF DRUG EDUCATION 20(1):77-94, 1990

Behavioral risks: mother knows best, by M. D. Decker. NEW YORK STATE JOURNAL OF MEDICINE 90(7):346-347, July 1990

Can we love our battering fathers?, by H. Gordon. CHANGING MEN Winter 1990, p. 7

Changes in family perception in a group of chronic alcoholics in treatment, by M. Campigli, et al. MINERVA PSICHIATRICA 31(2):97-101, April/June 1990

Characteristics of the development of children of alcoholic mothers, by I. N. Usov, et al. SOVIET NEUROLOGY AND PSYCHIATRY 22(3):82-89, Fall 1989

Child maltreatment and alcohol abuse: comparisons and perspectives for treatment, by S. J. Bavolek, et al. JOURNAL OF CHEMICAL DEPENDENCY TREATMENT 3(1):165-184, 1989

Children of alcoholics, by R. Maynard. HOMEMAKER'S MAGAZINE 24(8):128-130+, November/December 1989

Codependency: a view from women married to alcoholics, by R. Asher, et al. INTERNATIONAL JOURNAL OF THE ADDICTIONS 23(4):331-350, 1988

Communicative competence in sons of alcoholics, by C. Carter, et al. BRITISH JOURNAL OF ADDICTION 85(9):1157-1164, 1990

Comparison of familial and nonfamilial male alcoholic patient without a coexisting psychiatric disorder, by E. C. Penick, et al. JOURNAL OF STUDIES ON ALCOHOL 51(5):443-447, September 1990

Depression in homicidal adolescents, by C. P. Malmquist. BULLETIN OF THE AMERICAN ACADEMY OF PSYCHIATRY AND THE LAW 18(1):23-36, 1990

Effect of parental symptoms, parental relationships, and parenting practices on the intergenerational transmission of alcoholism and depression, by S. J. Holmes. DAI A 50(10):3371-3372, April 1990

Event-related potential characteristics in children of alcoholics from high density families, by S. Y. Hill, et al. ALCOHOLISM: CLINICAL AND EXPERIMENTAL RESEARCH 14(1):6-16, February 1990

Familial and personality correlates of alcohol-related problems, by E. E. Knowles, et al. ADDICTIVE BEHAVIORS 14(5):537-543, 1989

Familial transmission of alcohol use norms and expectancies and reported alcohol use, by R. C. Johnson, et al. ALCOHOLISM 14(2):216-220, April 1990

Familial transmission of alcohol use: I—parent and adult offspring alcohol use over 17 years; Tecumseh, Michigan, by D. W. Webster, et al. JOURNAL OF STUDIES ON ALCOHOL 50(6):557-566, November 1989

Familial transmission of alcohol use: II—imitation of and aversion to parent drinking by adult offspring: 1960-1977, Tecumseh, Michigan, by E. Harburg, et al. JOURNAL OF STUDIES ON ALCOHOL 51(3):245-256, May 1990

Families of drug addicts, by A. F. Radchenko, et al. ZHURNAL NEVROPATOLOGII I PSIKHIATRII IMENI S. S. KORSAKOVA 90(2):38-42, 1990

Family cohesion, expressiveness and conflict in alcoholic families, by K. L. Barry, et al. BRITISH JOURNAL OF ADDICTION 85(1):81-87, January 1990

Family environment of married male pathological gamblers, alcoholics, and dually addicted gamblers, by J. Clarrocchi, et al. JOURNAL OF GAMBLING BEHAVIOR 5(4):283-291, Winter 1989

Family hero in Black alcoholism families, by F. L. Brisbane. JOURNAL OF ALCOHOL AND DRUG EDUCATION 34(3):29-37, Spring 1989

Family history of depression and alcoholism in Alzheimer patients and age-matched controls, by B. A. Lawlor, et al. INTERNATIONAL JOURNAL OF GERIATRIC PSYCHOLOGY 4(6):321-326, November/December 1989

Help for families and friends of alcoholics. AGING (361):49-50, 1990

Helping children of alcoholics, by E. Nishioka. JOURNAL OF SCHOOL HEALTH 59(9):404-405, November 1989

Human resistance to alcoholism as a function of the structure of marriages, by L. A. Atramentova, et al. TSITOLOGIYA I GENETIKA 23(6):19-21, 1989

Identifying and helping children of alcoholics, by K. Scheitlin. NURSE PRACTITIONER 15(2):34-36+, February 1990

Impact of family stress-regulating variables on recovery from alcoholism, by C. Captain. MILITARY MEDICINE 154(11):539-546, November 1989

Individual and adult children of alcoholics, by G. Transeau, et al. PSYCHOLOGICAL REPORTS 67(1):137-142, 1990

Labeling the child of an alcoholic: stereotyping by mental health professionals and peers, by J. P. Burk, et al. JOURNAL OF STUDIES ON ALCOHOL 51(2):156-163, March 1990

Life style and family history in medical students with arterial hypertension, by S. Guemez, et al. ARCHIVOS DE INSTITUTO DE CARDIOLOGIA DE MEXICO 60(3):283-287, 1990

Mother-infant interaction in a multirisk population, by H. L. Johnson, et al. AMERICAN JOURNAL OF ORTHOPSYCHIATRY 60(2):281-288, April 1990

ALCOHOL AND THE FAMILY

Offspring of parents with drinking problems: drinking and drug-taking as young adults, by J. Orford, et al. BRITISH JOURNAL OF ADDICTION 85(6):770-784, June 1990

One big happy family and other myths, by N. P. Johnson, et al. JOURNAL OF THE SOUTH CAROLINA MEDICAL ASSOCIATION 86(1):38-41, January 1990

Other side of the street: non-alcoholic adults from alcoholic homes, by E. M. Scott. ALCOHOLISM TREATMENT QUARTERLY 6(3-4):63-74, 1989

Parents as alcohol pushers, by W. Pedersen. TIDSSKRIFT FOR DEN NORSKE LAEGEFORENING 110(14):1834-1837, May 30, 1990

Parents reach for the bottle. TIMES HIGHER EDUCATION SUPPLEMENT 931:9, September 7, 1990

Personality and object relational pathology in young adult children of alcoholics, by S. Hibbard. PSYCHOTHERAPY 26(4):504-509, Winter 1989

Personality charcteristics of sons of alcohol abusers, by E. E. Knowles, et al. JOURNAL OF STUDIES ON ALCOHOL 51(2):142-147, March 1990

Personality profiles of children of alcoholics, by P. Calder, et al. PROFESSIONAL PSYCHOLOGY: RESEARCH AND PRACTICE 20(6):417-418, December 1989

Psychiatric illnesses in adolescents of alcoholic parents, by K. Suzuki. PSYCHIATRIA ET NEUROLOGIA JAPONICA 92(2):79-88, 1990

Psychological damage to children by the alcohol dependence of their parents, by M. Metzler. ZEITSCHRIFT FUR ARZTLICHE FORTBILDUNG 83(16):825-826, 1989

Relationship between child and adult psychopathology in children of alcoholics, by J. J. Giglio, et al. INTERNATIONAL JOURNAL OF THE ADDICTIONS 25(3):263-290, 1990

Risk for hypertension in female members of multigenerational male-limited alcoholic families, by S. B. Miller, et al. ALCOHOLISM: CLINICAL AND EXPERIMENTAL RESEARCH 13(4):505-507, August 1989

Role of family formation and dissolution in shaping drinking behaviour in early adulthood, by C. Power, et al. BRITISH JOURNAL OF ADDICTION 85(4):521-530, April 1990

Role of the family in alcohol education and alcohol abuse in Poland, by W. Tryzno, et al. MEDICINE AND LAW 8(3):267-273, 1989

Social support network of adolescents: relation to family alcohol abuse, by M. G. Holden, et al. AMERICAN JOURNAL OF DRUG AND ALCOHOL ABUSE 14(4): 487-498, December 1988

Somatic symptoms in alcohol abusers' families, by E. Nordlie. TIDSSKRIFT FOR DEN NORSKE LAEGEFORENING 110(6):725-726, February 28, 1990

ALCOHOL AND THE FAMILY

Women married to alcoholics: help and home for nonalcoholic partners (book review), by M. Kokin. QUILL AND QUIRE 56(1):27, January 1990; also in ANGLICAN JOURNAL 116(4):16, April 1990

ALCOHOL AND HEALTH CARE PROFESSIONALS
Assessment and referral service for Ontario's health professionals with alcohol, drug and related problems, by E. J. Larkin, et al. CANADA'S MENTAL HEALTH 38(1): 5-8, March 1990

ALCOHOL AND HIGH SCHOOL STUDENTS
Alcohol use among high school athletes: a comparison of alcohol use and intoxication in male and female high school athletes and non-athletes, by C. N. Carr, et al. JOURNAL OF ALCOHOL AND DRUG EDUCATION 36:39-43, Fall 1990

Codependency and self-esteem among high school students, by D. Fisher, et al. PSYCHOLOGICAL REPORTS 66(3 Pt 1):1001-1002, June 1990

Comparison of smoking and drinking among Asian and white schoolchildren in Glasgow, by H. S. Kohli. PUBLIC HEALTH 103(6):433-439, November 1989

Relationship between alcohol dependency and suicide ideation among high school students, by J. Beer, et al. PSYCHOLOGICAL REPORTS 66(3):1363-1366, 1990

Self-esteem, depression, and alcohol dependency among high school students, by M. Workman, et al. PSYCHOLOGICAL REPORTS 65(2):451-455, October 1989

Survey of alcohol and psychoactive drug consumption in a sample of high school students of the 9th and 19th local health units in the Marche Region, by F. Donato, et al. ANNALI DI IGIENE 1(3-4):693-708, May/June 1989

Use of alcohol among high school students in Lesotho, by K. Meursing, et al. BRITISH JOURNAL OF ADDICTION 84(11):1337-1342, November 1989

Use of alcohol among high school students in Lesotho: a health promotion perspective, by A. Amos. BRITISH JOURNAL OF ADDICTION 84(12):1447-1449, December 1989

ALCOHOL AND THE HOMELESS
Alameda County Department of Alcohol and Drug Programs Comprehensive Homeless Alcohol Recovery Services: CHARS, by R. W. Bennett, et al. ALCOHOLISM TREATMENT QUARTERLY 7(1):111-128, 1990

Alcohol and drug abuse among the homeless population: a national response, by B. Lubran. ALCOHOLISM TREATMENT QUARTERLY 7(1):11-23, 1990

Alcohol-free living centers: hope for homeless alcoholics, by N. M. Koroloff, et al. SOCIAL WORK 34(6):497-504, November 1989

Alcohol, homelessness, and public policy, by J. Baumohl. CONTEMPORARY DRUG PROBLEMS 16(3):281-300, Fall 1989

ALCOHOL AND THE HOMELESS

Alcohol problems and homelessness: history and research, by G. R. Garrett. CONTEMPORARY DRUG PROBLEMS 16(3):301-322, 1989

Alcohol use and abuse among homeless adolescents in Hollywood, by M. J. Robertson, et al. CONTEMPORARY DRUG PROBLEMS 16(3):415-452, Fall 1989

Alcoholic elderly subset of homeless, by E. Hauschildt. JOURNAL OF THE ADDICTION RESEARCH FOUNDATION 19(7-8):10, July/August 1990

Alcoholism and homelessness, by N. Shanks. PRACTITIONER 233(1477):1364+, October 22, 1989

Deviance and dwelling space: notes on the resettlement of homeless persons with drug and alcohol problems, by K. Hopper. CONTEMPORARY DRUG PROBLEMS 16(3):391-416, 1989

Elderly on street need honest, candid care, by E. Hauschildt. JOURNAL OF THE ADDICTION RESEARCH FOUNDATION 19(7-8):10, July/August 1990

Estimating the prevalence of alcohol, drug and mental health problems in the contemporary homeless population: a review of the literature—paper presented at the National Conference on Homelessness, Alcohol, and Other Drugs, San Diego, California, February 2-4, 1989, by P. J. Fischer. CONTEMPORARY DRUG PROBLEMS 16(3):333-339, 1989

Factors affecting the use of medical, mental health, alcohol, and drug treatment services by homeless adults, by D. Padgett, et al. MEDICAL CARE 28(9):805-821, September 1990

Family treatment for homeless alcohol/drug-addicted women and their preschool children, by M. Comfort, et al. ALCOHOLISM TREATMENT QUARTERLY 7(1): 129-147, 1990

Homeless women, by S. C. Anderson, et al. AFFILIA 3:62-70, Summer 1988

Homelessness among participants in residential alcohol problems in a Northern California county: the commitment and organization of social resources, by R. Speiglman. CONTEMPORARY DRUG PROBLEMS 16(3):453-482, Fall 1989

Housing models for alcohol programs serving homeless people, by F. D. Wittman. CONTEMPORARY DRUG PROBLEMS 16(3):483-504, Fall 1989

Louisville's Project Connect for the homeless alcohol and drug abuser, by G. S. Bonham, et al. ALCOHOLISM TREATMENT QUARTERLY 7(1):57-78, 1990

Outreach and engagement for homeless women at risk of alcoholism, by S. Ridlen, et al. ALCOHOLISM TREATMENT QUARTERLY 7(1):99-109, 1990

Return of skid row, by D. Whitman. US NEWS AND WORLD REPORT 108:27-29, January 15, 1990

Stabilization services for homeless alcoholics and drug addicts, by D. McCarty, et al. ALCOHOLISM TREATMENT QUARTERLY 7(1):31-45, 1990

ALCOHOL AND THE HOMELESS

Thiamin status of a sample of homeless clinic attenders in Sydney, Australia, by I. Darnton-Hill, et al. MEDICAL JOURNAL OF AUSTRALIA 152(1):5-9, 1990

Treatment and research with homeless alcoholics, by T. E. Shipley, Jr., et al. CONTEMPORARY DRUG PROBLEMS 16:505-526, Fall 1989

Wrong battle in a noble cause: removing access to fortified wine for homeless alcoholics is no solution, by R. B. Slater. BUSINESS AND SOCIETY REVIEW (72):52-53, Winter 1990

ALCOHOL AND HOMOSEXUALS
AA spiritual issues, and the treatment of lesbian and gay alcoholics, Michigan State University, by S. L. Berg. DAI A 50(7):2121, 1990

Alcohol and drug experiences in criminal justice higher education, by N. R. Montgomery, Jr., et al. JOURNAL OF ALCOHOL AND DRUG EDUCATION 36:35-38, Fall 1990

Bibliotherapy and gay American men of Alcoholics Anonymous, by R. J. Kus. JOURNAL OF GAY AND LESBIAN PSYCHOTHERAPY 1(2):73-86, 1989

Drinking patterns and drinking problems in a community sample of gay men, by J. L. Martin. PROGRESS IN CLINICAL AND BIOLOGICAL RESEARCH 325:27-34, 1990

Gay men in recovery. LAMBDA RISING BOOK REPORTS 2(4):15, April 1990

Support choices and abstinence in gay-lesbian and heterosexual alcoholics, by P. R. Holleran, et al. ALCOHOLISM TREATMENT QUARTERLY 6(2):71-83, 1989

Treatment of homosexual alcoholics in government-funded agencies: provider training and attitudes, by R. E. Hellman, et al. HOSPITAL AND COMMUNITY PSYCHIATRY 40(11):1163-1168, November 1989

Use of drugs and alcohol by homosexually active men in relation to sexual practices, by J. McCusker, et al. JOURNAL OF THE ACQUIRED IMMUNE DEFICIENCY SYNDROME 3(7):729-736, 1990

Walk on the sober side: one gay man's story, by L. Grant. ADVOCATE (541):26, January 2, 1990

ALCOHOL AND INFANTS
see also: Alcohol: Fetal Alcohol Syndrome

Effect of prenatal alcohol exposure on growth and morphology of offspring at 8 months of age, by N. L. Day, et al. PEDIATRICS 85(5):748-752, 1990

Maternal use of alcohol and breast-fed infants, by B. Lindmark. NEW ENGLAND JOURNAL OF MEDICINE 322(5):338-339, February 1, 1990

Maternal use of alcohol and breast-fed infants, by R. E. Little. NEW ENGLAND JOURNAL OF MEDICINE 322(5):229, February 1990

ALCOHOL AND INFANTS

Prediction of subsequent motor and mental retardation in newborn infants exposed to alcohol in utero by computerized EEG analysis, by S. Ioffe, et al. NEUROPEDI-ATRICS 21(1):11-17, February 1990

Small-for-gestational age infants, by J. G. Bryson. NEW ZEALAND MEDICAL JOUR-NAL 102(878):564, October 25, 1989

ALCOHOL AND LAWYERS
Lawyer impairment: more common than you might think; Denver survey suggests, by S. B. Goldberg. ABA JOURNAL 76:32, February 1990

Lawyers at risk, by R. H. Gordon, et al. NEW YORK STATE BAR JOURNAL 62(4):22-24+, May 1990

Would you tell a lawyer he or she's a drunk?, by M. G. Crawford. CANADIAN LAWYER 14(2):5, March 1990

ALCOHOL AND THE MEDIA
Cosby on chemicals: mistreatment of youthful drinking on an episode of The Cosby Show, by G. Vandal. PHIL DELTA KAPPAN 71:632-633, April 1990

Reducing alcohol consumption through television advertising, by J. G. Barber, et al. JOURNAL OF CONSULTING AND CLINICAL PSYCHOLOGY 57(5):613-618, October 1989

Using national news events to stimulate local awareness of public policy issues, by R. B. Convissor, et al. PUBLIC HEALTH REPORTS 105(3):257-260, May/June 1990

Youth and alcohol in television stories, with suggestions to the industry for alternative protrayals, by J. E. De Foe, et al. ADOLESCENCE 25:533-550, Fall 1988

ALCOHOL AND THE MILITARY
Boozy boomers get banned from the bar: artillerymen trigger troubles at a Roger Pass hotel, by D. Powell. BC REPORT 1(26):42, March 5, 1990

Changes in the use of alcohol and tobacco during introductory military services, by G. Bovim, et al. TIDSSKRFIT FOR DEN NORSKE LAEGEFORENING 110(13):1705-1706, May 20, 1990

Legal aspects of alcohol abuse in the Navy, by L. H. Kallen, et al. BEHAVIORAL SCI-ENCES AND THE LAW 7(3):355-377, Summer 1989

Occupational outcome after military treatment for alcoholism, by C. Wright, et al. JOURNAL OF OCCUPATIONAL MEDICINE 32(1):24-32, January 1990

Physical activity, smoking, alcohol consumption, body mass index, and plasma lipid profiles of military reserve officers, by P. F. Kokkinos, et al. MILITARY MEDICINE 154(12):600-603, December 1989. Erratum. 155(2):51, February 1990

ALCOHOL AND THE MILITARY

Traumatism among naval personnel associated with alcoholic intoxication in the north, by K. A. Shapovalov. ORTOPEDIIA TRAVMATOLOGIIA I PROTEZIROVANIE (1): 42-45, January 1990

Twin study of the effects of the Vietnam conflict on alcohol drinking patterns, by J. Goldberg, et al. AMERICAN JOURNAL OF PUBLIC HEALTH 80(5):570-574, May 1990

VA moves ahead in alcoholism treatment and research. AGING (361):51, 1990

ALCOHOL AND MINORITIES
Alcohol intakes and deficiencies in thiamine and vitamin B6 in black patients with cardiac failure, by S. L. Tobias, et al. SOUTH AFRICAN MEDICAL JOURNAL 76(7): 299-302, October 7, 1989

Alcohol use among Latino adolescents: what we know and what we need to know, by M. J. Gilberg. DRUGS AND SOCIETY 3(1-2):35-53, 1988

Alcoholism among blacks, by J. E. Franklin, Jr. HOSPITAL AND COMMUNITY PSYCHIATRY 40(11):1120-1122+, November 1989

Alcoholism in elderly native Americans, focus of AOA grants. AGING (361):53-54, 1990

Alcoholism in minority populations (book review), by T. D. Watts, et al. JOURNAL OF THE ADDICTION RESEARCH FOUNDATION 19(4):10, April 1, 1990

American Indians, stress, and alcohol, by P. D. Mail. AMERICAN INDIAN AND ALASKA NATIVE MENTAL HEALTH RESEARCH 3(2):7-26, Fall 1989

Asians, Asian-Americans and alcohol, by R. C. Johnson, et al. JOURNAL OF PSYCHOACTIVE DRUGS 22(1):45-52, January/March 1990

Band leadership: of Samson Cree Nation, committed to solving the problems of drug and alcohol abuse. WINDSPEAKER 8(17):22, November 9, 1990

Children in peril: A. Kayitah, Apache child with fetal alcohol syndrome, by M. Brower. PEOPLE WEEKLY 33:86-89, April 16, 1990

Ethnic differences in the consequences of alcohol misuse, by M. Clarke, et al. ALCOHOL AND ALCOHOLISM 25(1):9-11, 1990

Fighting ads in the inner city: alcohol and tobacco ads targeted to blacks, by M. Mabry. NEWSWEEK 115:46, February 5, 1990

Indian health threat: fetal alcohol syndrome, by L. Plunkett. UTNE READER (37):62, January 1990

Level and extent of rehabilitation needs of black alcohol abuse clients in an outpatient treatment program, by E. R. Smith. DAI A 50(9):3069, 1990

Native American alcoholism: a transcultural counseling perspective, by L. French. COUNSELLING PSYCHOLOGY QUARTERLY 2(2):153-166, 1989

ALCOHOL AND MINORITIES

Peyotism and the control of heavy drinking: the Nebraska Winnebago in the early 1990s, by T. W. Hill. HUMAN ORGANIZATION 49(3):255-265, 1990

Point of view: Indian sobriety must come from Indian solutions, by P. D. Mail, et al. HEALTH EDUCATION 20:19-22, December 1989

Profile of abused and neglected American Indian children in the Southwest, by C. Lujan, et al. CHILD ABUSE AND NEGLECT 13(4):449-461, 1989

Psychosocial correlates of alcohol consumption among black college students, by D.S. Ford, et al. JOURNAL OF ALCOHOL AND DRUG EDUCATION 36:45-51, Fall 1990

Tilting at billboards: opposition to alcohol and tobacco ads targeted to blacks, by B. Wildavsky. NEW REPUBLIC 203:19-20, August 20-27, 1990

To be young in Indian country, by R. A. Warrior. CHRISTIANITY AND CRISIS 50:65-67, March 5, 1990

Working solutions for Indian alcoholism. UTNE READER (37):63, January 1990

ALCOHOL AND MUSIC
Alcohol themes within country-western songs, by G. J. Connors, et al. INTERNATIONAL JOURNAL OF THE ADDICTIONS 24(5):445-451, May 1989

ALCOHOL AND NURSES
Addiction to drugs and alcohol among physicians and nurses, by A. S. Sorensen, et al. UGESKRIFT FOR LAEGER 151(41):2660-2664, October 9, 1989

Alcohol knowledge and drinking patterns of nursing students over time, by R. C. Engs, et al. EDUCATION 110:179-185, Winter 1989

ALCOHOL AND NUTRITION
Alcoholism and associated malnutrition in the elderly, by F. L. Iber. PROGRESS IN CLINICAL AND BIOLOGICAL RESEARCH 326:157-173, 1990

Alcoholism and biosynthesis of phosphatidylethanol. NUTRITION REVIEWS 48:186-187, April 1990

Alcoholism-induced zinc deficiency in mother and fetus, by A. Jendryczko, et al. WIADOMSCI LEKARSKIE 42(19-21):1052-1054, October 1-November 1, 1989

Alcoholism treatment under scrutiny: disulfiram/serotonin-rich foods, by R. Cowen. SCIENCE NEWS 137:254, April 21, 1990

Biochemical and anthropometric evaluation of the nutritional status of 35-year-old Dutch men with reference to smoking and drinking habits, by G. van Poppel, et al. INTERNATIONAL JOURNAL OF VITAMIN AND NUTRITION RESEARCH 59(4): 381-387, 1989

ALCOHOL AND NUTRITION

Changes in the fatty acid composition of erythrocyte membranes in patients with chronic alcoholism under the effect of a diet enriched with linoleic acid, by V. U. Buko, et al. VOPROSY PITANIIA (6):10-13, November/December 1989

Concentration of vitamin B6 and activities of enzymes of B6 metabolism in the blood of alcoholic and nonalcoholic men, by M. L. Fonda, et al. ALCOHOLISM 13(6): 804-809, December 1989

Contribution of a long-term prospective cohort study to the issue of nutrition and cancer with special reference to the role of alcohol drinking, by T. Hirayama. PROGRESS IN CLINICAL AND BIOLOGICAL RESEARCH 346:179-187, 1990

Ethanol induced malnutrition: a potential cause of immunosuppression during AIDS, by M. E. Mohs, et al. PROGRESS IN CLINICAL AND BIOLOGICAL RESEARCH 325:433-444, 1990

Lasting nutritional imbalance following abstinence in patients with alcoholic cirrhosis, by A. Watanabe, et al. JOURNAL OF MEDICINE 20(5-6):331-336, 1989

Moderate alcohol intake and spontaneous eating patterns of humans: evidence of unregulated supplementation, by J. M. De Castro, et al. AMERICAN JOURNAL OF CLINICAL NUTRITION 52(2):246-253, August 1990

Natural killer cell activity in alcoholic cirrhosis: influence of nutrition, by F. Ledesma, et al. EUROPEAN JOURNAL OF CLINICAL NUTRITION 44:733-740, October 1990

Recommended amounts of nutrients do not debate the toxic effects of an alcohol dose that sustains significant blood levels of ethanol, by C. S. Lieber, et al. JOURNAL OF NUTRITION 119(12):2038-2040, December 1989

Social, circadian, nutritional, and subjective correlates of the spontaneous patterns of moderate alcohol intake of normal humans, by J. M. de Castro. PHARMACOL-OGY, BIOCHEMISTRY AND BEHAVIOR 35(4):923-931, April 1990

ALCOHOL AND PHYSICIANS

Addiction to drugs and alcohol among physicians and nurses, by A. S. Sorensen, et al. UGESKRIFT FOR LAEGER 151(41):2660-2664, October 9, 1989

Alcohol misuse and the hospital doctor, by A. Paton. BRITISH JOURNAL OF HOSPI-TAL MEDICINE 42(5):394-400, November 1989

Alcohol-related problems of future physicians prior to medical training, by J. A. Rich-man, et al. JOURNAL OF STUDIES ON ALCOHOL 51(4):296-300, July 1990

Alcoholic doctors can recover, by A. Allibone. BMJ 300(6730):1014, April 14, 1990

Alcoholic doctors can recover, by G. Lloyd. BMJ 300(6726):728-730, March 17, 1990

Combined Alcoholics Anonymous and professional care for addicted physicians, by M. Galanter, et al. AMERICAN JOURNAL OF PSYCHIATRY 147(1):64-68, January 1990

Impaired doctor: ensuring patient safety. NURSING 90 20:110+, April 1990

ALCOHOL AND PHYSICIANS

Impaired small town physicians and their spouses, by R. Estep, et al. JOURNAL OF DRUG ISSUES 19(3 Pt 1):351-367, Summer 1989

PWI: practicing while intoxicated addictions and the State Board of Medical Examiners, by J. E. Lathem, et al. JOURNAL OF THE SOUTH CAROLINA MEDICAL ASSOCIATION 86(1):15-16, January 1990

Treatment for GPs with a drink probem. PRACTITIONER 233(1477):1353, October 22, 1989

Youthful precusors of alcohol abuse in physicians, by R. D. Moore, et al. AMERICAN JOURNAL OF MEDICINE 88(4):332-336, April 1990

ALCOHOL AND THE POLICE

Alcohol-drug dependence in police forces: a community health policy for the 1990s, by J. Dietrich. RCMP GAZETTE 51(6):5-15, 1989

Deputy was justified in shooting drunken man who took his night stick and was advancing on him with night stick upraised. AELE LIABILITY REPORTER 200:118-119, August 1989

Drunk while off duty: fatal auto accident—Los Angeles. POLICE OFFICER GRIEVANCES BULLETIN April 1990, pp. 5-6

Recovering alcoholic police officer and the danger of professional emotional suppression, by D. F. Machell. ALCOHOLISM TREATMENT QUARTERLY 6(2):85-92, 1989

ALCOHOL AND POLITICIANS

High—and mighty: J. M. Post elaborated on some famous historical political figures with substance abuse problems in Washington Post. SECURITY MANAGEMENT 34:16+, April 1990

Scandal in Monte Porzio: mayor's son gets drunk on communion wine, by N. Hazelon. NATIONAL REVIEW 42:57-58, December 17, 1990

Ted Kennedy on the rocks, by M. Kelly. GENTLEMEN'S QUARTERLY 60:200-209+, February 1990

ALCOHOL AND PREGNANCY
see also:　　Alcohol and Infants
　　　　　　　Fetal Alcohol Syndrome

36- and 48-month neurobehavioral follow-ups of children prenatally exposed to marijuana, cigarettes, and alcohol, by P. A. Fried, et al. JOURNAL OF DEVELOPMENTAL AND BEHAVIORAL PEDIATRICS 11(2):49-58, April 1990

Alcohol and pregnancy, by B. G. Barbour. JOURNAL OF NURSE-MIDWIFERY 35(2): 78-85, March/April 1990

ALCOHOL AND PREGNANCY

Alcohol consumption, cigarette smoking and fetal outcome in Victoria, 1985, by R. Bell, et al. COMMUNITY DENTISTRY AND ORAL EPIDEMIOLOGY 13(4):484-491, 1989

Alcoholism-induced zinc deficiency in mother and fetus, by A. Jendryczko, et al. WIADOMSCI LEKARSKIE 42(19-21):1052-1054, October 1-November 1, 1989

Can maternal alcoholism cause spasmus nutans in offspring?, by P. F. Bray. NEW ENGLAND JOURNAL OF MEDICINE 322(8):554, February 22, 1990

Changing smoking, drinking, and eating behaviour among pregnant women in Denmark: evaluation of a health campaign in a local region, by J. Olsen, et al. SCANDINAVIAN JOURNAL OF SOCIAL MEDICINE 17(4):277-280, 1989

Disorders in the development of the brain of embryos from alcohol-dependent mothers, by G. N. Konovalov, et al. SOVIET NEUROLOGY AND PSYCHIATRY 22(4): 60-71, Winter 1989/1990

Effect of prenatal alcohol exposure on growth and morphology of offspring at 8 months of age, by N. L. Day, et al. PEDIATRICS 85(5):748-752, 1990

Fetal rights: a new assault on feminism, by K. Pollitt. NATION 250(12):409, March 26, 1990

Hormonal function of the fetoplacental system in pregnant women with chronic alcoholic intoxication, by G. I. Gerasimovich, et al. AKUSHERSTVO I GINEKOLOGIIA (12):18-22, December 1989

IQ at age 4 in relation to maternal alcohol use and smoking during pregnancy, by A. P. Streissguth, et al. DEVELOPMENTAL PSYCHOLOGY 25:3-11, January 1989

Labor in a drunk mother: fatal risk for the neonate, by R. Uzel, et al. CESKOSLO-VENSKA GYNEKOLOGIE 55(2):132-134, March 1990

Maternal alcohol abuse is associated with elevated fetal erythropoietin levels, by E. Halmesmaki, et al. OBSTETRICS AND GYNECOLOGY 76(2):219-222, August 1990

Maternal alcohol and pentazocine abuse: neonatal behavior and morphology in an opposite-sex twin pair, by M. L. Riese. ACTA GENETICAE MEDICAE E GEMEL-LOLOGIAE 38(1-2):49-56, 1989

Maternal and paternal moderate daily alcohol consumption and unexplained miscarriages, by F. Parazzini, et al. BRITISH JOURNAL OF OBSTETRICS AND GYNAE-COLOGY 97(7):618-622, July 1990

Pregnancy outreach program in British Columbia: the prevention of alcohol-related birth defects, by K. O. Asante, et al. CANADIAN JOURNAL OF PUBLIC HEALTH 81(1):76-77, January/February 1990

Prevalence of illicit-drug or alcohol use during pregnancy and discrepancies in mandatory reporting in Pinellas County, Florida, by I. J. Chasnoff, et al. NEW ENGLAND JOURNAL OF MEDICINE 322(17):1202-1206, April 26, 1990

ALCOHOL AND PREGNANCY

Preventing alcohol related birth damage: a review, by E. J. Waterson, et al. SOCIAL SCIENCE AND MEDICINE 30(3):349-364, 1990

Recall of alcohol consumption during pregnancy, by N. Robles, et al. JOURNAL OF STUDIES ON ALCOHOL 51:403-407, September 1990

Serum lipids and liproproteins in alcoholic women during pregnancy, by M. Valimaki, et al. METABOLISM 39(5):486-493, May 1990

Smoking and alcohol consumption by Flemish pregnant women: 1966-1983, by E. Lodewijckx, et al. JOURNAL OF BIOSOCIAL SCIENCE 22(1):43-51, January 1990

ALCOHOL AND PRISONS
Consistency of alcohol self-report measures In a male young offender population, by M. McMurran, et al. BRITISH JOURNAL OF ADDICTION 85(2):205-208, February 1990

ALCOHOL AND PUBLIC HEALTH
Alcohol and public health: implications for New York State, by M. T. Saunders. NEW YORK STATE JOURNAL OF MEDICINE 90(1):41, January 1990

Alcohol and tobacco as public health challenges in a democracy, by D. E. Beauchamp. BRITISH JOURNAL OF ADDICTION 85(2):251-254, February 1990

Alcohol as a public health problem: how to continue, by P. Allebeck. LAKARTIDNINGEN 86(40):3388-3389, October 4, 1989

Alcohol: a public health problem—is there a role for the general practitioner, by C. Robertson. JOURNAL OF THE ROYAL SOCIETY OF MEDICINE 83(4):232-236, April 1990

HHS releases special report on alcoholism and health. PUBLIC HEALTH REPORTS 105:214-215, March/April 1990

ALCOHOL AND RELIGION
Characteristics of alcoholism among Catholic sisters: results of a national survey, by V. M. Spiegel. COUNSELING AND VALUES 34(1):51-56, October 1989

Demon rum on the run, by H. A. Snyder. CHRISTIANITY TODAY 34:24-26, June 18, 1990

Religiosity, social class, and alcohol use: an application of reference group theory, by L. Clarke, et al. SOCIOLOGICAL PERSPECTIVES 33(2):201-218, Summer 1990

Spirituality and recovery: relationships between levels of spirituality, contentment and stress during recovery from alcoholism in AA, by J. E. Corrington. ALCOHOL AND ALCOHOLISM 6(3-4):151-165, 1989

ALCOHOL AND SEX (AND SEXUALITY)

Alcohol, AIDS risk and commercial sex: some preliminary results from a Scottish study, by M. L. Plant, et al. DRUG AND ALCOHOL DEPENDENCE 25(1):51-55, February 1990

Alcohol and unsafe sex: an overview of research and theory, by B. C. Leigh. PROGRESS IN CLINICAL AND BIOLOGICAL RESEARCH 325:35-46, 1990

Alcohol, sex and AIDS, by M. A. Plant. ALCOHOL AND ALCOHOLISM 25(2-3):293-301, 1990

Alcohol use and sexual arousal research: application of the health belief model, by D. I. Frank, et al. NURSE PRACTITIONER 15(5):32-35, May 1990

Alcohol use and sexual risk-taking among adolescents: methodological approaches for addressing causal issues, by M. L. Cooper, et al. PROGRESS IN CLINICAL AND BIOLOGICAL RESEARCH 325:11-19, 1990

Alcohol use as a situational influence on young women's pregnancy risk-taking behaviors, by B. Flanigan, et al. ADOLESCENCE 25(97):205-214, Spring 1990

Alcoholism and sex abuse in the family: incest and marital rape, by C. P. Barnard. JOURNAL OF CHEMICAL DEPENDENCY TREATMENT 3(1):131-144, 1989

Beliefs about AIDS, use of alcohol and drugs, and unprotected sex among Massachusetts adolescents, by R. W. Hingson, et al. AMERICAN JOURNAL OF PUBLIC HEALTH 80(3):295-299, March 1990

Chronic alcoholism and low testosterone levels, by D. M. Gallant. ALCOHOLISM 13(5):721, October 1989

Chronic alcoholism and male sexual dysfunction, by R. C. Schiavi. JOURNAL OF SEX AND MARITAL THERAPY 16(1):23-33, Spring 1990

Cigarettes, alcohol and marijuana are related to pyospermia in infertile men, by C. E. Close, et al. JOURNAL OF UROLOGY 144(4):900-903, October 1990

Comparison of AIDS and STD knowledge between sexually active alcohol consumers and abstainers, by S. Nagy, et al. JOURNAL OF SCHOOL HEALTH 60:276-279, August 1990

Prompting bar patrons with signs to take free condoms, by T. J. Honnen, et al. JOURNAL OF APPLIED BEHAVIOR ANALYSIS 23(2):215-217, Summer 1990

Relationship of sex-related alcohol expectancies to alcohol consumption and sexual behavior, by B. C. Leigh. BRITISH JOURNAL OF ADDICTION 85(7):919-928, July 1990

Sex, booze and videotape. MARKETING 95(49):8, December 3, 1990

Sexual relationship of male alcoholics and their female partners during periods of drinking and abstinence, by T. D. Nirenberg, et al. JOURNAL OF STUDIES ON ALCOHOL 51:565-568, November 1990

ALCOHOL AND SEX (AND SEXUALITY)

Social context of alcohol consumption prior to female sexual intercourse, by B. J. Flanigan. JOURNAL OF ALCOHOL AND DRUG EDUCATION 36:97-113, Fall 1990

Use of drugs and alcohol by homosexually active men in relation to sexual practices, by J. McCusker, et al. JOURNAL OF THE ACQUIRED IMMUNE DEFICIENCY SYNDROME 3(7):729-736, 1990

ALCOHOL AND SPORTS

Alcohol advertising and sport: a role for preventive medicine, by G. W. Sivyer. MEDICAL JOURNAL OF AUSTRALIA 153(4):230-231, August 20, 1990

Alcohol and the athlete: a university's response, by J. E. Gay, et al. JOURNAL OF ALCOHOL AND DRUG EDUCATION 35(2):81-86, Winter 1990

Alcohol use among high school athletes: a comparison of alcohol use and intoxication in male and female high school athletes and non-athletes, by C. N. Carr, et al. JOURNAL OF ALCOHOL AND DRUG EDUCATION 36:39-43, Fall 1990

And the loser is: the drinking athlete, by K. M. Porterfield. CURRENT HEALTH 2 17:18-19, October 1990

From the Centers for Disease Control: alcohol use and aquatic activities—Massachusetts. JAMA 264(1):19-20, July 4, 1990

Pete Rose disease, by L. P. Solursh. CMAJ 142(3):209-210, February 1, 1990

Pilot survey of aquatic activities and related consumption of alcohol, with implications for drowning, by J. Howland, et al. PUBLIC HEALTH REPORTERS 105(4):415-419, July/August 1990

Sex-role conflict in female athletes: a possible marker for alcoholism, by D. L. Wetzig. JOURNAL OF ALCOHOL AND DRUG EDUCATION 35(3):45-53, Spring 1990

Sober facts: drinking and skiing do not mix, by S. Bayley. SKI CANADA 18(5):62-63, February 1990

ALCOHOL AND SUICIDE

Alcohol as a provoking factor of suicidal behavior, by A. V. Stoliarov, et al. ZHURNAL NEVROPATOLOGII I PSIKHIATRII IMENI S. S. KORSAKOVA 90(2):55-58, 1990

Alcohol consumption and rates of personal violence, suicide and homicide, by D. Lester. ACTIVITAS NERVOSA SUPERIOR 31(4):248-251, December 1989

Alcoholism and suicide, by H. Hugler. ZEITSCHRIFT FUR ARCHTLICHE FORTBILDUNG 83(16):823-824, 1989

Cerebrospinal fluid monoamine metabolies in alcoholic patients who attempt suicide, by A. Roy, et al. ACTA PSYCHIATRICA SCANDINAVICA 81(1):58-61, January 1990

ALCOHOL AND SUICIDE

Changes in suicide rates after reductions in alcohol consumption and problems in Ontario, 1975-1983, by R. G. Smart, et al. BRITISH JOURNAL OF ADDICTION 85(4): 463-468, April 1990

Characteristics of alcoholics who attempt suicide, by A. Roy, et al. AMERICAN JOURNAL OF PSYCHIATRY 147(6):761-765, June 1990

Lifetime risk of suicide in alcoholism, by G. E. Murphy, et al. ARCHIVES OF GENERAL PSYCHIATRY 47(4):383-392, April 1990

Relationship between alcohol dependency and suicide ideation among high school students, by J. Beer, et al. PSYCHOLOGICAL REPORTS 66(3):1363-1366, 1990

Suicidal alcoholic patients: profile, risk factors and review of the literature from 1955 to 1988, by L. Theret, et al. ANNALES MEDICO-PSYCHOLOGIQUES 147(10): 1092-1094, December 1989

ALCOHOL AND TEENS

Adolescent drinking problem: urban vs. rural differences in Nova Scotia, by W. R. Mitic. CANADIAN JOURNAL OF COMMUNITY MENTAL HEALTH 8(1):5-14, Spring 1989

Adolescent health status, behaviors, and cardiovascular diseases, by M. Adeyanju. ADOLESCENCE 25:155-169, Spring 1990

Adolescents who kill, by J. Arbit, et al. JOURNAL OF CLINICAL PSYCHOLOGY 46(4): 472-485, 1990

Alcohol attitude scale for teen-agers: a short form, by M. R. Torabi. JOURNAL OF SCHOOL HEALTH 59(9):385-388, November 1989

Alcohol consumption of the juvenile population of Cadiz, by M. A. Ruiz Jimenez, et al. ANALES ESPANOLES DE PEDIATRIA 32(5):438-440, May 1990

Alcohol in the life of a teen. CURRENT HEALTH 2 17:4-16+, October 1990

Alcohol use among Latino adolescents: what we know and what we need to know, by M. J. Gilberg. DRUGS AND SOCIETY 3(1-2):35-53, 1988

Alcohol use and abuse among homeless adolescents in Hollywood, by M. J. Robertson, et al. CONTEMPORARY DRUG PROBLEMS 16(3):415-452, Fall 1989

Alcohol use and sexual risk-taking among adolescents: methodological approaches for addressing causal issues, by M. L. Cooper, et al. PROGRESS IN CLINICAL AND BIOLOGICAL RESEARCH 325:11-19, 1990

Beliefs about AIDS, use of alcohol and drugs, and unprotected sex among Massachusetts adolescents, by R. W. Hingson, et al. AMERICAN JOURNAL OF PUBLIC HEALTH 80(3):295-299, March 1990

Biological maturation in adolescence and the development of drinking habits and alcohol abuse among young males: a prospective longitudinal study, by T. Andersson, et al. JOURNAL OF YOUTH AND ADOLESCENCE 19(1):33-41, February 1990

Comparison of alcohol, tobacco, and illicit drug use among students and delinquents in the Bahamas, by R. G. Smart, et al. BULLETIN OF THE PAN AMERICAN HEALTH ORGANIZATION 24(1):39-45, 1990

Contributions of delinquency and substance use to school dropout among inner-city youths, by J. Fagan, et al. YOUTH AND SOCIETY 21(3):306-354, March 1990

Cross-cultural and cognitive factors examined in groups of adolescent drinkers, by J. C. Brannock, et al. JOURNAL OF DRUG ISSUES 20(3):427-442, Summer 1990

Development of psychosocial scales for the assessment of adolescents involved with alcohol and drugs, by G. A. Henly, et al. INTERNATIONAL JOURNAL OF THE ADDICTIONS 24(10):973-1001, October 1989

Differences between white and black youth who drink heavily, by C. L. Ringwalt, et al. ADDICTIVE BEHAVIORS 15(5):455-460, 1990

Drinking in America: portrait of a teenage alcoholic— I, by A. N. LeBlanc. SEVENTEEN 49:179-183, March 1990

Drinking in America: portrait of a teenage alcoholic—II, by A. N. LeBlanc. SEVENTEEN 49:77-80, April 1990

Drunk driving, sensation seeking, and egocentrism among adolescents, by J. Arnett. PERSONALITY AND INDIVIDUAL DIFFERENCES 11(6):541-546, 1990

Juvenile alcohol use and self-destructive behaviour in northern populations: a cross-cultural comparison, by L. Jilek-Aall. ARCTIC MEDICAL RESEARCH 47(Suppl)1:604-610, 1988

Problem of teenage drinking, by M. C. McClellan. PHI DELTA KAPPAN 71:810-813, June 1990

Relationship of physical activity to alcohol consumption in youths 15-16 years of age, by R. A. Faulkner, et al. CANADIAN JOURNAL OF PUBLIC HEALTH 81(2):168-169, March/April 1990

Review of correlates of alcohol use and alcohol problems in adolescence, by K. K. Bucholz. RECENT DEVELOPMENTS IN ALCOHOLISM 8:111-123, 1990

Skin resistance reaction to alcohol-related verbal stimuli in alcoholic adolescents, by A. V. Nemtsov. ZHURNAL NEVROPATOLOGII I PSIKHIATRII IMENI S. S. KORSAKOVA 89(8):112-117, 1989

Sleep loss hits teen tipplers, by B. Thompson. JOURNAL OF THE ADDICTION RESEARCH FOUNDATION 19(11):4, November 1, 1990

Teenage heavy drinkers: alcohol-related knowledge, beliefs, experiences, motivation and the social context of drinking, by M. A. Plant, et al. ALCOHOL AND ALCOHOLISM 25(6):691-698, 1990

ALCOHOL AND TEENS

Validating and improving the validity of self-reports in adolescent substance misuse surveys, by H. Swadi. JOURNAL OF DRUG ISSUES 20:473-486, Summer 1990

Young people and drinking: results of an English national survey, by M. Plant, et al. ALCOHOL AND ALCOHOLISM 25(6):685-690, 1990

Youths and alcohol: drinking behavior of young people, by M. Reissig. ARZTLICHE JUGENDKUNDE 81(2):117-127, 1990

ALCOHOL AND TRANSPLANTS
In vino veritas: alcoholics and liver transplantation, by K. Schwartzman. CMAJ 141(12):1262-1265, December 15, 1989

Influence of cyclosporine on abstinence from alcohol in transplant patients, by H. G. Giles, et al. TRANSPLANTATION 49(6):1201-1202, June 1990

Liver transplantation: an update for physicians, by K. Powell. AUSTRALIAN AND NEW ZEALAND JOURNAL OF MEDICINE 20(1):100-101, February 1990

ALCOHOL AND WOMEN
Alcohol and women's health: a cause for concern, by A. Wodak. HEALTHRIGHT 9:17-22, May 1990

Alcohol consumption and cancers of hormone-related organs in females, by I. Kato, et al. JAPANESE JOURNAL OF CLINICAL ONCOLOGY 19(3):202-207, September 1989

Alcohol consumption and menstrual distress in women at higher and lower risk for alcoholism, by L. Charette, et al. ALCOHOLISM 14(2):152-157, April 1990

Alcohol effects on cognitive and personality style in women with special reference to primary and secondary process, by R. Gustafson, et al. ALCOHOLISM 13(5):644-648, October 1989

Alcohol effects on plasma estradiol levels following LHRH administration to women, by J. H. Mendelson, et al. NIDA RESEARCH MONOGRAPH SERIES 95:425, 1989

Alcohol gender gap: women feel it faster—effect of having less of enzyme alcohol dehydrogenase, by J. Seligmann. NEWSWEEK 115:53, January 22, 1990

Alcohol use and premenstrual symptoms in social drinkers, by N. K. Mello, et al. PSYCHOPHARMACOLOGY 101(4):448-455, 1990

Alcohol use as a situational influence on young women's pregnancy risk-taking behaviors, by B. Flanigan, et al. ADOLESCENCE 25(97):205-214, Spring 1990

Alcoholic housewives and role satisfaction, by B. Farid, et al. ALCOHOL AND ALCOHOLISM 24(4):331-337, 1989

Anterior pituitary, gonadal and adrenal hormones in women with alcohol and polydrug abuse, by S. K. Teoh, et al. NIDA RESEARCH MONOGRAPH SERIES 95:481-482, 1989

ALCOHOL AND WOMEN

Are women drinking more like men: an empirical examination of the convergence hypothesis, by P. W. Mercer, et al. ALCOHOLISM: CLINICAL AND EXPERIMENTAL RESEARCH 14(3):461-466, June 1990

Characteristics of women receiving mandated treatment for alcohol and polysubstance dependence in Massachusetts, by B. W. Lex, et al. DRUG AND ALCOHOL DEPENDENCE 25(1):13-20, February 1990

Cheers: the sobering news about women and alcohol: diminished levels of alcohol dehydrogenase means women get drunk faster than men, by D. Sobel. MADEMOISELLE 96:138, May 1990

Clinical and neurohumoral indicators in women-alcoholics of reproductive and climacteric age, by V. Semke, et al. ZHURNAL NEVROPATOLOGII I PSIKHIATRII IMENI S. S. KORSAKOVA 90(2):71-73, 1990

Clinical characteristics of female alcoholics with low platelet monoamine oxidase activity, by J. Hallman, et al. ALCOHOLISM: CLINICAL AND EXPERIMENTAL RESEARCH 14(2):227-231, April 1990

Comparison of 7-day retrospective and prospective alcohol consumption diaries in a female population in Perth, Western Australia: methodological issues, by B. Corti, et al. BRITISH JOURNAL OF ADDICTION 85(3):379-388, March 1990

Could you stop drinking for a month, by S. Jacoby. GLAMOUR 88:288-289+, April 1990

Delinquency, childhood violence, and the development of alcoholism in women, by B. A. Miller, et al. CRIME AND DELINQUENCY 35:94-108, January 1989

Drinking and smoking at 3 months postpartum by lactation history, by R. E. Little, et al. PAEDIATRIC AND PERINATAL EPIDEMIOLOGY 4(3):290-302, July 1990

Drinking in America: portrait of a teenage alcoholic— I, by A. N. LeBlanc. SEVENTEEN 49:179-183, March 1990

Drowning the sorrow: treating alcoholism and depression in women—research by Deborah Goldman, by J. Newman. AMERICAN HEALTH 9:32, June 1990

Family treatment for homeless alcohol/drug-addicted women and their preschool children, by M. Comfort, et al. ALCOHOLISM TREATMENT QUARTERLY 7(1): 129-147, 1990

Female alcohol abuser: vulnerability to multiple organ damage, by D. M. Gallant. ALCOHOLISM 14(2):260, April 1990

Female alcoholics: II—the expression of alcoholism in relation to gender and age, by A. Blankfield. ACTA PSYCHIATRICA SCANDINAVICA 81(5):448-452, May 1990

Female alcoholics: III—some clinical associations of the Michigan Alcoholism Screening Test and diagnostic implications, by A. Blankfield, et al. ACTA PSYCHIATRICA SCANDINAVICA 81(5):483-487, May 1990

Health and other characteristics of employed women and homemakers in Tecumseh, 1959-1978: I—demographic characteristics, smoking habits, alcohol consumption, and pregnancy outcomes and conditions, by M. H. Higgins, et al. WOMEN AND HEALTH 16(2):5-21, 1990

Marijuana and alcohol effects on mood states in young women, by B. W. Lex, et al. NIDA RESEARCH MONOGRAPH SERIES 95:462, 1989

Operant acquisition of alcohol by women, by N. K. Mello, et al. JOURNAL OF PHAR-MACOLOGY AND EXPERIMENTAL THERAPEUTICS 253(1):237-245, April 1990

Outreach and engagement for homeless women at risk of alcoholism, by S. Ridlen, et al. ALCOHOLISM TREATMENT QUARTERLY 7(1):99-109, 1990

Patriarchy and recovery in AA: discussion of December 6, 1989 article, "Twelve Steps for Women Alcoholics," by G. Unterberger. CHRISTIANITY TODAY 107:338-340, April 4, 1990

Pituitary-gonadal hormones and adrenal androgens in non-cirrhotic female alcoholics after cessation of alcohol intake, by M. Valimaki, et al. EUROPEAN JOURNAL OF CLINICAL INVESTIGATION 20(2):177-181, April 1990

Providing services for women with difficulties with alcohol or other drugs: the current United Kingdom situation as seen by women practitioners, researchers and policy makers in the field, by J. Waterson, et al. DRUG AND ALCOHOL DEPENDENCE 24(2):119-125, October 1989

Psychologists and alcoholic women, by J. B. Murray. PSYCHOLOGICAL REPORTS 64:627-644, April 1989

Psychosocial correlates of alcohol intake among women aged 45 to 64 years: the Framingham study, by K. Hamlett, et al. JOURNAL OF BEHAVIORAL MEDICINE 12(6):525-542, December 1989

Relation of moderate alcohol consumption and risk of systemic hypertension in women, by J. C. Witteman, et al. AMERICAN JOURNAL OF CARDIOLOGY 65(9): 633-637, March 1, 1990

Review and analysis of literature on indicators of women's drinking problems, by C. Schmidt, et al. BRITISH JOURNAL OF ADDICTION 85(2):179-182, February 1990

Rhetorical dimensions of institutional language: a case study of women alcoholics, by L. M. Hallberg. DAI A 50(4):1113, October 1989

Self-esteem and purpose in life: a comparative study of women alcoholics, by S. Schlesinger, et al. JOURNAL OF ALCOHOL AND DRUG EDUCATION 36:127-141, Fall 1990

Sex-role conflict in female athletes: a possible marker for alcoholism, by D. L. Wetzig. JOURNAL OF ALCOHOL AND DRUG EDUCATION 35:45-53, Spring 1990

Social context of alcohol consumption prior to female sexual intercourse, by B. J. Flanigan. JOURNAL OF ALCOHOL AND DRUG EDUCATION 36:97-113, Fall 1990

ALCOHOL AND WOMEN

Structure of depression in alcoholic women, by J. E. Turnbull, et al. JOURNAL OF STUDIES ON ALCOHOL 51(2):148-155, March 1990

Structure of psychological defense mechanisms in women as a function of alcohol intoxication, by R. Gustafson, et al. ALCOHOLISM 13(6):772-775, December 1989

Tradeswoman: and addicted, by K. Barbara. TRADESWOMAN 9(3):28, Summer 1990

Treatment failures: the role of sexual victimization in women's addictive behavior, by M. P. P. Root. AMERICAN JOURNAL OF ORTHOPSYCHIATRY 59(4):542-549, October 1989

True blue: former addict's relationship with cat, by E. Drenick. NEW YORK TIMES MAGAZINE October 7, 1990, p. 24+

Why liquor is quicker for women: gastric system has less of enzyme alcohol dehydrogenase. US NEWS AND WORLD REPORT 108:13, January 22, 1990

Why men can outdrink women: it's not a matter of macho, but of enzymes, by A. Toufexis. TIME 135(4):53, January 22, 1990

Why men can outdrink women: less enzyme alcohol dehydrogenase in women's gastric system, by A. Toufexis. TIME 135:61, January 22, 1990

Women and alcohol: a gastric disadvantage: role of alcohol dehydrogenase, by J. Raloff. SCIENCE NEWS 137(3):39, January 20, 1990

Women and alcohol: mother's ruin: society's attitude to female drinkers, by M.C. Mason. GUARDIAN May 1, 1990, p. 21

Women and alcohol: trends in Australia, by B. Corti, et al. MEDICAL JOURNAL OF AUSTRALIA 152(12):625-632, June 18, 1990

Women for sobriety: a qualitative analysis, by L. Kaskutas. CONTEMPORARY DRUG PROBLEMS 16(2):177-200, Summer 1989

Women with alcohol problems, by S. Fauske, et al. TIDSSKRIFT FOR DEN NORSKE LAEGEFORENING 110(13):1700-1703, May 20, 1990

ALPRAZOLAM

Alprazolam use and dependence: a retrospective analysis of 30 cases of withdrawal, by B. Dickinson, et al. WESTERN JOURNAL OF MEDICINE 152(5):604-608, May 1990

Detoxification with phenobarbital of alprazolam-dependence polysubstance abusers, by N. V. Ravi, et al. JOURNAL OF SUBSTANCE ABUSE TREATMENT 7(1):55-58, 1990

AMANTADINE

Acute psychosis after amantadine overdose, by E. R. Snoey, et al. ANNALS OF EMERGENCY MEDICINE 19(6):668-670, June 1990

AMERICAN BAR ASSOCIATION (ABA)

ABA fights the drug war, by C. E. Anderson. ABA JOURNAL 76:63, February 1990

ABA toughens marijuana stand, by S. B. Goldberg. ABA JOURNAL 76:105, April 1990

AMERICAN CIVIL LIBERTIES UNION (ACLU)
ACLU challenges traffic check lanes in court. CRIME CONTROL DIGEST 23(40):9, October 9, 1989

ACLU philosophy and the right to abuse the unborn, by P. E. Johnson. CRIMINAL JUSTICE ETHICS 9(1):48-51, 1990

AMINEPTINE
Case of amineptine dependence, by J. C. Perez de los Cobos, et al. ENCEPHALE 16(1):41-42, January/February 1990

AMITRIPTYLINE
Accidental amitriptyline poisoning in a toddler, by D. W. Beal, et al. SOUTHERN MEDICAL JOURNAL 82(12):1588-1589, December 1989

Amitriptyline overdose complicated by intestinal pseudo-obstruction and caecal per-foration, by A. J. McMahon. POSTGRADUATE MEDICAL JOURNAL 65(770):948-949, December 1989

Case of amitriptyline abuse, by J. D. Delisle. AMERICAN JOURNAL OF PSYCHIATRY 147(10):1377-1378, October 1990

Toxicological findings after fatal amitriptyline self-poisoning, by A. Tracqui, et al. HU-MAN AND EXPERIMENTAL TOXICOLOGY 9(4):257-261, July 1990

Why do amitriptyline and dothiepin appear to be so dangerous in overdose?, by S. A. Montgomery, et al. ACTA PSYCHIATRICA SCANDINAVICA 354(Suppl):47-53, 1989

AMPHETAMINES
Administration of laughing gas during labor may cause later amphetamine addiction in the offspring, by K. A. Salvesen. TIDSSKRIFT FOR DEN NORSKE LAEGE-FORENING 109(32):3363-3364, November 20, 1989

Amphetamine and cocaine induce drug-specific activation of the *c-fos* gene in strio-some-matrix compartments and limbic subdivisions of the striatum, by A. M. Gray-biel, et al. PROCEEDINGS OF THE NATIONAL ACADEMY OF SCIENCES USA 87(17):6912-6916, September 1990

Amphetamines: aggressive and social behavior, by K. A. Miczek, et al. NIDA RE-SEARCH MONOGRAPH SERIES 94:68-100, 1989

Effect of haloperidol in cocaine and amphetamine intoxication, by R. W. Derlet, et al. JOURNAL OF EMERGENCY MEDICINE 7(6):633-637, November/December 1989

AMPHETAMINES

Impurities in illicit drug preparations: amphetamine and methamphetamine, by A. M. A.Verweij. FORENSIC SCIENCE REVIEW 1(1):1-11, 1989

Complications

Acute myocardial infarction caused by intravenous amphetamine abuse, by G. E. Packe, et al. BRITISH HEART JOURNAL 64(1):23-24, July 1990

Bladder outflow obstruction secondary to intravenous amphetamine abuse, by J. Worsey, et al. BRITISH JOURNAL OF UROLOGY 64(3):320-321, September 1989

Case of amphetamine poisoning manifesting rhabdomyolysis and reversible cardio-cyopathy, by F. Yamazaki, et al. NIPPON NAIKA GAKKAI ZASSHI 79(1):100-101, January 10, 1990

Case of hypertrophic cardiomyopathy associated with amphetamine abuse, by Y. Tanaka, et al. NIPPON NAIKA GAKKAI ZASSHI 78(7):944-948, July 1989

Intracranial haemorrhage caused by amphetamine abuse, by M. P. Lessing, et al. JOURNAL OF THE ROYAL SOCIETY OF MEDICINE 82(12):766-767, December 1989

Intraventricular hemorrhage following amphetamine abuse, by J. Imanse, et al. NEU-ROLOGY 40(8):1318-1319, August 1990

Neurologic complications caused by use of cocaine, amphetamines and sympatho-mimetics, by E. Diez-Tejedor, et al. ARCHIVOS DE NEUROBIOLOGIA 52 (Suppl)1:162-182, 1989

Stroke from alcohol and drug abuse: a current social peril, by P. B. Goerlick. POST-GRADUATE MEDICINE 88(2):171-174+, August 1990

Research

Alpha-methyl-p-tyrosine partially attenuates p-chloroamphetamine-induced 5-hydroxytryptamine depletions in the rat brains, by K. J. Axt, et al. PHARMACOL-OGY, BIOCHEMISTRY AND BEHAVIOR 35(4):995-997, April 1990

Behavioral effects of cocaine and its interaction with d-amphetamine and morphine in rats, by G. R. Wenger, et al. PHARMACOLOGY, BIOCHEMISTRY AND BEHAV-IOR 35(3):595-600, March 1990

Central action of psychomotor stimulants on glucose utilization in extrapyramidal mo-tor areas of the rat brain, by E. D. London, et al. BRAIN RESEARCH 512(1):155-158, March 26, 1990

Characteristics of the binding of N-isopropyl-p-[125I]iodoamphetamine in the rat brain synaptosomal membranes, by H. Mori, et al. NUCLEAR MEDICINE COMMUNI-CATIONS 11(4):327-331, April 1990

Chronic amphetamine intoxication and the blood-brain barrier permeability to inert polar molecules studied in the vascularly perfused guinea pig brain, by L. M. Rakic, et al. JOURNAL OF THE NEUROLOGICAL SCIENCES 94(1-3):41-50, December 1989

Novel and neurotoxic tetrahydroisoquinoline derivative in vivo: formation of 1,3-dimethyl-1,2,3,4-tetrahydroisoquinoline, a condensation product of amphetamines, in brains of rats under chronic ethanol treatment, by Y. Makino, et al. JOURNAL OF NEUROCHEMISTRY 55(3):963-969, September 1990

Stimulus effects of N-monoethyl-1-[3,4-methylenedioxyphenyl]-2-aminopropane (MDE) and N-hydroxy-1-[3,4-methylenedioxyphenyl]-2-aminopropane (N-OH MDA) in rats trained to discriminative MDMA from saline, by R. A. Glennon, et al. PHARMACOLOGY, BIOCHEMISTRY AND BEHAVIOR 33(4):909-912, August 1989

Structure-affinity study of the binding of 4-substituted analogues of 1-[2,5-dimethoxyphenyl]-2-aminopropane at 5-HT2 serotonin receptors, by M. R. Seggel, et al. JOURNAL OF MEDICINAL CHEMISTRY 33(3):1032-1036, March 1990

ANALEPTICS
Narcolepsy, paranoid psychosis, and analeptic abuse, by G. B. Leong, et al. PSYCHIATRIC JOURNAL OF THE UNIVERSITY OF OTTAWA 14(3):481-483, September 1989

ANALGESIA/ANALGESICS
Compound analgesics, by A. H. Dawson, et al. MEDICAL JOURNAL OF AUSTRALIA 152(6):334, March 19, 1990

Consumption of, overdose and fatal poisoning with analgesics in Denmark 1979-1986, by P. Ott, et al. UGESKRIFT FOR LAEGER 152(4):250-252, January 22, 1990

Topical anesthetic abuse, by G. O. Rosenwasser, et al. OPHTHALMOLOGY 97(8):967-972, August 1990

Complications
Analgesic abuse and hypertension, by G. Kuster, et al. LANCET 2(8671):1105, November 4, 1989

ANTICHOLINERGIC DRUGS
Abuse of anticholinergic agents, by B. P. Dieleman, et al. NEDERLANDS TIJDSCHRIFT VOOR GENEESKUNDE 134(13):625-627, March 31, 1990

Anticholinergic drug abuse, by H. A. Hidalgo, et al. DICP 24(1):40-41, January 1990

Characterizing anticholinergic abuse in community mental health, by B. G. Wells, et al. JOURNAL OF CLINICAL PSYCHOPHARMACOLOGY 9(6):431-435, December 1989

ANTIDEPRESSANTS
Antidepressant toxicity, by A. K. Banerjee. BRITISH JOURNAL OF PSYCHIATRY 155:267-268, August 1989

ANTIDEPRESSANTS

Norweigian data on death due to overdose of antidepressants, by N. Retterstol. ACTA PSYCHIATRICA SCANDINAVICA 354(Suppl):61-68, 1989

Suicide and antidepressant overdosage in general practice, by G. Beaumont. BRITISH JOURNAL OF PSYCHIATRY (6):27-31, October 1989

Toxicity of antidepressants, by G. Beaumont. BRITISH JOURNAL OF PSYCHIATRY 154:454-458, April 1989

Toxicity of antidepressants, by K. Matthews, et al. BRITISH JOURNAL OF PSYCHIATRY 155:420, September 1989

Why do fatal overdose rates vary between antidepressants?, by R. D. Farmer, et al. ACTA PSYCHIATRICA SCANDINAVICA 354(Suppl):25-35, 1989

ANTITUSSIVES
Clinical reports on recent abuse of an antitussive, by E. Tempesta, et al. BRITISH JOURNAL OF ADDICTION 85(6):815-816, June 1990

ANXIOLYTICS
Abuse liability of anxiolytics and sedative-hypnotics: methods assessing the likelihood of abuse, by J. D. Roache, et al. NIDA RESEARCH MONOGRAPH SERIES 92:123-146, 1989

Addiction potential of benzodiazepines and non-benzodiazepine anxiolytics, by J. D. Roache. ADVANCES IN ALCOHOL AND SUBSTANCE ABUSE 9(1-2):103-128, Spring 1990

ARF   (ADDICTION RESEARCH FOUNDATION)
Addiction Research Foundation: a voyage of discovery (book review), by H. D. Archibald. JOURNAL OF THE ADDICTION RESEARCH FOUNDATION 19(10):10, October 1, 1990

ARF recommends ban on all drink ads. JOURNAL OF THE ADDICTION RESEARCH FOUNDATION 19(12):11-12, December 1, 1990

ARF to move on liver drug: propylithiouracil (PTU), by J. Hollobon. JOURNAL OF THE ADDICTION RESEARCH FOUNDATION 19(4):1-2, April 1, 1990

ATTITUDES
ACLU philosophy and the right to abuse the unborn, by P. E. Johnson. CRIMINAL JUSTICE ETHICS 9(1):48-51, 1990

American drug panic of the 1980s: social construction or objective threat, by E. Goode. VIOLENCE, AGGRESSION AND TERRORISM 3(4):327-348, 1989

Blacks see racism at bottom of Barry bust, by C. Hardy. GUARDIAN 42(16):4, February 14, 1990

Canadians accuse United States of "hysteria" over drugs, by L. Dayton. NEW SCIENTIST 125:19, February 24, 1990

ATTITUDES

Critical analysis of drug war alternatives: the need for a shift in personal and social values, by L. S. Wong. JOURNAL OF DRUG ISSUES 20:679-688, Fall 1990

Drug and alcohol attitudes and usage among elementary and secondary students, by G. P. Fournet, et al. JOURNAL OF ALCOHOL AND DRUG EDUCATION 35(3):81-92, Spring 1990

Drug problems in perspective: legal and easily-obtainable drugs cause more problems than illicit substances. HEALTH NEWS 8(3):1-10, June 1990

Drug use, crime, and the attitudes of magistrates, by A. Johns, et al. MEDICINE, SCIENCE AND THE LAW 30(3):263-270, July 1990

Drug use "unfashionable" for United States high-school seniors, by H. McConnell. JOURNAL OF THE ADDICTION RESEARCH FOUNDATION 19(4):8, April 1, 1990

Drugs, consciousness and self-control: popular and medical conceptions, by R. Room. INTERNATIONAL REVIEW OF PSYCHIATRY 1(1-2):63-70, March 1989

Instrument for the measurement of individual and societal attitudes toward drugs, by D. Green. INTERNATIONAL JOURNAL OF THE ADDICTIONS 25(2):141-158, 1990

Legalization of illicit drugs: a law enforcement response, by E. J. Tully, et al. CANADIAN POLICE COLLEGE JOURNAL 13(4):283-291, 1989

Legalization too simplistic, by A. MacLennan. JOURNAL OF THE ADDICTION RESEARCH FOUNDATION 19(6):1, June 1, 1990

Legalizing drug use: is it the only realistic solution: no, by E. Koch. ABA JOURNAL 75:37, January 1989

Legalizing drug use: is it the only realistic solution: yes, by K. Schmoke. ABA JOURNAL 75:36, January 1989

Legalizing drugs: a few simple questions, by D. A. Zohn. VIRGINIA MEDICINE 117(6): 250-251, June 1990

Legally bombed: many respectable thinkers now believe that a society hooked on drugs should simply legalize them, by G. Jonas. SATURDAY NIGHT 105(7):34-39+, September 1990

Letter to President George Bush from a summer neighbor on drugs in our schools, by D. M. McConnell. EDUCATION 111:214-221, Winter 1990

New York Times/CBS drug poll supports Bush's strategy. NARCOTICS DEMAND REDUCTION DIGEST 1(5):3-4, October 1989

Nosologic objections to the criminal defense of pathological intoxication: what do the doubters doubt?, by L. P. Tiffany, et al. INTERNATIONAL JOURNAL OF LAW AND PSYCHIATRY 13(1-2):49-75, 1990

Not one cent for defense either: an appeal for more public indifference, by R. R. Korn. SOCIAL JUSTICE 16(2):188-191, Summer 1989

ATTITUDES

Notes and comment: symmetry between drug war and cold war. NEW YORKER 65: 21-22, January 1, 1990

Our national drug policy: drugs have created an environment of terror in our country, yet we lack a coherent national policy to fight the drug war, by C. Rangel. STANFORD LAW AND POLICY REVIEW 1:43-56, Fall 1989

Perception of drugs and support for social policy, by W. L. Grichting, et al. JOURNAL OF ALCOHOL AND DRUG EDUCATION 36:7-21, Fall 1990

Pet theories intoxicate drug legalization advocates, by J. J. Kilpatrick. HUMAN EVENTS 50:16, June 13, 1990

Pharmacy students attitudes toward the need for university implemented policies regarding alcohol and drug use, by S. L. Szeinbach, et al. AMERICAN JOURNAL OF PHARMACEUTICAL EDUCATION 54(2):155-158, Summer 1990

Poles now hostile to drug users. JOURNAL OF THE ADDICTION RESEARCH FOUNDATION 19(6):4, June 1, 1990

Professional vs. personal factors related to physicians' attitudes toward drug testing, by L. S. Linn, et al. JOURNAL OF DRUG EDUCATION 20(2):95-109, 1990

"Public enemy no. 1": police appear unhappy with the leniency of the courts, by E. Saenger. BC REPORT 1(39):24, June 4, 1990

Racial differences in attitudes toward crime control, by P. E. Secret, et al. JOURNAL OF CRIMINAL JUSTICE 17(5):361-375, 1989

Researchers say debate over drug war and legalization is tied to Americans' cultural and religious values, by C. Raymond. CHRONICLE OF HIGHER EDUCATION 36:6-7+, March 7, 1990

SAG's take stand on youth death penalty-drug abuse. JUVENILE JUSTICE DIGEST 17(19):6, October 4, 1989

Saying "no" to legalized drugs, by M. Parenti. POLITICAL AFFAIRS 68:8-10, November 1989

Scholars are irked by Bennett speech criticizing their approaches to nation's drug problems, by S. Jaschik. CHRONICLE OF HIGHER EDUCATION 36:1+, January 3, 1990

Schoolchildren's views on drug use and abuse, by V. V. Gul'dman, et al. SOTSIO-LOGICHESKIE ISSLEDOVANIYA 16(3):66-71, 1989

Should some illegal drugs be legalized: three experts debate whether current law enforcement and public health policies ought to be extended, improved or replaced. ISSUES IN SCIENCE AND TECHNOLOGY 6:43-49, Summer 1990

Student attitudes toward a campus drug-testing program, by D. Thombs, et al. JOURNAL OF COLLEGE STUDENT DEVELOPMENT 31:283-284, May 1990

Student attitudes toward drug testing of college athletes, by L. S. Hamilton, et al. PHYSICAL EDUCATION 47:33-36, Spring 1990

ATTITUDES

Survey of general practitioners' opinion and attitude to drug addicts and addiction, by R. T. Abed, et al. BRITISH JOURNAL OF ADDICTION 85(1):131-136, January 1990

When boundaries disappear: how will Europe be policed when its frontiers are removed in 1992?, by S. R. Baker. POLICING 4(4):281-292, 1988

Whipping up that drug-war spirit, by M. Reiss. IN THESE TIMES 14(9):5, January 17, 1990

Why we must win the war against drugs: education is crucial in changing attidudes, by R. B. Walton. UPDATE ON LAW-RELATED EDUCATION 14(1):3-5, Winter 1990

Widespread public opposition to drug legalization: a majority of Americans consider education the answer, by D. Colasanto. GALLUP POLE MONTHLY January 1990, pp. 2-8

Worthless crusade: drug prohibition, by R. King. NEWSWEEK 115(1):4-5, January 1, 1990   BARBITURATES Abuse liability of barbiturates and other sedative-hyponotics, by W. W. Morgan. ADVANCES IN ALCOHOL AND SUBSTANCE ABUSE 9(1-2):67-82, Spring 1990

BARBITURATES
Pulmonary embolism complicating barbiturate overdose, by J. Toscano, et al. CRITICAL CARE MEDICINE 18(7):777-778, July 1990

Research
Effects of acute barbiturate administration, tolerance and dependence on brain GABA system: comparison to alcohol and benzodiazepines, by S. Yu, et al. ALCOHOL 7(3):261-272, May/June 1990

Increased response of cellular cGMP to kainate but not NMDA or quisqualate following barbital withdrawal from dependent rats, by P. P. McCaslin, et al. EUROPEAN JOURNAL OF PHARMACOLOGY 173(2-3):127-132, December 7, 1989

BARRY, MARION
Apartheid on the Potomac: M. Barry's trial, by F. Bruning. MACLEAN'S 103:11, July 30, 1990

Barry beats the rap, by J. N. Baker. NEWSWEEK 116:43-44, August 20, 1990

Barry bust: Mayor M. Barry arrested on drug charge in Washington, D.C. NEW REPUBLIC 202:8-10, February 12, 1990

Barry calls for "healing" in D.C. after his victory in drug and perjury trial. JET 78:16-18, August 27, 1990

Barry makes heroic return to D.C. as loyalists raise funds for his legal defense. JET 77:8, April 2, 1990

Barry: the mayor's last-ditch strategy? NEWSWEEK 115:19, June 25, 1990

Barry: new charges, new pressures. NEWSWEEK 115:44, February 26, 1990

Barry to appeal six-month prison term, $5,000 fine in D.C. drug case sentence. JET 79:4-5, November 12, 1990

Barry's decision not to seek re-election ignites political scramble for D.C. mayorship. JET 78:8, July.2, 1990

Barry's free ride: Mayor M. Barry. NEW REPUBLIC 202:7, May 7, 1990

Blacks see racism at bottom of Barry bust, by C. Hardy. GUARDIAN 42(16):4, February 14, 1990

Busting the mayor: Marion Barry is arrested on a cocaine charge in Washington, by T. Morganthau. NEWSWEEK 115(5):24-28, January 29, 1990

Bye-bye, Barry. TIME 135:23, June 25, 1990

Capital scandal: Washington Mayor M. Barry faces cocaine charge, by H. Mackenzie. MACLEAN'S 103:30-31, January 29, 1990

Case of Marion Barry: political persuasion and self-denial—attempt by mayor to blame alcoholism for his problems, by R. E. Vatz, et al. USA TODAY 119:88-89, September 1990

Colombains angry about Mayor Barry trial verdict. CRIME CONTROL DIGEST 24(23): 1-4, August 20, 1990

Crack in the Washington culture: M. Barry's drug arrest, by J. Morley. NATION 250: 221+, February 19, 1990

Effi Barry reveals: mayor wanted her skin darkened to protect his image as a black man. JET 78:12-15+, July 23, 1990

Effi Barry stands by Mayor Barry through thick and thin, by R. L. Haywood. JET 72:12-13+, February 19, 1990

FBI video tape becomes key element in Barry trial. JET 78:14-16, July 16, 1990

"I guess you all figured that I couldn't resist that lady": videotape shown at M. Barry trial, by M. Riley. TIME 136:19, July 9, 1990

Indicted for perjury and cocaine possession, Barry declares he'll be cleared. JET 77:13, March 5, 1990

Looking for a pattern: new drug charges against Mayor Barry, by J. N. Baker. NEWS-WEEK 115:33, May 21, 1990

Mayor Barry: lurid tales of the tape, by G. Hackett. NEWSWEEK 116:25, July 9, 1990

Mixed verdict divided city: M. Barry's trial ends. TIME 136:48, August 20, 1990

Model and the mayor: R. Moore's involvement with M. Barry, by M. Miller. NEWS-WEEK 115:21, February 5, 1990

BARRY, MARION

Old flame draws Mayor Marion Barry into the fire: role of R. Moore in Washington drug bust, by M. Brower. PEOPLE WEEKLY 33:38-49, February 5, 1990

Racial injustice: questioning Judge T. P. Jackson's stiff sentence for M. Barry. TIME 136:42, November 12, 1990

Rough justice: verdict in M. Barry trial, by H. Schwartz. NATION 251:224-225, September 10, 1990

Run, Barry, run: aftermath of Mayor M. Barry's indictment for drug use, by J. Johnson. TIME 135:19-20, February 5, 1990

Tearful Mayor Barry delegates duties and leaves for Florida to heal "mind, body, soul," by D. M. Cheers. JET 77:4-5+, February 5, 1990

Thoughts on Mayor Barry, by M. Greenfield. NEWSWEEK 115:66, June 25, 1990

Wife Effi and loyal staff help Marion Barry hold on to leadership in D.C., by S. Booker. JET 77:4-6+, February 12, 1990

Wife endures trial by scandal: E. Barry, wife of Washington mayor M. Barry, by M. Brower. PEOPLE WEEKLY 34:34-36, July 16, 1990

You set me up: a drug bust could be the last straw for Washington's mayor, by M. Riley. TIME 135(5):30, January 29, 1990

BENNETT, WILLIAM J.

Bennett anti-drug plan would expand criminal justice system. CRIMINAL JUSTICE NEWSLETTER 20(17):1-3, September 1, 1989

Bennett calls for shooting down drug smuggling aircraft. CORPORATE SECURITY DIGEST 3(37):3, September 18, 1989

Bennett explains drug plan, by R. O'Connell. CRIME CONTROL DIGEST 23(37):2-4, September 18, 1989

Curbing the drug supply requires reducing demand, swift, certain punishment, by W. J. Benentt. NARCOTICS CONTROL DIGEST 19(22):2-4, June 7, 1989

Just say whoa: J. Bennett resigns as drug czar. TIME 136:91, November 19, 1990

Just say whoa: United States antidrug czar says his job is done, but critics are skeptical. TIME 136(22):64, November 19, 1990

Notes and comment: W. Bennett's comment that drug war will increase need for orphanages. NEW YORKER 66:21-22, July 23, 1990

"People are resisting": interview with drug czar W. J. Bennett. US NEWS AND WORLD REPORT 108:18-19, February 19, 1990

Two William Bennetts, by M. Massing. NEW YORK REVIEW OF BOOKS 37:29-33, March 1, 1990

William Bennett: drug policy coordinator, by J. S. Podesta. PEOPLE WEEKLY 33: 97+, June 11, 1990

BENZODIAZEPINES

Abuse liability and the regulatory control of therapeutic drugs: untested assumptions, by J. H. Woods. DRUG AND ALCOHOL DEPENDENCE 25(2):229-233, April 1990

Addiction potential of benzodiazepines and non-benzodiazepine anxiolytics, by J. D. Roache. ADVANCES IN ALCOHOL AND SUBSTANCE ABUSE 9(1-2):103-128, Spring 1990 .

Anxiety disorders and the use and abuse of drugs, by S. M. Roth. JOURNAL OF CLINICAL PSYCHIATRY 50(Suppl):30-35, November 1989

Are there differences in the dependence potential of benzodiazepines?, by W. E. Muller. ACTA PSYCHIATRICA SCANDINAVICA 80(5):526, November 1989

Association between non-recreational benzodiazepine use and other substance abuse, by L. B. Cottler. NIDA RESEARCH MONOGRAPH SERIES 95:370-371, 1989

Benzodiazepine dependence, by J. Holden. PRACTITIONER 233(1478):1479-1480+, November 8, 1989

Benzodiazepine dependence and the problems of withdrawal, by J. G. Edwards, et al. POSTGRADUATE MEDICAL JOURNAL 66(Suppl)2:27-35, 1990

Benzodiazepine use, by P. England. AUSTRALIAN FAMILY PHYSICIAN 19(5):782, May 1990

Benzodiazepines: addictional effects of the triplicate program. NEW YORK STATE JOURNAL OF MEDICINE 90(5):273-275, May 1990

Benzodiazepines: an extensive collection of mass spectra, by J. Zamecnik, et al. CANADIAN SOCIETY OF FORENSIC SCIENCE JOURNAL 22(3):233-259, 1989

Benzodiazepines in a health-catolog product, by R. L. DuPont, et al. JAMA 264(6): 695, August 8, 1990

Benzodiazepines: reconsidered, by N. S. Miller, et al. ADVANCE IN ALCOHOL AND SUBSTANCE ABUSE 8(3-4):67-84, Spring 1990

Benzodiazepines: tolerance, dependence, abuse, and addiction, by N. S. Miller, et al. JOURNAL OF PSYCHOACTIVE DRUGS 22(1):23-33, January/March 1990

Cognitive cues for use in a case of amphetamine sulfate abuse, by K. P. O'Connor, et al. JOURNAL OF NERVOUS AND MENTAL DISEASE 178(4):271-272, April 1990

Effect of minimal interventions by general practitioners on long-term benzodiazepine use, by M. A. Cormack, et al. JOURNAL OF THE ROYAL COLLEGE OF GEN-ERAL PRACTITIONERS 39(327):408-411, October 1989

Effects of cannabis smoked together with a substance sold as Mandrax, by D. Wilson, et al. SOUTH AFRICAN MEDICAL JOURNAL 76(11):636, December 2, 1989

Patients' attitudes to benzodiazepine dependence, by I. Hamilton. PRACTITIONER 233(1469):722+, May 22, 1989

BENZODIAZEPINES

Use and abuse of benzodiazepines: issues relevant to prescribing, by J. H. Woods, et al. JAMA 260:3476-3480, December 16, 1988

Complications
Congenital malformations and maternal consumption of benzodiazepines: a case-control study, by L. Laegreid, et al. DEVELOPMENTAL MEDICINE AND CHILD NEUROLOGY 32(5):431-441, May 1990

Research
But what if a patient gets hooked: fallacies about long-term use of benzodiazpeines, by J. H. Talley. POSTGRADUATE MEDICINE 87(1):187-203, January 1990

Effects of acute barbiturate administration, tolerance and dependence on brain GABA system: comparison to alcohol and benzodiazepines, by S. Yu, et al. ALCOHOL 7(3):261-272, May/June 1990

History of benzodiazepine dependence: a review of animal studies, by S. E. File. NEUROSCIENCE AND BEHAVIORAL PHYSIOLOGY 14(2):135-146, Summer 1990

BETAL NUTS
Observations on betel-nut use, habituation, addiction and carcinogenesis in Papua New Guineans, by N. T. Talonu. PAPUA NEW GUINEA MEDICAL JOURNAL 32(3):195-197, September 1989

BISEXUALS
AIDS and chemical dependency: special issues and treatment barriers for gay and bisexual men, by R. P. Cabaj. JOURNAL OF PSYCHOACTIVE DRUGS 21(4): 387-393, October/December 1989

AIDS-related illness and AIDS risk in male homo-bisexual substance abusers: case reports and clinical issues, by J. Westermeyer, et al. AMERICAN JOURNAL OF DRUG AND ALCOHOL ABUSE 15(4):443-461, December 1989

BODY PACKING
Body-packing: detection of incorporated drug packets using ultrasound technics, by A. Freislederer, et al. BEITRAGE ZUR GERICHTLICHEN MEDIZIN 47:187-191, 1989

"Cocaine body packer" syndrome: case report and review of the literature, by P. Geyskens, et al. ACTA CHIRURGICA BELGICA 89(4):201-203, July/August 1989

Cocaine body-packer syndrome: evaluation of a method of contrast study of the bowel, by B. Marc, et al. JOURNAL OF FORENSIC SCIENCES 35(2):245-255, March 1990

Cocaine body packer with normal abdominal plain radiograms: value of drug detection in urine and contrast study of the bowel, by R. Gheradi, et al. AMERICAN JOURNAL OF FORENSIC MEDICINE AND PATHOLOGY 11(2):154-157, June 1990

BODY PACKING

CT demonstration of ingested cocaine packets, by W. J. Vanarthos, et al. AJR 155(2): 419-420, August 1990

Detecting packages of narcotics ingested at arrest, by U. Wagner, et al. ARCHIV FUR KRIMINOLOGIE 183(3-4):101-107, 1989

Perfected, professional body-packing, by K. Wehr, et al. ZEITSCHRIFT FUR RECHTSMEDIZIN 103(1):63-68, 1989

Procedures and findings in the study of "body-packing" in Hannover, by J. Eidam, et al. BEITRAGE ZUR GERICHTLICHEN MEDIZIN 47:193-202, 1989

Successful endoscopic retrieval of a cocaine packet from the stomach, by A. Sherman, et al. GASTROINTESTINAL ENDOSCOPY 36(2):152-154, March/April 1990

Why teenagers put rocks in their ears: hidden drugs and confidentiality, by R. E. Morris. JOURNAL OF ADOLESCENT HEALTH CARE 10(6):548-550, November 1989

BUPRENORPHINE
Buprenorphine and temazepam: abuse, by R. Hammersley, et al. BRITISH JOURNAL OF ADDICTION 85(2):301-303, February 1990

Emergence of buprenorphine dependence, by R. G. Gray, et al. BRITISH JOURNAL OF ADDICTION 84(11):1373-1374, November 1989

BUSPIRONE
Abuse potential of buspirone and related drugs, by R. L. Balster. JOURNAL OF CLINICAL PSYCHOPHARMACOLOGY 10(Suppl)3:31-37, June 1990

Buspirone: potentials for abuse, by F. R. Raleigh. DICP 23(12):1035, December 1989

Comment: lack of abuse potential with buspirone, by J. R. Steinberg. DICP 24(7-8): 785-786, July/August 1990

BUTANE
Clinical study of butane gas abuse: in comparison with toluene-based solvent and marihuana, by S. Tohhara, et al. ARUKORU KENKYUTO YAKUBUTSU ISON 24(6):504-510, December 1989

Sniffers using butane, propane: 11 year old and 15 year old die suddenly after use, by K. Fournis. JOURNAL OF THE ADDICTION RESEARCH FOUNDATION 19 (12):3, December 1, 1990

CAFFEINE
Caffeine consumption, expectancies of caffeine-enhanced performance, and caffeinism symptoms among university students, by J. R. Bradley, et al. JOURNAL OF DRUG EDUCATION 20(4):319-328, 1990

CAFFEINE

How much caffeine is too much in athletes?, by K. O. Price, et al. AMERICAN JOURNAL OF HOSPITAL PHARMACY 47(2):303, February 1990

Physical dependence on and toxicity from caffeine, by J. R. Hughes, et al. NIDA RESEARCH MONOGRAPH SERIES 95:437, 1989

Complications

Caffeine and heart disease, by R. Gilbert. JOURNAL OF THE ADDICTION RESEARCH FOUNDATION 19(11):9, January 1, 1990

Caffeine assaults your body causing irritating results: moderation, the key to avoid adverse reactions, by E. Skutezsky. FORESIGHT 9(4):21-22, July/August 1990

Effects of dietary caffeine on renal handling of minerals in adult women, by E. A. Bergman, et al. LIFE SCIENCES 47(6):557-564, 1990

Massive caffeine ingestion resulting in death, by R. M. Mrvos, et al. VETERINARY AND HUMAN TOXICOLOGY 31(6):571-572, December 1989

Research

Caffeine and human cerebral blood flow: a positron emission tomography study, by O. G. Cameron, et al. LIFE SCIENCES 47(13):1141-1146, 1990

Caffeine: a double-blind, placebo-controlled study of its thermogenic, metabolic, and cardiovascular effects in healthy volunteers, by A. Astrup, et al. AMERICAN JOURNAL OF CLINICAL NUTRITION 51:759-767, May 1990

CANNABIS

Acculturation amd marijuana and cocaine use: findings from HHANES 1982-1984, by H. Amaro, et al. AMERICAN JOURNAL OF PUBLIC HEALTH 80(Suppl):54-60, December 1990

Adolescent marijuana use: risk factors and implications, by M. Rob, et al. AUSTRALIAN AND NEW ZEALAND JOURNAL OF PSYCHIATRY 24(1):45-56, March 1990

Adolescents initiating cannabis use: cultural opposition or poor mental health, by W. Pederson. JOURNAL OF ADOLESCENCE 13(4):327-339, 1990

Alcohol, tobacco and cannabis: 12-year longitudinal associations with antecedent social context and personality, by M. F. Sieber, et al. DRUG AND ALCOHOL DEPENDENCE 25(3):281-292, June 1990

Analysis of the aged processes in hashish samples from different geographic origin, by G. Martone, et al. FORENSIC SCIENCE INTERNATIONAL 47(2):147-155, 1990

Breathhold duration and response to marijuana smoke, by J. P. Zacny, et al. PHARMACOLOGY, BIOCHEMISTRY AND BEHAVIOR 33(2):481-484, June 1989

CANNABIS

Cannabis and human social behaviour, by D. F. Marks, et al. HUMAN PSYCHO-
PHARMACOLOGY: CLINICAL AND EXPERIMENTAL 4(4):283-290, December
1989

Cannabis and mortality among young men: a longitudinal study of Swedish conscripts, by S. Andreasson, et al. SCANDINAVIAN JOURNAL OF SOCIAL MEDI-
CINE 18(1):9-15, 1990

Cannabis comprehended: the "assassin of youth" points to a new pharmacology, by
T. M. Beardsley. SCIENTIFIC AMERICAN 263(4):38, October 1990

Cannabis comprehended: cannabinoid receptor cloned by Lisa A. Matsuda, by T.
Beardsley. SCIENTIFIC AMERICAN 263:38, October 1990

Cannabis dependence and tolerance production, by D. R. Compton, et al. AD-
VANCES IN ALCOHOL AND SUBSTANCE ABUSE 9(1-2):129-147, Spring 1990

Cannabis most used illicit drug in Canada: RCMP 1988-1989 estimate. JOURNAL OF
THE ADDICTION RESEARCH FOUNDATION 19(10):5, October 1, 1990

Cannabis poisoning in a young child: don't ask about drugs, by M. L. de Sonnaville-
de Roy van Zuidewijn, et al. NEDERLANDS TIJDSCHRIFT VOOR GENEES-
KUNDE 133(35):1752-1753, September 2, 1989

Cannabis-ressin foreign body in the ear, by A. C. Thompson, et al. NEW ENGLAND
JOURNAL OF MEDICINE 320(26):1758, June 1989

Cigarettes and marijuana: are there measurable long-term neurobehavioral teratogenic effects?, by P. A. Fried. NEUROTOXICOLOGY 10(3):577-583, Fall 1989

Cocaine and marijuana use by medical students before and during medical school, by
R. H. Schwartz, et al. ARCHIVES OF INTERNAL MEDICINE 150(4):883-886, April
1990

Consequences of marijuana use on intrapersonal and interpersonal functioning in
black and white adolescents, by J. S. Brook, et al. GENETIC, SOCIAL, AND
GENERAL PSYCHOLOGY MONOGRAPHS 115(3):349-369, August 1989

Developmental variations in the context of marijuana initiation among adolecents, by
S. L. Bailey, et al. JOURNAL OF HEALTH AND SOCIAL BEHAVIOR 31(1):58-70,
March 1990

Divided attention performance in cannabis users and non-users following alcohol and
cannabis separately and in combination, by D. F. Marks, et al. PSYCHOPHAR-
MACOLOGY 99(3):397-401, November 1989

Domestic marijuana growers: mainstreaming deviance, by R. A. Weisheit. DEVIANT
BEHAVIOR 11(2):107-129, April/June 1990

Drug self-administration procedures: alcohol and marijuana, by N. K. Mello, et al. NIDA
RESEARCH MONOGRAPH SERIES 92:147-170, 1989

Effect of cannabis use on oral candidal carriage, by M. R. Darling, et al. JOURNAL OF
ORAL PATHOLOGY AND MEDICINE 19(7):319-321, 1990

Effect of hashish-smoking on serum levels of pancreatic lipase: RV 3.1.1.3, in man, by A. Dionyssiou-Asteriou, et al. JOURNAL OF TOXICOLOGY: CLINICAL TOXICOLOGY 28(2):263-265, 1990

Effects of cannabis smoked together with a substance sold as Mandrax, by D. Wilson, et al. SOUTH AFRICAN MEDICAL JOURNAL 76(11):636, December 2, 1989

Effects of the combination of cocaine and marijuana on the task-elicited physiological response, by R. W. Foltin, et al. NIDA RESEARCH MONOGRAPH SERIES 95: 359-360, 1989

Effects of combinations of intranasal cocaine, smoked marijuana, and task performance on heart rate and blood pressure, by R. W. Foltin, et al. PHARMACOLOGY, BIOCHEMISTRY AND BEHAVIOR 36(2):311-315, June 1990

Effects of food deprivation on subjective responses to d-amphetamine and marijuana in humans, by J. Zacny, et al. NIDA RESEARCH MONOGRAPH SERIES 95:490-491, 1989

Effects of smoked marijuana on interpersonal distances in small groups, by J. J. Rachlinski, et al. DRUG AND ALCOHOL DEPENDENCE 24(3):183-186, December 1989

Effects of tetrahydrocannabinol content on marijuana smoking behavior, subjective reports, and performance, by S. J. Heishman, et al. PHARMACOLOGY, BIOCHEMISTRY AND BEHAVIOR 34(1):173-179, September 1989

Going to pot: a grassroots movement touts hemp's environmental virtues, by J. Horgan. SCIENTIFIC AMERICAN 263(6):23-24, December 1990

Hemperors' new clothes. DOLLARS AND SENSE (159):5, September 1990

Higher and higher: why Western Canada leads in hydroponic pot production, by P. MacDonald. ALBERTA (WESTERN) REPORT 17(23):44, May 21, 1990

Identifying and helping patients who use marijuana, by R. H. Schwartz. POSTGRADUATE MEDICINE 86(6):91-95, November 1, 1989

Indoor marihuana cultivation, by M. W. Pearson. RCMP GAZETTE 51(1):1-6, 1989

Initiation, continuation or discontinuation of cannabis use in the general population, by T. Hammer, et al. BRITISH JOURNAL OF ADDICTION 85(7):899-909, July 1990

International news: Canada—marijuana unpopular, by A. Harman. LAW AND ORDER 37(10):8, October 1989

Journal of a harvest, by K. Tibershraney. RFD (63):45, Fall 1990

Justified paternalism in adolescent health care: cases of anorexia nervosa and substance abuse, by T. J. Silber. JOURNAL OF ADOLESCENT HEALTH CARE 10(6):449-453, November 1989

CANNABIS

Living with prohibition: regular cannabis users, legal sanctions, and informal controls, by P. G. Erickson. INTERNATIONAL JOURNAL OF THE ADDICTIONS 24(3):175-188, March 1989

Manufacture of marijuana: consumption of electricity—Oregon. NARCOTICS LAW BULLETIN January 1990, pp. 3-4

Marijuana, by B. S. Selden, et al. EMERGENCY MEDICINE CLINICS OF NORTH AMERICA 8(3):527-539, August 1990

Marijuana, aging, and task difficulty effects on pilot performance, by V. O. Leirer, et al. AVIATION, SPACE AND ENVIRONMENTAL MEDICINE 60(12):1145-1152, December 1989

Marijuana and alcohol effects on mood states in young women, by B. W. Lex, et al. NIDA RESEARCH MONOGRAPH SERIES 95:462, 1989

Marijuana and immunity: tetrahydrocannabinol mediated inhibition of lymphocyte blastogenesis, by S. Spector, et al. INTERNATIONAL JOURNAL OF IMMUNOPHARMACOLOGY 12(3):261-267, 1990

Marijuana as medicine, by D. E. Anderson. CHRISTIANITY AND CRISIS 50:241-243, August 6, 1990

Marijuana bigger threat than cocaine: study—effects of illicit drugs in the workplace, by M. A. Hofmann. BUSINESS INSURANCE 24:71-72, September 3, 1990

Marijuana: can't say no. NURSING 90 20:82, November 1990

Marijuana makes a comeback, by J. Malone. MADEMOISELLE 96:184-187, October 1990

Marijuana manufacturing: definition—Missouri. NARCOTICS LAW BULLETIN March 1990, p. 7

Marijuana use and abuse in psychiatric outpatients, by R. A. Weller, et al. ANNALS OF CLINICAL PSYCHIATRY 1(2):87-91, June 1989

Marijuana use in pregnancy and pregnancy outcome, by F. R. Witter, et al. AMERICAN JOURNAL OF PERINATOLOGY 7(1):36-38, January 1990

Marijuana: where there's smoke. NURSING 90 20:76+, February 1990

Mental state of marijuana-smoking adolescents, by J. Rabe-Jablonska, et al. PRZEGLAD LEKARSKI 46(12):802-805, 1989

Model proposing three processes of adolescent marijuana use, by S. L. Bailey. DAI A 50(9):3071, March 1990

Motivational effects of smoked marijuana: behavioral contingencies and high-probability recreational activities, by R. W. Foltin, et al. PHARMACOLOGY, BIOCHEMISTRY AND BEHAVIOR 34(4):871-877, December 1989

Motivational effects of smoked marijuana: behavioral contingencies and low-probability recreational activities, by R. W. Foltin, et al. JOURNAL OF THE EXPERIMENTAL ANALYSIS OF BEHAVIOR 53(1):5-19, January 1990

Off the pot, by C. P. Wohlforth. NEW REPUBLIC 203:9, December 3,1990

Over the top. NEW STATESMAN AND SOCIETY 2(70):4, 1989

Pharmacology: planning for serendipity, by S. H. Snyder. NATURE 346:508, August 9, 1990

Phenomenological analysis of African adolescents' meaning of dagga use within changing social relations, by H. Mkhize. MEDICINE AND LAW 8(2):149-156, 1989

Plasma delta-9-THC levels as a predictive measure of marijuana use by women, by J. H. Mendelson, et al. NIDA RESEARCH MONOGRAPH SERIES 95:152-158, 1989

Pot production, price surge despite 1988 eradication campaign. LAW ENFORCE-MENT NEWS 15(295):3, June 30, 1989

Prevalence of marijuana (cannabis) use and dependence in cocaine dependence, by N. S. Miller, et al. NEW YORK STATE JOURNAL OF MEDICINE 90(10):491-492, 1990

Reefer madness, by C. Goldfinch. HEALTH 22:21+, September 1990

Saving trees with grass, by A. Ozols. CHAIN REACTION (62):12, October 1990

Smoked marijuana effects on tobacco cigarette smoking behavior, by T. H. Kelly, et al. JOURNAL OF PHARMACOLOGY AND EXPERIMENTAL THERAPEUTICS 252(3):934-944, March 1990

Survey shows marijuana, cocaine, heroin emergencies soar for third straight year. NARCOTICS CONROL DIGEST 19(23):9-10, November 8, 1989 ; also in CRIME CONTROL DIGEST 23(45):4, November 13, 1989

Symptomatology of chronic and acute marijuana poisoning, by G. Marmajewska. PSYCHIATRIA POLSKA 22(6):474-482, November/December 1988

Terminal elimination plasma half-life of delta 1-tetrahydrocannabinol (delta 1-THC) in heavy users of marijuana, by E. Johansson, et al. EUROPEAN JOURNAL OF CLINICAL PHARMACOLOGY 37(3):273-277, 1989

Withdrawal sequelae to cannabis use, by J. M. Rohr, et al. INTERNATIONAL JOUR-NAL OF THE ADDICTIONS 24(7):627-631, July 1989

Complications

Association of spontaneous pneumomediastinum with substance abuse, by L. L. Fajardo. WESTERN JOURNAL OF MEDICINE 152(3):301-304, March 1990

Cannabis and psychosis: is there epidemiological evidence for an association?, by G. Thornicroft. BRITISH JOURNAL OF PSYCHIATRY 157:25-33, July 1990

Cannabis-schizophrenia linked, by K. Birchard. JOURNAL OF THE ADDICTION RE-SEARCH FOUNDATION 19(9):5, September 1, 1990

Cholinergic syndrome patient abusing marijuana, by R. Tandon, et al. BRITISH JOURNAL OF PSYCHIATRY 154:712-714, May 1989

Cigarettes, alcohol and marijuana are related to pyospermia in infertile men, by C. E. Close, et al. JOURNAL OF UROLOGY 144(4):900-903, October 1990

Effect of marijuana use during pregnancy on newborn cry, by B. M. Lester, et al. CHILD DEVELOPMENT 60:765-771, August 1989

Genotoxicity of heroin and cannabinoids in humans, by E. Piatti, et al. PHARMACO-LOGICAL RESEARCH 21(Suppl)1:59-60, November/December 1989

Ingestion of cannabis: a cause of coma in children, by A. Macnab, et al. PEDIATRIC EMERGENCY CARE 5(4):238-239, December 1989

Marijuana smoking and carcinoma of the tongue: is there an association?, by G. A. Caplan, et al. CANCER 66(5):1005-1006, September 1, 1990

Marijuana use and memory loss. AMERICAN FAMILY PHYSICIAN 41:930-931, March 1990

Marijuana use linked to schizophrenia, by B. Boxerman. ST. LOUIS JOURNALISM REVIEW 20(129):4, September 1990

Marijuana uvula, by L. M. Haddad. AMERICAN JOURNAL OF EMERGENCY MEDI-CINE 8(2):179, March 1990

Maternal marijuana use during lactation and infant development at one year, by S. J. Astley, et al. NEUROTOXICOLOGY AND TERATOLOGY 12(2):161-168, March/April 1990

Mental performance long-term heavy cannabis use: a preliminary report, by J. Leon-Carrion. PSYCHOLOGICAL REPORTS 67(3):947-952, 1990

Neurologic complications of drug addiction: general aspects—complications caused by cannabis, designer drugs and volatile substances, by M. Farre Albaladejo. ARCHIVES DE NEUROGIOLOGIA 52(Suppl)1:143-148, 1989

Psychopharmacological effects of cannabis, by B. A. Johnson. BRITISH JOURNAL OF HOSPITAL MEDICINE 43(2):114-116+, February 1990

Psychosis and cannabis consumption: study of the psychopathologic differences and risk factors, by M. D. Crespo, et al. ACTAS LUSO-ESPANOLAS DE NEU-ROLOGIA, PSYIQUIATRIA Y CIENCIAS AFINES 18(2):120-124, March/April 1990

Pulmonary complications of smoked substance abuse, by D. P. Tashkin. WESTERN JOURNAL OF MEDICINE 152(5):525-530, May 1990

Short-term memory impairment in cannabis-dependent adolescents, by R. H. Schwartz, et al. AMERICAN JOURNAL OF DISEASES OF CHILDREN 143(10): 1214-1219, October 1989

Short-term memory impairment in chronic cannabis abusers. LANCET 2(8674):1254-1255, November 25, 1989

Subjective and behavioral effects of marijuana the morning after smoking, by L. D. Chait. PSYCHOPHARMACOLOGY 100(3):328-330, March 1990

Ulcerative colitis and marijuana, by J. A. Baron, et al. ANNALS OF INTERNAL MEDICINE 112(6):471, March 15, 1990

Visual illusions associated with previous drug abuse, by L. Levi, et al. JOURNAL OF CLINICAL NEURO-OPHTHALMOLOGY 10(2):103-110, June 1990

Research
Aggressive behaviour: basic and clinical frontiers, by S. K. Bhattachaya, et al. INDIAN JOURNAL OF MEDICAL RESEARCH 90:387-406, December 1989

Comparison of pharmacological effects of tetrahydrocannabinols and their 11-hydroxy metabolites in mice, by Z. Watanabe, et al. CHEMICAL AND PHARMACEUTICAL BULLETIN 38(8):2317-2319, 1990

Effect of marijuana smoke exposure on murine sarcoma 180 survival in Fisher rats, by E. S. Watson. IMMUNOPHARMACOLOGY AND IMMUNOTOXICOLOGY 11(2-3): 211-222, 1989

Marijuana (cannabis) use is anecdotally said to precipitate anxiety symptoms in patients with panic disorder: is there any research evidence to support this—also, can marijuana use precipitate or expose paranoia in patients with an underlying bipolar disorder?, by J. P. Seibyl, et al. JOURNAL OF CLINICAL PSYCHOPHARMACOLOGY 10(1):78, February 1990

Marijuana receptor gene cloned: THC receptor—work of Lisa Matsuda, by J. L. Marx. SCIENCE 249:624-626, August 10, 1990

Method for exposing primates to marihuana smoke that simulates the method used by human marihuana smokers, by G. T. Pryor, et al. PHARMACOLOGY, BIOCHEMISTRY AND BEHAVIOR 34(3):521-525, November 1989

Political implications of scientific research in the field of drug abuse: the case of cannabis, by J. C. Negrete. DRUG AND ALCOHOL DEPENDENCE 25(2):225-228, April 1990

Receptor for cannabinoids discovered in brain, by S. Borman. CHEMICAL ENGINEERING NEWS 68:5, August 13, 1990

Selective inactivation of mouse liver cytochrome P-450IIIA by cannabidiol, by L. M. Bornheim, et al. MOLECULAR PHARMACOLOGY 38(3):319-326, 1990

Structure of a cannabinoid receptor and functional expression of the cloned cDNA, by L. A. Matsuda, et al. NATURE 346:561-564, August 9, 1990

Switch that turns the brain on to cannabis, by A. Abbott. NEW SCIENTIST 127:31, August 11, 1990

CARE
United States care providers face rough weather, by M. Korcok. JOURNAL OF THE ADDICTION RESEARCH FOUNDATION 19(11):5, November 1, 1990

Addicts' search: Canadians seek treatment in United States hospitals, by N. Underwood. MACLEAN'S 103(22):51, May 28, 1990

Children in peril: nurse K. Jorgenson's work with crack babies at Boston City Hospital, by W. Plummer. PEOPLE WEEKLY 33:84-85, April 16, 1990

Comparative effectiveness of alpha-2 adrenergic agonists clonidine-guanfacine, in the hospital detoxification of opiate addicts, by R. Muga, et al. MEDICINA CLINICA 94(5):169-172, February 10, 1990

Drug abuse treatment at the San Martin General Hospital, Buenos Aires, by R. Fahrer, et al. MEDICINE AND LAW 8(4):365-367, 1989

Evaluation of a hospital based substance abuse intervention and referral service for HIV affected patients, by J. Guydish, et al. GENERAL HOSPITAL PSYCHIATRY 12(1):1-7, January 1990

Hospitalization of adolescents for psychiatric and substance abuse treatment: legal and ethical issues, by I. M. Schwartz. JOURNAL OF ADOLESCENT HEALTH CARE 10(6):473-478, November 1989

Hospitalized with a double stigma, by C. A. de Jong. NEDERLANDS TIJDSCHRIFT VOOR GENEESKUNDE 134(27):1289-1291, July 7, 1990

Natural history of parenteral drug addicts treated in a general hospital, by R. Muga, et al. BRITISH JOURNAL OF ADDICTION 85(6):775-778, June 1990

Rehabilitation hospital's approach to the problem of substance abuse, by H. E. Irby, et al. JOURNAL OF THE MISSISSIPPI STATE MEDICAL ASSOCIATION 31(6):189-191, June 1990

Towards freedom: treatment approaches to drug dependence at TTK Hospital, by R. R. Cherian. BRITISH JOURNAL OF ADDICTION 84(12):1401-1407, December 1989

Nurses

Children in peril: nurse K. Jorgenson's work with crack babies at Boston City Hospital, by W. Plummer. PEOPLE WEEKLY 33:84-85, April 16, 1990

Cocaine use during pregnancy: research findings and clinical implications, by M. Lynch, et al JOURNAL OF OBSTETRIC, GYNECOLOGIC, AND NEONATAL NURSING 19(4):285-292, July/August 1990

Consumption of alcohol and tobacco during pregnancy by health advisors: an investigation of nurses, nurses' aides, physicians and school teachers, by J. G. Frische, et al. UGESKRIFT FOR LAEGER 152(9):2101-2104, July 16, 1990

Helping people to stop smoking: a study of the nurse's role, by J. M. Clark, et al. JOURNAL OF ADVANCED NURSING 15(3):357-363, March 1990

Nurses' knowledge of opioid analgesic drugs and psychological dependence, by M. McCaffery, et al. CANCER NURSING 13(1):21-27, February 1990

Nursing at the front—of the cocaine wars, by M. B. Mallison. AMERICAN JOURNAL OF NURSING 90(4):7, April 1990

Perinatal substance abuse and public health nursing intervention, by B. A. Rieder. CHILDREN TODAY 19:33-35, July/August 1990

Weaning infants from sedation, by P. Gordin. MCN 15(2):74+, March/April 1990

Physicians

AIDS and cocaine: a deadly combination facing the primary care physician, by S. P. Weinstein, et al. JOURNAL OF FAMILY PRACTICE 31(3):253-254, September 1990

Cocaine use during pregnancy: implications for physicians, by R. A. Aronson, et al. WISCONSIN MEDICAL JOURNAL 89(3):105-110, March 1990

Cocaine use in pregnancy: physicians urged to look for problem where they least expect it, by A. Skolnick. JAMA 264(3):306+, July 18, 1990

Cocaine users may not fit MDs' stereotype, FPs warned, by B. Trent. CMAJ 143(11): 1239-1240, December 1, 1990

Consumption of alcohol and tobacco during pregnancy by health advisors: an investigation of nurses, nurses' aides, physicians and school teachers, by J. G. Frische, et al. UGESKRIFT FOR LAEGER 152(9):2101-2104, July 16, 1990

Drug overdose: how to handle it as a replacement family physician, by G. H. Brussel, et al. NEDERLANDS TIDJSCHRIFT VOOR GENEESKUNDE 134(21):1043-1045, May 26, 1990

Educational factors in substance abuse for physicians, by N. P. Johnson, et al. JOURNAL OF THE SOUTH CAROLINA MEDICAL ASSOCIATION 86(1):64-65, January 1990

Evaluation of substance-abusing adolescents by primary care physicians, by L. S. Friedman, et al. JOURNAL OF ADOLESCENT HEALTH CARE 11(3):227-230, May 1990

General practitioner management of drug misusers, by J. Cohen, et al. PRACTITIONER 233(1478):1471-1474, November 8, 1989

Heroin misusers: what they think of their general practitioners, by I. Telfer, et al. BRITISH JOURNAL OF ADDICTION 85(1):137-140, January 1990

Patient-phyician communications as a determination of medication misuse in older, minority women, by T. F. Garrity, et al. JOURNAL OF DRUG ISSUES 19(2):245-259, Spring 1989

Physicians' attitudes toward drug-use evaluation interventions, by J. F. Pierson, et al. AMERICAN JOURNAL OF HOSPITAL PHARMACY 47(2):388-390, February 1990

Physicians' attitudes toward substance abuse and drug testing, by L. S. Linn, et al. INTERNATIONAL JOURNAL OF THE ADDICTIONS 25(4):427-444, 1990

Physicians, cancer control and the treatment of nicotine dependence: defining success, by T. J. Glynn, et al. HEALTH EDUCATION RESEARCH 4(4):479-487, December 1989

Physicians have been drafted for the "war on drugs," by H. Martin. RHODE ISLAND MEDICAL JOURNAL 73(6):230-231, June 1990

Physicians' primer on the toxicology of adolescent drug abuse, by M. Thoman. VETERINARY AND HUMAN TOXICOLOGY 31(4):384-391, August 1989

Physician's responsibilities in drug rehabilitation, by F. Bschor. FORSCHRITTE DER MEDIZIN 108(13):259-261, April 30, 1990

Physician's role in rehabilitating chemically dependent patients, by J. Femino, et al. RHODE ISLAND MEDICAL JOURNAL 73(6):259-263, June 1990

Pregnancy and drugs: physicians face new testing and reporting law, by T. Jopke. MINNESOTA MEDICINE 73(4):29-32, April 1990

Recommended core educational guidelines on alcoholism and substance abuse for family practice residents. AMERICAN FAMILY PHYSICIAN 42:1437-1438, November 1990

Support for GPs caring for drug misusers, by J. Mack. PRACTITIONER 233(1478): 1491-1495, November 8, 1989

Survey of general practitioners' opinion and attitude to drug addicts and addiction, by R. T. Abed, et al. BRITISH JOURNAL OF ADDICTION 85(1):131-136, January 1990

Use of services of the physician-on-call by chronic morphine users, by V. M. Schmidt. UGESKRIFT FOR LAEGER 152(35):2482-2485, August 27, 1990

What practicing physicians need to know about self-help for chemical dependents, by B. E. Donovan. RHODE ISLAND MEDICAL JOURNAL 72(12):443-449, December 1989

CARISOPRODOL
Mail-order: veterinary drug dependence—carisoprodol, by J. G. Luehr, et al. JAMA 263:657, February 2, 1990

CASE STUDIES
Case reports and the assessment of drug abuse liability, by E. C. Senay. NIDA RESEARCH MONOGRAPH SERIES (92):231-240, 1989

Sweet and sour: profile of Rafaella Fletcher, author of personal account of teenage heroin addiction, by G. Troupp. GUARDIAN September 25, 1990, p. 38

CELEBRITIES

see also: Alcohol and Celebrities

Bill Cosby: living with heartbreak—relationship with daughter Erinn and views on parenting, by M. Southgate. REDBOOK 175:52+, June 1990

Chuck Berry surrenders on drug, child abuse charges. JET 78:38, August 20, 1990

CSNY honors its former drummer: D. Taylor, by J. Ressner. ROLLING STONE May 17, 1990, p. 18

DEA targets Chuck Berry, by J. Neely. ROLLING STONE August 23, 1990, p. 34

Down at the end of Lonely Street: evidence that E. Presley committed suicide, by A. H. Goldman. LIFE 13:96-98+, June 1990

Dual drug busts turn a painful spotlight on two children of Hollywood: arrests of C. Feldman and D. Bonaduce, by W. Plummer. PEOPLE WEEKLY 33:51-52, March 26, 1990

Falling down: and getting back up again—D. Barrymore, by J. Park. PEOPLE WEEKLY 33:56-61, January 29, 1990

Finally drug-free, drummer Dallas Taylor hopes for one more miracle: a new liver, by C. Sanz. PEOPLE WEEKLY 33:84-86, April 2, 1990

Great sax: F. Morgan, by E. Pooley. NEW YORK 23:44-49, February 12, 1990

In his most arresting performance: Cheers star Kelsey Grammer runs afoul of booze, coke and Los Angeles law, by M. Neill. PEOPLE WEEKLY 33:101-102, June 4, 1990

Soul star on ice: divorced by Tina, Ike Turner pays for his romance with cocaine in a California prison, by S. Dougherty. PEOPLE WEEKLY 34:57+, September 3, 1990

Trial of Hunter S. Thompson, by M. Sager. ROLLING STONE June 28, 1990, pp. 64-65+

CHILDREN
see also: Alcohol and Children

36- and 48-month neurobehavioral follow-ups of children prenatally exposed to marijuana, cigarettes, and alcohol, by P. A. Fried, et al. JOURNAL OF DEVELOPMENTAL AND BEHAVIORAL PEDIATRICS 11(2):49-58, April 1990

Accidental amitriptyline poisoning in a toddler, by D. W. Beal, et al. SOUTHERN MEDICAL JOURNAL 82(12):1588-1589, December 1989

Acute toxicity from oral ingestion of crack cocaine: a report of four cases, by D. Riggs, et al. PEDIATRIC EMERGENCY CARE 6(1):24-26, March 1990

Age of first use of drugs among rural midwestern youth, by P. D Sarvela, et al. HUMAN SERVICES IN THE RURAL ENVIRONMENT 13(3):9-15, Winter 1990

CHILDREN

Children at multiple risk: treatment and prevention, by R. J. Johnson, et al. JOURNAL OF CHEMICAL DEPENDENCY TREATMENT 3(1):145-163, 1989

Children of the damned: North Philadelphia crack neighborhood, by E. Barnes. LIFE 13:30-36+, June 1990

Children of substance abusers in New York State, by S. Deren, et al. NEW YORK STATE JOURNAL OF MEDICINE 90(4):179-184, April 1990

Clonidine poisoning in children, by G. P. Wedin, et al. AMERICAN JOURNAL OF DISEASES OF CHILDREN 144(8):853-854, August 1990

Consider the children, drug workers urged, by J. Hollobon. JOURNAL OF THE AD-DICTION RESEARCH FOUNDATION 19(9):3, September 1, 1990

"Crack babies" in school, by M. C. Rist. EDUCATIONAL DIGEST 55:30-33, May 1990

Crack babies: ready or not here they come, by D. A. Laderman. AMERICAN TEACHER 75:10-11+, November 1990

Crack babies: the schools' new high-risk students, by Y. Bellisimo. THRUST 19:23-26, January 1990

Crack children: as cocaine babies grow up, health and social workers are discovering a whole new set of drug-related problems, by B. Kantrowitz. NEWSWEEK 115(7): 62-63, February 12, 1990

Crack children in foster care, by D. J. Besharov. CHILDREN TODAY 19:21-25+, July/August 1990

Crack cocaine: a new danger for children, by M. C. Heagarty. AMERICAN JOURNAL OF DISEASES OF CHILDREN 144(7):756-757, July 1990

Epidemiology of pediatric paracetamol poisoning: retrospective analysis of calls received by the Poison Control Centre of Tours, by A. P. Jonville, et al. JOURNAL DE TOXICOLOGIE CLINIQUE ET EXPERIMENTALE 10(1):21-25, January/February 1990

Esophagitis, epiglottitis, and cocaine alkaloid (crack): "accidental" poisoning or child abuse, by S. Kharasch, et al. PEDIATRICS 86(1):117-119, July 1990

Examination attainments of secondary school pupils who abuse solvents, by O. Chadwick, et al. BRITISH JOURNAL OF EDUCATIONAL PSYCHOLOGY 60 (Pt 2):180-181, June 1990

Fatal attraction of a 5-minute fix: increase in solvent abuse by school children in Great Britain, by E. Heron. TIMES EDUCATIONAL SUPPLEMENT 3882:10, November 23, 1990

Fetal drug exposure and its possible implications for learning in the preschool and school-age population, by D. C. Van Dyke, et al. JOURNAL OF LEARNING DIS-ABILITIES 23(3):160-163, March 1990

Grandparents get 10-year-old drug suspect. JUVENILE JUSTICE DIGEST 17(18):7-8, September 20, 1989

Health and development of 8-year-old children whose mothers abused amphetamine during pregnancy, by M. Eriksson, et al. ACTA PAEDIATRICA SCANDINAVICA 78(6):944-949, November 1989

Identity failure: heroin addiction in preadolescents, by A. Magoudi, et al. NEURO-PSYCHIATRIE DE l'ENFANCE ET DE l'ADOLESCENCE 36(2-3):69-73, February/March 1988

Ingestion of cannabis: a cause of coma in children, by A. Macnab, et al. PEDIATRIC EMERGENCY CARE 5(4):238-239, December 1989

Is your child hooked on drugs or alcohol?, by P. Krantz. BETTER HOMES AND GARDENS 68:41-43, February 1990

NCJFCJ response to children and drugs: part I, by G. E. Radcliffe. JUVENILE JUSTICE DIGEST 18(10):4-5, May 16, 1990

NCJFCJ response to children and drugs: part II, by G. E. Radcliffe. JUVENILE JUSTICE DIGEST 18(11):1+, June 6, 1990

Nicotine abuse by elementary school children: a comparison of urban versus rural children and correlates associated with use, by J. P. Martin, et al. NORTH CAROLINA MEDICAL JOURNAL 51(7):328-330, July 1990

Onset of drug abuse in children, by L. Chvila, et al. CESKOSLOVENSKA PSYCHIATRIE 85(4):256-259, August 1989

Prenatal marijuana exposure remains evident in early childhood, by R. E. Dahl. AMERICAN FAMILY PHYSICIAN 41:596, February 1990

Psychological study in children addicted to inhalation of volatile substances, by L. M. Rojas, et al. REVISTA DE INVESTIGACION CLINICA 41(4):361-365, October/December 1989

School performance, academic aspirations, and drug use among children and adolescents, by M. J. Paulson, et al. JOURNAL OF DRUG EDUCATION 20(4):289-303, 1990

Social and medical problems in children of heroin-addicted parents: a study of 75 patients, by J. Casado-Flores, et al. AMERICAN JOURNAL OF DISEASES OF CHILDREN 144(9):977-979, September 1990

South Florida schools brace for influx of crack babies. JUVENILE JUSTICE DIGEST 18(10):10, May 16, 1990

Startling statistics about children. ABA JOURNAL 76:8, February 1990

Thousands of drug-exposed children to start school. JUVENILE JUSTICE DIGEST 18(12):3-4, June 20, 1990; also in NARCOTICS CONTROL DIGEST 2(6):1+, June 1990

Ultrastructural characteristics of embryonic brain cells in the offspring of alcoholic mothers, by A. V. Solonskii, et al. ZHURNAL NEVROPATOLOGII I PSIKHIATRII IMENI S. S. KORSAKOVA 89(7):41-45, 1989

CHLORAL HYDRATE

Chloral hydrate: 2 cases of fatal poisoning, by G. Finini, et al. REVUE MEDICALE DE LA SUISSE ROMANDE 109(9):759-760, September 1989

CINNAMON OIL
Cinnamon oil abuse by adolescents, by P. A. Perry, et al. VETERINARY AND HUMAN TOXICOLOGY 32(2):162-164, April 1990

Cinnamon oil: kids use it to get high, by R. H. Schwartz. CLINICAL PEDIATRICS 29(3):196, March 1990

CLONIDINE
Clonidine poisoning in children, by G. P. Wedin, et al. AMERICAN JOURNAL OF DISEASES OF CHILDREN 144(8):853-854, August 1990

COCAINE
Acculturation amd marijuana and cocaine use: findings from HHANES 1982-1984, by H. Amaro, et al. AMERICAN JOURNAL OF PUBLIC HEALTH 80(Suppl):54-60, December 1990

Acute toxicity from oral ingestion of crack cocaine: a report of four cases, by D. Riggs, et al. PEDIATRIC EMERGENCY CARE 6(1):24-26, March 1990

Adolescent cocaine abuse: addictive potential, behavioral and psychiatric effects, by T. W. Estroff, et al. CLINICAL PEDIATRICS 28(12):550-555, December 1989

AIDS and cocaine: a deadly combination facing the primary care physician, by S. P. Weinstein, et al. JOURNAL OF FAMILY PRACTICE 31(3):253-254, September 1990

Aloha from "ice" land, by S. Albrecht. LAW AND ORDER 37(12):55-57, December 1989

America's forgotten drug war: early use of cocaine, by D. Musto. READER'S DIGEST 136:147-150, April 1990

Amphetamine and cocaine induce drug-specific activation of the *c-fos* gene in strio-some-matrix compartments and limbic subdivisions of the striatum, by A. M. Graybiel, et al. PROCEEDINGS OF THE NATIONAL ACADEMY OF SCIENCES USA 87(17):6912-6916, September 1990

Anatomy of a high, by L. Martz. MADEMOISELLE 96:161+, May 1990

Antagonism of behavioral effects of cocaine by selective dopamine receptor blockers, by R. D. Spealman. PSYCHOPHARMACOLOGY 101(1):142-145, 1990

Bag of cocaine: abandonment of property—Los Angeles. SEARCH AND SEIZURE BULLETIN April 1990, pp. 5-6

Behind the cocaine war, by R. Santero. LUCHA 13(6):7, November 1989

Between a "rock" and a hard place: perinatal drug abuse, by W. Chavkin, et al. PEDIATRICS 85(2):223-225, February 1990

Black adolescent crack users in Oakland: no quick fix, by B. G. Silverman. JAMA 264(3):337, July 18, 1990

Callus of crack cocaine, by R. F. Larkin. NEW ENGLAND JOURNAL OF MEDICINE 323(10):685, September 6, 1990

Carcinogenic potential of cocaine, by H. S. Rosenkranz, et al. CANCER LETTERS 52(3):243-246, 1990

Careful assessment and quick action for overdose, by D. Unkle. RN 53:86+, January 1990

Changes in mood, craving, and sleep during short-term abstinence reported by male cocaine addicts: a controlled residential study, by W. W. Weddington, et al. ARCHIVES OF GENERAL PSYCHIATRY 47(9):861-868, September 1990

Characterization of a cocaine binding protein in human placenta, by M. A. Ahmed, et al. LIFE SCIENCES 46(8):553-561, 1990

Chasing the dragon: the smoking of heroin and cocaine, by T. H. Kramer, et al. JOURNAL OF SUBSTANCE ABUSE TREATMENT 7(1):65, 1990

Chauvin: "help cocaine babies." ABA JOURNAL 76:99, February 1990

Children of the damned: North Philadelphia crack neighborhood, by E. Barnes. LIFE 13:30-36+, June 1990

Cocaine, by L. Van Beylen. OFFICIER DE POLICE 9:5-18+, 1988

Cocaine, by M. A. House. AMERICAN JOURNAL OF NURSING 90(4):40-45, April 1990

Cocaine abuse and acquired immunodeficiency syndrome: a tale of two epidemics, by W. D. Lerner. AMERICAN JOURNAL OF MEDICINE 87(6):661-663, December 1989

Cocaine abuse and addiction. AMERICAN FAMILY PHYSICIAN 41:636+, February 1990

Cocaine abuse and dependence, by R. M. Swift, et al. RHODE ISLAND MEDICAL JOURNAL 73(6):265-270, June 1990

Cocaine abuse and its treatment, by R. D. Hicks. HAWAII MEDICAL JOURNAL 48(11): 462+, November 1989

Cocaine abuse and its treatment, by W. C. Hall, et al. PHARMACOTHERAPY 10(1): 47-65, 1990

Cocaine abuse and violent death, by R. D. Budd. AMERICAN JOURNAL OF DRUG AND ALCOHOL ABUSE 15(4):375-382, December 1989

Cocaine abuse during pregnancy: correlation between prenatal care and perinatal outcome, by S. N. MacGregor, et al. OBSTETRICS AND GYNECOLOGY 74(6): 882-885, December 1989

Cocaine abuse in pregnancy. AMERICAN FAMILY PHYSICIAN 40:232, August 1989

COCAINE

Cocaine addiction. AMERICAN FAMILY PHYSICIAN 42(Suppl):78, November 1990

Cocaine and cocaine poisoning: pharmacology, symptoms and treatment, by R. Rossi. DEUTSCHE MEDIZINISCHE WOCHENSCHRIFT 115(22):868-873, June 1, 1990

Cocaine and crack, by A. R. Patel, et al. BMJ 299(6703):856, September 30, 1989

Cocaine and crack, by C. Brewer. BMJ 299(6702):792, September 23, 1989

Cocaine and crack, by J. Strang, et al. BMJ 299(6695):337-338, August 5, 1989

Cocaine and crack, by N. Retterstol. UGESKRIFT FOR LAEGER 151(49):3292-3294, December 4, 1989

Cocaine and marijuana use by medical students before and during medical school, by R. H. Schwartz, et al. ARCHIVES OF INTERNAL MEDICINE 150(4):883-886, April 1990

Cocaine- and methamphetamine-related deaths in San Diego County: 1987: homicides and accidental overdoses, by D. N. Bailey, et al. JOURNAL OF FORENSIC SCIENCES 34(2):407-422, 1989

Cocaine and the nervous system, by R. Cowen. SCIENCE NEWS 137:238, April 14, 1990

Cocaine and polysubstance abuse by psychiatric inpatients, by F. Miller, et al. HOSPITAL AND COMMUNITY PSYCHIATRY 41(11):1251-1253, 1990

Cocaine cases down in United States. JOURNAL OF THE ADDICTION RESEARCH FOUNDATION 19(7-8):1, July/August 1990

Cocaine-"crack" dependence among psychiatric inpatients, by G. Bunt, et al. AMERICAN JOURNAL OF PSYCHIATRY 147:1542-1546, November 1990

Cocaine danger on the road: study of fatal New York City motor vehicle accidents by Peter M. Marzuk and J. John Mann. SCIENCE NEWS 137:23, January 13, 1990

Cocaine epidemic: a comprehensive review of use, abuse and dependence, by N. M. Chychula, et al. NURSE PRACTITIONER 15(7):31-39, July 1990

Cocaine: European "drug of the year" also available in Arabic, French and Spanish. INTERNATIONAL CRIMINAL POLICE REVIEW 418:23-27, 1989

Cocaine-HIV alert is raised in study, by K. Fournis. JOURNAL OF THE ADDICTION RESEARCH FOUNDATION 19(12):1, December 1, 1990

Cocaine intoxication, by R. W. Derlet. POSTGRADUATE MEDICINE 86(5):245-248+, October 1989

Cocaine: maternal use during pregnancy and its effect on the mother, the fetus, and the infant, by D. Rosenak, et al. OBSTETRICAL AND GYNECOLOGICAL SURVEY 45(6):348-359, June 1990

Cocaine overdose, by D. Dubiel. NURSING 90 20:33, March 1990

COCAINE

Cocaine: recognizing, treating the abuser, by P. Coleman. VIRGINIA MEDICINE 117 (6):251-255, June 1990

Cocaine smokers excrete a pyrolysis product, anhydroecgonine methyl ester, by P. Jacob, 3d, et al. JOURNAL OF TOXICOLOGY: CLINICAL TOXICOLOGY 28(1): 121-125, 1990

Cocaine update: abuse and therapy, by G. J. DiGregorio. AMERICAN FAMILY PHYSICIAN 41(1):247-250, January 1990

Cocaine users may not fit MDs' stereotype, FPs warned, by B. Trent. CMAJ 143(11): 1239-1240, December 1, 1990

Cocaine's defenseless victims. AMERICAN JOURNAL OF NURSING 90:32, February 1990

Competing theoretical explanations of cocaine use: differential association versus control theory, by P. T. MacDonald. JOURNAL OF CONTEMPORARY CRIMINAL JUSTICE 5(2):73-88, 1989

Crack and cocaine use in south London drug addicts: 1987-1989, by J. Strang, et al. BRITISH JOURNAL OF ADDICTION 85(2):193-196, February 1990

Crack and kids, by D. J. Besharov. SOCIETY 27(5):25-26, July/August 1990

Crack cocaine: a new danger for children, by M. C. Heagarty. AMERICAN JOURNAL OF DISEASES OF CHILDREN 144(7):756-757, July 1990

CRACK: the death of our children, by J. Muther. DIE NEUE POLIZEI 44(8):441+, 1990

Crack: girls like you on drugs like that, by M. Massing. MADEMOISELLE 96:158-161, May 1990

Crack of doom: crack abuse in the United States and Britain, by P. Gillman. SUNDAY TIMES MAGAZINE April 1, 1990, p. 24+

Crack troops. NEW SCIENTIST 125:26, March 3, 1990

Dirty drug secret: hyping instant addiction doesn't help, by L. Martz. NEWSWEEK 115(8):74+, February 19, 1990

Down to cocaine hell. READER'S DIGEST 137:183-185+, December 1990

Dr. Sone: condensed from the book, by C. Saline. READER'S DIGEST (CANADA) 136(813):149-168+, January 1990

Drug dilemma: manipulating the demand—cocaine, by M. E. Jarvick. SCIENCE 250:387-392, October 19, 1990

Drug market position of cocaine among young adults in Sydney, New South Wales, Australia, by P. Homel, et al. BRITISH JOURNAL OF ADDICTION 85(7):891-898, July 1990

Drug use, health, family and social support in "crack" cocaine users, by C. J. Boyd, et al. ADDICTIVE BEHAVIORS 15(5):481-486, 1990

Drugs: goodbye, cocaine. ECONOMIST 316:28+, September 8, 1990

Drugs, women's work and ecology: questions, by J. Ucelli. SOCIALISM AND DEMOC-
RACY (10):103, Spring 1990

Effect of haloperidol in cocaine and amphetamine intoxication, by R. W. Derlet, et al.
JOURNAL OF EMERGENCY MEDICINE 7(6):633-637, November/December
1989

Effective use of search warrants in the war on crack: Denver, Coloraro, by P. Mahoney. POLICE CHIEF 57:50-52, May 1990

Effects of cadmium on the self-administration of ethanol as an isocaloric-isohedonic
equivalent, by J. R. Nation, et al. NEUROTOXICOLOGY AND TERATOLOGY
11(5):509-514, September/October 1989

Effects of cocaine and morphine on IgG production by human peripheral blood lymphocytes in vitro, by F. Martinez, et al. LIFE SCIENCES 47(15):59-64, 1990

Effects of the combination of cocaine and marijuana on the task-elicited physiological
response, by R. W. Foltin, et al. NIDA RESEARCH MONOGRAPH SERIES 95:
359-360, 1989

Effects of combinations of intranasal cocaine, smoked marijuana, and task performance on heart rate and blood pressure, by R. W. Foltin, et al. PHARMACOL-
OGY, BIOCHEMISTRY AND BEHAVIOR 36(2):311-315, June 1990

Effects of fetal exposure to cocaine and heroin. AMERICAN FAMILY PHYSICIAN
41:1595+, May 1990

Esophagitis, epiglottitis, and cocaine alkaloid (crack): "accidental" poisoning or child
abuse, by S. Kharasch, et al. PEDIATRICS 86(1):117-119, July 1990

Explaining the recent decline in cocaine use among young adults: further evidence
that perceived risks and disapproval lead to reduced drug use, by J. G. Bachman,
et al. JOURNAL OF HEALTH AND SOCIAL BEHAVIOR 31(2):173-184, June
1990

Federal study finds drinking down; cocaine use up. CRIME CONTROL DIGEST
24(20):6, May 21, 1990

From crackhouse to freakhouse, by D. P. Hamilton. SCIENCE 249:982, August 31,
1990

Good news in the drug war: prices up, purity down—cocaine, by G. Hackett. NEWS-
WEEK 116(1):24, July 2, 1990

Goodbye, cocaine: cocaine's price has risen and cocaine-related admissions to hospitals are falling. ECONOMIST 316:28+, September 8, 1990

Great crack attack. CURRENT HEALTH 2 16:6, February 1990

Harrisburg cocaine case embarrassing Thornburgh. CRIME CONTROL DIGEST 24
(23):1-2, August 20, 1990

High affinity dopamine reuptake inhibitors as potential cocaine antagonists: a strategy for drug development, by R. B. Rothman. LIFE SCIENCES 46(20):17-21, 1990

History of cocaine toxicity, by S. B. Karch. HUMAN PATHOLOGY 20(11):1037-1039, November 1989

Holding mom accountable, by M. Curriden. ABA JOURNAL 76:50-53, March 1990

"Hop and hubbas": a tough new mix—a research note on cocaine use among methadone maintenance clients, by D. McDonnell, et al. CONTEMPORARY DRUG PROBLEMS 17:145-156, Spring 1990

Human psychopharmacology of intranasal cocaine, by S. T. Higgins, et al. NIDA RESEARCH MONOGRAPH SERIES 95:357-358, 1989

Illicit price of cocaine in two eras: 1908-1914 and 1982-1989, by D. F. Musto. CONNECTICUT MEDICINE 54(6):321-326, June 1990

Immunomodulation by cocaine: a neuroendocrine mediated response, by B. Watzl, et al. LIFE SCIENCES 46(19):1391-1329, 1990

Initiation into crack and cocaine: a tale of two epidemics, by J. Fagan, et al. CONTEMPORARY DRUG PROBLEMS 16(4):579-617, 1989

Intelligence survey: DEA reports on status of crack. NARCOTICS CONTROL DIGEST 19(17):2-3, August 16, 1989; also in 19(18):10, August 30, 1989 and 19(20):7, September 27, 1989

Isolation, identification and separation of isomeric truxillines in illicit cocaine, by I. S. Lurie, et al. JOURNAL OF CHROMATOGRAPHY 504(2):391-402, 1990

It's a lovely job and some people die, by R. Gordon. LESBIAN CONTRADICTION (30):3, Spring 1990

Maternal abuse of cocaine and heroin, by E. C. Maynard. AMERICAN JOURNAL OF DISEASES OF CHILDREN 144(5):520-521, May 1990

Maternal cocaine use during pregnancy: effect on the newborn infant, by M. Abdeljaber, et al. PEDIATRICS 85(4):630, April 1990

Mechanisms responsible for the cardiotoxic effects of cocaine, by G. E. Billman. FASEB JOURNAL 4:2469-2475, May 1990

Ophthalmic use of cocaine and the urine test for benzoylecgonine, by B. B. Bralliar, et al. NEW ENGLAND JOURNAL OF MEDICINE 320:1757-1758, June 29, 1989

Overall illegal drug use dealing at a rapid rate. NARCOTICS CONTROL DIGEST August 2, 1989, p. 12

Patterns of alcohol and drug abuse in an urban trauma center: the increasing role of cocaine abuse, by G. A. Lindenbaum, et al. JOURNAL OF TRAUMA 29(12): 1654-1658, December 1989

Patterns of cocaine abuse in an inner city emergency psychiatric service setting, by A. Y. Ghali, et al. MEDICINE AND LAW 8(2):165-170, 1989

COCAINE

Pharmacology of cocaine related to its abuse, by C. E. Johanson, et al. PHARMACO-LOGICAL REVIEWS 41(1):3-52, March 1989

Potentiality risk factors for cocaine abuse, by W. R. Yates, et al. JAMA 262:2654, November 17, 1989

Prenatal substance abuse: an overview of the problem, by J. Gittler, et al. CHILDREN TODAY 19:3-7, July/August 1990

Presidential address of the SSCI: metabolic and social consequences of cocaine abuse, by J. P. Kokko. AMERICAN JOURNAL OF MEDICAL SCIENCES 299(6): 361-365, June 1990

Prevalence and self-reported consequences of cocaine use, by A. M. Trinkoff, et al. NIDA RESEARCH MONOGRAPH SERIES 95:329, 1989

Prevalence of marijuana (cannabis) use and dependence in cocaine dependence, by N. S. Miller, et al. NEW YORK STATE JOURNAL OF MEDICINE 90(10):491-492, 1990

Prevalence of recent cocaine use among motor vehicle fatalities in New York City, by P. M. Marzuk, et al. JAMA 263(2):250-256, January 12, 1990

Prospective evaluation of "crack-vial" ingestions, by R. S. Hoffman, et al. VETERI-NARY AND HUMAN TOXICOLOGY 32(2):164-167, April 1990

Snowed in: cocaine, by M. A. R. Kleiman. NEW REPUBLIC 202:14-16, April 23, 1990

Statewide prevalence of cocaine use during the perinatal period. RHODE ISLAND MEDICAL JOURNAL 73(6):272, June 1990

Streets are filled with coke, by D. Whitman. US NEWS AND WORLD REPORT 108: 24-26, March 5, 1990

Survey shows marijuana, cocaine, heroin emergencies soar for third straight year. NARCOTICS CONROL DIGEST 19(23):9-10, November 8, 1989 ; also in CRIME CONTROL DIGEST 23(45):4, November 13, 1989

Trading sex for crack among juvenile drug users: a research note, by J. A. Inciardi. CONTEMPORARY DRUG PROBLEMS 16(4):689-700, Winter 1989

Tragedy unfolds. IOWA MEDICINE 80(5):282, May 1990

Undeterred cocaine user: intention to quit and its relationship to perceived legal and health threats, by P. G. Erickson, et al. CONTEMPORARY DRUG PROBLEMS 16(2):141-156, Summer 1989

What crack can do: Texas user slays three family members, holds man hostage. NAR-COTICS CONTROL DIGEST 19(14):3-4, July 5, 1989

Women and crack addiction, by J. Sher. JOURNAL OF THE AMERICAN MEDICAL WOMEN'S ASSOCIATION 44(6):166, November/December 1989

Acute cocaine abuse associated with cerebral infarction, by M. E. Seaman. ANNALS OF EMERGENCY MEDICINE 19(1):34-37, January 1990

Acute gastroduodenal perforations associated with use of crack, by H. S. Lee, et al. ANNALS OF SURGERY 211(1):15-17, January 1990

Acute myocardial infarct in a cocaine-addicted young man, by I. Laynez Cardena, et al. REVISTA ESPANOLA DE CARDIOLOGIA 43(3):198-200, March 1990

Acute renal failure and rhabdomyolysis following cocaine abuse, by F. Ahijado, et al. NEPHRON 54(3):268, 1990

Angiographic and histologic study of cocaine-induced chest pain, by P. A. Majid, et al. AMERICAN JOURNAL OF CARDIOLOGY 65(11):812-814, March 15, 1990

Application of a model of exertional heatstroke pathophysiology to cocaine intoxication, by L. E. Armstrong, et al. AMERICAN JOURNAL OF EMERGENCY MEDICINE 8(2):178, March 1990

Association of cocaine use with sperm concentration, motility, and morphology, by M. B. Bracken, et al. FERTILITY AND STERILITY 53(2):315-322, February 1990

Association of spontaneous pneumomediastinum with substance abuse, by L. L. Fajardo. WESTERN JOURNAL OF MEDICINE 152(3):301-304, March 1990

Bias against the null hypothesis: the reproductive hazards of cocaine, by G. Koren, et al. LANCET 2(8677):1440-1442, December 16, 1989

Biopsy-proven cerebral vasculitis associated with cocaine abuse, by D. A. Krendel, et al. NEUROLOGY 40(7):1092-1094, July 1990

Cardiologic complications related to cocaine, by H. Van Viet, et al. ANNALES DE MEDECINE INTERNE 140(8):702-708, 1989

Cardiopulmonary abnormalities after smoking cocaine, by T. Christou, et al. SOUTHERN MEDICAL JOURNAL 83(3):335-338, March 1990

Central mechanisms of action involved in cocaine-induced tachycardia, by L. F. Jones, et al. LIFE SCIENCES 46(10):723-728, 1990

Cerebral abnormalities in cocaine abusers: demonstration by SPECT perfusion brain scintigraphy—work in progress, by S. S. Tumeh, et al. RADIOLOGY 176(3):821-824, September 1990

Cerebral hemorrhage caused by cocaine consumption, by L. Vicens, et al. REVISTA CLINICA ESPANOLA 186(1):43-44, January 1990

Cerebral infarction and cocaine abuse. AMERICAN FAMILY PHYSICIAN 42:797, September 1990

Cerebrovascular complications of the use of the "crack" form of alkaloidal cocaine, by S. R. Levine, et al. NEW ENGLAND JOURNAL OF MEDICINE 323(11):699-704, September 13, 1990

Chronic cocaine abuse associated with dilated cardiomyopathy, by P. T. Hogya, et al. AMERICAN JOURNAL OF EMERGENCY MEDICINE 8(3):203-204, May 1990

Cocaine, by P. D. Mueller, et al. EMERGENCY MEDICINE CLINICS OF NORTH AMERICA 8(3):481-493, August 1990

Cocaine and disturbances of adrenergic neurotransmission, by G. Nahas, et al. BULETIN DE l'ACADEMIE NATIONALE DE MEDICINE 173(9):1199-1206, December 1989

Cocaine and pregnancy: effects on the pregnant woman, the fetus and the newborn infant, by A. Garcia Perez, et al. MEDICINA CLINICA 93(14):538-542, November 4, 1989

Cocaine and pregnancy: a lethal combination, by K. S. Pitts, et al. JOURNAL OF PERINATOLOGY 10(2):180-182, June 1990

Cocaine and the risk of low birth weight: Alameda County, California, by D. B. Petitti, et al. AMERICAN JOURNAL OF PUBLIC HEALTH 80(1):25-28, January 1990

Cocaine and scleroderma, by H. D. Kerr. SOUTHERN MEDICAL JOURNAL 82(10): 1275-1276, October 1989

Cocaine and sudden cardiac death, by T. J. Pallasch, et al. JOURNAL OF ORAL AND MAXILLOFACIAL SURGERY 47(11):1188-1191, November 1989

Cocaine and traffic accident fatalities in New York City. JAMA 263(21):2887-2888, June 6, 1990

Cocaine-associated asthma, by R. B. Rubin, et al. AMERICAN JOURNAL OF MEDICINE 88(4):438-439, April 1990

Cocaine-associated multifocal ties, by A. Pascual-Leone, et al. NEUROLOGY 40(6): 999-1000, 1990

Cocaine-associated rhabdomyolysis and hemoptysis mimicking pulmonary embolism, by F. R. Justiniani, et al. AMERICAN JOURNAL OF MEDICINE 88(3):316-317, March 1990

Cocaine cardiac toxicity, by T. S. Rummel. JOURNAL OF THE TENNESSEE MEDICAL ASSOCIATION 82(10):541, October 1989

Cocaine-induced acute aortic dissection, by D. Gadaleta, et al. CHEST 96(5):1203-1205, November 1989

Cocaine-induced delirium versus delusional disorder, by G. D. Pearlson, et al. BIOLOGICAL PSYCHIATRY 26(8):847-848, December 1989

Cocaine-induced dental erosions, by D. J. Krutchkoff, et al. NEW ENGLAND JOURNAL OF MEDICINE 322:408, February 8, 1990

Cocaine-induced ischemic myocardial disease, by L. S. Roh, et al. AMERICAN JOURNAL OF FORENSIC MEDICINE AND PATHOLOGY 11(2):130-135, June 1990

Cocaine-induced small-bowel perforation, by C. Endress, et al. AJR 154(6):1346-1347, June 1990

Cocaine-related maternal death, by G. Burkett, et al. AMERICAN JOURNAL OF OB-
STETRICS AND GYNECOLOGY 163(1 Pt 1):40-41, July 1990

Cocaine-related medical problems: consecutive series of 233 patients, by S. L.
Brody, et al. AMERICAN JOURNAL OF MEDICINE 88(4):325-331, April 1990

Cocaine, rhabdomyolysis and metastic calcifications, by A. M. Castelao, et al.
NEPHROLOGY, DIALYSIS, TRANSPLANTATION 4(7):675, 1989

Cocaine threat, by F. Brown. MCN 14(5):308, September/October 1989

Cocaine use and cerebrovascular disease: two cases of ischemic stroke in young
adults, by M. Guidotti, et al. ITALIAN JOURNAL OF NEUROLOGICAL SCIENCES
11(2):153-155, April 1990

Cocaine use and its effect on umbilical artery prostacyclin production, by H. E. Cejtin,
et al. PROSTAGLANDINS 40(3):249-258, 1990

Cocaine use during pregnancy, by D. R. Coustan, et al. RHODE ISLAND MEDICAL
JOURNAL 73(6):249-252, June 1990

Cocaine use during pregnancy: implications for physicians, by R. A. Aronson, et al.
WISCONSIN MEDICAL JOURNAL 89(3):105-110, March 1990

Cocaine use during pregnancy may result in birth defects, by R. Hume, Jr. AMERI-
CAN FAMILY PHYSICIAN 41:928, March 1990

Cocaine use during pregnancy: research findings and clinical implications, by M.
Lynch, et al JOURNAL OF OBSTETRIC, GYNECOLOGIC, AND NEONATAL
NURSING 19(4):285-292, July/August 1990

Cocaine use in pregnancy: physicians urged to look for problem where they least expect it, by A. Skolnick. JAMA 264(3):306+, July 18, 1990

Cocaine use may severely weaken the immune system, by J. Delafuente. AMERICAN
FAMILY PHYSICIAN 40:149, December 1989

Cocaine user: the potential problem patient for rhinoplasty, by S. A. Slavin, et al.
PLASTIC AND RECONSTRUCTIVE SURGERY 86(3):436-442, September 1990

Cocaine withdrawal dystonia, by K. Kumor. NEUROLOGY 40(5):863-864, May 1990

Complex partial status epilepticus provoked by "crack" cocaine, by A. O. Ogunyemi,
et al. ANNALS OF NEUROLOGY 26(6):785-786, December 1989

Complications of cocaine use, by C. E. Emory. CLINICAL PHARMACY 8(10):689-
690, October 1989

Congenital renal abnormalities in infants with in utero cocaine exposure, by B. J.
Rosenstein, et al. JOURNAL OF UROLOGY 144(1):110-112, 1990

Corneal epithelial defects after smoking crack cocaine, by J. G. McHenry, et al.
AMERICAN JOURNAL OF OPHTHALMOLOGY 108(6):732, December 15, 1989

Crack abuse: do you know enough about it?, by D. J. Hannan, et al. POSTGRADU-
ATE MEDICINE 88(1):141-143+, July 1990

Crack-induced rhadbdomyolysis, by J. S. Steingrub, et al. CRITICAL CARE MEDI-CINE 17(10):1073-1074, October 1989

Crack lung: an acute pulmonary syndrome with a spectrum of clinical and histopatho-logic findings, by J. M. Forrester, et al. AMERICAN REVIEW OF RESPIRATORY DISEASE 142(2):462-467, August 1990

Crack users: the new AIDS risk group, by R. E. Fullilove, et al. CANCER DETECTION AND PREVENTION 14(3):363-368, 1990

Decreased cardiac output in infants of mothers who abused cocaine, by M. van de Bor, et al. PEDIATRICS 85(1):30-32, January 1990

Desperate crack legacy: fetal alcohol syndrome and crack babies, by M. Dorris. NEWSWEEK 114(26):8, June 25, 1990

Diaplacental poisoning with narcotics and alcohol in newborn infants, by A. Kloppel, et al. BEITRAGE ZUR GERICHTLICHEN MEDIZIN 47:77-79, 1989

Dopaminergic mechanisms in idiopathic and drug-induced psychoses, by J. A. Lieberman, et al. SCHIZOPHRENIA BULLETIN 16(1):97-110, 1990

Dopaminergic sensitivity and cocaine abuse: response to apomorphine, by E. Hol-lander, et al. PSYCHIATRY RESEARCH 33(2):161-170, 1990

Effect of maternal cocaine use on the fetus and newborn: review of the literature, by E. H. Roland, et al. PEDIATRIC NEUROSCIENCE 15(2):88-94, 1989

Effects of chronic cocaine abuse on postsynaptic dopamine receptors, by N. D. Volkow, et al. AMERICAN JOURNAL OF PSYCHIATRY 147(6):719-724, June 1990

Effects of cocaine on the human fetus: a review of clinical studies, by P. L. Doering, et al. DICP 23(9):639-645, September 1989

Effects of maternal cocaine abuse on perinatal and infant outcome, by L. Cordero, et al. OHIO MEDICINE 86(5):410-412, May 1990

Endocarditis in intravenous drug abusers, by R. Roberts, et al. EMERGENCY MEDI-CINE CLINICS OF NORTH AMERICA 8(3):665-681, August 1990

Eosinophilic myocarditis and pulmonary hypertension in a drug-addict: anatomo-clini-cal study and brief review of the literature, by V. C. Talebzadeh, et al. ANNALES DE PATHOLOGIE 10(1):40-46, 1990

Freebase cocaine and memory, by T. C. Manschreck, et al. COMPREHENSIVE PSY-CHIATRY 31(4):369-375, July/August 1990

Heart defects now seen in cocaine babies: most critical period is first 28 weeks of pregnancy, by J. McCann. JOURNAL OF THE ADDICTION RESEARCH FOUN-DATION 19(3):5, March 1, 1990

Hemolytic-uremic syndrome following "crack" cocaine inhalation, by J. A. Tumlin, et al. AMERICAN JOURNAL OF MEDICAL SCIENCES 299(6):366-371, June 1990

Histopathology of cocaine hepatotoxicity: report of four patients, by I. R. Wanless, et al. GASTROENTEROLOGY 98(2):497-501, February 1990

Hypoatremia in a neonate of a cocaine abusing mother, by S. Dollberg, et al. JOURNAL OF TOXICOLOGY: CLINICAL TOXICOLOGY 27(4-5):287-292, 1989

Hypodermic needle aspiration in a freebase cocaine abuser, by S. Lacagnina, et al. CHEST 97(5):1275-1276, May 1990

Hyponatremia in a neonate of a cocaine abusing mother, by S. Dollberg, et al. JOURNAL OF TOXICOLOGY: CLINICAL TOXICOLOGY 27(4-5):287-292, 1989

Increased cerebral blood flow velocity in infants of mothers who abuse cocaine, by M. van de Bor, et al. PEDIATRICS 85(5):733-736, May 1990

Infants exposed to cocaine in utero: implications for developmental assessment and intervention, by J. W. Schneider, et al. INFANTS AND YOUNG CHILDREN 2(1): 25-36, July 1989

Intravenous cocaine abuse and subarachnoid haemorrhage: effect on outcome, by R. K. Simpson, Jr., et al. BRITISH JOURNAL OF NEUROSURGERY 4(1):27-30, 1990

Investigation of cocaine-related seizures showing unsuspected brain tumors, by M. Seaman, et al. 19(6):733-734, June 1990

Lack of specific placental abnormality associated with cocaine use, by W. M. Gilbert, et al. AMERICAN JOURNAL OF OBSTETRICS AND GYNECOLOGY 163(3):998-999, September 1990

Maternal cocaine abuse and effects on the mother, fetus and newborn, by D. Rosenak, et al. HAREFAUH 116(21):600-603, June 1, 1989

Medical complications of cocaine and other illicit drug abuse simulating rheumatic disease, by J. T. Lie. JOURNAL OF RHEUMATOLOGY 17(6):736-737, June 1990

Medical complications of the use of cocaine, by S. J. Wallach. HAWAII MEDICAL JOURNAL 48(11):461-462, November 1989

More on rhabdomyolysis associated with cocaine intoxication, by A. W. Fox. NEW ENGLAND JOURNAL OF MEDICINE 321(18):1271, November 2, 1989

Multiple intracerebral hemorrhages after smoking "crack" cocaine, by R. M. Green, et al. STROKE 21(6):957-962, June 1990

Mycoardial infarction during cocaine withdrawal, by C. Del Aguila, et al. ANNALS OF INTERNAL MEDICINE 112(9):712, May 1, 1990

Myocardial ischemia during cocaine withdrawal, by K. Nademanee, et al. ANNALS OF INTERNAL MEDICINE 111(11):876-880, December 1, 1989

Nasal cocaine abuse causing an aggressive midline intranasal and pharyngeal destructive process mimicking midline reticulosis and limited Wegener's granulomatosis, by R. B. Daggett, et al. JOURNAL OF RHEUMATOLOGY 17(6):838-840, June 1990

Neonatal cocaine-related seizures, by L. D. Kramer, et al. JOURNAL OF CHILD NEU-
ROLOGY 5(1):60-64, January 1990

Neonatal intestinal perforation: the "crack" connection, by B. M. Miller, et al. AMERI-
CAN JOURNAL OF GASTROENTEROLOGY 85(6):767-769, June 1990

Neonatal ultrasound casebook: antenatal brain injury and maternal cocaine use, by M.
E. Sims, et al. JOURNAL OF PERINATAL 9(3):349-350, September 1989

Neurobiology of abused drugs: opioids and stimulants, by T. R. Kosten. JOURNAL
OF NERVOUS AND MENTAL DISEASE 178(2):217-227, April 1990

Neurologic complications caused by use of cocaine, amphetamines and sympathomimetics, by E. Diez-Tejedor, et al. ARCHIVOS DE NEUROBIOLOGIA 52
(Suppl)1:162-182, 1989

Neurologic complications of cocaine abuse, by H. Van Viet, et al. PRESSE MEDI-
CALE 19(22):1045-1049, June 2, 1990

Neurologic consequences of cocaine use, by M. C. Rowbotham, et al. ANNUAL RE-
VIEW OF MEDICINE 41:417-422, 1990

Noradrenergic mechanisms appear not to be involved in cocaine-induced seizures
and lethality, by H. C. Jackson, et al. LIFE SCIENCES 47(4):353-359, 1990

Opsoclonus-myoclonus following the intranasal usage of cocaine, by D. Scharf.
JOURNAL OF NEUROLOGY, NEUROSURGERY AND PSYCHIATRY 52(12):
1447-1448, December 1989

Personality disorders classification and symptoms in cocaine and opioid addicts, by R.
M. Malow, et al. JOURNAL OF CONSULTING AND CLINICAL PSYCHOLOGY
57(6):765-757, December 1989

Postpartum cardiovascular complications after bromocriptine and cocaine use, by F.
R. Bakht, et al. AMERICAN JOURNAL OF OBSTETRICS AND GYNECOLOGY
162(4):1065-1066, April 1990

Prenatal cocaine exposure and fetal vascular disruption, by H. E. Hoyme, et al. PEDI-
ATRICS 85(5):743-747, 1990

Prenatal cocaine use: effects of perinatal outcome, by J. R. Janke, et al. JOURNAL
OF NURSE-MIDWIFERY 35(2):74-77, March/April 1990

Priapism associated with intranasal cocaine abuse, by R. L. Fiorelli, et al. JOURNAL
OF UROLOGY 143(3):584-585, March 1990

Pulmonary artery medial hypertrophy in cocaine users without foreign particle mi-
croembolization, by R. J. Murray, et al. CHEST 96(5):1050-1053, November
1989

Pulmonary edema after freebase cocaine smoking: not due to an adulterant, by J. N.
Kline, et al. CHEST 97(4):1009-1010, April 1990

Pulmonary talc granulomatosis in a cocaine sniffer, by M. Oubeid, et al. CHEST 98(1):
237-239, July 1990

Quantitative analysis of amounts of coronary arterial narrowing in cocaine addicts, by F. A. Dressler, et al. AMERICAN JOURNAL OF CARDIOLOGY 65(5):303-308, February 1, 1990

Report offers new insights on cocaine and heart risk. NARCOTICS DEMAND REDUCTION DIGEST 1(7):8, December 1989

Reversible cardiomyopathy associated with cocaine intoxication, by S. K. Chokshi, et al. ANNALS OF INTERNAL MEDICINE 111(12):1039-1040, December 15, 1989

Review of the respiratory effects of smoking cocaine, by N. A. Ettinger, et al. AMERICAN JOURNAL OF MEDICINE 87(6):664-668, December 1989

Rupture of unscarred uterus in primigravid woman in association with cocaine abuse, by W. Gonsoulin, et al. AMERICAN JOURNAL OF OBSTETRICS AND GYNECOLOGY 163(2):526-527, August 1990

Severe acid-base abnormalities associated with cocaine abuse, by T. R. Drake, et al. JOURNAL OF EMERGENCY MEDICINE 8(3):331-334, May/June 1990

Severe thrombocytopenia associated with cocaine use, by C. A. Leissinger. ANNALS OF INTERNAL MEDICINE 112(9):708-710, May 1, 1990

Shadow children: crack babies, by M. C. Rist. AMERICAN SCHOOL BOARD JOURNAL 177:18-24, January 1990

Sickle cell disease and cocaine abuse: a deadly mixture, by A. Strauss, et al. SOUTHERN MEDICAL JOURNAL 82(11):1455-1456, November 1989

Spinal cord infarction after cocaine use, by G. R. Sawaya, et al. SOUTHERN MEDICAL JOURNAL 83(5):601-602, May 1990

Stroke associated with cocaine use, by P. M. Deringer, et al. ARCHIVES OF NEUROLOGY 47(5):502, May 1990

Stroke from alcohol and drug abuse: a current social peril, by P. B. Goerlick. POSTGRADUATE MEDICINE 88(2):171-174+, August 1990

Sudden death from acute cocaine intoxication in Virginia in 1988, by R. McKelway, et al. AMERICAN JOURNAL OF PSYCHIATRY 147:1667-1669, December 1990

Thrombocytopenic purpura in HIV-seronegative users of intravenous cocaine, by M. J. Koury. AMERICAN JOURNAL OF HEMATOLOGY 35(2):134-135, October 1990

Unrecognized left ventricular dysfunction in an apparently healthy cocaine abuse population, by B. D. Bertolet, et al. CLINICAL CARDIOLOGY 13(5):323-328, May 1990

Upper extremity deep venous thrombosis: increased prevalence due to cocaine abuse, by J. R. Lisse, et al. AMERICAN JOURNAL OF MEDICINE 87(4):457-458, October 1989

Utero exposure to cocaine and the risk of SIDS, by B. Lounsbury, et al. NIDA RESEARCH MONOGRAPH SERIES 95:352, 1989

Vascular changes in the nasal submucosa of chronic cocaine addicts, by J. M. Chow, et al. AMERICAN JOURNAL OF FORENSIC MEDICINE AND PATHOLOGY 11(2): 136-143, June 1990

Research

5-HT3 receptor antagonists attenuate cocaine-induced locomotion in mice, by M. E. A. Reith. EUROPEAN JOURNAL OF PHARMACOLOGY 186(2-3):327-330, 1990

Acute and chronic effects of cocaine on isolation-induced aggression in mice, by N. A. Darmani, et al. PSYCHOPHARMACOLOGY 102(1):37-40, 1990

Behavioral and EEG studies of acute cocaine administration: comparisons with morphine, amphetamine, pentobarbital, nicotine, ethanol and marijuana, by S. E. Lukas, et al. NIDA RESEARCH MONOGRAPH SERIES 95:146-151, 1989

Behavioral effects of cocaine and its interaction with d-amphetamine and morphine in rats, by G. R. Wenger, et al. PHARMACOLOGY, BIOCHEMISTRY AND BEHAVIOR 35(3):595-600, March 1990

Bromocriptine antagonizes behavioral effects of cocaine in the rat, by A. Campbell, et al. NEUROPSYCHOPHARMACOLOGY 2(3):209-224, September 1989

Bromocriptine produces decreases in cocaine self-administration in the rat, by C. B. Hubner, et al. NEUROPSYCHOPHARMACOLOGY 3(2):101-108, April 1990

Bromocriptine self-administration and bromocriptine-reinstatement of cocaine-trained and heroin-trained lever pressing in rats, by R. A. Wise, et al. PSYCHOPHARMACOLOGY 100(3):355-360, 1990

Buprenorphine and naltrexone effects on cocaine self-administration by rhesus monkeys, by N. K. Mello, et al. JOURNAL OF PHARMACOLOGY AND EXPERIMENTAL THERAPEUTICS 254(3):926-939, September 1990

Chlordiazepoxide alters intravenous cocaine self-administration in rats, by N. E. Goeders, et al. PHARMACOLOGY, BIOCHEMISTRY AND BEHAVIOR 33(4):859-866, August 1989

Chronic cocaine and rat brain catecholamines: long-term reduction in hypothalamic and frontal cortex dopamine metabolism, by F. Karoum, et al. EUROPEAN JOURNAL OF PHARMACOLOGY 186(1):1-8, 1990

Chronic cocaine treatment decreases levels of the G protein subunits Gia in discrete regions of rat brain, by E. J. Nestler, et al. JOURNAL OF NEUROCHEMISTRY 55(3):1079-1082, 1990

Cocaine and body temperature in the rat: effects of ambient temperature, by P. Lomax, et al. PHARMACOLOGY 40(2):103-109, 1990

Cocaine and level of arousal: effects on vigilance task performance of rats, by D. M. Grilly, et al. PHARMACOLOGY, BIOCHEMISTRY AND BEHAVIOR 35(1):269-271, January 1990

Cocaine and local anesthetics: stimulants in rats with nigral lesions, by P. B. Silverman. PSYCHOPHARMACOLOGY 102(2):269-272, 1990

Cocaine as a cause of congenital malformations of vascular origin: experimental evidence in the rat, by W. S. Webster, et al. TERATOLOGY 41(6):689-697, June 1990

Cocaine attenuates opiate withdrawal in human and rat, by T. A. Kosten, et al. NIDA RESEARCH MONOGRAPH SERIES 95:361-362, 1989

Cocaine: effect on spinal projection neurons in the rat, by A. Pertovaara, et al. BRAIN RESEARCH BULLETIN 25(1):1-6, 1990

Cocaine effects on pulsatile secretion of anterior pituitary, gonadal, and adrenal hormones, by J. H. Mendelson, et al. JOURNAL OF CLINICAL ENDOCRINOLOGY AND METABOLISM 69(6):1256-1260, December 1989

Cocaine enhances memory storage in mice, by I. B. Introini-Collison, et al. PSYCHO-PHARMACOLOGY 99(4)537-541, December 1989

Cocaine hepatotoxicity in cultured liver slices: a species comparison, by S. Connors, et al. TOXICOLOGY 61(2):171-184, 1990

Cocaine increases benzodiazepine receptors labeled in the mouse brain in vivo with [3H]Ro 15-1788, by M. E. Jung, et al. NIDA RESEARCH MONOGRAPH SERIES 95:512-513, 1989

Cocaine-induced cerebral vascular damage can be ameliorated by Mg2+ in rat brain, by Q. F. Huang, et al. NEUROSCIENCE LETTERS 109(1-2):113-116, February 5, 1990

Cocaine-induced reduction of glucose utilization in human brain: a study using positron emission tomography and [fluorine 18]-fluorodeoxyglucose, by E. D. London, et al. ARCHIVES OF GENERAL PSYCHIATRY 47(6):567-574, June 1990

Cocaine inhibition of ligand binding at dopamine, norepinephrine and serotonin transporters: a structure-activity study, by M. C. Ritz, et al. LIFE SCIENCES 46(9): 635-639, 1990

Cocaine inhibits baroreflex control of blood pressure by action at arterial baroreceptors, by M. C. Andresen, et al. AMERICAN JOURNAL OF PHYSIOLOGY 258(pt 2):1244-1249, April 1990

Cocaine produces locomotor stimulation in SS but not LS mice: relationship to dopaminergic function, by F. R. George, et al. PSYCHOPHARMACOLOGY 101(1):18-22, 1990

Comparison of the effects of cocaine and other inhibitors of dopamine uptake in rat striatum, nucleus accumbens, olfactory tubercle, and medial prefrontal cortex, by S. Izenwasser, et al. BRAIN RESEARCH 520(1-2):303-309, 1990

Comparison of responses by neuropeptide systems in rat to the psychotropic drugs, methamphetamine, cocaine, and PCP, by G. R. Hanson, et al. NIDA RESEARCH MONOGRAPH SERIES 95:348, 1989

Correlation between cocaine-induced locomotion and cocaine disposition in the brain among four inbred strains of mice, by H. L. Wiener, et al. PHARMACOLOGY, BIO-CHEMISTRY AND BEHAVIOR 36(3):699-702, 1990

D1 receptor gene cloned: clue to cocaine addiction, by K. Fournis. JOURNAL OF THE ADDICTION RESEARCH FOUNDATION 19(10):2, October 1, 1990

Effect of acute cocaine administration on the cholinergic enzyme levels of specific brain regions in the rat, by L. H. Claye, et al. PHARMACOLOGY 40(4):218-223, 1990

Effect of chronic cocaine administration and cocaine withdrawal flow rate and heart rate responses to epinephrine and cocaine in isolated perfused rat hearts, by E. V. Avakian, et al. LIFE SCIENCES 46(22):1569-1574, 1990

Effect of cocaine and cocaine metabolites on cerebral arteries in vitro, by J. A. Madden, et al. LIFE SCIENCES 47(13):1109-1114, 1990

Effect of cocaine on responses of mouse phrenic nerve-diaphragm preparation, by M. K. Pagala, et al. LIFE SCIENCES 48(8):795-802, 1991

Effect of intravenous infusion and oral self-administration of cocaine on plasma and adrenal catecholamine levels and cardiovascular parameters in the conscious rat, by W. R. Dixon, et al. NIDA RESEARCH MONOGRAPH SERIES 95:335-336, 1989

Effects of acute and chronic administration of cocaine on striatal uptake, compartmentalization and release of [3H]dopamine, by S. J. Yi, et al. NEUROPHARMACOLOGY 29(5):475-486, May 1990

Effects of acute and chronic cocaine administration on somatostatin level and blading in the rat brain, by M. N. Rodriguez-Sanchez, et al. NEUROPEPTIDES 16(1):1-8, 1990

Effects of acute and subacute cocaine administration on the CNS dopaminergic system in Wistar-Kyoto rats and spontaneously hypertensive rats: I—levels of dopamine and metabolities, by Z. J. Yu, et al. NEUROCHEMICAL RESEARCH 15(6):613-620, 1990

Effects of acute and subacute cocaine administration on the CNS dopaminergic system in Wistar-Kyoto rats and spontaneously hypertensive rats: II—dopamine receptors, by D. K. Lim, et al. NEUROCHEMICAL RESEARCH 15(6):621-628, 1990

Effects of acute and subacute cocaine administration on the CNS dopaminergic system in Wistar-Kyoto rats and spontaneously hypertensive rats: III—dopamine uptake, by D. K. Lim, et al. NEUROCHEMICAL RESEARCH 15(6):629-634, 1990

Effects of bromocriptine and desipramine on behavior maintained by cocaine or food presentation in rhesus monkeys, by M. S. Kleven, et al. PSYCHOPHARMACOLOGY 101(2):208-213, June 1990

Effects of capsaicin treatment of self-administration of amphetamine vapor in rats, by L. G. Sharpe, et al. NIDA RESEARCH MONOGRAPH SERIES 95:539, 1989

Effects of cocaine and d-amphetamine on sustained and selective attention in rats, by D. M. Grilly, et al. PHARMACOLOGY, BIOCHEMISTRY AND BEHAVIOR 33(4): 733-739, August 1989

Effects of cocaine and related drugs in nonhuman primates: II—stimulant effects on schedule-controlled behavior, by R. D. Spealman, et al. JOURNAL OF PHARMACOLOGY AND EXPERIMENTAL THERAPEUTICS 251(11):142-149, October 1989

Effects of cocaine on conflict behavior in the rat, by D. J. Fontana, et al. LIFE SCIENCES 45(9):819-827, 1989

Effects of prenatal exposure to cocaine or related drugs on rat developmental and neurological indices, by M. G. Henderson, et al. BRAIN RESEARCH BULLETIN 24(2):207-212, February 1990

Energy substrate metabolism in testis of rats treated with delta-9-tetrahydrocannabinol (THC) and cocaine (COC), by S. Husain. NIDA RESEARCH MONOGRAPH SERIES 95:509-510, 1989

Extracellular concentrations of cocaine and dopamine are enhanced during chronic cocaine administration, by H. O. Pettit, et al. JOURNAL OF NEUROCHEMISTRY 55(3):789-804, 1990

Facile procedure for the synthesis of pseudococaine from cocaine, by W. W. Sy, et al. FORENSIC SCIENCE INTERNATIONAL 43(1):93-95, 1989

Failure of magnesium to maintain self-administration in cocaine-naive rats, by K. M. Kantak, et al. PHARMACOLOGY, BIOCHEMISTRY AND BEHAVIOR 36(1):9-12, May 1990

Fluoxetine lowers rat cocaine use, by F. K. Goodwin. JAMA 263:1610, March 23-30, 1990

Fluoxetine reduces intravenous cocaine self-administration in rats, by M. E. Carroll, et al. PHARMACOLOGY, BIOCHEMISTRY AND BEHAVIOR 35(1):237-244, January 1990

Frontiers in cocaine research: symposium of the Canadian Federation of Biological Societies, Quebec, Canada, June 15, 1988. CANADIAN JOURNAL OF PHYSIOLOGY AND PHARMACOLOGY 67(9):1153-1181, September 1989

Influence of cocaine self-administration on in vivo dopamine and acetylcholine neurotransmission in rat caudate-putamen, by Y. L. Hurd, et al. NEUROSCIENCE LETTERS 109(1-2):227-233, February 5, 1990

Influence of housing conditions on the acquisition of intravenous heroin and cocaine self-administration in rats, by M. A. Bozarth, et al. PHARMACOLOGY, BIOCHEMISTRY AND BEHAVIOR 33(4):903-907, August 1989

Inhibition of rat fibroblast cell proliferation at specific cell cycle stages by cocaine, by P. Di Francesco, et al. CELL BIOLOGY AND INTERNATIONAL REPORTS 14(6): 549-558, 1990

Multiple, but not acute, infusions of cocaine alter the release of prolactin in male rats, by N. S. Pilotte, et al. BRAIN RESEARCH 512(1):107-112, March 26, 1990

Neurobehavioral and immunological effects of prenatal cocaine exposure in rat, by S. K. Sobrian, et al. PHARMACOLOGY, BIOCHEMISTRY AND BEHAVIOR 35(3): 617-629, March 1990

Neuroendocrine measures of dopaminergic function in chronic cocaine users, by M. A. Lee, et al. PSYCHIATRY RESEARCH 33(2):151-160, 1990

New perspectives on cocaine addiction: recent findings from animal research, by M. A. Bozarth. CANADIAN JOURNAL OF PHYSIOLOGY AND PHARMACOLOGY 67(9):1158-1167, September 1989

New, potent cocaine analogs: ligand binding and transport studies in rat striatum, by J. W. Boja, et al. EUROPEAN JOURNAL OF PHARMACOLOGY 184(2-3):329-332, 1990

Persistence of neurochemical changes in dopamine systems after repeated cocaine administration, by J. Peris, et al. JOURNAL OF PHARMACOLOGY AND EXPERI-MENTAL THERAPEUTICS 253(1):38-44, April 1990

Pharmacological characterization of the discriminative stimulus effects of cocaine in rhesus monkeys, by M. S. Kleven, et al. JOURNAL OF PHARMACOLOGY AND EXPERIMENTAL THERAPEUTICS 254(1):312-317, 1990

Prefrontal cortex lesions differentially disrupt cocaine-reinforced conditioned place preference but not conditioned taste aversion, by W. L. Isaac, et al. BEHAV-IORAL NEUROSCIENCE 103:345-355, April 1989

Preliminary evidence for a cocaine-induced embryopathy in mice, by R. H. Finnell, et al. TOXICOLOGY AND APPLIED PHARMACOLOGY 103(2):228-237, April 1990

Prenatal cocaine exposure in the Long-Evans rat: I—dose-dependent effects on gestation, mortality, and postnatal maturation, by M. W. Church, et al. NEURO-TOXICOLOGY AND TERATOLOGY 12(4):327-334,1990

Prenatal cocaine exposure in the Long-Evans rat: II—dose-dependent effects on off-spring behavior, by M. W. Church, et al. NEUROTOXICOLOGY AND TERATOL-OGY 12(4):335-344, 1990

Prenatal cocaine exposure in the Long-Evans rat: III—developmental effects on the brainstem auditory-evoked potential, by M. W. Church. NEUROTOXICOLOGY AND TERATOLOGY 12(4):345-352, 1990

Prenatal cocaine exposure induces deficits in Pavalovian conditioning and sensory preconditioning among infant rat pups, by C. J. Heyser, et al. BEHAVIORAL NEUROSCIENCES 104:955-963, December 1990

Prenatal exposure to cocaine in rats: lack of long-term effects on locomotion and stereotypy, by M. Giordano, et al. BULLETIN OF THE PSYCHONOMIC SOCIETY 28(1):51-54, January 1990

Presence of cocaine and benzoylecgonine in rat parotid saliva, plasma, and urine after the intravenous administration of cocaine, by A. P. Ferko, et al. RESEARCH COMMUNICATIONS IN SUBSTANCE ABUSE 11(1-2):11-26, 1990

Probing cocaine in the heart and the brain, by R. Cowen. SCIENCE NEWS 137(26): 406-407, June 30, 1990

Rate altering effects of magnesium on cocaine self-administration, by K. M. Kantak, et al. NIDA RESEARCH MONOGRAPH SERIES 95:339-340, 1989

Research on crack, by J. Fagan. CONTEMPORARY DRUG PROBLEMS 16:527-700, Winter 1989

Role of calcium homeostasis hormones in the development of tolerance following drug and alcohol consumption, by S. Balabanova, et al. BEITRAGE ZUR GERICHTLICHEN MEDIZIN 47:379-383, 1989

Strain, sex and developmental profiles of cocaine metabolizing enzymes in mice, by D. Leibman, et al. PHARMACOLOGY, BIOCHEMISTRY AND BEHAVIOR 37(1): 161-166, 1990

Ventral pallidum plays a role in mediating cocaine and heroin self-administration in the rat, by C. B. Hubner, et al. BRAIN RESEARCH 508(1):20-29, January 29, 1990

CODEINE
Codeine abuse, by M. S. Sakol, et al. LANCET 2(8674):1282, November 25, 1989

Codeine abuse from co-codarpin, by J. R. Paterson, et al. LANCET 335(8683):224, January 27, 1990

Detection of codeine abuse by hair analysis, by M. Scheller. DEUTSCHE MEDIZINIS-CHE WOCHENSCHRIFT 115(35):1313-1315, August 31, 1990

Dihydrocodeine in substance dependence, by A. Ulmer. FORSCHRITTE DER MEDI-ZIN 108(13):261, April 30, 1990

Research
Pharmacokinetics of codeine after parenteral and oral dosing in the rat, by J. Shah, et al. DRUG METABOLISM AND DISPOSITION 18(5):670-673, 1990

CODEPENDENCY
Codependency and self-esteem among high school students, by D. Fisher, et al. PSYCHOLOGICAL REPORTS 66(3 Pt 1):1001-1002, June 1990

Codependency: a view from women married to alcoholics, by R. Asher, et al. INTER-NATIONAL JOURNAL OF THE ADDICTIONS 23(4):331-350, 1988

Problems for profit, by H. G. Lerner. WOMEN'S REVIEW OF BOOKS 7:15-16, April 1990

COLLEGE STUDENTS

see also: Alcohol and College Students

Alcohol and drug experiences in criminal justice higher education, by N. R. Montgomery, Jr., et al. JOURNAL OF ALCOHOL AND DRUG EDUCATION 36:35-38, Fall 1990

Alcohol and drug use by college males as a function of family alcoholism history, by M. E. McCaul, et al. ALCOHOLISM: CLINICAL AND EXPERIMENTAL RESEARCH 14(3):467-471, June 1990

Alcohol, drug, and mental health problems among Jewish and Christian men at a university, by M. G. Monteiro, et al. AMERICAN JOURNAL OF DRUG AND ALCOHOL ABUSE 15(4):403-412, December 1989

Bogus-pipeline effects on self-reported college student drug use, problems, and attitudes, by C. E. Werch, et al. INTERNATIONAL JOURNAL OF THE ADDICTIONS 24(10):1003-1010, October 1989

Caffeine consumption, expectancies of caffeine-enhanced performance, and caffeinism symptoms among university students, by J. R. Bradley, et al. JOURNAL OF DRUG EDUCATION 20(4):319-328, 1990

Campus crime linked to students' use of drugs and alcohol, by S. Dodge. CHRONICLE OF HIGHER EDUCATION 36:33+, January 17, 1990

Cocaine and marijuana use by medical students before and during medical school, by R. H. Schwartz, et al. ARCHIVES OF INTERNAL MEDICINE 150(4):883-886, April 1990

Comparison of alcohol and illicit drug use between pharmacy students and the general college population, by C. J. Miller, et al. AMERICAN JOURNAL OF PHARMACEUTICAL EDUCATION 54(1):27-30, Spring 1990

Myths and heroes: visions of the future, by L. C. Whitaker. JOURNAL OF COLLEGE STUDENT PSYCHOTHERAPY 4(2):13-33, 1989

Nebraska governor proposes that students guilty of drug offenses be expelled from state colleges, by C. Myers. CHRONICLE OF HIGHER EDUCATION 36:25+, January 17, 1990

Perceptions of risk as predictors of alcohol, marijuana, and cocaine use among college students, by G. M. Gonzalez, et al. JOURNAL OF COLLEGE STUDENT DEVELOPMENT 31(4):313-318, July 1990

Pre-examination psychotropic drug use by 5th-year medical students at the University of Cape Town, by A. J. Flisher. SOUTH AFRICAN MEDICAL JOURNAL 76(10): 541-543, November 18, 1989

Relationshp between stress and substance use among first-year medical students: an exploratory investigation, by M. A. Forney, et al. JOURNAL OF ALCOHOL AND DRUG EDUCATION 35(3):54-65, Spring 1990

COMMISSIONS AND COMMITTEES

American Academy of Pediatrics Provisional Committee on Substance Abuse: selection of substance abuse treatment programs. PEDIATRICS 86(1):139-140, July 1990

More freedom for SADAC: Saskatchewan Alcohol and Drug Abuse Commission. JOURNAL OF THE ADDICTION RESEARCH FOUNDATION 19(6):2, June 1, 1990

President Bush names 27 to drug advisory panel. NARCOTICS DEMAND REDUCTION DIGEST 1(7):8-9, December 1989

Problems of drug dependence: proceedings of the 50th annual scientific meeting of the Committee on Problems of Drug Dependence, Inc., North Falmouth, Massachusetts, June 1988. NIDA RESEARCH MONOGRAPH SERIES 90:1-550, 1988

Problems of drug dependence: proceedings of the 51st annual scientific meeting of the Committee on Problems of Drug Dependence, Inc., Keystone, Colorado, June 1989. NIDA RESEARCH MONOGRAPH SERIES 95:1-679, 1989

Report of the Expert Advisory Committee on the use of drugs in the treatment of abuse and dependence to narcotic and controlled drugs. CMAJ 143(9):861-865, November , 1990

Report: Privacy Commissioner's Report, *Drug Testing and Privacy*, slams drug testing. OCCUPATIONAL HEALTH AND SAFETY CANADA 6(5):13, September/October 1990

Royal commission suggests realignment of Nova Scotia agency: proposed merger of Nova Scotia Commission on Drug Dependency and Provincial Health Ministry. JOURNAL OF THE ADDICTION RESEARCH FOUNDATION FOUNDATION 19 (2):3, February 1, 1990

Symposium on drug testing in the workplace: Committee on Public Health and the Section on Occupational Medicine, New York Academy of Medicine: February 3, 1988. BULLETIN OF THE NEW YORK ACADEMY OF MEDICINE 65(2):163-242, February 1989

COMPLICATIONS
see also: AIDS
Parenteral Administration: Intravenous—Complications
Pregnancy: Complications
the specific drug (such as Alcohol: Complications)

Acute effects of drug abuse in schizophrenic patients: clinical observations and patients' self-reports, by L. Dixon, et al. SCHIZOPHRENIA BULLETIN 16(1):69-79, 1990

After lights: flashbacks, by S. J. Nadis. OMNI 12:24+, February 1990

Alcohol and drug abuse in treated alcoholics: a comparison of men and women, by H. E. Ross. ALCOHOLISM: CLINICAL AND EXPERIMENTAL RESEARCH 13(6): 810-816, December 1989

COMPLICATIONS

Alcoholism and drug addiction among patients with active tuberculosis, by G. T. Khauadamova, et al. PROBLEMY TUBERKULIOZA (10):7-10, 1989

Antisocial personality disorder in patients with substance abuse disorders: a problematic diagnosis, by L. J. Gerstley, et al. AMERICAN JOURNAL OF PSYCHIATRY 147(2):173-178, February 1990

Anxiety disorders and the use and abuse of drugs, by S. M. Roth. JOURNAL OF CLINICAL PSYCHIATRY 50(Suppl):30-35, November 1989

Bronchopulmonary diseases in drug-dependent pateints, by J. Lorenz. PNEUMOLOGIE 44(3):675-680, March 1990

Delta infection and drug abuse in Merseyside, by G. C. Turner, et al. JOURNAL OF INFECTION 19(2):113-118, September 1989

Drug abuse, psychiatric disorders, and AIDS: dual and triple diagnosis, by S. L. Batki. WESTERN JOURNAL OF MEDICINE 152(5):547-552, May 1990

Drug-induced myopathy: clofibrate, succinylcholine, heroin, L-dopa, steroid hormone, by S. Shoji. NIPPON RINSHO 48(7):1517-1521, July 1990

Drugs that brake the brain. SCIENCE NEWS 137:78, February 3, 1990

Dual disorders: substance abuse and mental illness—getting closer look, by B. Blackadar. JOURNAL OF THE ADDICTION RESEARCH FOUNDATION 19(11):2, January 1, 1990

Dual mental health and substance use problems: a model of four subtypes, by K. K. White, et al. PSYCHOSOCIAL REHABILITATION JOURNAL 13(1):93-98, July 1989 and PSYCHOSOCIAL REHABILITATION JOURNAL 13(2):8, October 1989

Economic toll of mental problems, by D. P. Hamilton. SCIENCE 250:1085, November 23, 1990

Effects of drug abuse on maturation. AMERICAN FAMILY PHYSICIAN 42:1123, October 1990

Epidemiological analysis of alcohol and drug use as risk factors for psychotic experiences, by A. Y. Tien, et al. JOURNAL OF NERVOUS AND MENTAL DISEASE 178(8):473-480, August 1990

Exogenous factors and schizophrenia, by L. de Groot, et al. NEDERLANDS TIDJSCHRIFT VOOR GENEESKUNDE 133(34):1673-1675, August 26, 1989

Eye manifestations in drug addicts, by P. Gastaud, et al. ANNEE THERAPEUTIQUE E CLINIQUE EN OPHTHALMOLOGIE 39:113-124, 1988

Factors in hepatitis A transmission, by C. P. Schade, et al. AMERICAN JOURNAL OF PUBLIC HEALTH 79(11):1571, November 1989

Hypoxic cardiomyopathy: acute myocardial dysfunction after severe hypoxia, by F. Smith, et al. AUSTRALIAN AND NEW ZEALAND JOURNAL OF MEDICINE 19(5):488-492, October 1989

Illicit drug use and the risk of new-onset seizures, by S. K. Ng, et al. AMERICAN JOURNAL OF EPIDEMIOLOGY 132(1):47-57, July 1990

Incidence of alcoholism and drug addiction among patients with active tuberculosis, by G. T. Khauadamova, et al. PROBLEMY TUBERKULIOZA (10):7-10, 1989

Increase of infectious syphilis among heterosexuals in Amsterdam: its relationship to drug use and prostitution, by J. A. van den Hoek, et al. GENITOURINARY MEDICINE 66(1):31-32, February 1990

Learning handicaps linked to drug exposure. OHIO MEDICINE 86(1):14, January 1990

Medical complications of drug abuse, by W. Chiang, et al. MEDICAL JOURNAL OF AUSTRALIA 152(2):83-88, January 15, 1990

Morbidity at an Amsterdam inner city clinic in relation to drug use, by L. Van Trigt, et al. FAMILY PRACTICE 6(4):299-302, December 1989

Morbidity of the drug addict, by M. Staak. VERSICHERUNGSMEDIZEN 42(4):106-109, August 1, 1990

Nutritional effects of marijuana, heroin, cocaine, and nicotine, by M. E. Mohs, et al. JOURNAL OF THE AMERICAN DIETETIC ASSOCIATION 90(9):1261-1267, September 1990

Nutritional implications of medication use and misuse in elderly, by M. C. Cook, et al. JOURNAL OF THE FLORIDA MEDICAL ASSOCIATION 77(6):606-613, June 1990

Pain management in the chemically dependent patients, by R. D. Hicks. HAWAII MEDICAL JOURNAL 48(11):491-492+, November 1989

Predictors of the initiation of psychotherapeutic medicine use, by A. M. Trinkoff, et al. AMERICAN JOURNAL OF PUBLIC HEALTH 80(1):61-65, January 1990

Prevention of acute renal failure in rhabdomyolysis caused by alcohol and drug intoxication, by I. Karpati, et al. ORVOSI HETILAP 131(21):1147-1150, May 27, 1990

Psychiatric complications of Erimin abuse, by L. H. Peh, et al. SINGAPORE MEDICAL JOURNAL 30(1):72-73, February 1989

Psychiatric diagnostic challenge in patients with drug abuse, by E. N. Shulman, et al. HAREFUAH 116(11):597-600, June 1, 1989

Psychiatric disorders in a Dutch addict population: rates and correlates of DSM-III diagnosis, by V. M. Hendriks. JOURNAL OF CONSULTING AND CLINICAL PSYCHOLOGY 58(2):158-162, April 1990

Psychotogenic drug use and neuroleptic response, by M. B. Bowers, Jr., et al. SCHIZOPHRENIA BULLETIN 16(1):81-85, 1990

Pulmonary reactions from illicit substance abuse, by J. E. Heffner, et al. CLINICS IN CHEST MEDICINE 11(1):151-162, March 1990

COMPLICATIONS

Renal damage in drug abusers, by G. Barbiano di Belgiojoso, et al. CONTRIBUTIONS TO NEPHROLOGY 77:142-156, 1990

Renal failure caused by chemicals, foods, plants, animal venoms, and misuse of drugs: an overview, by J. G. Abuelo. ARCHIVES OF INTERNAL MEDICINE 150(3):505-510, March 1990

Researchers seek MDs' help to study link between substance abuse, injury, by N. Giesbrecht, et al. CMAJ 142(10):1108, May 15, 1990

Seizures associated with recreational drug abuse, by B. K. Alldredge, et al. NEUROLOGY 39(8):1037-1039, August 1989

Self-reported negative consequences of drug use among rural adolescents, by D. R. Holcomb, et al. HEALTH EDUCATION 21:36-40, July/August 1990

Serum beta-2-microglobulin values in drug addicts with persistent generalized lymphadenopathy, by R. De Mercato, et al. MINERVA MEDICA 81(4):271-274, April 1990

Solvent abuse psychosis, by A. Byrne, et al. BRITISH JOURNAL OF PSYCHIATRY 155:132, July 1989

Somatic disorders in drug addiction: a review of the literature, by B. I. Rudyk. VRACHEBNOE DELO (1):97-101, January 1990

Splenic abscess, by M. A. Cohen, et al. WORLD JOURNAL OF SURGERY 14(4):513-517, 1990

Stability of psychological symptoms: drug use consequences and intervening processes, by R. J. Johnson, et al. JOURNAL OF HEALTH AND SOCIAL BEHAVIOR 31:277-291, September 1990

Sternal osteomyelitis in drug addicts, by K. L. Boll, et al. JOURNAL OF BONE AND JOINT SURGERY. BRITISH VOLUME 72(2):328-329, March 1990

Substance abuse and mental disorders: the dual diagnoses concept, by N. el-Guebaly. CANADIAN JOURNAL OF PSYCHIATRY 35(3):261-267, April 1990

Substance abuse and psychoses, by F. K. Goodwin. JAMA 264:2495, November 21, 1990

Substance abuse comorbidity in schizophrenia: editors' introduction, by J. A. Leiberman, et al. SCHIZOPHRENIA BULLETIN 16(1):29-30, 1990

Survey shows marijuana, cocaine, heroin emergencies soar for third straight year. NARCOTICS CONTROL DIGEST 19(23):9-10, November 8, 1989

Sympathomimetics, by C. K. Aaron. EMERGENCY MEDICINE CLINICS OF NORTH AMERICA 8(3):513-526, August 1990

Talc lung in a drug abuser, by A. D. Hill, et al. IRISH JOURNAL OF MEDICAL SCIENCES 159(5):147-148, May 1990

COMPLICATIONS

Transition between apnoea and spontaneous ventilation in patients with coma due to voluntary intoxication with barbiturates and carbamates, by S. Launois, et al. EUROPEAN RESPIRATORY JOURNAL 3(5):573-578, 1990

CONFERENCES

Aruba drug money laundry conference will launch tough new sanctions. NARCOTICS CONTROL DIGEST 20(11):6-7, May 23, 1990

As Americans unite, drug crisis will end: keynote address, 120th Congress of Correction, by R. B. Walton. CORRECTIONS TODAY 52:50+, October 1990

Beating back the cocaine kings: drug summit in Colombia, by G. F. Gugliotta. US NEWS AND WORLD REPORT 108:18-20, February 19, 1990

Bush plays macho man: attending drug summit in Colombia, by T. M. DeFrank, et al. NEWSWEEK 115:20, February 5, 1990

Bush scores diplomatic gain at summit in Colombia, by P. Fessler. CONGRESSIONAL QUARTERLY WEEKLY REPORT 48:537-538, February 17, 1990

Chat about drugs: the Andean summit's main agenda will be salving wounded egos, by J. Smolowe. TIME 135(8):34-35, February 19, 1990

Cocaine abuse among schizophrenic patients: paper presented at the 143rd Annual Meeting of the American Psychiatric Association, New York, NY, May 12-17, 1990, by K. Brady, et al. AMERICAN JOURNAL OF PSYCHIATRY 147(9):1164-1167, 1990

Colombia: in the lion's den—Bush attends a drug summit in Cartagena, by M. Nemeth. MACLEAN'S 103(9):30-31, February 26, 1990

Conference looks at few anti-crack success stories. LAW ENFORCEMENT NEWS 16(313):7+, April 30, 1990

Congress, international narcotics policy, and the Anti-Drug Abuse Act 1988: paper presented at a conference on drug trafficking in the Americas held September 30, 1988 in Washington, DC, by R. F. Perl. JOURNAL OF INTERAMERICAN STUDIES AND WORLD AFFAIRS 30(2-3):19-51, Summer/Fall 1988

Developed nations promised aid to curtail drug demand: London summit. UN CHRONICLE 27:61-64, September 1990

Dimensions of the South American cocaine industry: paper presented at a conference on drug trafficking in the Americas held September 30, 1988 in Washington, DC, by R. Lee, III. JOURNAL OF INTERAMERICAN STUDIES AND WORLD AFFAIRS 30(2):87-103, 1988

DOT sponsoring conference to help transport industries implement drug test programs. CORPORATE SECURITY DIGEST 3(50):8, December 18, 1989

Drug abuse and brain development: proceedings of the Sixth International Neurotoxicology Conference, October 10-14, 1988, Little Rock, Arkansas. NEUROTOXICOLOGY 10(3):305-634, Fall 1989

CONFERENCES

Drug menace to be focus of special session. UN CHRONICLE 27:82-83, March 1990

Drug war: going after supply—a commentary paper presented at a conference on drug trafficking in the Americas held September 30, 1988 in Washington, DC, by K. E. Sharpe. JOURNAL OF INTERAMERICAN STUDIES AND WORLD AFFAIRS 30(2-3):77-85, 1988

Drug war issues debate at ASIS seminar. CORPORATE SECURITY DIGEST 3(37):1+, September 18, 1989

EC forms computer net to foil cocaine traffic, by T. Land. JOURNAL OF THE ADDICTION RESEARCH FOUNDATION 19(10):9, October 1, 1990

Estimating the prevalence of alcohol, drug and mental health problems in the contemporary homeless population: a review of the literature—paper presented at the National Conference on Homelessness, Alcohol, and Other Drugs, San Diego, California, February 2-4, 1989, by P. J. Fischer. CONTEMPORARY DRUG PROBLEMS 16(3):333-339, 1989

Functions of punishment and drug addiction: introductory report presented at the 24th Congress of the French Criminological Association, Montpellier, March 24-25, 1988 on the theme; "responses to drug addictions," by C. Lazerges. REVUE DE SCIENCE CRIMINELLE ET DE DROIT PENAL COMPARE 4:857-864, 1988

Gold medal athlete attends addictions' conference. WINDSPEAKER 8(13):6, September 14, 1990

In the lion's den: summit in Cartagena, by M. Nemeth. MACLEAN'S 103:30-31, February 26, 1990

Integrating systematic cue exposure with standard treatment in recovering drug dependent patients: paper presented at the Behavior Therapy World Congress, Edinburgh, Scotland, September 1988, by C. P. O'Brien, et al. ADDICTIVE BEHAVIORS 15(4):355-365, 1990

International Narcotics Research Conference (INRC) '89, Ste-Adele, Quebec, Canada, July 9-14, 1989. PROGRESS IN CLINICAL AND BIOLOGICAL RESEARCH 328:1-534, 1990

Jamaican OC Conference helps "spread the word." CRIME CONTROL DIGEST 23(37):4-5, September 18, 1989

Kidnapping drug lords: United States practice foreign countries, by S. J. Hedges, et al. US NEWS AND WORLD REPORT 108:28-30, May 14, 1990

Licit and illicit drug policies: a typology: paper presented at the seminar on tobacco use—a perspective for alcohol and drug researchers, Addiction Research Foundation, Toronto, Canada, April 14, 1988, by K. E. Warner, et al. BRITISH JOURNAL OF ADDICTION 85(2):255-262, February 1990

Mission to nowhere: at the Cartagena summit, Bush will try to persuade Latin American nations to step up the drug war, by T. Morganthau. NEWSWEEK 115(8):32-34, February 19, 1990

CONFERENCES

Narcotics and politicos: the politics of drug trafficking in Honduras—paper presented at a conference on drug trafficking in the Americas held September 30, 1988 in Washington, DC, by M. D. Rosenberg. JOURNAL OF INTERAMERICAN STUDIES AND WORLD AFFAIRS 30(2-3):143-165, 1988

National drug abuse confab about black family and crack cocaine held in San Francisco. JET 78:11, May 21, 1990

NBRB workshop on the neurochemical bases of alcohol-related behavior, Bethesda, Maryland, August 31-September 1, 1989: proceedings. ALCOHOL 7(3):181-278, May/June 1990

Ninth District Medical Society workshop focuses on illegal drug use, by W. A. Check. JOURNAL OF THE MEDICAL ASSOCIATION OF GEORGIA 79(6):367-372, June 1990

Prohibition or regulation: an economist's view of Australian heroin policy: paper presented at the Fifth Annual Conference of the Australian and New Zealand Society of Criminology, University of Sydney, Sydney, July 1989, by R. Marks. AUSTRALIAN AND NEW ZEALAND JOURNAL OF CRIMINOLOGY 23(2):65-87, 1990

Seaside chat about drugs: summit in Cartagena, by J. Smolowe. TIME 135:62-63, February 19, 1990

Seventh World Conference on tobacco and health, by J. Crofton. THORAX 45(7): 560-562, July 1990

Sixth International Caffeine Workshop, Hong Kong, 7-10 August 1989, by J. J. Barone, et al. FOOD AND CHEMICAL TOXICOLOGY 28(4):279-283, April 1990

Testing for abuse liability of drugs in humans: proceedings of a conference: November 5-6, 1988, by N. J. Princeton. NIDA RESEARCH MONOGRAPH SERIES 92:1-376, 1989

United States department's narcotics control policy in the Americas: paper presented at a conference on drug trafficking in the Americas held September 30, 1988, in Washington, DC, by J. M. Van Wert. JOURNAL OF INTERAMERICAN STUDIES AND WORLD AFFAIRS 30(2):1-18, 1988

Worker drug use poses challenges for insurers: Drug Free Workplace Conference in New York City, by E. Gilbert. NATIONAL UNDERWRITER. LIFE AND HEALTH/ FINANCIAL SERVICES EDITION 94:12, December 10, 1990

World ministerial drug summit targets demand, reduction, by H. McConnell. JOURNAL OF THE ADDICTION RESEARCH FOUNDATION 19(5):1, May 1, 1990

COUNSELING

Alcohol and drug abuse: a needs assessment of rural counselors, by D. J. Hawes, et al. SCHOOL COUNSELOR 38:40-45, September 1990

Barriers face pregnant women seeking drug-treat, by M. Garb. IN THESE TIMES 14(12):7, February 7, 1990

COUNSELING

Counseling addiction a paradoxical consistency: powerlessness and control theory—correction, by A. Honeyman. JOURNAL OF REALITY THERAPY 9(2):59, Spring 1990

Effectiveness of two smoking cessation programmes for use in general practice: a randomised clinical trial, by K. Slama, et al. BMJ 300(6741):1707-1709, June 30, 1990

HIV infection and drug users: setting up support groups, by G. Mulleady, et al. COUNSELLING PSYCHOLOGY QUARTERLY 2(1):53-57, 1989

Mandela House gives women and babies second chance, by M. Thomas. CALIFOR-NIA PRISONER 18(8):11, February 1990

More job mobility for counsellors. JOURNAL OF THE ADDICTION RESEARCH FOUNDATION 19(6):4, June 1, 1990

Requiem for a counselor training program: the history and development of the Veterans Administration's Alcohol and Drug Counselor Training Program, by L. S. Stephen. JOURNAL OF ALCOHOL AND DRUG EDUCATION 35(2):55-60, Winter 1990

CRIME AND CRIMINOLOGY

Addiction and crime: an investigation, by E. Leuw. JUSTITIELE VERKENNINGEN 15(5):8-22, 1989

Alcohol and drug use by college males as a function of family alcoholism history, by M. E. McCaul, et al. ALCOHOLISM: CLINICAL AND EXPERIMENTAL RESEARCH 14(3):467-471, June 1990

Alcohol and drug use by rapists and their victims, by J. M. Rodenas, et al. MEDICINE AND LAW 8(2):157-164, 1989

Alcohol, drugs and murder: a study of convicted homicide offenders, by W. F. Wieczorek, et al. JOURNAL OF CRIMINAL JUSTICE 18(3):217-227, 1990

Americans blame drugs for nation's crime problems. SECURITY 26(10):11, October 1989

Belated justice: another conviction in the murder of a DEA agent. TIME 136(7):39, August 13, 1990

Belated justice: Los Angeles jury convicts: R. Zuno Arce for abetting murder of DEA agent E. Camarean. TIME 136:36, August 13, 1990

Campus crime linked to students' use of drugs and alcohol, by S. Dodge. CHRONI-CLE OF HIGHER EDUCATION 36:33+, January 17, 1990

Can medical treatment reduce crime amongst young heroin users?, by G. Jarvis, et al. HOME OFFICE RESEARCH AND STATISTICS DEPARTMENT RESEARCH BULLETIN 28:29-32, 1990

Chinese laundry: international drug trafficking and Hong Kong's banking industry, by M. S. Gaylord. CONTEMPORARY CRISIS 14(1):23-37, 1990

Cleaning up: how a big drug cartel laundered $1.2 billion with aid of United States firms: many banks, others raised few questions about piles of cash, authorities says, by J. J. Fialka. WALL STREET JOURNAL 215:1+, March 1, 1990

Cocaine- and methamphetamine-related deaths in San Diego County: 1987: homicides and accidental overdoses, by D. N. Bailey, et al. JOURNAL OF FORENSIC SCIENCES 34(2):407-422, 1989

Cocaine mafia, by R. W. Lee. SOCIETY 27(2):53-62, January/February 1990

Courting disaster: a rapidly rising number of drug cases, new sentencing rules and the impact of the Speedy Trial Act are threatening to bury the already short-handed judicial system, by W. J. Moore. NATIONAL JOURNAL 22:502-507, March 3, 1990

Crack and homicide in New York City, 1988: a conceptually based event analysis, by P. J. Goldstein, et al. CONTEMPORARY DRUG PROBLEMS 16(4):651-687, 1989

Criminality of female narcotics addicts: a causal modeling approach, by Y. I. Hser, et al. JOURNAL OF QUANTITATIVE CRIMINOLOGY 6(2):207-208, June 1990

Criminality of heroin users presenting to an Australian hospital-based drug and alcohol unit, by M. Desland, et al. BRITISH JOURNAL OF ADDICTION 85(6):795-801, June 1990

Criminalization approach to the illegal drug problem: a descriptive analysis of the processing of felony drug arrestees, by P. B. Kraska. DAI A 50(3):769, September 1989

Criminalization of drugs, by A. Burr. NATURE 342(6245):12, November 2, 1989

Crips, bloods: more than 170 gang members arrested in 11-state sweep. NARCOTICS CONTROL DIGEST 20(13):8, June 20, 1990

D.C. retailers find drug-related thefts at epidemic levels. CORPORATE SECURITY DIGEST 3(52):8, December 29, 1989

Delinquency and substance use among inner-city students, by J. Fagan, et al. JOURNAL OF DRUG ISSUES 20:351-402, Summer 1990

Does addiction excuse thieves and killers from criminal responsibility?, by S. Peele. INTERNATIONAL JOURNAL OF LAW AND PSYCHIATRY 13(1-2):95-101, 1990

Drug crimes pushing caseloads of federal courts to new highs. CRIMINAL JUSTICE NEWSLETTER 20(19):2-3, October 2, 1989

Drug-positive homicides in Virginia 1987 through 1989. MEDICO-LEGAL BULLETIN 39(1):1-9, January/February 1990

Drug-related bombings nearly doubled in 1989. NARCOTICS CONTROL DIGEST 20(14):8, July 4, 1990

Drug-related slayings of police officers increasing, by E. Wiener. CRIMINAL JUSTICE NEWSLETTER 20(18):5, September 15, 1989

Drug trafficking and related serious crime. CRIMINAL LAW REVIEW February 1990, p. 73

Drug use and felony crime: biochemical credibility and unsettled questions, by N. J. Pallone. JOURNAL OF OFFENDER COUNSELING, SERVICES AND REHABILI- TATION 15(1):85-110, January 1990

Drug use and pretrial misconduct in New York City, by D. A. Smith, et al. JOURNAL OF QUANTITATIVE CRIMINOLOGY 5(2):101-126, June 1989

Drugs, alcohol and crime: abstracts of the Society for the Study of Addiction to Alco- hol and Other Drugs annual symposium, 16th and 17th November 1989, Leices- ter. BRITISH JOURNAL OF ADDICTION 84(11):1387-1392, November 1989

Drugs and crime data. FBI LAW ENFORCEMENT BULLETIN 59(9):12, September 1990

Drugs, crime, and the failure of American organized crime models, by T. Mieczkowski. INTERNATIONAL JOURNAL OF COMPARATIVE AND APPLIED CRIMINAL JUSTICE 14(1):97-106, 1990

Follow-up study of psychiatrically examined arsonists, by K. Noreik, et al. TIDSSKRIFT FOR DEN NORSKE LAEGEFORNING 110(14):1820-1822, 1990

Gun-toting students commonplace. JUVENILE JUSTICE DIGEST 27(22):7-8, November 15, 1989

Heroin use, crime, and the "main hustle," by G. S. Kowalski, et al. DEVIANT BEHAV- IOR 11(1):1-16, January/March 1990

Homicide and near-homicide by anabolic steroid users, by G. H. Pope, Jr., et al. JOURNAL OF CLINICAL PSYCHIATRY 51(1):28-31, January 1990

Homicide in the Nordic countries, by G. H. Guthjonsson, et al. ACTA PSYCHIATRICA SCANDINAVICA 82(1):49-54, 1990

House Bill would require mandatory death penalty for police killers in drug cases. CRIME CONTROL DIGEST 23(40):1+, October 9, 1989; also in NARCOTICS CONTROL DIGEST 19(21):6, October 11, 1989

In a frenzy of evil: C. Hill, police officer killed in drug-related incident in Alexandria, Virginia, by M. McConnell. READER'S DIGEST 136:65-71, February 1990

International news: Canada murder linked to drugs, by A. Harman. LAW AND ORDER 37(12):6, December 1989

Intoxication and criminal responsibility, by C. Mitchell, et al. INTERNATIONAL JOUR- NAL OF LAW AND PSYCHIATRY 13(1-2):1-161, 1990

Laundering drug money: Colombian money laundering organizations, by C. P. Flo- rez, et al. FBI LAW ENFORCEMENT BULLETIN 59(4):22-25, April 1990

Links between drug misuse and crime, by T. Bennett. BRITISH JOURNAL OF AD- DICTION 85(7):833-835, July 1990

Making sense of the heroin-crime link, by I. Dobinson. AUSTRALIAN AND NEW ZEALAND JOURNAL OF CRIMINOLOGY 22(4):259-275, 1989

Murder in a "model" city: Washington, D.C. US NEWS AND WORLD REPORT 108: 13-14, April 16, 1990

Murdered to the music of Bob Dylan, by J. E. Goodyear. AMERICAN JOURNAL OF FORENSIC MEDICINE AND PATHOLOGY 10(4):349-352, December 1989

Myth of narcoterrorism in Latin America, by D. C. Meyer. MILITARY REVIEW 70(3):64-70, March 1990

Narcotics and violence: the consequences of a disorganized market—part I, by N. B. Checket. ORGANIZED CRIME DIGEST 10(19):8-10, October 11, 1989

Narcotics and violence: the consequences of a disorganized market—part II. ORGA-NIZED CRIME DIGEST 10(20):5-7, October 25, 1989

Perspective. LAW OFFICER'S BULLETIN 14(11):66, December 21, 1989

Police file no. 37, by N. Fielding, et al. HOWARD JOURNAL OF CRIMINAL JUSTICE 29(2):130-142, May 1990

Political economy of crack-related violence, by A. Hamid. CONTEMPORARY DRUG PROBLEMS 17(1):31-78, 1990

Re-examining the black on black crime issue: a theoretical essay, by R. L. Perry. WESTERN JOURNAL OF BLACK STUDIES 13(2):66-71, Summer 1989

Reducing heroin related crime, by J. Mott. HOME OFFICE RESEARCH AND STATIS-TICS DEPARTMENT RESEARCH BULLETIN 26:30-33, 1989

Relationship between crime and opioid use, by R. Hammersley, et al. BRITISH JOUR-NAL OF ADDICTION 84(9):1029-1043, September 1989

Relationship between substance abuse and crime among Native American inmates in the Nebraska Department of Corrections, by E. S. Grobsmith. HUMAN ORGANI-ZATION 48(4):285-298, Winter 1989

Sex role egalitarianism and marital violence, by R. K. Crossman, et al. SEX ROLES 22:293-304, March 1990

Snaring the smurfs: the war on drugs is heating up, and the banks are playing a key role in efforts to catch the launderers of illicit drug money, by M. Tobin. US BANKER 98:27-28+, November 1989

Snatching "Dr. Mengele": DEA agents capture H. Alvarez Machain, wanted in con-nection with E. Camarena murder, by E. Shannon. TIME 135:27, April 23, 1990

Spousal violence and alcohol-drug problems among parolees and their spouses, by B. A. Miller, et al. WOMEN AND CRIMINAL JUSTICE 1(2):55-72, 1990

Spouse battering and chemical dependency: dynamics, treatment, and service deliv-ery, by A. J. Levy, et al. JOURNAL OF CHEMICAL DEPENDENCY TREATMENT 3(1):81-97, 1989

Street gangs are big business—and growing, by D. Harrington-Lueker. EXECUTIVE EDUCATOR 12(7):14, July 1990

Syringes in soup kettles: two charged with tampering at grocery salad bars. CRIME CONTROL DIGEST 24(13):4-5, April 2, 1990

Terrorism in the '90s: the skull and crossbones still files— narcoterrorism, by D. F. Williams. POLICE CHIEF 57:47-51, September 1990

Two veteran New York City Police Department officers murdered because they were careless: commissioner says. TRAINING AIDS DIGEST 14(12):1+, December 1989

War on drugs: Kentucky program shows we need treatment and rehabilitation in our arsenal, by G. F. Vito. CORRECTIONS TODAY 51:34+, June 1989

What can be done to stop Crips and Blood advance across the United States? CRIME CONTROL DIGEST 23(49):3-7, December 11, 1989

What crack can do: Texas user slays three family members, holds man hostage. NAR-COTICS CONTROL DIGEST 19(14):3-4, July 5, 1989

Youth gangs and public policy, by C. R. Huff. CRIME AND DELINQUENCY 35(4):524-537, 1989

DARE   (DRUG ABUSE RESISTANCE EDUCATION)
DARE: selecting the right officer—Drug Abuse Resistance Education Program, Los Angeles, California. FBI LAW ENFORCEMENT BULLETIN 59:11-12, May 1990

First honorary Ohio D.A.R.E. officer. ENFORCEMENT JOURNAL 29(1):28, January-March 1990

DEA   (UNITED STATES DRUG ENFORCEMENT AGENCY)
see also: Narcotics Agents

Choice to head DEA strongly supports demand reduction. NARCOTICS DEMAND REDUCTION DIGEST 2(6):4-5, June 1990

Crime in the 1990's: a federal perspective, by M. J. Seng, et al. FEDERAL PROBA-TION 53(4):36-40, December 1989

DEA declines to certify marijuana as acceptable for medical applications. CRIMINAL LAW REPORTER: COURT DECISIONS 46(14):1307-1308, January 10, 1990

DEA in Latin America: dealing with institutionalized corruption, by E. A. Nadelmann. JOURNAL OF INTERAMERICAN STUDIES AND WORLD AFFAIRS 29(4):1-39, 1987-1988

DEA offers free guidelines on how to safely clean up clandestine drug labs. CRIME CONTROL DIGEST 24(26):4, July 2, 1990; also in NARCOTICS CONTROL DI-GEST 20(14):4, July 4, 1990

DEA targets Chuck Berry, by J. Neely. ROLLING STONE August 23, 1990, p. 34

DEA

Drugs enforcement agency in Latin America: I—dealing with institutionalized corruption; II—the ins and outs of working around corruption, by E. A. Nadelmann. JOURNAL OF INTERAMERICAN STUDIES AND WORLD AFFAIRS 62(1):31-42, 1989

In the cocaine war, the jungle is winning: Drug Enforcement Agency efforts, by M. Massing. NEW YORK TIMES MAGAZINE March 4, 1990, pp. 26-27+

Interview: Robert M. Stutman—special agent in charge of the Drug Enforcement Administration's New York field office, by M. S. Rosen. LAW ENFORCEMENT NEWS 15(296):9-11, July 15, 1989

Narcoterrorism: the new unconventional war, by M. P. Hertling. MILITARY REVIEW 70(3):16-28, March 1990

New DEA chief is veteran prosecutor of big drug cases. CRIME CONTROL DIGEST 24(20):1+, May 21, 1990; also in NARCOTICS CONTROL DIGEST 20(11):1-2, May 23, 1990

DENTISTS
Chemical dependency: there are 18,000 dentists who need our special attention—part II, by S. W. Oberg. JOURNAL OF THE AMERICAN COLLEGE OF DENTISTS 56(3):10-13, Fall 1989

Dentist was a junkie: case of M. Cohen. NEW YORK 23:26-32, July 30, 1990

DESIGNER DRUGS
Comparison of the behavioral and neurochemical effects of 5,7-DHT, MDMA and D,L-fenfluramine, by S. A. Lorens, et al. NIDA RESEARCH MONOGRAPH SERIES 95:347, 1989

Contamination of clandestinely prepared drugs with synthetic by-products, by W. H. Soine. NIDA RESEARCH MONOGRAPH SERIES 95:44-50, 1989

Design and synthesis of mimetics of peptides beta-turns, by M. Kahn, et al. JOURNAL OF MOLECULAR RECOGNITION 1(2):75-79, April 1988

Designer drugs: a silver lining. ECONOMIST 310:84+, January 21, 1989

Designer drugs: the "whats" and the "why," by G. Chesher. MEDICAL JOURNAL OF AUSTRALIA 153(3):157-161, August 6, 1990

Fight designer drugs, by J. D. Durrant. LAW AND ORDER 38(2):71, February 1990

Ice can freeze out cocaine. LAW AND ORDER 37(10):4, October 1989

"Ice" lab cracked. NARCOTICS CONTROL DIGEST 20(7):4, March 28, 1990

Ice: a new designer drug, by F. Ornskov. UGESKRIFT FOR LAEGER 152(15):1100-1101, April 9, 1990

Ice: a new dosage form of an old drug, by A. K. Cho. SCIENCE 249:631-634, August 10, 1990

DESIGNER DRUGS

Ice overdose. ECONOMIST 313:29-30, December 2, 1989

Ice storm is coming. NARCOTICS CONTROL DIGEST 19(20):1+, September 27, 1989; also in CRIME CONTROL DIGEST 23(39):1-2, October 2, 1989

Identification of two new "designer" amphetamines by NMR techniques, by B. A. Dawson, et al. CANADIAN SOCIETY OF FORENSIC SCIENCE JOURNAL 22(2): 195-202, 1989

Junkie culture: super-charged speed is scourge of Manilla's smart set—ice, by J. Mc-Beth. FAR EASTERN ECONOMIC REVIEW 146:44+, November 23, 1989

Neurochemical mechanisms involved in behavioral effects of amphetamines and related designer drugs, by L. H. Gold, et al. NIDA RESEARCH MONOGRAPH SERIES 94:101-126, 1989

Pharmacology and toxicology of amphetamine and related designer drugs. NIDA RESEARCH MONOGRAPH SERIES 94:1-357, 1989

Structure-activity relationships of MDMA-like substances, by D. E. Nichols, et al. NIDA RESEARCH MONOGRAPH SERIES 94:1-29, 1989

Synthesis of fentanyl analogs, by F. I. Carroll, et al. NIDA RESEARCH MONOGRAPH SERIES 95:497-498, 1989

Synthesis reduction in clandestine amphetamine and metamphetamine laboratories: a review, by A. Allen, et al. FORENSIC SCIENCE INTERNATIONAL 42(3):183-199, 1989

Synthetic drugs of abuse, the second generation: designer drugs, 1—amphetamine and other arylalkane amines, by K. A. Kovar, et al. PHARMAZIE IN UNSERER ZEIT 19(3):99-107, May 1990

Complications
Neurologic complications of drug addiction: general aspects—complications caused by cannabis, designer drugs and volatile substances, by M. Farre Albaladejo. ARCHIVES DE NEUROGIOLOGIA 52(Suppl)1:143-148, 1989

Opioids and designer drugs, by M. Ford, et al. EMERGENCY MEDICINE CLINICS OF NORTH AMERICA 8(3):495-511, August 1990

Research
Recommendations for future research on amphetamines and related designer drugs, by R. W. Fuller. NIDA RESEARCH MONOGRAPH SERIES (94):341-357, 1989

Role of dopamine in the neurotoxicity induced by amphetamines and related designer drugs, by J. W. Gibb, et al. NIDA RESEARCH MONOGRAPH SERIES 94: 161-178, 1989

Self-injection in baboons of amphetamines and related designer drugs, by C. A. Sannerud, et al. NIDA RESEARCH MONOGRAPH SERIES 94:30-42, 1989

DESIGNER DRUGS—Research

Stimulus properties of hallucinogenic phenalkylamines and related designer drugs: formation of structure-activity relationships, by R. A. Glennon. NIDA RESEARCH MONOGRAPH SERIES 94:43-67, 1989

DEXTROMORAMIDE
Dextromoramide-related fatality, by E. Brewer. JOURNAL OF FORENSIC SCIENCES 35(2):483-489, March 1990

DIAGNOSIS
Anabolic steroid dependence, by L. R. Hays, et al. AMERICAN JOURNAL OF PSYCHIATRY 147(1):122, January 1990

Application of the Tridimensional Personality Questionaire to a population of alcoholics and other substance abusers, by S. J. Nixon, et al. ALCOHOLISM: CLINICAL AND EXPERIMENTAL RESEARCH 14(4):513-517, 1990

Assessment and classification of patient with psychiatric and substance abuse syndromes, by A. F. Lehman, et al. HOSPITAL AND COMMUNITY PSYCHIATRY 40(10):1019-1025, October 1989

Assessment of the transferrin index in screening heavy drinkers from a general practice, by R. E. Poupon, et al. ALCOHOLISM 13(4):549-553, August 1989

Callus of crack cocaine, by R. F. Larkin. NEW ENGLAND JOURNAL OF MEDICINE 323(10):685, September 6, 1990

Carrier Addiction Severity Index for Adolescents (CASI-A), by K. Meyers, et al. NIDA RESEARCH MONOGRAPH SERIES 95:467-468, 1989

Characterizing anticholinergic abuse in community mental health, by B. G. Wells, et al. JOURNAL OF CLINICAL PSYCHOPHARMACOLOGY 9(6):431-435, December 1989

Cocaine intoxication, by R. W. Derlet. POSTGRADUATE MEDICINE 86(5):245-248+, October 1989

Cocaine: recognizing, treating the abuser, by P. Coleman. VIRGINIA MEDICINE 117 (6):251-255, June 1990

Conjunctival naloxone is no decision aid in opioid addiction, by N. Loimer, et al. LANCET 335:1107-1108, May 5, 1990

Convergence of DSM-III diagnoses and self reported symptoms in child and adolescent inpatients, by S. R. Weinstein, et al. JOURNAL OF THE AMERICAN ACADEMY OF CHILD AND ADOLESCENT PSYCHIATRY 29(4):627-634, July 1990

Cross-reactivity of amphetamine analogues with Roche Abuscreen radioimmunoassay reagents, by J. T. Cody. JOURNAL OF ANALYTICAL TOXICOLOGY 14(1): 50-53, January/February 1990

Detection of codeine abuse by hair analysis, by M. Scheller. DEUTSCHE MEDIZINISCHE WOCHENSCHRIFT 115(35):1313-1315, August 31, 1990

DIAGNOSIS

Diagnosis of alcohol and cannabis dependence in cocaine dependence, by N. S. Miller, et al. ADVANCES IN ALCOHOL AND SUBSTANCE ABUSE 8(3-4):33-42, 1990

Diagnostic and behavioral characteristics of psychiatric patients who abuse substances, by S. R. Kay, et al. HOSPITAL AND COMMUNITY PSYCHIATRY 40(10): 1062-1064, October 1989

Diagnostic disorders, by L. B. Cottler, et al. NIDA RESEARCH MONOGRAPH SERIES 95:380-381, 1989

Drug abuse recognition: local enforcement strategy for effective user-accountability, by R. De Pompa. JOURNAL OF CALIFORNIA LAW ENFORCEMENT 24(1):19-24, 1990

Evaluation of the psychoactive substance dependence syndrome in its application to opiate users, by A. M. Stripp, et al. BRITISH JOURNAL OF ADDICTION 85(5): 621-627, May 1990

Evaluation of substance-abusing adolescents by primary care physicians, by L. S. Friedman, et al. JOURNAL OF ADOLESCENT HEALTH CARE 11(3):227-230, May 1990

Evidence for physical and psychological dependence on anabolic androgenic steroids in weight weight lifters, by K. J. Brower, et al. AMERICAN JOURNAL OF PSYCHIATRY 147(4):510-512, April 1990

From basic concepts to clinical reality: unresolved issues in the diagnosis of dependence, by T. F. Babor, et al. RECENT DEVELOPMENTS IN ALCOHOLISM 8:85-104, 1990

Human abuse liability assessment by measurement of subjective and physiological effects, by D. R. Jasinski, et al. NIDA RESEARCH MONOGRAPH SERIES 92:73-100, 1989

Identifying and helping patients who use marijuana, by R. H. Schwartz. POSTGRADUATE MEDICINE 86(6):91-95, November 1, 1989

Identifying drug use prenatally, by G. Luggiero. TRUSTEE 43(9):6, September 1990

Motivation and drug dependency: a preliminary evaluation of an assessment tool, by D. J. Harper. JOURNAL OF ADVANCED NURSING 15(2):176-179, February 1990

Operationalization of alcohol and drug dependence criteria by means of a structured interview, by L. B. Cottler, et al. RECENT DEVELOPMENTS IN ALCOHOLISM 8:69-83, 1990

Plasma delta-9-THC levels as a predictive measure of marijuana use by women, by J. H. Mendelson, et al. NIDA RESEARCH MONOGRAPH SERIES 95:152-158, 1989

Potential substance abuse: detection among adolescent patients using the Drug and Alcohol Problem (DAP) Quick Screen, a 30-item questionnaire, by R. H. Schwartz, et al. CLINICAL PEDIATRICS 29(1):38-43, January 1990

Prevalence of surreptitous laxative abuse in patients with diarrhoea of uncertain origin: a cost-benefit analysis of a screening procedure, by P. Bytzer, et al. GUT 30(10):1379-1384, October 1989

Problems of diagnosis and classification related to the improper use of substances in the DSM-III and DSM-III-R, by E. A. Mata. ACTA PSYCHIATRICA Y PSIOLOGICA DE AMERICA.LATINA 35(1-2):31-38, January/June 1989

Psychometric properties of the Drug Abuse Screening Test in a psychiatric patient population, by D. Staley, et al. ADDICTIVE BEHAVIORS 15(3):257-264, 1990

Question of responsibility, by R. H. Lewis, et al. AUSTRALIAN FAMILY PHYSICIAN 19(3):417-418, March 1990

Recognizing the cocaine addict, by K. I. Povenmire, et al. NURSING 90 20:46-48, May 1990

Screening for substance abuse in hospitalized psychiatric patients, by R. W. Kanwischer, et al. HOSPITAL AND COMMUNITY PSYCHIATRY 41(7):795-797, July 1990

Severity of opiate dependence in an Australian sample: further validation of SODQ, by P. M. Burgess, et al. BRITISH JOURNAL OF ADDICTION 84(12):1451-1459, December 1989

Specialized addictions assessment-referral services in Ontario: a review of their characteristics and roles of the addiction treatment system, by A. C. Ogborne, et al. BRITISH JOURNAL OF ADDICTION 85(2):197-204, February 1990

Substance abuse, by Y. Kaminer. JOURNAL OF THE AMERICAN ACADEMY OF CHILD AND ADOLESCENT PSYCHIATRY 28(5):798, September 1989

Substance abuse: a suitable case for testing, by C. Roythorne. JOURNAL OF THE SOCIETY OF OCCUPATIONAL MEDICINE 39(3):111-112, Autumn 1989

Teaching critical thinking in the context of substance abuse in a psychiatry clerkship, by M. G. Regan-Smith, et al. ACADEMIC MEDICINE 65(2):89, February 1990; Erratum. 65(4):233, April 1990

Teen Addiction Severity Index (T-ASI): clinical and research implications—a preliminary report, by Y. Kaminer, et al. NIDA RESEARCH MONOGRAPH SERIES 95: 363, 1989

Validity of the MCMI Drug Abuse Scale with drug abusing and psychiatric samples, by D. A. Calsyn, et al. JOURNAL OF CLINICAL PSYCHOLOGY 46(2):244-246, March 1990

What is an MRO?, by L. F. Weiler. NEBRASKA MEDICAL JOURNAL 75(7):163-164, July 1990

What'd he say: street drug terminology, by N. P. Johnson, et al. JOURNAL OF THE SOUTH CAROLINA MEDICAL ASSOCIATION 86(1):51-56, January 1990; Erratum. 86(3):166, March 1990

DIAZEPAM

Diazepam abuse in pregnant women on methadone maintenance: implications for the neonate, by L. R. Sutton, et al. CLINICAL PEDIATRICS 29(2):108-111, February 1990

DIHYDROCODEINE TARTRATE
Misuse of dihydrocodeine tartrate (DF 118) among opiate addicts, by H. Swadi, et al. BMJ 300(6735):1313, May 19, 1990

DIMENHYDRINATE
Dimenhydrinate addiction in a schizophrenic woman, by B. Bartlik, et al. JOURNAL OF CLINICAL PSYCHIATRY 50(12):476, December 1989

DIPHENHYDRAMINE
Abuse liability of diphenhydramine in sedative abusers, by B. Wolf, et al. NIDA RE-SEARCH MONOGRAPH SERIES 95:486-487, 1989

DOD (UNITED STATES DEPARTMENT OF DEFENSE)
DOD and its role in the war against drugs: based on news briefing at the Pentagon 18 September 1989, by R. B. Cheney. DEFENSE 89:2-7, November/December 1989

DOD now becoming a major player in national undertaking: drug interdiction, by J. C. Irwin. SEA POWER 33(1):74-79, January 1990

DOD plays in the drug war, by C. L. Diaz. US NAVAL INSTITUTE. PROCEEDINGS 116(5):76-80+, May 1990

DOD to provide more anti-drug training to state and local police. CRIME CONTROL DIGEST 24(11):10, March 19, 1990

DOJ (UNITED STATES DEPARTMENT OF JUSTICE)
DOJ establishing National Drug Intelligence Center. CRIME CONTROL DIGEST 24(24):8-9, June 18, 1990; also in NARCOTICS CONTROL DIGEST 20(13):1-2, June 20, 1990 and ORGANIZED CRIME DIGEST 11(12):1-3, June 27, 1990

DOT (UNITED STATES DEPARTMENT OF TRANSPORTATION)
DOT preempts state drug law: Vermont, by J. A. Calderwood. TRANSPORTATION AND DISTRIBUTION 31:40+, August 1990

DOT provides summary of industry drug police rules. CORPORATE SECURITY DI-GEST 4(5):3-5, February 5, 1990

DOT seeks comment on need for more action on alcohol abuse in transport industry. CORPORATE SECURITY DIGEST 3(47):7-8, November 27, 1989

DOT seeks legislation to continue drug testing in mass transit industry. CORPORATE SECURITY DIGEST 4(15):1+, April 16, 1990

DOT sponsoring conference to help transport industries implement drug test programs. CORPORATE SECURITY DIGEST 3(50):8, December 18, 1989

DOT to lower passive drug levels, expects go-ahead on random tests, by J. Schulz. TRAFFIC WORLD 224:37+, October 22, 1990

DOT to reimpose drug testing standards, by A. A. Anderson. MASS TRANSIT 17:14-16+, June 1990

DRIVING
see also: Alcohol—Drunk Driving

Cocaine and traffic accident fatalities in New York City. JAMA 263(21):2887-2888, June 6, 1990

Cocaine danger on the road: study of fatal New York City motor vehicle accidents, by P. M. Marzu, et al. SCIENCE NEWS 137:23, January 13, 1990

Contractual nature of a driver's license, by S. Sariola. JOURNAL OF ALCOHOL AND DRUG EDUCATION 35(1):35-41, Fall 1989

Detect drivers under influence of alcohol or drugs: New Jersey. SEARCH AND SEIZURE BULLETIN April 1989, p. 3

Drinking, drug use, and driving among rural midwestern youth, by P. D. Sarvela, et al. JOURNAL OF SCHOOL HEALTH 60(5):215-219, May 1990

Driving under the influence of toluene, by H. Gjerde, et al. FORENSIC SCIENCE INTERNATIONAL 44(1):77-83, January 1990

Drug evaluation and classification program sites being sought. POLICE CHIEF 56(7): 44, July 1989

Drug recognition experts, by R. Bocklet. LAW AND ORDER 37(9):105-112, September 1989

Drug recognition program, by W. H. Mann. JOURNAL OF TRAFFIC SAFETY EDUCATION 37:6-7+, July 1990

Drug use by tractor-trailer drivers, by A. K. Lund, et al. NIDA RESEARCH MONOGRAPH SERIES (91):47-67, 1989

Drugs and abuse and fatal automobile accidents, by I. Root. LEGAL MEDICINE 1989, pp. 25-38

Drugs: driving under the influence—proof of use of particular drug. CRIMINAL LAW REPORTER: COURT DECISIONS 46(15):1325, January 17, 1990

Effects of paroxetine and other antidepressants in combination with alcohol on psychomotor activity related to care driving, by I. Hindmarch, et al. ACTA PSYCHIATRICA SCANDINAVICA 350(Suppl):45, 1989

Effects of terfenadine with and without alcohol on an aspect of car driving performance, by J. Z. Bhatti, et al. CLINICAL AND EXPERIMENTAL ALLERGY 19(6): 609-611, November 1989

DRIVING

Get the drugged drivers off the roads, by R. C. Mayer. CRIMINAL JUSTICE 4(3):6-9+, Fall 1989

Illicit drugs take still another toll: death or injury from vehicle-associated trauma, by A. Skolnick. JAMA 263(23):2133+, June 20, 1990

Impaired driving: analysis of statistics for the city of Sherbrooke, by S. Brochu, et al. CANADIAN JOURNAL OF CRIMINOLOGY 32(2):279-290, 1990

Influence and use of drugs other than alcohol among drivers, by A. S. Christophersen, et al. TIDSSKRIFT FOR DEN NORSKE LAEGEFORENING 110(9):1103-1105, March 30, 1990

Not a tragedy if teens get the last act right, by P. O. Gonder. TRAFFIC SAFETY 89(5):14-15, September/October 1989

Prevalence of recent cocaine use among motor vehicle fatalities in New York City, by P. M. Marzuk, et al. JAMA 263(2):250-256, January 12, 1990

Report on the incidence of drugs and driving in Canada, by H. W. Peel, et al. CANADIAN SOCIETY OF FORENSIC SCIENCE JOURNAL 23(2-3):75-79, 1990

Screening for drug use among Norwegian drivers suspected of driving under influence of alcohol or drugs, by A. S. Christophersen, et al. FORENSIC SCIENCE INTERNATIONAL 45(1-2):5-14, March 1990

Subjective factors related to fatigue, by T. M. Nelson. ALCOHOL, DRUGS AND 5(3):193-214, July/September 1989

Substance abuse and driving: the physician's role, by H. Poole. CMAJ 141(12):1218+, December 15, 1989

Substance abuse and traffic deaths: report by National Transportation Safety Board. SAFETY AND HEALTH 141:32, April 1990

Traffic accidents and drivers suspected for drug influence, by L. Q. Christensen, et al. FORENSIC SCIENCE INTERNATIONAL 45(3):273-280, April 1990

Was he driving?, by N. Ansley. POLYGRAPH 19(2):147-149, 1990

DRUG ABUSE

1990s: new days, old problems, by E. J. Tully. POLICE CHIEF 57(1):34+, 1990

Adult drug abuse factor in Forster Home Placement. NARCOTICS DEMAND REDUCTION DIGEST 1(5):6, October 1989

Aerostat, by S. Harding. SOLDIERS 45(8):14-15+, August 1990

Alternative to the war on drugs, by B. K. Alexander, et al. JOURNAL OF DRUG ISSUES 20(4):509-700, 1990

Around the nation: Illinois. LAW ENFORCEMENT NEWS 16(313):2, April 30, 1990

Around the nation: Washington. LAW ENFORCEMENT NEWS 16(313):2, April 30, 1990

Biogenic amines, neuropeptides and substance abuse: Grand Forks, North Dakota, October 17, 1987. PHYSIOLOGY AND BEHAVIOR 46(1):1-104, July 1989

Breaking the language barrier, by E. D. Degnan. POLICE CHIEF 57(5):40-41, 1990

"British System": past, present and future, by J. Strang. INTERNATIONAL REVIEW OF PSYCHIATRY 1(1-2):109-120, March 1989

Bufo abuse: a toxic toad gets licked, boiled, by J. Horgan. SCIENTIFIC AMERICAN 263(2):26-27, August 1990

Canada wants drug data collected globally, by E. Hauschildt. JOURNAL OF THE ADDICTION RESEARCH FOUNDATION 19(4):5, April 1, 1990

"Caretaker generation," by J. France. NEWSWEEK 115:16, January 29, 1990

Coupons help fight drugs. LAW AND ORDER 38(5):4, May 1990

Dangerous liaisons: insurgency and drugs, by V. Dennison. INTERNATIONAL DEFENSE REVIEW (1):12-14, May 1990

DES threatens third generation. TRIAL 26(7):13-15, July 1990

Director, Eva Tongue, wants ICAA (International Council on Alcohol and Addictions) continually. JOURNAL OF THE ADDICTION RESEARCH FOUNDATION 19(9):5, September 1, 1990

Drug abuse in patients with chronic pain. AMERICAN FAMILY PHYSICIAN 42(Suppl): 79, November 1990

Drug file. LIAISONS 294:4-31, 1989

Drug referral schemes, by N. Dorn, et al. POLICING 6(2):482-492, 1990

Emergency aspects of drug abuse. EMERGENCY MEDICINE CLINICS OF NORTH AMERICA 8(3):467-723, August 1990

Fallacies and phobias about addiction and pain, by J. Lander. BRITISH JOURNAL OF ADDICTION 85(6):803-809, June 1990

Federal drugstore: interview with M. S. Gazzaniga. NATIONAL REVIEW 42:34+, February 5, 1990

Form and function of North Yemeni Qat Sessions, by P. A Frye. SOUTHERN COMMUNICATION JOURNAL 55(3):292-304, Spring 1990

Getting stoned the healthy way, by C. Holden. SCIENCE 249:120, July 13, 1990

Importance of cooperative enforcement programs, by S. E. Morris. POLICE CHIEF 56(11):11, November 1989

It's the right thing to do, by H. A. Nocella. SECURITY MANAGEMENT 34(5):8+, May 1990

Keeping tabs on addicts, by A. Blackwell. POLICE REVIEW 97(5015):1168-1169, 1989

DRUG ABUSE

Looking to the 90s: crisis-wise, by W. Howell. JOURNAL OF THE ADDICTION RE-
SEARCH FOUNDATION 19(11):1, January 1, 1990

Narrow battling drug-alcohol problems, by J. Morrow. WINDSPEAKER 8(3):3, April
27, 1990

NCCDN omission, by R. Bryson. AMERICAN JOURNAL OF NURSING 90(8):20, August 1990

"Not my son": G. Ferraro's account of son's cocaine arrest, by B. Gerbasi. MCCALLS
117:48+, February 1990

Open question. NATURAL REVIEW 42:42-44+, April 1, 1990

Perspective. LAW OFFICER'S BULLETIN 14(14):84, February 1, 1990

Perspective on the medical use of drugs of abuse, by D. P. Friedman. JOURNAL OF
PAIN AND SYMPTOM MANAGEMENT 5(Suppl)1:2-5, February 1990

Piece of my mind: predator and prey, by L. J. Purdy. JAMA 263(4):523, Janaury 26,
1990

Portmanteau lexicon, by W. Howell. JOURNAL OF THE ADDICTION RESEARCH
FOUNDATION 19(3):3, March 1, 1990

Problem of drug addiction and substance abuse, by M. P. Zakharchenko, et al.
VOENNO-MEDITSINSKII ZHURNAL (6):54-55, June 1989

Remembering history's lessons: avoiding its mistakes, by H. J. Miron. LAW EN-
FORCEMENT NEWS 16(313):8, April 30, 1990

Solvent abuse, by C. H. Ashton. BMJ 300(6718):135-136, January 20, 1990

Substance abuse. WINDSPEAKER 8(17):1-32, November 9, 1990

Substance abuse, by S. H. Schnoll, et al. JAMA 263(19):2682-2683, May 16, 1990

Taint of intoxication, by R. D. MacKay. INTERNATIONAL JOURNAL OF LAW AND
PSYCHIATRY 13(1-2):37-48, 1990

Teasing young minds with biology, by C. Holden. SCIENCE 248:167, April 13, 1990

This and that: cheap drinks and expensive drugs, by B. Max. TRENDS IN PHARMA-
COLOGICAL SCIENCES 11(2):56-60, February 1990

Tragedy of needless pain, by R. Malezack. SCIENTIFIC AMERICAN 262(2):27-33,
February 1990

Universal urge: brainstorming, by S. Snyder, et al. TIMES LITERARY SUPPLEMENT
January 19, 1990, p. 54

Up against the wall. TRIAL 26(4):8, April 1990

Were you always a criminal?, by G. Terry. RFD (62):559, Summer 1990

DRUG ABUSE

Will the parties soon be over?, by J. Morton. POLICE REVIEW 97(5034):2120-2121, 1989

Africa
Recent trends in drug abuse in southern Africa, by S. de Miranda. MEDICINE AND LAW 8(1):45-51, 1989

Argentina
Epidemiologic information on the improper use of psychoactive substances: some strategies applied in Argentina, by H. A. Miguez. BOLETIN DE LA OFICINA SANITARIA PANAMERICANA 107(6):541-560, December 1989

Australia
Severity of opiate dependence in an Australian sample: further validation of the SODQ, by P. M. Burgess, et al. BRITISH JOURNAL OF ADDICTION 84(12):1451-1459, December 1989

Belgium
Drugs in Belgium: current status and perspectives, by I. Pelc. BULLETIN ET MEMOIRS DE L'ACADEMIE ROYALE DE MEDECINE DE BELGIQUE 144(11):580-587, 1989

Bermuda
Bermuda developing national drug strategy. JOURNAL OF THE ADDICTION RESEARCH FOUNDATION 19(12):13, December 1, 1990

Brazil
Research is badly needed to improve programmes for the prevention and treatment of drug abuse and drug dependence in Brazil, by E. A. Carlini. DRUG AND ALCOHOL DEPENDENCE 25(2):169-173, April 1990

Canada
Canada faces problems: drugs, by A. Harman. LAW AND ORDER 37(9):122-123, September 1989

Drug abuse in Ontario, Canada, by R. G. Smart. BOLETIN DE LA OFICINA SANITARIA PANAMERICANA 107(6):495-503, December 1989

Drug use in Ontario, Canada, by R. G. Smart, et al. BULLETIN OF THE PAN AMERICAN HEALTH ORGANIZATION 24(1):22-29, 1990

International news: Canada—tougher on drugs, by A. Harman. LAW AND ORDER 38(1):8, January 1990

Through 1991: Canada and illicit drugs—summary from National Drug Intelligence Estimate 1988-1989. JOURNAL OF THE ADDICTION RESEARCH FOUNDATION 19(10):12, October 1, 1990

Epidemiologic report on the use and abuse of psychoactive substances in 16 countries of Latin America and the Caribbean. BULLETIN OF THE PAN AMERICAN HEALTH ORGANIZATION 24(1):97-139, 1990

China
China's drug problem, by C. Hong. WORLD PRESS REVIEW 37:70, January 1990

International news: China—increased drug use. LAW AND ORDER 38(1):8, January 1990

Colombia
Alcoholism and substance abuse, Colombia 1987. EPIDEMIOLOGICAL BULLETIN 9(4):11-15, 1988

Costa Rica
Adaptation and validity of the index of severity of addiction in a Costa Rican population group, by L. E. Sandi Esquivel, et al. BOLETIN DE LA OFICINA SANITARIA PANAMERICANA 107(6):561-567, December 1989

Drug abuse in Costa Rica: a review of several studies, by E. Alfaro Murillo. BULLETIN OF THE PAN AMERICAN HEALTH ORGANIZATION 24(1):30-34, 1990

Denmark
Drug abuse in Jutland, Denmark: an investigation based on narcotics and addict deaths examined at the Institute of Forensic Medicine, University of Aarhus during the period 1981-1988; 2—deaths among addicts, by E. Kaa. UGESKRIFT FOR LAEGER 152(15):1080-1083, 1990

Developing Countries
Impact of research on designing strategies for preventing and treating dependence on drugs: the case for developing countries, especially African countries, by T. Asuni. DRUG AND ALCOHOL DEPENDENCE 25(2):203-207, April 1990

Ecuador
Prevalence of the improper use of alcohol, tobacco and drugs in the Ecuadorian population, by E. Aguilar. BOLETIN DE LA OFICINA SANITARIA PANAMERICANA 107(6):510-513, December 1989

England
Crack and cocaine use in south London drug addicts: 1987-1989, by J. Strang, et al. BRITISH JOURNAL OF ADDICTION 85(2):193-196, February 1990

Crack of doom: crack abuse in the United States and Britain, by P. Gillman. SUNDAY TIMES MAGAZINE April 1, 1990, p. 24+

European patterns of alcohol use on AIDS and drug abuse, Stockholm 25-28 September 1989, by E. Segest. UGESKRIFT FOR LAEGER 152(6):406, February 5, 1990

France
French population and drugs, by F. Curtet. ANNALES MEDICO-PSYCHOLOGIQUES 147(8):841-849, October 1989

Germany
Death caused by drug addiction: a review of the experiences in Hamburg and the situation in the Federal Republic of Germany in comparison with the literature, by W. Janssen, et al. FORENSIC SCIENCE INTERNATIONAL 43(3):223-227, December 1989

Hashish in the eyes of West Germans: moral judgment, perceived dangerousness and desired sanctions 1970-1971, by K. H. Reuband. NEUE PRAXIS 18(6):480-495, 1988

Great Britain
Class A drug users: prevalence and characteristics in greater Nottingham, by J. Giggs, et al. BRITISH JOURNAL OF ADDICTION 84(12):1473-1480, December 1989

Thrills "n" pills "n" bellyaches: discusses revival of 1960s culture in 1990s Britain. OBSERVER November 18, 1990, pp. 52-53

India
Socio-demographic features of cannabis and heroin abuse in Bombay, by S. S. Shastri, et al. JOURNAL OF POSTGRADUATE MEDICINE 35(4):196-198, October 1989

Ireland
Drug problems in Dublin, by G. Bury. PRACTITIONER 233(1478):1486-1489, November 8, 1989

Israel
Israeli drug cases: field research, by A. Carmi. MEDICINE AND LAW 8(5):433-437, 1989

Japan
Addictions: what's happening in Japan?, by H. Suwaki. INTERNATIONAL REVIEW OF PSYCHIATRY 1(1-2):9-11, March 1989

Brief history of control, prevention and treatment of drug dependence in Japan, by M. Kato. DRUG AND ALCOHOL DEPENDENCE 25(2):213-214, April 1990

Epidemiologic report on the use and abuse of psychoactive substances in 16 countries of Latin America and the Caribbean. BULLETIN OF THE PAN AMERICAN HEALTH ORGANIZATION 24(1):97-139, 1990

Malaysia
Epidemiological assessment of drug dependence in Malaysia: a trend analysis, by V. Navaratnam, et al. MEDICAL JOURNAL OF MALAYSIA 44(2):92-103, June 1989

Mexico
Development of a system for registry of information on drug use in Mexico, by A. Ortiz. BULLETIN OF THE PAN AMERICAN HEALTH ORGANIZATION 24(1):46-52, 1990

Epidemiologic status of drug abuse in Mexico, by M. E. Medina-Mora, et al. BULLETIN OF THE PAN AMERICAN HEALTH ORGANIZATION 24(1):1-11, 1990

Epidemiological status of drug abuse in Mexico, by M. E. Medina-Mora, et al. BOLETIN DE LA OFICINA SANITARIA PANAMERICANA 107(6):475-484, December 1989

The Netherlands
Commentaries: Dutch policy on the management of drug-related problems: an Anglo-Dutch debate, by R. A. Zucker. BRITISH JOURNAL OF ADDICTION 84(9):989-997, September 1989

Do all junkies pinch: crime and drug use in the Netherlands, by D. J. Korf. TIJDSCHRIFT VOOR CRIMINOLOGIE 32(2):105-123, 1990

Drug problems in Amsterdam, by W. Scheele. PRACTITIONER 233(1478):1484-1485, November 8, 1989

Nigeria
Substance abuse, health, and social welfare in Africa: an analysis of the Nigerian experience, by I. S. Obot. SOCIAL SCIENCE AND MEDICINE 31(6):699-704, 1990

Scotland
Drug problems and patterns of service use among illicit drug users in Edinburgh, Scotland, United Kingdom, by V. Morrison, et al. BRITISH JOURNAL OF ADDICTION 85(4):547-554, April 1990

Soviet Union
Abuse of drugs other than alcohol and tobacco in the Soviet Union, by M. S. Conroy. SOVIET STUDIES 42:447-480, July 1990

Sweden
Current approaches to measurement of drug use and abuse in Sweden, by U. Bergman, et al. NIDA RESEARCH MONOGRAPH SERIES 92:267-286, 1989

Age of first use of drugs among rural midwestern youth, by P. D Sarvela, et al. HUMAN SERVICES IN THE RURAL ENVIRONMENT 13(3):9-15, Winter 1990

Crack of doom: crack abuse in the United States and Britain, by P. Gillman. SUNDAY TIMES MAGAZINE April 1, 1990, p. 24+

Epidemiology of drug abuse in the United States of America: summary of methods and findings, by N. J. Kozel. BOLETIN DE LAW OFICINA SANITARIA PANA-MERICANA 107(6):531-540, December 1989

THE DRUG TRADE
see also: Drug Trafficking
Noriega, Manuel

Clandestine manufacture of 3,4-methylenedioxymethylamphetamine (MDMA) by low pressure reductive amination: a mass spectrometric study of some reaction mixtures, by A. M. A. Verwey. FORENSIC SCIENCE INTERNATIONAL 45(1-2):91-96, 1990

Coke Inc.: inside the big business of drugs, by M. Stone. NEW YORK 23:20-29, July 16, 1990

Contradictions of cocaine capitalism, by J. Morley. ANARCHY (23):16, January 1990

Crack dealers' rotten lives, by S. Minerbrook. US NEWS AND WORLD REPORT 109: 36+, November 12, 1990

Deadly dilemma: what finally will stop drugs' threat to the American way of life? USA TODAY 119:15-37, July 1990

Developing a standard operating procedure for crime scene and identification processing of illicit methamphetamine labs, by D. L. Conner. JOURNAL OF FOREN-SIC IDENTIFICATION 38(6):299-302, November/December 1988

Diversion of chemicals and the clandestine manufacture of drugs. INTERNATIONAL CRIMINAL POLICE REVIEW 44(417):18-27, 1989

Drug-related bombings nearly doubled in 1989. NARCOTICS CONTROL DIGEST 20(14):8, July 4, 1990

Drug trade: attacking the mainline, by S. Dickman. NATURE 347:322, September 27, 1990

Drugs: the world picture, by M. E. Sullivan. CURRENT HEALTH 2 16:4-10, February 1990

Evidence links Medellin cartel to members of Sicilian mafia. ORGANIZED CRIME DI-GEST 10(22):5-6, November 22, 1989

Ex-drug cartel worker warns of terrorist attacks in United States. CRIME CONTROL DIGEST 23(37):5-6, September 18, 1989; also in NARCOTICS CONTROL DI-GEST 19(20):2, September 27, 1989

Gangs put $5,000 bounty on drug activist's life: G. Watson. JET 77:38, January 15, 1990

Illicit drug prices are at all-time low: production at all-time high, by M. Brosnahan. JOURNAL OF THE ADDICTION RESEARCH FOUNDATION 19(6):6, June 1, 1990

In search of Horatio Alger: culture and ideology in the crack economy, by P. Bourgois. CONTEMPORARY DRUG PROBLEMS 16:619-649, Winter 1989

In search of the ultimate high: B.C. police prepare for a new generation of speed merchants, by T. Gallagher. BC REPORT 1(36):47-48, May 14, 1990

Insider dope: Avianca plane crash victims carrying cocaine inside their bodies. TIME 135:24, February 12, 1990

King of hash: the rise and fall of Stanley Esser, by L. Elliott. READER'S DIGEST (CANADA) 137(821):113-117+, September 1990

Lawyers, drugs and money: the Crown prepares to confiscate a cocaine importer's mansion, by T. Gallagher. BC REPORT 1(35):54-55, May 7, 1990

Money laundering and the war on drugs, by H. K. Sinclair. CANADIAN SPEECHES 4(1):32-38, March 1990

Narco-guerrilla warfare: is the United States prepared?, by J. M. Skinner. DEFENSE AND DIPLOMACY 8(5):48-53, May 1990

Narco-terrorism, by S. Sen. POLICE JOURNAL 62(4):297-302, 1989

Narco-terrorism: the Soviet connection, by R. Ehrenfeld. DEFENSE AND DIPLOMACY 8(9):11-15, September 1990

Net tightening around drug money globally, by T. Land. JOURNAL OF THE ADDICTION RESEARCH FOUNDATION 19(11):8, November 1, 1990

New urgency in EC illicit-drug fight: borders disappear in 1992, by K. Birchard. JOURNAL OF THE ADDICTION RESEARCH FOUNDATION 19(4):5, April 1, 1990

No fight in this fish: an accused cocaine conspirator pleads guilty, by B. Hutchinson. ALBERTA (WESTERN) REPORT 17(49):45-46, November 19, 1990

On mobilization of moths, by W. Howell. JOURNAL OF THE ADDICTION RESEARCH FOUNDATION 19(4):7, April 1, 1990

Ounce of prevention in drug-lab raids, by E. F. Connors, III. LAW ENFORCEMENT NEWS 15(926):8, July 15, 1989

Proof of attempted manufacture: routine purchase of necessary items—Los Angeles. NARCOTICS LAW BULLETIN April 1990, p. 4

Reeking of excess and paying with cash: drug traffickers have big impact on luxury product sales, by W. Spain. ADVERTISING AGE 61:8, July 9, 1990

Russians and the Charter of Rights: arguments over media coverage delay a conspiracy case, by J. McDowell. BC REPORT 2(15):26, December 10, 1990

Search of Horatio Alger: culture and ideology in the crack economy, by P. Bourgois. CONTEMPORARY DRUG PROBLEMS 16(4):619-649, 1989

Supply-side bias failed to curb drug problem, by H. McConnell. JOURNAL OF THE ADDICTION RESEARCH FOUNDATION 19(5):2, May 1, 1990

Terry Williams takes drugs seriously, by P. Giddings. ESSENCE 20:42, February 1990

Too many holes in the fence, by R. Schneiderman. MICROWAVES AND RF 29:35-37+, March 1990

Turning oil into drugs: Hobbema's royalty money helps fuel a serious drug problem, by B. Clark. ALBERTA (WESTERN) REPORT 17(48):51-52, November 12, 1990

Tussle over drug-war money, by L. Parham. AMERICAN CITY AND COUNTY 105:12, March 1990

United States assualt weapons reaching drug cartels. CRIME CONTROL DIGEST 23 (45):2-3, November 13, 1989

Weapons detector sniffs out illegal drugs, by J. Hart. NEW SCIENTIST 127:28, August 18, 1990

Whose conspiracy was it: an alleged drug importer's lawyer claims the Mounties were duped, by J. McDowell. BC REPORT 1(41):24-25, June 18, 1990

Burma

For a heroin king in the Golden Triangle, death and taxes rule: drug lord Khun Sa, by K. Petersen. PEOPLE WEEKLY 33:95-96, June 25, 1990

Head on a plate: Khun Sa begins to outlive his usefulness, by B. Lintner. FAR EASTERN ECONOMIC REVIEW 148:26, June 28, 1990

Legendary Burma drug lord tough to bump, by T. Gillotte. IN THESE TIMES 15(3):6, November 21, 1990

New dealer: Rangoon generals groom a new drugs kingpin, by B. Lintner. FAR EASTERN ECONOMIC REVIEW 148:22-23, June 28, 1990

Seeds of destruction: if you can afford a beer, you can afford heroin, by R. Tasker. FAR EASTERN ECONOMIC REVIEW 146:46+, November 23, 1989

Canada

Billion $$$ high: the drug invasion of Canada (book review), by P. Appleton, et al. QUILL AND QUIRE 56(10):21+, October 1990

Budding crime problem: pot-growing is on the rise in B.C. and so are drug busts, by T. Gallagher. BC REPORT 2(13):48-49, November 26, 1990

Canadian connection: the drug cartel tries to open a new route, by H. F. Waters. NEWSWEEK 115(2):60, January 8, 1990

Hydroponic hierarchy: police believe they have uncovered a massive pot-growing operation, by M. McCullough. BC REPORT 1(38):44, May 28, 1990

Colombia

Ballot and the gun barrel: Colombian election campaign—political violence; medellin drug cartel killings, by M. Reig. GUARDIAN (Supp):20-21, May 26, 1990

Barons who bomb the press: murderous vendetta by cocaine traffickers against newspapers of Colombia, by M. Reid. GUARDIAN February 12, 1990, p. 23

Cocaine trade's up-and-comers: Cali cartel, by C. Poole. FORBES 146:182, July 23, 1990

Colombia: a capo's death—Rodriguez Gacha gets it. TIME 134(26):19, December 25, 1989

Colombia: President Barco's noble battle, terrible toll—the narcos lash back by terrorizing the innocent, by J. Moody. TIME 134(25):36+, December 18, 1989

Colombia under siege: drug-fueled violence tears country apart, by D. Chepsiuk. DEFENSE AND DIPLOMACY 7(12):41-45, December 1989

Colombian cocaine production has dropped 20 percent. NARCOTICS CONTROL DIGEST 20(11):4, May 23, 1990

Colombian journalists vs. drug terrorists: interview with J. Salgar, by C. D. Van de Stadt. WORLD PRESS REVIEW 37:38-41, January 1990

Colombia's drug busting journalist, by M. J. Duzan. MS July/August 1990, p. 12

Godfathers of cocaine cry uncle. US NEWS AND WORLD REPORT 108:11, January 29, 1990

Narco terrorists: warring factions in Medellin—gangs of assassins who kill for drugs, cash, power or survival; institutionalised violence and corruption, by R. Gott. GUARDIAN (Suppl):4-6, July 28, 1990

War that will not end: despite the government's costly campaign and the pain inflicted on the drug empire, the cocaine cartels are holding their own against government forces, by J. Moody. TIME 136(4):13-14, July 23, 1990

Weep for Medellin, by O. Calle. READER'S DIGEST (CANADA) 136(814):143-144+, February 1990

Cuba

Castro, cocaine and the A-bomb connection: Cuban defector J. A. Rodriguez exposes Cuba's link with narcotics, by J. Barron. READER'S DIGEST (CANADA) 136(817):65-71, March 1990

Castro connection, by B. Crozier. NATIONAL REVIEW 42:31, March 5, 1990

Can Britain cope with the Euro-drug barons?, by J. Boothroyd. POLICE REVIEW 97(5000):390-391, 1989

How Europe keeps the cocaine cartel in business, by D. Charles. NEW SCIENTIST 127:18, August 11, 1990

Great Britain
United Kingdom to act on drug chemical trade. CHEMICAL INDUSTRY (24):810, December 18, 1989

Italy
Sicilian Mafia's secret invasion: C. Sterling's Octopus reveals link with narcotics trade, by E. H. Methvin. READER'S DIGEST 136:111-116, April 1990

Latin America
By keeping the chemicals flowing: American industry kept the cocaine cartels in business, by L. Feldman. ROLLING STONE November 1, 1990, p. 44

Drug lords vs. the press in Latin America, by R. Chepesiuk. NEW LEADER 73:9-11, April 30, 1990

Meanwhile, in Latin America: with whole economics at stake, the drug war rages on, by A. L. Sanders. TIME 136(24):41, December 3, 1990

When economies get hooked on coke. US NEWS AND WORLD REPORT 108:13-14, February 26, 1990

Peru
Next nasty war: you can't do counternarcotics in Peru without fighting the Shining Path, by H. Anderson. NEWSWEEK 115(21):36-37, May 21, 1990

One valley, two wars: police and army battle drugs and rebels, by L. Lopez. TIME 135(2):5+, January 8, 1990

Peru's addiction to coca dollars, by P. Andreas. NATION 250(15):515-518, April 16, 1990

Snorting Peru's rain forest: world demand for cocaine is leaving a massive trail of destruction in a jungle, by S. Joyce. INTERNATIONAL WILDLIFE 20(3):20-23, May/June 1990

South America
Are drug kingdoms South America's new wave?, by R. B. Craig. WORLD AND I November 1989, p. 160-165

Coca and cocaine: their role in "traditional" cultures in South America, by A. R. Henman. JOURNAL OF DRUG ISSUES 20:577-588, Fall 1990

Attempted manufacture of narcotics: discovery of necessary materials—overt step toward manufacturing, Oklahoma. NARCOTICS LAW BULLETIN January 1990, pp. 2-3

High times: crack house in Washington Heights, N.Y., by M. Stone. NEW YORK 23: 107-108, April 30, 1990

DRUG TRAFFICKING
see also: Body Packing
The Drug Trade
Narcotics Control

ADPA opposed to shooting down drug smuggling aircraft, by R. O'Connell. CORPORATE SECURITY DIGEST 3(42):2, October 23, 1989

Air traffic controller sentenced in drug case. CORPORATE SECURITY DIGEST 3(46): 9, November 20, 1989

Airport arrest: possession of cocaine. SEARCH AND SEIZURE BULLETIN April 1989, pp. 1-2

Airport neighborhood watch program. AIR PROGRESS 52:24, March 1990

American Airlines: United States customs agree to keep drugs off jets. CORPORATE SECURITY DIGEST 4(30):2, July 30, 1990

Ann Arbor: house them in jails. GUARDIAN 42(31):9, May 30, 1990

Attorneys do try to smuggle drugs into jails and officers do have right to search them. CORRECTIONS DIGEST 21(1):2+, January 10, 1990

Brady says United States wants to work with Mexico to stop laundries. NARCOTICS CONTROL DIGEST 19(18):3, August 30, 1989

Capitalism and the "war on drugs," by C. Brant. MONTHLY REVIEW 41(9):40, February 1990

Chinese laundry: international drug trafficking and Hong Kong's banking industry, by M. S. Gaylord. CONTEMPORARY CRISIS 14(1):23-37, 1990

Clandestine drug laboratories, by A. T. Laszlo. NATIONAL SHERIFF 41(4):9-10+, August/September 1989

Coca: an alternative to cocaine, by A. Henman. CRITIQUE OF ANTHROPOLOGY 10(1):65, Summer 1990

Cocaine flow at border a "national disgrace." NARCOTICS CONTROL DIGEST 19(21):9, October 11, 1989; also in CRIME CONTROL DIGEST 23(42):4, October 23, 1989

Cocaine purity declines. NARCOTICS CONTROL DIGEST 20(12):9, June 6, 1990

Combined assault aimed at junior black mafia. NARCOTICS CONTROL DIGEST 19(20):5, September 27, 1989

DRUG TRAFFICKING

Cure that went too far: Dr. Ann Dally's book about struggle with medical establishment over prescribing of controlled drugs to addicts, by S. Boseley. GUARDIAN April 20, 1990, p. 29

Customs service target Chinese heroin smuggling. ORGANIZED CRIME DIGEST 10(17):5-6, September 13, 1989; also in NARCOTICS CONTROL DIGEST 19(20):5-6, September 27, 1989

Customs signs super carrier agreement with steamship lines and airlines. CORPO-RATE SECURITY DIGEST 3(38):9-10, September 25, 1989; also in NARCOTICS CONTROL DIGEST 19(20):6-7, September 27, 1989

DEA agent arrested in cocaine trafficking sting confessed, federal prosecuters say. NARCOTICS CONTROL DIGEST 19(18):9-10, August 30, 1989

DEA agents move to seize millions from Florida banks. NARCOTICS CONTROL DI-GEST 20(11):5-6, May 23, 1990

Domestic cocaine seizures indicate cartel changing methods. NARCOTICS CON-TROL DIGEST 19(21):10-11, October 11, 1989

Drug dealer allegedly conspired to blow up nuke power plant; USN vessel. CORPO-RATE SECURITY DIGEST 4(8):8-9, February 26, 1990

Drug dealers find uses for caller ID equipment. CRIME CONTROL DIGEST 24(22):10, June 4, 1990; also in NARCOTICS CONTROL DIGEST 20(12):1-2, June 6, 1990

Drug lab king sentenced. CRIME CONTROL DIGEST 23(24):4-5, August 28, 1989 ; also in NARCOTICS CONTROL DIGEST 19(18):3-4, August 30, 1989

Drug peddler: did arrest occur during parole? ARREST LAW BULLETIN 1:8, December 1989

Drug planes out of action. NARCOTICS CONTROL DIGEST 20(1):5, January 3, 1990

Drug-related seizures to exceed one billion dollars. CRIME CONTROL DIGEST 23(18):4-5, May 8, 1989; also in NARCOTICS CONTROL DIGEST 19(10):5-6, May 10, 1989

Drug traffickers' bid for power, by J. Tutuy. WORLD MARXIST REVIEW 32:71-75, November 1989

Drug trafficking: then and now, by H. Shea. ATLANTIC ADVOCATE 81(1):46, September 1990

Drug warriors march to different drums, by K. Dermota. IN THESE TIMES 14(9):2, January 17, 1990

Drug wars and the empire, by P. Drucker. AGAINST THE CURRENT 5(3):24, July 1990

Ecstasy making inroads in Florida: authorities say. NARCOTICS CONTROL DIGEST 20(13):7-8, June 20, 1990

Entrepreneurial spirit: ticket to future, by S. Milsom. NEW MARITIMES 9(1):2, September 1990

DRUG TRAFFICKING

Ex-police chief faces 20-year sentence in drug case. CRIME CONTROL DIGEST 24(23):10, August 20, 1990

Express mail evidence: illegal steroid dealer, by B. L. Arlen. FDA CONSUMER 24:36, November 1990

Farace's sister nabbed. ORGANIZED CRIME DIGEST 10(20):4, October 25, 1989

FBI agent shot, suspect killed in drug shootout. CRIME CONTROL DIGEST 23(18):7, May 7, 1990

FBI arrests officers selling cocaine. LAW AND ORDER 38(4):4, April 1990

Federal agents raid cross-border drug tunnel. NARCOTICS CONTROL DIGEST 20(11):4-5, May 23, 1990

Feds arrest reputed No. 1 "China White" heroin dealer. ORGANIZED CRIME DIGEST 10(20):5+, October 25, 1989

Female pushers: dangerous and deadly deals—high school students, by W. Woodward. TEEN 34:28+, February 1990

Firearms: use during drug crime—nexus between gun and offense. CRIMINAL LAW REPORTER: COURT DECISIONS 46(17):1364-1365, January 31, 1990

First small fish from a big haul: an RCMP undercover agent stars at Operation Deception's initial trial, by J. McDowell. BC REPORT 1(30):19, April 2, 1990

From the valleys to a prison cell, with a high life in between: profile of cannabis smuggler Howard Marks, now in Miami Correction Center awaiting sentencing, by L. Barber. INDEPENDENT ON SUNDAY August 5, 1990, pp. 8-9+

Has treasury pushed drug money laundering problem to back burner? ORGANIZED CRIME DIGEST 11(5):1+, March 14, 1990

Hiding United States drug profits in Canada? LAW AND ORDER 37(12):4-5, December 1989

Ice storm is coming. NARCOTICS CONTROL DIGEST 19(20):1+, September 27, 1989; also in CRIME CONTROL DIGEST 23(39):1-2, October 2, 1989

Indian scouts track drug "mules." LAW ENFORCEMENT NEWS 15(296):5+, July 15, 1989

Information relayed by another officer: controlled delivery— North Carolina. SEARCH AND SEIZURE BULLETIN March 1990, p. 8

International news: Japan—gangsters a United States problem, by A. Harman. LAW AND ORDER 38(2):8, February 1990

Knowledge of quantity or quality: identity of informant—New Jersey. NARCOTICS CONTROL DIGEST June 1990, p. 8

La Penca's scattered shrapnel beats path to CIA, by K. Brown. IN THESE TIMES 14(35):6, September 19, 1990

Living dangerously, by A. Small. CANADIAN LAWYER 13(8):18-20, November 1989

Los Angeles gang member charged in Idaho drug case. CRIME CONTROL DIGEST 24(3):7, January 22, 1990; also in JUVENILE JUSTICE DIGEST 18(22):7-8, January 24, 1990

Marijuana kingpin convicted. NARCOTICS CONTROL DIGEST 20(1):6-7, January 3, 1990

Marijuana selling wholesale for up to $1,800 per pound. NARCOTICS CONTROL DIGEST 19(10):6-7, May 10, 1989

More than 170 gang members arrested in 11-state sweep. CRIME CONTROL DIGEST 24(25):5, June 25, 1990

Mutual assistance to combat drug trafficking. CRIMINAL LAW REVIEW November 1989, p. 765

Narcotics and violence: the consequences of a disorganized market—part I, by N. B. Checket. ORGANIZED CRIME DIGEST 10(19):8-10, October 11, 1989

Narcotics and violence: the consequences of a disorganized market—part II. ORGANIZED CRIME DIGEST 10(20):5-7, October 25, 1989

Narcotics and violence: the consequences of a disorganized market—part III. ORGANIZED CRIME DIGEST 10(21):5-9, November 8, 1989

New national drug strategy includes intensified focus on money laundering activities. ORGANIZED CRIME DIGEST 10(17):1+, September 13, 1989

New space program, by J. T. Moore. LAW ENFORCEMENT NEWS 15(298):8, September 15, 1989

Not a smart move. CORRECTIONS DIGEST 20(22):4, November 1, 1989

Penal policy file No. 36, by N. Fielding, et al. HOWARD JOURNAL OF CRIMINAL JUSTICE 29(1):42-51, February 1990

Possession: defendant thought he had marijuana, not cocaine—California. NARCOTICS LAW BULLETIN March 1990, pp. 6-7

Problems of tourism in "America's paradise," by B. Johnston. CULTURAL SURVIVAL QUARTERLY 14(2):31, 1990

Profile of a drug dealer in the act, by T. Kleine. ZETA MAGAZINE 3(9):42, September 1990

Public safety endangered as never before: says New York's Mayor Dinkins. CRIME CONTROL DIGEST 24(17):1+, April 30, 1990

Record haul in Los Angeles money laundry. LAW ENFORCEMENT NEWS 15(288): 7, March 15, 1989

Retail price of LSD averages $2-$8 per hit: PCP selling for $30-$70 per cigarette. NARCOTICS CONTROL DIGEST 19(11):9-10, May 24, 1989

Security wrap-up: cellular, biometrics, discharge suits. SECURITY 27(6):13, June 1990

Social structure of street drug dealing, by J. H. Skolnick, et al. AMERICAN JOURNAL OF POLICE 9(1):1-41, 1990

Sonography for intracorporeal drug smuggling, by W. Sauer, et al. DEUTSCHE MEDIZINISCHE WOCHENSCHRIFT 114(48):1865-1868, December 1, 1989

Special report: an electronic picket faces smugglers, by S. Bidman, Jr. AIR FORCE TIMES 50(45):14-15+, June 18, 1990

Studying heroin retailers: a research note, by T. Mieczkowski. CRIMINAL JUSTICE REVIEW 13(1):39-44, Spring 1988

Supreme Court report: the drug exception, by D. O. Stewart. ABA JOURNAL 76:42+, May 1990

Suspect indicted in major heroin trafficking operation. ORGANIZED CRIME DIGEST 10(24):9-10, December 20, 1989

Suspected Hong Kong drug king indicted in Boston. ORGANIZED CRIME DIGEST 10(22):7, November 22, 1989

Terror of international violence hits home, by C. McLeod. CANADIAN LAWYER 13(8): 20, November 1989

Tom-Tom's story, by C. E. Anderson. ABA JOURNAL 76:62, February 1990

Towards an etiology of drug trafficking and insurgent relations: the phenomenon of narco-terrorism, by P. A. Lupsha. INTERNATIONAL JOURNAL OF COMPARATIVE AND APPLIED CRIMINAL JUSTICE 13(2):61-75, Winter1989

Tracing drug money: Thornburgh vows prosecution of money launderers, by C. E. Anderson. ABA JOURNAL 76:23, January 1990

Trading tips for immunity. LAW ENFORCEMENT NEWS 15(294):3, June 15, 1989

Trafficking on a small scale, by A. Moya. POLICIA 59:20-23, 1990

United States addiction to national security: Panama, by R. Matthews. COVERT ACTION INFORMATION BULLETIN (34):6, Summer 1990

United States foreign policy and the war on drugs: analysis failure—paper presented at a conference on drug trafficking in the Americas held September 30, 1988 in Washington, DC, by B. M. Bagley. JOURNAL OF INTERAMERICAN STUDIES AND WORLD AFFAIRS 30(2-3):189-212, 1988

Up from the streets: Detroit gangs—research by C. S. Taylor, by S. C. Gwynne. TIME 135:34, April 3, 1990

Usual suspects: drug courier profiles, by B. Ehrenreich. MOTHER JONES 15:7-8, September/October 1990

Watch visitors' pens. CORRECTIONS DIGEST 21(9):4, May 2, 1990

Well-heeled drug runner: inner city sneaker business, by J. Leo. US NEWS AND WORLD REPORT 108:20, April 30, 1990

Who's really getting paid?, by M. DiLeonardo. NATION 250(19):672, May 14, 1990

Youth gang intervention strategies, by C. Baca. JUVENILE JUSTICE DIGEST 18(4):6-7, February 21, 1990

Africa
Heroin trafficking in Africa: its impact on Europe. INTERNATIONAL CRIMINAL PO-LICE REVIEW 420:25-28, 1989

Argentina
Argentina ready to fight. NARCOTICS CONTROL DIGEST 19(21), October 11, 1989

Asia
New routes for heroin, by B. Lintner. WORLD PRESS REVIEW 37:65, September 1990

Australia
Freer market for heroin in Australia: alternatives to subsidizing organized crime, by R. Marks. JOURNAL OF DRUG ISSUES 20(1):131-176, 1990

International news: Australia—police-mafia drug links studies. LAW AND ORDER 38(8):6, August 1990

Burma
Hugh opium crop being harvested in golden triangle. CRIME CONTROL DIGEST 24(9):10, March 5, 1990

Indigenous people mixed in "foreign mud": Burma, by E. Mirante. CULTURAL SUR-VIVAL QUARTERLY 13(4):18, 1989

Roads from Mandalay: heroin traffickers exploit new land, sea routes, by B. Lintner. FAR EASTERN ECONOMIC REVIEW 148:27, June 28, 1990

Colombia
Cartel hitman killed. NARCOTICS CONTROL DIGEST 20(14):6, July 4, 1990

Civil war in cartel expected in Colombia. NARCOTICS CONTROL DIGEST 20(1):4-5, January 3, 1990

Colombia cocaine war sends the trade elsewhere, but supplies in United States re-main stable. NARCOTICS CONTROL DIGEST 20(12):1+, June 6, 1990

Colombia: gunship diplomacy—United States plans raise alarms, by J. Bierman. MACLEAN'S 103(4):22, January 22, 1990

Colombian organized crime, by C. P. Florez, et al. POLICE STUDIES 13(2):81-88, 1990

De Greiff's Miami retreat. ABA JOURNAL 76:42, April 1990

Drug war: Colombia's elite and drug cartels, by M. Chernick. NACLA'S REPORT ON THE AMERICAS 23(6):30, April 1990

EC will assist Colombia in fight against drugs. NARCOTICS CONTROL DIGEST 20 (14):9, July 4, 1990

"I fought the drug lords": Justice Minister battles cocaine traffickers, by G. F. Gugliotta, et al. LADIES HOME JOURNAL 107:22+, February 1990

International news: Colombia—bounty for police chief. LAW AND ORDER 38(8):6, August 1990

International news: Colombia—crackdown on police, by A. Harman. LAW AND ORDER 37(12):6, December 1989

Judiciary under fire: in Bogota, bullets and hard questions about United States drug policies, by R. L. Fricker. ABA JOURNAL 76:54-58, February 1990

King Coke: attempts to arrest Pablo Escobar, Colombian drug baron, by T. Ross. IN-DEPENDENT July 21, 1990, p. 27

Long winding road to the Colombian dirty war: struggle against drug cartels, and their use of terrorist and guerrila tactics. INDEX ON CENSORSHIP 19:8-12, May 1990

New battle to break the link between assault guns and drugs, by G. Witkin. US NEWS AND WORLD REPORT 108:26, March 5, 1990

Sherrif of cocaine city: Thomas Cash, leading United States drug traffic investigator—Colombian drug cartels, by G. Sereny. TIMES January 2, 1990, p. 9

United States anti-cocaine blockade of Colombia by using aircraft carrier. NARCOTICS CONTROL DIGEST 20(1):1+, January 3, 1990

Costa Rica

Oliver North and Co. banned from Costa Rica. EXTRA 3(1):1, October 1990

Cuba

Cuba's policy against drug trafficking. COVERT ACTION INFORMATION BULLETIN (33):62, Winter 1990

Dealing with drugs in Cuba, by D. Evenson. COVERT ACTION INFORMATION BUL-LETIN (33):59, Winter 1990

It's time to expose the "Cuban connection": Castro running drugs, weapon, by M. S. Evans. HUMAN EVENTS 50:9, January 20, 1990

Ochoa's legacy-Cuba: government officials and drugs, by E. Quint. NACLA 24(2):30, August 1990

When the walls come tumbling down: money laundering crackdown, by B. Zagaris, et al. SECURITY MANAGEMENT 34(5):69-72, May 1990

Great Britain

British travel agents on alert to help catch drug smugglers. JOURNAL OF THE ADDICTION RESEARCH FOUNDATION 19(10):9, October 1, 1990

Case and comment: conspiracy, by L. Knapman, et al. CRIMINAL LAW REVIEW October 1989, pp. 712-717

Case and comment: sentence. CRIMINAL LAW REVIEW October 1989, pp. 750-762

Drug trafficking and related serious crime. CRIMINAL LAW REVIEW February 1990, p. 73

Moss Side mob: violent crime and drug dealing in Manchester's Moss Side, by S. Kelly. GUARDIAN December 15, 1990, pp. 20-21

Pawns in drug traffickers' game of chance: interviews with nine women in Holloway prison, serving long sentences for conviction as foreign couriers importing drugs into United Kingdom, by J. Carvel. GUARDIAN July 30, 1990, p. 3

Jamaica

Going for ganja: how Jamaicans evade American anti-drug measures, by G. Kennaway. SPECTATOR August 18, 1990, p. 18

Laos

Laos: a country hooked on opium, by S. Helm. INDEPENDENT March 28, 1990, p. 15

Latin America

Funny, dirty little drug war: interview with M. Levine, by R. Szykowny. HUMANIST 50: 15-26+, September/October 1990

Kickback from cocaine. ECONOMIST 316:40, July 21, 1990

Laws

Asset forfeiture and third party rights: the need for further law reform, by M. Goldsmith, et al. DUKE LAW JOURNAL 5:1254-1301, 1989

Assisting drug kingpin: aiding and abetting. NARCOTICS LAW BULLETIN October 1989, p. 2

Attempted trafficking: possession not required—contingent informant fee allowed, Florida. NARCOTICS LAW BULLETIN May 1990, p. 6

Bag of cocaine: abandonment of property—Los Angeles. SEARCH AND SEIZURE BULLETIN April 1990, pp. 5-6

Closing down the launderette: attempts by European community to pass laws against money laundering. ECONOMIST October 27, 1990, p. 130

Consent: package of cocaine—Florida. SEARCH AND SEIZURE BULLETIN June 1989, p. 8

Conspiracy: intent to deliver—North Carolina. NARCOTICS LAW BULLETIN June 1990, pp. 7-8

Conspiracy to possess marijuana: four separate seizures involving similar circumstances—New York. NARCOTICS LAW BULLETIN August 1990, p. 6

Conspiracy to traffic: constructive possession—North Carolina. NARCOTICS LAW BULLETIN June 1990, pp. 3-4

Constructive possession of cocaine: Los Angeles. NARCOTICS LAW BULLETIN September 1989, pp. 4-5

Constructive possession of marijuana: Wisconsin. NARCOTICS LAW BULLETIN September 1989, p. 4

Constructive possession: use of firearms in drug trafficking—Alabama. NARCOTICS LAW BULLETIN April 1990, p. 5

Constructive transfer of drugs: Texas. NARCOTICS LAW BULLETIN September 1989, p. 3

Cracked windshield: plain view—drugs; New York. SEARCH AND SEIZURE BULLETIN April 1989, pp. 3-4

Delivery of marijuana: actions by codefendant—Texas. NARCOTICS LAW BULLETIN October 1989, p. 2

Determining weight of LSD seized: sentencing guidelines—Iowa. NARCOTICS LAW BULLETIN November 1989, p. 2

Distribution: circumstantial evidence by layman—Nebraska. NARCOTICS LAW BULLETIN February 1990, p. 7

Distribution of cocaine to minors: proof of age—Virginia. NARCOTICS LAW BULLETIN June 1990 p. 4-5

Double jeopardy: multiple convictions based on single act—construction of statutes. CRIMINAL LAW REPORTER: COURT DECISIONS 45(23):2431-2432, September 23, 1989

Double jeopardy: multiple convictions for possessing and distributing same drug. CRIMINAL LAW REPORTER: COURT DECISIONS 47(8):1154-1155, May 23, 1990

"Drug profile" use gets mixed Florida Supreme Court ruling. CRIME CONTROL DIGEST 24(23):9, June 11, 1990; also in NARCOTICS CONTROL DIGEST 20(13): 5, June 20, 1990

Drug smuggling conspiracy: use of house as depot—Puerto Rico. NARCOTICS LAW BULLETIN December 1989, p. 3

Drug trafficking and use: French legislation, practice and perspectives, by J. Borricand. REVUE DE DROIT PENAL ET DE CRIMINOLOGIE 3:245-272, 1989

Drug trafficking with a firearm: evidence of separate crime—Washington. NARCOTICS LAW BULLETIN June 1990, p. 2

Drug transactions: photographic records—New York. ARREST LAW BULLETIN 3:4, March 1990

Drugs: possession with intent to distribute and conspiracy—sufficiency of evidence. CRIMINAL LAW REPORTER: COURT DECISIONS 45(20):2367-2368, August 23, 1989

Drugs: sales within 100 feet of school—relevant measure of distance. CRIMINAL LAW REPORTER: COURT DECISIONS 46(6):1129-1130, November 8, 1989

Drugs: "schoolyard" statute—constitutionality. CRIMINAL LAW REPORTER: COURT DECISIONS 47(2):1035, April 11, 1990

Drugs: "schoolyard" statute—equal protection; due process. CRIMINAL LAW REPORTER: COURT DECISIONS 47(5):1097, May 2, 1990

Drugs: "schoolyard" statutes—sale of contraband after school hours. CRIMINAL LAW REPORTER: COURT DECISIONS 46(2):1036, October 11, 1989

Federal jurisdiction: foreign vessel outside United States waters—maritime drug law enforcement act; applicability of fourth amendment. CRIMINAL LAW REPORTER: COURT DECISIONS 47(10):1200, June 6, 1990

Federal law on using minors in drug trade establishes separate crime CA 9 says. CRIMINAL LAW REPORTER: COURT DECISIONS 46(16):1329-1330, January 24, 1990

Forfeiture: drug offenses—dentist's office; illegal prescriptions written on premises. CRIMINAL LAW REPORTER: COURT DECISIONS 46(22):1480-1481, March 7, 1990

Forfeiture: money found on premises of drug seizure—Massachusetts. NARCOTICS LAW BULLETIN April 1990, p. 8

Forfeiture of realty doesn't require proof of "substantial" link to underlying crimes. CRIMINAL LAW REPORTER: COURT DECISIONS 47(12):1229-1230, June 20, 1990

Forfeiture: property used to facilitate drug-trafficking offense. CRIMINAL LAW REPORTER: COURT DECISIONS 45(25):2474, September 27, 1989

Gambling big to nail Noriega: money laundering case against Bank of Credit and Commerce International, by G. DeGeorge. BUSINESS WEEK February 19, 1990, pp. 116-117

Grabbing dirty money: and horses, yachts, planes, cars, by G. DeGeorge. BUSINESS WEEK June 4, 1990, pp. 152+

House passes asset forfeiture legislation. CRIME CONTROL DIGEST 23(43):1-2, October 30, 1989

Immigration officials in west cracking down on illegal aliens who commit crimes. CRIME CONTROL DIGEST 23(18):7, May 8, 1989; also in NARCOTICS CONTROL DIGEST 19(10):5, May 10, 1989

Inferred intent to distribute: Los Angeles. NARCOTICS LAW BULLETIN September 1989, pp. 5-6

Intent to distribute: quantity is indication—Los Angeles. NARCOTICS LAW BULLETIN April 1990, p. 3

Intent to distribute: quantity of drugs seized—identity of informant; Indiana. NARCOTICS LAW BULLETIN June 1990, p. 3

Intent to distribute: sufficiency of evidence—what constitutes possession; Maine. NARCOTICS LAW BULLETIN January 1990, pp. 6-7

Intent to sell cocaine: circumstantial evidence—Florida. NARCOTICS LAW BULLETIN October 1989

Joint trial: selling and possession of cocaine—severance denied; Georgia. NARCOTICS LAW BULLETIN April 1990, p. 6

No excuses for narcotics offenders under tough new anti-drug proposal. CRIME CONTROL DIGEST 23(34):1+, August 28, 1989; also in NARCOTICS CONTROL DIGEST 19(18):4-5, August 30, 1989

Possession: cohabitation of apartment—delivery lesser-included offense; Illinois. NARCOTICS LAW BULLETIN March 1990, pp. 5-6

Possession: Warner and S. 28, by I. H. E. Patient. JOURNAL OF CRIMINAL LAW 53(1):105-116, 1989

Possession with intent to abandon or destroy: methamphetamine—California. NARCOTICS LAW BULLETIN August 1990, pp. 4-5

"Schoolyard" law applied only if defendant intented distribution within protected area. CRIMINAL LAW REPORTER: COURT DECISIONS 46(21):1443-1444, February 28, 1990

Specificity: "no knock" provision—Minnesota. SEARCH AND SEIZURE BULLETIN January 1990, p. 8

Statutes and ordinances: effective date—"no parole" provision. CRIMINAL LAW REPORTER: COURT DECISIONS 46(9):1198-1199, November 29, 1989

Statutes and ordinances: use of telephone to facilitate drug felony—ordering drugs for personal use. CRIMINAL LAW REPORTER: COURT DECISIONS 47(12):1243-1244, June 20, 1990

Statutes and ordinances: use of telephone to facilitate felony—ordering drugs for personal use. CRIMINAL LAW REPORTER: COURT DECISIONS 46(11):1239, December 13, 1989

Supreme Court upholds federal forfeiture law. NARCOTICS CONTROL DIGEST 19 (14):2-3, July 5, 1989

Whom to search: drug courier profiles, by W. F. Buckley. NATIONAL REVIEW 42:62-63, April 30, 1990

Legal Issues

ACLU challenges traffic check lanes in court. CRIME CONTROL DIGEST 23(40):9, October 9, 1989

Aider and abettor liability: the continuing criminal enterprise, and street gangs: a new twist in an old war on drugs, by W. G. Skalitzky. JOURNAL OF CRIMINAL LAW AND CRIMINOLOGY 81(2):348-397, 1990

Aiding and abetting in sale: sufficient evidence of involvement—Texas. NARCOTICS LAW BULLETIN May 1990, p. 2

Airport surveillance: stop of suspected drug smuggler based on reasonable suspicion—Indiana. ARREST LAW BULLETIN 1:5, November 1989

Baltimore fuming over reversal of drug conviction. CRIME CONTROL DIGEST 23(45): 9, November 13, 1989

CA 8 condemns judge's refusal to let defendants go under cover while on bond. CRIMINAL LAW REPORTER: COURT DECISIONS 47(5):1083-1084, May 2, 1990

CA DC sets minimum nexus for showing that defendant "used" gun in drug crime. CRIMINAL LAW REPORTER: COURT DECISIONS 47(14):1271-1272, July 4, 1990

California gives restrictive reading to felony-murder doctrine in drug deaths. CRIMINAL LAW REPORTER: COURT DECISIONS 46(1):1007-1008, October 4, 1989

Case and comment: extradition, by N. P. Metcalfe. CRIMINAL LAW REVIEW March 1990, pp. 196-197

Case and comment: sentence. CRIMINAL LAW REVIEW November 1989, pp. 837-847

Compromised Russians: media reports may have jeopardized a drug case, by J. McDowell. ALBERTA (WESTERN) REPORT 17(40):30-31, September 17, 1990

Court to consider mandatory life sentence for drug possession. CORRECTIONS DIGEST 21(12):8, June 13, 1990

Deception on the high seas: a ship's crew of drug agents produces a precedent-setting trial, by J. McDowell. BC REPORT 1(27):27, May 21, 1990

Dispatches from the drug war: tough drug sentences, by G. Fitzgerald. COMMON CAUSE 16(1):13, January/February 1990

Distribution: sentence excessive if grossly disproportionate to crime—Los Angeles. NARCOTICS LAW BULLETIN February 1990, p. 2

Dragon Lady's revenge: Brooklyn-based United States attorney C. Palmer prosecutes Asian heroin traffickers, by S. J. Hedges. US NEWS AND WORLD REPORT 109:23-25+, July 2, 1990

Drug courier profile: organizer—offense level determines sentencing, Illinois. NARCOTICS LAW BULLETIN April 1990, p. 2

Drug courier profile: search of abandoned baggage—DC. SEARCH AND SEIZURE BULLETIN February 1990, p. 6-7

Drug dealer's smile cannot be used against him. CRIME CONTROL DIGEST 24(23):9-10, June 11, 1990

Drug paraphernalia as evidence of trafficking in marijuana: Ohio. NARCOTICS LAW BULLETIN December 1989, p. 7

Evidence doesn't support lawyer's conviction for aiding client in drug trafficking. CRIMINAL LAW REPORTER: COURT DECISIONS 46(4):1066-1068, October 25, 1989

Evidence: drug-courier profile—admissibility as substantive evidence on drug trafficking. CRIMINAL LAW REPORTER: COURT DECISIONS 46(11):1236, December 13, 1989

Expectation of privacy: automobile stop—crack cocaine; New York. SEARCH AND SEIZURE BULLETIN August 1990, p. 7

Florida: getting caught in the middle—B. Everett caught in drug ring asset disposal, by P. Katel. NEWSWEEK 115:20, April 23, 1990

Hong Kong: banking centre freezes, seizes profits from drugs, by L. MacQuarrie. JOURNAL OF THE ADDICTION RESEARCH FOUNDATION 19(2):9, February 1, 1990

Hong Kong freezes $38 million in drug money, by L. MacQuarrie. JOURNAL OF THE ADDICTION RESEARCH FOUNDATION 19(12):13, December 1, 1990

Mandatory life term without parole isn't disproportionate to heroin trafficking crime. CRIMINAL LAW REPORTER: COURT DECISIONS 45(23):2427-2428, September 13, 1989

Marijuana in tractor-trailer: circumstantial evidence—Texas. NARCOTICS LAW BULLETIN October 1989, p. 3

Marijuana possession: helicopter search held legal. SEARCH AND SEIZURE BULLETIN April 1989, pp. 7-8

Michigan appeals court rules on mandatory life terms for selling drugs. CORRECTIONS DIGEST 21(18):5, September 5, 1990

Officers lacked basis to detain bags of air traveler who fit courier profile. CRIMINAL LAW REPORTER: COURT DECISIONS 46(9):1190-1192, November 29, 1989

Presumptive sentencing: first offender—Arkansas. NARCOTICS LAW BULLETIN March 1990, pp. 7-8

Probable cause: arrest afer a controlled buy—Alabama. ARREST LAW BULLETIN June 1990, pp. 4-5

Probable cause for forfeiture was established by claimant's state conviction. CRIMINAL LAW REPORTER: COURT DECISIONS 47(5):1082-1083, May 2, 1990

Proving intent to distribute: circumstantial evidence—Los Angeles. NARCOTICS LAW BULLETIN April 1990, pp. 3-4

Reasonable suspicion of weapon: rock cocaine—California. SEARCH AND SEIZURE BULLETIN November 1989, pp. 2-3

Reliability: heroin transaction—Montana. SEARCH AND SEIZURE BULLETIN December 1989, pp. 7-8

Sale: agent or under cover officer—New York. NARCOTICS LAW BULLETIN February 1990, p. 2

Sale and distribution of cocaine: errors in deputy sheriff's testimony not enough to reverse conviction—Georgia. NARCOTICS LAW BULLETIN June 1990, p. 5

Sale of narcotics: defense of agency—New York. NARCOTICS LAW BULLETIN December 1989, pp. 5-6

Search wasn't 100% pure, so alleged trafficker gets off. CRIME CONTROL DIGEST 23(42):5-6, October 23, 1989

Selling cocaine: mandatory imprisonment—sentence reasonable; Illinois. NARCOTICS LAW BULLETIN November 1989, p. 3

Sentencing: considerations for sentencing first-time marijuana seller. CRIMINAL LAW REPORTER: COURT DECISIONS 45(23):2433, September 13, 1989

Sentencing: cruel and unusual punishment—proportionality; consensual sexual intercourse with minors; distributing marijuana to minors. CRIMINAL LAW REPORTER: COURT DECISIONS 47(6):1118, May 9, 1990

Sentencing: federal guidelines—adjustment for possessing weapon during drug crime. CRIMINAL LAW REPORTER: COURT DECISIONS 47(14):1279, July 4, 1990

Sentencing: federal guidelines—disparate penalties for ordinary cocaine and "crack." CRIMINAL LAW REPORTER: COURT DECISIONS 46(18):1388, February 7, 1990

Sentencing: trafficking—Ohio. NARCOTICS LAW BULLETIN August 1990, p. 7

Supreme Court to consider mandatory life sentence for drug possession. CRIMINAL LAW REPORTER: COURT DECISIONS 46(18):1388, February 7, 1990; also in NARCOTICS CONTROL DIGEST 20(13):5, June 20, 1990

United States indicts alleged sicilian heroin kingping, but faces difficulties with extradition. NARCOTICS CONTROL DIGEST 20(11):8-9, May 23, 1990

Mexican heroin haul is largest in its history. NARCOTICS CONTROL DIGEST 19(17): 10, August 16, 1989

The Netherlands
International news: the Netherlands—drug trade enters European ports. LAW AND ORDER 38(6):7, June 1990

Panama
Dealing with the maxium leader, by R. L. Fricker. ABA JOURNAL 76:54-58, April 1990

Drug links of Panama's new rulers. ST. LOUIS JOURNALISM REVIEW 20(129):19, September 1990

Panama connection: laundering drug money, by C. Bryon. NEW YORKER 23:19-20, January 22, 1990

Peru
International news: Peru—massive drug effort, by A. Harman. LAW AND ORDER 37(10):8, October 1989

Peruvian coffee growers turn to coca leaf. NARCOTICS CONTROL DIGEST 20(11): 10, May 23, 1990

Poor Peru, by W. Rosenau. AMERICAN SPECTATOR 23:16-18, December 1990

Spain
International news: Spain—drug agreement with Italy. LAW AND ORDER 38(6):7, June 1990

Thailand
International news: Thailand—warrant issued, by A. Harman. LAW AND ORDER 37(11):6, November 1989

Paradise in limbo—conflicting pressures in Thailand's industrializing society, by D. Tonkin. NATO'S SIXTEEN NATIONS 35(4):30-33, July/August 1990

Turkey
United States and Turkey revise agreement. NARCOTICS CONTROL DIGEST 19(21):9, October 11, 1989

United States
$15.5 million drug cash seizure called largest on west coast. ORGANIZED CRIME DIGEST 11(15):3-4, August 8, 1990

Around the nation: Alabama. LAW ENFORCEMENT NEWS 16(313):2, April 30, 1990

Around the nation: Hawaii. LAW ENFORCEMENT NEWS 16(313):2, April 30, 1990

Around the nation: Michigan. LAW ENFORCEMENT NEWS 16(313):2, April 30, 1990

Around the nation: New Jersey. LAW ENFORCEMENT NEWS 16(313):2, April 30, 1990

Around the nation; Texas. LAW ENFORCEMENT NEWS 16(313):2, April 30, 1990

Around the nation: Washington. LAW ENFORCEMENT NEWS 16(313):2, April 30, 1990

Asian heroin floods United States, DEA official says. CRIME CONTROL DIGEST 23(48):2, December 4, 1989

Black males and the drug trade: new enterpreneurs of new illusions—Joint Center Conferences report that urban drug dealers are largely addicts who earn little by their trade and fear street violence more than jail, by K. McFate. FOCUS 18:5-6, May 1990

Buffalo, New York: police see first large amounts of crack in their city. CRIME CONTROL DIGEST 24(17):4-5, April 30, 1990

California Attorney General says state now is leading entry point for Colombian cocaine. NARCOTICS CONTROL DIGEST 19(17):9-10, August 16, 1989

Chinese gangsters fill a narcotics gap left by United States on Mafia: Johnny Kon and his "Eagles" hit pay dirt as the market for quality heroin surges, by S. Penn. WALL STREET JOURNAL 215:1+, March 22, 1990

Crack distribution in Detroit, by T. Mieckowski. CONTEMPORARY DRUG PROBLEMS 17:9-30, Spring 1990

Crack lingo in Detroit, by T. Mieczkowski. AMERICAN SPEECH 65:284-288, Fall 1990

Drug trafficking in world capitalism: a perspective on Jamaican posses in the United States, by F. V. Harrison. SOCIAL JUSTICE 16(4):115-131, Winter 1989

Fling of a high roller: Los Angeles cocaine dealer B. Bennett, by J. Beaty, et al. TIME 136:51-52, December 3, 1990

From rocks to riches: crack dealing Chambers brothers in Detroit, by W. M. Adler. ESQUIRE 113:104-106+, January 1990

Growing up in East Harlem, by J. Van Dyk. NATIONAL GEOGRAPHIC 177:52-75, May 1990

Ice headed for Oregon. NARCOTICS CONTROL DIGEST 19(21):6, October 11, 1989; also in CRIME CONTROL DIGEST 23(41):4, October 16, 1989

Ice hits Washington. CRIME CONTROL DIGEST 23(43):2-3, October 30, 1989

Los Angeles gang members charged in nationwde cocaine-PCP ring. NARCOTICS CONTROL DIGEST 20(14):10, July 4, 1990

Los Angeles seen challenging Miami as nation's drug-distribution capital. LAW EN-FORCEMENT NEWS 15(291):1+, April 30, 1989

Marijuana: conspiracy to possess—possession and intent to distribute; Texas. NAR-COTICS LAW BULLETIN June 1990, pp. 3-4

Marshals oust DC druggies. LAW ENFORCEMENT NEWS 15(296):1+, July 15, 1989

New drug trends adding to United States problems. LAW ENFORCEMENT NEWS 15(298):7, September 15, 1989

Nine alleged Chicago OC members nabbed for drugs. ORGANIZED CRIME DIGEST 11(12):9-10, June 27, 1990

Out there: I—involvement of black youth in drug trade in New Haven, Connecticut, by W. Finnegan. NEW YORKER 66:51-52+, September 10, 1990

Out there: II—involvement of black youth in drug trade in New Haven, Connecticut, by W. Finnegan. NEW YORKER 66:60-64+, September 17, 1990

Pen register on phone reveals many calls to known traffickers: New York. SEARCH AND SEIZURE BULLETIN April 1990, p. 8

Philadelphia's project fishnet scares dealers, but doesn't halt drug trafficking. LAW ENFORCEMENT NEWS 15(294):3+, June 15, 1989

Search for drugs: furs in plain view—Wyoming. SEARCH AND SEIZURE BULLETIN March 1990, p. 5

Searfo-backed meth ring busted in Pennsylvania, New Jersey. ORGANIZED CRIME DIGEST 10(18):7-8, September 17, 1989

Trafficking in cocaine: Georgia. NARCOTICS LAW BULLETIN December 1989, p. 6

Trafficking in cocaine: sampling—not in possession of entire amount, Florida. NAR-COTICS LAW BULLETIN June 1990, pp. 2-3

Trafficking: participation—Georgia. NARCOTICS LAW BULLETIN May 1990, pp. 2-3

Undercover money laundering: Florida. NARCOTICS LAW BULLETIN January 1990, pp. 7-8

EATING DISORDERS

Correlates of laxative abuse in bulimia, by D. A. Waller, et al. HOSPITAL AND COM-MUNITY PSYCHIATRY 41(7):797-799, July 1990

Covert drug abuse in patients with eating disorders, by R. C. Hall, et al. PSYCHIATRY IN MEDICINE 7(4):247-255, 1989

Eating disorders: a primer for the substance abuse specialist: I—clinical features, by J. L. Katz. JOURNAL OF SUBSTANCE ABUSE TREATMENT 7(3):143-150, 1990

Influence of prior alcohol and drug abuse problems on bulimia nervosa treatment out-come, by J. E. Mitchell, et al. ADDICTIVE BEHAVIORS 15(2):169-173, 1990

EATING DISORDERS

Inpatient care of the substance-abusing patient with a concomitant eating disorder, by R. N. Marcus, et al. HOSPITAL AND COMMUNITY PSYCHIATRY 41(1):59-63, January 1990

Justified paternalism in adolescent health care: cases of anorexia nervosa and substance abuse, by T. J. Silber. JOURNAL OF ADOLESCENT HEALTH CARE 10(6):449-453, November 1989

Laxative abuse in eating disorders, by S. G. Willard, et al. PSYCHIATRY IN MEDICINE 7(3):75-87, 1989

Opiate addiction and anorexia nervosa: a case report, by D. D. Krahn, et al. INTERNATIONAL JOURNAL OF 9(4):453-456, July 1990

Sorbitol abuse among eating-disordered patients, by E. S. Ohlrich, et al. PSYCHOSOMATICS 30(4):451-453, Fall 1989

EC   (EUROPEAN COMMISSION)

EC bans all ads for alcohol, beer. JOURNAL OF THE ADDICTION RESEARCH FOUNDATION 19(11):1, November 1, 1990

EC forms computer net to foil cocaine traffic, by T. Land. JOURNAL OF THE ADDICTION RESEARCH FOUNDATION 19(10):9, October 1, 1990

EC moving on alcohol, tobacco advertising, by S. Milmo. JOURNAL OF THE ADDICTION RESEARCH FOUNDATION 19(7-8):1+, July/August 1990

EC to reexamine cocaine precursors policy, by K. Sternberg. CHEMICAL WEEK 147:18, August 15, 1990

EC too soft on hard-drug chemicals: plans to impose strict regulations, by K. Sternberg. CHEMICAL WEEK 146:18, June 13, 1990

EC will assist Colombia in fight against drugs. NARCOTICS CONTROL DIGEST 20(14):9, July 4, 1990

ECONOMICS

ADAMHA awards record total of alcohol and drug grants. PUBLIC HEALTH REPORTS 105:213-214, March/April 1990

Alcohol, tobacco and public policy: the contribution of economics, by K. Hartley. BRITISH JOURNAL OF ADDICTION 84(10):1113-1121, October 1989

Cost of maternal drug abuse drawing notice, by L. Wagner. MODERN HEALTHCARE 20(12):21, March 26, 1990

Curbing mental health and chemical dependency costs, by H. Rendell-Baker. PENSION WORLD 26:24-26, November 1990

Drug-dealing danger money: Rand Corporation study—money from crime; a study of the economics of drug-dealing in Washington, D.C. ECONOMIST 316:29-30, July 14, 1990

ECONOMICS

Drug use in the 1990s, by D. L. Heerema. BUSINESS HORIZONS 33:127-132, January/February 1990

Economic aspects of illicit drug markets and drug enforcement policies, by A. Wagstaff. BRITISH JOURNAL OF ADDICTION 84(10):1173-1182, October 1989

Economics of addiction: the role of the economist in addictions research, by C. Godfrey, et al. BRITISH JOURNAL OF ADDICTION 84(10):1109-1112, October 1989

Economics plays role in alcohol and drug abuse. ENFORCEMENT JOURNAL 28(3): 82, July-September 1989

Federal courts have a drug problem: delays caused by narcotics are boosting corporate legal bills, by T. Smart. BUSINESS WEEK March 26, 1990, pp. 76-77

Foundation funding for health promotion and disease prevention, by L. G. Greenberg. HEALTH AFFAIRS 9(2):209-214, Summer 1990

Health benefits of increases of alcohol and cigarette taxes, by M. Grossman. BRITISH JOURNAL OF ADDICTION 84(10):1193-1204, October 1989

Health policy implications of international trade in alcohol and tobacco products, by M. Powell. BRITISH JOURNAL OF ADDICTION 84(10):1151-1162, October 1989

Kansas City doesn't just talk: voters raise their sales tax to fight the drug war, by D. A. Kaplan. NEWSWEEK 115(6):62, February 5, 1990

Nice place to visit, but you might not want to run a hospital in New York City, by D. Weber. HEALTHCARE FORUM JOURNAL 32(6):69-75, November/December 1989

Radical insights on drug-taking, by W. F. Buckley, Jr. JOURNAL OF THE FLORIDA MEDICAL ASSOCIATION 76(4):409, April 1989

Rancor, ill will pits justice agency, House panel over crime grants. JUVENILE JUSTICE DIGEST 18(11):1-3, June 6, 1990

Senate panel rejects funding for drug intelligence center. ORGANIZED CRIME DIGEST 11(15):1+, August 8, 1990; also in CRIME CONTROL DIGEST 24(32):3, August 13, 1990

EDUCATION
see also: Prevention

Administration presents parents' anti-drug handbook. JUVENILE JUSTICE DIGEST 18(5):8, March 7, 1990

Booklets useful in drug fight. ENFORCEMENT JOURNAL 28(3):7, July/September 1989

Cavazos issue drug prevention curriculum. JUVENILE JUSTICE DIGEST 18(15):1-2, August 1, 1990

Communication and health education research: potential sources for education for prevention of drug use, by N. Maccoby. NIDA RESEARCH MONOGRAPH SERIES 93:1-23, 1990

Consumption of alcohol and tobacco during pregnancy by health advisors: an investigation of nurses, nurses' aides, physicians and school teachers, by J. G. Frische, et al. UGESKRIFT FOR LAEGER 152(9):2101-2104, July 16, 1990

Country collaboration creates a unique drug treatment program for adolescents: Santa Clara County, by J. Carey, et al. THRUST 19:27-29, January 1990

Creating an educational comic book, by L. F. Sawicki. ETC 46:248-249, Fall 1989

Credibility and drug education: a critique and reformulation, by J. E. Buckley. INTERNATIONAL JOURNAL OF THE ADDICTIONS 24(6):489-497, June 1989

Dealer and reality: drug education and the anti-hero, by W. Howell. JOURNAL OF THE ADDICTION RESEARCH FOUNDATION 19(2):3, February 1, 1990

Detours on the road to drugs: award-winning anti-drug programs, by E. Ficklen. AMERICAN SCHOOL BOARD JOURNAL 177(2):18-22, February 1990

Drug education, by F. Roberts. PARENTS 65:52-53, October 1990

Drug-free zones: winning the war on drugs, by C. A. Murray. CURRENT 326:19-24, October 1990

Drug problem: films-videos for children, by E. A. Eddowes. CHILDHOOD 66:349-350, 1990

Education—not legislation—resolves benzodiazepine abuse, by J. J. Rodos. JOURNAL OF THE AMERICAN OSETOPATHIC ASSOCIATON 90(1):26+, January 1990

Effectiveness of anti-smoking advice from doctors who smoke, by P. A. Wilson. JOURNAL OF THE ROYAL COLLEGE OF GENERAL PRACTITIONERS 39(326): 388, September 1989

Effectiveness of video instruction in educating teenagers about the health risks of smokeless tobacco use, by R. O. Greer, Jr. JOURNAL OF CANCER 4(1):33-37, 1989

Effects of a theory-based, peer-focused drug education course, by G. M. Gonzalez. JOURNAL OF COUNSELING AND DEVELOPMENT 68:446-449, March/April 1990

Efficacy of social-influence prevention programs versus "standard care": are new initiatives needed?, by D. V. Ary, et al. JOURNAL OF BEHAVIORAL MEDICINE 13(3):281-296, 1990

Evaluation of an antismoking educational programme among adolescents in Italy, by I. Figa-Talamanca, et al. HYGIE 8(3):24-28, September 1989

EDUCATION

Experts beg to disagree on success of anti-drug efforts, notably cocaine. JUVENILE JUSTICE DIGEST 18(12):1-3, June 20, 1990; also in NARCOTICS CONTROL DIGEST 2(6):1-3, June 1990

Factors in smoking cessation among participants in a televised intervention, by R. B. Warnecke, et al. PREVENTIVE MEDICINE 18(6):833-846, November 1989

First honorary Ohio D.A.R.E. officer. ENFORCEMENT JOURNAL 29(1):28, January-March 1990

Getting high: components of successful drug education programs, by P. A. Winters. JOURNAL OF ALCOHOL AND DRUG EDUCATION 35(2):20-23, Winter 1990

Global approach in the prevention of drug addiction, by M. E. Servais. ARCHIVES BELGES 46(11-12):476-479, 1988

Health education and tobacco prevention, by R. Masironi. HYGIE 9(1):3-4, March 1990

How to win the war on drugs, by C. A. Murray. NEW REPUBLIC 202:19-21+, May 21, 1990

Ideas in practice: developing critical thinkers—content and process, by N. R. Stone. JOURNAL OF DEVELOPMENTAL EDUCATION 13:20-22+, Spring 1990

Incentives and competition in a worksite smoking cessation intervention, by L. A. Jason, et al. AMERICAN JOURNAL OF PUBLIC HEALTH 80(2):205-206, February 1990

Influence of education and advertising on the uptake of smoking by children, by B. K. Armstrong, et al. MEDICAL JOURNAL OF AUSTRALIA 152(3):117-124, February 5, 1990

"Just say no" is not enough, by S. D. Kelly. EDUCATIONAL DIGEST 56:66-68, January 1991

Juvenile drug offenders create powerful brochure. ENFORCEMENT JOURNAL 28(4):1, October/December 1989

Long-term effectiveness of mass media led antismoking campaigns in Australia, by J. P. Pierce, et al. AMERICAN JOURNAL OF PUBLIC HEALTH 80(5):565-569, May 1990

Marihuana perception inventory: the effects of substance abuse instruction, by S. G. Gabany, et al. JOURNAL OF DRUG EDUCATION 20(3):235-245, 1990

Medical education for alcohol and other drug abuse in the United States, by D. C. Lewis. CMAJ 143(10):1091-1096, November 15, 1990

Mobile talking robot teaches United States children. ENFORCEMENT JOURNAL 28(3):49, July-September 1989

New antidrug video program, by F. George. FLYING 117:89, May 1990

Office of Justice Programs Review, by R. Abell. NATIONAL SHERIFF 41(4):34-34+, August/September 1989

OJJDP plan for 1990 maintains focus on drugs. CRIMINAL JUSTICE NEWSLETTER 21(3):7, February 1, 1990

PBS launches an anti-drug series of its own: Traffik, by D. Hudson. TV GUIDE 38:6-7, April 21-27, 1990

P.L. 99-252 and the roles of state and local governments in decreasing smokeless tobacco use, by E. M. Capwell. JOURNAL OF PUBLIC HEALTH DENTISTRY 50(1):70-76, Winter 1990

P.L. 99-252: implications for dentists and their clinical practice, by K. L. Schroeder. JOURNAL OF PUBLIC HEALTH DENTISTRY 50(1):84-89, Winter 1990

Police agencies find "Drugs: a Deadly Game" useful in teaching about drug dangers. CRIME CONTROL DIGEST 24(16):2-3, April 23, 1990

Police and Brownies say no. LAW AND ORDER 37(12):30, December 1989

Police try hand at referrals. LAW ENFORCEMENT NEWS 16(313):3+, April 30, 1990

Preparing community educational presentations on ergogenic drug use, by B. J. Isetts. AMERICAN JOURNAL OF HOSPITAL PHARMACY 46(10):2028-2030, October 1989

Preventing drug use among young adolescents: Project ALERT, by P. L. Ellickson, et al. EDUCATION DIGEST 56:63-67, November 1990

Prevention of smoking in young children in Holland: education and changing attitudes, by B. Basan. LUNG 168(Suppl):320-326, 1990

Prevention: the other war on drugs, by R. G. Schlaadt. HEALTH EDUCATION 21:58-60, May/June 1990

Primary preventive approach to children's drug refusal behavior: the impact of rehearsal-plus, by R. T. Jones, et al. JOURNAL OF PEDIATRIC PSYCHOLOGY 15(2):211-224, April 1990

Psychiatric education and substance problems: a slow response to neglect, by I. B. Glass. INTERNATIONAL REVIEW OF PSYCHIATRY 1(1-2):17-19, March 1989

S.M.A.R.T. choices. SLJ 36:58, May 1990

S.M.A.R.T. choices, by C. Kinnamon. EDUCATION INSTRUCTOR 100:54, October 1990

Safety and survival offers new drug awareness program for teenagers. CRIME CONTROL DIGEST 24(15):8, April 16, 1990; also in JUVENILE JUSTICE DIGEST 18(8):5, April 18, 1990

Second annual drug test for members of Congress: educational tool about America's current drug war. PLAYBOY 37:48, January 1990

Serendipity in drug education, by J. Rue, et al. MOMENTUM 21:58, September 1990

Smoking, drugs and alcohol: educating your child about the dangers, by R. Maynard. CHATELAINE 63(2):132, February 1990

Social influences approach to smoking prevention: the effects of videotape delivery with and without same-age peer leader participation, by M. J. Telch, et al. ADDICTIVE BEHAVIORS 15(1):21-28, 1990

Social worker and drug abuse prevention education, by S. S. U. D. Ahmad. SOCIETES 20:5-6, October 1988

Special section on National Addictions' Awareness Week activities. WINDSPEAKER 8(12):1-24, August 31, 1990

Substance abuse education in pediatrics, by H. Adger, Jr., et al. PEDIATRICS 86(4): 555-560, 1990

Task force leads in war on drug abuse, by R. L. Schneider. PENNSYLVANIA MEDICINE 92(10):30, October 1989

Teens hear if you'll listen: morality-based judgments just not helpful, by B. Thompson. JOURNAL OF THE ADDICTION RESEARCH FOUNDATION 19(11):1, November 1, 1990

Television, school and family smoking prevention-cessation project: IV—controlling for program success expectancies across experimental and control conditions, by S. Sussman, et al. ADDICTIVE BEHAVIORS 14(6):601-610, 1989

Television, school, and family smoking prevention-cessation project: V—the impact of curriculum delivery format on program acceptance, by B. R. Brannon, et al. PREVENTIVE MEDICINE 18(4):492-502, July 1989

Ten juvenile court judges launch community anti-drug efforts. CRIMINAL JUSTICE NEWSLETTER 21(9):3-4, May 1, 1990

Texas will see red during Drug Free America Week, by D. B. Jones. TEXAS MEDICINE 85(10):40-41, October 1989

Tobacco use trends and control strategies in the United States, by T. J. Glynn, et al. HYGIE 9(1):6-12, March 1990

Use of time-series: ARIMA designs to assess program efficacy, by J. P. Braden, et al. SCHOOL PSYCHOLOGY REVIEW 19(2):224-231, 1990

Voices from within. JUVENILE JUSTICE DIGEST 18(22):2-3, January 24, 1990

Colleges

Comments regarding alcohol knowledge, drug use and drinking practices: implications for programming on a college campus, by J. W. Lammers, et al. HEALTH 21:27-31, July/August 1990

Development of medical education on alcohol- and drug-related problems at the University of Toronto, by J. G. Rankin. CMAJ 143(10):1083-1091, November 15, 1990

Model curriculum for substance abuse education in child and adolescent psychiatry training program, by J. A. Halikas. JOURNAL OF THE AMERICAN ACADEMY OF CHILD AND ADOLESCENT PSYCHIATRY 29:817-820, September 1990

Alcoholism and substance abuse teaching in child psychiatry residency programs, by J. A. Steg, et al. JOURNAL OF THE AMERICAN ACADEMY OF CHILD AND ADOLESCENT PSYCHIATRY 29(5):813-816, September 1990

Computer-assisted curriculum for medical students on early diagnosis of substance abuse, by R. L. Brown, et al. FAMILY MEDICINE 22(4):288-292, July/August 1990

Drug and alcohol medical education in Australia: on the map at last, by A. M. Roche. MEDICAL JOURNAL OF AUSTRALIA 152(9):503, May 7, 1990

Experiential training program and medical students' attitudes toward patients with chemical dependency, by S. B. Oldham, et al. ACADEMIC MEDICINE 65(6):421-422, June 1990

Medical profession has achieved a major change in its smoking behaviour: how might undergraduate medical education achieve a similar change in doctors' drinking habits?, by K. Talbot. ALCOHOL AND ALCOHOLISM 24(4):339-345, 1989

Substance abuse education in residency training programs in emergency medicine: NIAAA Task Force of the American College of Emergency Physicians, by E. H. Taliaferro, et al. ANNALS OF EMERGENCY MEDICINE 18(12):1344-1347, December 1989

Undergraduate medical school training in psychoactive drugs and rational prescribing in the United Kingdom, by J. Fallowski, et al. BRITISH JOURNAL OF ADDICTION 84(12):1539-1542, December 1989

Schools

Bumpy road to drug-free schools, by R. A. Hawley. PHI DELTA KAPPAN 72:310-314, December 1990

Can one teacher really fight the war on drugs? INSTRUCTOR 99:40-46, January 1990

Can school program prevent adolescent drug abuse? AMERICAN JOURNAL OF NURSING 90:33, April 1990

Dilemma in drug abuse prevention, by R. Paisley, et al. SCHOOL COUNSELOR 38:113-122, November 1990

Drug-free success story: program at Roosevelt Vocational School, Lake Wales, Florida, by H. Macready. VOCATIONAL JOURNAL 65(2):23-25+, March 1990

Drug intervention program that works: Student Assistance Program, by P. King. PRINCIPAL 69:57-58, March 1990

Drugs and schools, by W. Kindermann. PADAGOGIK HEUTE 41(12):8-10, December 1989

Effect of an anabolic steroid education program on knowledge and attitudes of high school football players, by L. Goldberg, et al. JOURNAL OF ADOLESCENT HEALTH CARE 11(3):210-214, May 1990

Effects on students of teacher training in use of a drug education curriculum, by K. R. Allison, et al. JOURNAL OF DRUG 20(1):31-46, 1990

Elementary schools get drug prevention package. JUVENILE JUSTICE DIGEST 18(5):6, March 7, 1990

Evaluation of a comprehensive elementary school curriculum-based drug education program, by R. Ambtman, et al. JOURNAL OF DRUG 20(3):199-225, 1990

Exposing the drug trade's evil face, by A. Trotter. AMERICAN SCHOOL BOARD JOURNAL 177:24-28+, August 1990

Extraordinary teen talk: T. Ferguson helps tackle drug problem at her school. TEEN 34:111, November 1990

Helping schools say no, by M. Johnson. VOCATIONAL JOURNAL 65:24-25, March 1990

How do school-based prevention programs work and for whom?, by D. P. MacKinnon, et al. DRUGS AND SOCIETY 3(1-2):125-143, 1988

Meta-analysis of the California school-based risk reduction program, by W. H. Bruvold. JOURNAL OF DRUG 20(2):139-152, 1990

New support for the drug fight, by N. Penning. SCHOOL ADMINISTRATOR 47(3):32-33, March 1990

Planning for the appropriate analysis in school-based drug-use prevention studies: United States, by D. M. Murray, et al. JOURNAL OF CONSULTING AND CLINICAL PSYCHOLOGY 85(4):458-468, 1990

Prevention of cigarette smoking in school: a prospective controlled study, by H. Gohlke, et al. DEUTSCHE MEDIZINISCHE WOCHENSCHRIFT 114(46):1780-1784, November 17, 1989

Prevention of drug abuse: examination of the effectiveness of a program with elementary school children, by P. Church, et al. BEHAVIOURAL THERAPEUTICS 21(3):339-348, 1990

Prevention of substance dependence in primary school: work implement, by C. Sonda, et al. ARCHIVES BELGES 47(1-4):49-52, 1989

Project Impact: a national study of high school substance abuse intervention training, by B. D. Caudill, et al. JOURNAL OF ALCOHOL AND DRUG EDUCATION 35(2):61-74, Winter 1990

Public schools: learning for living—a place to stop drug abuse, by S. L. Channon. EDUCATION 109:409-410+, Summer 1989

Role of schools in community-based approaches to prevention of AIDS and intravenous drug use, by L. D. Gilchrist. NIDA RESEARCH MONOGRAPH SERIES 93:150-166, 1990

School program cuts adolescent drug use: effect of Project ALERT on junior high school students, by B. Bower. SCIENCE NEWS 137(11):165, March 17, 1990

Schooled in steroids: an educational package targets teenagers, by B. Clark. AL-BERTA (WESTERN) REPORT 17(49):59, November 19, 1990

Schools to get drug prevention videos. JUVENILE JUSTICE DIGEST 16(20):8-9, October 18, 1988

Smoke-free class of 2000 project, by B. Olsen. JOURNAL OF THE FLORIDA MEDICAL ASSOCIATION 77(4):442-443, April 1990

Soft sell for drug attack: drug education in schools, by D. Tytler. TIMES February 19, 1990, p. 31

Software to help students understand the effects of drugs, by A. Safer. ELECTRONIC LEARNING 9:58-59, September 1989

Substance abuse prevention program for student-athletes, by P. W. Meilman, et al. JOURNAL OF COLLEGE STUDENT DEVELOPMENT 31:477-379, September 1990

Team approach to drug-abuse prevention, by R. D. Hayes. SCHOLASTIC COACH 59:5-7, May/June 1990

Three-pronged approach to substance abuse prevention in a school system, by M. Gonet. SOCIAL WORK AND EDUCATION 12(3):208-216, April 1990

EMPLOYMENT
see also: Testing—Employment
Therapy—Employee Assistance Programs

Addiction in a coworker: getting past the denial, by H. Miller. AMERICAN JOURNAL OF NURSING 90(5):72-75, May 1990

Alcohol and drug abuse in the workplace in broad perspective, by C. Weiss, et al. BULLETIN OF THE NEW YORK ACADEMY OF MEDICINE 65(2):173-184, February 1989

Alcohol and drugs in the workplace: major problem or myth, by B. A. Campbell, et al. BUSINESS QUARTERLY 55(2):60-63, Autumn 1990

Alternative solutions to the workplace drug problem: results of a survey of personnel managers, by J. G. Rosse, et al. JOURNAL OF EMPLOYMENT COUNSELING 27(2):60-75, June 1990

Antibodies to morphine in workers exposed to opiates at a narcotics manufacturing facility and evidence for similar antibodies in heroin abusers, by R. E. Biagini, et al. LIFE SCIENCES 47(10):897-908, 1990

Around the ABA. ABA JOURNAL 76:99, February 1990

Bad day on Chicago-area rivers. CORPORATE SECURITY DIGEST 4(30):10, July 30, 1990

EMPLOYMENT

Building a cumulative knowledge base about drugs and the workplace, by D. R. Gerstein, et al. NATIONAL INSTITUTE ON DRUG ABUSE: RESEARCH MONOGRAPH SERIES (91):319-333, 1989

Bush drug strategy targets drugs in the workplace. CORPORATE SECURITY DIGEST 3(36):10, September 11, 1989

Business can help keep drugs out of a community. CORPORATE SECURITY DIGEST July 1990, p. 7

Business crime increases, security responses diversify as budgets flatten in 1990. CORPORATE SECURITY DIGEST 4(9):1+, March 5, 1990

Can we stop drug abuse in the workplace?, by R. M. Stutman. USA TODAY 119:18-20, July 1990

Case of the mangled magazines, by R. Wentzler. PIMA MAGAZINE 71:10+, November 1989

Chemical dependency: denial, and the academic lifestyle, by B. E. Donovan. ACADEME 76(1):20-24, January/February 1990

Confronting drug abuse on the job, by J. Brice. HEALTHCARE FORUM JOURNAL 33(1):25-29, January/February 1990

Controversy continues, by W. D. Farina. SECURITY MANAGEMENT 34(2):65-66+, February 1990

Critical evaluation of the Utah Power and Light Company's Substance Abuse Management Program: absenteeism, accidents and costs, by D. J. Crouch, et al. NIDA RESEARCH MONOGRAPH SERIES 91:169-193, 1989

D.C. retailers find drug-related thefts at epidemic levels. CORPORATE SECURITY DIGEST 3(52):8, December 29, 1989

Disability pension: addiction in the line of duty—Washington. POLICE OFFICER GRIEVANCES BULLETIN December 1989, pp. 2-3

DOT provides summary of industry drug police rules. CORPORATE SECURITY DIGEST 4(5):3-5, February 5, 1990

Drawing the line: when is an ex-coke addict fit to practice law?, by S. B. Goldberg. ABA JOURNAL 76:48-52, February 1990

Drug and alcohol policies, by R. A. Marinucci. FIRE ENGINEERING 142:9-10, October 1989

"Drug-free America" exposition planned for September. CORPORATE SECURITY DIGEST 4(32):4, August 13, 1990

Drug-Free Workplace Act and related federal antidrug rules, by D. S. Tatel. PUBLIC MANAGEMENT 71:20-22, July 1989

Drug problems in the workplace: somewhere between three to five per cent of the workforce is impaired on the job at some time. HEALTH NEWS 8(4):10-11, August 1990

EMPLOYMENT

Drugs in the workplace: research and evaluation data. NIDA RESEARCH MONO-GRAPH SERIES 91:1-333, 1989

Federal agencies don't fire for drug use. CORPORATE SECURITY July 1990, p. 4

Federal contractors maintain drug-free workplace, by P. L. Vaccaro, et al. PROVIDER 16(3):26-27, March 1990

Fighting workplace drug use. SECURITY 26(8):20, August 1989

Fired-up employee "fires" himself, by R. Wentzler. PIMA MAGAZINE 72:10, July 1990

Former DEA agents battle drug war on corporate front. CORPORATE SECURITY DI-GEST 4(9):9-10, March 5, 1990

Hidden signs of abuse, by P. M. Leckinger. SECURITY MANAGEMENT 34(5):50, May 1990

"Human factor" needs greater emphasis in safety probes. CORPORATE SECURITY DIGEST 4(10):3, March 12, 1990

IACP develops model policy on workplace drug abuse. CRIME CONTROL DIGEST 23(43):3, October 30, 1989; also in CORPORATE SECURITY DIGEST 3(44):7, November 6, 1989

Individualized suspicion: police officers—Massachusetts. SEARCH AND SEIZURE BULLETIN March 1990, pp. 7-8

International news: Canada—drugs and hiring. LAW AND ORDER 37(12):6, Decem-ber 1989

Is it libelous to call an employee a "drug addict"? CORPORATE SECURITY March 1990, p. 8

Knocking out drugs in the workplace, by B. S. Harrison, et al. SECURITY MANAGE-MENT 33(11):99-102, November 1989

Labor force experiences of a national sample of young adult men: the role of drug in-volvement, by D. B. Kandel, et al. YOUTH AND SOCIETY 21(4):411-445, June 1990

Look at the past: a step toward the future. POLICE CHIEF 56(8):16, August 1989

Managing conflict in the workplace. ELECTRICAL WORLD 203:21-22, December 1989

Marijuana, aging, and task difficulty effects on pilot performance, by V. O. Leirer, et al. AVIATION, SPACE AND ENVIRONMENTAL MEDICINE 60(12):1145-1152, De-cember 1989

Marijuana bigger threat than cocaine: study—effects of illicit drugs in the workplace, by M. A. Hofmann. BUSINESS INSURANCE 24:71-72, September 3, 1990

New national drug strategy targets workplace users. CORPORATE SECURITY DI-GEST 4(5):1-3, February 5, 1990

EMPLOYMENT

One-third of employees say drugs sold at work. CORPORATE SECURITY DIGEST 3(51):8, December 25, 1989

Private security and law enforcement: responding to drugs in corporate America, by J. W. Corry. NATIONAL SHERIFF 41(4):31+, August/September 1989

Research on the prevalence, impact, and treatment of drug abuse in the workplace, by S. W. Gust, et al. NIDA RESEARCH MONOGRAPH SERIES 91:3-13, 1989

Security wrap up: ATMS, drugs, references, shoplifting. SECURITY 27(3):13, March 1990

Skinner says DOT safety and security workers drug use far below general population. CORORATE SECURITY DIGEST 3(41):6-7, October 16, 1989

Small firms enlist to fight drugs, by B. A. McKee. NATION'S BUSINESS 78:49-50, February 1990

Start workplace drug policy with help from professionals. SECURITY 27(1):18, January 1990

Supervisor's role in workplace drug abuse, by J. Mazzoni. HEALTH CARE MANAGE-MENT REVIEW 8(2):35-39, January 1990

Survey identifies greater drug problem in California workplace than United States average. CORPORATE SECURITY DIGEST 4(25):1-3, June 25, 1990

TACP develops model policy on workplace drug abuse. CORRECTIONS DIGEST 20(22):2, November 1, 1989

Teacher drug use: a response to occupational stress, by W. D. Watts, et al. JOURNAL OF DRUG EDUCATION 20(1):47-65, 1990

Termination: "unbecoming conduct"—Missouri. POLICE OFFICER GRIEVANCES BULLETIN March 1990, p. 4

War on drugs at work, by C. R. Carroll. SECURITY MANAGEMENT 34(2):54-58, February 1990

War on drugs in the workplace. TRADESWOMAN 9(3):20, Summer 1990

What proves worker drug possession? CORPORATE SECUIRTY August 1989, p. 8

When is a drug not a drug?, by C. E. King. SECURITY MANAGEMENT 34(2):59+, February 1990

When will we ever learn?, by R. J. O'Connell. CRIME CONTROL DIGEST 23(45):1+, November 13, 1989

Workers' views on drugs are tougher than anticipated. NATION'S BUSINESS 78:87, March 1990

Workplace drug use drops. CORPORATE SECURITY DIGEST 4(28):6, July 16, 1990

EMPLOYMENT—Legal Issues

Alcoholism and drug abuse: some legal issues for employers, by G. Howard. BRITISH JOURNAL OF ADDICTION 85(5):593-603, May 1990

Alleged drug abuse: coerced resignation/wrongful termination—Illinois. POLICE OFFICER GRIEVANCES BULLETIN February 1990, pp. 3-4

Federal employees: random and reasonable suspicion: DC. SEARCH AND SEIZURE BULLETIN November 1989, pp. 6-7

ENFLURANE

Fatal accidental enflurane intoxication, by B. Jacob, et al. JOURNAL OF FORENSIC SCIENCES 34(6):1408-1412, November 1989

Fatal recreational inhalation of enflurane, by F. B. Walker, et al. JOURNAL OF FORENSIC SCIENCES 35(1):197-198, January 1990

EPIDEMIOLOGY

Adaptation and validity of the index of severity of addiction in a Costa Rican population group, by L. E. Sandi Esquivel, et al. BOLETIN DE LA OFICINA SANITARIA PANAMERICANA 107(6):561-567, December 1989

Addiction to drugs and alcohol among physicians and nurses, by A. S. Sorensen, et al. UGESKRIFT FOR LAEGER 151(41):2660-2664, October 9, 1989

Adolescent substance abuse survey: statewide findings for 1988, by R. J. Marshall, Jr. RHODE ISLAND MEDICAL JOURNAL 72(12):464, December 1989

Adolescent use of narcotics and toxic substances, by G. Lukacher, et al. SOVIET MEDICINE (6):105-109, 1990

Alcoholism and other drug abuse: the South Carolina story—introduction, by G. L. Phelps, et al. JOURNAL OF THE SOUTH CAROLINA MEDICAL ASSOCIATION 86(1):6-7, January 1990

Alcoholism and other substance abuse: preventive programs in Santiago, Chile, by R. Florenzano. BULLETIN OF THE PAN AMERICAN HEALTH ORGANIZATION 24(1):86-96, 1990

Analysis of regional trends in narcotic studies between 1980 and 1986, by K. Wehr, et al. ZEITSCHRIFT FUR RECHTSMEDIZIN 102(8):509-519, 1989

Antidrug message gets its facts wrong, by J. Horgan. SCIENTIFIC AMERICAN 262(5): 36, May 1990

Association between non-recreational benzodiazepine use and other substance abuse, by L. B. Cottler. NIDA RESEARCH MONOGRAPH SERIES 95:370-371, 1989

Biological evaluation of compounds for their physical dependence potential and abuse liability: XIII—Drug Testing Program of the Committee on Problems of Drug Dependence, Inc., 1989, by A. E. Jacobson. NIDA RESEACH MONOGRAPH SERIES 95:556-577, 1989

Children of substance abusers in New York State, by S. Deren, et al. NEW YORK STATE JOURNAL OF MEDICINE 90(4):179-184, April 1990

Class A drug users: prevalence and characteristics in greater Nottingham, by J. Giggs, et al. BRITISH JOURNAL OF ADDICTION 84(12):1473-1480, December 1989

Cocaine abuse and acquired immunodeficiency syndrome: a tale of two epidemics, by W. D. Lerner. AMERICAN JOURNAL OF MEDICINE 87(6):661-663, December 1989

Cocaine in the cradle: a hidden epidemic, by G. P. Giacoia. SOUTHERN MEDICAL JOURNAL 83(8):947-951, August 1990

Cocaine in Wayne County, Michigan, USA: medical examiner's cases, by I. Hood, et al. JOURNAL OF FORENSIC SCIENCES 35(3):591-600, May 1990

Comorbidity of mental disorder with alcohol and other drug abuse: results from the Epidemiologic Catchment Area (ECA) study, by D. A. Regier, et al. JAMA 264:2511-2518, November 21, 1990

Comparison of the abuse of alcohol, tobacco and drugs between students and delinquents in the Bahamas, by R. G. Smart, et al. BOLETIN DE LA OFICINA SANITARIA PANAMERICANA 107(6):514-522, December 1989

Consumption of dependency-producing substances in Colombia, by Y. Torres de Galvis, et al. BOLETIN DE LA OFICINA SANITARIA PANAMERICANA 107(6): 485-494, December 1989

Could Britain inherit the American nightmare, by S. MacGregor. BRITISH JOURNAL OF ADDICTION 85(7):863-872, July 1990

Crack cocaine: a new danger for children, by M. C. Heagarty. AMERICAN JOURNAL OF DISEASES OF CHILDREN 144(7):756-757, July 1990

Data on buprenorphine consumption in drug addicted individuals, by J. Segui, et al. REVISTA CLINICA ESPANOLA 185(5):271-272, October 1989

Development of a drug information registry system in Mexico, by A. Ortiz. BOLETIN DE LA OFICINA SANITARIA PANAMERICANA 107(6):523-530, December 1989

Drug abuse among residents of Beijing: an epidemiologic survey of 1,822 households, by Z. Jiang. CHUNG HUA SHEN CHING CHING SHEN KO TSA CHIH 23(2):66-68+, April 1990

Drug consumption patterns in 2 villages of Bahia, by H. Haak. REVISTA DE SAUDE PUBLICA 23(2):143-151, April 1989

Drug dependence: defining the issues, by C. K. Erickson, et al. ADVANCES IN ALCOHOL AND SUBSTANCE ABUSE 9(1-2):1-7, Spring 1990

Drug dependence in patients in psychiatric hospitals in Switzerland: a survey conducted in nine psychiatric hospitals from 1983-1986, by D. Ladewig, et al. PHARMACOPSYCHIATRY 23(4):182-186, July 1990

EPIDEMIOLOGY

Drug market position of cocaine among young adults in Sydney, New South Wales, Australia, by P. Homel, et al. BRITISH JOURNAL OF ADDICTION 85(7):891-898, July 1990

Drug use among working adults: prevalence rates and estimation methods, by R. F. Cook. NIDA RESEARCH MONOGRAPH SERIES 91:17-32, 1989

Drug use and life style among college undergraduates in 1989: a comparison with 1969 and 1978, by H. G. Pope, Jr., et al. AMERICAN JOURNAL OF PSYCHIA-TRY 147(8):998-1001, August 1990

Epidemiologic information on the improper use of psychoactive substances: some strategies applied in Argentina, by H. A. Miguez. BOLETIN DE LA OFICINA SANITARIA PANAMERICANA 107(6):541-560, December 1989

Epidemiologic report on the use and abuse of psychoactive substances in 16 countries of Latin America and the Caribbean. BULLETIN OF THE PAN AMERICAN HEALTH ORGANIZATION 24(1):97-139, 1990

Epidemiologic status of drug abuse in Mexico, by M. E. Medina-Mora, et al. BULLETIN OF THE PAN AMERICAN HEALTH ORGANIZATION 24(1):1-11, 1990

Epidemiological assessment of drug dependence in Malaysia: a trend analysis, by V. Navaratnam, et al. MEDICAL JOURNAL OF MALAYSIA 44(2):92-103, June 1989

Epidemiological status of drug abuse in Mexico, by M. E. Medina-Mora, et al. BO-LETIN DE LA OFICINA SANITARIA PANAMERICANA 107(6):475-484, December 1989

Epidemiology of drug abuse in the United States: a summary of methods and findings, by N. J. Kozel, et al. BULLETIN OF THE PAN AMERICAN HEALTH ORGANIZATION 24(1):53-62, 1990

Epidemiology of substance dependence, by A. Uchtenhagen. SCHWEIZER ARCHIV FUR NEUROLOGIE UND PSYCHIATRIE 140(5):407-419, 1989

From the Assistant Secretary for Health, by J. O. Mason. JAMA 263(4):494, January 26, 1990

Heroin users' careers and perceptions of drug use: a comparison of smokers and injectors in the Mersey region, by P. Cousins, et al. BRITISH JOURNAL OF ADDICTION 84(12):1467-1472, December 1989

Initiation into crack and cocaine: a tale of two epidemics, by J. Fagan, et al. CONTEMPORARY DRUG PROBLEMS 16(4):579-617, 1989

Methodological issues in the epidemiological study of alcohol-drug problems: sources of confusion and misunderstanding, by J. Westermeyer. AMERICAN JOURNAL OF DRUG AND ALCOHOL ABUSE 16(1-2):47-55, March/June 1990

Nicotine dependence and alcoholism epidemiology and treatment, by J. K. Bobo. JOURNAL OF PSYCHOACTIVE DRUGS 21(3):323-329, July/September 1989

Notification of drug addicts, by D. Acheson. BMJ 300(6735):1343, May 19, 1990

EPIDEMIOLOGY

Obtaining epidemiologic information on the improper use of psychoactive substances: strategies applied in Argentina, by H. A. Miguez, et al. BULLETIN OF THE PAN AMERICAN HEALTH ORGANIZATION 24(1):63-69, 1990

Opiate dependence: the role of benzodiazepines, by V. Navaratnam, et al. CURRENT MEDICAL RESEARCH AND OPINION 11(10):620-630, 1990

Prevalence and self-reported consequences of cocaine use, by A. M. Trinkoff, et al. NIDA RESEARCH MONOGRAPH SERIES 95:329, 1989

Prevalence of alcohol dependence and cocaine dependence in an inpatient population, by N. S. Miller, et al. ANNALS OF CLINICAL PSYCHIATRY 1(2):93-97, June 1989

Prevalence of substance abuse in schizophrenia: demographic and clinical correlates, by K. T. Mueser, et al. SCHIZOPHRENIA BULLETIN 16(1):31-56, 1990

Psychoactive abuse potential of Robitussin-DM, by J. Helfer, et al. AMERICAN JOURNAL OF PSYCHIATRY 147(5):672-673, May 1990

Relative abuse liability of benzodiazepines in methadone maintained populations in three cities, by M. Y. Iguchi, et al. NIDA RESEARCH MONOGRAPH SERIES 95:364-365, 1989

Reliability of drug use responses in a longitudinal study, by W. Pedersen. SCANDINAVIAN JOURNAL OF PSYCHOLOGY 31(1):28-33, 1990

Research on drug use: a review of problems, needs and future perspectives, by K. H. Reuband. DRUG AND ALCOHOL DEPENDNECE 25(2):149-152, April 1990

Sequence of onset of different drug use among opiate addicts, by V. Navaratnam, et al. CURRENT MEDICAL RESEARCH AND OPINION 11(9):600-609, 1989

Social impact of crack dealing in the inner-city, by B. D. Johnson, et al. NIDA RESEARCH MONOGRAPH SERIES 95:326-327, 1989

Substance abuse and mental health status of homeless and domiciled low-income users of a medical clinic, by L. S. Linn, et al. HOSPITAL AND COMMUNITY PSYCHIATRY 41(3):306-310, March 1990

Toxicology, screening in urban trauma patterns: drug prevalence and its relationship to trauma severity and management, by E. P. Sloan, et al. JOURNAL OF TRAUMA 29(12):1647-1653, December 1989

Trends in substance abuse, by H. A. DeFord. TEXAS MEDICINE 86(7):132, July 1990

United States epidemiologic data on drug use and abuse: how are they relevant to testing abuse liability of drugs, by J. C. Anthony, et al. NIDA RESEARCH MONOGRAPH SERIES (92):241-266, 1989

Use of alcohol and drugs in the transitional phase from adolescence to young adulthood, by T. Hammer, et al. JOURNAL OF ADOLESCENCE 13(2):129-142, June 1990

ERGOTAMINE

Reduced serotonin vascular sensivity in ergotamine abusers, by A. Panconesi, et al. CEPHALAGIA 9(4):259-264, December 1989

ERIMIN
Psychiatric complications of Erimin abuse, by L. H. Peh, et al. SINGAPORE MEDICAL JOURNAL 30(1):72-73, February 1989

ERYTHROPOIETIN
Abuse of erythropoietin to enhance athletic performance, by W. C. Scott. JAMA 264 (13):1660, October 3, 1990

ETIOLOGY
Addiction potential of abused drugs, by J. E. Raper, Jr., et al. ADVANCES IN ALCO-HOL AND SUBSTANCE ABUSE 9(1-2):191-201, Spring 1990

Addiction potential of benzodiazepines and non-benzodiazepine anxiolytics, by J. D. Roache. ADVANCES IN ALCOHOL AND SUBSTANCE ABUSE 9(1-2):103-128, Spring 1990

Addictions: what does biology have to tell?, by J. H. Jaffe. INTERNATIONAL REVIEW OF PSYCHIATRY 1(1-2):51-61, March 1989

Administration of laughing gas during labor may cause later amphetamine addiction in the offspring, by K. A. Salvesen. TIDSSKRIFT FOR DEN NORSKE LAEGE-FORENING 109(32):3363-3364, November 20, 1989

Are there differences in the dependence potential of benzodiazepines?, by W. E. Muller. ACTA PSYCHIATRICA SCANDINAVICA 80(5):526, November 1989

Biological evaluation of compounds for their physical dependence potential and abuse liability: XII—drug testing program of the Committee on Problems of Drug Dependence, Inc., 1988, by A. E. Jacobson. NIDA RESEARCH MONOGRAPH SERIES 90:392-420, 1988

Characteristics of premorbid conditions in drug addicts, by S. P. Genailo. ZHURNAL NEVROPATOLOGII I PSIKHIATRII IMENI S. S. KORSAKOVA 90(2):42-47, 1990

Chasing the dragon: the smoking of heroin and cocaine, by T. H. Kramer, et al. JOURNAL OF SUBSTANCE ABUSE TREATMENT 7(1):65, 1990

Childhood of drug addicts, by A. Charles-Nicolas, et al. ANNALES MEDICO-PSYCHOLOGIQUES 147(2):241-244, March/April 1989

Clinical reports on recent abuse of an antitussive, by E. Tempesta, et al. BRITISH JOURNAL OF ADDICTION 85(6):815-816, June 1990

Comment: lack of abuse potential with buspirone, by J. R. Steinberg. DICP 24(7-8): 785-786, July/August 1990

Comparison of the dependence capacity of amphetamine: MK-306 and (-)deprenyl, by S. Yasar, et al. ACTA PHYSIOLOGICA HUNGARICAE 75(Suppl):299-300, 1990

ETIOLOGY

Consumption of dependence-producing substances in Colombia, by Y. De Galvis, et al. BULLETIN OF THE PAN AMERICAN HEALTH ORGANIZATION 24(1):12-21, 1990

Crack cocaine smoker as adult children of alcoholics: the dysfunctional family link, by B. C. Wallace. JOURNAL OF SUBSTANCE ABUSE TREATMENT 7(2):89-100, 1990

Disease and adaptive models of addiction: a re-evaluation, by N. S. Miller, et al. JOURNAL OF DRUG ISSUES 20(1):29-35, Winter 1990

I am a chemical, by M. H. Zwerling. JOURNAL OF THE SOUTH CAROLINA MEDICAL ASSOCIATION 86(1):71-72, January 1990

"Paradoxical" analgesia and aggravated morphine dependence induced by opioid antagonists, by T. Suzuki, et al. LIFE SCIENCES 47(6):515-521, 1990

Peregrinations among drugs of dependence: Nathan B. Eddy Memorial Award lecture, by L. E. Hollister. NIDA RESEARCH MONOGRAPH SERIES 95:36-43, 1989

Psychosocial etiology of adolescent drug use: a family interactional approach, by J. S. Brook, et al. GENETIC, SOCIAL, AND GENERAL PSYCHOLOGY MONOGRAPHS 116(2):111-267, May 1990

Rational use of narcotic analgesics, benzodiazepines and psychostimulants in medical practice: a response to the paper "prescribing addictive medication," by C. B. Nemeroff. NORTH CAROLINA MEDICAL JOURNAL 51(5):240-243, May 1990

Relative addiction potential of major centrally-active drugs and drug classes: inhalants and anesthetics, by T. G. Pollard. ADVANCES IN ALCOHOL AND SUBSTANCE ABUSE 9(1-2):149-165, Spring 1990

What does exposure to nitrous oxide during labor mean for the development of amphetamine abuse in children?, by B. Jacobson. TIDSSKRIFT FOR DEN NORSKE LAEGEFORENING 109(33):3477, November 30, 1989

EUROPEAN COMMISSION see: EC

FAA (Federal Aviation Administration)

FAA adopts rule grounding pilots who drive drunk. CORPORATE SECURITY DIGEST 4(31):9, August 6, 1990

FAA charges pilots with alcohol abuse, revamps inspectors' response procedures: Northwest Airlines pilots. AVIATION WEEK AND SPACE TECHNOLOGY 132: 220, March 19, 1990

FAA's random drug tests upheld: DOT seeks change in procedures, by J. D. Schulz. TRAFFIC WORLD 223:41-42, July 23, 1990

FAMILY
see also: Therapy—Family

Adolescent substance use and perceived family functioning, by L. S. Smart, et al. JOURNAL OF FAMILY ISSUES 11(2):208-227, June 1990

Anguished father recounts the battle he lost: trying to rescue a teenage son from drugs, by R. G. Shafer. PEOPLE WEEKLY 33:81-82+, March 12, 1990

Children of substance abusers in New York State, by S. Deren, et al. NEW YORK STATE JOURNAL OF MEDICINE 90(4):179-184, April 1990

Contributing to neglect: drug use—Indiana. JUVENILE AND FAMILY LAW DIGEST 22(5):180-181, May 1990

"Did I do the right thing?" Bradley O'Hara loves his mother most of all, that's why he turned her in for using drugs, by M. Capuzzo. LIFE 13(5):28-29+, April 1990

Divorce, remarriage, and adolescent substance use: a prospective longitudinal study, by R. H. Needle, et al. JOURNAL OF MARRIAGE AND THE FAMILY 52:157-169, Fall 1990

Effects of familial risk factors on social-cognitive abilities in children, by E. F. Walker, et al. CHILD PSYCHIATRY AND HUMAN DEVELOPMENT 20(4):253-257, Summer 1990

Families of drug addicts, by A. F. Radchenko, et al. ZHURNAL NEVROPATOLOGII I PSIKHIATRII IMENI S. S. KORSAKOVA 90(2):38-42, 1990

Family and peer effects upon adolecent chemical use and abstinence, by J. R. McBroom. DAI A 50(9):3064+, March 1990

Family history of alcoholism in depressed patients: DST and REM latency findings, by G. Zammit, et al. AMERICAN JOURNAL OF PSYCHIATRY 146(8):1077, August 1989

Family life cycle and substance abuse, by M. Goldner-Vukov, et al. SOCIJALNA PSI-HIJATRIJA 17(4):327-338, 1989

Family structure as a predictor of initial substance use and sexual intercourse in early adolescence, by R. L. Flewelling, et al. JOURNAL OF MARRIAGE AND THE FAMILY 52:171-181, February 1990

Family systems and adolescent drug abuse, by R. J. Volk. DAI A 50(11):3764, May 1990

Highs and lows: importance of good mother-daughter relationship in dealing with substance abuse, by G. Slick. NEWSWEEK 115:58-59, Summer/Fall 1990

Impact of quality of family life on drug consumption, by W. L. Grichting, et al. INTER-NATIONAL JOURNAL OF THE ADDICTIONS 24(10):963-971, October 1989

Involving families in substance abuse prevention, by P. T. Nelson. FAMILY RELA-TIONS 38(3):306-310, July 1989

Maternal abuse of cocaine and heroin, by E. C. Maynard. AMERICAN JOURNAL OF DISEASES OF CHILDREN 144(5):520-521, May 1990

Mother versus child, by K. Jost. ABA JOURNAL 75:84-88, April 1989

FAMILY

Multi-family groups, by C. S. Albretsen. TIDSSKRIFT FOR DEN NORSKE LAEGE-FORENING 110(9):1094-1095, 1990

Narcotics addicts: effect of family and parental risk factors on timing of emancipation, drug use onset, pre-addiction incarcerations and educational achievement, by W. J. McCarthy, et al. JOURNAL OF DRUG ISSUES 20(1):99-123, Winter 1990

Neglect: mother's drug use. JUVENILE JUSTICE DIGEST 21(10):339-341, October 1989

Parent-adolescent congruence for adolescent substance use, by J. Langhinrichsen, et al. JOURNAL OF YOUTH AND ADOLESCENCE 19:623-635, December 1990

Parenting styles, drug use, and children's adjustment in families of young adults, by D. B. Kandel. JOURNAL OF MARRIAGE AND THE FAMILY 52:192-196, February 1990

Perceived family relationships in drug abusing adolescents, by A. Stoker, et al. DRUG AND ALCOHOL DEPENDENCE 25(3):293-297, June 1990

Role of older brothers in younger brothers' drug use viewed in the context of parent and peer influences, by J. S. Brook, et al. JOURNAL OF GENETIC PSYCHOLOGY 151(1):59-75, March 1990

Spousal violence and alcohol-drug problems among parolees and their spouses, by B. A. Miller, et al. WOMEN AND CRIMINAL JUSTICE 1(2):55-72, 1990

Substance abuse and child abuse: impact of addiction on the child, by J. Bays. PEDIATRIC CLINICS OF NORTH AMERICA 37(4):881-904, August 1990

FEDERAL AVIATION ADMINISTRATION *see*: FAA

FLUOXETINE
Ritualistic use of fluoxetine by a former substance abuser, by M. J. Goldman, et al. AMERICAN JOURNAL OF PSYCHIATRY 147(10):1377, October 1990

GENETICS
Alcohol and drug use by college males as a function of family alcoholism history, by M. E. McCaul, et al. ALCOHOLISM: CLINICAL AND EXPERIMENTAL RESEARCH 14(3):467-471, June 1990

Can genetic constitution affect the "objective" diagnosis of nicotine dependence?, by J. E. Henningfield. AMERICAN JOURNAL OF PUBLIC HEALTH 80(9):1040-1041, September 1990

Degree of familial alcoholism: effects on substance use by college males, by M. E. McCaul, et al. NIDA RESEARCH MONOGRAPH SERIES 95:273-273, 1989

Dependency: a legacy of generations, by E. Hauschildt. JOURNAL OF THE ADDICTION RESEARCH FOUNDATION 19(5):3, May 1, 1990

GENETICS

Diagnosis of alcohol and cannabis dependence in their families, by N. S. Miller, et al. BRITISH JOURNAL OF ADDICTION 84(12):1491-1498, December 1989

Families of drug addicts, by A. F. Radchenko, et al. ZHURNAL NEVROPATOLOGII I PSIKHIATRII IMENI S. S. KORSAKOVA 90(2):38-42, 1990

Genetic approaches to studying drug abuse: correlates of drug self-administration, by F. R. George. ALCOHOL 7(3):207-211, May/June 1990

Heritability of substance abuse and antisocial behavior: a study of monozygotic twins reared apart, by W. M. Grove, et al. BIOLOGICAL PSYCHIATRY 27(12):1293-1304, June 15, 1990

Heritability of substance use in the NAS-NRC Twin Registry, by D. Carinelli, et al. ACTA GENETICAE MEDICAE E GEMELLOLOGIAE 39(1):91-98, 1990

Serious alcohol and drug problems among adolescents with a family history of alcoholism, by R. J. Pandina, et al. JOURNAL OF STUDIES ON ALCOHOL 51(3):278-282, May 1990

GROWTH HORMONES
Growth hormone: physiology, therapeutic use, and potential for abuse, by A. D. Rogol. EXERCISE AND SPORT SCIENCES REVIEW 17:353-377, 1989

HALLUCINOGENIC DRUGS
Carbamazepine adjunct for nonresponsive psychosis with prior hallucinogenic abuse, by M. Scher, et al. JOURNAL OF NERVOUS AND MENTAL DISEASE 177(12): 755-757, December 1989

Research
Multidimensional scaling of subjective judgements of drug similarities among ketocyclazocine, morphine, cyclazocine, naloxone and placebo, by C. A. Haertzen. PHARMACOLOGY, BIOCHEMISTRY AND BEHAVIOR 35(2):397-404, February 1990

HEALTH CARE PROFESSIONALS
Assessment and referral service for Ontario's health professionals with alcohol, drug and related problems, by E. J. Larkin, et al. CANADA'S MENTAL HEALTH 38(1): 5-8, March 1990

Impaired health care professional, by J. A. Pauwels, et al. JOURNAL OF FAMILY PRACTICE 29(5):477-479+, November 1989

HEROIN
Alcohol use by heroin addicts 12 years after drug abuse treatment, by W. E. Lehman, et al. JOURNAL OF STUDIES ON ALCOHOL 51(3):233-244, May 1990

Changing trends in drug use: the second follow-up of a local heroin using community, by M. George, et al. BRITISH JOURNAL OF ADDICTION 84(12):1461-1466, December 1989

HEROIN

Chasing the dragon: the smoking of heroin and cocaine, by T. H. Kramer, et al. JOURNAL OF SUBSTANCE ABUSE TREATMENT 7(1):65, 1990

Chronic intoxication by heroin: histopathological effects on seminiferous tubules, by A. Gomez, et al. FORENSIC SCIENCE INTERNATIONAL 43(1):97-101, September 1989

Deaths of heroin addicts starting on methadone maintenance, by C. H. Wu, et al. LANCET 335(8686):424, February 17, 1990

Deaths of heroin addicts starting on a methadone maintenance programme, by O. H. Drummer, et al. LANCET 335(8681):108, January 13, 1990

Effects of fetal exposure to cocaine and heroin. AMERICAN FAMILY PHYSICIAN 41: 1595+, May 1990

Grains of truth: life of long-term heroin addict and Second World War ex-serviceman Barry Ellis, by M. Kohn. GUARDIAN (Suppl):14-15, September 1, 1990

Hello, heroin: may be making a comeback. ECONOMIST 316:33, September 8, 1990

Heroin comes back. TIME 135:63, February 19, 1990

Heroin use, crime, and the "main hustle," by G. S. Kowalski, et al. DEVIANT BEHAVIOR 11(1):1-16, January/March 1990

Identity failure: heroin addiction in preadolescents, by A. Magoudi, et al. NEUROPSYCHIATRIE DE l'ENFANCE ET DE l'ADOLESCENCE 36(2-3):69-73, February/March 1988

Maternal abuse of cocaine and heroin, by E. C. Maynard. AMERICAN JOURNAL OF DISEASES OF CHILDREN 144(5):520-521, May 1990

Pharmaceutical heroin and "chasing the dragon," by M. Battersby, et al. BRITISH JOURNAL OF ADDICTION 85(1):151, January 1990

Poland's tragic harvest: "Kompot:" lethal home-made brew of raw heroin and chemical additives, is destroying lives in Poland, by A. Ross. OBSERVER MAGAZINE November 4, 1990, pp. 16-20+

Potent form of "black tar" heroin surfaces in Calfornia. NARCOTICS CONTROL DIGEST 19(21):7, October 11, 1989

Role of ethanol abuse in the etiology of heroin-related death, by A. J. Ruttenber, et al. JOURNAL OF FORENSIC SCIENCES 35(4):891-900, July 1990

Smokeable heroin use will increase, by H. McConnell. JOURNAL OF THE ADDICTION RESEARCH FOUNDATION 19(4):3, April 1, 1990

Survey shows marijuana, cocaine, heroin emergencies soar for third straight year. NARCOTICS CONROL DIGEST 19(23):9-10, November 8, 1989 ; also in CRIME CONTROL DIGEST 23(45):4, November 13, 1989

Acute myoglobinuria as a fatal complication of heroin addiction, by Y. F. Chan, et al. AMERICAN JOURNAL OF FORENSIC MEDICINE AND PATHOLOGY 11(2):160-164, June 1990

Acute unilateral edema of the lung in a patient with heroin overdose and treated with intravenous naloxone, by A. Navarro Beynes, et al. MEDICINA CLINICA 94(16): 637, April 28, 1990

Candidal infection of bone: assessment of serologic tests in diagnosis and management, by G. Quindos, et al. DIAGNOSTIC MICROBIOLOGY AND INFECTIOUS DISEASE 13(4):297-302, 1990

Case of embolism caused by metallic mercury in a drug addict, by M. A. De Ruggieri, et al. ANNALI DI IGIENE 1(3-4):673-678, May/August 1989

Cervical osteomyelitis due to i.v. heroin use: radiologic findings in 14 patients, by C. Endress, et al. AJR 155(2):333-335, August 1990

Chondrocostal and chondrosternal tuberculosis in 2 heroin addicts infected with the human immunodeficiency virus, by J. A. Martos, et al. MEDICINA CLINICA 93(12): 467-470, October 21, 1989

Dyschromatopsia in heroin addicts, by P. L. Dias. BRITISH JOURNAL OF ADDICTION 85(2):241-244, February 1990

Endocarditis in heroin addicts: incidence in the Vaal d 'Hebron General Hospital, by X. Martinez-Costa, et al. MEDICINA CLINICA 92(20):794, May 27, 1989

Enhanced assays detect increased chromosome damage and sister-chromatid exchanges in heroin addicts, by D. A. Shafer, et al. MUTATION RESEARCH 234(5): 327-336, 1990

Eosinophilic myocarditis and pulmonary hypertension in a drug-addict: anatomo-clinical study and brief review of the literature, by V. C. Talebzadeh, et al. ANNALES DE PATHOLOGIE 10(1):40-46, 1990

Gluteal compartment syndrome with normal interstitial pressure in a drug addict, by X. Nogues, et al. MEDICINA CLINICA 94(8):316-317, March 3, 1990

Immunological aspects in anti-HIV seronegative drug addicts: correlation with the duration of heroin addiction and other viral infections, by P. Farci, et al. MINERVA MEDICA 80(11):1193-1198, November 1989

Impaired ACTH and beta-endorphin response to sauna-induced hyperthermia in heroin addicts, by P. P. Vescovi, et al. ACTA ENDOCRINOLOGICA 121(4):484-488, October 1989

Infection by HTLV-1 in heroin addicts in Barcelona, by V. Soriano, et al. MEDICINA CLINICA 92(20):799, May 27, 1989

Infective endocarditis in heroin addicts in the province of Cadiz, by M. Torres Tortosa, et al. MEDICINA CLINICA 93(9):356-367, September 30, 1989

Internuclear ophthalmoplegia related to opiate overdose, by C. Gomez Manzano, et al. MEDICINA CLINICA 94(16):637, April 28, 1990

Lyell's syndrome induced by heroin contaminants, by L. M. Llibre, et al. MEDICINA CLINICA 94(20):799, May 26, 1990

Maternal and fetal effects of heroin addiction during pregnancy, by B. B. Little, et al. JOURNAL OF REPRODUCTIVE MEDICINE 35(2):159-162, February 1990

Myocardial infarct in young drug addicts: apropos of 2 clinical cases, by D. Pereira, et al. REVISTA PORTUGEUSA DE CARDIOLOGIE 7(5):505-509, September/October 1988

Non-infective neurologic complications associated to heroin use, by J. Pascual Calvet, et al. ARCHIVOS DE NEUROBIOLOGIA 52(Suppl)1:155-161, 1989

Personality disorders classification and symptoms in cocaine and opioid addicts, by R. M. Malow, et al. JOURNAL OF CONSULTING AND CLINICAL PSYCHOLOGY 57(6):765-757, December 1989

Resolution of nephrotic syndrome secondary heroin-associated renal amyloidosis, by J. Soler Amigo, et al. NEPHROLOGY, DIALYSIS, TRANSPLANTATION 5(2):158, 1990

Severe non-occlusive ischemic stroke in young heroin addicts, by R. Jensen, et al. ACTA NEUROLOGICA SCANDINAVICA 81(4):354-357, 1990

Research

Brain catecholamine system in narcotic-dependent rats under the action of oxytoxin, by R. Ibragimov, et al. FIZIOLOGICHESKII ZHURNAL SSSR 75(12):1657-1663, December 1989

Buprenorphine-induced pupillary effects in human volunteers, by W. B. Pickworth, et al. LIFE SCIENCES 47(14):1269-1277, 1990

Effect of oxytocin on the activity of the brain serotoninergic systems in narcotic-dependent rats, by R. Ibragimov, et al. FIZIOLOGICHESKII ZHURNAL SSSR 75(10):1355-1360, October 1989

Effect of vasopressin on the concentration of regulatory peptides in the hippocampus of opiate-dependent animals, by G. G. Gasanov, et al. DOKLADY AKADEMII NAUK SSSR 310(6):1501-1503, 1990

Effects of D1 and D2 dopamine antagonists on heroin-trained drug discrimination, by W. A. Corrigall, et al. NIDA RESEARCH MONOGRAPH SERIES 95:499, 1989

Heroin-induced myopathy in rat skeletal muscle, by J. Pena, et al. ACTA NEUROPATHOLOGICA 80(1):72-76, 1990

Heroin self-administration by rats: influence of dose and physical dependence, by S. Dai, et al. PHARMACOLOGY, BIOCHEMISTRY AND BEHAVIOR 32(4):1009-1015, April 1989

Influence of housing conditions on the acquisition of intravenous heroin and cocaine self-administration in rats, by M. A. Bozarth, et al. PHARMACOLOGY, BIOCHEMISTRY AND BEHAVIOR 33(4):903-907, August 1989

Selective D1 and D2 dopamine antagonists decrease response rats of food-maintained behavior and reduce the discriminative stimulus produced by heroin, by W. A. Corrigall, et al. PHARMACOLOGY, BIOCHEMISTRY AND BEHAVIOR 35(2): 351-355, February 1990

Ventral pallidum plays a role in mediating cocaine and heroin self-administration in the rat, by C. B. Hubner, et al. BRAIN RESEARCH 508(1):20-29, January 29, 1990

Withdrawal
Modification of the pain threshold and beta-endorphin level in heroin addicts undergoing withdrawal, by M. Matera, et al. RIVISTA EUROPEA PER LE SCIENZE MEDICHE E FARMACOLOGICHE 10(1):73-77, February 1988

Neonatal heroin withdrawal syndrome: evaluation of different pharmacological treatment, by P. Pacifico, et al. PHARMACOLOGICAL RESEARCH 21(Suppl)1:63-64, November/December 1989

Opiate withdrawal presenting as posttraumatic stress disorder, by S. Salloway, et al. HOSPITAL AND COMMUNITY PSYCHIATRY 41(6):666-667, June 1990

HIGH SCHOOL STUDENTS
Annual NIDA survey shows continuing declines in drug use by high school seniors. CRIME CONTROL DIGEST 24(8):1+, February 26, 1990; also in JUVENILE JUSTICE DIGEST 18(5):2-3, March 7, 1990

Drug use "unfashionable" for United States high-school seniors, by H. McConnell. JOURNAL OF THE ADDICTION RESEARCH FOUNDATION 19(4):8, April 1, 1990

Licit and illicit drug consumption in the school environment: results of a cross-sectional epidemiologic survey carried out among 663 high school students in Le Havre, by D. Bourderont, et al. ARCHIVES FRANCAISE DE PEDIATRIE 46(8): 617-621, October 1989

Prediction of risk for drug use in high school students, by C. E. Climent, et al. INTERNATIONAL JOURNAL OF THE ADDICTIONS 24(11):1053-1064, November 1989

Resisting or acquiescing to peer pressure to engage in misconduct: adolescents' expectations of probable consequences, by R. Pearl, et al. JOURNAL OF YOUTH AND ADOLESCENCE 19(1):43-56, 1990

Social and school factors in predicting cannabis use among Ontario high school students, by K. R. Allison, et al. CANADIAN JOURNAL OF PUBLIC HEALTH 81(4): 301-306, July/August 1990

Sources of information about drugs and alcohol for black and white suburban high school students, by K. H. Beck, et al. HEALTH EDUCATION 21:20-24+, March/April 1990

Survey of alcohol and psychoactive drug consumption in a sample of high school students of the 9th and 19th local health units in the Marche Region, by F. Donato, et al. ANNALI DI IGIENE 1(3-4):693-708, May/August 1989

HIGH SCHOOL STUDENTS

To whom would adolescents turn with drug problems: implications for school professionals, by J. L. Naginey, et al. HIGH SCHOOL JOURNAL 73:80-85, December 1989/January 1990

HISTORY

Acculturation amd marijuana and cocaine use: findings from HHANES 1982-1984, by H. Amaro, et al. AMERICAN JOURNAL OF PUBLIC HEALTH 80(Suppl):54-60, December 1990

America's forgotten drug war: early use of cocaine, by D. Musto. READER'S DIGEST 136:147-150, April 1990

Brief history of control, prevention and treatment of drug dependence in Japan, by M. Kato. DRUG AND ALCOHOL DEPENDENCE 25(2):213-214, April 1990

Drug use in historical perspective: continuities and dicontinuities, by I. Vogt. CONTEMPORARY DRUG PROBLEMS 16:123-139, Summer 1989

Historical perspectives on the use of subjective effects measures in assessing the abuse potential of drugs, by J. H. Jaffe, et al. NIDA RESEARCH MONOGRAPH SERIES 92:43-72, 1989

Historical studies and strategies against alcohol and drug abuse, by T. Baasher. DRUG AND ALCOHOL DEPENDENCE 25(2):215-219, April 1990

Illicit price of cocaine in two eras: 1908-1914 and 1982-1989, by D. F. Musto. CONNECTICUT MEDICINE 54(6):321-326, June 1990

India and the Anglo-Chinese opium agreements, 1907-1014, by R. K. Newman. MODERN ASIAN STUDIES 23:525-560, July 1989

Kung fu kerosene drinking: extension of Amotz Zahavi's sexual selection theory to human abuse of chemicals, by J. Diamond. NATURAL HISTORY July 1990, pp. 20+

Opium and the Indonesian revolution, by R. Cribb. MODERN ASIAN STUDIES 22: 701-722, October 1988

THE HOMELESS

Alameda County Department of Alcohol and Drug Programs Comprehensive Homeless Alcohol Recovery Services: CHARS, by R. W. Bennett, et al. ALCOHOLISM TREATMENT QUARTERLY 7(1):111-128, 1990

Alcohol and drug abuse among the homeless population: a national response, by B. Lubran. ALCOHOLISM TREATMENT QUARTERLY 7(1):11-23, 1990

Crime, drug abuse and mental illness: a comparison of homeless men and women, by B. B. Benda. JOURNAL OF SOCIAL SERVICE RESEARCH 13(3):39-60, 1990

Deviance and dwelling space: notes on the resettlement of homeless persons with drug and alcohol problems, by K. Hopper. CONTEMPORARY DRUG PROBLEMS 16(3):391-416, 1989

Estimating the prevalence of alcohol, drug and mental health problems in the contemporary homeless population: a review of the literature—paper presented at the National Conference on Homelessness, Alcohol, and Other Drugs, San Diego, California, February 2-4, 1989, by P. J. Fischer. CONTEMPORARY DRUG PROBLEMS 16(3):333-339, 1989

Factors affecting the use of medical, mental health, alcohol, and drug treatment services by homeless adults, by D. Padgett, et al. MEDICAL CARE 28(9):805-821, September 1990

Family treatment for homeless alcohol/drug-addicted women and their preschool children, by M. Comfort, et al. ALCOHOLISM TREATMENT QUARTERLY 7(1): 129-147, 1990

Homeless: chemical dependency and mental health problems, by B. E. Cohen, et al. SOCIAL WORK RESEARCH AND ABSTRACTS 26(1):8-17, 1990

Homeless intravenous drug abuser and the AIDS epidemic, by H. Joseph, et al. NIDA RESEARCH MONOGRAPH SERIES 93:210-253, 1990

Homeless women, by S. C. Anderson, et al. AFFILIA 3:62-70, Summer 1988

Homeless women and men: their problems and use of service, by B. B. Benda, et al. AFFILIA 5:50-82, Fall 1990

Louisville's Project Connect for the homeless alcohol and drug abuser, by G. S. Bonham, et al. ALCOHOLISM TREATMENT QUARTERLY 7(1):57-78, 1990

Outreach efforts with dually diagnosed homeless persons: mental health problems coupled with substance abuse: CEU test included, by L. E. Blankertz, et al. FAMILIES IN SOCIETY 71:387-397, September 1990

Services for the homeless, by R. J. Koshes, et al. HOSPITAL AND COMMUNITY PSYCHIATRY 41(3):331-332, March 1990

Stabilization services for homeless alcoholics and drug addicts, by D. McCarty, et al. ALCOHOLISM TREATMENT QUARTERLY 7(1):31-45, 1990

Substance abuse and mental health status of homeless and domiciled low-income users of a medical clinic, by L. S. Linn, et al. HOSPITAL AND COMMUNITY PSYCHIATRY 41(3):306-310, March 1990

Substance abuse: a growing problem among homeless families, by L. F. Weinreb, et al. FAMILY AND COMMUNITY HEALTH 13(1):55-64, May 1990

Treating homeless and mentally ill substance abusers in Alaska, by R. A. Dexter. ALCOHOLISM TREATMENT QUARTERLY 7(1):25-30, 1990

HOMOSEXUALS
AIDS and chemical dependency: special issues and treatment barriers for gay and bisexual men, by R. P. Cabaj. JOURNAL OF PSYCHOACTIVE DRUGS 21(4):387-393, October/December 1989

HOMOSEXUALS

AIDS-related illness and AIDS risk in male homo-bisexual substance abusers: case reports and clinical issues, by J. Westermeyer, et al. AMERICAN JOURNAL OF DRUG AND ALCOHOL ABUSE 15(4):443-461, December 1989

Alcohol and drug use among homosexual men and women: epidemiology and population characteristics by D. J. McKirnan, et al. ADDICTIVE BEHAVIORS 14(5):545-553, 1989

Drug use and unprotected anal intercourse among gay men, by J. L. Martin. HEALTH PSYCHOLOGY 9(4):450-465, 1990

Homosexuality and illegal residency status in relation to substance abuse and personality triats among Mexican nationals, by C. D. Tori. JOURNAL OF CLINICAL PSYCHOLOGY 45(5 Suppl):814-821, September 1989

Psychosocial and cultural factors in alcohol and drug abuse: an analysis of a homosexual community, by D. J. McKirnan, et al. ADDICTIVE BEHAVIORS 14(5):555-563, 1989

Use of drugs and alcohol by homosexually active men in relation to sexual practices, by J. McCusker, et al. JOURNAL OF THE ACQUIRED IMMUNE DEFICIENCY SYNDROME 3(7):729-736, 1990

HOSPITALS
see also: Care—Hospitals

Chicago hospitals: no drug abusers need apply, by P. Eubanks. HOSPITALS 64(13): 79, July 5, 1990

HOTLINES
279-DOPE hotline heats drug war. ENFORCEMENT JOURNAL 28(3):49, July-August 1989

HYPNOTICS
Actions and interactions of hypnotics on human performance: single doses of zopiclone, triazolam and alcohol, by T. Kuitunen, et al. INTERNATIONAL CLINICAL PSYCHOPHARMACOLOGY 5(Suppl)2:115-130, April 1990

Dependence on sedative-hypnotics, by J. S. Templeton. BRITISH JOURNAL OF ADDICTION 85(2):301, February 1990

Effect of controls on sedatives and hypnotics on their use for suicide, by D. Lester, et al. JOURNAL OF TOXICOLOGY: CLINICAL TOXICOLOGY 27(4-5):299-303, 1989

Sedatives-hypnotics for abuse, by J. Dobson. NEW ZEALAND MEDICAL JOURNAL 102(881):651, December 13, 1989

IACP (INTERNATIONAL ASSOCIATION OF CHIEFS OF POLICE)

IACP board urges Bush to strengthen role of drug czar. NARCOTICS CONTROL DIGEST August 2, 1989, pp. 7-8; also in CRIME CONTROL DIGEST 23(31):1+, August 7, 1989

IACP conference speakers focus on drug war issues. CRIME CONTROL DIGEST 23(42):1+, October 23, 1989

IACP develops model policy on workplace drug abuse. CRIME CONTROL DIGEST 23(43):3, October 30, 1989; also in CORPORATE SECURITY DIGEST 3(44):7, November 6, 1989

IACP report examines integrity and drug-related corruption in United States police agencies. CRIME CONTROL DIGEST 23(44):5-6, November 6, 1989; also in NARCOTICS CONTROL DIGEST 19(23):7-8, November 8, 1989

IACP urges President to give stronger powers to "drug czar." CRIMINAL JUSTICE NEWSLETTER 20(16):2-3, August 15, 1989

IMMUNOLOGY

Basic immunology issues in drug abuse, by P. Kind. NIDA RESEARCH MONOGRAPH SERIES 90:72-76, 1988

Biochemical correlates of abuse and addiction, by N. P. Westhoff. AMERICAN FAMILY PHYSICIAN 42(3):588+, September 1990

Drug abuse and immune-neuroendocrine connections, by D. Habour, et al. NIDA RESEARCH MONOGRAPH SERIES 90:87-98, 1988

Immunologic effect of drugs of abuse, by R. Weber. NIDA RESEARCH MONOGRAPH SERIES 90:99-104, 1988

Immunological approaches to clinical issues in drug abuse, by M. J. Kreek. NIDA RESEARCH MONOGRAPH SERIES 90:77-86, 1988

Rubella immunity in chemically dependent adolescent females, by D. J. Mersy, et al. JOURNAL OF SUBSTANCE ABUSE TREATMENT 7(1):59-60, 1990

IMOVANE

Imovane addiction potential, by S. H. Thompson. NEW ZEALAND MEDICAL JOURNAL 103(891):276, June 13, 1990

Imovane; zopiclone, by R. J. Crawford. NEW ZEALAND MEDICAL JOURNAL 102 (879):595, November 8, 1989

INFANTS

Addict babies better off with mums on methadone, by B. I. Lee. JOURNAL OF THE ADDICTION RESEARCH FOUNDATION 19(2):4, February 1, 1990

Between a "rock" and a hard place: perinatal drug abuse, by W. Chavkin, et al. PEDIATRICS 85(2):223-225, February 1990

Chauvin: "help cocaine babies." ABA JOURNAL 76:99, February 1990

Childhood's end: babies born to crack-addicted mothers, by E. Hopkins. ROLLING STONE October 18, 1990, pp. 66-69+

Children in peril: nurse K. Jorgenson's work with crack babies at Boston City Hospital, by W. Plummer. PEOPLE WEEKLY 33:84-85, April 16, 1990

Cocaine and pregnancy: effects on the pregnant woman, the fetus and the newborn infant, by A. Garcia Perez, et al. MEDICINA CLINICA 93(14):538-542, November 4, 1989

Cocaine and the risk of low birth weight: Alameda County, California, by D. B. Petitti, et al. AMERICAN JOURNAL OF PUBLIC HEALTH 80(1):25-28, January 1990

Cocaine babies in Oklahoma, by G. P. Giacoia. JOURNAL OF THE OKLAHOMA STATE MEDICAL ASSOCIATON 83(2):64-67, February 1990

Cocaine's defenseless victims. AMERICAN JOURNAL OF NURSING 90:32, February 1990

Congenital renal abnormalities in infants with in utero cocaine exposure, by B. J. Rosenstein, et al. JOURNAL OF UROLOGY 144(1):110-112, 1990

Crack and kids, by D. J. Besharov. SOCIETY 27(5):25-26, July/August 1990

Crack babies and the Constitution: threatening chemically dependent, pregnant women with legal prosecution, by J. C. Rosen. PLAYBOY 37:50+, May 1990

Damage to the newborns. NEW DIRECTIONS FOR WOMEN 19(2):8, March 1990

Decreased cardiac output in infants of mothers who abused cocaine, by M. van de Bor, et al. PEDIATRICS 85(1):30-32, January 1990

Descriptive study of infants and toddlers exposed prenatally to substance abuse, by T. Free, et al. MCN 15(4):245-249, July/August 1990

Desperate crack legacy: fetal alcohol syndrome and crack babies, by M. Dorris. NEWSWEEK 114(26):8, June 25, 1990

Development of infants of drug dependent mothers, by A. Van Baar. JOURNAL OF CHILD PSYCHOLOGY AND PSYCHIATRY AND ALLIED DISCIPLINES 31(6):911-920, 1990

Developmental decline in infants born to HIV-infected intravenous drug-using mothers, by R. Kletter, et al. NIDA RESEARCH MONOGRAPH 95:409-410, 1989

Diaplacental poisoning with narcotics and alcohol in newborn infants, by A. Kloppel, et al. BEITRAGE ZUR GERICHTLICHEN MEDIZIN 47:77-79, 1989

Drug babies, by J. V. Greer. EXCEPTIONAL CHILDREN 56(5):382-384, February 1990

Drug-exposed neonates, by G. Hoegerman, et al. WESTERN JOURNAL OF MEDICINE 152(5):559-564, May 1990

Echoencephalographic findings in neonates associated with maternal cocaine and methamphetamine use: incidence and clinical correlates, by S. D. Dixon, et al. JOURNAL OF PEDIATRICS 115(5 Pt 1):770-778, November 1989

Effect of marijuana use during pregnancy on newborn cry, by B. M. Lester, et al. CHILD DEVELOPMENT 60:765-771, August 1989

Effect of maternal cocaine use on the fetus and newborn: review of the literature, by E. H. Roland, et al. PEDIATRIC NEUROSCIENCE 15(2):88-94, 1989

Effects of maternal cocaine abuse on perinatal and infant outcome, by L. Cordero, et al. OHIO MEDICINE 86(5):410-412, May 1990

Gallbladder sludge and lithiasis in an infant born to a morphine user mother, by R. Figuerosa-Colon, et al. JOURNAL OF PEDIATRIC GASTROENTEROLOGY AND NUTRITION 10(2):234-238, February 1990

Healing lessons from cocaine babies, by J. Adolph. NEW AGE 7(6):9, December 1990

Heart defects now seen in cocaine babies: most critical period is first 28 weeks of pregnancy, by J. McCann. JOURNAL OF THE ADDICTION RESEARCH FOUN-DATION 19(3):5, March 1, 1990

Hemolytic disease of the newborn as an unusual consequence of drug abuse: a case report, by I. Williamson, et al. JOURNAL OF REPRODUCTIVE MEDICINE 35(1): 46-48, January 1990

Hyponatremia in a neonate of a cocaine abusing mother, by S. Dollberg, et al. JOUR-NAL OF TOXICOLOGY: CLINICAL TOXICOLOGY 27(4-5):287-292, 1989

I gave birth to an addicted baby, by M. A. Grand. GOOD HOUSEKEEPING 210:130-131+, April 1990

Increased cerebral blood flow velocity in infants of mothers who abuse cocaine, by M. van de Bor, et al. PEDIATRICS 85(5):733-736, May 1990

Infants exposed to cocaine in utero: implications for developmental assessment and intervention, by J. W. Schneider, et al. AND YOUNG CHILDREN 2(1):25-36, July 1989

Infrequent neonatal opiate withdrawal following maternal methadone detoxification during pregnancy, by U. Maas, et al. JOURNAL OF PERINATAL MEDICINE 18(2): 111-118, 1990

Kallikdrein-kinin system in newborns of the drug addicted, by E. Salvaggio, et al. AD-VANCES IN EXPERIMENTAL MEDICINE AND BIOLOGY 247:471-476, 1989

Lower serum osteocalcin levels in pregnant drug users and their newborns at the time of delivery, by H. Rico, et al. OBSTETRICS AND GYNECOLOGY 75(6):998-1000, June 1990

Management of maternal and neonatal substance abuse problems, by L. Finnegan. NIDA RESEARCH MONOGRAPH SERIES 90:177-182, 1988

INFANTS

Maternal alcohol and pentazocine abuse: neonatal behavior and morphology in an opposite-sex twin pair, by M. L. Riese. ACTA GENETICAE MEDICAE E GEMEL-LOLOGIAE 38(1-2):49-56, 1989

Maternal cocaine abuse and effects on the mother, fetus and newborn, by D. Rosenak, et al. HAREFAUH 116(21):600-603, June 1, 1989

Maternal cocaine use during pregnancy: effect on the newborn infant, by M. Abdel-jaber, et al. PEDIATRICS 85(4):630, April 1990

Maternal marijuana use during lactation and infant development at one year, by S. J. Astley, et al. NEUROTOXICOLOGY AND TERATOLOGY 12(2):161-168, March/April 1990

Mending small cracked lives: fostering programmes for "crack" and HIV-positive babies in New York, by M. Pye. INDEPENDENT ON SUNDAY September 30, 1990, p. 25

Motor development of infants subject to maternal drug use: current evidence and future research strategies, by B. J. Cratty. ADAPTED PHYSICAL ACTIVITY QUARTERLY 7(2):110-125, April 1990

Neonatal cocaine-related seizures, by L. D. Kramer, et al. JOURNAL OF CHILD NEUROLOGY 5(1):60-64, January 1990

Neonatal heroin withdrawal syndrome: evaluation of different pharmacological treatment, by P. Pacifico, et al. PHARMACOLOGICAL RESEARCH 21(Suppl)1:63-64, November/December 1989

Neonatal intestinal perforation: the "crack" connection, by B. M. Miller, et al. AMERICAN JOURNAL OF GASTROENTEROLOGY 85(6):767-769, June 1990

Newborn infant of the drug addicted mother: clinical and therapeutic problems, by J. Gonzalez-Hachero, et al. ANALES ESPANOLES DE PEDIATRIA 31(3):205-209, September 1989. Erratum. 31(6):608, December 1989

Pediatrics: innocent addicts. NURSING 90 20:92, November 1990

Pregnant, addicted—and guilty: prosecution of K. Hardy and L. Bremer in Muskegon County, Michigan, by J. Hoffman. NEW YORK TIMES MAGAZINE August 19, 1990, pp. 32-35+

Prenatal cocaine exposure and fetal vascular disruption, by H. E. Hoyme, et al. PEDIATRICS 85(5):743-747, 1990

Problem of the drug-exposed newborn: a return to principled intervention, by B. I. Robbin-Vergeer. STANDARD LAW REVIEW 42(3):745-809, February 1990

Protecting fetuses from prenatal hazards: whose crimes, what punishment?, by K. Nolan. CRIMINAL JUSTICE ETHICS 9(1):13-23, 1990

Risk of febrile seizures in childhood in relation to prenatal maternal cigarette smoking and alcohol intake, by P. A. Cassano, et al. AMERICAN JOURNAL OF EPIDEMIOLOGY 132(3):462-473, September 1990

Shadow children, by M. C. Rist. AMERICAN SCHOOL BOARD JOURNAL 177(1):18-24, January 1990

Should cocaine moms be prosecuted for addicting their babies?, by M. McCalope. JET 78:54-55, July 16, 1990

Social worker's agony: working with children affected by crack-cocaine, by D. Priddy. SOCIAL WORK 35(3):197-199, May 1990

Special issue on prenatal substance abuse. CHILDREN TODAY 19:1-36 July/August 1990

Trends in reporting of maternal drug abuse in infant mortality drug-exposed infants in New York City, by L. Habel, et al. WOMEN AND HEALTH 16(2):41-58, 1990

Utero exposure to cocaine and the risk of SIDS, by B. Lounsbury, et al. NIDA RESEARCH MONOGRAPH SERIES 95:352, 1989

We are so lucky to have him: adoption of drug-exposed baby, by C. Breslin. LADIES HOME JOURNAL 107:136+, December 1990

INTERACTIONS

Acetaminophen hepatotoxicity in the alcoholic, by F. T. Wootton, et al. SOCIAL SCIENCE AND MEDICINE 83(9):1047-1049, September 1990

Behavioral aspects of alcohol-tobacco interactions, by I. F. Zacny. RECENT DEVELOPMENTS IN ALCOHOLISM 8:205-209, 1990

Caffeine and cigarette smoking: behavioral, cardiovascular, and metabolic interactions, by C. R. Brown, et al. PHARMACOLOGY, BIOCHEMISTRY AND BEHAVIOR 34(3):565-570, November 1989

Case in which carbamazepine attenuated cocaine "rush," by M. A. Sherer, et al. AMERICAN JOURNAL OF PSYCHIATRY 147(7):950, July 1990

Effects of cannabis smoked together with a substance sold as Mandrax, by D. Wilson, et al. SOUTH AFRICAN MEDICAL JOURNAL 76(11):636, December 2, 1989

Effects of the combination of cocaine and marijuana on the task-elicited physiological response, by R. W. Foltin, et al. NIDA RESEARCH MONOGRAPH SERIES 95:359-360, 1989

Effects of combinations of intranasal cocaine, smoked marijuana, and task performance on heart rate and blood pressure, by R. W. Foltin, et al. PHARMACOLOGY, BIOCHEMISTRY AND BEHAVIOR 36(2):311-315, June 1990

Effects of paroxetine and other antidepressants in combination with alcohol on psychomotor activity related to care driving, by I. Hindmarch, et al. ACTA PSYCHIATRICA SCANDINAVICA 350(Suppl):45, 1989

Effects of terfenadine with and without alcohol on an aspect of car driving performance, by J. Z. Bhatti, et al. CLINICAL AND EXPERIMENTAL ALLERGY 19(6):609-611, November 1989

INTERACTIONS

Fatal interaction of methocarbamol and ethanol in an accidental poisoning, by K. E. Ferslew, et al. JOURNAL OF FORENSIC SCIENCES 35(2):477-482, March 1990

Interactions between alcohol and benzodiazepines, by L. E. Hollister. RECENT DEVELOPMENTS IN ALCOHOLISM 8:233-239, 1990

Interactions between alcohol and drugs, by J. Marland. TIDSSKRIFT FOR DEN NORSKE LAEGEFORENING 110(9):1106-1109, March 30, 1990

Management of paracetamol poisoning complicated by enzyme induction due to alcohol or drugs, by B. M. McClements, et al. LANCET 335(8704):1526, June 23, 1990

Nifedipine overdose accompanied by ethanol intoxication in a patient with congenital heart disease, by R. D. Welch, et al. JOURNAL OF EMERGENCY MEDICINE 8(2):169-172, March/April 1990

Pharmacokinetic and pharmacodynamic drug interactions: implications for abuse liability testing, by E. M. Sellers, et al. NIDA RESEARCH MONOGRAPH SERIES (92):287-306, 1989

Vascular lesions in intestinal ischemia induced by cocaine-alcohol abuse: report of a fatal case due to overdose, by A. Garfia, et al. JOURNAL OF FORENSIC SCIENCES 35(3):740-745, May 1990

INTERNATIONAL ASSOCIATION OF CHIEFS OF POLICE see: IACP

KETAMINE
Ketamine: can chronic use impair memory?, by K. L. Jansen. INTERNATIONAL JOURNAL OF THE ADDICTIONS 25(2):133-140, 1990

KHAT
Khat: a dangerous drug, by P. Kalix. HAREFUAH 118(9):555-556, May 1, 1990

Khat: a plant with amphetamine effects, by C. Pantelis, et al. JOURNAL OF SUBSTANCE ABUSE TREATMENT 6(3):205-206, 1989

Use and abuse of khat (catha edulis): a review of the distribution, pharmacology, side effects and a description of psychosis attributed to khat chewing, by C. Pantelis, et al. PSYCHOLOGICAL MEDICINE 19(3):657-668, August 1989

LAWS
ABA toughens marijuana stand, by S. B. Goldberg. ABA JOURNAL 76:105, April 1990

Administration's drug war can reduce demand: views of H. Kleber, by E. Kaye. VOGUE 180:354+, March 1990

Adoptive forfeitures and the 1988 Anti-Drug Abuse Act. POLICE CHIEF 56:65, May 1989

Advocating drug decriminalization: a tough stand, by S. Muwakkil. IN THESE TIMES 14(10):6, January 24, 1990

Against the legalization of drugs, by J. Q. Wilson. COMMENTARY 89:21-28, February 1990

Alternative to "war on drugs," by P. Kurtz. ST. LOUIS JOURNALISM REVIEW 20 (129):2, September 1990

Anti-crime war heats up in congress as republicans push "National Emergency Act." CRIME CONTROL DIGEST 24(3):1-5, January 22, 1990; also in NARCOTICS CONTROL DIGEST 20(3):6-8, January 31, 1990

Anti-drug appropriations bills struggling in congress, by R. O'Connell. CRIME CONTROL DIGEST 23(44):1-5, November 6, 1989; also in NARCOTICS CONTROL DIGEST 19(23):1+, November 8, 1989

Ban all drug paraphernalia. NARCOTICS CONTROL DIGEST 19(18):5, August 30, 1989

Bennett's new optimism: the evidence is mixed—United States drug czar upbeat about war on drugs, by M. Miller. NEWSWEEK 115(11):32, March 12, 1990

Bill Bennett can't lose the drug war, by J. Weisberg. ESQUIRE 114:138-140+, September 1990

Bill of rights: war on drugs—address, September 14, 1990, by E. E. Sterling. VITAL SPEECHES OF THE DAY 57:40-46, November 1, 1990

Body count: Operation Democracy launched by the military. NATION 251:5, July 2, 1990

Bush administration proposes wider anti-drug powers. NARCOTICS CONTROL DIGEST 20(11):9, May 23, 1990

By keeping the chemicals flowing: American industry kept the cocaine cartels in business, by L. Feldman. ROLLING STONE November 1, 1990, p. 44

Case and comment: drugs, by T. Rees, et al. CRIMINAL LAW REVIEW April 1990, pp. 261-263, April 1990

Charges dropped against Hunter Thompson, by M. Sager. ROLLING STONE July 12-26, 1990, pp. 12+

Chemical industry, drug agency sort out chemical diversion issues: exports of chemicals for manufacture of narcotics, by D. J. Hanson. CHEMICAL ENGINEERING NEWS 68:18-19, January 29, 1990

Child neglect statute applies to mothers who abused drugs during pregnancy. FAMILY LAW REPORTER: COURT OPINIONS 16(32):1377-1379, June 19, 1990

Constitutional law conference address Supreme Court's 1978-1989 term. CRIMINAL LAW REPORTER: COURT DECISIONS 46(2):1039-1043, October 11, 1989

Crime bill near death, but a compromise could save it. CRIME CONTROL DIGEST 24(24):1+, June 18, 1990

LAWS

Czar is hooked: substituting the war on drugs for the cold war, by M. Ivins. PRO-GRESSIVE 54:38, February 1990

D.C.'s war on drugs: why Bennett is losing, by M. Massing. NEW YORK TIMES MAGAZINE September 23, 1990, pp. 36-37+

Dirty business: money laundering and the war on drugs: address, February 19, 1990, by H. K. Sinclair. VITAL SPEECHES OF THE DAY 56:395-398, April 15, 1990

Don't legalize drugs, by M. M. Kondracke. DRUGS AND SOCIETY 3(3-4):209-215, March/April 1989

Draft Narcotics Crime Control Act and organized crime, by K. Handel. DIE NEUE POLIZEI 44(8):403-406, 1990

Drug czar attacks calls for legalization of drugs. CRIMINAL LAW REPORTER: COURT DECISIONS 46(12):1262-1263, December 20, 1989

Drug-Free Workplace Act and related federal antidrug rules, by D. S. Tatel. PUBLIC MANAGEMENT 71:20-22, July 1989

Drug laws are immoral, by J. C. Marquis. US CATHOLIC 55:14-19, May 1990

Drug legalization: now or never? WORLD AND I 5:108-119, May 1990

Drug use during pregnancy: new Minnesota law requires doctors to test and report, by D. M. Fortney. MINNESOTA MEDICINE 73(4):41-43, April 1990

Drug war. HUMANIST 50:5-30+, September/October 1990

Drug war's over: guess who won—America has lost the war against drugs, by M. Royco. PLAYBOY 37:46, January 1990

Drug wars: why legalization won't work, by T. A. Constantine. POLICE CHIEF 57(5): 37-39, May 1990

Drugs: amount needed to constitute a crime. CRIMINAL LAW REPORTER: COURT DECISIONS 47(11):1220, June 13, 1990

Drugs and the law, by G. Kellens. JOURNAL DE PHARMACIE DE BELGIQUE 44(5): 362-365, September/October 1989

Drugs: classification of marijuana as schedule I controlled substance: freedom of religion. CRIMINAL LAW REPORTER: COURT DECISIONS 46(15):1324-1325, January 17, 1990

Drugs: device adopted for production containers. CRIMINAL LAW REPORTER 46(24):1519-1520, March 21, 1990

Drugs: is legislation the last resort?, by S. Tandler. POLICE REVIEW 97(5029):1866-1867, 1989

Economics of legalizing drugs, by R. J. Dennis. ATLANTIC 266(5):126-130+, November 1990

LAWS

Education Department sets deadline for colleges to comply with drug law, by T. J. DeLoughry. CHRONICLE OF HIGHER EDUCATION 36:18, May 30, 1990

Expert debunks drive to legalize drugs: Dr. Arnold M. Washton, founding director of the Washton Institute on Addictions in Manhattan. HUMAN EVENTS 50:6, June 13, 1990

Experts who want the legalisation of drugs, by L. Hunt. INDEPENDENT April 5, 1990, p. 29

Extraterritorial applicability of the fourth amendment. HARVARD LAW REVIEW 102(7):1672-1694, 1989

Fear and loathing and the forfeiture laws, by M. Schecter. CORNELL LAW REVIEW 75(5):1151-1183, 1990

Fighting the drug "war." COMMONWEAL 117:173, March 23, 1990

"Get tough" Maryland plan actually heavily focused on prevention, treatment. NARCOTICS DEMAND REDUCTION DIGEST 1(7):3-4, December 1989

Golden lie, by D. Reynolds. HUMANIST 50:10-14+, September/October 1990

Hemp: outlawing a miracle product. UTNE READER (40):122, July 1990

House Bill would require mandatory death penalty for police killers in drug cases. CRIME CONTROL DIGEST 23(40):1+, October 9, 1989; also in NARCOTICS CONTROL DIGEST 19(21):6, October 11, 1989

House passes drug bills. CRIME CONTROL DIGEST 23(46):1+, November 20, 1989

House steroids bill gains support. NARCOTICS CONTROL DIGEST 19(21):12, October 11, 1989

How to legalize drugs: E. Nadelmann, by E. Yoffe. MOTHER JONES 15(2):18, February 1990

How to win the war on drugs, by L. Kraar. FORTUNE 121:70-71+, March 12, 1990

Ideology, agency and the limits of power: the social construction of marihuana decriminalization, by A. DiChiara. DAI A 50(11):3746, May 1990

Implication for research of the 1988 Anti-Drug Abuse Act, by C. R. Schuster. NIDA RESEARCH MONOGRAPH SERIES 95:16-22, 1989

Industry rebuts chemical diversion charges, by D. Hanson. CHEMICAL ENGINEERING NEWS 68:5-6, February 12, 1990

Intoxicated mistakes, by K. L. Campbell. CRIMINAL LAW QUARTERLY 32(1):110-134, December 1989

Latest reform of Spanish criminal law on drugs, by A. R. Reeg. ZEITSCHRIFT FUR DIE GESAMTE STRAFRECHTSWISSENSCHAFT 39(3):756-770, 1989

Legal drugs: a view from neuroscience. SCIENCE 247:919, February 23, 1990

LAWS

Legalising drugs: a soft option or necessary evil?, by B. Appleyard. SUNDAY TIMES MAGAZINE 3:5, July 29, 1990

Legalization of drugs, by N. Taub. DELAWARE MEDICAL JOURNAL 61(11):637-638, November 1989

Legalization of drugs socially irresponsible, by W. E. Arnado. LAW AND ORDER 38(4):71, April 1990

Legislation proposed to protect physician "whistle blowers," by C. A. Marvinney. COLORADO MEDICINE 87(5):144-145, May 1990

Lure of masterstrokes: drug legalization, by M. Farrell, et al. BRITISH JOURNAL OF ADDICTION 85(1):5-7, January 1990

MADD endorses mandatory random drug testing bill. CORPORATE SECURITY DIGEST 4(9):8-9, March 5, 1990

Measuring the impact of P.L. 99-252: an economist's view, by R. J. Caswell. JOURNAL OF PUBLIC HEALTH DENTISTRY 50(1):77-83, Winter 1990

Money laundering: address, May 11, 1990, by D. Thornburgh. VITAL SPEECHES OF THE DAY 56:578-580, July 15, 1990

New York legalization bill pushed. LAW ENFORCEMENT NEWS 16(306):6, January 15, 1990

Off the pot, by C. P. Wohlforth. NEW REPUBLIC 203:9, December 3,1990

Plan for Michigan to legalize marijuana, by Z. Ferency. IN THESE TIMES 14(20):17, April 11, 1990

Recent developments in the law: primary and secondary education: miscellaneous. JOURNAL OF LAW AND EDUCATION 19(1):120-121, Winter 1990

Remembering last year's war, by M. Barone, et al. US NEW AND WORLD REPORT 109:32, September 17, 1990

Representative Gilman supports far-reaching drug legislation. CRIME CONTROL DIGEST 24(29):8, July 23, 1990

Representative Wise pushing new anti-drug legislation. CRIME CONTROL DIGEST 24(20):8-9, May 21, 1990; also in NARCOTICS CONTROL DIGEST 20(11):7, May 23, 1990

Republicans introduce new anti-drug, crime legislation. NARCOTICS CONTROL DIGEST 20(13):8-10, June 20, 1990; also in CRIME CONTROL DIGEST 24(25):1-3, June 25, 1990

Saint Valentine's Day: the massacre continues: the 1920's alcohol prohibition and today's drug prohibition both made substance abuse worse, by W. J. Helmer. PLAYBOY 37:46, March 1990

Security briefs. SECURITY LETTER. PART I 19(13):4, July 1, 1989

LAWS

Sentencing: federal guidelines—drug calculations. CRIMINAL LAW REPORTER: COURT DECISIONS 46(17):1367, January 31, 1990

Sentencing: federal guidelines—drugs; "blotter acid." CRIMINAL LAW REPORTER: COURT DECISIONS 46(18):1388, February 7, 1990; also in CRIMINAL LAW RE-PORTER: COURT DECISIONS 46(19):1414, February 14, 1990

Sentencing: federal guidelines—inclusion of "carrier medium" in determining weight of LSD. CRIMINAL LAW REPORTER: COURT DECISIONS 45(23):2433-2434, September 13, 1989

Sentencing: federal guidelines—inconsistency between drug quantity table and penalty statute. CRIMINAL LAW REPORTER: COURT DECISIONS 47(15):1302-1303, July 18, 1990

State legislation: effects on drug programs in industry, by R. T. Angarola, et al. NIDA RESEARCH MONOGRAPH SERIES 91:305-317, 1989

Steroids and the Controlled Substances Act, by L. Uzych. BIOLOGICAL PSYCHIA-TRY 27(6):561-562, March 15, 1990

Taking drugs seriously, by J. Kaplan. DRUGS AND SOCIETY 3(3-4):187-208, March/April 1989

Taxonomy as politics, by S. Gould. DISSENT 37(1):73, Winter 1990

To legalize or not to legalize, by D. J. Cashman. SECURITY MANAGEMENT 34(2):63-64, February 1990

User accountability: a long-overdue concept, by J. C. Lawn. POLICE CHIEF 56(8):49-50, August 1989

War on some drugs, by S. J. Gould. HARPERS 280:24-26, April 1990

Was legalization a bad idea: Alaska—one state's war on drugs, by R. Roth. HUMAN RIGHTS 17:29, Summer 1990

We don't need to give up our constitutional protections to fight the war on drugs, by S. Dash, et al. CRIMINAL JUSTICE 5(1):2-5+, Spring 1990

Yesterday's drug war, prohibition, by D. Lazare. UTNE READER (39):117, May 1990

LAWYERS

Attorneys do try to smuggle drugs into jails and officers do have right to search them. CORRECTIONS DIGEST 21(1):2+, January 10, 1990

Drawing the line: when is an ex-coke addict fit to practice law?, by S. B. Goldberg. ABA JOURNAL 76:48-52, February 1990

Evidence doesn't support lawyer's conviction for aiding client in drug trafficking. CRIMINAL LAW REPORTER: COURT DECISIONS 46(4):1066-1068, October 25, 1989

Fighting the drug war: lawyers should enlist in this synergism of efforts, by L. S. Chauvin, Jr. ABA JOURNAL 75:8, October 1989

LAWYERS

Illegal insurance: Florida lawyer convicted for conspiring to import marijuana, by C. E. Anderson. ABA JOURNAL 75:34, November 1989

Prevalence of depression, alcohol abuse, and cocaine abuse among United States lawyers, by G. A. H. Benjamin, et al. INTERNATIONAL JOURNAL OF LAW AND PSYCHIATRY 13(3):233-246, 1990

Staying clean: substance abuse is becoming a major problem in the legal profession—here, one lawyer tells of his cocaine addiction, by L. Aisenberg. CANADIAN LAWYER 142(2):14-17, March 1990

LAXATIVES
Abuse of laxatives as the cause of obscure prolonged diarrhea, by L. Blomquist, et al. LAKARTIDNINGEN 86(41):3467-3470, October 11, 1989

Correlates of laxative abuse in bulimia, by D. A. Waller, et al. HOSPITAL AND COMMUNITY PSYCHIATRY 41(7):797-799, July 1990

Laxative abuse as a cause of ammonium urate renal calculi, by W. H. Dick, et al. JOURNAL OF UROLOGY 143(2):244-247, February 1990

Laxative abuse in eating disorders, by S. G. Willard, et al. PSYCHIATRY IN MEDICINE 7(3):75-87, 1989

Prevalence of surreptitous laxative abuse in patients with diarrhoea of uncertain origin: a cost-benefit analysis of a screening procedure, by P. Bytzer, et al. GUT 30(10):1379-1384, October 1989

LEGAL ISSUES
Belated justice: another conviction in the murder of a DEA agent. TIME 136(7):39, August 13, 1990

Belated justice: Los Angeles jury convicts: R. Zuno Arce for abetting murder of DEA agent E. Camarean. TIME 136:36, August 13, 1990

Container crime. INTERNATIONAL CRIMINAL POLICE REVIEW 44(416):18-23, 1989

Courts and the "war on drugs." JUDICATURE 73(5):236+, February/March 1990

Crack babies and the Constitution: threatening chemically dependent, pregnant women with legal prosecution, by J. C. Rosen. PLAYBOY 37:50+, May 1990

Drug cases clog the courts: civil suits suffer, prisons overcrowded in 43 states, by D. C. Moss. ABA JOURNAL 76:34+, April 1990

Drug panel named to study impact on courts. JUVENILE JUSTICE DIGEST 17(19):8, October 4, 1989

Effective use of search warrants in the war on crack: Denver, Coloraro, by P. Mahoney. POLICE CHIEF 57:50-52, May 1990

LEGAL ISSUES

Evidence: impeachment with prior convictions—crime of "moral torpitude"; cocaine possession. CRIMINAL LAW REPORTER: COURT DECISIONS 47(2):1035, April 11, 1990

Evidence: impeachment—witness's history of drug use. CRIMINAL LAW RE-PORTER: COURT DECISIONS 45(25):2473-2474, September 27, 1989

Evidence: parental fitness—psychotherapist-patient privilege; drug counselor. FAMILY LAW REPORTER: COURT OPINIONS 16(27):1322, May 15, 1990

Evidence: presence in house and possible acid burns in jeans not enough—Oregon. NARCOTICS LAW BULLETIN September, 1989. p. 2

Expectation of privacy: evidence of marijuana held admissible—Georgia. SEARCH AND SEIZURE BULLETIN April 1989, p. 4

"Fetal abuse": should we recognize it as a crime—no, by L. Paltrow. ABA JOURNAL 75:39, August 1989

"Fetal abuse": should we recognize it as a crime—yes. by J. Robertson. ABA JOUR-NAL 75:38, August 1989

Fetal alcohol syndrome: liability for failure to warn—should liquor manufacturers pick up the tab?, by R. Goble. JOURNAL OF FAMILY LAW 28(1):71-85, 1989-1990

Filling the gaps: police get an unexpected ally—the courts, by R. Burnham. BC RE-PORT 2(1):27, September 3, 1990

Forfeiture of attorney's fees, by K. A. Kingston. FBI LAW ENFORCEMENT BULLE-TIN 59:27-32, April 1990

Forfeiture of attorneys fees: the right remaining to the accused and his attorney after *Caplin and Drysdale and United States v. Monsanto*, by A. Y. Castillo. AMERICAN JOURNAL OF CRIMINAL LAW 17(2):123-142, 1990

From the Supreme Court: court to review need for warnings before seeking voice ex-emplar. LAW OFFICER'S BULLETIN 14(7):41, October 26, 1989

Impact of drug cases on case processing in urban trial courts, by J. A. Goerdt, et al. STATE COURT JOURNAL 13(4):4-12, Fall 1989

In Michigan, drugs thrown away in chase may be used as evidence. CRIME CON-TROL DIGEST 24(23):8-9, August 20, 1990

Jail terms, harsher fines for inhalant sales to kids, by M. Brosnahan. JOURNAL OF THE ADDICTION RESEARCH FOUNDATION 19(3):3, March 1, 1990

Judicial response to the drug crisis, by R. D. Lipscher. STATE COURT JOURNAL 13(4):13-17, Fall 1989

Just say no: Thornburgh promises to get tough on crime, by G. A. Hengsler. ABA JOURNAL 75:126, April 1989

Legal alternatives for fetal injury, by A. M. Rhodes. MCN 15(2):111, March/April 1990

LEGAL ISSUES

Maryland court of appeals throws out drug convictions. CRIME CONTROL DIGEST 23(42):9, October 23, 1989

Mayor Jackson wants son arrested for marijuana treated same as others. JET 77:24, January 29, 1990

Negligence: marijuana and alcohol—sufficiency of evidence; Oregon. NARCOTICS LAW BULLETIN June 1990, p. 7

Panel recommends shifting drug cases to state courts, by E. Wiener. CRIMINAL JUSTICE NEWSLETTER 21(8):1-3, April 16, 1990

Privacy and teens: student T. McClary sues after drug search in Miami high school, by L. Tarshis. SCHOLASTIC UPDATE 123:9-10, September 21, 1990

Repeat player police officers and prosecutorial charge reduction decisions: a note, by J. J. Sloan, et al. AMERICAN JOURNAL OF POLICE 9(1):163-168, 1990

Revitalizing the drug decriminalization debate, by K. A. Farr. CRIME AND DELIN-QUENCY 36:223-237, April 1990

Should we fight or switch?, by S. France. ABA JOURNAL 76:42-46, February 1990

State judiciary news: New York, by S. Wachtler. STATE COURT JOURNAL 14(2):27-35, Spring 1990

Supreme Court recommends adjustments for drugs. JUVENILE JUSTICE DIGEST 18(22):8, January 24, 1990

Survival model of pretrial failure, by C. A. Visher, et al. JOURNAL OF QUANTITATIVE CRIMINOLOGY 6(2):153-184, June 1990

Text of United States Supreme Court decision: Employment Division, Department of Human Resources of Oregon, et al. v. Alfred L. Smith, et al. JOURNAL OF CHURCH AND STATE 32:691-718, Summer 1990

To jail or not to jail, by B. Flicker. ABA JOURNAL 76:64-67, February 1990

Variation found in how courts handle alcohol and drug cases. CRIMINAL JUSTICE NEWSLETTER 21(6):5, March 15, 1990

You be the judge: Dane County v. Sharpee. LAW OFFICER'S BULLETIN 14(18):106, March 29, 1990

You be the judge: State v. Rode. LAW OFFICER'S BULLETIN 14(24):142, June 21, 1990

LESBIANS

Epidemiology of reported cases of AIDS in lesbians: United States, 1980-1989, by S. Y. Chu, et al. AMERICAN JOURNAL OF PUBLIC HEALTH 80:1380-1381, November 1990

Substance use as a correlate of violence in intimate lesbian relationships, by R. Schilit, et al. JOURNAL OF HOMOSEXUALITY 19(3):51-65, 1990

LICORICE

Case from practice, 171: pseudohyperaldosteronism in licorice abuse, by C. Ghiel-mini, et al. SCHWEIZERISCHE RUNDSCHAU FUR MEDIZIN PRAXIS 79(15):472-743, April 10, 1990

LITERATURE

Dr. Sone: condensed from the book, by C. Saline. READER'S DIGEST (CANADA) 136(813):149-168+, January 1990

Getting straight: K. Wozencarft's novel, by C. S. Smith. NEW YORK 23:48-50+, March 26, 1990

Help in fighting the war against drugs. CHILDREN TODAY 19:2-3, March/April 1990

Narcotic dependence in the light of the publications of the International Agency for Narcotic Control 1987, by J. Kubalski, et al. POLSKI TYGODNIK LEKARSKI 43(51-52):1691-1695, December 19-26, 1988

Out from undercover, an ex-cop, ex-con writes a million-dollar novel about drugs and corruption: K. Wozencraft, by K. McMurran. PEOPLE WEEKLY 33:75-76+, April 23, 1990

Selective guide to current reference sources on topics discussed in this issue, by L. K. Morgan, et al. ADVANCES IN ALCOHOL AND SUBSTANCE ABUSE 8(1):125-133, Spring 1989

Substance problems: what books do the experts recommend?, by R. J. Hodgson, et al. INTERNATIONAL REVIEW OF PSYCHIATRY 1(1-2):181-190, March 1989

Truth too often lost in drug debate: bogeyman images cheapen legitimate concerns—(excerpt from *Peaceful measures: Canada's Way Out of the War on Drugs*). JOURNAL OF THE ADDICTION RESEARCH FOUNDATION 19(11):12, November 1, 1990

Book Reviews

Addiction Research Foundation: a voyage of discovery (book review), by H. D. Archibald. JOURNAL OF THE ADDICTION RESEARCH FOUNDATION 19(10):10, October 1, 1990

Billion $$$ high: the drug invasion of Canada (book review), by P. Appleton, et al. QUILL AND QUIRE 56(10):21+, October 1990

Illicit drugs in Canada: a risky business (book review), by J. C. Blackwell, et al. CANADIAN JOURNAL OF CRIMINOLOGY 32(3):556-558, July 1990

Kids, drugs and booze: survival strategies for parents (book review), by S. Moynihan, et al. QUILL AND QUIRE 55(12):27, December 1989; also in PRESBYTERIAN RECORD 14(4):32-33, April 1990

Merchants of misery: inside Canada's illegal drug scene (book review), by V. Malarek. PRESBYTERIAN RECORD 114(4):33-34, April 1990

Peaceful measures: Canada's way out of the "war on drugs" (book review), by B. K. Alexander. QUILL AND QUIRE 56(7):58, July 1990

Speed trap: inside the biggest scandal in Olympic history (book review), by C. Francis, et al. QUILL AND QUIRE 56(11):23, November 1990

Statistics on alcohol and drug use in Canada and other countries (book review), by M. Adrian, et al. JOURNAL OF THE ADDICTION RESEARCH FOUNDATION 19(3):8, March 1, 1990

When society becomes an addict (book review), by A. Wilson Schaef. CITY MAGA-ZINE 11(2-3):58, Winter/Spring 1990

LITHIUM
Lithium in drinking water and the incidences of crimes, suicides, and arrests related to drug addictions, by G. N .Schrauzer, et al. BIOLOGICAL TRACE ELEMENT RE-SEARCH 25(2):105-114, 1990

LSD   (LYSERGIC ACID DIETHYLAMIDE)
Class A drug users: prevalence and characteristics in greater Nottingham, by J. Giggs, et al. BRITISH JOURNAL OF ADDICTION 84(12):1473-1480, December 1989

LSD, by K. Kulig. EMERGENCY MEDICINE CLINICS OF NORTH AMERICA 8(3):551-558, August 1990

LSD and psychotherapy, by K. Bliss. CONTEMPORARY DRUG PROBLEMS 15:519-563, Winter 1988

Complications
Syndrome identical to the neuroleptic malignant syndrome induced by LSD and alco-hol, by A. M. Bakheit, et al. BRITISH JOURNAL OF ADDICTION 85(1):150-151, January 1990

MARIHUANA/MARIJUANA   *see*: Cannabis

MDA   (METHYLENEDIOXYAMPHETAMINE)
Abuse of smoking methamphetamine mixed with tobacco: II—the formation mecha-nism of pyrolysis products, by H. Sekine, et al. JOURNAL OF FORENSIC SCIENCES 35(3):580-590, May 1990

Characteristics of some 3,4-methylenedioxypheny lisopropylamine (MDA) analogs, by T. A. Dal Cason. JOURNAL OF FORENSIC SCIENCES 34(4):928-961, 1989

Characterization of brain interactions with methylenedioxyamphetamine and methyl-enedioxymethamphetamine, by R. Zaczek, et al. NIDA RESEARCH MONO-GRAPH SERIES 94:223-239, 1989

MDMA   (METHYLENEDIOXYMETHAMPHETAMINE)
Characterization of brain interactions with methylenedioxyamphetamine and methyl-enedioxymethamphetamine, by R. Zaczek, et al. NIDA RESEARCH MONO-GRAPH SERIES 94:223-239, 1989

Ecstasy making inroads in Florida: authorities say. NARCOTICS CONTROL DIGEST 20(13):7-8, June 20, 1990

Neurochemistry and neurotoxicity of 3,4-methylenedioxymethamphetamine (MDMA), "ecstasy," by D. J. McKenna, et al. JOURNAL OF NEUROCHEMISTRY 54(1):14-22, January 1990

Psychostimulant properties of MDMA, by L. H. Gold, et al. NIDA RESEARCH MONOGRAPH SERIES 95:345-346, 1989

Responses to i.v. L-tryptophan in MDMA users, by L. H. Price, et al. NIDA RESEARCH MONOGRAPH SERIES 95:421-422, 1989

Second thoughts on 3,4-methylenedioxymethamphetamine (MDMA) neurotoxicity, by C. Grob, et al. ARCHIVES OF GENERAL PSYCHIATRY 47(3):288-289, March 1990

Research

Acute and long-term neurochemical effects of methylenedioxymethamphetamine in the rat, by C. J. Schmidt. NIDA RESEARCH MONOGRAPH SERIES 94:179-195, 1989

Acute and subchronic effects of methylenedioxymethamphetamine [(+/-)MDMA] on locomotion and serotonin syndrome behavior in the rat, by L. J. Spanos, et al. PHARMACOLOGY, BIOCHEMISTRY AND BEHAVIOR 32(4):835-840, April 1989. Erratum. 34(3):679, November 1989

Antinociceptive effects of 3,4-methylenedioxymethamphetamine (MDMA) in the rat, by T. Crisp, et al. PHARMACOLOGY, BIOCHEMISTRY AND BEHAVIOR 34(3):497-501, November 1989

Behavioral and neurochemical effects of orally administered MDMA in the rodent and nonhuman primate, by W. Slikker, Jr., et al. NEUROTOXICOLOGY 10(3):529-542, Fall 1989

Effects of MDMA, "ecstasy," on firing rates of serotonergic, dopaminergic, and noradrenergic neurons in the rat, by M. F. Piercey, et al. BRAIN RESEARCH 526(2):203-206, 1990

Effects of optical isomers of 3,4-methylenedioxymethamphetamine (MDMA) on stereotyped behavior in rats, by M. Hiramatsu, et al. PHARMACOLOGY, BIOCHEMISTRY AND BEHAVIOR 33(2):343-347, June 1989

Long-term central 5-HT depletions resulting from repeated administration of MDMA enhances the effects of single administration of MDMA on schedule-controlled behavior of rats, by A. A. Li, et al. PHARMACOLOGY, BIOCHEMISTRY AND BEHAVIOR 33(3):641-648, July 1989

MDMA (ecstasy) effects on cultured serotonergic neurons: evidence for Ca2[+]-dependent toxicity linked to release, by E. C. Azmitia, et al. BRAIN RESEARCH 510(1):97-103, February 26, 1990

MDMA transiently alters biogenic amines and metabolites in mouse brain and heart, by T. D. Steele, et al. PHARMACOLOGY, BIOCHEMISTRY AND BEHAVIOR 34(2):223-227, October 1989

Reserpine does not prevent 3,4-methylenedioxymethamphetamine-induced neuro-toxicity in the rat, by C. R. Hekmatpanah, et al. NEUROSCIENCE LETTERS 104 (1-2):178-182, September 25, 1989

Studies of MDMA-induced neurotoxicity in nonhuman primates: a basis for evaluating long-term effects in humans, by G. A. Ricaurte. NIDA RESEARCH MONOGRAPH SERIES 94:306-322, 1989

THE MEDIA
Ad industry helps fight war on drugs in a full-blown, multi-media campaign, by J. McEl-gunn. MARKETING 95(39):2-3, September 24, 1990

Crack and the box: television as cause of drug addiction, by P. Hamill. ESQUIRE 113: 63-64+, May 1990

Drug wars, news casualties: NBC news involvement with TV movie Drug Wars: the Camarena story, by M. Brown. CHANNELS 10:22, March 1990

Drugbusters: miniseries on the E. Camarena case, by M. Massing. NATION 250:152-153, February 5, 1990

Drugs, blood and money: M. Mann's TV miniseries on the E. Camarena case, by M. Leahy. TV GUIDE 38:18-20, January 6-12, 1990

Mediacom campaign helps fight war on drugs. MARKETING 95(10):13, March 5, 1990

Movies on drugs, by F. T. Thompson. AMERICAN FILM 15:54-57, November 1990

PBS launches an anti-drug series of its own: Traffik, by D. Hudson. TV GUIDE 38:6-7, April 21-27, 1990

Rallying 'round Mayor Barry: coverage of trial by black press, by P. Ruffins. NATION 251:121-122+, July 30-August 6, 1990

Use of mass media in substance abuse prevention, by W. DeJong, et al. HEALTH AFFAIRS 9(2):30-46, Summer 1990

Were the Russians compromised: media reports may have jeopardized a Vancouver drug case, by J. McDowell. BC REPORT 2(3):28-29, September 17, 1990

When TV enlists in the war on drugs: loss of objectivity in Dallas station's advocacy programming for Texas crackdown, by D. Holder. CHANNELS 10:8, May 7, 1990

THE MENTALLY HANDICAPPED
Drug abuse among mentally retarded people: an overlooked problem, by D. Delaney, et al. JOURNAL OF ALCOHOL AND DRUG EDUCATION 35(2):48-54, Winter 1990

METHADONE

Methadone and edema, by W. Macfadden, et al. JOURNAL OF CLINICAL PSYCHIA-TRY 51(1):36-37, January 1990

Research

Actions and side effects of methadone, by J. Jade. DEUTSCHE MEDIZINISCHE WOCHENSCHRIFT 115(14):552-555, April 6, 1990

Effect of methadone in vitro on natural killer (NK) activity, by M. Ochshorn, et al. NIDA RESEARCH MONOGRAPH SERIES 95:522-523, 1989

Effects of methadone on alternative fixed-ratio fixed-interval performance: latent influences on schedule-controlled responding, by M. Egli, et al. JOURNAL OF THE

METHAMPHETAMINE

Cocaine-and methamphetamine-related deaths in San Diego County: 1987: homicides and accidental overdoses, by D. N. Bailey, et al. JOURNAL OF FORENSIC SCIENCES 34(2):407-422, 1989

"Crystal meth": ice age in Hawaii. CRIME CONTROL DIGEST 23(39):2-4, October 2, 1989

Dexamphetamine for "speed" addiction, by J. P. Sherman. MEDICAL JOURNAL OF AUSTRALIA 153(5):306, September 3, 1990

Iceman cometh and killeth: smokable methamphetamine, by R. B. Mack. NORTH CAROLINA MEDICAL JOURNAL 51(6):276-278, June 1990

Impurities in illicit drug preparations: amphetamine and methamphetamine, by A. M. A.Verweij. FORENSIC SCIENCE REVIEW 1(1):1-11, 1989

Complications

Clinical course of chronic methamphetamine psychoses, by H. Fujimori, et al. FORT-SCHRITTE DER NEUROLOGIE-PSYCHIATRIE 57(9):383-394, September 1989

Crystal methamphetamine-induced acute pulmonary edema: a case report, by T. A. Nestor, et al. HAWAII MEDICAL JOURNAL 48(11):457-458+, November 1989

Lead poisoning associated with intravenous-methamphetamine use: Oregon, 1988. MMWR 39(48):830-831, December 8, 1989

Methamphetamine psychosis in Japan: a survey, by Y. Nakatani, et al. BRITISH JOUR-NAL OF ADDICTION 84(12):1548-1549, December 1989

Reversible dilated cardiomyopathy induced by methamphetamine, by L. J. Jacobs. CLINICAL CARDIOLOGY 12(12):725-727, December 1989

Research

Comparison of responses by neuropeptide systems in rat to the psychotropic drugs, methamphetamine, cocaine, and PCP, by G. R. Hanson, et al. NIDA RESEARCH MONOGRAPH SERIES 95:348, 1989

METHAMPHETAMINE—Research

Methamphetamine and related drugs: toxicity and resulting behavioral changes in response to pharmacological probes, by L. S. Seiden, et al. NIDA RESEARCH MONOGRAPH SERIES 94:146-160, 1989

Methamphetamine synthesis via hydriodic acid-red phosphorus reduction of ephedrine, by H. F. Skinner. FORENSIC SCIENCE INTERNATIONAL 48(2):123-134, 1990

METHANOL

Case of thinner sniffing: part 2—urinary excretion of cresols and methanol after inhalation of toluene and methanol, by S. Kira, et al. INDUSTRIAL HEALTH 27(4): 175-180, 1989

METHOCARBAMOL

Assessment of the abuse potential of methocarbamol in primates, by B. A. Hayes, et al. NIDA RESEARCH MONOGRAPH SERIES 95:506, 1989

METHOMYL

Fatal and non-fatal methomyl intoxication in an attempted double suicide, by T. Miyazaki, et al. FORENSIC SCIENCE INTERNATIONAL 42(3):263-270, August 1989

METHYLENEDIOXYAMPHETAMINE *see*: MDA

METHYLENEDIOXYMETHAMPHETAMINE *see*: MDMA

THE MILITARY

see also: The Military and Narcotics Control
Testing—The Military

Drugs in the army, by B. F. Kalachev, et al. SOTSIOLOGICHESKIE ISSLEDOVANIYA 16(4):56-61, 1989

Traumatogenicity: effects of self-reported noncombat trauma on MMPIs of male Vietnam combat and noncombat veterans treated for substance abuse, by E. Berk, et al. JOURNAL OF CLINICAL PSYCHOLOGY 45(5):704-708, September 1989

War on drugs gets a general: beginning of United States Army drug and alcohol program, by E. K. Jeffer. ARMY 40(1):36-39, January 1990

THE MILITARY AND NARCOTICS CONTROL

AFOSI's role in drug interdiction and enforcement: Air Force Office of Special Investigations, by S. F. Minger. POLICE CHIEF 57:124-126, October 1990

Andean drug trafficking and the military option, by D. J. Mabry. MILITARY REVIEW 70(3):29-40, March 1990

Army Mohawks join the anti-drug effort. SOLDIERS 45(8):16, August 1990

Army's drug war role expanding, by G. High. SOLDIERS 45(1):14-15, January 1990

AWACS to play larger role in Bush antidrug effort. AVIATION WEEK AND SPACE TECHNOLOGY 132:45, April 2, 1990

Bill introduced to create anti-drug command structure in defense department. NARCOTICS CONTROL DIGEST 19(11):8-9, May 24, 1989

Body count: Operation Democracy launched by the military. NATION 251:5, July 2, 1990

California Guard: California National Guard stopping flow of illegal drugs, by W. H. McMichael. SOLDIERS 45(7):37-41, July 1990

Changing roles for military intelligence in the 21st century, by R. B. Davis. MILITARY INTELLIGENCE 16(2):32-35, April/June 1990

Coast Guard announces new zero tolerance procedure. NARCOTICS CONTROL DIGEST 19(23):10, November 8, 1989; also in CORPORATE SECURITY DIGEST 3(45):5, November 13, 1989

Coast Guard: changing technologies, budgetary pressures, by P. A. Yost, Jr. SEA TECHNOLOGY 31:21-22, January 1990

Coast Guard tests Lockheed's strap-on surveillance pod against drug smugglers. AVIATION WEEK AND SPACE TECHNOLOGY 132:76, March 5, 1990

Colombian outcry hurts United States naval intervention, by H. Fried. GUARDIAN 42(14):12, January 31, 1990

Combating the Colombian drug cartels, by R. J. Kolton. Maj. MILITARY REVIEW 70(3):49-63, March 1990

D.C. National Guard as "force multiplier" in war on drugs, by D. Steele. ARMY 40(2):50-52, February 1990

Drugs: the military's new unwinnable war, by J. Kitfield. GOVERNMENT EXECUTIVE 22(3):10-14, March 1990

E-3 flights to increase in drug-war plan, by J. Longo. AIR FORCE TIMES 50(32):3, March 19, 1990

F-16s in Panama in anti-drug fight, by D. Fulghum. AIR FORCE TIMES 50(22):4, January 8, 1990

Fighting drugs with the military, by M. T. Klare. NATION 250:8-10+, January 1, 1990

Let the military shoot down the drug smugglers. NARCOTICS CONTROL DIGEST 19(21):1+, October 11, 1989

Military labs build high-tech drug weapons, by W. Matthews. AIR FORCE TIMES 50(34):20, April 2, 1990

Military role to remain strong in drug war. NARCOTICS CONTROL DIGEST 20(12):10, June 6, 1990

THE MILITARY AND NARCOTICS CONTROL

More and more, a real war: in search of a mission, the military is stepping up its battle against drugs, by E. Magnuson. TIME 135(4):32-33, January 22, 1990

National Guard develops interagency countenarcotics program, by J. M. Beall. NATIONAL GUARD 44(10):34-36+, October 1990

National Guard drug mission help to law enforcement, by R. Bocklet. LAW AND ORDER 38(6):71-77, June 1990

National Guard in the war on drugs, by H. R. Temple, Jr. MILITARY REVIEW 70(3):41-48, March 1990

Navy units to monitor drug lanes, by G. Willis. AIR FORCE TIMES 50(22):4, January 8, 1990

NSC to recommend greater military role in drug war. NARCOTICS CONTROL DIGEST 19(14):10, July 5, 1989

Revisiting the war on drugs: after one year, military's impact hard to measure, by W. Matthews. AIR FORCE TIMES 51(13):16+, November 5, 1990

Sending out for reinforcements: National Guard called in to aid nationwide anti-drug efforts. LAW ENFORCEMENT NEWS 15(296):1+, July 15, 1989

Smuggler beware: Texas National Guard fights drugs. SOLDIERS 45(6):28-33, June 1990

Stamping out domestic drugs: Florida National Guard, by D. Miles. SOLDIERS 45(11):37-40, November 1990

Terrors on patrol: Navy's PHM Squadron is the refleetest of the fleet, by V. C. Thomas. SEA POWER 33(5):21-22, May 1990

MINORITIES

African-American youth and AIDS high-risk behavior: the social context and barriers to prevention, by B. P. Bowser, et al. YOUTH AND SOCIETY 22:54-66, September 1990

Application of psychological knowledge for American Indians and Alaska natives, by J. E. Trimble. JOURNAL OF TRAINING AND PRACTICE IN PROFESSIONAL PSYCHOLOGY 4(1):45-63, Spring 1990

Band leadership: of Samson Cree Nation, committed to solving the problems of drug and alcohol abuse. WINDSPEAKER 8(17):22, November 9, 1990

Black adolescent crack users in Oakland: no quick fix, by B. G. Silverman. JAMA 264 (3):337, July 18, 1990

Black intravenous drug users: prospects for intervening in the transmission of human immunodeficiency virus infection, by L. S. Brown, Jr. NIDA RESEARCH MONOGRAPH SERIES 93:53-67, 1990

Black males and the drug trade: new enterpreneurs of new illusions—Joint Center Conferences report that urban drug dealers are largely addicts who earn little by their trade and fear street violence more than jail, by K. McFate. FOCUS 18:5-6, May 1990

Drugs and the black community: the other side of the picture, by W. J. Bennett. USA TODAY 119:35-37, July 1990

Drugs and Native-American youth, by E. R. Oetting, et al. DRUGS AND SOCIETY 3(1-2):1-34, 1988

Ethnic differences in narcotics addiction: I—characteristics of Chicano and Anglo methadone maintenance clients, by M. D. Anglin, et al. INTERNATIONAL JOURNAL OF THE ADDICTIONS 23(2):125-149, 1988

Ethnicity and drug use: a critical look, by E. M. Adlaf, et al. INTERNATIONAL JOURNAL OF THE ADDICTIONS 24(1):1-18, January 1989

Farrakhan's mission: fighting the drug war, by L. Wright. NEWSWEEK 115:25, March 19, 1990

Interdisciplinary treatment of drug misuse among older people of color: ethnic considerations for social work practice, by P. R. Raffoul, et al. JOURNAL OF DRUG ISSUES 19(2):297-313, Spring 1989

Out there: I—involvement of black youth in drug trade in New Haven, Connecticut, by W. Finnegan. NEW YORKER 66:51-52+, September 10, 1990

Out there: II—involvement of black youth in drug trade in New Haven, Connecticut, by W. Finnegan. NEW YORKER 66:60-64+, September 17, 1990

Peyotism and the control of heavy drinking: the Nebraska Winnebago in the early 1990s, by T. W. Hill. HUMAN ORGANIZATION 49(3):255-265, 1990

Puerto Rican intravenous drug user, by Y.Serrano. NIDA RESEARCH MONOGRAPH SERIES 93:24-34, 1990

Racial differences in attitudes toward crime control, by P. E. Secret, et al. JOURNAL OF CRIMINAL JUSTICE 17(5):361-375, 1989

Social learning theory, drug use and American Indian youths: a cross-cultural test, by I. T. Winfree, et al. JUSTICE QUARTERLY 6(3):395-417, September 1989

Study: news depicts blacks in drug stories unfairly. JET 79:24, November 12, 1990

Substance abuse among American Indians in an urban treatment program, by C. G. Gurnee, et al. AMERICAN INDIAN AND ALASKA NATIVE MENTAL HEALTH RESEARCH 3(3):17-26, Spring 1990

Substance abuse among Native-American youth, by M. S. Moncher, et al. JOURNAL OF CONSULTING AND CLINICAL PSYCHOLOGY 58(4):408-415, 1990

Substance abuse: the toll on blacks— facts and figures. BLACK ENTERPRISE 20: 39, July 1990

Tobacco, alcohol, and marijuana use among black adolescents: a comparison across gender, grade, and school environment, by S. M. Thomas, et al. JOURNAL OF THE LOUISIANA STATE MEDICAL SOCIETY 142(4):37-42, April 1990

MINORITIES

Triple jeopardy: child abuse, drug abuse, and the minority client, by J. N. Thomas. JOURNAL OF INTERPERSONAL VIOLENCE 4(3):351-355, September 1989

MORPHINE

Acute opioid physical dependence in humans: effect of naloxone at 6 and 24 hours postmorphine,.by S. J. Heishman, et al. PHARMACOLOGY, BIOCHEMISTRY AND BEHAVIOR 36(2):393-399, June 1990

Acute opioid physical dependence in humans: maximum morphine-naloxone interval, by K. C. Kirby, et al. NIDA RESEARCH MONOGRAPH SERIES 95:393-394, 1989

Effects of cocaine and morphine on IgG production by human peripheral blood lymphocytes in vitro, by F. Martinez, et al. LIFE SCIENCES 47(15):59-64, 1990

Functional role of the oxytocin-sensitive hippocampal system in organizing the mechanisms of morphine addiction, by R. Ibragimov. FIZIOLOGICHESKII ZHURNAL SSSR 75(6):752-758, June 1989

Immune system and morphine dependence, by N. Dafny, et al. NIDA RESEARCH MONOGRAPH SERIES 95:293-295, 1989

Intensification and attenuation of morphine dependence by D-aspartic acid and PLG, by H. Koyuncuoglu, et al. PHARMACOLOGY, BIOCHEMISTRY AND BEHAVIOR 35(1):47-50, January 1990

Modification of morphine-induced analgesia, tolerance and dependence by bromocriptine, by A. A. Gomaa, et al. EUROPEAN JOURNAL OF PHARMACOLOGY 170(3):129-135, November 7, 1989

Morphine analgesia and acute physical dependence: rapid onset of two opposing, dose-related processes, by D. H. Kim, et al. BRAIN RESEARCH 516(1):37-40, May 14, 1990

"Paradoxical" analgesia and aggravated morphine dependence induced by opioid antagonists, by T. Suzuki, et al. LIFE SCIENCES 47(6):515-521, 1990

Complications

Gallbladder sludge and lithiasis in an infant born to a morphine user mother, by R. Figuerosa-Colon, et al. JOURNAL OF PEDIATRIC GASTROENTEROLOGY AND NUTRITION 10(2):234-238, February 1990

Suppression of small intestinal motility and morphine withdrawal diarrhoea by clonidine: peripheral site of action, by M. Thollander, et al. ACTA PHYSIOLOGICA SCANDINAVICA 137(3):385-392, November 1989

Research

Automated method for the evaluation of jumping activity in mice: effects of clonidine on morphine withdrawal, by L. F. Alguacil, et al. METHODS AND FINDINGS IN EXPERIMENTAL AND CLINICAL PHARMACOLOGY 11(11):677-681, November 1989

Binding of 3H-[3-MeHis2] thyrotropin releasing hormone to brain and pituitary membranes of morphine tolerant-dependent and abstinent rats, by H. N. Bhargava, et al. PHARMACOLOGY, BIOCHEMISTRY AND BEHAVIOR 34(1):7-12, September 1989

Brain and spinal cord 5-HT2 receptor of morphine-tolerant-dependent and -abstinent rats, by A. Gulati, et al. EUROPEAN JOURNAL OF PHARMACOLOGY 167(2): 185-192, August 22, 1989

Butorphanol precipitates abstinence in morphine dependent rats, by P. Horan, et al. EUROPEAN JOURNAL OF PHARMACOLOGY 170(3):265-268, November 7, 1989

Cardiovascular responses to acute myocardial ischaemia in morphine-dependent rats, by W. W. Ko, et al. CLINICAL AND EXPERIMENTAL PHARMACOLOGY AND PHYSIOLOGY 15(1):23-31, January 1988

Context-specific morphine withdrawal in rats: duration and effects of clonidine, by J. E. Kelsey, et al. BEHAVIORAL NEUROSCIENCE 104:704-710, October 1990

Cortical dihydropyridine binding sites and a behavioral syndrome in morphine-abstinent rats, by L. Antkiewicz-Michaluk, et al. EUROPEAN JOURNAL OF PHARMACOLOGY 180(1):129-135, May 3, 1990

Dependence and withdrawal following intracerebroventricular and systemic morphine administration: functional anatomy and behavior, by R. E. Adams, et al. BRAIN RESEARCH 518(1-2):6-10, June 4, 1990

Discriminative stimulus effects of opioid agonists in morphine-dependent pigeons, by C. P. France, et al. JOURNAL OF PHARMACOLOGY AND EXPERIMENTAL THERAPEUTICS 254(2):626-632, August 1990

Effects of antihistaminics on naloxone-induced withdrawal in morphine-dependent mice, by J. C. Leza, et al. PSYCHOPHARMACOLOGY 102(1):106-111, 1990

Effects of chronic treatment with specific antagonists on analgesia and physical dependence on morphine in rats, by Y. Fukagawa, et al. PROGRESS IN CLINICAL AND BIOLOGICAL RESEARCH 328:527-530, 1990

Effects of a selective kappa-opioid agonist, U-50,488H, on morphine dependence in rats, by Y. Fukagawa, et al. EUROPEAN JOURNAL OF PHARMACOLOGY 170(1-2):47-51, October 24, 1989

Enhanced affinity of mu-opioid receptors in morphine-dependent mice, by E. E. Abdelhamid, et al. PROGRESS IN CLINICAL AND BIOLOGICAL RESEARCH 328: 523-526, 1990

Enhancement of morphine withdrawal signs in the rat after chronic treatment with naloxone, by T. Suzuki, et al. EUROPEAN JOURNAL OF PHARMACOLOGY 178(2):239-242, March 20, 1990

Evidence that physical dependence on morphine is mediated by the ventral midbrain, by A. A. Baumeister, et al. NEUROPHARMACOLOGY 28(11):1151-1157, November 1989

Functional role of the oxytocin-sensitive hippocampal system in organizing the mechanisms of morphine addiction, by R. Ibragimov. FIZIOLOGICHESKII ZHURNAL SSSR 75(6):752-758, June 1989

Intrathecal pertussis toxin attenuates the morphine withdrawal syndrome in normal but not in arthritic rats, by M. Lerida, et al. LIFE SCIENCES 46(5):329-334, 1990

Is there a genetic control of morphine preference in the rat?, by L. Ronnback. PHARMACOLOGY, BIOCHEMISTRY AND BEHAVIOR 35(1):15-20, January 1990

Maintenance of morphine dependence by naloxone in acutely dependent mice, by M. Sofuoglu, et al. JOURNAL OF PHARMACOLOGY AND EXPERIMENTAL THERAPEUTICS 254(3):841-846, September 1990

Method for evaluating the reinforcing properties of morphine in a model of addictive behavior, by L. A. Surkova, et al. FARMAKOLOGIYA I TOKSIKOLOGIYA 52(4): 93-94, July/August 1989

Modification of brain and spinal cord dopamine D1 receptors labeled with [3H]SCH 23390 after morphine withdrawal from tolerant and physically dependent rats, by H. N. Bhargava, et al. JOURNAL OF PHARMACOLOGY AND EXPERIMENTAL THERAPEUTICS 252(3):901-907, March 1990

Modification of the effects of naloxone in morphine-dependent mice, by T. Suzuki, et al. LIFE SCIENCES 45(14):1237-1246, 1989

Modulation of synaptosomal free intracellular calcium in naive and morphine-tolerant mice: correlation of calcium modulation in vitro and in vivo to tolerance development, by S. P. Welch, et al. NIDA RESEARCH MONOGRAPH SERIES 95:552-553, 1989

Opiate withdrawal and the rat locus coeruleus: behavioral, electrophysiological, and biochemical correlates, by K. Rasmussen, et al. JOURNAL OF NEUROSCIENCE 10(7):2308-2317, July 1990

Phosphodiesterase inhibitors potentiate opiate-antagonist discrimination by morphine-dependent rats, by S. G. Holtzman. PHARMACOLOGY, BIOCHEMISTRY AND BEHAVIOR 33(4):875-879, August 1989

Physical dependence induced by the voluntary consumption of morphine in inbred mice, by J. K. Belknap. PHARMACOLOGY, BIOCHEMISTRY AND BEHAVIOR 35(2):311-315, February 1990

Physical dependence on morphine using the mu receptor deficient CXBK mouse, by T. Suzuki, et al. PROGRESS IN CLINICAL AND BIOLOGICAL RESEARCH 328: 519-522, 1990

Release of oxytocin but not corticotrophin-releasing factor-41 into rat hypophysial portal vessel blood can be made opiate dependent, by W. J. Sheward, et al. JOURNAL OF ENDOCRINOLOGY 124(1):141-150, January 1990

Responses of morphine dependent opioid neurones to stressors, by J. E. Olley, et al. PROGRESS IN CLINICAL AND BIOLOGICAL RESEARCH 328:511-514, 1990

Role of plasma catecholamines in eliciting cardiovascular changes seen during naloxone-precipitated withdrawal in conscious, unrestrained morphine-dependent rats, by A. P. Chang, et al. JOURNAL OF PHARMACOLOGY AND EXPERIMENTAL THERAPEUTICS 254(3):857-863, September 1990

Tolerance and dependence after continuous morphine infusion from osmotic pumps measured by operant responding in rats, by J. U. Adams, et al. PSYCHOPHARMACOLOGY 100(4):451-458, 1990

Trans-cranial electrical stimulation attenuates abrupt morphine withdrawal in rats assayed by remote computerized quantification of multiple motor behavior indices, by P. M. Dougherty, et al. EUROPEAN JOURNAL OF PHARMACOLOGY 175(2): 187-195, January 10, 1990

Vascular adrenergic responses in morphine-dependent rats, by H. Gustafsson, et al. ACTA PHYSIOLOGICA SCANDINAVICA 139(2):333-339, June 1990

MORTALITY
see also: Suicide

Acute myoglobinuria as a fatal complication of heroin addiction, by Y. F. Chan, et al. AMERICAN JOURNAL OF FORENSIC MEDICINE AND PATHOLOGY 11(2):160-164, June 1990

Cannabis and mortality among young men: a longitudinal study of Swedish conscripts, by S. Andreasson, et al. SCANDINAVIAN JOURNAL OF SOCIAL MEDICINE 18(1):9-15, 1990

Causes of death in hospitalized intravenous drug abusers, by E. C. Klatt, et al. JOURNAL OF FORENSIC SCIENCES 35(5):1143-1148, 1990

Cocaine abuse and violent death, by R. D. Budd. AMERICAN JOURNAL OF DRUG AND ALCOHOL ABUSE 15(4):375-382, December 1989

Cocaine- and methamphetamine-related deaths in San Diego County: 1987: homicides and accidental overdoses, by D. N. Bailey, et al. JOURNAL OF FORENSIC SCIENCES 34(2):407-422, 1989

Cocaine and sudden cardiac death, by T. J. Pallasch, et al. JOURNAL OF ORAL AND MAXILLOFACIAL SURGERY 47(11):1188-1191, November 1989

Cocaine in Wayne County, Michigan, USA: medical examiner's cases, by I. Hood, et al. JOURNAL OF FORENSIC SCIENCES 35(3):591-600, May 1990

Cocaine-related maternal death, by G. Burkett, et al. AMERICAN JOURNAL OF OBSTETRICS AND GYNECOLOGY 163(1 Pt 1):40-41, July 1990

Comparison of drug-related deaths in Oslo, Norway and Aarhus, Denmark, by B. Teige, et al. JOURNAL OF THE FORENSIC SCIENCE SOCIETY 28(5-6):311-319, 1988

DEA agent dies of heroin overdose: first for agency. NARCOTICS CONTROL DIGEST 19(17):8-9, August 16, 1989

MORTALITY

Death caused by drug addiction: a review of the experiences in Hamburg and the situation in the Federal Republic of Germany in comparison with the literature, by W. Janssen, et al. FORENSIC SCIENCE INTERNATIONAL 43(3):223-227, December 1989

Death from overdose and rapid intervention by local units, by P. Testa. CLINICA TERAPEUTICA 133(5):275-288, June 15, 1990

Death on a frozen street: Edmonton youth dies after drugged romp in the snow, by B. Clark. ALBERTA (WESTERN) REPORT 17(52):34, December 10, 1990

Death takes a ride: alcohol-associated single vehicle fatalities revisited, by M. J. Hyland, et al. NEW YORK STATE JOURNAL OF MEDICINE 90(7):349-351, July 1990

Deaths of heroin addicts starting on methadone maintenance, by C. H. Wu, et al. LANCET 335(8686):424, February 17, 1990

Deaths of heroin addicts starting on a methadone maintenance programme, by O. H. Drummer, et al. LANCET 335(8681):108, January 13, 1990

Dextromoramide-related fatality, by E. Brewer. JOURNAL OF FORENSIC SCIENCES 35(2):483-489, March 1990

Drug abuse in Jutland, Denmark: an investigation based on narcotics and addict deaths examined at the Institute of Forensic Medicine, University of Aarhus during the period 1981-1988; 2—deaths among addicts, by E. Kaa. UGESKRIFT FOR LAEGER 152(15):1080-1083, 1990

Drug-positive homicides in Virginia 1987 through 1989. MEDICO-LEGAL BULLETIN 39(1):1-9, January/February 1990

Factors in mortality by drug dependence among Puerto Ricans in New York City, by D. Shai, et al. AMERICAN JOURNAL OF DRUG AND ALCOHOL ABUSE 16(1-2):97-107, March/June 1990

Fatal abuse of nitrous oxide in the workplace, by A. J. Suruda, et al. JOURNAL OF OCCUPATIONAL MEDICINE 32(8):682-684, August 1990

Fatal accidental enflurane intoxication, by B. Jacob, et al. JOURNAL OF FORENSIC SCIENCES 34(6):1408-1412, November 1989

Fatal interaction of methocarbamol and ethanol in an accidental poisoning, by K. E. Ferslew, et al. JOURNAL OF FORENSIC SCIENCES 35(2):477-482, March 1990

Fatal intoxications in the age group 15-34 years in Denmark in 1984 and 1985: a forensic study with special reference in drug addicts, by A. Steentoft, et al. ZEITSCHRIFT FUR RECHTSMEDIZIN 103(2):93-100, 1989

Fatal poisoning among narcotic addicts in Denmark in 1984-1986, by E. Kaa, et al. UGESKRIFT FOR LAEGER 151(41):2650-2652, October 9, 1989

Fatal poisoning with antidepressants in Finland, 1985-1987, by E. Vuori, et al. ACTA PSYCHIATRICA SCANDINAVICA 354(Suppl):55-60, 1989

Fatal recreational inhalation of enflurane, by F. B. Walker, et al. JOURNAL OF FOREN-SIC SCIENCES 35(1):197-198, January 1990

Fatal staphylococcus saprophyticus native valve endocartitis in an intravenous drug addict, by V. R. Singh, et al. JOURNAL OF INFECTIOUS DISEASES 162(3):783-784, September 1990

Fatal variceal haemorrhage after paracetamol overdose, by J. R. Thornton, et al. GUT 30(10):1424-1425, October 1989

Fatalities in drug dependent patients: suicide or accident?, by M. Graw, et al. VER-SICHERUNGSMEDIZEN 41(6):188-191, November 1, 1989

HIV-1 prevalence in deaths caused by drug overdose in various large cities of West Germany and West Berlin between 1985 and 1988, by K. Puschel, et al. ZEITSCHRIFT FUR RECHTSMEDIZIN 103(6):407-414, 1990

HTLV-I-II seropositivity and death from AIDS among HIV-1 seropositive intravenous drug users, by J. B. Page, et al. LANCET 355(8703):1439-1441, June 16, 1990

Iceman cometh and killeth: smokable methamphetamine, by R. B. Mack. NORTH CAROLINA MEDICAL JOURNAL 51(6):276-278, June 1990

Incidence and toxicological aspects of cannabis and ethanol detected in 1394 fatally injured drivers and pedestrians in Ontario: Canada: 1982-1984, by G. Cimbura, et al. JOURNAL OF FORENSIC SCIENCES 35(5):1035-1041, 1990

Increase in deaths from deliberate inhalation of fuel gases and pressurised aerosols, by H. R. Anderson. BMJ 301(6742):41, July 7, 1990

Intravenous abuse of crushed tablets: a case with fatal outcome, by M. Roger, et al. TIDSSKRIFT FOR DEN NORSKE LAEGEFORENING 110(16):2080-2081, June 20, 1990

Massive caffeine ingestion resulting in death, by R. M. Mrvos, et al. VETERINARY AND HUMAN TOXICOLOGY 31(6):571-572, December 1989

Modes of death and types of cardiac diseases in opiate addicts: analysis of 168 necropsy cases, by F. A. Dressler, et al. AMERICAN JOURNAL OF CARDIOLOGY 64(14):909-920, October 15, 1989

Mortality and aggressiveness in a 30-year follow-up study in child guidance clinics in Stockholm, by P. de Chateau. ACTA PSYCHIATRICA SCANDINAVICA 81(5): 472-576, May 1990

Mortality following releasing from prison, by D. Harding-Pink. MEDICINE, SCIENCE AND THE LAW 30(1):12-16, January 1990

Mortality in heroin addiction: impact of methadone treatment, by L. Gonbladh, et al. ACTA PSYCHIATRICA SCANDINAVICA 82(3):223-227, 1990

Narcotic abuse in Jylland: a study based on narcotics and deaths of addicts examined at the Institute of Forensic Medicine, University of Aarhus during the period 1981-1988: 1—narcotics, by E. Kaa. UGESKRIFT FOR LAEGER 152(15):1077-1080, April 1990

MORTALITY

Narcotic abuse in Jylland: a study based on narcotics and deaths of addicts examined at the Institute of Forensic Medicine, University of Aarhus during the period 1981-1988: 2—deaths among addicts, by E. Kaa. UGESKRIFT FOR LAEGER 152(15): 1080-1083, April 9, 1990

New trend in solvent abuse deaths, by P. McBride, et al. MEDICINE, SCIENCE AND THE LAW 30(3):207-213, July 1990

Norweigian data on death due to overdose of antidepressants, by N. Retterstol. ACTA PSYCHIATRICA SCANDINAVICA 354(Suppl):61-68, 1989

Patterns of rates of mortality from narcotics and cocaine overdose in Texas: 1976-1987, by K. C. Harlow. PUBLIC HEALTH REPORT 105:455-462, October/September 1990

Prevalence of HIV-1 among deaths connected with drug abuse in various West German cities and in West Berlin between 1985 and 1988, by K. Pueschel, et al. ZEITSCHRIFT FUR RECHTSMEDIZIN 103(6):407-414, 1990

Prevalence of recent cocaine use among motor vehicle fatalities in New York City, by P. M. Marzuk, et al. JAMA 263(2):250-256, January 12, 1990

Sniffers using butane, propane: 11 year old and 15 year old die suddenly after use, by K. Fournis. JOURNAL OF THE ADDICTION RESEARCH FOUNDATION 19(12):3, December 1, 1990

Steroids claimed our son's life: with commentary by Harrison G. Pope, Jr., by G. Elofson, et al. PHYSICIAN AND SPORTSMEDICINE 18:15-16, August 1990

Substance abuse and traffic deaths: report by National Transportation Safety Board. SAFETY AND HEALTH 141:32, April 1990

Sudden death from acute cocaine intoxication in Virginia in 1988, by R. McKelway, et al. AMERICAN JOURNAL OF PSYCHIATRY 147:1667-1669, December 1990

Sudden death in a drug milieu following use of an appetite suppressant, by H. W. Raudonat, et al. BEITRAGE ZUR GERICHTLICHEN MEDIZIN 47:539-540, 1989

Sudden sniffing deaths. JOURNAL OF THE ADDICTION RESEARCH FOUNDATION 19(11):4, November 1, 1990

Toxicological findings after fatal amitriptyline self-poisoning, by A. Tracqui, et al. HUMAN AND EXPERIMENTAL TOXICOLOGY 9(4):257-261, July 1990

Vascular lesions in intestinal ischemia induced by cocaine-alcohol abuse: report of a fatal case due to overdose, by A. Garfia, et al. JOURNAL OF FORENSIC SCIENCES 35(3):740-745, May 1990

NALOXONE

Naloxone induces miosis in normal subjects, by N. Loimer, et al. PSYCHOPHARMACOLOGY 101(2):282-283, 1990

Adolescent use of narcotics and toxic substances, by G. Lukacher, et al. SOVIET MEDICINE (6):105-109, 1990

Analysis of regional trends in narcotic studies between 1980 and 1986, by K. Wehr, et al. ZEITSCHRIFT FUR RECHTSMEDIZIN 102(8):509-519, 1989

Biological evaluation of compounds for their physical dependence potential and abuse liability: XII—drug testing program of the Committee on Problems of Drug Dependence, Inc., 1988, by A. E. Jacobson. NIDA RESEARCH MONOGRAPH SERIES 90:392-420, 1988

Clinical notes for evaluating soundness of mind and compliance to drug preventive measures in cases of narcotic use, by R. Rutkowski. PSYCHIATRIA POLSKA 23(2):146-153, March/April 1989

Drugs of abuse: opiates, by W. Ling, et al. WESTERN JOURNAL OF MEDICINE 152 (5):565-572, May 1990

Ghosts from "stagnation," by A. M. Presman, et al. SOTSIOLOGICHESKIE ISSLE-DOVANIYA 16(5):77-79, 1989

Implications of the mulitplicity of opioid receptors for the problem of addiction, by A. Herz. DRUG AND ALCOHOL DEPENDENCE 25(2):125-127, April 1990

Interactions of the opioid and immune systems, by R. M. Donahoe. NIDA RESEARCH MONOGRAPH SERIES 95:186-191, 1989

Narcotic abuse in Jylland: a study based on narcotics and deaths of addicts examined at the Institute of Forensic Medicine, University of Aarhus during the period 1981-1988: 1—narcotics, by E. Kaa. UGESKRIFT FOR LAEGER 152(15):1077-1080, April 1990

Narcotic abuse in Jylland: a study based on narcotics and deaths of addicts examined at the Institute of Forensic Medicine, University of Aarhus during the period 1981-1988: 2—deaths among addicts, by E. Kaa. UGESKRIFT FOR LAEGER 152(15): 1080-1083, April 9, 1990

Opiate dependence: the role of benzodiazepines, by V. Navaratnam, et al. CUR-RENT MEDICAL RESEARCH AND OPINION 11(10):620-630, 1990

Opioid drug discrimination in humans: stability, specificity and relation to self-reported drug effect, by W. K. Bickel, et al. JOURNAL OF PHARMACOLOGY AND EXPER-IMENTAL THERAPEUTICS 251(3):1053-1063, December 1989

Opioids: abuse liability and treatments for dependence, by J. W. Ternes, et al. AD-VANCES IN ALCOHOL AND SUBSTANCE ABUSE 9(1-2):27-45, Spring 1990

Pavlovian conditioning to morphine in opiate abusers, by D. B. Newlin, et al. NIDA RESEARCH MONOGRAPH SERIES 95:390-391, 1989

Premorbid characteristics in patients with narcomanias, by S. P. Genailo. ZHURNAL NEVROPATOLOGII I PSIKHIATRII IMENI S. S. KORSAKOVA 90(2):42-47, 1990

Study of the motor and sensory neuron conduction velocity and of the H reflex in
subjects with chronic opiate poisoning, by A. Appiotti. MINERVA MEDICA 80(10):
1073-1077, October 1989

Complications
Case of right-sided infective endocarditis in a drug addict, by H. Ohshima, et al.
KOKYU TO JUNKAN 38(3):277-281, March 1990

Diagnosis of toxic lesions of the brain using computerized tomography, by I. Bushev,
et al. ZHRUNAL NEVROPATOLOGII I PSIKHIATRII IMENI S. S. KORSAKOVA
90(2):107-109, 1990

Fatal poisoning among narcotic addicts in Denmark in 1984-1986, by E. Kaa, et al.
UGESKRIFT FOR LAEGER 151(41):2650-2652, October 9, 1989

Health and development of 8-year-old children whose mothers abused amphetamine
during pregnancy, by M. Eriksson, et al. ACTA PAEDIATRICA SCANDINAVICA
78(6):944-949, November 1989

Opiate addiction and anorexia nervosa: a case report, by D. D. Krahn, et al. INTER-
NATIONAL JOURNAL OF EATING DISORDERS 9(4):453-456, July 1990

Opioids and designer drugs, by M. Ford, et al. EMERGENCY MEDICINE CLINICS OF
NORTH AMERICA 8(3):495-511, August 1990

Pathology mimicking distal intestinal obstruction syndrome in cystic fibrosis, by A. M.
Dalzell, et al. ARCHIVES OF GENERAL PSYCHIATRY 65(5):540-541, 1990

Post-education in clinical problems of narcotics abuse, by S. Fauske. TIDSSKRIFT
FOR DEN NORSKE LAEGEFORENING 110(8):973-975, March 20, 1990

Research
1989 annual report: evaluation of new compounds for opioid activity, by J. H. Woods,
et al. NIDA RESEARCH MONOGRAPH SERIES 95:632-679, 1989

Changes in the level of regulatory peptides and serotonin in the hippocampus of opiate-dependent animals treated with oxytocin, by G. G. Gasanov, et al. DOKLADY
AKADAMII NAUK SSSR 311(1):235-237, 1990

Effect of oxytocin on changes in the level of regulatory peptides and serotonin in the
hippocampus of opiate-dependent animals, by G. G. Gasanov, et al. DOKLADY
AKADAMII NAUK SSSR 311(1):235-237, 1990

FMRF-amide-like mammalian octapeptide: possible role in opiate dependence and
abstinence, by D. H. Malin, et al. PEPTIDES 11(5):969-972, 1990

Magnitude of opioid dependence after continuous intrathecal infusion of mu- and
delta-selective opioids in the rat, by C. W. Stevens, et al. EUROPEAN JOURNAL
OF PHARMACOLOGY 166(3):467-472, August 2, 1989

Mechanisms of cellular adaptive sensitivity changes: applications to opioid tolerance
and dependence, by S. M. Johnson, et al. PHARMACOLOGICAL REVIEWS
41(4):435-488, December 1989

New rules for clinical trials in the USA will introduce new drugs on the market earlier, by L. Bergstrom. LAKARTIDNINGEN 86(50):4461, December 13, 1989

Opiate dependence alters central reward of nalbuphine or pentazocine plus tripelennamine, by D. Huston-Lyons, et al. EUROPEAN JOURNAL OF PHARMACOLOGY 169(1):153-157, October 4, 1989

Opioid dependence after continuous intrathecal infusion of mu and delta opioids in the rat, by C. W. Stevens, et al. NIDA RESEARCH MONOGRAPH SERIES 95: 544-545, 1989

Opponent process theory of motivation: neurobiological evidence from studies of opiate dependence, by G. F. Koob, et al. NEUROSCIENCE AND BIOBEHAVIORAL REVIEWS 13(2-3):135-140, Summer/Fall 1989

Pharmacological studies on drug dependence in rodents: dependence on opioids and CNS depressants, by T. Suzuki. JAPANESE JOURNAL OF PHARMACOLOGY 52(1):1-10, January 1990

Preferences for opioids by the weight pulling methods in rats, by T. Suzuki, et al. PHARMACOLOGY, BIOCHEMISTRY AND BEHAVIOR 35(2):413-418, February 1990

Supersensitivity to electrical stimulation for assessing physical dependence on opioids in isolated tissues, by A. Rezvani, et al. JOURNAL OF PHARMACOLOGY AND EXPERIMENTAL THERAPEUTICS 254(1):52-57, July 1990

NARCOTICS AGENTS
see also: DEA
             The Police

Chamber honors DEA agent shot during drug bust. NARCOTICS CONTROL DIGEST 19(10):9, May 10, 1989

DEA agent arrested in cocaine trafficking sting confessed, federal prosecuters say. NARCOTICS CONTROL DIGEST 19(18):9-10, August 30, 1989

DEA agent dies of heroin overdose: first for agency. NARCOTICS CONTROL DIGEST 19(17):8-9, August 16, 1989

DEA agents move to seize millions from Florida banks. NARCOTICS CONTROL DIGEST 20(11):5-6, May 23, 1990

DEA surpervisor indicted on tax evasion charges. NARCOTICS CONTROL DIGEST 19(21):7-8, October 11, 1989

FBI agent shot, suspect killed in drug shootout. CRIME CONTROL DIGEST 23(18):7, May 7, 1990

Interview: Robert M. Stutman—special agent in charge of the Drug Enforcement Administration's New York field office, by M. S. Rosen. LAW ENFORCEMENT NEWS 15(296):9-11, July 15, 1989

NARCOTICS AGENTS

Peruvian drug recon plane crashes: kills 6 Americans. NARCOTICS CONTROL DI-
GEST 19(22):2, June 7, 1989

Two California officers overcome by PCP fumes. CRIME CONTROL DIGEST 24(26):
9, July 2, 1990; also in NARCOTICS CONTROL DIGEST 20(14):3, July 4, 1990

Undercover negotiating: dealing for your life—undercover narcotics officers, by M. D.
Moriarty. POLICE CHIEF 57:44-47, November 1990

Veteran DEA agent arrested. NARCOTICS CONTROL DIGEST 19(17):5, August 16,
1989

NARCOTICS CONTROL
see also: Bennett, William
           Drug Trafficking
           The Military and Narcotics Control
           The Police and Narcotics Control

279-DOPE hotline heats drug war. ENFORCEMENT JOURNAL 28(3):49, July-
August 1989

Adios to the Andean strategy: Washington drug-war allies are losing heart, by S.
Reiss. NEWSWEEK 116(11):32, September 10, 1990

Amsterdam's subtle war on drugs, by C. Tyler. FINANCIAL POST 83(50):11, December 11, 1989

Anti-drugs programs: the Hamburg Senate initiative. DIE NEUE POLIZEI 44(2):91-
93+, 1990

Anti-narcotics alliance urged at Colombia "drug summit": transcript of news conference following Cartagena summit. CONGRESSIONAL QUARTERLY WEEKLY
REPORT 48:543-544, February 17, 1990

Attorney General addresses anti-drug concerns. CRIME CONTROL DIGEST 23(34):
10, August 28, 1989

Attorney subpoenas imperil choice of counsel, by J. B. Zimmermann, et al. TRIAL
26:51-55, April 1990

Bennett says anti-drug efforts are cutting cocaine supply. NARCOTICS CONTROL
DIGEST 20(13):10, June 20, 1990; also in CRIME CONTROL DIGEST 24(25):6,
June 25, 1990

Body-packing: detection of incorporated drug packets using ultrasound technics, by
A. Freislederer, et al. BEITRAGE ZUR GERICHTLICHEN MEDIZIN 47:187-191,
1989

Bonner plans few changes in direction of drug war for the immediate future, by R. H.
Feldkamp. CRIME CONTROL DIGEST 24(28):1+, July 16, 1990

Bush drug strategy targets drugs in the workplace. CORPORATE SECURITY DIGEST
3(36):10, September 11, 1989

Bush sends United Nations Narcotics Convention to Senate. NARCOTICS CONTROL DIGEST 19(14):10, July 5, 1989

Bush wants chemical companies to help fight drugs by curbing product sales. NARCOTICS CONTROL DIGEST 19(10):10, May 10, 1989

Clandestine drug lab raid, by S. Hermann. LAW AND ORDER 38(9):142-147, 1990

Coca eradication: a remedy for independence, by A. L. Spedding. ANTHROPOLOGY TODAY 5(5):4-9, October 1989

Coca price dropping. NARCOTICS CONTROL DIGEST 20(7):10, March 28, 1990

Cocaine price, purity signal shortage and possible end of epidemic, by R. H. Feldkamp. CRIME CONTROL DIGEST 24(29):1-2, July 23, 1990

Cocaine seizures fail to disrupt market. LAW AND ORDER 38(4):4, April 1990

Combatting the $300-billion drug smuggling empire. INTERNATIONAL PERSPECTIVES 19(5):57, May 1990

Comprehensive pharmaceutical services in the outpatient surgery center of a health maintenance organization, by K. M. Kollar, et al. AMERICAN JOURNAL OF HOSPITAL PHARMACY 47(2):343-346, February 1990

Contraband: the hidden risk, by L. R. Pelletier, et al. QRB 16(1):9-14, January 1990

Cooperation, coordination, intelligence, and hard work: interview with Joint Task Force 4 commander VADM James C. Irwin. SEA POWER 33(3):7-9+, March 1990

Cultural teams attack "Air America," defend CIA, by A. Cockburn. IN THESE TIMES 14(35):17, September 19, 1990

Customs initiates commercial carrier program to curb flow of smuggled narcotics. NARCOTICS CONTROL DIGEST 19(10):4, May 10, 1989

Cutting cocaine's cord: chemical export laws, by K. Sternberg. CHEMICAL WEEK 146:10, April 18, 1990

DARPA cries "help" in the drug war, by D. Harvey. DEFENSE SCIENCE 9(4):23-24+, April 1990

DCA faces expanding challenges to systems interoperability: Defense Communications Agency. AVIATION WEEK AND SPACE TECHNOLOGY 132:72-73, June 4, 1990

DEA offers free guidelines on how to safely clean up clandestine drug labs. CRIME CONTROL DIGEST 24(26):4, July 2, 1990; also in NARCOTICS CONTROL DIGEST 20(14):4, July 4, 1990

Demand reduction boss named. NARCOTICS CONTROL DIGEST August 2, 1989, p. 7

Disillusionment in the face of false antidrug Messiahs, by R. R. Korn. LAW ENFORCEMENT NEWS 15(288):8+, March 15, 1989

Does the administration really want to win the war on drugs: interference by the State Department. UTNE READER September/October 1990, p. 108

Don't let corrections be the scapegoat in the war on drugs, by A. P. Travisono. CORRECTIONS DIGEST 20(19):1-2+, September 20, 1989

Drug intelligence network formed in South. CRIME CONTROL DIGEST 23(38):10, September 25, 1989; also in NARCOTICS CONTROL DIGEST 19(20):2, September 27, 1989

Drug interdiction: the air war takes off. AVIATION WEEK AND SPACE TECHNOLOGY 132:1-15, February 5, 1990

Drug interdiction programs target cocaine-carrying trucks, by B. James. TRAFFIC WORLD 224:27-28, November 19, 1990

Drug plan would shift burden to local level critics say. CRIMINAL JUSTICE NEWSLETTER 20(18):1-2, September 15, 1989

Drug seizure program ended. LAW AND ORDER 38(4):5, April 1990

Drug seizures dropping along south Texas border. NARCOTICS CONTROL DIGEST 20(14):10, July 4, 1990

Drug war, by A. DeCrosta. LEARNING 89 17(6):58-63, February 1989

Drug war, by S. France, et al. ABA JOURNAL 76:42-67, February 1990

Drug war is only make-believe, by R. E. Burns. US CATHOLIC 55:2, June 1990

Drug war of words, by R. Brauer. NATION 250:705-706, May 21, 1990

Drug war revisited, by G. I. Wilson, et al. MARINE CORPS GAZETTE 74(3):18-20, March 1990

Drug war victory not in sight, says retiring DEA chief. CRIME CONTROL DIGEST 24(13):5+, April 2, 1990; also in NARCOTICS CONTROL DIGEST 20(7):1-4, March 28, 1990

Drug wars: breaking the language barrier, by E. D. Degnan. POLICE CHIEF 57(5):40-41, May 1990

Drug wars, turf wars, by M. L. Goldstein. GOVERNMENT EXECUTIVE 22(1):22-26+, January 1990

Drug wars: what history teaches us, by J. C. Lawn. POLICE CHIEF 57(5):53-55, May 1990

Drug wars: the word from the trenches— controlling drugs in Dallas, by M. M. Vines. POLICE CHIEF 57(5):44+, May 1990

Drug wars: the word from the trenches—drug abatements, an effective tool in the wars on narcotics, by H. Ferguson. POLICE CHIEF 57(5):46-49, May 1990

Drugs: consequences and confrontation. POLICE CHIEF 56(8):53+, August 1989

Drugs: goodbye, cocaine. ECONOMIST 316:28+, September 8, 1990

Dutch policy on the management of drug-related problems: an Anglo-Dutch debate. BRITISH JOURNAL OF ADDICTION 84(9):989-997, September 1989

Dutch soft-drug policy, by M. Dean. LANCET 2(8669):993-994, October 21, 1989

EC to reexamine cocaine precursors policy, by K. Sternberg. CHEMICAL WEEK 147:18, August 15, 1990

EC too soft on hard-drug chemicals: plans to impose strict regulations, by K. Sternberg. CHEMICAL WEEK 146:18, June 13, 1990

Ex-BINM head under Carter suggests ways of dealing with nation's drug problem. NARCOTICS CONTROL DIGEST 19(14):9, July 5, 1989

Experts plotting international war on money laundering. NARCOTICS CONTROL DIGEST 19(20):8, September 27, 1989

Faster access to controlled substances, by M. Trauernicht, et al. NURSING 20(2):32, February 1990

FBI needs more manpower. LAW AND ORDER 38(8):5, August 1990

Former DEA executive is in Bush's doghouse. NARCOTICS DEMAND REDUCTION DIGEST 2(4):10, April 1990

From Milken to the Mafia: a talk with Rudy Giuliani, who led a broad-based war on crime—interview. BARRONS 70:12-13+, November 26, 1990

Good clinical practice: necessity or fashion, by J. M. Keppel Gesselink. NEDERLANDS TIJDSCHRIFT VOOR GENEESKUNDE 133(43):2108-2111, October 28, 1989

Governing body report: IACP supports drug control strategy. POLICE CHIEF 56(10):16, October 1989

Halcion: the overdue truth, by M. N. Dukes. NEDERLANDS TIJDSCHRIFT VOOR GENEESKUNDE 133(44):2155-2157, November 4, 1989

Half-hearted war on drugs. NATURE 344(6268):689, April 19, 1990

History repeats itself: why do we need another drug intelligence center, by J. Warner. NARCOTICS CONTROL DIGEST 20(14):1+, July 4, 1990

Hospital pharmacy-based service for patient-controlled analgesia, by E. Y. Wong, et al. AMERICAN JOURNAL OF HOSPITAL PHARMACY 47(2):364-369, February 1990

Hospitals investigate suspected drug abuse, by J. Nemes. MODERN HEALTHCARE 19(39):34-35, September 29, 1989

IACP conference speakers focus on drug war issues. CRIME CONTROL DIGEST 23(42):1+, October 23, 1989

NARCOTICS CONTROL

Improved system for narcotic control in the operating room, by J. A. Johnson, et al. CANADIAN JOURNAL OF ANAESTHESIOLOGY 37(4 Pt 2):83, May 1990

In war on drugs, will technology work. DEFENSE SCIENCE 9(4):35, April 1990

Interdicting drugs in the big pond: Pacific Ocean, by W. J. Lahnemann. US NAVAL INSTITUTE. PROCEEDINGS 116(7):56-63, July 1990

International crime requires international punishment, by A. Spector. USA TODAY 118:28-31, May 1990

INTERPOL inaugurates new communications network. CRIME CONTROL DIGEST 23(47):2, November 27, 1989

Laundering drug money: whitewash— or crackdown? ECONOMIST 310:76, March 4, 1989

Law enforcement successes point for need for stronger demand reduction programs. NARCOTICS DEMAND REDUCTION DIGEST 1(5):1-3, October 1989

Little battles, by R. Malcolm. JAMA 263:90, January 5, 1990

Local drug enforcement, prosecutors and case attrition: theoretical perspectives for the drug war, by T. C. Castellano, et al. AMERICAN JOURNAL OF POLICE 9(1): 133-162, 1990

Long arm of radar: Pentagon warriors enlist the ionosphere against smugglers, by B. Van Voorst. TIME 135(19):77, May 7, 1990

Malodorous: narcotics vapor detector developed by Thermedics Inc., by B. Weber. NEW YORK TIMES MAGAZINE July 1, 1990, p. 42

Managing controlled drugs in the office. OHIO MEDICINE 86(4):315, April 1990

Managing drug dealers who swallow the evidence, by B. Marc, et al. BMJ 299(6707): 1082, October 28, 1989

Managing the war on drugs, by D. T. Dingle. BLACK ENTERPRISE 20:43-44+, July 1990

Mexico-United States: agreement on cooperation in combatting narcotics trafficking and drug dependency—done at Mexico City, February 23, 1989. INTERNA-TIONAL LEGAL MATERIALS 29:58-61, January 1990

More questions, few answers on drug war strategy. CRIME CONTROL DIGEST 23 (40):1+, October 9, 1989

Multidiciplinary approach to patient controlled analgesia, by K. A. Michael, et al. HOSPITAL PHARMACY 24(10):829-834, October 1989

NCEL's "stealth" balloon for war on drugs. SEA TECHNOLOGY 31:51, February 1990

New anti-drug program. NARCOTICS CONTROL DIGEST 19(20):6, September 27, 1989

New DEA chief is veteran prosecutor of big drug cases. CRIME CONTROL DIGEST 24(20):1+, May 21, 1990; also in NARCOTICS CONTROL DIGEST 20(11):1-2, May 23, 1990

New drug strategy continues expansion of justice system. CRIMINAL JUSTICE NEWSLETTER 21(3):5-6, February 1, 1990

New drug warriors: lasers, labs and coke-eating bugs, by G. Witkin. US NEWS AND WORLD REPORT 108:20-21, February 19, 1990

New frontier in the war on drugs: blocking Colombian cocaine traffic at Mexican-United States border, by G. Witkin, et al. US NEWS AND WORLD REPORT 109:52+, December 3, 1990

NIJ announces special initiative on drug program evaluation. CRIME CONTROL DIGEST 24(7):7, February 19, 1990; also in CORRECTIONS DIGEST 21(4):4-5, February 21, 1990 and JUVENILE JUSTICE DIGEST 18(4):5, February 21, 1990

Now, more than ever, where is the drug czar? LAW ENFORCEMENT NEWS 15(295): 8+, June 30, 1989

OCDETF program is making "significant inroad" against traffickers, Thornburgh says. NARCOTICS CONTROL DIGEST 19(17):1+, August 16, 1989

On the beat with Customs' Air Branch. SOLDIERS 45(8):18-19, August 1990

Opiate prescribing debate, by A. Johns. BRITISH JOURNAL OF PSYCHIATRY 156: 129, January 1990

Opiate prescribing debate, by R. F. Hill. BRITISH JOURNAL OF PSYCHIATRY 154: 888-889, June 1989

Perspective. LAW OFFICER'S BULLETIN 14(4):24, September 14, 1989

Pharmacy practice in a chemical-dependency treatment center, by T. J. Ives, et al. AMERICAN JOURNAL OF HOSPITAL PHARMACY 47(5):1080-1083, May 1990

Phoney war, by B. Lintner. FAR EASTERN ECONOMIC REVIEW 148:20-21, June 28, 1990

Playing the home field: a problem-oriented approach to drug control, by D. L Weisel. AMERICAN JOURNAL OF POLICE 9(1):75-95, 1990

Police-prosecutor drug enforcement teams: innovations in three jurisdictions, by J. Buchanan. AMERICAN JOURNAL OF POLICE 9(1):117-131, 1990

Politicians and scientists in the combat against drug abuse, by L. M. Gunne. DRUG AND ALCOHOL DEPENDENCE 25(2):241-244, April 1990

Prescribing issues grant report to the Board of Medical Examiners: II—Minnesota Medical Association. MINNESOTA MEDICINE 73(8):36-42, August 1990

Prescription drug abuse and control: 1990, by B. B. Wilford. HOSPITAL PHARMACY 25(8):796, August 1990

Prescription drug control and dispensing. MARYLAND MEDICAL JOURNAL 39(1): 47-52, January 1990

Problem-oriented policing and drug enforcement in Newport News, by W. P. Mitchell. PUBLIC MANAGEMENT 72:13-16, July 1990

Public support needed for victory against drugs, by W. S. Sessions. POLICE CHIEF 56(9):11, September 1989

Radiography of suspected drug smugglers, by J. O. Craig. CLINICAL RADIOLOGY 41(4):228, April 1990

Record drug busts fail to dent market. CRIME CONTROL DIGEST 24(7):7, February 19, 1990

Rehnquist: without more judges, war against drugs will be lost. CRIMINAL JUSTICE NEWSLETTER 21(2):6, January 16, 1990

Reporter's notebook: drugs—another wrong war; the president's war on drugs, by R. Scheer. PLAYBOY 37:51+, January 1990

Risky business: as its involvement in the drug war grows, the Pentagon outlines a plan to crush the cartels, by D. Waller. NEWSWEEK 116(3):16-19, July 16, 1990

Risky business: Pentagon plan for drug raid, by D. C. Waller. NEWSWEEK 116:16-19, July 16, 1990

Role of abuse liability testing in drug control procedures, by H. McClain, Jr., et al. NIDA RESEARCH MONOGRAPH SERIES 92:21-42, 1989

Rules of the game: United States drug war-Latin America, by J. Kawell. NACLA'S RE-PORT ON THE AMERICAS 23(6):9, April 1990

Scientists are essential for war on drugs, by R. Johnson. FASEB JOURNAL 3(12): 2333-2334, October 1989

Search of train roomette: sniff by narcotics dog—DC. SEARCH AND SEIZURE BUL-LETIN July 1989, p. 1

Search tactics come under new scrutiny. LAW AND ENFORCEMENT NEWS 16(306): 13+, January 15, 1990

Senator Biden offers President a strategy for fighting the war against drugs. NAR-COTICS CONTROL DIGEST August 2, 1989, pp. 8-12; also in CRIME CONTROL DIGEST 23(32):6-10, August 14, 1989

Senator Biden proposes high-tech war on drugs. CRIME CONTROL DIGEST 24(17): 9, April 30, 1990

Senator Grassley calls for drug war programming changes. NARCOTICS CONTROL DIGEST 20(1):5-6, January 3, 1990

Should mind-altering substances be legalized?, by L. L. Alexander. JOURNAL OF THE NATIONAL MEDICAL ASSOCIATION 82(1):15-16, January 1990

South can win the drug war. CRIME CONTROL DIGEST 24(30):10, July 30, 1990

Spend more on the drug war: GOP task force says. NARCOTICS CONTROL DIGEST 19(14):10, July 5, 1989

State, local officals ask for more resources in drug war. CRIME CONTROL DIGEST 23(39):9, October 2, 1989

States starting to target Rx drugs sold on the streets, by M. F. Conlan. DRUG TOPICS 134:44, August 6, 1990

Still flying blind in the war on drugs. SCIENCE 250:28, October 5, 1990

Sullivan releases drug report: disputes conflicting studies. NARCOTICS CONTROL DIGEST 20(12):7-8, June 6, 1990

Sweet sours on war. ABA JOURNAL 76:44-45, February 1990

Systems for verifying use of controlled substances in anesthesia, by G. B. Satterlee. AMERICAN JOURNAL OF HOSPITAL PHARMACY 46(12):2506-2508, December 1989

Taking back the property: front-line dispatches from the drug wars—discovering and eradicating drug problems, by C. Rategan. JOURNAL OF PROPERTY MANAGEMENT 55:30-33, May/June 1990

Technology: high-tech drugbusters—with an increasingly sophisticated arsenal, our anti-drug forces seek to stem a deadly tide, by A. Dane. POPULAR MECHANICS 167(2):49-52, February 1990

Tennessee state senator calls on congress to consider impact of National Drug Control Policy. CRIME CONTROL DIGEST 24(22):2-3, June 4, 1990; also in NARCOTICS CONTROL DIGEST 20(12):4-5, June 6, 1990

Thornburgh's views on drugs, by O. P. Burden. NARCOTICS CONTROL DIGEST 19(10):2-3, May 10, 1989

Time for a progressive attack on drugs, by M. Ridley-Thomas. CHRISTIANITY AND CRISIS 49:259-261, September 11, 989

Treasury inaugurates financial crime intelligence anti-drug network system. NARCOTICS CONTROL DIGEST 20(11):1-3, May 23, 1990; also in CRIME CONTROL DIGEST 24(21):2-3, May 28, 1990

Trojan horse: anti-communism and the war on drugs, by B. Bullington, et al. CONTEMPORARY DRUG PROBLEMS 14(1):39-55, 1990

Uncle Sam gets serious: a report from the front line, by C. E. Anderson. ABA JOURNAL 76:60-63, February 1990

United Nations report shows world drug situation deteriorating. CRIME CONTROL DIGEST 24(2):9-10, January 15, 1990

United Nations' role in fight against illicit drugs is under-valued. JOURNAL OF THE ADDICTION RESEARCH FOUNDATION 19(6):1, June 1, 1990

USCG shifts drug interdiction from Virginia to Florida. NARCOTICS CONTROL DIGEST 19(20):10, September 27, 1989

Veterinary medicines and the European Parliament, by K. Collins. VETERINARY RECORD 125(10):281, September 2, 1989

View from the nation's Capital: "off-label" uses of approved drugs—limits on physicians' prescribing behavior, by W. D. Appler, et al. JOURNAL OF CLINICAL PSYCHOPHARMACOLOGY 9(5):368-370, October 1989

Von Raab exists, gun blazing. LAW ENFORCEMENT NEWS 15(298):4, September 15, 1989

Washington parole officer initiates drug crackdown. CORRECTIONS DIGEST 20(22): 8, November 1, 1989

Why legislation won't work, by T. A. Constantine. POLICE CHIEF 57(5):3-39, 1990

Why we are losing the war on drugs, by J. Skirrow. CANADIAN SPEECHES 4(5):30-37, August/September 1990

"Zero tolerance" program operational at the border. NARCOTICS CONTROL DIGEST 19(17):7, August 16, 1989

Afghanistan
Fume of poppies: efforts to end opium cultivation hit new snags, by J. Jennings. FAR EASTERN ECONOMIC REVIEW 148:22-23, June 14, 1990

Bolivia
Dependence on drugs: unemployment, migration and an alternative path to development in Bolivia, by A. LaBrousse. INTERNATIONAL LABOUR REVIEW 129(3): 333-348, 1990

Burma
Dateline drug wars: Burma—the wrong enemy, by W. H. Overholt. FOREIGN POLICY 77:172-191, 1989/1990

International news: Myanmar—United Nations and United States officials watch burning, by A. Harman. LAW AND ORDER 38(4):9, April 1990

Canada
International news: Canada—drug war fought in air. LAW AND ORDER 38(8):6, August 1990

Tracking the dealers: Canada adds new zeal to its drug enforcement, by G. Allen. MACLEAN'S 103(36):42-43, September 3, 1990

War on drugs: address, May 8, 1990, by J. Skirrow. VITAL SPEECHES OF THE DAY 56:601-605, July 15, 1990

China
China toughens drug enforcement. ORGANIZED CRIME DIGEST 10(21):2, November 8, 1989

China trying to beef up drug enforcement efforts. NARCOTICS CONTROL DIGEST 19(21):7, October 11, 1989

Colombia
Ardean initiative: what's in the works?, by R. O'Connell. NARCOTICS CONTROL DIGEST 20(3):11-12, January 31,1990

Cocaine crossfire, by M. J. Duzan. NEW STATESMAN AND SOCIETY 3(124):10-12, October 26, 1990

Colombia: cocaine and friends—Patriotic Union party. ECONOMIST 314:38-39, March 31, 1990

Colombia in a state of seige as drug cartel bosses protest extradition pact with United States. NARCOTICS CONTROL DIGEST 19(18):1+, August 30, 1989

Colombia's president-elect seeks special drug courts. NARCOTICS CONTROL DIGEST 20(12):9-10, June 6, 1990

Dateline drug wars: Colombia—the wrong strategy, by B. M. Bagely. FOREIGN POLICY 77:154-171, 1989/1990

Gunship diplomacy: United States plans to patrol off Colombia raise alarms, by J. Bierman. MACLEAN'S 103:22, January 22, 1990

Muzziest of wars: the United States is becoming involved in the drugs wars on Colombia and Peru. ECONOMIST 315:15-16, May 5, 1990

Economics
15 communities get grants to fight drugs and alcohol. PUBLIC HEALTH REPORTS 105:323-324, May/June 1990

$40-million cut at OJJDP sought to help finance drug strategy. CRIMINAL JUSTICE NEWSLETTER 20(18):3-4, September 15, 1989

Bennett's draft anti-drug proposal would allocate up to $350 million to states, cities. CRIME CONTROL DIGEST 23(32):2, August 14, 1989

Biden introduces legislation to aid hard-hit drug areas. NARCOTICS CONTROL DIGEST 20(7):8-9, March 28, 1990; also in CRIME CONTROL DIGEST 24(13):1-2, April 2, 1990

Bradley calls federal aid "pittance" in war on drugs. CRIME CONTROL DIGEST 24(28): 2, July 16, 1990

Bush budget seeks $10.6B for drug control: includes $492M for state-local aid. NARCOTICS CONTROL DIGEST 20(3):1+, January 31, 1990; also in CRIME CONTROL DIGEST 24(5):1+, February 5, 1990 and CORRECTIONS DIGEST 21(3):1-4, February 7, 1990

Bush drug strategy seeks $350 million in state-local anti-drug grants for FY '90, by B. B. Bosarge. CORRECTIONS DIGEST 20(18):1+, September 6, 1989; also in CRIME CONTROL DIGEST 23(36):1+, September 11, 1989

Bush says he will back increased federal spending for waging the war on drugs. NARCOTICS CONTROL DIGEST 23(23):1-2, August 21, 1989

Bush team remains vague on funding for war on drugs. NARCOTICS CONTROL DIGEST 19(18):1+, August 30, 1989; also in CRIME CONTROL DIGEST 23(35):3-4, September 4, 1989

Bush's $10.6 billion strategy targets enforcement again, by P. Fessler. CONGRESSIONAL QUARTERLY WEEKLY REPORT 48:242-244, January 27, 1990

Communities push reinvestment of drug assets, by D. Baron. NEIGHBORHOOD WORKS 13(3):1, June 1990

Competition to be Cracktown, U.S.A.: federal aid to target cities. US NEWS AND WORLD REPORT 108:10-11, February 5, 1990

Comprehensive economic development: an alternative measure to reduce cocaine supply, by E. Morales. JOURNAL OF DRUG ISSUES 20:629-637, Fall 1990

Congress approves only $75 million in FY 1989 supplemental drug funds. CRIME CONTROL DIGEST 23(26):4, July 3, 1989; also in NARCOTICS CONTROL DIGEST 19(14):6, July 5, 1989

Democrats question financing. CRIME CONTROL DIGEST 23(36):10, September 11, 1989

Does the war on drugs need a new strategy: the United States government will spend more than $9 billion this year on the war against drugs, by M. H. Cooper. EDITORIAL RESEARCH REPORTS February 23, 1990, pp. 110-123

Drug enforcement economics, by J. A. Schnepper. USA TODAY 118:71, March 1990

Economic aspects of the illicit drug market and drug enforcement policies in the United Kingdom: summary of the report, by A. Wagstaff, et al. BRITISH JOURNAL OF ADDICTION 84(5):461-467, May 1989

Economic aspects of illicit drug markets and drug enforcement policies, by A. Wagstaff. BRITISH JOURNAL OF ADDICTION 84(10):1173-1182, October 1989

Entire criminal justice system must receive drug war funds. CRIME CONTROL DIGEST 23(50):1+, December 18, 1989

Federal drug enforcement grants: direct pass-through a recurring issue. POLICE CHIEF 57:22+, October 1990

Federal grants funding anti-drug efforts in 7 cities. CRIMINAL JUSTICE NEWSLETTER 20(16):6-7, August 15, 1989

Funding against crime and drugs: an intergovernmental partnership, by M. Box. JUVENILE JUSTICE DIGEST 18(8):1-5, April 18, 1990

Grants awarded to fight drugs. LAW AND ORDER 37(12):4, December 1989

Justice Department budget climbs, but FBI agents may be fewer. CRIMINAL JUSTICE NEWSLETTER 21(4):5-7, February 15, 1990

Law enforcement leaders praise drug strategy but question shortage of funds. CRIME CONTROL DIGEST 23(36):9-10, September 11, 1989

Local officials want to talk drug money with Bush. CRIME CONTROL DIGEST 24(2):9, January 15, 1990

Mayors and chiefs laud "first step" in drug war, but rap lack of funding. CRIME CONTROL DIGEST 23(38):1-3, September 25, 1989

Mayors call for direct federal funding, again. CRIME CONTROL DIGEST 24(4):1+, January 29, 1990; also in NARCOTICS CONTROL DIGEST 20(3):2-3, January 31, 1990 and JUVENILE JUSTICE DIGEST 18(3):2-3, February 7, 1990

Mayors meet with Thornburgh to ask for anti-drug funds. CRIME CONTROL DIGEST 24(10):4-5, March 12, 1990

Nearly $1 billion Ok'd for demand reduction in FY '90. NARCOTICS CONTROL DIGEST 1(7):6-7, December 1989

New federal drug plan may funnel more money to state, local law enforcement. CRIME CONTROL DIGEST 24(3):9-10, January 22, 1990

OJP program plan focuses on drugs, with most money targeted for formula grants. NARCOTICS CONTROL DIGEST 20(7):1+, March 28, 1990; also in TRAINING AIDS DIGEST 15(4):1+, April 1990

OMB director opposes state-local drug funds, trying to undercut Bennett. CRIME CONTROL DIGEST 23(49):1-3, December 11, 1989

Opportunities and strategies for grantmakers in the war on drugs, by J. S. Dolan, et al. HEALTH AFFAIRS 9(2):202-208, Summer 1990

Philly residents seek share of drug assets. LAW ENFORCEMENT NEWS 15(291):3+, April 30, 1989

President's new drug control strategy seeks $10.6 billion: focuses on state-local aid. CRIME CONTROL DIGEST 24(4):1-7, January 29, 1990; also in JUVENILE JUSTICE DIGEST 18(3):1+, February 7, 1990, and CORRECTIONS DIGEST 21(3): 1+, February 7, 1990

Representative Staggers says rural communities deserve more federal anti-drug money. CRIME CONTROL DIGEST 23(46):2, November 20, 1989

Representative Wise wants DOJ to improve drug funding policy. CRIME CONTROL DIGEST 24(17):2, April 30, 1990

Senate approves $450 million for drug enforcement grants. CRIMINAL JUSTICE NEWSLETTER 20(20):1-3, October 16, 1989

Senate debating plan to add $2.2 billion more to drug war. CRIME CONTROL DIGEST 23(37):4, September 18, 1989

Senate democrats aim to add $2.2 billion to Bush drug plan. CRIMINAL JUSTICE NEWSLETTER 20(18):3, September 15, 1989

Senate judiciary committee passes proposal to double state-local anti-drug money. CRIME CONTROL DIGEST 24(11):1+, March 19, 1990

Senate OK's bill to beef up aid to rural law enforcement. CRIME CONTROL DIGEST 23(41):1-2, October 16, 1989

Senate says "no" to supplemental drug funds. NARCOTICS CONTROL DIGEST 19(22):1+, June 7, 1989

Senate votes $1.7 billion for FY '89 drug spending. CRIME CONTROL DIGEST 23(32):1-2, August 14, 1989; also in NARCOTICS CONTROL DIGEST 19(17): 10, August 16, 1989

Senator Biden offers alternative drug strategy with more aid for state, local programs. CRIME CONTROL DIGEST 24(4):10-12, January 29, 1990; also in NARCOTICS CONTROL DIGEST 20(3):3-5, January 31, 1990

States receive more drug grants. LAW AND ORDER 38(5):4, March 1990

Thornburgh says DOJ will award over $395 million in anti-drug grants this year. CRIME CONTROL DIGEST 24(13):1+, April 2, 1990; also in CORRECTIONS DIGEST 21(7):2, April 4, 1990

Europe
Breaking the connection, by B. Zagaris, et al. SECURITY MANAGEMENT 34(6):46-52, June 1990

Policies on drugs in the new Europe, by R. D. Mann. BMJ 301(6743):122, July 14, 1990

Policies on drugs in the new Europe, by T. D. Griffin. BMJ 301(6745):238-239, July 28, 1990

Policing and prevention of drug traffick in Europe in post 1992, by D. A. Jordan. NATIONAL SECURITY March/April 1989, pp. 14-15

Great Britain
United Kingdom will reward tips on drug crimes, by H. McConnell. JOURNAL OF THE ADDICTION RESEARCH FOUNDATION 19(9):8, September 1, 1990

Italy
Italians seize pure heroin, crack coke smuggling ring. ORGANIZED CRIME DIGEST 11(5):3-4, March 14, 1990

Jamaica
Jamaica's P.M. explains anti-drug force concept to United States Senate panel, by R. O'Connell. NARCOTICS CONTROL DIGEST 19(23):1-3, November 8, 1989

United States national security and the war on drugs in Latin America. JOURNAL OF INTERAMERICAN STUDIES AND WORLD AFFAIRS 30(1):161-186, 1988

Laws

Bennett sends Hill a bill to implement anti-drug plan. NARCOTICS CONTROL DIGEST 19(20):1+, September 27, 1989; also in CRIME CONTROL DIGEST 23(39):4-5, October 2, 1989

Biden sponsors bill to control steroid abuse. NARCOTICS DEMAND REDUCTION DIGEST 1(7):3, December 1989

Bill introduced to create anti-drug command structure in defense department. NARCOTICS CONTROL DIGEST 19(11):8-9, May 24, 1989

Bill introduced to shoot down drug smuggling planes operating in Carribean basin. CORPORATE SECURITY DIGEST 4(31):7-8, August 6, 1990

Bills boost anti-drug efforts of schools, Andean nations: provisions of legislation. CONGRESSIONAL QUARTERLY WEKELY REPORT 47:3328-3329, December 2, 1989

Bush wins, Andean initiative: two narcotics bills falter, by P. Fessler. CONGRESSIONAL QUARTERLY WEEKLY REPORT 47:3246, November 25, 1989

Cartagena: call for war on three fronts. UN CHRONICLE 27:60, June 1990

Cartagena high, by C. Black. NATION 250:260-261, February 26, 1990

Colombia's next president wants a gentler drug war: C. Gaviria, by L. S. Robinson. US NEWS AND WORLD REPORT 109:27, July 30, 1990

Compatibility of cosmetics and toiletries, by L. Motitschke. ZEITSCHRIFT FUR HAUTKRANKHEITEN 64(12):1111-1117, December 15, 1989

Converts to curiosity: legalization of drugs. ECONOMIST 313:33, November 18, 1989

Douglas bill would force colleges to get tough on drugs. CORPORATE SECURITY DIGEST 3(41):10, October 16, 1989

"Drug scene": how will it be in the next century?, by J. Masur. BRITISH JOURNAL OF ADDICTION 85(1):9-11, January 1990

Drug user penalties: denial of eligibility for federal benefits, by L. Harris, et al. TRIAL 26(4):31-32+, April 1990

Drug wars: drug policy and the intellectuals, by W. J. Bennett. POLICE CHIEF 57(5): 30-33+, May 1990

Effect of controls on sedatives and hypnotics on their use for suicide, by D. Lester, et al. JOURNAL OF TOXICOLOGY: CLINICAL TOXICOLOGY 27(4-5):299-303, 1989

Failed "test case": Washington's drug war, by M. Miller. NEWSWEEK 115(5):28-29, January 29, 1990

Frontal asault on drugs: police chief R. Greenberg, by V. E. Smith. NEWSWEEK 115(18):26, April 30, 1990

Justice Department asks Supreme Court for wider overseas search powers. CRIME CONTROL DIGEST 23(47):6, November 27, 1989

Legal and ethical matters, by K. Palmer. PRACTITIONER 233(1466):500-501, April 8, 1989

Legislative and legal developments: federal. CRIMINAL JUSTICE 5(1):25-27, Spring 1990

Medical quackery in Rhode Island: the perspective of state and federal drug control agencies, by P. B. Fairfield, et al. RHODE ISLAND MEDICAL JOURNAL 73(4): 145-147, April 1990

Modeling the longitudinal impact of legal sanctions on narcotics use and property crime, by G. M. Speckart, et al. JOURNAL OF QUANTITATIVE CRIMINOLOGY 5(1):33-56, March 1989

New rules for physicians implement sample drug bill. TEXAS MEDICINE 86(6):58-59, June 1990

Senate approves sweeping anti-drug bill. NARCOTICS CONTROL DIGEST 19(21): 1+, October 11, 1989

Senate bill would improve counter-narcotics technology. NARCOTICS CONTROL DIGEST 20(11):10, May 23, 1990

Senate OK's drug funding beyond Bush's proposal. NARCOTICS CONTROL DIGEST 1(5):1+, October 1989

War on drugs—or the Constitution, by N. R. Sonnett. TRIAL 26(4):1-5+, April 1990

Legal Issues

Cocaine supplier: inventory search—Indiana. SEARCH AND SEIZURE BULLETIN December 1989, p. 3

Constructive possession: four large marijuana patches found in dense, wooded area: Alabama. NARCOTICS LAW BULLETIN August 1990, p. 2

Detention of parcel while police fetched drug-sniffing dog wasn't unreasonable. CRIMINAL LAW REPORTER: COURT DECISIONS 45(18):2321-2322, August 9, 1989

Detention of suitcase: canine sniff. ARREST LAW BULLETIN September 1989, pp. 2-3

Indictment unsealed against Southeast Asian drug lord. NARCOTICS CONTROL DIGEST 20(7):7, March 28, 1990; also in ORGANIZED CRIME DIGEST 11(6):6, March 28, 1990

Marijuana cultivation: probable cause—sufficiency of evidence; Oklahoma. NARCOTICS LAW BULLETIN June 1990, pp. 6-7

Marijuana spotted during seatbelt stop. SEARCH AND SEIZURE BULLETIN July 1989, p. 7

Phoenix-area drug users are offered a way out of felony raps. LAW ENFORCEMENT NEWS 15(294):1+, June 15, 1989

Physical examinations based on criminal process regulations: exemplified by suspected intracorporeal drug smuggle, by W. Weissauer, et al. CHIRURG 60 (Suppl)10:160-162, October 1989

Plain view: inadvertent discovery of marijuana plants in home—Washington. SEARCH AND SEIZURE BULLETIN June 1990, p. 5

Uncivil liberties: debating whether drug-war tactics are eroding constitutional rights, by T. Morganthau. NEWSWEEK 115(17):18-20, April 23, 1990

Malaysia
Noose for an American: Malaysia's stiff justice for possession of pot, by D. A. Kaplan. NEWSWEEK 116(16):42, October 15, 1990

Mexico
Mexican President calls for joint efforts to fight drugs. NARCOTICS CONTROL DIGEST 19(10):8-9, May 10, 1989

Mexican standoff: yacht Rusalka searched for drugs by Mexican drug agents, by P. A. Janssen. MOTOR BOATING AND SAILING 166:17, July 1990

The Netherlands
Criminal law and drugs control in the Netherlands: a kingdom going it along—paper presented at the Max-Planck-Institute for Foreign and International Criminal Law, Freiburg, June 29, 1987, by C. E. Ruter. ZEITSCHRIFT FUR DIE GASAMTE STRAFRECHTSWISSENSCHAFT 100(2):385-404, 1988

Dutch plan tighter export regulations. CHEMICAL INDUSTRY (5):114, March 5, 1990

War by other means: Dutch have abolished most drug-related crime, and may be reducing drug-taking too. ECONOMIST 314:50, February 10, 1990

Panama
Case against Noriega, by S. J. Hedges. US NEWS AND WORLD REPORT 108:18-20, January 15, 1990

Peru
America's deadly drug war in the jungle, by L. S. Robinson, et al. US NEWS AND WORLD REPORT 108:26, April 30, 1990

General and the cocaleros. ECONOMIST 313:40-41, December 9, 1989

In the cocaine war, the jungle is winning: Drug Enforcement Agency efforts, by M. Massing. NEW YORK TIMES MAGAZINE March 4, 1990, pp. 26-27+

Muzziest of wars: the United States is becoming involved in the drugs wars on Colombia and Peru. ECONOMIST 315:15-16, May 5, 1990

Peru's drug war: Vietnam-era methods won't net narco-guerrillas, by T. Arbuckle, et al. INTERNATIONAL DEFENSE REVIEW 23(4):373-374, April 1990

Political economy of cocaine production: an analysis of the Peruvian case, by E. Morales. LATIN AMERICAN PERSPECTIVES 17(4):91-109, Fall 1990

What are we doing in Peru?, by M. D. Wilde. CHRISTIAN CENTURY 107:724-725, August 8-15, 1990

The Philippines

Echo of gunshots: drug killings rattle Aquino government, by R. Tiglao, et al. FAR EASTERN ECONOMIC REVIEW 149:13, August 16, 1990

Quick and the dead: drug-busters get out after shootings, by J. McBeth. FAR EASTERN ECONOMIC REVIEW 149:19, August 9, 1990

South Africa

Regulation of medicines in South Africa: does it control costs, by P. I. Folb, et al. SOUTH AFRICAN MEDICAL JOURNAL 76(12):643-645, December 16, 1989

Soviet Union

Drug abuse control in the USSR, by A. M. Kotlyarov. POLICE CHIEF 57:22+, August 1990

International policing: drug abuse control in the USSR, by A. M. Kotlyarov. POLICE CHIEF 57(8):22-28, 1990

Thailand

Fix in the making: a drug warlord may be sacrificed to placate United States, by B. Lintner. FAR EASTERN ECONOMIC REVIEW 148:20-23, June 28, 1990

Hooked. ECONOMIST 315:35-36, May 29, 1990

Seeds of destruction: if you can afford a beer, you can afford heroin, by R. Tasker. FAR EASTERN ECONOMIC REVIEW 146:46+, November 23, 1989

Thailand's drug war: hooked. ECONOMIST 315:35-36, May 26, 1990

Trinidad

International news: Trinidad steps up drug fight, by A. Harman. LAW AND ORDER 37(9):6, September 1989

United States

Accentuate the positive: winning the war against drugs. ECONOMIST 314:28, February 24, 1990

Accuracy and time requirements of a bar-code inventory system for controlled substances, by K. C. Dinklage, et al. AMERICAN JOURNAL OF HOSPITAL PHARMACY 46(11):2304-2307, November 1989

Administration outlines details of national drug control strategy. CRIMINAL LAW REPORTER: COURT DECISIONS 46(18):1391, February 7, 1990

Arguments for a harmfulness tax, by L. Grinspoon, et al. JOURNAL OF DRUG ISSUES 20:599-604, Fall 1990

ASIS responds to drug czar on national drug control strategy. NARCOTICS CONTROL DIGEST 19(14):7-9, July 5, 1989

Atlantic Coast governors sign historic pact to expand cooperation in drug war. NARCOTICS CONTROL DIGEST August 2, 1989, pp. 1+; also in CRIME CONTROL DIGEST 23(31):6, August 7, 1989

Bennett warns Colorado about growth of drug labs. CRIME CONTROL DIGEST 24(17):3-4, April 30, 1990

Blowing smoke: an evaluation of marijuana eradication in Kentucky, by G. Potter, et al. AMERICAN JOURNAL OF POLICE 9(1):97-116, 1990

Border wars, by A. N. Sabrosky. JOURNAL OF SOCIAL, POLITICAL AND ECONOMIC STUDIES 14:433-442, Winter 1989

Bundle of peaceful compromises, by A. S. Trebach. JOURNAL OF DRUG ISSUES 20:515-531, Fall 1990

Bush administration unveils plan to combat drugs. CRIMINAL LAW REPORTER: COURT DECISIONS 45(23):2434-2436, September 13, 1989

Bush scores diplomatic gain at summit in Colombia, by P. Fessler. CONGRESSIONAL QUARTERLY WEEKLY REPORT 48:537-538, February 17, 1990

Can the borders be sealed?, by P. Reuter. PUBLIC INTEREST (92):51-65, 1988

Cocaine crossfire, by M. J. Duzan. NEW STATESMAN AND SOCIETY 3(124):10-12, October 26, 1990

Combating America's drug problem. FBI LAW ENFORCEMENT BULLETIN 59:2-32, April 1990

Cooperation with interdiction in the eye of the beholder, by P. Fessler. CONGRESSIONAL QUARTERLY WEEKLY REPORT 48:686, March 3, 1990

Crack in context: politics and media in the making of a drug scare, by C. Reinarman, et al. CONTEMPORARY DRUG PROBLEMS 16(4):535-577, Winter 1989

Decriminalizing drug use, by P. J. Imperato. JOURNAL OF COMMUNITY HEALTH 15:225-226, August 1990

Developing strategies in the war on drugs, by C. A. Gruber. POLICE CHIEF 57:8, March 1990

Drug wars in the United States, by R. J. Epstein. BMJ 299(6710):1275-1276, November 18, 1989

Drug wars: the word from the trenches—patrol NET in Suffolk County, by K. Rau. POLICE CHIEF 57(5):42-43, May 1990

Drugs and the warlike administration of justice, by E. H. Czajkoski. JOURNAL OF DRUG ISSUES 20:125-129, Winter 1990

Drugs: follow the money—money laundering investigation procedures. ECONOMIST 313:29, October 21, 1989

Drugs in America: special report. HUMAN RIGHTS 17:14-29+, Summer 1990

Essential factors of a rational policy on intoxicant use, by N. E. Zinberg, et al. JOURNAL OF DRUG ISSUES 20:619-627, Fall 1990

FBI's continuing war against drugs, by W. S. Sessions. POLICE CHIEF 57(5):16, May 1990

Fee forfeiture: apocalypse now or business as usual, by B. Tarlow. TRIAL 26:44-50, April 1990

Fight evil, forget freedom: our Bill of Rights is becoming a pointless piece of paper in the war against drugs, by E. M. Kennedy. HUMAN RIGHTS 17:36-37+, Fall/Winter 1990

Fighting the drug wars: rhetoric and reality, by S. G. Koven. PUBLIC ADMINISTRATION REVIEW 49:580-583, November/December 1989

Fix in the making: a drug warlord may be sacrificed to placate United States, by B. Lintner. FAR EASTERN ECONOMIC REVIEW 148:20-23, June 28, 1990

Fourth Amendment: using the drug courier profile to fight the war on drugs: United States v. Sokolow, 109 S. Ct. 1581: 1989, by S. K. Bernstein. JOURNAL OF CRIMINAL LAW AND CRIMINOLGOY 80:996-1017, Winter 1990

Getting their hands dirty: American-Burmese anti-narcotics program, by S. Awanohara. FAR EASTERN ECONOMIC REVIEW 148:26-27, June 28, 1990

Governors from four states sign anti-drug pact. NARCOTICS CONTROL DIGEST 20(7):10, March 28, 1990

Great unveiling: hints of Bennett's anti-drug plan suggest more emphasis on street-level enforcement. LAW ENFORCEMENT NEWS 15(298):1+, September 15, 1989

High noon in Alexandria: how we ran the crack dealers out of public housing, by J. P. Moran, Jr. POLICY REVIEW (53):78-81, Summer 1990

IACP board urges Bush to strengthen role of drug czar. NARCOTICS CONTROL DIGEST August 2, 1989, pp. 7-8; also in CRIME CONTROL DIGEST 23(31):1+, August 7, 1989

IACP urges President to give stronger powers to "drug czar." CRIMINAL JUSTICE NEWSLETTER 20(16):2-3, August 15, 1989

Implications of United States border and immigration incidents for federal and state law enforcement agencies, by T. W. Foster. AMERICAN JOURNAL OF POLICE 8(2):93-122, 1989

League of cities official says Bush drug plan will hurt state, local governments. CRIME CONTROL DIGEST 23(37):9, September 18, 1989

Losing battle: despite billions of dollars and more than a million arrests, the United States war on drugs has barely dented addiction or violent crime, by E. Shannon. TIME 136(24):36-40, December 3, 1990

Marijuana crop: moonshine again. ECONOMIST 317:25-26, October 20, 1990

Marijuana seized in open field: helicopter surveillance—Oregon. SEARCH AND SEIZURE BULLETIN September 1989, p. 8

Michigan's triplicate prescription program now in effect, by L. D. Wagenknecht. MICHI-GAN MEDICINE 88(8):32-33, August 1989

Morris joining Bennett's staff. NARCOTICS CONTROL DIGEST August 2, 1989, p. 2

Narcotics committee meets with Bush, Bennett: Representative Rangel pleased with progress. NARCOTICS CONTROL DIGEST 19(10):1+, May 10, 1989

Narcotics: the problem and the solution, by E. J. Mishan. POLITICAL QUARTERLY 61:441-462, October/December 1990

Narcotics trafficking and United States law enforcement policies: bibliography-in-brief, 1984-1986, by E. Sutterlin. JOURNAL OF INTERAMERICAN STUDIES AND WORLD AFFAIRS 30(2-3):213-218, 1988

National town meeting: expert panel tackles drug issue. CORRECTIONS TODAY 52:60-61, October 1990

Noriega's trial: smokescreen. ECONOMIST 314:28-29, January 13, 1990

Oklahoma opts for black box instead of triplicate forms to send data on Schedule II Rxs electronically to Bureau of Narcotics and Dangerous Drugs Control, by K. Gannon. DRUG TOPICS 134:66-67, July 23, 1990

Other war: some thoughts for Bob Martinez, America's new head of drug policy. ECONOMIST 317:13-14, December 8, 1990

Pennsylvania training electric utility workers to look for illegal drug laboratories. COR-PORATE SECURITY DIGEST 3(50):8-9, December 18, 1989

President Bush details drug strategy. CORRECTIONS TODAY 52(2):207+, April 1990

Problem of drugs is nothing new in America: commentary, by D. F. Musto. HUMAN RIGHTS 17, Summer 1990

Special focus: drug wars. POLICE CHIEF 57:30-33+, May 1990

Undercover negotiating: flashroll management—undercover narcotics officers and the purchase money, by G. E. Wade. POLICE CHIEF 57:48-49+, November 1990

United States Attorney General Thornburgh urges incarceration alternatives, by D. Thornburgh. CORRECTIONS TODAY 52:132+, August 1990

United States claims "clear signs of progress" on drugs, by H. McConnell. JOURNAL OF THE ADDICTION RESEARCH FOUNDATION 19(10):3, October 1, 1990

United States customs service spearheads the drug war, by R. H. Williams. SIGNAL 45(4):52-54, December 1990

United States customs still working on smuggling problem guidelines. CORPORATE SECURITY DIGEST 3(47):6, November 27, 1989

United States drug interdiction programme, by P. Edgerton. MILITARY TECHNOLOGY 14(10):133+, October 1990

United States should modernize its aviation information systems to stop crime: need of FAA for system to track known terrorists and stop drug smuggling, by R. H. Jones. AVIATION WEEK AND SPACE TECHNOLOGY 132:61, April 2, 1990

United States war on drugs claims medical victims, too, by K. Kelley. IN THESE TIMES 14(35):6, September 1, 1990

United States west leaps backward to curb drug dealers. CRIME CONTROL DIGEST 24(15):7, April 16, 1990

War on drugs: American democracy under assault, by M. J. Blachman, et al. WORLD POLICY JOURNAL 7:135-163, Winter 1989/1990

War on drugs: prospects for success, by J. D. Douglass. JOURNAL OF SOCIAL, POLITICAL AND ECONOMIC STUDIES 15:43-57, Spring 1990

Why aren't NASDEA, IACP Narcotics Committee helping to design United States drug strategy?, by B. S. Allsbrok. CRIME CONTROL DIGEST 23(40):2-4, October 9, 1989; also in NARCOTICS CONTROL DIGEST 19(21):2-4, October 11, 1989

NATIONAL COLLEGIATE ATHLETIC ASSOCIATION *see*: NCAA

NATIONAL FOOTBALL LEAGUE *see*: NFL

NATIONAL INSTITUTE OF JUSTICE *see*: NIJ

NATIONAL INSTITUTE ON DRUG ABUSE *see*: NIDA

NCAA   (NATIONAL COLLEGIATE ATHLETIC ASSOCIATION)
NCAA drug program: out of bounds but still in play, by J. M. Evans, et al. JOURNAL OF LAW AND EDUCATION 19(2):161-191, Spring 1990

NCAA

NCAA tightens drug rules for collegiate gridders. JET 77:48, February 12, 1990

NEEDLE EXCHANGE/FREE NEEDLE PROGRAMS
Bridge to treatment: the needle exchange pilot program in New York City, by S. C. Joseph. AIDS EDUCATION AND PREVENTION 1(4):340-345, Winter 1989

Effect of a needle and syringe exchange on a methadone maintenance unit, by A. Wodak, et al. BRITISH JOURNAL OF ADDICTION 85(11):1445-1450, 1990

Genesis of New York City's experimental needle exchange program: getting a denigrated group on the government agenda, by C. L. Gillman. NIDA RESEARCH MONOGRAPH SERIES 95:419-420, 1989

Help-seeking and referrals in a needle exchange: a comprehensive service to injecting drug users, by A. M. Carvell, et al. BRITISH JOURNAL OF ADDICTION 85(2): 235-240, February 1990

How to "sell" a needle exchange program, by J. Blatherwick. CANADIAN JOURNAL OF PUBLIC HEALTH 80(Suppl)1:26-27, May/June 1989

Impact of the needle and syringe-exchange programme in Amsterdam on injecting risk behaviour, by C. Hartgers, et al. AIDS 3(9):571-576, September 1989

National survey of syringe exchange schemes in England, by G. V. Stimson, et al. BRITISH JOURNAL OF ADDICTION 85(11):1433-1443, 1990

Needles and syringes for IVDUs, by R. M. Mullins. MEDICAL JOURNAL OF AUSTRALIA 152(12):672, June 18, 1990

New York City AIDS needle policy draws activists' fire, by B. Day. GUARDIAN 42(30):9, May 23, 1990

Preventing the spread of HIV injecting drug users: the experience of syringe-exchange schemes in England and Scotland, by G. Stimson, et al. NIDA RESEARCH MONOGRAPH SERIES 90:302-310, 1988

Prevention of AIDS transmission by syringes and needles in France and Africa, by J. C. Petithory, et al. BULLETIN DE l'ACADEMIE NATIONALE DE MEDECINE 173(4):415-419, April 1989

Provision of injecting equipment to drug users, by D. Goldberg. JOURNAL OF THE ROYAL COLLEGE OF GENERAL PRACTITIONERS 38(317):572, December 1988

Sunday in the park: syringe distribution program in Zurich, by L. Shavelson. MOTHER JONES 15:36-38, February/March 1990

Syringe exchange schemes: a report and some commentaries. BRITISH JOURNAL OF ADDICTION 84(11):1283-1290, November 1989

Vancouver's needle exchange program, by J. Bardsley, et al. CANADIAN JOURNAL OF PUBLIC HEALTH 81(1):39-45, January/February 1990

Women and AIDS: too little, too late, by N. Bell. HYPATIA 4(3):3, Fall 1989

NFL (NATIONAL FOOTBALL LEAGUE)

NFL battles steroid use, by D. L. Black. PHYSICIAN AND SPORTSMEDICINE 18:25-26, August 1990

NFL creates tempest in a pee pot, by S. Muwakkil. IN THESE TIMES 14(13):6, February 14, 1990

NFL drug problem faces allegations of racism. JET 77:46+, February 12, 1990

Testing your rights: random drug testing—views of NFL players, by W. Ladson. SPORT 81:16, April 1990

We can clean in up: Atlanta Falcon Bill Fralic is making it his business to rid the NFL of steroids, by P. King. SPORTS ILLUSTRATED 73(2):34-36+, July 9, 1990

NICOTINE

Addiction Research Unit of the Institute of Psychiatry, University of London: II—the work of the unit's smoking section, by M. A. Russell. BRITISH JOURNAL OF ADDICTION 84(8):853-863, August 1989

Adolescents' first and most recent use situations of smokeless tobacco and cigarettes: similarities and differences, by G. Hahn, et al. ADDICTIVE BEHAVIORS 15(5):439-448, 1990

Affective regulation, nicotine addiction, and smoking cessation, by T. P. Carmody. JOURNAL OF PSYCHOACTIVE DRUGS 21(3):331-342, July/September 1989

Alcohol and tobacco as public health challenges in a democracy, by D. E. Beauchamp. BRITISH JOURNAL OF ADDICTION 85(2):251-254, February 1990

Analysis of the addiction liability of nicotine, by A. C. Collins. ADVANCES IN ALCOHOL AND SUBSTANCE ABUSE 9(1-2):83-101, Spring 1990

Behavioral and physiologic aspects of nicotine dependence: the role of nicotine dose, by J. E. Henningfield, et al. PROGRESS IN BRAIN RESEARCH 79:303-312, 1989

Beneficial effects of treatment of nicotine dependence during an inpatient substance abuse treatment program, by A. M. Joseph, et al. JAMA 263(22):3043-3046, June 13, 1990

Caffeine and cigarette smoking: behavioral, cardiovascular, and metabolic interactions, by C. R. Brown, et al. PHARMACOLOGY, BIOCHEMISTRY AND BEHAVIOR 34(3):565-570, November 1989

Can genetic constitution affect the "objective" diagnosis of nicotine dependence?, by J. E. Henningfield. AMERICAN JOURNAL OF PUBLIC HEALTH 80(9):1040-1041, September 1990

Cigarette smoking, nicotine dependence, and treatment, by K. L. Sees. WESTERN JOURNAL OF MEDICINE 152(5):578-584, May 1990

Cigarettes and marijuana: are there measurable long-term neurobehavioral teratogenic effects?, by P. A. Fried. NEUROTOXICOLOGY 10(3):577-583, Fall 1989

Drug treatment of nicotine dependence, by M. Fellhauer. MEDIZINISCHE MONATS-SCHRIFT FUR PHARMAZEUTEN 13(6):184-186, June 1990

Effect of parental smoking classification on the association between parental and adolescent smoking, by K. E. Bauman, et al. ADDICTIVE BEHAVIORS 15(5):413-422, 1990

Fight against tobacco addiction moving into international arena, by M. F. Goldsmith. JAMA 263(22):2989-2990, June 13, 1990

Human aggressive and non-aggressive responding during acute tobacco abstinence, by D. R. Cherek, et al. NIDA RESEARCH MONOGRAPH SERIES 95:435-436, 1989

Influence of behavior analysis on the Surgeon General's Report: the health consequences of smoking—nicotine addiction, by J. E. Henningfield, et al. BEHAVIOR ANALYST 12(1):99-101, Spring 1989

Information on nicotine abuse, by J. C. Moore, Jr. PEDIATRICS 86(2):329-330, August 1990

Ingestion of cigarettes: risks and management, by E. C. Joekes, et al. TIJDSCHRIFT VOOR KINDERGENEESKUNDE 57(4):149-150, August 1989

Nicotine abstinence effects, by J. R. Hughes. NIDA RESEARCH MONOGRAPH SERIES 95:123, 1989

Nicotine abuse by elementary school children: a comparison of urban versus rural children and correlates associated with use, by J. P. Martin, et al. NORTH CAROLINA MEDICAL JOURNAL 51(7):328-330, July 1990

Nicotine addiction, by J. Slade. HAWAII MEDICAL JOURNAL 48(11):485-486+, November 1989

Nicotine addiction trap: a 40-year sentence for four cigarettes, by M. A. Russell. BRITISH JOURNAL OF ADDICTION 85(2):293-300, February 1990

Nicotine: an addictive substance or a therapeutic agent?, by D. M. Warburton. PROGRESS IN DRUG RESEARCH 33:9-41, 1989

Nicotine dependence and alcoholism epidemiology and treatment, by J. K. Bobo. JOURNAL OF PSYCHOACTIVE DRUGS 21(3):323-329, July/September 1989

Nicotine dependence and tolerance in man: pharmacokinetic and pharmacodynamic investigations, by N. L. Benowitz, et al. PROGRESS IN BRAIN RESEARCH 79:279-287, 1989

No smoking: punitive words for addicted patients, by T. Droste. HOSPITALS 63(23):54, December 5, 1989

Offers treatment plan for "the most dangerous drug," by C. G. Smith. VIRGINIA MEDICINE 116(11):451, November 1989

Paced puffing as a method for administering fixed doses of nicotine, by C. S. Pomerleau, et al. ADDICTIVE BEHAVIORS 14(5):571-575, 1989

Pack size, reported cigarette smoking rates, and the heaviness of smoking, by L. T. Kozlowski, et al. CANADIAN JOURNAL OF PUBLIC HEALTH 80(4):266-270, July/August 1989

Physical dependence and attributions of addiction among cigarette smokers, by D. S. Martin. ADDICTIVE BEHAVIORS 15(1):69-72, 1990

Smoking history, instructions and the effects of nicotine: two pilot studies, by J. R. Hughes, et al. PHARMACOLOGY, BIOCHEMISTRY AND BEHAVIOR 34(1):149-155, September 1989

Time for cigarette reclassfication, by G. B. Gori. NATURE 344(6269):821, April 26, 1990

Tobacco ingestions in children, by W. A. Bonadio, et al. CLINICAL PEDIATRICS 28(12):592-593, December 1989

Tobacco: the neglected addiction, by E. B. Bogolub. SOCIAL WORK 35(1):77-78, January 1990

Total particulate matter and nicotine in Indian bidis and cigarettes: a comparative study of standard machine estimates and exposure levels in smokers in Bombay, by S. S. Pakhale, et al. INDIAN JOURNAL OF CANCER 26(4):227-232, December 1989

Typology and correlates of smokeless tobacco use, by W. T. Riley, et al. JOURNAL OF ADOLESCENT HEALTH CARE 10(5):357-362, September 1989

Understanding nicotine addiction and physical withdrawal process, by J. E. Henningfield. JOURNAL OF THE AMERICAN DENTAL ASSOCIATION (Suppl):2-6, January 1990

Use of smokeless tobacco in a group of professional baseball players, by K. M. Cummings, et al. JOURNAL OF BEHAVIORAL MEDICINE 12(6):559-567, December 1989

Worldwide smoking epidemic: tobacco trade, use, and control: Council on Scientific Affairs. JAMA 263(24):3312-3318, June 27, 1990

Complications

Apnea and seizures caused by nicotine ingestion, by J. Singer, et al. PEDIATRIC EMERGENCY CARE 6(2):135-137, June 1990

Occurrence of oral mucosal lesions: the influence of tobacco habits and an estimate of treatment time in an adult Swedish population, by L. Salonen, et al. JOURNAL OF ORAL PATHOLOGY AND MEDICINE 19(4):170-176, April 1990

Relation between ischemic heart disease and tobacco smoking, by J. Kuch, et al. WIADOMSCI LEKARSKIE 42(8):489-492, April 30, 1989

Site predilection of oral cancer and its correlation with chewing and smoking habit: a study of 103 cases, by F. Ahmed, et al. BANGLADESH MEDICAL RESEARCH COUNCIL BULLETIN 16(1):17-25, June 1990

Study of patients with diabetes mellitus, type 1, and end-stage renal failure: tobacco usage may increase risk of nephropathy and death, by B. G. Stegmayr. JOURNAL OF INTERNAL MEDICINE 228(2):121-124, August 1990

Tobacco use in Alzheimer's disease, by L. Barclay, et al. PROGRESS IN CLINICAL AND BIOLOGICAL RESEARCH 317:189-194, 1989

Research

Acute exposure to cigarette smoke induces airway hyperresponsiveness without airway inflammation in guinea pigs: dose-response characteristics, by M. Nishikawa, et al. AMERICAN REVIEW OF RESPIRATORY DISEASE 142(1):177-183, July 1990

Alcohol or tobacco research versus alcohol and tobacco research, by L. C. Sobell, et al. BRITISH JOURNAL OF ADDICTION 85(2):263-269, February 1990

Analysis of cytogenetic effects in bone-marrow cells of rats subchronically exposed to smoke from cigarettes which burn or only heat tobacco, by C. K. Lee, et al. MUTATION RESEARCH 240(4):251-257, April 1990

Are smokers trying to stop and smokers not trying to stop the same experimental model, by D. P. Sachs, et al. NIDA RESEARCH MONOGRAPH SERIES 95:366-367, 1989

Aversion instead of preference learning indicated by nicotine place conditioning in rats, by D. E. Jorenby, et al. PSYCHOPHARMACOLOGY 101(4):533-538, 1990

Behavioral effects in the mouse during and following withdrawal from ethanol ingestion and/or nicotine administration, by E. S. Onaivi, et al. DRUG AND ALCOHOL DEPENDENCE 24(3):205-211, December 1989

Comparison of 3 methods of exposing rats to cigarette smoke, by J. L. Mauderly, et al. EXPERIMENTAL PATHOLOGY 37(1-4):194-197, 1989

Constituents of tobacco smoke and their biological effects, by J. Kagawa, et al. KOKYU TO JUNKAN 38(1):11-16, January 1990

Effect of dose on nicotine's reinforcing, withdrawal-suppression and self-reported effects, by J. R. Hughes, et al. JOURNAL OF PHARMACOLOGY AND EXPERIMENTAL THERAPEUTICS 252(3):1175-1183, March 1990

Effect of dose on nicotine's withdrawal-suppressing, adverse and discriminative stimulus effects in humans, by J. R. Huges, et al. NIDA RESEARCH MONOGRAPH SERIES 95:428, 1989

Effect of nicotine and tobacco-specific nitrosamines on the metabolism of N'-nitrosonornicotine and 4-[methylnitrosamino]-1-[3-pyridyl]-1-butanone by rat oral tissue, by S. E. Murphy, et al. CARCINOGENESIS 11(9):1663-1664, September 1990

Effect of smoking on the hypophyseo-adrenal axis, by M. Sellini, et al. MEDICINA 9(2):194-196, April/June 1989

Effects of a 24-hour fast on cigarette smoking in humans, by J. P. Zacny, et al. BRITISH JOURNAL OF ADDICTION 85(4):555-560, 1990

Effects of low-yield cigarettes on electroencephalographic dynamics, by V. J. Knott. NEUROPSYCHOBIOLOGY 21(4):216-222, 1989

Effects of nicotine and cigarette smoke extracts on plasma level of complement C3a and C5a, thromboxane B2 and 6-keto PGF1 alpha in rabbits, by Y. Kirhira, et al. NIPPON KYOBU SHIKKAN GAKKAI ZASSHI 27(12):1495-1501, December 1989

Effects of smoking on the mood, cardiovascular and adrenergic reactivity of heavy and light smokers in a non-stressful environment, by P. M. Cincirpini, et al. BIOLOGICAL PSYCHIATRY 29(3):273-289, December 1989

Ethanol-nicotine interactions in long-sleep and short-sleep mice, by C. M. de Fiebre, et al. ALCOHOL 7(3):249-257, May/June 1990

Interpretative review of smokeless tobacco research in the United States: part II, by E. D. Glover, et al. JOURNAL OF DRUG EDUCATION 19(1):1-19, 1989

Liquid membrane electrodes for the selective determination of nicotine in cigarette smoke, by S. S. Hassan, et al. ANALYST 114(9):1033-1037, September 1989

Measurements of certain environmental tobacco smoke components on long-range flights, by J. W. Drake, et al. AVIATION, SPACE AND ENVIRONMENTAL MEDICINE 61(6):531-542, June 1990

Mechanism of the mutagenic-carcinogenic action of cigarette smoke at the pulmonary level: enzymatic induction, activation and detoxification, by G. Scassellati Sforzoloini, et al. ANNALI DI IGIENE 1(1-2):295-311, January/April 1989

Metabolic effects of nicotine after consumption of a meal in smokers and nonsmokers, by K. A. Perkins, et al. AMERICAN JOURNAL OF CLINICAL NUTRITION 52(2):228-233, August 1990

Metabolic effects of nicotine in smokers and non-smokers, by K. A. Perkins, et al. NIDA RESEARCH MONOGRAPH SERIES 95:469-470, 1989

Model of cigarette smoke particle deposition, by W. J. Muller, et al. AMERICAN INDUSTRIAL HYGIENE ASSOCIATION JOURNAL 51(5):245-256, May 1990

Neuropsychopharmacology of smoking, by D. M. Warburton. YAKUBUTSU SEISHIN KODO 992):245-256, June 1989

Nicotine-induced tolerance and dependence in rats and mice: studies involving schedule-controlled behavior, by J. A. Rosecrans, et al. PROGRESS IN BRAIN RESEARCH 79:239-248, 1989

Preference among research cigarettes with varying nicotine yields, by J. J. Boren, et al. PHARMACOLOGY, BIOCHEMISTRY AND BEHAVIOR 36(1):191-193, May 1990

Smoking research: basic research, intervention, prevention, and new trends, by L. H. Epstein, et al. HEALTH PSYCHOLOGY 8(6):705-712, 1989

Spontaneous EEG changes during tobacco abstinence and nicotine substitution in human volunteers, by W. B. Pickworth, et al. JOURNAL OF PHARMACOLOGY AND EXPERIMENTAL THERAPEUTICS 251(3):976-982, December 1989

Tobacco use among adolescents: directions for research, by E. W. Bonaguro, et al. AMERICAN JOURNAL OF HEALTH PROMOTION 4(1):37-41+, September/ October 1989

Tobacco use research program at Oregon Research Institute, by E. Lichtenstein, et al. BRITISH JOURNAL OF ADDICTION 85(6):715-724, June 1990

Withdrawal

Effect of tobacco withdrawal on sustained attention, by J. R. Hughes, et al. ADDIC-TIVE BEHAVIORS 14(5):577-580, 1989

Evidence for a behavioral deficit during withdrawal from chronic nicotine treatment, by W. A. Corrigall, et al. PHARMACOLOGY, BIOCHEMISTRY AND BEHAVIOR 33(3): 559-562, July 1989

Intravenous nicotine replacement suppresses nicotine intake from cigarette smoking, by N. L. Benowitz, et al. JOURNAL OF PHARMACOLOGY AND EXPERIMENTAL THERAPEUTICS 254(3):1000-1005, September 1990

Mania after nicotine withdrawal, by S. B. Cohen. AMERICAN JOURNAL OF PSYCHI-ATRY 147(9):1254-1255, September 1990

Severe mania following abrupt nicotine withdrawal, by F. Benazzi. AMERICAN JOUR-NAL OF PSYCHIATRY 146(12):1641, December 1989

Severity of withdrawal symptoms as a predictor of outcome of an attempt to quit smoking, by R. J. West, et al. PSYCHOLOGICAL MEDICINE 19(4):981-985, November 1989

Transdermal nicotine facilitaties smoking cessation, by J. E. Rose, et al. CLINICAL PHARMACOLOGY AND THERAPEUTICS 47(3):323-330, March 1990

Use of transdermal nicotine in smoking cessation, by P. Muller, et al. LUNG 168 (Suppl):445-453, 1990

NICOTINE CHEWING GUM

Coming off long-term nicotine gum, by R. Bitoun. LANCET 2(8672):1164, November 11, 1989

Competition-cooperation in worksite smoking cessation using nicotine gum, by M. M. Maheu, et al. PREVENTIVE MEDICINE 18(6):867-876, November 1989

Dependence on nicotine in chewing gum, by W. Poser. DEUTSCHE MEDIZINISCHE WOCHENSCHRIFT 114(42):1633, October 20, 1989

Development of a psychologically founded program for smoking cessation with adju-vant use of nicotine-containing chewing gum, by E. Meier-Lammermann, et al. PNEUMOLOGIE 44(Suppl)1:116-117, February 1990

NICOTINE CHEWING GUM

Effect of instructions and nicotine on smoking cessation, withdrawal symptoms and self-administration of nicotine gum, by J. R. Hughes, et al. PSYCHOPHARMA-COLOGY 99(4):486-491, December 1989

Effects of nicotine gum on psychomotor performance in smokers and non-smokers, by I. Hindmarch, et al. PSYCHOPHARMACOLOGY 100(4):535-541, 1990

Evaluation of a treatment approach combining nicotine gum with self-guided behavioral treatments for smoking relapse prevention, by J. D. Killen, et al. JOURNAL OF CONSULTING AND CLINICAL PSYCHOLOGY 58(1):85-92, February 1990

Side effects of nicotine chewing gum, by M. L. Lopez Gonzalez, et al. MEDICINA CLINICA 94(8):319, March 3, 1990

Smoking cessation using in smokers with chronic diseases, by J. Kozak. CASOPIS LEKARU CESKYCH 129(1):26-29, January 5, 1990

Smoking cessation with nicotine gum, by P. Scholdborg. TIDSSKRIFT FOR DEN NORSKE LAEGEFORENING 110(10):1199-1201, 1990

NIDA (NATIONAL INSTITUTE ON DRUG ABUSE)

National Institute on Drug Abuse may join in anabolic steroid research, by V. S. Cowart. JAMA 261:1855-1856, April 7, 1989

NIDA, HRSA join forces in studies of AIDS risk behavior by i.v. drug users, by P. Delaney. PUBLIC HEALTH REPORTS 105(3):323, May/June 1990

NIDA (National Institute on Drug Abuse) stops lab's drug tests. JOURNAL OF THE ADDICTION RESEARCH FOUNDATION 19(12):5, December 1, 1990

NIDA's Medication Development Program: 1989, by C. R. Schuster, et al. NIDA RESEARCH MONOGRAPH SERIES 95:64-73, 1989

NIFEDIPINE

Nifedipine overdose accompanied by ethanol intoxication in a patient with congenital heart disease, by R. D. Welch, et al. JOURNAL OF EMERGENCY MEDICINE 8(2): 169-172, March/April 1990

NIJ (NATIONAL INSTITUTE OF JUSTICE)

Federal file: National Institute of Justice. LAW ENFORCEMENT NEWS 16(313):3, April 30, 1990

NITRITE

Nitrite inhalant abuse and AIDS-related Kaposi's sarcoma, by H. W. Haverkos. JOURNAL OF THE ACQUIRED IMMUNE DEFICIENCY SYNDROME 3(Suppl)1:47-50, 1990

Search for cofactors in AIDS: including an analysis of the association of nitrite inhalant abuse and Kaposi's sarcoma, by H. W. Haverkos. PROGRESS IN CLINICAL AND BIOLOGICAL RESEARCH 325:93-102, 1990

NITROUS OXIDE

Fatal abuse of nitrous oxide in the workplace, by A. J. Suruda, et al. JOURNAL OF OCCUPATIONAL MEDICINE 32(8):682-684, August 1990

Nitrous oxide abuse presenting as premature exhaustion of sodasorb, by S. M. Yudenfreud-Sujka. ANESTHESIOLOGY 73(3):580, September 1990

Suicide by nitrous oxide poisoning, by A. Chadly, et al. AMERICAN JOURNAL OF FORENSIC MEDICINE AND PATHOLOGY 10(4):330-331, December 1989

Complications
Subacute myeloneuropathy after abuse of nitrous oxide: an electron microscopic study on the peripheral nerve, by T. Shimizu, et al. RINSHO SHINKEIGAKU 29(9):1129-1135, September 1989

NORIEGA, MANUEL
Happy New Year, Noriega your money is being seized. NARCOTICS CONTROL DIGEST 20(1):7-10, January 3, 1990

Man who knows too much: J. Blandon's inside knowledge of M. A. Noriega's drug connection, by J. Klein. NEW YORK 23:11-12, January 15, 1990

New evidence that could nail Noriega, by D. Harbrecht. BUSINESS WEEK January 15, 1990, p. 35

Noriega can be successfully prosecuted, by J. E. DiGenova. TRIAL 26(4):104-105, April 1990

Noriega on ice, by R. Lacayo. TIME 135:24-27, January 15, 1990

Noriega on trial: surrender, by J. Bierman. MACLEAN'S 103:4+, January 15, 1990

Noriega "treasure chest": money laundering, by G. DeGeorge, et al. BUSINESS WEEK January 22, 1990, pp. 32-33

Noriega's trial: smokescreen. ECONOMIST 314:28-29, January 13, 1990

NURSES AND NURSING
see also: Alcohol and Nurses
Care—Nurses

Addiction to drugs and alcohol among physicians and nurses, by A. S. Sorensen, et al. UGESKRIFT FOR LAEGER 151(41):2660-2664, October 9, 1989

Confessions of an impaired nurse about drug addiction. NURSING 90 20:57, August 1990

Helping the addicted nurse, by D. S. Sherman. CONTEMPORARY LONGTERM CARE 13(6):81-83, June 1990

When nurses are addicted to drugs: confronting an impaired co-worker, by D. Alexander, et al. NURSING 90 20:54-58, August 1990

NUTRITION

Indicators of nutritional status among clients from New York City, New York, USA, by J. R. Hebert, et al. JOURNAL OF SUBSTANCE ABUSE TREATMENT 7(3):161-166, 1990

Nutritional effects of marijuana, heroin, cocaine, and nicotine, by M. E. Mohs, et al. JOURNAL OF THE AMERICAN DIETETIC ASSOCIATION 90(9):1261-1267, September 1990

Nutritional implications of medication use and misuse in elderly, by M. C. Cook, et al. JOURNAL OF THE FLORIDA MEDICAL ASSOCIATION 77(6):606-613, June 1990

Nutritional status assessment of HIV-positive drug addicts, by P. Varela, et al. EUROPEAN JOURNAL OF CLINICAL NUTRITION 44(5):415-418, May 1990

OPIUM
Opium of the masses, by A. Blackwell. POLICE REVIEW 97(4995):139, 1989

Opium wars revisited as United States forces tobacco exports in Asia, by T. T. Chen, et al. AMERICAN JOURNAL OF PUBLIC HEALTH 80(6):659-662, June 1990

Under the influence: marching through the opium fog, by J. Street, Jr. CIVIL WAR TIMES ILLUSTRATED 27(3):30-35, 1988

OVER-THE-COUNTER DRUGS
Are you an unwitting addict: you may be if you are not careful when using prescription and over-the-counter medication, by S. Curson. GOOD TIMES 1(9):32-34, October 1990

Over-the-counter drug abuse: research by Charles Seifert. USA TODAY 118:9, February 1990

OVERDOSE
General practice consultation patterns before and after intentional overdose: a matched control study, by D. Gorman, et al. BRITISH JOURNAL OF GENERAL PRACTICE 40(332):102-105, March 1990

PARACETAMOL
see also: Acetaminophen

Consumption, overdose and death from analgesics during a period of over-the-counter availability of paracetamol in Denmark, by P. Ott, et al. JOURNAL OF INTERNAL MEDICINE 227(6):423-428, June 1990

Disposition and kinetics of intravenous N-acetylcysteine in patients with paracetamol overdosage, by L. F. Prescott, et al. EUROPEAN JOURNAL OF CLINICAL PHARMACOLOGY 37(5):501-506, 1989

Epidemiology of pediatric paracetamol poisoning: retrospective analysis of calls received by the Poison Control Centre of Tours, by A. P. Jonville, et al. JOURNAL

DE TOXICOLOGIE CLINIQUE ET EXPERIMENTALE 10(1):21-25, January/ February 1990

Intravenous N-acetylcysteine, hepatotoxicity and plasma glutathione S-transferase in patients with paracetamol overdosage, by G. J. Beckett, et al. HUMAN AND EX-PERIMENTAL TOXICOLOGY 9(3):183-186, May 1990

Management of paracetamol poisoning complicated by enzyme induction due to alcohol or drugs, by B. M. McClements, et al. LANCET 335(8704):1526, June 23, 1990

Paracetamol poisoning in pregnancy: an analysis of the outcomes of cases referred to the Teratology Information Service of the National Poisons Information Service, by P. R. McElhatton, et al. HUMAN AND EXPERIMENTAL TOXICOLOGY 9(3): 147-153, May 1990

Safety of late acetylcysteine treatment in paracetamol poisoning, by D. Parker, et al. HUMAN AND EXPERIMENTAL TOXICOLOGY 9(1):25-27, January 1990

Complications
Fatal variceal haemorrhage after paracetamol overdose, by J. R. Thornton, et al. GUT 30(10):1424-1425, October 1989

Improved outcome of paracetamol-induced fulminant hepatic failure by late administration of acetylcysteine, by P. M. Harrison, et al. LANCET 335(8705):1572-1573, June 30, 1990

Plasma glutathione S-transferase and F protein are more sensitive than alanine aminotransferase as markers of paracetamol: acetaminophen-induced liver damage, by G. J. Beckett, et al. CLINICAL CHEMISTRY 35(11):2186-2189, November 1989

Research
Electron transport and protection of liver slices in the late stage of paracetamol injury of the liver, by M. Mourelle, et al. BRITISH JOURNAL OF PHARMACOLOGY 98(Suppl):825, December 1989

PARAPHERNALIA
Ban all drug paraphernalia. NARCOTICS CONTROL DIGEST 19(18):5, August 30, 1989

Chicago's drug-busting "God Squad": Catholic priests G. Clements and M. Pfleger pressure stores, by J. G. Hubbell. READER'S DIGEST 137:98-102, November 1990

Drug paraphernalia as evidence of trafficking in marijuana: Ohio. NARCOTICS LAW BULLETIN December 1989, p. 7

Mail order drug paraphernalia act: probable cause—vagueness; New York. SEARCH AND SEIZURE BULLETIN September 1989, pp. 6-7

PARAPHERNALIA

Mountains of vile vials: the United States tries to crush the lucrative trade in drug paraphernalia, by R. Behar. TIME 135(23):66, June 4, 1990

Possession of drug paraphernalia: Colorado. NARCOTICS LAW BULLETIN May 1990, pp. 6-7

Smoking pipe: intent to use for marijuana—Indiana. NARCOTICS LAW BULLETIN February 1990, p. 3

PARENTERAL ADMINISTRATION

Inhalants

Abuse of smoking methamphetamine mixed with tobacco: II—the formation mechanism of pyrolysis products, by H. Sekine, et al. JOURNAL OF FORENSIC SCIENCES 35(3):580-590, May 1990

Alcohol intoxication in teenagers using inhalant stupefacients, by J. W. Tomczak, et al. POLISH JOURNAL OF PHARMACOLOGY AND PHARMACY 41(3):203-206, May/June 1989

Anesthetic care of a patient intoxicated with thinner, by J. Aono, et al. MASUI 39(3): 388-390, March 1990

Case of thinner sniffing: part 2—urinary excretion of cresols and methanol after inhalation of toluene and methanol, by S. Kira, et al. INDUSTRIAL HEALTH 27(4): 175-180, 1989

Chronic solvent abuse: 1—cognitive sequelae, by J. Zur, et al. CHILD: CARE, HEALTH AND DEVELOPMENT 16(1):1-20, January/February 1990

Chronic solvent abuse: 2—relationship with depression, by J. Zur, et al. CHILD: CARE, HEALTH AND DEVELOPMENT 16(1):21-34, January/February 1990

Cinnamon oil abuse by adolescents, by P. A. Perry, et al. VETERINARY AND HUMAN TOXICOLOGY 32(2):162-164, April 1990

Cinnamon oil: kids use it to get high, by R. H. Schwartz. CLINICAL PEDIATRICS 29(3):196, March 1990

Clinical study of butane gas abuse: in comparison with toluene-based solvent and marihuana, by S. Tohhara, et al. ARUKORU KENKYUTO YAKUBUTSU ISON 24(6):504-510, December 1989

Cocaine smokers excrete a pyrolysis product, anhydroecgonine methyl ester, by P. Jacob, 3d, et al. JOURNAL OF TOXICOLOGY: CLINICAL TOXICOLOGY 28(1): 121-125, 1990

Driving under the influence of toluene, by H. Gjerde, et al. FORENSIC SCIENCE INTERNATIONAL 44(1):77-83, January 1990

Effect of hashish-smoking on serum levels of pancreatic lipase: RV 3.1.1.3, in man, by A. Dionyssiou-Asteriou, et al. JOURNAL OF TOXICOLOGY: CLINICAL TOXICOLOGY 28(2):263-265, 1990

Effects of cannabis smoked together with a substance sold as Mandrax, by D. Wilson, et al. SOUTH AFRICAN MEDICAL JOURNAL 76(11):636, December 2, 1989

Effects of combinations of intranasal cocaine, smoked marijuana, and task performance on heart rate and blood pressure, by R. W. Foltin, et al. PHARMACOLOGY, BIOCHEMISTRY AND BEHAVIOR 36(2):311-315, June 1990

Effects of smoked marijuana on interpersonal distances in small groups, by J. J. Rachlinski, et al. DRUG AND ALCOHOL DEPENDENCE 24(3):183-186, December 1989

Examination attainments of secondary school pupils who abuse solvents, by O. Chadwick, et al. BRITISH JOURNAL OF EDUCATIONAL PSYCHOLOGY 60(Pt 2):180-181, June 1990

Fatal attraction of a 5-minute fix: increase in solvent abuse by school children in Great Britain, by E. Heron. TIMES EDUCATIONAL SUPPLEMENT 3882:10, November 23, 1990

Iceman cometh and killeth: smokable methamphetamine, by R. B. Mack. NORTH CAROLINA MEDICAL JOURNAL 51(6):276-278, June 1990

Inhalant abuse is a hidden epidemic among youth. CRIME CONTROL DIGEST 24(30):8-9, July 30, 1990; also in JUVENILE JUSTICE DIGEST 18(15):6-7, August 1, 1990

Inhalant and alcohol use go hand in hand: beer doesn't hurt you, is the common belief. JOURNAL OF THE ADDICTION RESEARCH FOUNDATION 19(6):5, June 1, 1990

Inhalants: boredom and frustration at heart of use, by H. McConnell. JOURNAL OF THE ADDICTION RESEARCH FOUNDATION 19(5):5, May 1, 1990

Method for delivery of precise doses of smoked cocaine-base to humans, by D. Hatsukami, et al. PHARMACOLOGY, BIOCHEMISTRY AND BEHAVIOR 36(1):1-7, May 1990

New trend in solvent abuse deaths, by P. McBride, et al. MEDICINE, SCIENCE AND THE LAW 30(3):207-213, July 1990

Nitrous oxide abuse presenting as premature exhaustion of sodasorb, by S. M. Yudenfreud-Sujka. ANESTHESIOLOGY 73(3):580, September 1990

Problem that won't go away, by A. Busuttil. POLICE REVIEW 98:1726-1727, 1990

Psychological study in children addicted to inhalation of volatile substances, by L. M. Rojas, et al. REVISTA DE INVESTIGACION CLINICA 41(4):361-365, October/December 1989

Smokeable heroin use will increase, by H. McConnell. JOURNAL OF THE ADDICTION RESEARCH FOUNDATION 19(4):3, April 1, 1990

Smoked marijuana effects on tobacco cigarette smoking behavior, by T. H. Kelly, et al. JOURNAL OF PHARMACOLOGY AND EXPERIMENTAL THERAPEUTICS 252 (3):934-944, March 1990

Sniffers using butane, propane: 11 year old and 15 year old die suddenly after use, by K. Fournis. JOURNAL OF THE ADDICTION RESEARCH FOUNDATION 19(12):3, December 1, 1990

White matter dementia in chronic toluene abuse, by C. M. Filley, et al. NEUROLOGY 40(3 Pt 1):532-534, March 1990

Inhalants—Complications

Barotrauma related to inhalational drug abuse, by M. E. Seaman. JOURNAL OF EMERGENCY MEDICINE 8(2):141-149, March/April 1990

Cardiopulmonary abnormalities after smoking cocaine, by T. Christou, et al. SOUTHERN MEDICAL JOURNAL 83(3):335-338, March 1990

Fatal accidental enflurane intoxication, by B. Jacob, et al. JOURNAL OF FORENSIC SCIENCES 34(6):1408-1412, November 1989

Fatal recreational inhalation of enflurane, by F. B. Walker, et al. JOURNAL OF FORENSIC SCIENCES 35(1):197-198, January 1990

Freebase cocaine and memory, by T. C. Manschreck, et al. COMPREHENSIVE PSYCHIATRY 31(4):369-375, July/August 1990

Hemolytic-uremic syndrome following "crack" cocaine inhalation, by J. A. Tumlin, et al. AMERICAN JOURNAL OF MEDICAL SCIENCES 299(6):366-371, June 1990

Human psychopharmacology of intranasal cocaine, by S. T. Higgins, et al. NIDA RESEARCH MONOGRAPH SERIES 95:357-358, 1989

Increase in deaths from deliberate inhalation of fuel gases and pressurised aerosols, by H. R. Anderson. BMJ 301(6742):41, July 7, 1990

Methanol poisoning as a result of inhalational solvent abuse, by M. J. McCormick, et al. ANNALS OF EMERGENCY MEDICINE 19(6):639-642, June 1990

Multiple intracerebral hemorrhages after smoking "crack" cocaine, by R. M. Green, et al. STROKE 21(6):957-962, June 1990

Nasal cocaine abuse causing an aggressive midline intranasal and pharyngeal destructive process mimicking midline reticulosis and limited Wegener's granulomatosis, by R. B. Daggett, et al. JOURNAL OF RHEUMATOLOGY 17(6):838-840, June 1990

Nitrite inhalant abuse and AIDS-related Kaposi's sarcoma, by H. W. Haverkos. JOURNAL OF THE ACQUIRED IMMUNE DEFICIENCY SYNDROME 3(Suppl)1:47-50, 1990

Opsoclonus-myoclonus following the intranasal usage of cocaine, by D. Scharf. JOURNAL OF NEUROLOGY, NEUROSURGERY AND PSYCHIATRY 52(12): 1447-1448, December 1989

Priapism associated with intranasal cocaine abuse, by R. L. Fiorelli, et al. JOURNAL OF UROLOGY 143(3):584-585, March 1990

Pulmonary complications of smoked substance abuse, by D. P. Tashkin. WESTERN JOURNAL OF MEDICINE 152(5):525-530, May 1990

Pulmonary edema after freebase cocaine smoking: not due to an adulterant, by J. N. Kline, et al. CHEST 97(4):1009-1010, April 1990

Pulmonary talc granulomatosis in a cocaine sniffer, by M. Oubeid, et al. CHEST 98(1): 237-239, July 1990

Pulmonary toxicity of inhaled and intravenous talc, by M. A. Hollinger. TOXICOLOGY LETTERS 52(2):121-127, July 1990

Review of the respiratory effects of smoking cocaine, by N. A. Ettinger, et al. AMERICAN JOURNAL OF MEDICINE 87(6):664-668, December 1989

Search for cofactors in AIDS: including an analysis of the association of nitrite inhalant abuse and Kaposi's sarcoma, by H. W. Haverkos. PROGRESS IN CLINICAL AND BIOLOGICAL RESEARCH 325:93-102, 1990

Sudden sniffing deaths. JOURNAL OF THE ADDICTION RESEARCH FOUNDATION 19(11):4, November 1, 1990

Suicide by nitrous oxide poisoning, by A. Chadly, et al. AMERICAN JOURNAL OF FORENSIC MEDICINE AND PATHOLOGY 10(4):330-331, December 1989

Tobacco chewing, alcohol and nasal snuff in cancer of the gingiva in Kerala, India, by R. Sankaranarayanan, et al. BRITISH JOURNAL OF CANCER 60(4):638-643, October 1989

Toluene dementia, by S. M. Gospe, Jr. NEUROLOGY 40(8):1320-1321, August 1990

Vascular changes in the nasal submucosa of chronic cocaine addicts, by J. M. Chow, et al. AMERICAN JOURNAL OF FORENSIC MEDICINE AND PATHOLOGY 11(2): 136-143, June 1990

Intravenous

Accessing intravenous drug users via the health care system, by P. E. Evans. NIDA RESEARCH MONOGRAPH SERIES 93:277-287, 1990

Anatomical distribution of soft tissue sepsis sites in intravenous drug misusers attending an accident and emergency department: Scotland, by M. H. Stone, et al. BRITISH JOURNAL OF ADDICTION 85(11):1495-1496, 1990

Association between intravenous drug use and early misbehavior, by J. M. Tomas, et al. DRUG AND ALCOHOL DEPENDENCE 25(1):79-89, February 1990

Blood and plasma donations among a cohort of intravenous drug users, by K. E. Nelson, et al. JAMA 263(16):2194-2197, April 25, 1990

Class A drug users: prevalence and characteristics in greater Nottingham, by J. Giggs, et al. BRITISH JOURNAL OF ADDICTION 84(12):1473-1480, December 1989

Cleaning injecting equipment: a message gone wrong, by J. Herrod, et al. BMJ 299(6699):601, September 2, 1989

Close relationship between neopterin and beta-2-microglobulin levels in intravenous drug abusers, by R. Y. Lin, et al. INTERNATIONAL ARCHIVES OF ALLERGY AND APPLIED IMMUNOLOGY 91(4):389-393, 1990

Cocaine injection and ethnicity in parenteral drug users during the early years of the human immunodeficiency virus (HIV) epidemic in New York City, by D. M. Novick, et al. JOURNAL OF MEDICAL VIROLOGY 29(3):181-185, November 1989

Demographic characteristics, risk behaviors, and HIV seroprevalence among intravenous drug users by site of contact: results from a community-wide HIV surveillance project, by J. McCusker, et al. AMERICAN JOURNAL OF PUBLIC HEALTH 80(9):1062-1067, September 1990

Detection of intravenous drug use, by M. Farrell, et al. BMJ 300(6724):612-613, March 3, 1990

Dihydrocodeine in substance dependence, by A. Ulmer. FORSCHRITTE DER MEDIZIN 108(13):261, April 30, 1990

Effects of bromocriptine pretreatment on subjective and physiological responses to IV cocaine, by K. Kumor, et al. PHARMACOLOGY, BIOCHEMISTRY AND BEHAVIOR 33(4):829-837, August 1989

Gallium-67 detection of intramammary injection sites secondary to intravenous drug abuse, by L. C. Swayne. CLINICAL NUCLEAR MEDICINE 14(9):693-694, September 1989

Initiation into intravenous drug abuse, by M. Stenbacka. ACTA PSYCHIATRICA SCANDINAVICA 81(5):459-462, May 1990

Injection drug use and needle sharing among Ontario students, by R. G. Smart, et al. CANADIAN JOURNAL OF PUBLIC HEALTH 81(4):295-296, July/August 1990

Intravenous drug abuse and one academic health center, by P. E. Dans, et al. JAMA 263(23):3173-3176, June 20, 1990

Mobility of injecting drug users, by D. Goldberg. JOURNAL OF THE ROYAL COLLEGE OF GENERAL PRACTITIONERS 39(319):83, February 1989

Natural history of parenteral drug addicts treated in a general hospital, by R. Muga, et al. BRITISH JOURNAL OF ADDICTION 85(6):775-778, June 1990

Primary medical care for IVDU's: model for future care, by R. S. Schottenfeld, et al. NIDA RESEARCH MONOGRAPH SERIES 95:403-404, 1989

Puerto Rican intravenous drug user, by Y.Serrano. NIDA RESEARCH MONOGRAPH SERIES 93:24-34, 1990

Sexual minority needle users, by A. B. Jones. NIDA RESEARCH MONOGRAPH SERIES 93:108-119, 1990

Talc of three cities: risk taking among intravenous drug users, by R. Booth, et al. NIDA RESEARCH MONOGRAPH SERIES 95:378-379, 1989

Variables influencing condom use among intravenous drug users, by S. Magura, et al. AMERICAN JOURNAL OF PUBLIC HEALTH 80(1):82-84, January 1990

Venous envy: the importance of having functional veins, by J. B. Page, et al. JOURNAL OF DRUG ISSUES 20(2):291-308, Spring 1990

Intravenous—Complications
see also: AIDS

Acute femoral neuropathy and iliopsoas infarction in intravenous drug abusers, by D. A. Kaku, et al. NEUROLOGY 40(8):1317-1318, August 1990

Acute myocardial infarction caused by intravenous amphetamine abuse, by G. E. Packe, et al. BRITISH HEART JOURNAL 64(1):23-24, July 1990

Acute pleurisy in an intravenous drug abuser, by A. E. Glatt. HOSPITAL PRACTICE 25(2):155+, February 15, 1990

Acute viral hepatitis B, reported to the Public Health Laboratory Service, by S. Polakoff. JOURNAL OF INFECTION 20(2):163-168, March 1990

Addict beliefs about access to HIV test results, by D. A. Calsyn, et al. NIDA RESEARCH MONOGRAPH SERIES 95:417, 1989

Alloimmunization and intravenous drug abuse, by J. M. Bowman, et al. CMAJ 142(5): 439, March 1, 1990

Aspergillus endophthalmitis in intravenous-drug users: Kentucky. MMWR 39(3):48-49, January 26, 1990; also in JAMA 263:941, February 16, 1990

Association of hepatitis delta virus and hepatitis B virus in parenteral drug abusers: 1971 to 1972 and 1986 to 1987, by W. R. Lange, et al. ARCHIVES OF INTERNAL MEDICINE 150(2):365-368, February 1990

Bladder outflow obstruction secondary to intravenous amphetamine abuse, by J. Worsey, et al. BRITISH JOURNAL OF UROLOGY 64(3):320-321, September 1989

Cardiac screening for pregnant intravenous drug abusers, by C. E. Henderson, et al. AMERICAN JOURNAL OF PERINATOLOGY 6(4):397-399, October 1989

Causes of death in hospitalized intravenous drug abusers, by E. C. Klatt, et al. JOURNAL OF FORENSIC SCIENCES 35(5):1143-1148, 1990

Changes in needle sharing behavior among intravenous drug users: San Francisco, 1986-1988, by J. R. Guydish, et al. AMERICAN JOURNAL OF PUBLIC HEALTH 80(8):995-997, August 1990

Changes in New York City, by R. E. Harris, et al. NEW YORK STATE JOURNAL OF MEDICINE 90(3):123-126, March 1990

Clinical, hematologic, and immunologic analysis of 21 HTLV-II-infected intravenous drug users, by J. D. Rosenblatt, et al. BLOOD 76(2):409-417, July 15, 1990

Contrasting prevalence of delta hepatitis markers in parenteral drug abusers with and without AIDS, by M. J. Kreek, et al. JOURNAL OF INFECTIOUS DISEASES 162(2):538-541, August 1990

Correlation of hepatitis C virus antibodies with HIV-1 seropositivity in intravenous drug addicts, by H. P. Huemer, et al. INFECTION 18(2):122-128, March/April 1990

"Cotton fever": a benign febrile syndrome in intravenous drug abusers, by D. W. Harrison, et al. JOURNAL OF EMERGENCY MEDICINE 8(2):135-139, March/April 1990

CT manifestation of sternoclavicular pyarthrosis in patients with intravenous drug abuse, by P. W. Alexander, et al. JOURNAL OF COMPUTER ASSISTED TOMOGRAPHY 14(1):104-106, January/February 1990

Developmental decline in infants born to HIV-infected intravenous drug-using mothers, by R. Kletter, et al. NIDA RESEARCH MONOGRAPH 95:409-410, 1989

Endocarditis in heroin addicts: incidence in the Vaal d 'Hebron General Hospital, by X. Martinez-Costa, et al. MEDICINA CLINICA 92(20):794, May 27, 1989

Endocarditis in intravenous drug abusers, by R. Roberts, et al. EMERGENCY MEDICINE CLINICS OF NORTH AMERICA 8(3):665-681, August 1990

False-positive serology of rickettsial disease in parenteral drug addicts, by M. E. Jimenez-Mejias, et al. JOURNAL OF INFECTIOUS DISEASES 160(6):1088-1089, December 1989

Fatal staphylococcus saprophyticus native valve endocartitis in an intravenous drug addict, by V. R. Singh, et al. JOURNAL OF INFECTIOUS DISEASES 162(3):783-784, September 1990

Fine needle aspiration cytology of talc granulomatosis in a peripheral lymph node in a case of suspected intravenous drug abuse, by I. Housini, et al. ACTA CYTOLOGICA 34(3):342-344, May/June 1990

From the Centers for Disease Control: aspergillus endophthalmitis in intravenous-drug users—Kentucky. JAMA 263(7):941, February 16, 1990

From the Centers for Disease Control: lead poisoning associated with intravenous-methamphetamine use—Oregon, 1988. JAMA 263(6):797-798, February 9, 1990

Gastrointestinal hemorrhage from an internal jugular abscess in an intravenous drug addict, by S. F. Ippolito, et al. AMERICAN JOURNAL OF FORENSIC MEDICINE AND PATHOLOGY 11(2):158-159, June 1990

Genamicin-resistant enterococcal endocarditis: the need for routine screening for high-level resistance to aminoglycosides, by C. R. Libertin, et al. SOUTHERN MEDICAL JOURNAL 83(4):458-460, April 1990

Granulocyte abnormalities in parenteral drug-addicts: the influence of HIV infection, by J. Gutierrez, et al. ALLERGOLOGIA ET IMMUNOPATHOLOGIA 17(5):251-255, September/October 1989

Group A beta-hemolytic streptococcal bacteremia and intravenous substance abuse: a growing clinical problem, by A. L. Lentnek, et al. ARCHIVES OF INTERNAL MEDICINE 150(1):89-93, January 1990

Haematogenous Serratia marcescens endophthalmitis in an HIV-infected intravenous drug addict, by R. Alvarez, et al. INFECTION 18(1):29-30, January/February 1990

Hepatitis B: transmission by sexual contact and needle sharing, by P. Piot, et al. VACCINE 8(Suppl):37-40, March 1990

Hepatitis C infection in two urban hemodialysis units, by L. J. Jeffers, et al. KIDNEY INTERNATIONAL 38(2):320-322, 1990

Hepatitis C virus in intravenous drug users, by J. Bell, et al. MEDICAL JOURNAL OF AUSTRALIA 153(5):274-276, September 3, 1990

Hepatitis C virus in Italian drug addicts, by B. Guida, et al. ANNALS OF INTERNAL MEDICINE 113(7):559-560, October 1, 1990

Hepatitis C virus: the main cause of the non-A, non-B hepatitis, by Z. Schaff, et al. ORVOSI HETILAP 131(35):1903-1906, 1990

Hepatitis D virus infection among intravenous drug abusers in Taiwan: analysis of risk factors and liver function tests, by H. M. Hsu, et al. JOURNAL OF MEDICAL VIROLOGY 31(2):76-81, June 1990

Hepatitis delta virus infections in intravenous drug abusers with hepatitis B in the west of Scotland, by E. A. McCruden, et al. JOURNAL OF MEDICAL VIROLOGY 29(1):59-62, September 1989

High prevalence of HTLV-II among intravenous drug abusers: PCR confirmation and typing, by S. Kwok, et al. AIDS RESEARCH: HUMAN RETROVIRUSES 6(4):561-565, April 1990

High *staphylococcus aureus* nasal carriage rate in patients with acquired immunodeficiency syndrome or AIDS-related complex, by M. C. Raviglione, et al. AMERICAN JOURNAL OF INFECTION CONTROL 18(2):64-69, 1990

HIV-related disorders, needle users, and the social services, by L. C. Schulman, et al. NIDA RESEARCH MONOGRAPH SERIES 93:254-276, 1990

HIV-related risk behaviour among a non-clinic sample of injecting drug users, by N. McKeganey, et al. BRITISH JOURNAL OF ADDICTION 84(12):1481-1490, December 1989

HIV-related severe thrombocytopenia in intravenous drug users: prevalence, response to therapy in a medium-term follow-up, and pathogenetic, by G. Landonio, et al. AIDS 4(1):29-34, January 1990

HIV risk behavior: antisocial personality disorders, drug use patterns, and sexual behavior among methadone maintanence admissions, by D. Nolimal, et al. NIDA RESEARCH MONOGRAPH SERIES 95:401-402, 1989

HIV-1-related and nonrelated diseases among IV drug users and sexual partners, by E. J. Trapido, et al. JOURNAL OF DRUG ISSUES 20(2):245-266, Spring 1990

Hodgkin's disease in HIV-infected intravenous drug abusers, by S. Roithmann, et al. NEW ENGLAND JOURNAL OF MEDICINE 323(4):275-276, July 26, 1990

Hodgkin's disease in patients with antibodies to human immunodeficiency virus: a study of 22 patients, by M. Serrano, et al. CANCER 65(10):2248-2254, 1990

Hospitalization decision in febrile intravenous drug users, by J. H. Samet, et al. AMERICAN JOURNAL OF MEDICINE 89(1):53-57, July 1990

HTLV-1 in drug addicts in Andalucia, by E. Pujol de la Llave, et al. MEDICINA CLINICA 93(12):476, October 21, 1989

HTLV-II infection in Italian drug abusers, by D. Zella, et al. LANCET 336(8714):575-576, September 1, 1990

Human immunodeficiency virus and viral hepatitis seroepidemiology in New York City intravenous drug abusers, by L. S. Brown, Jr., et al. NIDA RESEARCH MONO-GRAPH SERIES 95:443-444, 1989

Incidence of acute hepatitis B in injecting drug users as a indicator of continuing HIV transmission: international implications, by A. Mele, et al. AIDS 4(6):598-599, June 1990

Infected false aneurysms in the groin of intravenous drug abusers, by G. H. Welch, et al. BRITISH JOURNAL OF SURGERY 77(3):330-333, March 1990

Infection with hepatitis viruses HAV, HBV and HCV as well as with AIDS virus HIV in drug addicts of the Zurich street scene: a prevalence study, by S. Rohrig, et al. SCHWEIZERISCHE MEDIZINISCHE WOCHENSCHRIFT 120(17):621-629, April 28, 1990

Infections caused by gram positive bacteria: a new epidemic in patients with positive anti-HIV antibodies and drug addicts, by M. A. Gelabert. ARCHIVES ES-PANOLES DE UROLOGIA 43(2):103-105, March 1990

Infections secondary to intravenous drug abuse, by F. A. Reyes. HAND CLINICS 5(4):629-633, November 1989

Infective complications of the central nervous system (CNA) in addicts to parenterally administered drugs, by J. M. Garces. ARCHIVOS DE NEUROBIOLOGIA 52 (Suppl)1:149-154, 1989

Infective endocarditis in intravenous drug users: a comparison of human immunodeficiency virus type 1-negative and -positive patients, by R. G. Nahass, et al. JOURNAL OF INFECTIOUS DISEASES 162(4):967-970, October 1990

Injecting and sexual behaviour of intravenous drug users in Sydney, by A. Dinnen. MEDICAL JOURNAL OF AUSTRALIA 152(12):672, June 18, 1990

Injecting and sexual behaviour of intravenous drug users in Sydney, by S. Darke, et al. MEDICAL JOURNAL OF AUSTRALIA 152(8):446, April 16, 1990

Injection of illicit drugs into the granulation tissue of chronic ulcers, by M. R. Abidin, et al. ANNALS OF PLASTIC SURGERY 44(3):268-270, March 1990

Injuries of the vascular system in drug addicts in Kladno, by J. Horesovsky, et al. CASOPIS LEKARU CESKYCH 128(48):1528-1529, November 24, 1989

Intravenous abuse of crushed tablets: a case with fatal outcome, by M. Roger, et al. TIDSSKRIFT FOR DEN NORSKE LAEGEFORENING 110(16):2080-2081, June 20, 1990

Intravenous cocaine abuse and subarachnoid haemorrhage: effect on outcome, by R. K. Simpson, Jr., et al. BRITISH JOURNAL OF NEUROSURGERY 4(1):27-30, 1990

Intravenous drug abusers with antisocial personality disorder: increased HIV risk behavior, by R. K. Brooner, et al. DRUG AND ALCOHOL DEPENDENCE 26(1):39-44, 1990

Intravenous drug use and hepatitis A: an investigation of an outbreak, by A. Jin, et al. CANADIAN JOURNAL OF PUBLIC HEALTH 81(1):79-81, January/February 1990

Intravenous drug users: the only important reservoir of delta virus in Spain, by E. Perez-Trallero, et al. JOURNAL OF INFECTIOUS DISEASES 161(1):152, January 1990

Intravenous heroin use: its association with HIV infection in patients in methadone treatment, by A. Chu, et al. NIDA RESEARCH MONOGRAPH SERIES 95:447-448, 1989

Intravenous nasal decongestant use, by M. Edlund, et al. JOURNAL OF CLINICAL PSYCHIATRY 50(10):392, October 1989

Intravenous substance abuse and a presacral mass, by L. Nathan, et al. JAMA 263 (11):1496, March 16, 1990

Lead poisoning associated with intravenous-methamphetamine use: Oregon, 1988. MMWR 39(48):830-831, December 8, 1989

Levels of soluble CD8 antigen and circulating immune complexes in intravenous drug abusers: relationships to HIV antibody serology, by R. Y. Lin, et al. AIDS RESEARCH: HUMAN RETROVIRUSES 5(6):655-661, December 1989

Lexington addicts, 1971-1972: demographic characteristics, drug use patterns, and selected infectious disease experience, by W. R. Lange, et al. INTERNATIONAL JOURNAL OF THE ADDICTIONS 24(7):609-626, July 1989

Low-back pain and intravenous drug abusers, by P. H. Chandrasekar. ARCHIVES OF INTERNAL MEDICINE 150(5):1125+, May 1990

Low incidence of bleeding from HIV-related thrombocytopenia in drug addicts and hemophiliacs: implications for therapeutic strategies, by G. Finazzi, et al. EUROPEAN JOURNAL OF HAEMATOLOGY 45(2):82-85, 1990

Mathematical model to describe the risk of infection from sharing injection equipment, by R. Allard. JOURNAL OF THE ACQUIRED IMMUNE DEFICIENCY SYNDROME 3(10):1010-1016, 1990

Medical complications of intravenous drug use. AMERICAN FAMILY PHYSICIAN 42: 1367-1368, November 1990

Medical complications of intravenous drug use, by M. D. Stein. JOURNAL OF GENERAL INTERNAL MEDICINE 5(3):249-257, May/June 1990

Mixed bacterial endocarditis in an intravenous drug misuser, by D. Nathwani, et al. POSTGRADUATE MEDICAL JOURNAL 66(771):70, January 1990

Model of the sexual relations of young i.v. drug users, by M. L. Williams. JOURNAL OF THE ACQUIRED IMMUNE DEFICIENCY SYNDROME 3(2):192-193, 1990

Mondor's disease secondary to intravenous drug abuse, by R. A. Cooper. ARCHIVES OF SURGERY 125(6):807-808, June 1990

More on rhabdomyolysis associated with cocaine intoxication, by A. W. Fox. NEW ENGLAND JOURNAL OF MEDICINE 321(18):1271, November 2, 1989

Mucor cerebral abscess associated with intravenous drug abuse, by K. M. Fong, et al. AUSTRALIAN AND NEW ZEALAND JOURNAL OF MEDICINE 20(1):74-77, February 1990

Multiple small opacities of metallic density in the lung, by B. A. Shaffer, et al. CHEST 96(5):1179-1181, November 1989

Needle obtainment and cleaning habits of addicts, by A. J. Saxon, et al. NIDA RESEARCH MONOGRAPH SERIES 95:418, 1989

Needle sharing among male prostitutes: preliminary findings of the Prospero Project—San Francisco, by D. Waldorf, et al. JOURNAL OF DRUG ISSUES 20(2): 309-334, Spring 1990

Needle sharing in residential drug treatment units, by M. J. Bloor, et al. BRITISH JOURNAL OF ADDICTION 84(12):1547-1548, December 1989

Needle-sharing patterns as a predictor of HIV seroprevalence among New York City intravenous drug users (IVDUs), by K. Yee, et al. NIDA RESEARCH MONOGRAPH SERIES 95:488-489, 1989

Neurobiology of abused drugs: opioids and stimulants, by T. R. Kosten. JOURNAL OF NERVOUS AND MENTAL DISEASE 178(2):217-227, April 1990

New virus attacking drug users nationwide. CORRECTIONS DIGEST 20(19):10, September 9, 1989; also in JUVENILE JUSTICE DIGEST 17(18):6, September 20, 1989; CRIME CONTROL DIGEST 23(38):3-4, September 25, 1989 and NARCOTICS CONTROL DIGEST 19(20):4, September 27, 1989

NIDA, HRSA join forces in studies of AIDS risk behavior by i.v. drug users, by P. Delaney. PUBLIC HEALTH REPORTS 105(3):323, May/June 1990

Non-cardiogenic pulmonary oedema due to the intravenous administration of clove oil, by C. M. Kirsch, et al. THORAX 45(3):235-236, March 1990

Other infectious complications in intravenous drug users: the compromised host, by S. M. Shepherd, et al. EMERGENCY MEDICINE CLINICS OF NORTH AMERICA 8(3):683-692, August 1990

Parenteral pentazocine: cutaneous complications revisited, by B. B. Furner. JOURNAL OF THE AMERICAN ACADEMY OF DERMATOLOGY 22(4):694-695, April 1990

Patterns of HIV-1 and HTLV-I-II in intravenous drug abusers from the middle atlantic and central regions of the USA, by H. H. Lee, et al. JOURNAL OF INFECTIOUS DISEASES 162(2):347-352, August 1990

Prevalence, incidence, and risk factors of hepatitis C virus infection among drug users in Amsterdam, by J. A. van den Hoek, et al. JOURNAL OF INFECTIOUS DISEASES 162(4):823-826, October 1990

Prevalence of hepatitis B surface antigen (HBsAg) among parenteral drug abusers at Dhaka, by M. Mustafa, et al. BANGLADESH MEDICAL RESEARCH COUNCIL BULLETIN 15(1):1-7, June 1989

Prevalence of hepatitis B virus, delta agent and human immunodeficiency virus infections in drug addicts, by D. Bailly, et al. BIOMEDICINE AND PHARMACOTHERAPY 43(6):431-437, 1989

Prevalence of high-risk sexual behavior in male intravenous drug users with steady female partners, by D. K. Lewis, et al. AMERICAN JOURNAL OF PUBLIC HEALTH 80(4):465-468, April 1990

Prevalence of oral lesions among HIV-infected intravenous drug abusers and other risk groups, by R. Barone, et al. ORAL SURGERY, ORAL MEDICINE, ORAL PATHOLOGY 69(2):169-173, February 1990

Prevalence study of HAV, HBV, HCV and HIV infection among drug abusers on the Zurich: Switzerland, street scene, by S. Rohrig, et al. SCHWEIZERISCHE MEDIZINISCHE WOCHENSCHRIFT 120(17):621-629, 1990

Psoas abscess in a drug addict, by S. P. Kwok, et al. POSTGRADUATE MEDICAL JOURNAL 65(763):345, May 1989

Pulmonary needle embolism from intravenous drug abuse, by B. L. Hart, et al. CANADIAN ASSOCIATION OF RADIOLOGISTS JOURNAL 40(6):326-327, December 1989

Pulmonary toxicity of inhaled and intravenous talc, by M. A. Hollinger. TOXICOLOGY LETTERS 52(2):121-127, July 1990

Rh-negative women face added needle risk when they share intravenous drugs, by M. Brosnahan. JOURNAL OF THE ADDICTION RESEARCH FOUNDATION 19(5):3, May 1, 1990

Risk behavior of intravenous cocaine users: implications for intervention, by D. D. Chitwood, et al. NIDA RESEARCH MONOGRAPH SERIES 93:120-133, 1990

Role of HIV infection in alteration of pulmonary function in intravenous heroin addicts, by V. Foresti, et al. CHEST 97(1):254-255, January 1990

Septic pulmonary arteriovenous fistula: an unusual conduit for systemic embolization in right-sided valvular endocarditis, by D. J. Stagaman, et al. CHEST 97(6):1484-1486, June 1990

Serious infections caused by coagulase-negative staphylococci in intravenous drug users, by L. M. Baddour, et al. MISSOURI MEDICINE 87(6):363-366, June 1990

Seroepidemiology of hepatitis A, B, and D viruses and human T-lymphocyte tropic viruses in Japanese drug abusers, by K. Kiyosawa, et al. JOURNAL OF MEDICAL VIROLOGY 29(3):160-163, November 1989

Serologic investigations in a New York City cohort of parenteral drug users, by J. A. Bailey, et al. JOURNAL OF THE NATIONAL MEDICAL ASSOCIATION 82(6):405-408, June 1990

Severe non-occlusive ischemic stroke in young heroin addicts, by R. Jensen, et al. ACTA NEUROLOGICA SCANDINAVICA 81(4):354-357, April 1990

Skin changes in drug-dependent patients, by H. Rasokat. ZEITSCHRIFT FUR HAUTKRANKHEITEN 65(4):351-354+, April 1990

Spontaneous and nonspontaneous internal jugular vein thrombosis, by K. Chowdhury, et al. HEAD AND NECK SURGERY 12(2):168-173, 1990

Spontaneous pneumothorax as a complication of septic pulmonary embolism in intravenous drug addicts, by A. Olazabal, et al. EUROPEAN JOURNAL OF RADIOLOGY 10(1):56-58, January/February 1990

Surgical treatment of septic endocarditis in drug addicts, by I. Shevchenko, et al. VESTNIK KHIRURGII IMENI I. GREKOVA 144(3):18-20, March 1990

Talc in liver tissue of intravenous drug abusers with chronic hepatitis: a comparative study, by G. S. Allaire, et al. AMERICAN JOURNAL OF CLINICAL PATHOLOGY 92(5):583-588, November 1989

Thrombocytopenic purpura in HIV-seronegative users of intravenous cocaine, by M. J. Koury. AMERICAN JOURNAL OF HEMATOLOGY 35(2):134-135, October 1990

Treatment of right-sided staphylococcus aureus endocarditits in intravenous drug users with ciprofloxacin and rifampicin, by R. J. Dworkin, et al. LANCET 2(8671):1071-1073, November 4, 1989

Tuberculin skin reactivity in HIV-seropositive intravenous drug addicts, by C. F. Robert, et al. NEW ENGLAND JOURNAL OF MEDICINE 321(18):1268, November 2, 1989

Tuberculosis, AIDS and i.v. drug abuse, by R. J. Lamb, et al. NEW JERSEY MEDICINE 87(56):413-415, May 1990

Unusual pathogens in narcotic-associated endocarditis, by S. Szabo, et al. REVIEWS OF INFECTIOUS DISEASES 12(3):412-415, May/June 1990

Upper extremity deep venous thrombosis: increased prevalence due to cocaine abuse, by J. R. Lisse, et al. AMERICAN JOURNAL OF MEDICINE 87(4):457-458, October 1989

Vancomycin for staphylococcus aureus endocarditis in intravenous drug users, by P. M. Small, et al. ANTIMICROBIAL AGENTS AND CHEMOTHERAPY 34(6):1227-1231, June 1990

Vancomycin pharmacokinetics in burn patients and intravenous drug abusers, by M. J. Rybak, et al. ANTIMICROBIAL AGENTS AND CHEMOTHERAPY 34(5):792-795, May 1990

Vocal cord paralysis resulting from neck injections in the intravenous drug use population, by R. P. Hillstrom, et al. LARYNGOSCOPE 100(5):503-506, May 1990

Topical
Ocular drug abuse in Lagos, Nigeria, by A. O. Adefule-Ositelu. ACTA OPHTHALMOLOGICA 67(4):396-400, August 1989

Ophthalmic use of cocaine and the urine test for benzoylecgonine, by B. B. Bralliar, et al. NEW ENGLAND JOURNAL OF MEDICINE 320:1757-1758, June 29, 1989

Topical anesthetic abuse, by G. O. Rosenwasser, et al. OPHTHALMOLOGY 97(8): 967-972, August 1990

PCP (PHENCYCLIDINE)
PCP and hallucinogens, by M. E. Carroll. ADVANCES IN ALCOHOL AND SUBSTANCE ABUSE 9(1-2):167-190, Spring 1990

PCP: a relook at the chemistry intoxication, psychosis and treatment, by R. C. Frier. PSYCHIATRIC FORUM 14(2):52-57, Fall 1989

Phencyclidine, by E. B. Baldridge, et al. EMERGENCY MEDICINE CLINICS OF NORTH AMERICA 8(3):541-550, August 1990

Complications
Clinical implications of PCP, NMDA and opiate receptors, by J. Wilkins. NIDA RESEARCH MONOGRAPH SERIES 95:275-281, 1989

Non-competitive NMDA antagonists MK-801 and PCP, as well as the competitive NMDA antagonist SDZ EAA494: D-CPPene, interact synergistically with clonidine to promote locomotion in monoamine-depleted mice, by M. Carlsson, et al. LIFE SCIENCES 47(19):1729-1736, 1990

Research
Alterations in rat brain [3H]-TCP binding following chronic phencyclidine administration, by B. W. Massey, et al. LIFE SCIENCES 47(24):139-143, 1990

Comparison of responses by neuropeptide systems in rat to the psychotropic drugs, methamphetamine, cocaine, and PCP, by G. R. Hanson, et al. NIDA RESEARCH MONOGRAPH SERIES 95:348, 1989

Effects of terminating chronic phencyclidine on schedule-controlled behavior in rats, by B. W. Massey, et al. PHARMACOLOGY, BIOCHEMISTRY AND BEHAVIOR 36(1):117-121, May 1990

Facilitation of GABA-induced depression with PCP and sigma receptor agonists was mediated through catecholaminergic pathways, by Y. Wang, et al. LIFE SCIENCES 47(2):121-126, 1990

Mechanisms of phencyclidine (PCP) n-methyl-d-asparate (NMDA) receptor interaction: implications for drug abuse research, by S. R. Zukin, et al. NIDA RESEARCH MONOGRAPH SERIES 95:247-254, 1989

Novel photoaffinity ligand for the phencyclidine site of the N-methyl-D-asparate receptor labels a Mr 120,000 polypeptide, by M. S. Sonders, et al. JOURNAL OF BIOLOGICAL CHEMISTRY 265:6776-6781, April 25, 1990

Pathological changes induced in cerebrocortical neurons by phencyclidine and related drugs, by J. W. Olney, et al. SCIENCE 244:1360-1362, June 16, 1989

Pseudoallosteric modulation by [+]-MK801 of NMDA-coupled phencyclidine binding sites, by A. A. Reid, et al. LIFE SCIENCES 47(16):77-82, 1990

Structural and conformational aspects of the binding of aryl-alkyl amines to the phencyclidine binding site, by A. Thurkauf, et al. NIDA RESEARCH MONOGRAPH SERIES 95:51-56, 1989

PENTAZOCINE

Maternal alcohol and pentazocine abuse: neonatal behavior and morphology in an opposite-sex twin pair, by M. L. Riese. ACTA GENETICAE MEDICAE E GEMELLOLOGIAE 38(1-2):49-56, 1989

Complications

Parenteral pentazocine: cutaneous complications revisited, by B. B. Furner. JOURNAL OF THE AMERICAN ACADEMY OF DERMATOLOGY 22(4):694-695, April 1990

PENTOBARBITAL

Comparison of the behavioral effects and abuse liability of ethanol and pentobarbital in recreational sedative abusers, by J. J. Guarino, et al. NIDA RESEARCH MONOGRAPH SERIES 85:453-454, 1989

Research

Chronic ethanol and pentobarbital administration in the rat: effects on GABA receptor function and expression in brain, by A. L. Morrow, et al. ALCOHOL 7(3):237-244, May/June 1990

PEYOTE

Peyotism and the control of heavy drinking: the Nebraska Winnebago in the early 1990s, by T. W. Hill. HUMAN ORGANIZATION 49(3):255-265, 1990

THE PHARMACEUTICAL INDUSTRY

Bush wants chemical companies to help fight drugs by curbing product sales. NARCOTICS CONTROL DIGEST 19(10):10, May 10, 1989

Chemical industry, drug agency sort out chemical diversion issues: exports of chemicals for manufacture of narcotics, by D. J. Hanson. CHEMICAL ENGINEERING NEWS 68:18-19, January 29, 1990

Drug industry delusions, by R. M. Herman. TRIAL 25(12):7, December 1989

Halcion: waking up to the dangers of a sleeping pill, by D. W. Siegelman. TRIAL 25(11):38-40+, November 1989

PHARMACISTS

Programs for pharmacists impaired by substance abuse: a report, by G. E. McNees, et al. AMERICAN PHARMACY 30(5):33-37, May 1990

PHARMACOLOGY

Disruption of performance under titrating matching-to-sample schedule of reinforcement by drugs of abuse, by G. R. Wenger. JOURNAL OF PHARMACOLOGY AND EXPERIMENTAL THERAPEUTICS 254(1):258-269, 1990

Use of choice procedures for assessing the reinforcing properties of drugs in humans, by C. E. Johanson, et al. NIDA RESEARCH MONOGRAPH SERIES 92: 171-210, 1989

PHENACETIN

Twenty-year follow-up on phenacetin abuse, by U. C. Dubach. AGENTS ACTION 29(Suppl):101-102, 1990

PHENCYCLIDINE *see*: PCP

PHYSICIANS
see also: Care—Physicians

Addiction in doctors: hope and help, by H. Rakatansky. RHODE ISLAND MEDICAL JOURNAL 72(12):437-440, December 1989

Addiction to drugs and alcohol among physicians and nurses, by A. S. Sorensen, et al. UGESKRIFT FOR LAEGER 151(41):2660-2664, October 9, 1989

Diversion programs for impaired physicians, by R. Ikeda, et al. WESTERN JOURNAL OF MEDICINE 152(5):617-621, May 1990

From the Office of the General Counsel: drug testing of the physicians, by D. Orentlicher. JAMA 264(8):1039-1040, August 22-29, 1990

PHYSICIANS

Malpractice claims: experience of physicians investigated for inappropriate prescribing, by J. D. Bloom, et al. WESTERN JOURNAL OF MEDICINE 151(3):336-338, September 1989

Physicians with addictions: a doctor's drug overdose sparks criticism of hospital policy, by J. Bowman. BC REPORT 2(6):21, October 8, 1990

Who heals the healer: the history and purpose of the Physicians Assistance and Advocacy Committee, by H. V. Coleman. JOURNAL OF THE SOUTH CAROLINA MEDICAL ASSOCIATION 86(1):8-11, January 1990

PICENADOL
Evaluation of the abuse potential of picenadol, by D. R. Jasinski, et al. NIDA RESEARCH MONOGRAPH SERIES 95:387, 1989

THE POLICE
see also: Alcohol and The Police
             The Police and Narcotics Control

Alcohol-drug dependence in police forces: a community health policy for the 1990s, by J. Dietrich. RCMP GAZETTE 51(6):5-15, 1989

Alleged drug abuse: coerced resignation/wrongful termination—Illinois. POLICE OFFICER GRIEVANCES BULLETIN February 1990, pp. 3-4

Disability pension: addiction in the line of duty—Washington. POLICE OFFICER GRIEVANCES BULLETIN December 1989, pp. 2-3

Drug markets and law enforcement, by N. Dorn, et al. BRITISH JOURNAL OF CRIMINOLOGY 30(2):171-188, Spring 1990

Drug problem, methadone and the police: considerations to make a controversial discussion less emotional, by H. Gundlach. KRIMINALIST 21(4):178-182, 1989

Drug-related corruption of police officers: a contemporary typology, by D. L. Carter. JOURNAL OF CRIMINAL JUSTICE 18(2):85-98, March 1990

Emerging "ice" problem presents dangers for police, by D. G. Gibb. CRIME CONTROL DIGEST 23(43):1+, October 30, 1989

Have the good guys gone bad: police in Kinloch, Missouri accused of corruption, by K. Springen. NEWSWEEK 115(20):24, May 14, 1990

IACP report examines integrity and drug-related corruption in United States police agencies. CRIME CONTROL DIGEST 23(44):5-6, November 6, 1989; also in NARCOTICS CONTROL DIGEST 19(23):7-8, November 8, 1989

Two veteran New York City Police Department officers murdered because they were careless: commissioner says. TRAINING AIDS DIGEST 14(12):1+, December 1989

Who watches the watchers: and at what cost to morale? LAW ENFORCEMENT NEWS 15(294):5, June 15, 1989

Colombus anti-drug war is rated a draw by police. LAW ENFORCEMENT NEWS 15(288):3, March 15, 1989

Cooperative team approach: one Ohio sheriff's story on drugs, by J. Butterworth. NATIONAL SHERIFF 41(4):19, August/September 1989

Detention of parcel while police fetched drug-sniffing dog wasn't unreasonable. CRIMINAL LAW REPORTER: COURT DECISIONS 45(18):2321-2322, August 9, 1989

Detention of suitcase: canine sniff. ARREST LAW BULLETIN September 1989, pp. 2-3

DOD to provide more anti-drug training to state and local police. CRIME CONTROL DIGEST 24(11):10, March 19, 1990

East Coast police trying to crack phony prescription ring dealing in Dilaudid. NARCOTICS CONTROL DIGEST 20(11):3-4, May 23, 1990

In a frenzy of evil: C. Hill, police officer killed in drug-related incident in Alexandria, Virginia, by M. McConnell. READER'S DIGEST 136:65-71, February 1990

Injury to officer by arrestee: dram shop suit prohibited by officer—Iowa. POLICE OFFICER GRIEVANCES BULLETIN June 1989, pp. 6-7

LeRoy Martin: superintendent of the Chicago Police Department, by M. S. Rosen. LAW ENFORCEMENT NEWS 16(313):9-12+, April 30, 1990

Let our police take on the drug dealers: restrictions of the exclusionary rule, by G. Brandt. READER'S DIGEST 136:78-82, January 1990

Los Angeles police want permanent barricades in drug war. CRIME CONTROL DIGEST 23(48):2-3, December 4, 1989

Narc, narc: stories of police searches for drugs at the wrong houses, by J. Dentinger. PLAYBOY 37:49+, April 1990

National Drugs Intelligence Unit, by D. Stockley. POLICE JOURNAL 61(4):295-303, 1988

Old and new tools for the modern probation officer, by B. S. Erwin. CRIME AND DELINQUENCY 36(1):61-74, 1990

Police administrators exhorted to work together to combat drugs, violent crime. CRIMINAL LAW REPORTER: COURT DECISIONS 46(4):1084-1087, October 25, 1989

Police agencies find "Drugs: a Deadly Game" useful in teaching about drug dangers. CRIME CONTROL DIGEST 24(16):2-3, April 23, 1990

Police deaths rise in drug war: "buy-bust" the major killer. CRIME CONTROL DIGEST 23(37):1+, September 18, 1989; also in NARCOTICS CONTROL DIGEST 19(20):2-3, September 27, 1989 and TRAINING AIDS DIGEST 14(10):11-12, October 1989

THE POLICE AND NARCOTICS CONTROL

Police executives release law enforcement guide for public housing drug problem. NARCOTICS CONTROL DIGEST 20(14):5, July 4, 1990

Proactive policing against street-level drug trafficking, by L. Zimmer. AMERICAN JOURNAL OF POLICE 9(1):43-74, 1990

Tennessee sheriff-remembered for his war on drugs. CRIME CONTROL DIGEST 24(19):2, May 14, 1990

Virginia law enforcement officials admit "turf" fights hinder drug war efforts. CRIME CONTROL DIGEST 24(16):6-7, April 23, 1990

"Walled cities" of Los Angeles: citizens and cops gang up against the pushers, by E. Salholz. NEWSWEEK 115(20):24-25, May 14, 1990

Washington state patrol upgrading officers' weapons. CRIME CONTROL DIGEST 23(18):9-10, May 7, 1990

Welcome mat rolled out for North Carolina drug enforcers. LAW ENFORCEMENT NEWS 16(313):1+, April 30, 1990

POLICIES

Drug policy as a factor of trends in trade and use of different substances, by G. Arnao. JOURNAL OF DRUG ISSUES 20:443-449, Summer 1990

Drug policy: striking the right balance, by A. Goldstein, et al. SCIENCE 249:1513-1521, September 28, 1990

Forging strong drug policies, by L. Dogoloff. AMERICAN SCHOOL BOARD JOURNAL 177:29+, August 1990

IACP develops model policy on workplace drug abuse. CRIME CONTROL DIGEST 23(43):3, October 30, 1989; also in CORPORATE SECURITY DIGEST 3(44):7, November 6, 1989

Irrelevance of research to government policies on drugs, by D. S. Bell. DRUG AND ALCOHOL DEPENDENCE 25(2):221-224, April 1990

Position of the American Dietetic Association: nutrition intervention in treatment and recovery from chemical dependency, by L. M. Beckley-Barrett, et al. JOURNAL OF THE AMERICAN DIETITIC ASSOCIATION 90(9):1274-1277, September 1990

Preventing employee drug abuse starts with firm policy, awareness, by C. Thieme. OCCUPATIONAL HEALTH AND SAFETY 59:41+, September 1990

Prevention and research protocols for substance use, by N. Giesbrecht, et al. DIMENSIONS IN HEALTH SERVICE 67(4):12, May 1990

TACP develops model policy on workplace drug abuse. CORRECTIONS DIGEST 20(22):2, November 1, 1989

Toward an "Americanization" of Dutch drug policy, by I. H. Marshall, et al. JUSTICE QUARTERLY 7(2):391-420, 1990

POLICIES

United States drug policy: a bad export, by E. A. Nadelmann. FOREIGN POLICY (7)): 83-108, 1988

POLITICS AND GOVERNMENT
see also: Alcohol and Politicians
Barry, Marion

After a mudslinging primary, victor Ann Richards sets her sights on the Lone Star statehouse: controversy over alleged drug abuse, by W. Plummer. PEOPLE WEEKLY 33:85+, April 30, 1990

Declaration of Cartagena, February 15, 1990. WEEKLY COMPILATION OF PRESI-DENTIAL DOCUMENTS 26:248-254, February 19, 1990

Dope on Dana: views of California congressman D. Rohrabacher, by K. Lehrman. NEW REPUBLIC 203:17-18+, November 5, 1990

Foot in the other mouth: gubernatorial candidate A. Richards fails to answer questions on drug use, by G. Carroll. NEWSWEEK 115:27, March 19, 1990

Incredible friends of Marion Barry: convicted of cocaine possession. US NEWS AND WORLD REPORT 109:10, August 20, 1990

Jolt for Richards: refusal to answer drug use questions. TIME 135:19, March 19, 1990

Leak that fizzled: Senate leaks to the press concerning T. Ryan, Office of Thrift Supervision nominee, and his alleged use of drugs, by T. Eastland. AMERICAN SPECTATOR 23:28-30, June 1990

Mayor who couldn't just say no: impact of M. Barry's cocaine use on J. Jackson's political aspirations. US NEWS AND WORLD REPORT 108:8-9, January 29, 1990

Nation's drug abuse strategy, by C. G. Leukefeld. HEALTH AND SOCIAL WORK 15:87-90, May 1990

Nightmare on Main Street: George Bush's war on drugs, by J. R. Petersen. PLAYBOY 37:56, May 1990

Notes and comment: ineffectiveness of Bush administration's handling of the drug crisis. NEW YORKER 66:35-36, December 17, 1990

Political implications of scientific research in the field of drug abuse: the case of cannabis, by J. C. Negrete. DRUG AND ALCOHOL DEPENDENCE 25(2):225-228, April 1990

Politicians, and other immortal beings: Mayor M. Barry's drug use, by S. Budiansky. US NEWS AND WORLD REPORT 108:8-9, February 5, 1990

Prescription for a negative campaign: Florida gubernatorial candidate L. Chiles admits to taking Prozac, by S. Reiss. NEWSWEEK 115:22, April 30, 1990

Regrets only: confessions of past marijuana use, by M. Kinsley. NEW REPUBLIC 202:4+, April 30, 1990

POLITICS AND GOVERNMENT

Stan Moris confirmation hearing smooth sailing. CRIME CONTROL DIGEST 23(39):8, October 2, 1989

Thornburgh denies he's waging a "turf war" with drug czar Bennett. CRIME CONTROL DIGEST 24(13):3-4, April 2, 1990

POLYDRUG ABUSE

Adjunctive drug use among opiate addicts, by V. Navaratnam, et al. CURRENT MEDICAL RESEARCH AND OPINION 11(10):611-619, 1990

Analysis of the significance of performance errors on the Trail Making Test in polysubstance users, by R. J. McCaffery, et al. ARCHIVES OF CLINICAL NEUROPSYCHOLOGY 4(4):393-398, 1989

Anterior pituitary, gonadal and adrenal hormones in women with alcohol and polydrug abuse, by S. K. Teoh, et al. NIDA RESEARCH MONOGRAPH SERIES 95:481-482, 1989

Atypical course of combined cannabis-atropine abuse, by G. A. Wiesbeck, et al. NERVENARZT 60(8):516-517, August 1989

Characteristics of women receiving mandated treatment for alcohol and polysubstance dependence in Massachusetts, by B. W. Lex, et al. DRUG AND ALCOHOL DEPENDENCE 25(1):13-20, February 1990

Cocaine and polysubstance abuse by psychiatric inpatients, by F. Miller, et al. HOSPITAL AND COMMUNITY PSYCHIATRY 41(11):1251-1253, 1990

Combined alcohol and other drug dependence. RECENT DEVELOPMENTS IN ALCOHOLISM 8:1-327, 1990

Concurrent and simultaneous use of alcohol with cocaine: results of national survey, by B. F. Grant, et al. DRUG AND ALCOHOL DEPENDENCE 25(1):97-104, February 1990

Correlates of persisting drug use among former youth multiple drug abuse patients, by W. Feigelman, et al. JOURNAL OF PSYCHOACTIVE DRUGS 22(1):63-75, January/March 1990

Detoxication with phenobarbital of alprazolam-dependent polysubstance abusers, by N. V. Ravi, et al. JOURNAL OF SUBSTANCE ABUSE TREATMENT 7(1):55-58, 1990

Divided attention performance in cannabis users and non-users following alcohol and cannabis separately and in combination, by D. F. Marks, et al. PSYCHOPHARMACOLOGY 99(3):397-401, November 1989

Drug preferences of alcoholic polydrug abusers with and without panic, by C. F. Jensen, et al. JOURNAL OF CLINICAL PSYCHIATRY 51(5):189-191, May 1990

Inhalant and alcohol use go hand in hand: beer doesn't hurt you, is the common belief. JOURNAL OF THE ADDICTION RESEARCH FOUNDATION 19(6):5, June 1, 1990

POLYDRUG ABUSE

Levels of alcohol dependence in cocaine addicts: some clinical implications, by S. Walfish, et al. PSYCHOLOGY OF ADDICTIVE BEHAVIORS 3(2):65-68, 1989

Longitudinal patterns of alcohol use by narcotics addicts, by Y. I. Hser, et al. RECENT DEVELOPMENTS IN ALCOHOLISM 8:145-171, 1990

Multiple addictions: co-synchronous use of alcohol and drugs, by N. S. Miller, et al. NEW YORK STATE JOURNAL OF MEDICINE 90(12):596-600, 1990

Patterns of multiple substance abuse during pregnancy: implications for mother and fetus, by B. B. Little, et al. SOUTHERN MEDICAL JOURNAL 83(5):507-509+, May 1990

Sedative-tranquilizer use and abuse in alcoholics currently in outpatient treatment: incidence, pattern and preference, by B. Wolf, et al. NIDA RESEARCH MONOGRAPH SERIES 95:376-377, 1989

PREGNANCY
see also: Alcohol and Pregnancy

36- and 48-month neurobehavioral follow-ups of children prenatally exposed to marijuana, cigarettes, and alcohol, by P. A. Fried, et al. JOURNAL OF DEVELOPMENTAL AND BEHAVIORAL PEDIATRICS 11(2):49-58, April 1990

Barriers face pregnant women seeking drug-treat, by M. Garb. IN THESE TIMES 14(12):7, February 7, 1990

Child neglect statute applies to mothers who abuse drugs during pregnancy. FAMILY LAW REPORTER: COURT OPINIONS 16(32):1377-1379, June 19, 1990

Cocaine abuse during pregnancy: correlation between prenatal care and perinatal outcome, by S. N. MacGregor, et al. OBSTETRICS AND GYNECOLOGY 74(6): 882-885, December 1989

Cocaine abuse in pregnancy. AMERICAN FAMILY PHYSICIAN 40:232, August 1989

Cocaine: maternal use during pregnancy and its effect on the mother, the fetus, and the infant, by D. Rosenak, et al. OBSTETRICAL AND GYNECOLOGICAL SURVEY 45(6):348-359, June 1990

Cocaine use during pregnancy, by D. R. Coustan, et al. RHODE ISLAND MEDICAL JOURNAL 73(6):249-252, June 1990

Cocaine use during pregnancy: implications for physicians, by R. A. Aronson, et al. WISCONSIN MEDICAL JOURNAL 89(3):105-110, March 1990

Crime and pregnancy, by P. Marcotte. ABA JOURNAL 75:14+, August 1989

Drug abuse during pregnancy in an inner-city hospital: prevalence and patterns, by D. B. Land, et al. JOURNAL OF THE AMERICAN OSTEOPATHIC ASSOCIATION 90(5):421-425, May 1990

Drug abuse in pregnancy. AMERICAN FAMILY PHYSICIAN 42:506, August 1990

PREGNANCY

Drug-addicted women who have babies, by D. E. Roberts. TRIAL 26(4):56-58+, April 1990

Drug-addiction and pregnancy, by P. J. Parquet, et al. NEUROPSYCHIATRIE DE l'ENFANCE ET DE l'ADOLESCENCE 36(2-3):109-117, February/March 1988

Drug addiction and pregnancy: policy crossroads, by W. Chavkin. AMERICAN JOURNAL OF PUBLIC HEALTH 8(4):483-487, April 1990

Drug screening in prenatal care demands objective medical criteria, support services, by A. Skolnick. JAMA 264(3):309-310, July 18, 1990

Drug use among pregnant adolescents, by L. D. Gilchrist, et al. JOURNAL OF CONSULTING AND CLINICAL PSYCHOLOGY 58(4):402-407, August 1990

Drug use during pregnancy: new Minnesota law requires doctors to test and report, by D. M. Fortney. MINNESOTA MEDICINE 73(4):41-43, April 1990

Drugs in pregnancy and lactation: analysis of an information service in South Australia, by N. J. Hotham. AUSTRALIAN JOURNAL OF HOSPITAL PHARMACY 20(2): 153-159, 1990

Drugs in the womb: the newest battlefield in the war on drugs, by P. A. Logli. CRIMINAL JUSTICE ETHICS 9:23-29, Winter/Spring 1990

"Fetal abuse": should we recognize it as a crime—no, by L. Paitrow. ABA JOURNAL 75:39, August 1989

Issues of risk assessment: lessons from the use and abuse of drugs during pregnancy, by D. E. Hutchings. NEUROTOXICOLOGY AND TERATOLOGY 12(3): 183-189, May/June 1990

Kinin-kininase system in drug addicted woman in pregnancy and puerperium, by A. Virgolino, et al. ADVANCES IN EXPERIMENTAL MEDICINE AND BIOLOGY 247:463-469, 1989

Management of the pregnant opiate user, by C. Gerada, et al. BRITISH JOURNAL OF HOSPITAL MEDICINE 43(2):138-141, February 1990

Marijuana use in pregnancy and pregnancy outcome, by F. R. Witter, et al. AMERICAN JOURNAL OF PERINATOLOGY 7(1):36-38, January 1990

Maternal cocaine abuse and effects on the mother, fetus and newborn, by D. Rosenak, et al. HAREFAUH 116(21):600-603, June 1, 1989

Obstetric liaison. BRITISH JOURNAL OF PSYCHIATRY 155:264-265, August 1989

Pregnancy and drugs: physicians face new testing and reporting law, by T. Jopke. MINNESOTA MEDICINE 73(4):29-32, April 1990

Pregnancy, drugs, and the perils of prosecution, by W. K. Mariner, et al. CRIMINAL JUSTICE ETHICS 9:30-41, Winter/Spring 1990

Pregnancy police: if you're an addict, by J. B. Elshtain. PROGRESSIVE 54:26-28, December 1990

Pregnancy police: sending women to jail, by M. Graber. PROGRESSIVE 54(12):22, December 1990

Pregnant, addicted—and guilty: prosecution of K. Hardy and L. Bremer in Muskegon County, Michigan, by J. Hoffman. NEW YORK TIMES MAGAZINE August 19, 1990, pp. 32-35+

Pregnant drug users face jail, by E. J. Bader. NEW DIRECTIONS FOR WOMEN 19(2): 1+, March/April 1990

Prenatal substance abuse: an overview of the problem, by J. Gittler, et al. CHILDREN TODAY 19:3-7, July/August 1990

Prevalence of illicit-drug or alcohol use during pregnancy and discrepancies in mandatory reporting in Pinellas County, Florida, by I. J. Chasnoff, et al. NEW ENGLAND JOURNAL OF MEDICINE 322(17):1202-1206, April 26, 1990

Prevalence of use of cocaine and other substances in an obstetric population, by C. Matera, et al. AMERICAN JOURNAL OF OBSTETRICS AND GYNECOLOGY 163(3):797-801, September 1990

Proposal of a detoxification program for drug dependency in pregnancy, by P. Rosati, et al. MINERVA MEDICA 41(12):599-601, December 1989

Statement on drug use in pregnancy: an urgent problem for New York city Committee on Public Health: the New York Academy of Medicine. BULLETIN OF THE NEW YORK ACADEMY OF MEDICINE 66(2):193-197, March/April 1990

Statewide prevalence of illicit drug use by pregnant women: Rhode Island. MMWR 39(14):225-227, April 13, 1990; Erratum 39(16):280, April 27, 1990

Substance abuse during pregnancy, by J. T. Parente, et al. NEW YORK STATE JOURNAL OF MEDICINE 90(6):336-337, June 1990

Substance abuse during pregnancy, by K. Moss. HARVARD WOMENS LAW JOURNAL 13:278, Spring 1990

Substance abuse in pregnancy, by B. J. Dattel. SEMINARS IN PERINATOLOGY 14(2):179-187, April 1990

Treatment lacking for pregnant addicts, by M. H. Crawford. SCIENCE 247:285, January 19, 1990

Trends in reporting of maternal drug abuse and infant mortality among drug-exposed infants in New York City, by L. Habel, et al. WOMEN AND HEALTH 16(2):41-58, 1990

Validity of self-reporting of marijuana and cocaine use among pregnant adolescents, by B. Zuckerman, et al. JOURNAL OF PEDIATRICS 115(5 Pt 1):812-815, November 1989

Complications
see also: Alcohol and Pregnancy
Children
Infants

Cardiac screening for pregnant intravenous drug abusers, by C. E. Henderson, et al. AMERICAN JOURNAL OF PERINATOLOGY 6(4):397-399, October 1989

Cocaine and pregnancy: effects on the pregnant woman, the fetus and the newborn infant, by A. Garcia Perez, et al. MEDICINA CLINICA 93(14):538-542, November 4, 1989

Cocaine and pregnancy: a lethal combination, by K. S. Pitts, et al. JOURNAL OF PERINATOLOGY 10(2):180-182, June 1990

Cocaine and the risk of low birth weight: Alameda County, California, by D. B. Petitti, et al. AMERICAN JOURNAL OF PUBLIC HEALTH 80(1):25-28, January 1990

Cocaine use and its effect on umbilical artery prostacyclin production, by H. E. Cejtin, et al. PROSTAGLANDINS 40(3):249-258, 1990

Cocaine use during pregnancy may result in birth defects, by R. Hume, Jr. AMERI-CAN FAMILY PHYSICIAN 41:928, March 1990

Cocaine use during pregnancy: research findings and clinical implications, by M. Lynch, et al JOURNAL OF OBSTETRIC, GYNECOLOGIC, AND NEONATAL NURSING 19(4):285-292, July/August 1990

Cocaine use in pregnancy: physicians urged to look for problem where they least expect it, by A. Skolnick. JAMA 264(3):306+, July 18, 1990

Congenital malformations and maternal consumption of benzodiazepines: a case-control study, by L. Laegreid, et al. DEVELOPMENTAL MEDICINE AND CHILD NEUROLOGY 32(5):431-441, May 1990

Congenital renal abnormalities in infants with in utero cocaine exposure, by B. J. Rosenstein, et al. JOURNAL OF UROLOGY 144(1):110-112, 1990

Continuous wave Doppler umbilical artery blood flow velocity wave forms in drug addicted mothers, by M. S. Chatterjee. ARCHIVES OF GYNECOLOGY AND OB-STETRICS 247(3):117-119, 1990

Crack babies and the Constitution: threatening chemically dependent, pregnant women with legal prosecution, by J. C. Rosen. PLAYBOY 37:50+, May 1990

Criminalizing pregnancy: downside of kinder, by L. Maher. SOCIAL JUSTICE 17(3): 111, Fall 1990

Diazepam abuse in pregnant women on methadone maintenance: implications for the neonate, by L. R. Sutton, et al. CLINICAL PEDIATRICS 29(2):108-111, February 1990

Drug abuse in pregnancy: fetal growth and malformations, by P. Rosati, et al. PAN-MINERVA MEDICA 31(2):71-75, April/June 1989

Drug addiction and pregnancy: principal obstetrical and pediatric complications, by N. Ciraru-Vigneron, et al. JOURNAL DE GYNECOLOGIE, OBSTETRIQUE ET BI-OLOGIE DE LA REPRODUCTION 18(5):637-648, 1989

Effect of marijuana use during pregnancy on newborn cry, by B. M. Lester, et al. CHILD DEVELOPMENT 60:765-771, August 1989

Effect of maternal cocaine use on the fetus and newborn: review of the literature, by E. H. Roland, et al. PEDIATRIC NEUROSCIENCE 15(2):88-94, 1989

Effects of cocaine on the human fetus: a review of clinical studies, by P. L. Doering, et al. DICP 23(9):639-645, September 1989

Effects of fetal exposure to cocaine and heroin. AMERICAN FAMILY PHYSICIAN 41:1595+, May 1990

Effects of maternal cocaine abuse on perinatal and infant outcome, by L. Cordero, et al. OHIO MEDICINE 86(5):410-412, May 1990

"Fetal abuse": should we recognize it as a crime—yes. by J. Robertson. ABA JOURNAL 75:38, August 1989

Fetal drug exposure and its possible implications for learning in the preschool and school-age population, by D. C. Van Dyke, et al. JOURNAL OF LEARNING DISABILITIES 23(3):160-163, March 1990

Infrequent neonatal opiate withdrawal following maternal methadone detoxification during pregnancy, by U. Maas, et al. JOURNAL OF PERINATAL MEDICINE 18(2): 111-118, 1990

Lack of specific placental abnormality associated with cocaine use, by W. M. Gilbert, et al. AMERICAN JOURNAL OF OBSTETRICS AND GYNECOLOGY 163(3):998-999, September 1990

Legal alternatives for fetal injury, by A. M. Rhodes. MCN 15(2):111, March/April 1990

Lower serum osteocalcin levels in pregnant drug users and their newborns at the time of delivery, by H. Rico, et al. OBSTETRICS AND GYNECOLOGY 75(6):998-1000, June 1990

Management of maternal and neonatal substance abuse problems, by L. Finnegan. NIDA RESEARCH MONOGRAPH SERIES 90:177-182, 1988

Maternal alcohol and pentazocine abuse: neonatal behavior and morphology in an opposite-sex twin pair, by M. L. Riese. ACTA GENETICAE MEDICAE E GEMELLOLOGIAE 38(1-2):49-56, 1989

Maternal and fetal effects of heroin addiction during pregnancy, by B. B. Little, et al. JOURNAL OF REPRODUCTIVE MEDICINE 35(2):159-162, February 1990

Maternal liabilty for fetal injury, by A. M. Rhodes. MCN 15(1):41, January/February 1990

Neonatal ultrasound casebook: antenatal brain injury and maternal cocaine use, by M. E. Sims, et al. JOURNAL OF PERINATAL 9(3):349-350, September 1989

Obstetrics and neonatal effects of drugs of abuse, by M. Levy, et al. EMERGENCY MEDICINE CLINICS OF NORTH AMERICA 8(3):633-652, August 1990

Patterns of multiple substance abuse during pregnancy: implications for mother and fetus, by B. B. Little, et al. SOUTHERN MEDICAL JOURNAL 83(5):507-509+, May 1990

Perinatal drug abuse. PEDIATRICS 86(3):492-494, September 1990

Perinatal implications of cocaine exposure, by G. Burkett, et al. JOURNAL OF RE-PRODUCTIVE MEDICINE 35(1):35-42, January 1990

Perinatal outcome after recent cocaine usage, by D. S. Mastrogiannis, et al. OB-STETRICS AND GYNECOLOGY 76(1):8-11, July 1990

Perinatal outcome in HIV-infected pregnant women, by A. E. Semprini, et al. GYNE-COLOGIC AND OBSTETRIC INVESTIGATION 30(1):15-18, 1990

Perinatal substance abuse and public health nursing intervention, by B. A. Rieder. CHILDREN TODAY 19:33-35, July/August 1990

Prenatal cocaine use: effects of perinatal outcome, by J. R. Janke, et al. JOURNAL OF NURSE-MIDWIFERY 35(2):74-77, March/April 1990

Prenatal exposure to alcohol, caffeine, tobacco, and aspirin: effects on fine and gross motor performance in 4-year-old children, by H. M. Barr, et al. DEVELOPMENTAL PSYCHOLOGY 26(3):339-348, May 1990

Prenatal marijuana exposure remains evident in early childhood, by R. E. Dahl. AMERICAN FAMILY PHYSICIAN 41:596, February 1990

Prevalence of substance abuse in patients with suspected preterm labor, by J. A. Ney, et al. AMERICAN JOURNAL OF OBSTETRICS AND GYNECOLOGY 162(6): 1562-1565, June 1990

Prosecution of drug-addicted pregnant women being tested, by C. Fischer, et al. CRIMINAL JUSTICE NEWSLETTER 20(19):3-4, October 2, 1989

When becoming pregnant is a crime, by L. M. Paltrow. CRIMINAL JUSTICE ETHICS 9(1):41-47, Winter/Spring 1990

PRESCRIPTION DRUGS

Abuse of prescription drugs, by B. B. Wilford. WESTERN JOURNAL OF MEDICINE 152(5):609-612, May 1990

Are you an unwitting addict: you may be if you are not careful when using prescription and over-the-counter medication, by S. Curson. GOOD TIMES 1(9):32-34, October 1990

Beware the open house addict: prescription drug theft from real estate open house, by R. Springel. REAL ESTATE TODAY 23:24, August 1990

Malpractice claims: experience of physicians investigated for inappropriate prescrib-ing, by J. D. Bloom, et al. WESTERN JOURNAL OF MEDICINE 151(3):336-338, September 1989

PRESCRIPTION DRUGS

Opiate prescribing debate, by A. Johns. BRITISH JOURNAL OF PSYCHIATRY 156: 129, January 1990

Opiate prescribing debate, by R. F. Hill. BRITISH JOURNAL OF PSYCHIATRY 154: 888-889, June 1989

Patient-phyician communications as a determination of medication misuse in older, minority women, by T. F. Garrity, et al. JOURNAL OF DRUG ISSUES 19(2):245-259, Spring 1989

Portrayal of the elderly in drug advertisements: a factor in inappropriate prescribing, by J. Lexchin. CANADIAN JOURNAL OF AGING 9(3):296-303, Autumn 1990

Prescribing issues grant report to the Board of Medical Examiners: II—Minnesota Medical Association. MINNESOTA MEDICINE 73(8):36-42, August 1990

Prescription drug abuse and control: 1990, by B. B. Wilford. HOSPITAL PHARMACY 25(8):796, August 1990

Prescription drug abuse: patient, physician, and cultural responsibilities, by D. R. Wesson, et al. WESTERN JOURNAL OF MEDICINE 152(5):613-616, May 1990

Prescription drug control and dispensing. MARYLAND MEDICAL JOURNAL 39(1): 47-52, January 1990

Towards a sociology of tranquillizer prescribing, by J. Gabe. BRITISH JOURNAL OF ADDICTION 85(1):41-48, January 1990

PREVENTION
see also: Education
         Needle Exchange/Free Needle Programs

Ad industry helps fight war on drugs in a full-blown, multi-media campaign, by J. McEl-gunn. MARKETING 95(39):2-3, September 24, 1990

Addiction and primary prevention, by J. Bergeret. DRUG AND ALCOHOL DEPEN-DENCE 25(2):187-192, April 1990

Adlerian technique for substance-abuse prevention and intervention, by J. Linken-bach. INDIVIDUAL PSYCHOLOGY: JOURNAL OF ADLERIAN THEORY, RE-SEARCH AND PRACTICE 46(2):203-207, June 1990

Adolescent risk perception: a measure to further our understanding of tobacco and drug use, by H. Stevenson, et al. HYPIE 9(2):27-29, June 1990

Alternatives to the war on drugs, by B. K. Alexander. JOURNAL OF DRUG ISSUES 20(1):1-27, Winter 1990

Anabolic steroid use among high school athletes, by N. S. Engel. MCN 14(6):417, November/December 1989

Antidrug ads for dope fiends, by C. Holden. SCIENCE 250:1202, November 30, 1990

PREVENTION

Are they really serious?, by H. H. Frankel. WESTERN JOURNAL OF MEDICINE 151(5):562, November 1989

Are we too easy: do we care, by L. Hosto. JOURNAL OF THE ARKANSAS MEDICAL SOCIETY 87(3):122, August 1990

At last: some progress in the war on drugs, by P. Beatty. CANADIAN SPEECHES 3(8):72-77, December 1989

Being tested, by D. G. Sessions. MISSOURI MEDICINE 86(11):735-736, November 1989

Bennett says kids should be pulled from bad neighborhoods. JUVENILE JUSTICE DIGEST 18(10):7-8, May 16, 1990

Blunting "steroid epidemic" requires alternatives, innovative education, by V. S. Cowart. JAMA 264(13):1641, October 3, 1990

Bold stand against alcohol and drugs, by R. Maher, et al. NASSP BULLETIN 74:126-127, September 1990

"Booting" prevention info: E-Zoot, an electronic bulletin board for teenagers, by W. Howell. JOURNAL OF THE ADDICTION RESEARCH FOUNDATION 19(11):9, November 1, 1990

Campaigns on the go: drug awareness week—November 19-25, 1989. HEALTH PROMOTION 28(1):9, Summer 1989

Captain Kangaroo: Robert Keeshan nixes "just say no," by K. Fournis. JOURNAL OF THE ADDICTION RESEARCH FOUNDATION 19(12):5, December 1, 1990

Challenge of the nineties, by R. W. Frelick. DELAWARE MEDICAL JOURNAL 62(4): 961-962, April 1990

Changing trends in drug use: the second follow-up of a local heroin using community, by M. George, et al. BRITISH JOURNAL OF ADDICTION 84(12):1461-1466, December 1989

Cleaning injecting equipment: a message gone wrong, by J. Herrod, et al. BMJ 299(6699):601, September 2, 1989

Cognitive-behavioral approach to substance abuse prevention: one-year follow-up, by G. J. Botvin, et al. ADDICTIVE BEHAVIORS 15(1):47-63, 1990

Combatting the drug problem: a suggested bold legal experiment, by J. M. Bader. DELAWARE MEDICAL JOURNAL 61(11):637-638, November 1989

Communications teams aid substance abuse prevention. PUBLIC HEALTH REPORTS 105:261, May/June 1990

Community drug prevention programs show promise. PUBLIC HEALTH REPORTS 105:543, September/October 1990

Community psychology into the 1990s: capitalizing opportunity and promoting innovation, by J. A. Linney. AMERICAN JOURNAL OF COMMUNITY PSYCHOLOGY 18(1):1-17, February 1990

Computer-assisted drug prevention, by J. G. Barber. JOURNAL OF SUBSTANCE ABUSE TREATMENT 7(2):125-131, 1990

Computer-assisted strategies for substance abuse prevention: opportunities and barriers, by M. A. Orlandi, et al. JOURNAL OF CONSULTING AND CLINICAL PSYCHOLOGY 58:425-431, August 1990

Cooperative agreements for communications programs for the prevention of illegal drug use or the illegal use or abuse of alcohol: ADAMHA. FEDERAL REGISTER 55(59):11258-11263, March 27, 1990

Corporate crusading: multi-year, anti-drug campaign—alliance for a drug-free Canada, by J. McElgunn. MARKETING 94(3):3, January 15, 1990

Coupon assisted drug prevention, by J. G. Barber. JOURNAL OF SUBSTANCE ABUSE TREATMENT 7(2):125-131, 1990

Defining "success" in drug abuse prevention, by G. Botvin. NIDA RESEARCH MONOGRAPH SERIES 90:203-212, 1988

Designing substance abuse preventive interventions within a developmental framework, by R. Lorion. NIDA RESEACH MONOGRAPH SERIES 90:193-202, 1988

Drug abuse prevention. AMERICAN FAMILY PHYSICIAN 42:848+, September 1990

Drug abuse prevention begins in kindergarten, by E. Wasow, et al. PRINCIPAL 69(5): 24-27, May 1990

Drug abuse prevention in Western Canada and the North West Territories, Canada: a survey of students in grades 6-12, by H. W. Hindmarsh, et al. INTERNATIONAL JOURNAL OF THE ADDICTIONS 25(3):301-306, 1990

Drug abuse prevention programs: discussion of March 16, 1990 article, drug prevention in junior high—a multi-site longitudinal test, by P. L. Ellickson, et al. SCIENCE 250:739-740, November 9, 1990

Drug abuse: a step-by-step guide, by K. S. Skinner. NURSING MANAGEMENT 21(6): 14-15, June 1990

Drug abuse strategies, by W. R. Martin. DRUG AND ALCOHOL DEPENDENCE 25(2): 115-119, April 1990

Drug Awareness Week: Nechi leads campaign to reach non-natives. JOURNAL OF THE ADDICTION RESEARCH FOUNDATION 19(11):3, November 1, 1990

Drug prevention in junior high: a multi-site longitudinal test: assessing impact of Project ALERT, by P. Ellickson, et al. SCIENCE 247(4948):1299-1305, March 16, 1990

Drug use prevention programs, gender, and ethnicity: evaluation of three-seventh-grade Project SMART programs cohorts, by J. W. Graham, et al. PREVENTIVE MEDICINE 19(3):305-313, May 1990

Drug wars and drugstores, by D. Athy. OHIO MEDICINE 85(10):803-804, October 1989

PREVENTION

Drugs, hospitals and a quality assurance answer, by N. J. Galarza. BOLETIN-ASOCIACION MEDICAL DE PUERTO RICO 81(10):402-403, October 1989

Effects of program implementation on adolescent drug use behavior: the Midwestern Prevention Project (MPP), by M. A. Pentz, et al. EVALUATION REVIEW 14(3):264-289, June 1990

Evaluation of strategies developed to prevent substance abuse among student-athletes, by R. J. Marcello, et al. SPORT PSYCHOLOGIST 3(3):196-211, September 1989

Family, friends and neighbors: the role of primary groups in preventing the misuse of drugs, by B. L. Kail, et al. JOURNAL OF DRUG ISSUES 19(2):261-281, Spring 1989

Fighting a drug war together, by E. Zubrow. SCHOOL ADMINISTRATOR 47(5):24-27, May 1990

Fighting spread of drug abuse, by K. Pallarito. MODERN HEALTHCARE 19(44):60, November 3, 1989

Flemish Information System Drugfree Centers, by H. Vandenbroele, et al. ARCHIVES BELGES 47(1-4):142-145, 1989

FYI: help in fighting the war against drugs. CHILDREN TODAY 19(2):2-3, March/April 1990

Harmfulness tax: a new approach to drug control, by L. Grinspoon, et al. HOSPITAL AND COMMUNITY PSYCHIATRY 41(5):483, May 1990

Health-risk warning labels on smokeless tobacco products: are they effective?, by R. G. Brubaker, et al. ADDICTIVE BEHAVIORS 15(2):115-118, 1990

HIPP: a comprehensive school-based substance abuse program with cooperative community involvement, by C. E. Carlson. JOURNAL OF PRIMARY PREVENTION 10(4):289-302, 1990

Hospital quit-smoking consult service: clinical report and intervention guidelines, by C. T. Orleans, et al. PREVENTIVE MEDICINE 19(2):198-212, March 1990

ICAA (International Council on Alcohol and Addictions) hears youth, native voices. JOURNAL OF THE ADDICTION RESEARCH FOUNDATION 19(7-8):2, July/August 1990

Identification and management of drug-seeking behavior in a medical center, by L. Pankratz, et al. DRUG AND ALCOHOL DEPENDENCE 24(2):115-118, October 1989

Illicit drugs: a medical problem, by D. Platt. DELAWARE MEDICAL JOURNAL 61(10):571, October 1989

Info should be relevant, unbiased: parents are targets in NSW (New South Wales) program, by H. McConnell. JOURNAL OF THE ADDICTION RESEARCH FOUNDATION 19(6):8, June 1, 1990

Introducing the concept "community prevention," by Z. Amsel. NIDA RESEARCH MONOGRAPH SERIES 93:7-14, 1990

Is consent to antipsychotic meds the answer to drug abuse?, by L. Costa. CONTEMPORARY LONGTERM CARE 12(8):52-53, July 1989

Journal interview 27: conversation with Philip Connell. BRITISH JOURNAL OF ADDICTION 85(1):13-23, January 1990

Just say no, by H. J. Morowitz. HOSPITAL PRACTICE 24(12):49-50, December 15, 1989

"Just say no" campaign taking the pledge, by F. Andreae. JOURNAL OF THE FLORIDA MEDICAL ASSOCIATION 76(5):479, May 1989

Just say no: imaging effects of winning war on drugs, by C. P. Freund. ESQUIRE 113:187-199, April 1990

Legislative and humanitarian impetus for development of alcohol and other drug policy at an Australian university, by D. D. Blaze-Temple, et al. COMMUNITY HEALTH STUDIES 13(4):463-470, 1989

Let's make Texas drug-free, by B. Haisten. TEXAS MEDICINE 85(10):4, October 1989

McDonald's sponsors "historic" anti-drug program, by K. Riddell. MARKETING 95(21): 15, May 21, 1990

Mediacom campaign helps fight war on drugs. MARKETING 95(10):13, March 5, 1990

Medium isn't accurate "Ice Age" message, by P. Cotton. JAMA 263(20):2717, May 23-30, 1990

Missing component in substance abuse prevention efforts: a Native American sample, by L. Parker. CONTEMPORARY DRUG PROBLEMS 17(2):251-270, Summer 1990

Narcotics and their suppression, by K. Roepstorff. UGESKRIFT FOR LAEGER 151(44):2903-2904, October 30, 1989

National campaign against drug abuse, by D. S. Bell. MEDICAL JOURNAL OF AUSTRALIA 152(9):502, May 7, 1990

National health line, by C. G. Leukefeld. HEALTH AND SOCIAL WORK 15(2):87-90, May 1990

Nicotine addiction, by J. Slade. HAWAII MEDICAL JOURNAL 48(11):485-486+, November 1989

Ontario strategy is multi-faceted. JOURNAL OF THE ADDICTION RESEARCH FOUNDATION 19(6):10, June 1, 1990

Performance appraisal: an antidote for substance abuse, by M. A. Regan. BULLETIN OF THE NEW YORK ACADEMY OF MEDICINE 65(2):202-207, February 1989

PREVENTION

Perfussis toxin inhibits morphine analgesia and prevents opiate dependence, by D. Parolaro, et al. PHARMACOLOGY, BIOCHEMISTRY AND BEHAVIOR 35(1):137-141, January 1990

Pharmacists against drug abuse, by D. Cruikshank. MEDICINE AND LAW 8(6):641-644, 1989

Physician substance abuse: prevention through reeducation, by K. Martin, et al. JOURNAL OF CONTINUING EDUCATION IN THE HEALTH PROFESSIONS 10(1):35-46, 1990

Pittsburgh thrift' anti-drug program pays dividends in deposits and goodwill: Landmark Savings. BANK MARKETING 21:6, November 1989

Plan aimed at the prevention and treatment of drug dependence, by D. N. Nurco, et al. DRUG AND ALCOHOL DEPENDENCE 25(2):193-197, April 1990

Practical suggestions for drug prevention, by B. Weber-Hagedorn. PADAGOGIK HEUTE 41(12):16-19, December 1989

Preventing adolescent drug abuse through a multimodal cognitive-behavioral approach: results of a 3-year study, by G. J. Botvin, et al. JOURNAL OF CONSULTING AND CLINICAL PSYCHOLOGY 58:437-446, August 1990

Preventing drug use among young adolescents, by P. L. Ellickson, et al. EDUCATIONAL DIGEST 56:63-67, November 1990

Preventing drug use in adolescent through media interventions, by R. F. Schilling, et al. JOURNAL OF CONSULTING AND CLINICAL PSYCHOLOGY 58(4):416-424, August 1990

Preventing growth hormone abuse: an emerging health concern, by G. L. White, et al. HEALTH EDUCATION 20(4):4-7, August/September 1989

Preventing smoking and other drug use: let the buyers beware and the interventions be apt, by L. T. Kozlowski, et al. CANADIAN JOURNAL OF PUBLIC HEALTH 80(6):452-456, November/December 1989

Prevention and chemical dependence treatment needs of special target populations, by B. H. Chaffee. JOURNAL OF PSYCHOACTIVE DRUGS 21(4):371-379, October/December 1989

Prevention beginning at school of tobacco use and other addictive substances, by J. Abua Llambrich, et al. GACETA SANITARIA 4(17):70-75, March/April 1990

Prevention effort cuts cocaine use among teens. JUVENILE JUSTICE DIGEST 18(11):6, June 6, 1990; also in CRIME CONTROL DIGEST 24(23):4+, June 11, 1990

Primary prevention of adolescent substance abuse through the promotion of personal and social competence, by L. Dusenbury, et al. PREVENTION IN HUMAN SERVICES 7(1):201-224, 1989

Private foundations and the crisis of alcohol and drug abuse, by L. Renz. HEALTH AFFAIRS 9(2):193-201, Summer 1990

Problem of substance abuse, by V. B. Brown. NEW DIRECTIONS FOR STUDENT SERVICES (49):35-44, Spring 1990

Program of assistance to physicians of Quebec: a concerted effort, by C. Thaibault. UNION MEDICALE DU CANADA 119(4):149, July/August 1990

Progress toward achieving the 1990 national objectives for the misuse of alcohol and drugs. MMWR 39(15):256-258, April 20, 1990

Quicksand in the garden, by R. V. McIntyre. JOURNAL OF THE OKLAHOMA STATE MEDICAL ASSOCIATION 83(5):207-208, May 1990

Real options in the war on drugs, by G. G. Nahas. FASEB JOURNAL 4(2):256-257, February 1, 1990

Relapse prevention for the adolescent substance abuser, by G. Lima. MEDICINE AND LAW 8(4):375-378, 1989

Relative effectiveness of comprehensive community programming for drug abuse prevention with high-risk and low-risk adolescents, by C. A. Johnson, et al. JOURNAL OF CONSULTING AND CLINICAL PSYCHOLOGY 58(4):447-456, August 1990

Research needs and opportunities in severe intervention programs, by R. F. Saltz. HEALTH EDUCATION QUARTERLY 16(3):429-438, Fall 1989

Rhode Island program offers needy third graders free higher education in exchange for staying in school and off illegal drugs for 10 years, by M. C. Cage. CHRONICLE OF HIGHER EDUCATION 37:19+, November 7, 1990

Safe schools in Portland: protection of students and staff members from gang violence in Portland, Oregon, by M. Prophet. AMERICAN SCHOOL BOARD JOURNAL 177:28-30, October 1990

Safe streets in Tacoma: campaign in Pierce County, Washington, by M. K. Nebgen. AMERICAN SCHOOL BOARD JOURNAL 177:26-27, October 1990

Schools, parents, media in prevention mix, by H. McConnell. JOURNAL OF THE ADDICTION RESEARCH FOUNDATION 19(7-8):3, July/August 1990

Short-term outcome evaluation of the "I'm Special" drug abuse prevention program: a revisit using SCAT inventory, by S. Kim, et al. JOURNAL OF DRUG EDUCATION 20(2):127-138, 1990

Society too soft on users: "they're not okay, they're the problem," by J. Hollobon. JOURNAL OF THE ADDICTION RESEARCH FOUNDATION 19(6):1, June 1, 1990

State conditions for prevention and control of tobacco use. MMWR 39(28):476+, July 20, 1990

Street drugs: everyones business, by F. Su'a. HAWAII MEDICAL JOURNAL 48(11): 452+, November 1989

PREVENTION

Student athletes work toward a drug-free school, by J. P. Oberman. JOURNAL OF THE NEW YORK STATE SCHOOL BOARDS ASSOCIATION 19-20, October 1989

Targeted adolescent pregnancy substance abuse project, by T. S. Kerson. HEALTH AND SOCIAL WORK 15(1):73-74, February 1990

Teach approach to drug-abuse prevention, by R. D. Hayes. SCHOLASTIC COACH 59:5-7, May/June 1990

Teacher characteristics and competencies related to substance abuse prevention, by R. M. Jones, et al. JOURNAL OF DRUG EDUCATION 20(3):179-189, 1990

Technology of drug interdiction, by J. D. Shea. DEFENSE SCIENCE 9(4):32+, April 1990

Tele-direct publications to give $3M in anti-drug advertising space in *Yellow Pages* directories. MARKETING 95(27):2, July 2, 1990

There's nothing wrong with your TV set, it's only the cartoon war on drugs— cartoon all-stars to the rescue, by P. Karlak. TV GUIDE 38:4-7, April 21-27, 1990

To get at drug abuse, Alberta targets families: new Alberta Family Life and Drug Abuse Foundation, by D. Haynes. JOURNAL OF THE ADDICTION RESEARCH FOUNDATION 19(9):1, September 1, 1990

Towards a sociology of tranquillizer prescribing, by J. Gabe. BRITISH JOURNAL OF ADDICTION 85(1):41-48, January 1990

Truth too often lost in drug debate: bogeyman images cheapen legitimate concerns—(excerpt from *Peaceful measures: Canada's Way Out of the War on Drugs*). JOURNAL OF THE ADDICTION RESEARCH FOUNDATION 19(11):12, November 1, 1990

Twenty years on: two public initiatives to empower youth, by K. Low. JOURNAL OF DRUG ISSUES 20:589-598, Fall 1990

Understanding and preventing relapse. JOURNAL OF PSYCHOACTIVE DRUGS 22(2):113-260, April/June 1990

United States aid would motivate others. JOURNAL OF THE ADDICTION RESEARCH FOUNDATION 19(6):3, June 1, 1990

Use of mass media in substance abuse prevention, by W. DeJong, et al. HEALTH AFFAIRS 9(2):30-46, Summer 1990

Why a global policy on alcohol and drugs, by J. D. Sinclair. JOURNAL OF THE ADDICTION RESEARCH FOUNDATION 19(6):8, June 1, 1990

Working with heroin sniffers: clinical issues in preventing drug injection, by C. Casriel, et al. JOURNAL OF SUBSTANCE ABUSE TREATMENT 7(1):1-10, 1990

see also: Testing—Prisons and Prisoners
Therapy—Prisons and Prisoners

AIDS and the IV drug users in the criminal justice system, by D. C. McBride, et al. JOURNAL OF DRUG ISSUES 20(2):267-280, Spring 1990

Alleviating our prison crisis: national policy changes are needed. CORRECTIONS TODAY 51(6):38, October 1989

Crowding crisis: a national epidemic. CORRECTIONS TODAY 51(6):122, October 1989

Drug abusers in prisons: managing their health problems—report on a WHO meeting, the Hague, 16-18 May 1988. WHO REGIONAL PUBLICATIONS EUROPEAN SERIES 27:1-52, 1990

Drug sentences pinpointed as cause for rapid increase in federal prison population. CORRECTIONS DIGEST 20(24):5-6, November 29, 1989

Drugs: amount needed to constitute crime—prisons and jails. CRIMINAL LAW REPORTER: COURT DECISIONS 47(13):1256, June 27, 1990

Employee drug-testing policies in prison systems, by R. Guynes, et al. POLICE STRESS 9(1):21-24+, 1989

Hawaii State Department of Corrections substance abuse strategy, by H. Ichiho, et al. HAWAII MEDICAL JOURNAL 49(6):196+, June 1990

HIV seropositivity in a Yugoslav prison population, by Z. Radovanovic, et al. JOURNAL OF HYGIENE, EPIDEMIOLOGY, MICROBIOLOGY AND IMMUNOLOGY 34(1):7-29, 1990

HIV seroprevalence and the acceptance of voluntary HIV testing among newly incarcerated male prison inmates in Wisonsin, USA, by N. J. Hoxie, et al. AMERICAN JOURNAL OF PUBLIC HEALTH 80(9):1129-1131, 1990

Jail crisis underscores nation's drug problems, by H. Healey. NATIONAL SHERIFF 41(1):4-5, February/March 1989

Jail crowding puts Florida drug fugitives on the streets. CRIME CONTROL DIGEST 23(12):10, March 26, 1990

Justice's war on drug treatment, by D. Corn. NATION 250:659-662, May 14, 1990

Prison population increases 7.3 percent in six months. TRIAL 25(11):116, November 1989

Prison populations in 12 key states expected to increase about 68 percent by 1994. CORRECTIONS DIGEST 20(26):1+, December 27, 1989

Problem of co-occuring disorders among jail detainees: antisocial disorder, alcoholism, drug abuse, and depression, by K. A. Abram. LAW AND HUMAN BEHAVIOR 14(4):333-345, 1990

PRISONS AND PRISONERS

Research note: drug use in San Diego arrestees, by S. Pennell, et al. JOURNAL OF CONTEMPORARY CRIMINAL JUSTICE 5(2):61-72, 1989

Substance abuse and psychiatric disorders in prison inmates, by J. E. Chiles, et al. HOSPITAL AND COMMUNITY PSYCHIATRY 41(10):1132-1133, 1990

Watch visitors' pens. CORRECTIONS DIGEST 21(9):4, May 2, 1990

PROPANE
Sniffers using butane, propane: 11 year old and 15 year old die suddenly after use, by K. Fournis. JOURNAL OF THE ADDICTION RESEARCH FOUNDATION 19(12):3, December 1, 1990

PROSTITUTES
Escort services: a front for prostitution, by M. E. Biggs. FBI LAW ENFORCEMENT BULLETIN 57(8):17-22, 1988

Ethnographic approach to understanding HIV high-risk behaviors: prostitution and drug abuse, by M. G. Shedlin. NIDA RESEARCH MONOGRAPH SERIES 93:134-149, 1990

Fear of AIDS and risk reduction among heroin-addicted female street prostitutes: personal interviews with 72 southern California subjects, by D. J. Bellis. JOURNAL OF ALCOHOL AND DRUG EDUCATION 35:26-37, Spring 1990

If I have sex with a duck does that make me a drake: the Albion Street AIDS Centre, intravenous drug use and prostitution, by B. Donovan, et al. MEDICAL JOURNAL OF AUSTRALIA 152(9):498-499, May 7, 1990

Increase of infectious syphilis among heterosexuals in Amsterdam: its relationship to drug use and prostitution, by J. A. van den Hoek, et al. GENITOURINARY MEDICINE 66(1):31-32, February 1990

Needle sharing among male prostitutes: preliminary findings of the Prospero Project—San Francisco, by D. Waldorf, et al. JOURNAL OF DRUG ISSUES 20(2): 309-334, Spring 1990

PSILOCYBINE
Hallucinogenic psilocybine containing mushrooms: toxins contained in Danish wild mushrooms, by J. F. Lassen, et al. UGESKRIFT FOR LAEGER 152(5):314-317, January 29, 1990

Plants and mushrooms of abuse, by D. G. Spoerke, et al. EMERGENCY MEDICINE CLINICS OF NORTH AMERICA 8(3):579-593, August 1990

PSYCHIATRY AND PSYCHOLOGY
see also: Codependency

Addiction, helplessness, and narcissistic rage, by L. M. Dodes. PSYCHOANALYTICAL QUARTERLY 59(3):398-419, July 1990

Addiction in a coworker: getting past the denial, by H. Miller. AMERICAN JOURNAL OF NURSING 90(5):72-75, May 1990

Addiction Severity Index: predicting relationship to a hospital and a professional, by C. J. Rogalski. INTERNATIONAL JOURNAL OF THE ADDICTIONS 25(2):179-194, 1990

Addiction, time and value of Z indicators in Rorschachs of heroin users, by C. Cipolli, et al. PERCEPTUAL AND MOTOR SKILLS 70(3 pt 2):1105-1106, June 1990

Addictions as a challenge to general psychiatry, by G. Edwards. INTERNATIONAL REVIEW OF PSYCHIATRY 1(1-2):5-8, March 1989

Adolescent drug use and psychological health: a longitudinal inquiry, by J. Shedler, et al. AMERICAN PSYCHOLOGIST 45(5):612-630, May 1990

Adult literacy and drug addiction: what's the connection, by C. Neri. LEARNING 5(3): 16-17, 1990

Affective, substance use, and anxiety disorders in persons with arthritis, diabetes, heart disease, high blood pressure, or chronic lung conditions, by K. B. Wells, et al. GENERAL HOSPITAL PSYCHIATRY 11(5):320-327, September 1989

Age at onset of selected mental disorders in five community populations, by K. C. Burke, et al. ARCHIVES OF GENERAL PSYCHIATRY 47(6):511-518, June 1990

Aggression and violence associated with substance abuse, by M. M. Miller, et al. JOURNAL OF CHEMICAL DEPENDENCY TREATMENT 3(1):1-36, 1989

Aggressive behaviour: basic and clinical frontiers, by S. K. Bhattachaya, et al. INDIAN JOURNAL OF MEDICAL RESEARCH 90:387-406, December 1989

AIDS and drug abuse: some aspects of psychiatric consultation, by A. Musacchio de Zan, et al. MEDICINE AND LAW 8(2):119-123, 1989

AIDS and the social relations of intravenous drug users, by S. R. Friedman, et al. MILBANK QUARTERLY 68(Suppl)1:85-100, 1990

Alcohol, tobacco and cannabis: 12-year longitudinal associations with antecedent social context and personality, by M. F. Sieber, et al. DRUG AND ALCOHOL DEPENDENCE 25(3):281-292, June 1990

Analysis of the abstinence violation effect in a sample of illicit drug users, by S. A. Birke, et al. BRITISH JOURNAL OF ADDICTION 85(10):1299-1307, 1990

Antecedents of relapse and recent substance use, by L. Schonfeld, et al. COMMUNITY MENTAL HEALTH JOURNAL 25(3):245-249, Fall 1989

Antisocial personality and substance abuse disorders, by J. J. Collins, et al. BULLETIN OF THE AMERICAN ACADEMY OF PSYCHIATRY AND THE LAW 16(2): 187-198, 1988

Antisocial personality disorder in patients with substance abuse disorders: a problematic diagnosis, by L. J. Gerstley, et al. AMERICAN JOURNAL OF PSYCHIATRY 147(2):173-178, February 1990

Anxiety and anger among abusers of different substances, by S. Walfish, et al. DRUG AND ALCOHOL DEPENDENCE 25(3):253-256, June 1990

Approaching addiction as a symptom in psychiatry, by S. Brour, et al. TUNISIE MEDI-CALE 68(5):345-349, May 1990

Assessing depression in substance abusers: Beck Depression Inventory and SCL-90R, by L. A. Moffett, et al. ADDICTIVE BEHAVIORS 15(2):179-181, 1990

Assessing the reinforcing properties of drugs, by C. E. Johanson. NIDA RESEARCH MONOGRAPH SERIES 95:135-145, 1989

Assessment and classification of patient with psychiatric and substance abuse syndromes, by A. F. Lehman, et al. HOSPITAL AND COMMUNITY PSYCHIATRY 40(10):1019-1025, October 1989

Association between intravenous drug use and early misbehavior, by J. M. Tomas, et al. DRUG AND ALCOHOL DEPENDENCE 25(1):79-89, February 1990

Attention problems in first grade and shy and aggressive behaviors as antecedents to later heavy or inhibited substance use, by S. Kellam, et al. NIDA RESEARCH MONOGRAPH SERIES 95:368-369, 1989

Barriers to community treatment of patients with dual diagnosis, by R. H. Howland. HOSPITAL AND COMMUNITY PSYCHIATRY 41(10):1134-1135, 1990

Behavioral aspects of alcohol-tobacco interactions, by I. F. Zacny. RECENT DEVEL-OPMENTS IN ALCOHOLISM 8:205-209, 1990

Carcinogenicity and teratogenicity vs. psychogenicity: psychological charcteristics associated with self-reported Agent Orange exposure among Vietnam combat veterans who seek treatment for substance abuse, by R. Robinowitz, et al. JOURNAL OF CLINICAL PSYCHOLOGY 45(5):718-728, September 1989

Changes in drug involvement: a longitudinal study of childhood and adolescent determinants, by J. S. Brook, et al. PSYCHOLOGICAL REPORTS 65(3 Pt 1):707-726, December 1989

Characteristics of the autonomic nervous system test during group psychotherapy of patients with opioid dependence at the stage of induction of remission, by V. N. Mirtovskaia, et al. ZHURNAL NEVROPATOLOGII IPSIKHIATRII IMENI S. S. KOR-SAKOVA 89(10):33-35, 1989

Characteristics of narcotics and toxic substance abuse by adolescents: clinico-sociological study, by Gla Lukacher, et al. ZHURNAL NEVROPATOLOGII I PSIKHIATRII IMEN S. S. KORSAKOVA 89(8):117-121, 1989

Characteristics of non-referred cocaine abusing mothers, by I. E. Smith, et al. NIDA RESEARCH MONOGRAPH SERIES 95:330, 1989

Chronic medical conditions in a sample of the general population with anxiety, affective, and substance use disorders, by K. B. Wells, et al. AMERICAN JOURNAL OF PSYCHIATRY 146(11):1440-1446, November 1989

Chronic solvent abuse: 2—relationship with depression, by J. Zur, et al. CHILD: CARE, HEALTH AND DEVELOPMENT 16(1):21-34, January/February 1990

Clinical case management of the dually diagnosed patient, by D. Fariello, et al. HOSPITAL AND COMMUNITY PSYCHIATRY 40(10):1065-1067, October 1989

Clinical implications of PCP, NMDA and opiate receptors, by J. Wilkins. NIDA RESEARCH MONOGRAPH SERIES 95:275-281, 1989

Clinical notes for evaluating soundness of mind and compliance to drug preventive measures in cases of narcotic use, by R. Rutkowski. PSYCHIATRIA POLSKA 23(2):146-153, March/April 1989

Co-morbidity: lessons learned about post-traumatic stress disorder (PTSD) from developing PTSD scales for the MMPI, by W. E. Penk, et al. JOURNAL OF CLINICAL PSYCHOLOGY 45:709-717, September 1989

Cocaine and polysubstance abuse by psychiatric inpatients, by F. Miller, et al. HOSPITAL AND COMMUNITY PSYCHIATRY 41(11):1251-1253, 1990

Cocaine-"crack" dependence among psychiatric inpatients, by G. Bunt, et al. AMERICAN JOURNAL OF PSYCHIATRY 147:1542-1546, November 1990

Cocaine Expectancy Questionnaire (CEQ): its construction and predictive utility, by A. J. Jaffe, et al. NIDA RESEARCH MONOGRAPH SERIES 95:456, 1989

Comorbidity of substance abuse and other psychiatric disorders in adolescents, by M. J. Calache. AMERICAN JOURNAL OF PSYCHIATRY 147(5):681-682, May 1990

Comprehensive psychiatric emergency services, by J. M. Oldham, et al. PSYCHIATRIC QUARTERLY 61(1):57-67, Spring 1990

Consequences of marijuana use on intrapersonal and interpersonal functioning in black and white adolescents, by J. S. Brook, et al. GENETIC, SOCIAL, AND GENERAL PSYCHOLOGY MONOGRAPHS 115(3):349-369, August 1989

Correlates of self-reported early childhood aggression in subjects volunteering for drug studies, by C. Muntaner, et al. AMERICAN JOURNAL OF DRUG AND ALCOHOL ABUSE 15(4):383-402, 1989

Correlates of sexual abuse among boys in treatment for chemical dependency, by P. A. Harrison, et al. JOURNAL OF ADOLESCENT CHEMICAL DEPENDENCY 1(1):53-67, 1990

Correlations of substance abuse and self-image among socially diverse groups of adolescents and clinical implications, by V. M. Uribe, et al. HILLSIDE JOURNAL OF CLINICAL PSYCHIATRY 11(1):25-34, 1989

Depression in homicidal adolescents, by C. P. Malmquist. BULLETIN OF THE AMERICAN ACADEMY OF PSYCHIATRY AND THE LAW 18(1):23-36, 1990

Depressive symptoms during buprenorphine treatment of opioid abusers, by T. R. Kosten, et al. JOURNAL OF SUBSTANCE ABUSE TREATMENT 7(1):51-54, 1990

PSYCHIATRY AND PSYCHOLOGY

Depressive symptoms in opiate addicts on methadone maintenance, by H. Williams, et al. IRISH JOURNAL OF PSYCHOLOGICAL MEDICINE 7(1):45-46, March 1990

Determinants of neuropsychological impairment in antisocial substance abusers, by P. Malloy, et al. ADDICTIVE BEHAVIORS 15(5):431-438, 1990

Developmental variation in the context of marijuana initiation among adolecents, by S. L. Bailey, et al. JOURNAL OF HEALTH AND SOCIAL BEHAVIOR 31(1):58-70, March 1990

Dexamethasone Suppression Test applied to inpatients of a Brazilian psychiatric hospital, by F. Kerr-Correa, et al. BRAZILIAN JOURNAL OF MEDICAL AND BIO-LOGICAL RESEARCH 23(6-7):499-501, 1990

Diazepam and triazolam self-administration in sedative abusers: concordance of subject ratings, performance and drug self-administration, by J. D. Roache, et al. PSYCHOPHARMACOLOGY 99(3):309-315, November 1989

Differential anxiety symptoms in cocaine vs. alcoholic patients, by H. Pettinati, et al. NIDA RESEARCH MONOGRAPH SERIES 95:471-472, 1989

Differential diagnosis of physiological, psychiatric and sociocultural conditions associated with aggression and substance abuse, by R. T. Potter-Efron. JOURNAL OF CHEMICAL DEPENDENCY TREATMENT 3(1):37-59, 1989

Differential drug use patterns among sexually abused adolescent girls in treatment for chemical dependency, by P. A. Harrison, et al. INTERNATIONAL JOURNAL OF THE ADDICTIONS 24(6):499-514, June 1989

Differentiation of personality types among opiate addicts, by S. J. Blatt, et al. JOURNAL OF PERSONALITY ASSESSMENT 54(1-2):87-104, Spring 1990

Disease model of addiction: a biopsychiatrist's view, by N. S. Miller, et al. JOURNAL OF PSYCHOACTIVE DRUGS 22(1):83-85, January/March 1990

Does a relationship exist between stress and opioid dependence?, by P. Oehme, et al. PROGRESS IN CLINICAL AND BIOLOGICAL RESEARCH 328:429-431, 1990

Drug addiction and its individual psychological treatment, by R. Dreikurs. INDIVIDUAL PSYCHOLOGY: JOURNAL OF ADLERIAN THEORY, RESEARCH AND PRACTICE 46(2):209-215, June 1990

Drug and alcohol problems and the developing world, by T. Baasher. INTERNATIONAL REVIEW OF PSYCHIATRY 1(1-2):13-16, March 1989

Drug dilemma, by L. R. Marcos. HOSPITAL AND COMMUNITY PSYCHIATRY 41(8):929, August 1990

Drugs, delinquency and "nerds": are loners deviant?, by W. L. Tolone, et al. JOURNAL OF DRUG EDUCATION 20(2):153-162, 1990

Early onset of nonalcoholic cirrhosis in patients with familial alcoholism, by A. M. Arria, et al. ALCOHOLISM: CLINICAL AND EXPERIMENTAL RESEARCH 14(1):1-5, February 1990

Effect of co-occurring disorders on criminal careers: interaction of antisocial personality, alcoholism, and drug disorders, by K. M. Abram. INTERNATIONAL JOURNAL OF LAW AND PSYCHIATRY 12(2-3):133-148, 1989

Effect of d-amphetamine, secobarbital, and marijuana on choice behavior: social versus nonsocial options, by S. J. Heishman, et al. PSYCHOPHARMACOLOGY 99(2):156-162, October 1989

Effects of the combination of cocaine and marijuana on the task-elicited physiological response, by R. W. Foltin, et al. NIDA RESEARCH MONOGRAPH SERIES 95: 359-360, 1989

Effects of drug-related cues in current and former opiate users, by J. J. Legarda, et al. JOURNAL OF PSYCHOPHYSIOLOGY 4(1):25-31, 1990

Effects of exposure to drug-related cues in detoxified opiate addicts: a theoretical review and some data, by J. Powell, et al. ADDICTIVE BEHAVIORS 15(4):339-354, 1990

Effects of food deprivation on subjective responses to d-amphetamine and marijuana in humans, by J. Zacny, et al. NIDA RESEARCH MONOGRAPH SERIES 95:490-491, 1989

Effects of self-reported drug use and antisocial behavior on evoked potentials in adolescents, by W. B. Pickworth, et al. DRUG AND ALCOHOL DEPENDENCE 25(1):105-110, February 1990

Effects of smoked marijuana on interpersonal distances in small groups, by J. J. Rachlinski, et al. DRUG AND ALCOHOL DEPENDENCE 24(3):183-186, December 1989

Effects of tetrahydrocannabinol content on marijuana smoking behavior, subjective reports, and performance, by S. J. Heishman, et al. PHARMACOLOGY, BIOCHEMISTRY AND BEHAVIOR 34(1):173-179, September 1989

Evaluation of the abuse liability of drug, by C. E. Johanson. DRUG SAFETY 5(Suppl)1:46-57, 1990

Evidence for a behavioral deficit during withdrawal from chronic nicotine treatment, by W. A. Corrigall, et al. PHARMACOLOGY, BIOCHEMISTRY AND BEHAVIOR 33(3):559-562, July 1989

Examination of the stability of the MMPI personality disorder scales, by S. W. Hurt, et al. JOURNAL OF PERSONALITY AND SOCIAL PSYCHOLOGY 54(1-2):16-23, Spring 1990

Exploring the meanings of substance abuse: an important dimension of early work with borderline patients, by S. M. Southwick, et al. AMERICAN JOURNAL OF PSYCHOTHERAPY 44(1):61-67, January 1990

External validity of the new Devereux Adolescent Behavior Rating Scales, by C. L. Williams, et al. JOURNAL OF PERSONALITY ASSESSMENT 55(1-2):73-85, 1990

Five paragraphs for better care of mentally disturbed addicts, by M. Berglund, et al. LAKARTIDNINGEN 87(19):1649-1652, May 9, 1990

From one addiction to another: life after alcohol and drug abuse, by A. S. Hatcher. NURSE PRACTITIONER 14(11):13-14+, November 1989

General versus drug-specific coping skills and posttreatment drug use among adults, by E. A. Wells, et al. PSYCHOLOGY OF ADDICTIVE BEHAVIORS 3(1):8-21, 1989

Human d-amphetamine drug discrimination: testing with d-amphetamine and hydromorphone, by R. J. Lamb, et al. NIDA RESEARCH MONOGRAPH SERIES 94: 423-424, 1989

Human psychopharmacology of intranasal cocaine, by S. T. Higgins, et al. NIDA RESEARCH MONOGRAPH SERIES 95:357-358, 1989

Hypomanic personality trait in cocaine addiction, by F. Lemere, et al. BRITISH JOURNAL OF ADDICTION 85(4):575-576, April 1990

Idea of chemical and alcohol use is not registered, by H. McConnell. JOURNAL OF THE ADDICTION RESEARCH FOUNDATION 19(5):5, May 1, 1990

Illicit anabolic steroid use: a controlled personality study, by W. R. Yates, et al. ACTA PSYCHIATRICA SCANDINAVICA 81(6):548-550, June 1990

In-depth analysis of male adolescent smokeless tobacco users: interviews with users and their fathers, by D. V. Ary, et al. JOURNAL OF BEHAVIORAL MEDICINE 12(5):449-467, October 1989

In their own words: drugs and dependency in New York City's streets, by A. Waterston. NIDA RESEARCH MONOGRAPH SERIES 95:382-383, 1989

In what systems do alcohol-chemical addictions make sense: clinical ideologies and practices as cultural metaphors—disease model of chemical dependency, by H. F. Stein. SOCIAL SCIENCE AND MEDICINE 30(9):987-1000, 1990

Intoxication and responsibility, by R. A. Shiner. INTERNATIONAL JOURNAL OF LAW AND PSYCHIATRY 13(1-2):9-35, 1990

Intravenous drug abusers with antisocial personality disorder: increased HIV risk behavior, by R. K. Brooner, et al. DRUG AND ALCOHOL DEPENDENCE 26(1):39-44, 1990

Involvement of tobacco in alcoholism and illicit drug use, by J. E. Henningfield, et al. BRITISH JOURNAL OF ADDICTION 85(2):279-281, February 1990

Knowledge and experience of young people regarding drug abuse: 1969-1989, by J. D. Wright, et al. BMJ 300(6717):99-103, January 13, 1990

Maori elder-patient relationship as a therapeutic paradigm, by P. S. Sachdev. PSYCHIATRY 52(4):393-403, November 1989

MCMI comparison of cocaine abusers and heroin addicts, by R. J. Craig, et al. JOURNAL OF CLINICAL PSYCHOLOGY 46(2):230-237, March 1990

Mechanisms of addiction and reinforcement, by M. J. Lewis. ADVANCES IN ALCO-HOL AND SUBSTANCE ABUSE 9(1-2):47-66, Spring 1990

Mental state of marijuana-smoking adolescents, by J. Rabe-Jablonska, et al. PRZE-GLAD LEKARSKI 46(12):802-805, 1989

MMPI profiles of cocaine-addicted individuals in residential treatment: implications for practical treatment planning, by S. Walfish, et al. JOURNAL OF SUBSTANCE ABUSE TREATMENT 7(3):151-154, 1990

MMPI profiles of narcotics addicts: I—a review of the literature, by M. D. Anglin, et al. INTERNATIONAL JOURNAL OF THE ADDICTIONS 24(9):867-880, September 1989

MMPI profiles of narcotics addicts: II—ethnic and criminal history effects, by C. P. Weisman, et al. INTERNATIONAL JOURNAL OF THE ADDICTIONS 24(9):881-896, September 1989

Most label addicts "sick": Drug Policy Foundation survey. JOURNAL OF THE ADDIC-TION RESEARCH FOUNDATION 19(12):3, December 1, 1990

Motivational effects of smoked marijuana: behavioral contingencies and high-proba-bility recreational activities, by R. W. Foltin, et al. PHARMACOLOGY, BIOCHEM-ISTRY AND BEHAVIOR 34(4):871-877, December 1989

Motivational effects of smoked marijuana: behavioral contingencies and low-probabil-ity activities, by R. W. Foltin, et al. JOURNAL OF THE EXPERIMENTAL ANALY-SIS OF BEHAVIOR 53(1):5-19, January 1990

Multiple networks and substance use, by T. A. Wills. JOURNAL OF SOCIAL AND CLINICAL PSYCHOLOGY 9(1):78-90, Spring 1990

Narcotics addicts' hustling strategies: creation and manipulation of ambiguity, by B. W. Lex. JOURNAL OF CONTEMPORARY ETHNOGRAPHY 18:388-415, January 1990

Necessity and utility of abuse liability evaluations in human subjects: the FDA per-spective, by F. J. Vocci, Jr. NIDA RESEARCH MONOGRAPH SERIES 92:7-20, 1989

New revolving-door patients: results from a national cohort of first admissions, by L. T. Joyce, et al. ACTA PSYCHIATRICA SCANDINAVICA 82(2):130-135, 1990

Onset of drug abuse in children, by L. Chvila, et al. CESKOSLOVENSKA PSYCHIA-TRIE 85(4):256-259, August 1989

Patients' perceived service needs when seen in a psychiatric emergency room, by P. Solomon, et al. PSYCHIATRIC QUARTERLY 60(3):215-226, 1989

Pavlovian conditioning to morphine in opiate abusers, by D. B. Newlin, et al. NIDA RESEARCH MONOGRAPH SERIES 95:390-391, 1989

Personality of the drug problem, by J. Bertrand. JOURNAL DE PHARMACIE DE BELGIQUE 44(5):351-354, September/October 1989

Personality traits and addictive disease, by T. Ernst. AMERICAN JOURNAL OF PUB-LIC HEALTH 80(4):498-490, April 1990

Plasma cortisol correlates of impulsivity and substance abuse, by R. J. King, et al. PERSONALITY AND INDIVIDUAL DIFFERENCES 11(3):287-291, 1990

Predicting substance abuse in juvenile offenders: attention deficit disorder versus aggressivity, by J. A. Halikas, et al. CHILD PSYCHIATRY AND HUMAN DEVEL-OPMENT 21(1):49-55, Fall 1990

Premorbid characteristics in patients with narcomanias, by S. P. Genailo. ZHURNAL NEVROPATOLOGII I PSIKHIATRII IMENI S. S. KORSAKOVA 90(2):42-47, 1990

Prevalence of minor psychopathology in opioid users seeking treatment, by W. Swift, et al. BRITISH JOURNAL OF ADDICTION 85(5):629-634, May 1990

Psychiatric screening of alcohol and drug patients: the validity of the GHQ-60, by H. E. Ross, et al. AMERICAN JOURNAL OF DRUG AND ALCOHOL ABUSE 15(4): 42-442, December 1989

Psychological profile of young tobacco, alcohol and-or drug users, by G. Roger. ARCHIVES BELGES 47(1-4):107-109, 1989

Psychological study in children addicted to inhalation of volatile substances, by L. M. Rojas, et al. REVISTA DE INVESTIGACION CLINICA 41(4):361-365, October/ December 1989

Psychopathology among cocaine abusers entering treatment, by P. H. Kleinman, et al. JOURNAL OF NERVOUS AND MENTAL DISEASE 178(7):442-447, July 1990

Quest for identity, drug abuse, and identity crises, by R. N. Cassel. JOURNAL OF IN-STRUCTIONAL PSYCHOLOGY 17:155-158, September 1990

Reinforcing effects of a pentobarbital-ethanol combination relative to each drug alone, by R. A. Meisch, et al. PHARMACOLOGY, BIOCHEMISTRY AND BEHAV-IOR 35(2):443-450, February 1990

Relationship between attributional style and post-traumatic stress disorder in addicted patient, by R. A. McCormick, et al. JOURNAL OF TRAUMATIC STRESS 2(4):477-478, October 1989

Relationship between a diagnosis of antisocial personality and hostility: development of an antisocial hostility scale, by C. A. Haertzen, et al. JOURNAL OF CLINICAL PSYCHOLOGY 46:679-686, September 1990

Replication problems of substance abuser MMPI cluster types, by D. G. Fisher, et al. MULTIVARIATE BEHAVIORAL RESEARCH 24(3):335-352, July 1989

Reply: review of intoxication—life in pursuit of artificial paradise, by R. K. Siegel. JOURNAL OF PSYCHOACTIVE DRUGS 22(2):259-260, April/June 1990

Research on psychopathology and addiction: treatment implications, by G. E. Woody, et al. DRUG AND ALCOHOL DEPENDENCE 25(2):121-123, April 1990

Risk factors for depressive symptomatology in a drug using population, by J. C. Buckner, et al. AMERICAN JOURNAL OF PUBLIC HEALTH 80(5):580-585, May 1990

Risk taking and personality, by M. R. Levenson. JOURNAL OF PERSONALITY AND SOCIAL PSYCHOLOGY 58(6):1073-1080, June 1990

Sample attrition bias in a longitudinal study of young people, by A. H. Winefield, et al. AUSTRALIAN JOURNAL OF PSYCHOLOGY 42(1):75-86, 1990

Schizophrenia and assaultive behaviour: the role of alcohol and drug abuse, by P. Lindqvist, et al. ACTA PSYCHIATRICA SCANDINAVICA 82(3):191-195, 1990

Selected psychological characteristics of anabolic-androgenic steroid users, by M. S. Bahrke, et al. NEW ENGLAND JOURNAL OF MEDICINE 323(12):834-835, September 20, 1990

Self-report issues in substance abuse: state of the art and future directions, by S. A. Maisto, et al. BEHAVIORAL ASSESSMENT 12(1):117-134, 1990

Self-report vs. laboratory measures of aggression as predictors of substance abuse, by C. Muntaner, et al. DRUG AND ALCOHOL DEPENDENCE 25(1):1-11, February 1990

Sensitivity of 11 substance abuse scales from the MMPI to change in clinical status, by N. T. Gallucci, et al. PSYCHOLOGY OF ADDICTIVE BEHAVIORS 3(1):29-33, 1989

Severity of psychiatric symptoms as a predictor of benefits from psychotherapy: the Veterans Administration-Penn study, by G. E. Woody, et al. AMERICAN JOURNAL OF PSYCHIATRY 141:1651, December 1989

Sex difference in psychosocial consequences of alcohol and drug abuse, by C. Robbins. JOURNAL OF HEALTH AND SOCIAL BEHAVIOR 30:117-130, March 1989

Sexual abuse, eating disorder and addiction (SEA) triad: syndrome or coincidence?, by O. Minovitz, et al. MEDICINE AND LAW 8(1):59-61, 1989

Social and psychological aspects of pharmacodependence: Liege, January-March 1989. JOURNAL DE PHARMACIE DE BELGIQUE 44(5):345-371, September/October 1989

Social bonding-drug progression model of amphetamine use among young women, by D. E. Taub, et al. AMERICAN JOURNAL OF DRUG AND ALCOHOL ABUSE 16(1-2):77-95, March/June 1990

Social stress model of substance abuse, by J. E. Rhodes, et al. JOURNAL OF CONSULTING AND CLINICAL PSYCHOLOGY 58(4):395-401, 1990

Social support and substance use in early adolescence, by T. A. Wills, et al. JOURNAL OF BEHAVIORAL MEDICINE 12(4):321-339, August 1989

Some definitions and many questions, by A. Noirfalise. JOURNAL DE PHARMACIE DE BELGIQUE 44(5):347-350, September/October 1989

Some familial dynamic aspects in drug abusers, by O. A. D'Agnone, et al. MEDICINE AND LAW 8(5):431-432, 1989

Some personality correlates of drug use, by D. Lester, et al. PSYCHOLOGICAL REPORTS 62:1010, June 1988

Stress- and pharmacologically-induced behavioral sensitization increases vulnerability to acquisition of amphetamine self-administration, by P. V. Piazza, et al. BRAIN RESEARCH 514(1):22-26, April 23, 1990

Structure of problem behaviours among Irish adolescents, by J. W. Grube, et al. BRITISH JOURNAL OF ADDICTION 85(5):667-675, May 1990

Subjective and behavioral effects of marijuana the morning after smoking, by L. D. Chait. PSYCHOPHARMACOLOGY 100(3):328-333, 1990

Subjective dimensions of heroin urges: influence of heroin-related and affectively negative stimuli, by J. E. Sherman, et al. ADDICTIVE BEHAVIORS 14(6):611-623, 1989

Substance use in borderline personality disorder, by R. A. Dulit, et al. AMERICAN JOURNAL OF PSYCHIATRY 147:1002-1007, August 1990

Subtypes of substance abusers: personality differences associated with MacAndrew scores, by J. P. Allen, et al. PSYCHOLOGICAL REPORTS 66(2):691-698, April 1990

Thematic Apperception Test: psychodiagnosis of heroin-dependent patients, by J. C. Cabal Bravo, et al. ACTA LUSO-ESPANOLAS DE NEUROLOGIA, PSIQUIATRIA Y CIENCIAS AFINES 18(1):1-6, Janaury/February 1990

Theory of benzodiazepine dependence that can explain whether flumazenil will enhance or reverse the phenomena, by S. E. File, et al. PSYCHOPHARMACOLOGY 101(4):525-532, 1990

Types of self-reported psychopathology in Dutch and American heroin addicts, by R. A. Steer, et al. DRUG AND ALCOHOL DEPENDENCE 24(3):175-181, December 1989

Undeterred cocaine user: intention to quit and its relationship to perceived legal and health threats, by P. G. Erickson, et al. CONTEMPORARY DRUG PROBLEMS 16(2):141-156, Summer 1989

Validity of self-reports in clinical settings, by H. Rankin. BEHAVIORAL ASSESSMENT 12(1):107-116, 1990

Violence during pregnancy and substance use, by H. Amaro, et al. AMERICAN JOURNAL OF PUBLIC HEALTH 80(5):575-579, May 1990

Young chronic patients and substance abuse, by C. L. Caton, et al. HOSPITAL AND COMMUNITY PSYCHIATRY 40(10):1037-1040, October 1989

PSYCHOACTIVE DRUGS

Epidemiologic report on the use and abuse of psychoactive substances in 16 countries of Latin America and the Caribbean. BULLETIN OF THE PAN AMERICAN HEALTH ORGANIZATION 24(1):97-139, 1990

Survey of alcohol and psychoactive drug consumption in a sample of high school students of the 9th and 19th local health units in the Marche Region, by F. Donato, et al. ANNALI DI IGIENE 1(3-4):693-708, May/June 1989

Use of psychoactive drugs in the Amsterdam drug scene, by H. Nelen. JUSTITIELE VERKENNINGEN 15(5):47-66, 1989

Use of psychoactive substances among male secondary school pupils in Egypt: a study of a nationwide representative sample, by M. I. Soueif, et al. DRUG AND ALCOHOL DEPENDENCE 26(1):63-80, 1990

Complications
Mental and behavioural disorders due to psychoactive substance use: section F2—results of the ICD-10 field trial, by G. Winkler, et al. PHARMACOPSYCHIATRY 23(Suppl)4:151-154, June 1990

PSYCHOTROPIC DRUGS
Can overuse of psychotropic drugs by the elderly be prevented?, by R. W. Lyndon, et al. AUSTRALIAN AND NEW ZEALAND JOURNAL OF PSYCHIATRY 24(1):77-81, March 1990

Development of psychosocial scales for the assessment of adolescents involved with alcohol and drugs, by G. A. Henly, et al. INTERNATIONAL JOURNAL OF THE ADDICTIONS 24(10):973-1001, October 1989

Drug dependence defining the issues, by C. K. Erickson, et al. ADVANCES IN ALCOHOL AND SUBSTANCE ABUSE 9(1-2):1-7, Spring 1990

Emergency consultations for abuse of psychoactive substances in Buenos Aires hospitals, by H. A. Miguez, et al. BOLETIN DE LA OFICINA SANITARIA PANAMERICANA 107(4):296-306, October 1989

Epidemiologic information on the improper use of psychoactive substances: some strategies applied in Argentina, by H. A. Miguez. BOLETIN DE LA OFICINA SANITARIA PANAMERICANA 107(6):541-560, December 1989

Epidemiology of substance dependence, by A. Uchtenhagen. SCHWEIZER ARCHIV FUR NEUROLOGIE UND PSYCHIATRIE 140(5):407-419, 1989

Peregrinations among drugs of dependence: Nathan B. Eddy Memorial Award lecture, by L. E. Hollister. NIDA RESEARCH MONOGRAPH SERIES 95:36-43, 1989

Pharmacological treatment of substance-abusing schizophrenic patients, by S. G. Siris. SCHIZOPHRENIA BULLETIN 16(1):111-122, 1990

Prediction of risk for drug use in high school students, by C. E. Climent, et al. INTERNATIONAL JOURNAL OF THE ADDICTIONS 24(11):1053-1064, November 1989

PSYCHOTROPIC DRUGS

Pre-examination psychotropic drug use by 5th-year medical students at the University of Cape Town, by A. J. Flisher. SOUTH AFRICAN MEDICAL JOURNAL 76(10): 541-543, November 18, 1989

Preliminary investigation of alexithymia in men with psychoactive substance dependence, by G. J. Taylor, et al. AMERICAN JOURNAL OF PSYCHIATRY 147(9): 1228-1230, September 1990

Serotonergic responsivity and behavioral dimensions in antisocial personality disorder with substance abuse, by H. B. Moss, et al. BIOLOGICAL PSYCHIATRY 28(4):325-338, August 15, 1990

Should mind-altering substances be legalized?, by L. L. Alexander. JOURNAL OF THE NATIONAL MEDICAL ASSOCIATION 82(1):15-16, January 1990

Substance use and receipt of treatment in persons with recent spinal cord injuries, by S. H. Schnoll, et al. NIDA RESEARCH MONOGRAPH SERIES 95:426-427, 1989

Substance use in young adults with schizophrenic disorders, by M. A. Test, et al. SCHIZOPHRENIA BULLETIN 15(3):465-476, 1989

Trace elements in drug addicts, by M. Ruiz Martinez, et al. KLINISCHE WOCHEN-SCHRIFT 68(10):507-511, May 17, 1990

Treatment for psychoactive substance use disorder in social populations: issues in strategic planning, by J. Westermeyer. ADVANCES IN ALCOHOL AND SUBSTANCE ABUSE 8(3-4):1-8, Spring 1990

Use of psychotropic drugs and addiction: approaches to epidemiologic research, by F. Facy, et al. DRUG AND ALCOHOL DEPENDENCE 25(2):159-167, April 1990

Complications
Impact of substance abuse on the course and outcome of schizophrenia, by W. M. Turner, et al. SCHIZOPHRENIC BULLETIN 16(1):87-95, 1990

Psychoactive drug use and AIDS. JAMA 263(3):371-373, January 19, 1990

Research
Evaluation of nootropic drug effects in aging rats, by O. Benesova, et al. ACTIVITAS NERVOSA SUPERIOR 32(1):53-55, March 1990

PUBLIC HEALTH
Alcohol and tobacco as public health challenges in a democracy, by D. E. Beauchamp. BRITISH JOURNAL OF ADDICTION 85(2):251-254, February 1990

Comment on Stimson's "AIDS and HIV": the public health paradigm for AIDS and drug use—shifting the time frame, by D. C. des Jarlais, et al. BRITISH JOURNAL OF ADDICTION 85(3):348-350, March 1990

Health for all by the year 2000: alcohol and the Nordic countries, by E. Osterberg, et al. JOURNAL OF PUBLIC HEALTH POLICY 10(4):499-517, Winter 1989

PUBLIC HEALTH

Public health management of AIDS and drugs in Amsterdam, by G. van Brussel, et al. NIDA RESEARCH MONOGRAPH SERIES 90:295-301, 1988

PUBLIC RESPONSE TO DRUG ABUSE

Community action in the war against drugs, by S. Kernus. JUVENILE JUSTICE DIGEST 17(18):1+, September 20, 1989

Community drug prevention programs show promise. PUBLIC HEALTH REPORTS 105:543, September/October 1990

Community trauma and community interventions, by H. Macedo. ARCTIC MEDICAL RESEARCH 47(Suppl)1:94-96, 1988

Domestic volunteer corps eyed by Bennett drug aide for community programs, by R. H. Feldkamp. CRIME CONTROL DIGEST 23(50):3-4, December 18, 1989

Drug wars: the word from the trenches— community empowerment policing, by I. Fulwood, Jr. POLICE CHIEF 57(5):49-50, May 1990

Drug wars: the word from the trenches—the Narcotics Strike Force, a suburban community response, by R. Z. Voorhees. POLICE CHIEF 57(5):43-44, May 1990

Fighting back: what parents and schools can do—view of Geraldine Ferraro, et al. MCCALLS 117:52, February 1990

KKK joins drug war but police are wary. NARCOTICS CONTROL DIGEST 20(1):7, January 3, 1990; also in CRIME CONTROL DIGEST 24(1):3, January 8, 1990

Mr. Lee's side of the street: efforts of L. Lawrence to keep neighborhood in West Perrine, Florida drug-free, by K. Spivey. READER'S DIGEST 137:33-38, July 1990

Operation CLEAN: reclaiming city neighborhoods—Community and Law Enforcement Against Narcotics, Dallas, Texas, by R. W. Hatler. FBI LAW ENFORCEMENT BULLETIN 59(10):22-25, October 1990

PTA in action: plan an exciting drug and alcohol prevention program, by J. Koepsell. PTA TODAY 14(3):26-28, December/January 1988-1989

Shivaun: street-side fundraiser, by J. Gilden. IN THESE TIMES 14(22):4, April 25, 1990

"Walled cities" of Los Angeles: citizens and cops gang up against the pushers, by E. Salholz. NEWSWEEK 115(20):24-25, May 14, 1990

REHABILITATION
see also: Care
              Therapy

ABCs of awareness: a multimodal approach to relapse prevention and intervention: the College Hill Medical Center program, by D. R. Rioux, et al. JOURNAL OF SUBSTANCE ABUSE TREATMENT 7(1):61-63, 1990

REHABILITATION

Addict babies better off with mums on methadone, by B. I. Lee. JOURNAL OF THE ADDICTION RESEARCH FOUNDATION 19(2):4, February 1, 1990

Addict students re-enter school. JOURNAL OF THE ADDICTION RESEARCH FOUNDATION 19(6):2, June 1, 1990

Addict's search: Canadians seek treatment in United States hospitals, by N. Underwood. MACLEAN'S 103:51, May 28, 1990

Addiction in doctors: hope and help, by H. Rakatansky. RHODE ISLAND MEDICAL JOURNAL 72(12):437-440, December 1989

Alprazolam use and dependence: a retrospective analysis of 30 cases of withdrawal, by B. Dickinson, et al. WESTERN JOURNAL OF MEDICINE 152(5):604-608, May 1990

Anti-smoking programme for diabetic patients: the agony and the ecstasy, by P. M. Fowler, et al. DIABETIC MEDICINE 6(8):698-702, November 1989

Bouncing back from crack: Phoenix House, by N. S. Alexander. NEW YORK 23:38-43, February 12, 1990

Brief didactic treatment for alcohol and drug-related problems: an approach based on client choice, by M. Sanchez-Craig. BRITISH JOURNAL OF ADDICTION 85(2): 169-177, February 1990

Can kids on drugs be saved: Texas drug abuse programs for young people, such as the controversial straight, by S. Hollandsworth. TEXAS MONTHLY 18:106+, June 1990

Case for shorter residential alcohol and other drug abuse treatment: adolescents, by W. Van Meter, et al. JOURNAL OF PSYCHOACTIVE DRUGS 22(1):87-88, January/March 1990

Cash and carry plan shows good results. JOURNAL OF THE ADDICTION RESEARCH FOUNDATION 19(6):2, June 1, 1990

Characteristics of women receiving mandated treatment for alcohol and polysubstance dependence in Massachusetts, by B. W. Lex, et al. DRUG AND ALCOHOL DEPENDENCE 25(1):13-20, February 1990

Chemical dependency rehabilitation where fostering fitness is an integral part of the process, by R. N. Cassel, et al. JOURNAL OF INSTRUCTIONAL PSYCHOLOGY 17:202-207, December 1990

Clean break: Ben Johnson gets set to compete again, by N. Wood. MACLEAN'S 103(34):14-15, August 20, 1990

Client demographics and outcome in outpatient cocaine treatment, by L. B. Means, et al. INTERNATIONAL JOURNAL OF THE ADDICTIONS 24(8):765-783, August 1989

Cocaine and heroin use by methadone maintenance patients, by J. C. Ball, et al. NIDA RESEARCH MONOGRAPH SERIES 95:328, 1989

REHABILITATION

Cold turkey farms: drug addiction centres in United Kingdom, by L. Grant, et al. OBSERVER MAGAZINE July 15, 1990, pp. 32-38

"Colmate House," a residential experiment for the social rehabilitation of drug addicts: under direct public service management, by M. P. Bellomo, et al. MEDICINE AND LAW 8(4):399-401, 1989

Commitment to abstinence and acute stress in relapse to alcohol, opiates, and nicotine, by S. M. Hall, et al. JOURNAL OF CONSULTING AND CLINICAL PSYCHOLOGY 58(2):175-181, April 1990

Comprehensive psychiatric emergency services, by J. M. Oldham, et al. PSYCHIATRIC QUARTERLY 61(1):57-67, Spring 1990

Convergence of the mentally disordered and failed population, by K. H. Briar, et al. JOURNAL OF OFFENDER COUNSELING, SERVICES AND 15(1):147-162, 1990

Correlates of persisting drug use among former youth multiple drug abuse patients, by W. Feigelman, et al. JOURNAL OF PSYCHOACTIVE DRUGS 22(1):63-75, January/March 1990

Creating a new drug service in Edinburgh, by J. Greenwood. BMJ 300(6724):587-589, March 3, 1990

Detoxification of the chemically dependent patient, by A. A. Wartenberg. RHODE ISLAND MEDICAL JOURNAL 72(12):451-456, December 1989. Erratum. 73(6): 252, June 1990

Detoxification of the chemically dependent patient, by R. H. Woolard. RHODE ISLAND MEDICAL JOURNAL 73(3):93, March 1990

Diploma in addiction behaviour: update, by I. B. Glass. DRUG AND ALCOHOL DEPENDENCE 25(1):39-42, February 1990

Drug-dependent patients in general practice, by D. Ladewig. THERAPEUTISCHE UMSCHAU 47(3):209-213, March 1990

Drug problems and primary health care, by J. R. Robertson, et al. BRITISH JOURNAL OF ADDICTION 85(5):685-686, May 1990

Effect of impulsivity and empathy on abstinence of poly-substance abusers: a prospective study, by W. McCown. BRITISH JOURNAL OF ADDICTION 85(5): 635-637, May 1990

Effect of living arragement on the recovery of adolescent alcoholics: a research note, by C. Taffaro, et al. FREE INQUIRY IN CREATIVE SOCIOLOGY 17(2):163-164, November 1989

Effects of exposure to drug-related cues in detoxified opiate addicts: a theoretical review and some data, by J. Powell, et al. ADDICTIVE BEHAVIORS 15(4):339-354, 1990

REHABILITATION

Effects of in vivo behavioral rehearsal on the learning of assertive behaviors with a substance abusing population, by J. A. Ingram, et al. ADDICTIVE BEHAVIORS 15(2):189-194, 1990

Factors predicting outcome among opiate addicts after treatment, by M. Gossop, et al. BRITISH JOURNAL OF CLINICAL PSYCHOLOGY 29(Pt 2):209-216, May 1990

Fine tuning social control: electronic monitoring and surrogate homes for the using parolees—a research note, by F. P. Williams, III. JOURNAL OF CONTEMPORARY CRIMINAL JUSTICE 5(3):173-180, 1989

Follow-up study of drug abusers in a therapeutic community during periods of change, by M. Norris. INTERNATIONAL JOURNAL OF THERAPEUTIC COMMUNITIES 9(4):249-261, 1988

Health abuse marketing, by L. J. Coleman, et al. HEALTH MARKETING QUARTERLY 7(1-2):87-96, 1990

"Hello, may we help you:" a study of attrition prevention at the time of the first phone contact with substance-abusing clients, by M. J. Stark, et al. AMERICAN JOURNAL OF DRUG AND ALCOHOL ABUSE 16(1-2):67-76, March/June 1990

How to help addicts kick their habits, by J. Scognamiglio. USA TODAY 119:32-35, July 1990

Human Behavioral Pharmacology Laboratory: University of Vermont, by J. R. Hughes, et al. BRITISH JOURNAL OF ADDICTION 85(4):441-445, April 1990

Impact of HMO development on mental health and chemical dependency services, by M. Shadle, et al. HOSPITAL AND COMMUNITY PSYCHIATRY 40(11):1145-1151, November 1989

Improvement in psychological functioning among drug abusers: inpatient treatment compared to outpatient methadone maintenance, by R. J. Craig, et al. JOURNAL OF SUBSTANCE ABUSE TREATMENT 7(1):11-19, 1990

Integrating vocational rehabilitation into treatment programs: two case studies, by J. Randell, et al. JOURNAL OF APPLIED COUNSELING 21(2):38-44, Summer 1990

John Dewey Academy: a residential college preparatory therapeutic high school: a dialogue with Tom Brattler, by W. Glasser. JOURNAL OF COUNSELING AND DEVELOPMENT 68:582-585, May/June 1990

Kicking the habit: a social network to recovery from opiate addiction, by R. K. Price. DAI A 50(4):1110, October 1989

KIDS these days: a United States drug-treatment program meets opposition in Calgary, by P. MacDonald. ALBERTA (WESTERN) REPORT 17(14):41, March 19, 1990

REHABILITATION

Kuwait drug addiction scene: a changing pattern, by A. M. Bilal. INTERNATIONAL JOURNAL OF THE ADDICTIONS 24(12):1137-1144, December 1989

Lifesaving sounds: jazzman Frank Morgan swings away from prison and drugs, by J. Cocks. TIME 135(13):70, March 26, 1990

Many points to needle. LANCET 335(8680):20-21, January 6, 1990

Markers of the social network as criteria in the follow-up of patients of a therapeutic community, by B. Rohrle, et al. ZEITSCHRIFT FUR KLINISCHE PSYCHOLOGIE, PSYCHOPATHOLOGIE UND PSYCHOTERAPIE 37(3):291-302, 1989

Mobile treatment working well in the north, by D. Driver. JOURNAL OF THE ADDICTION RESEARCH FOUNDATION 19(9):10, September 1, 1990

National study of drug abuse treatment finds benefits include less drug use, fewer crimes. HOSPITAL AND COMMUNITY PSYCHIATRY 40(12):1309-1310, December 1989

Opiate maintenance and abstinence: attitudes, treatment modalities and outcome, by D. Ladewig. DRUG AND ALCOHOL DEPENDENCE 25(2):245-250, April 1990

Organization and implementation of the Australian methadone program and initial results, by D. Pfersmann, et al. NERVENARZT 61(7):438-443, July 1990

Ounce of prevention, by C. R. Talley. AMERICAN JOURNAL OF HOSPITAL PHARMACY 47(5):1031, May 1990

Outcome of a unique youth drug abuse program: a follow-up study of clients of Straight, Inc, by A. S. Friedman, et al. JOURNAL OF SUBSTANCE ABUSE TREATMENT 6(4):259-268, 1989

Pharmacy practice in a chemical-dependency treatment center, by T. J. Ives, et al. AMERICAN JOURNAL OF HOSPITAL PHARMACY 47(5):1080-1083, May 1990

Piece of my mind: little battles, by R. Malcolm. JAMA 263(1):90, January 5, 1990

Presence and integration of drug abuse intervention in human resource management, by T. C. Blum. NIDA RESEARCH MONOGRAPH SERIES 91:245-269, 1989

Prevalence of buprenorphine use by heroin addicts undergoing treatment, by L. San, et al. MEDICINA CLINICA 93(17):645-648, November 25, 1989

Primary health care and the addictions: where to start and where to go, by B. Pollak. BRITISH JOURNAL OF ADDICTION 84(12):1425-1432, December 1989

Primary medical care for IVDU's: model for future care, by R. S. Schottenfeld, et al. NIDA RESEARCH MONOGRAPH SERIES 95:403-404, 1989

Programs for pharmacists impaired by substance abuse: a report, by G. E. McNees, et al. AMERICAN PHARMACY 30(5):33-37, May 1990

Psychopathology, parent relations, and careers in vocational training: a prospective study, by E. Ravndal, et al. INTERNATIONAL JOURNAL OF THE ADDICTIONS 24(4):315-323, April 1989

Randomized controlled trial of recovery training and self-help for opioid addicts in New England and Hong Kong, by W. E. McAuliffe. JOURNAL OF PSYCHOACTIVE DRUGS 22(2):197-209, April/June 1990

Re: detoxification of the chemically dependent patient, by A. A. Wartenberg. RHODE ISLAND MEDICAL JOURNAL 73(4):139, April 1990

Relapse and recovery in drug abuse: research and practice, by C. G. Leukefeld, et al. INTERNATIONAL JOURNAL OF THE ADDICTIONS 24(3):189-201, March 1989

Relapse prevention in psychoeducational groups for compulsive crack cocaine smokers, by B. C. Wallace. JOURNAL OF SUBSTANCE ABUSE TREATMENT 6(4):229-239, 1989

Relapse prevention with adult chronic marijuana smokers, by R. A. Roffman, et al. JOURNAL OF CHEMICAL DEPENDENCY TREATMENT 2(2):241-257, 1989

Relapse treatment and prevention in an outpatient rehabilitation program, by D. L. Moyer. JOURNAL OF CHEMICAL DEPENDENCY TREATMENT 2(2):225-240, 1989

Risk and drug treatment: views of Beth Israel Medical Center's CEO R. Newman, N.Y.C., by H. J. Anderson. HOSPITALS 64:31-32, November 20, 1990

Scouting in adolescent treatment programs: building a foundation, by B. D. Austin. JOURNAL OF PSYCHOSOCIAL NURSING AND MENTAL HEALTH SERVICES 28(7):24-25, July 1990

Second change. JOURNAL OF THE SOUTH CAROLINA MEDICAL ASSOCIATION 86(1):12, January 1990

Self-efficacy and relapse among inpatient drug and alcohol abusers: a predictor of outcome, by T. A. Burling, et al. JOURNAL OF STUDIES ON ALCOHOL 50(4): 354-360, July 1989

Serum prolactin levels during extended cocaine abstinence, by C. M. Swartz, et al. AMERICAN JOURNAL OF PSYCHIATRY 147(6):777-779, June 1990

SHARP carwash: a community-oriented work program for substance abuse patients, by P. Stead, et al. SOCIAL WORK 35(1):79-80, January 1990

Should drug abusers be treated or convicted?, by M. McCalope. JET 78:30-32, May 28, 1990

Sleep: a relapse predictor, by B. L. Lee. JOURNAL OF THE ADDICTION RESEARCH FOUNDATION 19(11):9, January 1, 1990

Smoking control in a psychiatric setting, by H. H. Dawley, Jr., et al. HOSPITAL AND COMMUNITY PSYCHIATRY 40(12):1299-1301, December 1989

Social and drug-taking behavior of "maintained" opiate addicts, by J. Strang, et al. BRITISH JOURNAL OF ADDICTION 85(6):771-774, 1990

Some things work: it's never easy, but crack addicts can now be successfully treated, by D. Gelman. NEWSWEEK 116(13):78-79+, September 24, 1990

Specialized addictions assessment-referral services in Ontario: a review of their characteristics and roles in the addiction treatment system, by A. C. Ogborne, et al. BRITISH JOURNAL OF ADDICTION 85(2):197-204, February 1990

Specific treatment demand as a definitory trait of a typology in heroin addicts: differential profile of two subpopulations, by M. E. Herrero, et al. INTERNATIONAL JOURNAL OF THE ADDICTIONS 25(1):65-79, January 1990

Staying off the merry go round: prescribing habits for recovering patients, by B. Eames. JOURNAL OF THE SOUTH CAROLINA MEDICAL ASSOCIATION 86(1):42-45, January 1990

Structured outpatient treatment of alcohol vs. drug dependencies, by A. M. Washton. RECENT DEVELOPMENTS IN ALCOHOLISM 8:285-304, 1990

Subjective dimensions of heroin urges: influence of heroin-related and affectively negative stimuli, by J. E. Sherman, et al. ADDICTIVE BEHAVIORS 14(6):611-623, 1989

Substance abuse among the chronic mentally ill, by R. E. Drake, et al. HOSPITAL AND COMMUNITY PSYCHIATRY 40(10):1041-1046, October 1989

Substance abuse among the deaf population: an overview of current strategies, programs and barriers to recovery, by K. E. Lane. JOURNAL OF THE AMERICAN DEAFNESS AND ASSOCIATION 22(4):79-85, April 1989

Substance abuse treatment modalities in the age of HIV spectrum disease, by J. A. Nathan, et al. JOURNAL OF PSYCHOACTIVE DRUGS 21(4):423-429, October/December 1989

Success of reentry into anesthesiology training programs by residents with a history of substance abuse, by E. J. Menk, et al. JAMA 263(22):3060-3062, June 13, 1990

Therapeutic community model in the treatment of drug dependence: its advantages and disadvantages, by R. Sartor. MEDICINE AND LAW 8(4):337-341, 1989

Tolerated and forbidden addictive drugs: various effects on the management of adolescent drug dependent patients, by F. Vadasz. SCHWEIZER ARCHIV FUR NEUROLOGIE UND PSYCHIATRIE 141(1):73-87, 1990

Treating combined alcohol and drug abuse in community-based programs, by R. L. Hubbard. RECENT DEVELOPMENTS IN ALCOHOLISM 8:273-283, 1990

Treating crack cocaine dependence: the critical role of relapse prevention, by B. C. Wallace. JOURNAL OF PSYCHOACTIVE DRUGS 22(2):149-158, April/June 1990

Treatment for psychoactive substance use disorder in social populations: issues in strategic planning, by J. Westermeyer. ADVANCES IN ALCOHOL AND SUBSTANCE ABUSE 8(3-4):1-8, Spring 1990

Troubled waters at the bridge, by C. Saline. PHILADELPHIA MAGAZINE 81:114+, June 1990

REHABILITATION

Two ships in the night: physician usage of community drug and alcohol treatment centers, by G. L. Phelps, et al. JOURNAL OF THE SOUTH CAROLINA MEDICAL ASSOCIATION 86(1):22-23, January 1990

Untreated addicts do better: abstinence time longer, by K. Birchard. JOURNAL OF THE ADDICTION RESEARCH FOUNDATION 19(11):4, November 1, 1990

Use predicts treatment outcome, not opiate dependence or withdrawal, by T. A. Kosten, et al. NIDA RESEARCH MONOGRAPH SERIES 95:459-460, 1989

Various forms of chronicity in addicted patients at a psychiatric hospital, by G. Weithmann, et al. PSYCHIATRISCHE PRAXIS 16(5):171-178, September 1989

Vocational rehabilitation of substance abusers, by S. Deren, et al. JOURNAL OF APPLIED COUNSELING 21(2):4-6, Summer 1990

Who's the real victim of substance abuse? PROFILES IN HEALTHCARE MARKETING (38):18-21, 1990

RELIGION

Ask A.A.: dope and religion, by H. Ault. AMERICAN ATHEIST 31(9):10, September 1989

Chicago's drug-busting "God Squad": Catholic priests G. Clements and M. Pfleger pressure stores, by J. G. Hubbell. READER'S DIGEST 137:98-102, November 1990

Notes on the relationship between drugs and religion, by E. Long. LAW AND ORDER 37(9):101-103, September 1989

RESEARCH

Alberta does funding drug research chair. JOURNAL OF THE ADDICTION RESEARCH FOUNDATION 19(7-8):2, July/August 1990

Animals in research on addictive and mental disorders: foundation of the quest for knowledge, by F. K. Goodwin. NIDA RESEARCH MONOGRAPH SERIES 95:6-15, 1989

Applications "simply repay" cost of research, by J. Hollobon. JOURNAL OF THE ADDICTION RESEARCH FOUNDATION 19(2):7, February 1, 1990

Behavioral economics of drugs self-administration: I—functional equivalence of response requirements and drug dose—minireview, by W. K. Bickel, et al. LIFE SCIENCES 47(17):1501-1510, 1990

Cytochrome P-455 nm complex formation in the metabolism of phenylalkylamines: XI: peroxygenase versus monooxygenase function of cytochrome P-450 in rat liver microsomes, by K. H. Jonsson, et al. CHEMICO-BIOLOGICAL INTERACTIONS 75(3):267-279, 1990

Drug research: a comparison of ongoing research and perceived priorities, by S. Redman, et al. BRITISH JOURNAL OF ADDICTION 85(7):943-952, July 1990

RESEARCH

Drugs and adjustment: summary of research by J. Shedler and J. Block, by G. W. Bracey. PHI DELTA KAPPAN 72:246-247, November 1990

Drugs of choice: drug users who never suffer addiction attract scientific interest, by B. Bower. SCIENCE NEWS 136(25):392-393, December 16, 1989

Effect of ketotifen in rodent models of anxiety and on the behavioural consequences of withdrawing from treatment with drugs of abuse, by B. Costall, et al. NAUNYN-SCHMIEDEBERG'S ARCHIVES OF PHARMACOLOGY 341(6):547-551, June 1990

Empirical and theoretical bases for an adaptive model of addiction, by B. K. Alexander. JOURNAL OF DRUG ISSUES 20(1):37-65, Winter 1990

Impact of research on designing strategies for preventing and treating dependence on drugs and alcohol, by W. Feuerlein. DRUG AND ALCOHOL DEPENDENCE 25(2):199-202, April 1990

Investigations with the novel non-opioid analgesic flupirtine in regard to possible benzodiazepine-like abuse inducing potential, by B. Nickel, et al. ARZNEIMIT-TEL-FORSCHUNG 40(8):905-906, 1990

Liquid diet model of chlordiazepoxide dependence in mice, by A. W. Chan, et al. PHARMACOLOGY, BIOCHEMISTRY AND BEHAVIOR 34(4):839-845, December 1989

On terms used and abused: the concept of "codependency," by E. S. L. Gomberg. DRUGS AND SOCIETY 3(3-4):113-132, March/April 1989

"Point of no return" as a target of experimental research on drug dependence, by H. Coper, et al. DRUG AND ALCOHOL DEPENDENCE 25(2):129-134, April 1990

Scientists must own up when playing advocate role, by B. L. Lee. JOURNAL OF THE ADDICTION RESEARCH FOUNDATION 19(9):7, September 1, 1990

Social relevance of epidemiological research in drug use, abuse and dependence: a position paper, by W. I. Soueif. DRUG AND ALCOHOL DEPENDENCE 25(2): 153-157, April 1990

Studying crack users and their criminal careers: the scientific and artistic aspects of locating hard-to-reach subjects and interviewing them about sensitive topics, by E. Dunlap, et al. CONTEMPORARY DRUG PROBLEMS 17(1):121-144, Spring 1990

Substitution of temazepam and midazolam in pentobarbital-dependent rats, by G. J. Yutrzenka, et al. PHYSIOLOGY AND BEHAVIOR 46(1):55-60, July 1989

Tobacco use: a perspective for alcohol and drug researchers, by L. T. Kozlowski, et al. BRITISH JOURNAL OF ADDICTION 85(2):245, February 1990

What do opiate addicts and cigarette smokers mean by "craving": a pilot study, by M. Gossop, et al. DRUG AND ALCOHOL DEPENDENCE 26(1):85-88, 1990

SEDATIVES

Abuse liability of anxiolytics and sedative-hypnotics: methods assessing the likelihood of abuse, by J. D. Roache, et al. NIDA RESEARCH MONOGRAPH SERIES 92:123-146, 1989

Comparison of the behavioral effects and abuse liability of ethanol and pentobarbital in recreational sedative abusers, by J. J. Guarino, et al. NIDA RESEARCH MONOGRAPH SERIES 85:453-454, 1989

Dependence on sedative-hypnotics, by J. S. Templeton. BRITISH JOURNAL OF ADDICTION 85(2):301, February 1990

Diazepam and triazolam self-administration in sedative abusers: concordance of subject ratings, performance and drug self-administration, by J. D. Roache, et al. PSYCHOPHARMACOLOGY 99(3):309-315, November 1989

Effect of controls on sedatives and hypnotics on their use for suicide, by D. Lester, et al. JOURNAL OF TOXICOLOGY: CLINICAL TOXICOLOGY 27(4-5):299-303, 1989

Sedatives-hypnotics for abuse, by J. Dobson. NEW ZEALAND MEDICAL JOURNAL 102(881):651, December 13, 1989

SEX AND SEXUALITY

Are "sex-for-drugs" exchanges accelerating the risk of AIDS? OHIO MEDICINE 86(5):346, May 1990

Association of cocaine use with sperm concentration, motility, and morphology, by M. B. Bracken, et al. FERTILITY AND STERILITY 53(2):315-322, February 1990

Beliefs about AIDS, use of alcohol and drugs, and unprotected sex among Massachusetts adolescents, by R. W. Hingson, et al. AMERICAN JOURNAL OF PUBLIC HEALTH 80(3):295-299, March 1990

Cigarettes, alcohol and marijuana are related to pyospermia in infertile men, by C. E. Close, et al. JOURNAL OF UROLOGY 144(4):900-903, October 1990

Injecting and sexual behaviour of intravenous drug users in Sydney, by A. Dinnen. MEDICAL JOURNAL OF AUSTRALIA 152(12):672, June 18, 1990

Injecting and sexual behaviour of intravenous drug users in Sydney, by S. Darke, et al. MEDICAL JOURNAL OF AUSTRALIA 152(8):446, April 16, 1990

Model of the sexual relations of young i.v. drug users, by M. L. Williams. JOURNAL OF THE ACQUIRED IMMUNE DEFICIENCY SYNDROME 3(2):192-193, 1990

Prevalence of high-risk sexual behavior in male intravenous drug users with steady female partners, by D. K. Lewis, et al. AMERICAN JOURNAL OF PUBLIC HEALTH 80(4):465-468, April 1990

Relationship of substance use during sex to high-risk sexual behavior, by B. C. Leigh. JOURNAL OF SEX RESEARCH 27(2):199-213, May 1990

Sexual partners of injecting drug users: the risk of HIV infection, by H. Klee, et al. BRITISH JOURNAL OF ADDICTION 85(3):413-418, March 1990

SEX AND SEXUALITY

Survey of genitourinary organisms in a population of sexually active adolescent males admitted to a chemical dependency unit, by S. C. Jenkins, et al. JOURNAL OF ADOLESCENT HEALTH CARE 11(3):223-226, May 1990

Trading sex for crack among juvenile drug users: a research note, by J. A. Inciardi. CONTEMPORARY DRUG PROBLEMS 16(4):689-700, Winter 1989

Use of drugs and alcohol by homosexually active men in relation to sexual practices, by J. McCusker, et al. JOURNAL OF THE ACQUIRED IMMUNE DEFICIENCY SYNDROME 3(7):729-736, 1990

Variables influencing condom use among intravenous drug users, by S. Magura, et al. AMERICAN JOURNAL OF PUBLIC HEALTH 80(1):82-84, January 1990

SEXUALLY TRANSMITTED DISEASES
see also: Acquired Immune Deficiency Syndrome

Increase of infectious syphilis among heterosexuals in Amsterdam: its relationship to drug use and prostitution, by J. A. van den Hoek, et al. GENITOURINARY MEDICINE 66(1):31-32, February 1990

Relationship of cocaine use to syphilis and human immunodeficiency virus infections among inner city parturient women, by H. L. Minkoff, et al. AMERICAN JOURNAL OF OBSTETRICS AND GYNECOLOGY 163(2):521-526, August 1990

Risk factors for syphilis: cocaine use and prostitution, by R. T. Rolfs, et al. AMERICAN JOURNAL OF PUBLIC HEALTH 80(7):853-857, July 1990

Risk of sexually transmitted disease among black adolescent crack users in Oakland and San Francisco, California, by R. E. Fullilove, et al. JAMA 263(6):851-855, February 9, 1990

Syphilis among parturients at an inner city hospital: association with cocaine use and implications for congenital syphilis rates, United States, by D. Nanda, et al. NEW YORK STATE JOURNAL OF MEDICINE 90(10):488-490, 1990

SMOKELESS TOBACCO

Adolescents' first and most recent use situations of smokeless tobacco and cigarettes: similarities and differences, by G. Hahn, et al. ADDICTIVE BEHAVIORS 15(5):439-448, 1990

Here's something to chew on, by M. C. Taylor. CMAJ 142(1):1182-1183, June 1, 1990

In-depth analysis of male adolescent smokeless tobacco users: interviews with users and their fathers, by D. V. Ary, et al. JOURNAL OF BEHAVIORAL MEDICINE 12(5):449-467, October 1989

Licorice, tobacco chewing, and hypertension. NEW ENGLAND JOURNAL OF MEDICINE 322(12):849-850, March 22, 1990

SMOKELESS TOBACCO

Psychosocial factors in the use of smokeless tobacco and their implications for P.L. 99-252, by H. H. Severson. JOURNAL OF PUBLIC HEALTH DENTISTRY 50(1):90-97, Winter 1990

Smokeless tobacco addiction: a threat to the oral and systemic heath of a child and adolescent, by A. G. Christen, et al. PEDIATRICIAN 16(3-4):170-177, 1989

Smokeless tobacco use among Missouri youth, by R. C. Brownson, et al. MISSOURI MEDICINE 87(6):351-354, June 1990

Smokeless tobacco use among Native American school children, by B. Bruerd. PUBLIC HEALTH REPORTS 105(2):196-201, March/April 1990

Smokeless tobacco use and health effects among baseball players, by V. L. Ernster, et al. JAMA 264(2):218-224, July 11, 1990

Smokeless tobacco use by youth in Canadian Arctic, by W. J. Millar. ARCTIC MEDICAL RESEARCH 49(Suppl)2:39-47, 1990

Complications

Basal cell carcinoma of the scalp caused by contact with chewing tobacco, by B. Sassolas, et al. ANNALES DE DERMATOLGOIE ET DE VENEROLOGIE 116(9):663-665, 1989

Smokeless tobacco "time bomb," by A. G. Christen, et al. POSTGRADUATE MEDICINE 87(7):69-74, May 15, 1990

SOCIOLOGY

Cannabis and human social behaviour, by D. F. Marks, et al. HUMAN PSYCHO-PHARMACOLOGY: CLINICAL AND EXPERIMENTAL 4(4):283-290, December 1989

Crack in Spanish Harlem: culture and economy in the inner city, by P. Bourgois. ANTHROPOLOGY TODAY 5(4):6-11, August 1989

Cultural factors in the choice of drugs, by D. B. Heath. RECENT DEVELOPMENTS IN ALCOHOLISM 9:245-254, 1990

Culture and community: drink and soft drugs in Hebriedean youth culture, by A. Dean. SOCIOLOGICAL REVIEW 38(3):517-563, 1990

Exploratory study of social problems theory, by R. Peat. DAI A 50(7):2268, January 1990

Impact of drug abuse and addiction on society, by R. S. Hoffman, et al. EMERGENCY MEDICINE CLINICS OF NORTH AMERICA 8(3):467-480, August 1990

Lifestyle factors for drug users in relation to risks for HIV, by G. Mulleady, et al. AIDS CARE 1(1):45-50, 1989

One's coat cut according to one's cloth: drug use and economy of opiate addicts, by M. Grapendaal. JUSTITIELE VERKENNINGEN 15(5):23-46, 1989

SOCIOLOGY

Realistic local approach to controlling drug harms, by J. E. Eck. PUBLIC MANAGE-MENT 72:7-12, July 1990

Relationship between cultural values of Alaskan natives and substance abuse, by V. M. Jerrel. DAI A 50(2):471, 1989

Social class and its relationship to youth substance use and other delinquent behaviors, by B. D. Lorch. SOCIAL WORK RESEARCH AND ABSTRACTS 26(1):25-31, March 1990

Socio-cultural factors affecting drug addiction treatment in Italy: fear of treatment, by I. Maremmani, et al. DRUG AND ALCOHOL DEPENDENCE 25(2):235-239, April 1990

Struggle against drug addiction: the evidence of the object of work, by J. P. E. Baizieux. SOCIETES 20:32-36, October 1988

Study comparing demographic, economic, and family function characteristics, by D. R. Wood, et al. AMERICAN JOURNAL OF PUBLIC HEALTH 80(9):1049-1052, 1990

SOLVENTS

Examination attainments of secondary school pupils who abuse solvents, by O. Chadwick, et al. BRITISH JOURNAL OF EDUCATIONAL PSYCHOLOGY 60(Pt 2):180-181, June 1990

Fatal attraction of a 5-minute fix: increase in solvent abuse by school children in Great Britain, by E. Heron. TIMES EDUCATIONAL SUPPLEMENT 3882:10, November 23, 1990

New trend in solvent abuse deaths, by P. McBride, et al. MEDICINE, SCIENCE AND THE LAW 30(3):207-213, July 1990

Complications

Pattern of solvent consumption and neuropsychological damage associated with their use, by R. Sosa, et al. SALUD PUBLICA DE MEXICO 31(5):634-641, September/October 1989

SORBITOL

Sorbitol abuse among eating-disordered patients, by E. S. Ohlrich, et al. PSYCHO-SOMATICS 30(4):451-453, Fall 1989

SPORTS

see also: NCAA
NFL
Steroids and Sports
Testing—Sports

Abuse of drugs used to enhance athletic performance, by J. C. Wagner. AMERICAN JOURNAL OF HOSPITAL PHARMACY 46(10):2059-2067, October 1989

SPORTS

Abuse of erythropoietin to enhance athletic performance, by W. C. Scott. JAMA 264(13):1660, October 3, 1990

Athlete's guide to drug abuse, by J. K. Pate. SCHOLASTIC COACH 60:68-70+, December 1990

Banned and permitted drugs, by C. Smith. ATHLETICS November/December 1990, pp. 26-27

Black physician named to head NFL drug plan: L. S. Brown. JET 78:47, June 18, 1990

Blood doping: a literature review, by M. Jones, et al. BRITISH JOURNAL OF SPORTS MEDICINE 23(2):84-88, June 1989

David Thompson, back to earth, by M. Lupica. ESQUIRE 113:75+, March 1990

Doping and doping control, by N. Norman. TIDSSKRIFT FOR DEN NORSKE LAEGE-FORENING 110(13):1643-1644, May 20, 1990

Doping in sports, by B. Corrigan. AUSTRALIAN POLICE JOURNAL 43(3):105-110, 1989

Doping substances produced in Czechoslovakia, by I. Vodickova, et al. CESKOSLO-VENSKA FARMACIE 38(5):236-237, July 1989

Drug record: is the IAAF being fair in its treatment of Ben Johnson, by R. S. O'Neal. ATHLETICS February/March 1990, pp. 28-29

Drugs and the athlete, by G. I. Wadler, et al. CANADIAN JOURNAL OF PUBLIC HEALTH 81(2):171, March/April 1990

Drugs and cycling: the inside story, by P. Kimmage. BICYCLING 31:48-52, July 1990

Drugs: crack and field, by P. Gambaccini. RUNNER'S WORLD 25:86-90+, October 1990

Drugs, sport, and politics (book review), by R. Voy. ATHLETICS November/December 1990, p. 15

Dubin inquiry: the following are selected recommendations. ATHLETICS September 1990, pp. 6-8

Dubin Report, by S. Buffery. CHAMPION 14(2):8-13, November 1990

Dubin Report. JOURNAL OF THE ADDICTION RESEARCH FOUNDATION 19(9):12, September 1, 1990

Fear strikes out again: D. Gooden, by M. Lupica. ESQUIRE 113:71-73, May 1990

Fuhr shut out: ruling has many rethinking NHL's drug policy, by S. Morrison. HOCKEY NEWS 44(4):6, October 12, 1990

Fuhr's future in doubt as he admits to longtime substance abuse. HOCKEY NEWS 43(42):4, September 14, 1990

Games' drug stance undercut by finance. JOURNAL OF THE ADDICTION RE-SEARCH FOUNDATION 19(5):9, May 1, 1990

Grant Fuhr, by D. Staples. HOCKEY NEWS 44(12):20-21, 1990

GRD secrets are revealed: state-controlled drug use by athletes, by P. Nichols. OB-SERVER April 8, 1990, p. 21

Guilty: drug use in amateur sports, by Y. Dion. CHAMPION 13(4):59, April 1990

Hard time, hard questions: comeback hopes of C. Thompson, Oklahoma quarterback imprisoned for cocaine trafficking, by R. Telander. SPORTS ILLUSTRATED 73:118, December 24, 1990

"High" seas: patterns of drug use among southern California sport-boat operatives, by N. Curcione. DEVIANT BEHAVIOR 11(4):307-318, 1990

How did he do it: the best goalie in the world is exposed as a cocaine user, by M. Stevenson. ALBERTA (WESTERN) REPORT 17(40):49, September 17, 1990

How much caffeine is too much in athletes?, by K. O. Price, et al. AMERICAN JOUR-NAL OF HOSPITAL PHARMACY 47(2):303, February 1990

Hyperactivity, stimulants, and sports, by P. G. Dyment. PHYSICIAN AND SPORTS-MEDICINE 18:22, April 1990

Just say yes to NHL's drug policy, by S. Morrison. HOCKEY NEWS 44(5):47, October 19, 1990

Keeping cool with cocaine: the Oiler's goalie takes body blow from his ex-wife, by M. Stevenson. BC REPORT 3(2):50-51, September 17, 1990

Locker room pharmacology, by S. Heinzl. MEDIZINISCHE MONATSSCHRIFT FUR PHARMAZEUTEN 13(4):97, April 1990

Oiler's Grant Fuhr faces ban on coke use. JET 78:50, October 1, 1990

Olympic gold: the Dubin inquiry, by N. McCabe. CANADIAN LAWYER 14(1):22-26, February 1990

OTFA (Ontario Track and Field Association) response to the Dubin Report, by A. Buckstein. ATHLETICS September 1990, pp. 8+

Pharmaceutical services at the Tenth Pan American Games, by J. C. Wagner, et al. AMERICAN JOURNAL OF HOSPITAL PHARMACY 46(10):2023-2027, October 1989

Politics of sports policy in Britain: the examples of football hooliganism and drug abuse, by B. Houlihan. LEISURES STUDIES 9(1):55-69, January 1990

Presidential address of the American Orthopaedic Society for Sports Medicine: drug abuse in sports, by J. S. Cox. AMERICAN JOURNAL OF SPORTS MEDICINE 18:568-572, November/December 1990

Pro football's everyman: D. Manley with the Phoenix Cardinals after drug suspension, by T. Callahan. US NEWS AND WORLD REPORT 109:78, December 17, 1990

SPORTS

Rapport Dubin, by S. Buffery. CHAMPION 14(2):14-17, November 1990

Redskins Manley put on hold on return to NFL. JET 78:46, August 6, 1990

Reynolds disputes claim of illegal drug use. JET 79:49, November 26, 1990

Scandal and reform in collegiate athletics: implications from a national survey of head football coaches, by F. T. Cullen, et al. JOURNAL OF HIGHER EDUCATION 61(1):5-64, January/February 1990

Smokeless tobacco use and health effects among baseball players, by V. L. Ernster, et al. JAMA 264(2):218-224, July 11, 1990

Speed trap: inside the biggest scandal in Olympic history (book review), by C. Francis, et al. QUILL AND QUIRE 56(11):23, November 1990

Sporting life: is our ideal a mechanically tuned killer cyborg coming down the track or a full, vital, healthy human being?, by V. Burstyn. SATURDAY NIGHT 105(2):42-49, March 1990

Sports Minister, Marcel Danis, is not a good sport, by C. Smith. ATHLETICS October 1990, pp. 26-30

Survey finds drop in drug use by athletes, by C. Dervarics. BLACK ISSUES IN HIGHER EDUCATION 6(17):4-5, November 1989

Suspend Grand Fuhr: for what, being human, by B. McKenzie. HOCKEY NEWS 44(1):3, September 21, 1990

Use of smokeless tobacco in a group of professional baseball players, by K. M. Cummings, et al. JOURNAL OF BEHAVIORAL MEDICINE 12(6):559-567, December 1989

Vikings placekicker is indicted in drug probe: D. Igwebuike. JET 79:51, November 26, 1990

We can help student athletes fight substance abuse, by S. E. Scott. JOURNAL OF THE NEW YORK STATE SCHOOL BOARDS ASSOCIATION 21-23, October 1989

Winning and performance-enhancing drugs: our dual addiction, by C. E. Yesalis. PHYSICIAN AND SPORTSMEDICINE 18:161-163+, March 1990

STATISTICS
see also: Surveys

American and white American school dropouts' drug use, health status, and involvement in violence, by E. L. Chavez, et al. PUBLIC HEALTH REPORTS 104(6): 594-604, November/December 1989

Chemical people project: a case study analysis of three task forces from 1981 to 1989, University of Pittsburgh, 1989, by D. K. McCall. DAI A 50(7):2245, 1990

STATISTICS

Lies, damn lies, statistics, and the drug war, by C. M. Fuss, Jr. US NAVAL INSTITUTE. PROCEEDINGS 115(12):65-69, December 1989

One out of every 100 Americans is addicted to cocaine: Senate report finds. CRIME CONTROL DIGEST 24(19):5, May 14, 1990; also in NARCOTICS CONTROL DIGEST 20(11):8, May 23, 1990

Statistics on alcohol and drug use in Canada and other countries (book review), by M. Adrian, et al. JOURNAL OF THE ADDICTION RESEARCH FOUNDATION 19(3):8, March 1, 1990

United Kingdom Home Office notification statistics for 1989, by M. Farrell. BRITISH JOURNAL OF ADDICTION 85(7):971-972, July 1990

STEROIDS

Anabolic steroid dependence, by L. R. Hays, et al. AMERICAN JOURNAL OF PSYCHIATRY 147(1):122, January 1990

Anabolic steroids, by R. D. Daigle. JOURNAL OF PSYCHOACTIVE DRUGS 22(1):77-80, January/March 1990

Anabolic steroids and ergogenic aids, by D. O. Hough. AMERICAN FAMILY PHYSICIAN 41(4):1157-1164, April 1990

Are steroids muscling in on your patients?, by M. Carlson. OHIO MEDICINE 85(10): 777-779, October 1989

Express mail evidence: illegal steroid dealer, by B. L. Arlen. FDA CONSUMER 24:36, November 1990

Forensic issues arising from the use of anabolic steroids, by C. C. Kleinman. PSYCHIATRIC ANNALS 20(4):219-221, April 1990

Illicit anabolic steroid use: a controlled personality study, by W. R. Yates, et al. ACTA PSYCHIATRICA SCANDINAVICA 81(6):548-550, June 1990

Misuse of oral steroids by an asthmatic drug addict, by A. C. Dowell. BRITISH JOURNAL OF ADDICTION 84(12):1548, December 1989

Parents and steroid use by nonathletes, by P. S. Salva, et al. PEDIATRICS 84(5):940-941, November 1989

Phony steroid dealers receive real sentences: D. L. Tirado, by S. Snider. FDA CONSUMER 24:33-34, July/August 1990

Psychology of anabolic steroid use, by J. M. McGraw. JOURNAL OF CLINICAL PSYCHIATRY 51(6):260, June 1990

Steroids and the Controlled Substances Act, by L. Uzych. BIOLOGICAL PSYCHIATRY 27(6):561-562, March 15, 1990

Student steroid use way up, by H. McConnell. JOURNAL OF THE ADDICTION RESEARCH FOUNDATION 19(10):1, October 1, 1990

STEROIDS

Teenagers blase about steroid use: anabolic steroids. FDA CONSUMER 24:2-3, December 1990

Use of anabolic steroids, by P. D. Lee. AMERICAN JOURNAL OF DISEASES OF CHILDREN 144(9):954-955, September 1990

Was superman a junky: the fallacy of anabolic steroids, by N. P. Johnson. JOURNAL OF THE SOUTH CAROLINA MEDICAL ASSOCIATION 86(1):46-48, January 1990

Complications
Acne fulminas following use of anabolic steroids, by W. Mayerhausen, et al. ZEITSCHRIFT FUR HAUTKRANKHEITEN 64(10):875-876+, October 15, 1989

Anabolic steroid-associated hypogonadism in male hemodialysis patients, by Y. Maeda, et al. CLINICAL NEUROPHARMACOLOGY 32(4):198-201, October 1989

Anabolic steroid-induced hypogonadropic hypoganadism, by J. P. Jarow, et al. AMERICAN JOURNAL OF SPORTS MEDICINE 18(4):429-431, July/August 1990

Anabolic steroid-induced psychiatric reactions, by C. C. Oliva, et al. DICP 24(4):388, April 1990

Anabolic steroids and infarction, by S. Bowman. BMJ 300(6726):750, March 17, 1990

Cardiac effects of anabolic steroids, by Z. Herschman. ANESTHESIOLOGY 72(4): 772-773, April 1990

Drugs that build bodies but dismantle minds: evidence that anabolic steroids can cause psychiatric disorders and may be associated with violent crime, by B. Barr. INDEPENDENT October 5, 1990, p. 19

Homicide and near-homicide by anabolic steroid users, by G. H. Pope, Jr., et al. JOURNAL OF CLINICAL PSYCHIATRY 51(1):28-31, January 1990

Psychiatric symptoms from steroids abuse. SCHOLASTIC COACH 60:95, November 1990

Steroid-induced psychosis, by P. Turner. LANCET 2(8668):923, October 14, 1989

Research
National Institute on Drug Abuse may join in anabolic steroid research, by V. S. Cowart. JAMA 261:1855-1856, April 7, 1989

STEROIDS AND SPORTS
Acute metabolic effects of exercise in bodybuilders using anabolic steroids, by G. McKillop, et al. BRITISH JOURNAL OF SPORTS MEDICINE 23(3):186-187, September 1989

Anabolic-androgenic steroids in athletics, by M. B. Mellion, et al. AMERICAN FAMILY PHYSICIAN 41:1141-1142, April 1990

Anabolic steroid education for high school football players. AMERICAN FAMILY PHYSICIAN 42:1114, October 1990

Anabolic steroid use among high school athletes, by N. S. Engel. MCN 14(6):417, November/December 1989

Anabolic steroid use by male adolescents. AMERICAN FAMILY PHYSICIAN 41:267, January 1990

Anabolic steroids in athletics, by S. C. Holden, et al. TEXAS MEDICINE 86(3):32-36, March 1990

Analysis of anabolic steroids using GC-MS with selected ion monitoring, by B. C. Chung, et al. JOURNAL OF ANALYTICAL TOXICOLOGY 14(2):91-95, March/April1990

Ben Johnson predicts return to racing form. JET 78:52, July 16, 1990

Big muscles, big problems: anabolic steroids, by S. De Vore. CURRENT HEALTH 2 17:11-13, November 1990

Blunting "steroid epidemic" requires alternatives, innovative education, by V. S. Cowart. JAMA 264(13):1641, October 3, 1990

Canada OKs Johnson's return to competition. JET 78:46, September 3, 1990

Clean break: Ben Johnson gets set to compete again, by N. Wood. MACLEAN'S 103(34):14-15, August 20, 1990

Congress considers restricting steroids, by L. J. Dreyfuss. PHYSICIAN AND SPORTSMEDICINE 18:38, March 1990

Defying the laws of physiques: steroids join the list of illicit drugs in high schools, by B. Rempel. ALBERTA (WESTERN) REPORT 17(9):43, February 12, 1990

Dirty system: Stern magazine story on anabolic steroid use by East German athletes, by M. Noden. SPORTS ILLUSTRATED 73:27, December 17, 1990

Doping: also a problem in general practice, by H. H. Dickhuth, et al. FORTSCHRITTE DER MEDIZIN 107(28):585-588, September 30, 1989

Drug abuse in body builders: a questionnaire study, by A. Kisling, et al. UGESKRIFT FOR LAEGER 151(40):2582-2584, October 2, 1989

Effect of an anabolic steroid education program on knowledge and attitudes of high school football players, by L. Goldberg, et al. JOURNAL OF ADOLESCENT HEALTH CARE 11(3):210-214, May 1990

Effects of anabolic steroids on lipoprotein profiles of female weight lifters, by R. J. Moffatt, et al. PHYSICIAN AND SPORTSMEDICINE 18:106-110+, September 1990

STEROIDS AND SPORTS

Epidemiological and policy issues in the measurement of the long term health effects of anabolic-androgenic steroids, by C. E. Yesalis, 3d, et al. SPORTS MEDICINE 8(3):129-138, September 1989

Evidence for physical and psychological dependence on anabolic androgenic steroids in weight weight lifters, by K. J. Brower, et al. AMERICAN JOURNAL OF PSYCHIATRY 147(4):510-512, April 1990

Getting tough on anabolic steroids: can we win the battle?, by J. A. Shroyer. PHYSICIAN AND SPORTSMEDICINE 18:106-110+, February 1990

Illegal steroid use among fifty weightlifters, by J. R. Fuller, et al. SOCIOLOGY AND SOCIAL RESEARCH 73:19-21, October 1988

Illicit anabolic steroid use of athletes: a case series analysis, by P. J. Perry, et al. AMERICAN JOURNAL OF SPORTS MEDICINE 18(4):422-428, July/August 1990

Lipid and apoprotein modifications in body builders during and after self-administration of anabolic steroids, by G. Baldo-Enzi, et al. METABOLISM 39(2):203-208, February 1990

Lipid profile of body builders with and without self-administration of anabolic steroids, by J. Frohlich, et al. EUROPEAN JOURNAL OF APPLIED PHYSIOLOGY AND OCCUPATIONAL PHYSIOLOGY 59(1-2):98-103, 1989

New race for gold: Dubin report encouraging for B. Johnson, by D. Jenish. MACLEAN'S 103:18-19, July 9, 1990

NFL battles steroid use, by D. L. Black. PHYSICIAN AND SPORTSMEDICINE 18:25-26, August 1990

Of MDs, and muscles: lessons from two "retired steroid doctors," by D. L. Breo. JAMA 263(12):1697+, March 23-30, 1990

Prevalence of anabolic steroid use by male and female adolescents, by R. Windsor, et al. MEDICINE AND SCIENCE IN SPORTS AND EXERCISE 21(5):494-497, October 1989

Pushing for a clearer competition: a champion weightlifter, Richard Nowazek, fights steroid use, by S. Vanagas. BC REPORT 1(49):49, August 13, 1990

Schooled in steroids: an educational package targets teenagers, by B. Clark. ALBERTA (WESTERN) REPORT 17(49):59, November 19, 1990

Selected psychological characteristics of anabolic-androgenic steroid users, by M. S. Bahrke, et al. NEW ENGLAND JOURNAL OF MEDICINE 323(12):834-835, September 20, 1990

Steroid abuse in young athletes. AMERICAN FAMILY PHYSICIAN 41:682, February 1990

Steroid use by athletes shows poor judgment, lost integrity, by F. G. Corley. TEXAS MEDICINE 86(3):4, March 1990

STEROIDS AND SPORTS

Steroids claimed our son's life: with commentary by Harrison G. Pope, Jr., by G. Elofson, et al. PHYSICIAN AND SPORTSMEDICINE 18:15-16, August 1990

Steroids in athletics: one university's experience, by M. Lopez. JOURNAL OF COLLEGE STUDENT DEVELOPMENT 31:523-530, November 1990

Study of steroid use among athletes: knowledge, attitudes and use, by C. L. Chng, et al. HEALTH EDUCATION 21:12-17+, November/December 1990

Training volume, androgen use and serum creatine kinase activity, by K. Hakkinen, et al. BRITISH JOURNAL OF SPORTS MEDICINE 23(3):188-189, September 1989

United States, USSR join forces to combat steroid use, by M. Duda. PHYSICIAN AND SPORTSMEDICINE 17:16+, August 1989

University of Notre Dame says 5 of its football players tested positive for use of anabolic steroids, by D. Lederman. CHRONICLE OF HIGHER EDUCATION 37:37-38, September 5, 1990

Use of anabolic-androgenic steroids among body builders: frequency and attitudes, by M. Lindstrom, et al. JOURNAL OF INTERNAL MEDICINE 227(6):407-411, June 1990

Use of anabolic-androgenic steroids by athletes, by L. Goldberg, et al. NEW ENGLAND JOURNAL OF MEDICINE 322(11):775-776, March 15, 1990

Use of anabolic steroids in high school students, by R. Terney, et al. AMERICAN JOURNAL OF DISEASES OF CHILDREN 144(1):99-103, January 1990

We can clean in up: Atlanta Falcon Bill Fralic is making it his business to rid the NFL of steroids, by P. King. SPORTS ILLUSTRATED 73(2):34-36+, July 9, 1990

STIMULANTS

1990's: decade of the stimulants, by J. B. Davies, et al. BRITISH JOURNAL OF ADDICTION 85(6):811-813, June 1990

Addictiveness of central stimulants, by C. A. Dackis, et al. ADVANCES IN ALCOHOL AND SUBSTANCE ABUSE 9(1-2):9-26, Spring 1990

Hyperactivity, stimulants, and sports, by P. G. Dyment. PHYSICIAN AND SPORTSMEDICINE 18:22, April 1990

STREET DRUGS

Case study of illicit preparation of antirheumatic analgesic with phenylbutazone as active ingredient, by C. E. Thuan, et al. MEDICAL JOURNAL OF MALAYSIA 44(2): 160-166, June 1989

Drug abuse liability testing: human subject issues, by H. D. Kleber. NIDA RESEARCH MONOGRAPH SERIES 92:341-356, 1989

Drug discrimination: methods for drug characterization and classification, by G. E. Bigelow, et al. NIDA RESEARCH MONOGRAPH SERIES 92:101-122, 1989

Drugs and rhetorical devils, by T. Melia. JOURNAL OF CLINICAL PHARMACY AND THERAPEUTICS 14(6):415-418, December 1989

Evaluation of the potential of clandestine manufacture of 3,4-methylenedioxyamphetamine (MDA) analogs and homologs, by T. A. Dal Cason. JOURNAL OF FORENSIC SCIENCES 35(3):675-697, May 1990

Gender differences in initiation of psychotherapeutic medicine use, by A. M. Trinkoff, et al. ACTA PSYCHIATRICA SCANDINAVICA 81(1):32-38, January 1990

Hazardous chemicals from clandestine labs pose threat to law enforcement: drug laboratories, by E. F. Connors, III. POLICE CHIEF 57(1):37-41, January 1990

Lithium-ammonia reduction of ephedrine to methamphetamine: an ususual clandestine synthesis, by R. A. Ely, et al. JOURNAL OF FORENSIC SCIENCES 35(3): 720-723, May 1990

Molecular mechanisms of drug reinforcement: current status, by S. Dworkin, et al. NIDA RESEARCH MONOGRAPH SERIES 90:266-274, 1988

MST Continus: morphine, 100 mg: big dose—big money, by G. M. Robinson. NEW ZEALAND MEDICAL JOURNAL 103(897):435, September 12, 1990

Neurochemical effects of an acute treatment with 4-methylaminorex: a new stimulant of abuse, by C. F. Bunker, et al. EUROPEAN JOURNAL OF PHARMACOLOGY 180(1):103-111, May 3, 1990

"New drugs," by C. P. Bueaupere. OFFICIER DE POLICE 10:5-23+, 1990

Street drugs. HAWAII MEDICAL JOURNAL 48(11):448-495, November 1989

Street drugs: everyones business, by F. Su'a. HAWAII MEDICAL JOURNAL 48(11): 452+, November 1989

Testing and abuse liability of drugs in humans, by C. R. Schuster. NIDA RESEARCH MONOGRAPH SERIES 92:1-6, 1989

Tolerated and forbidden addictive drugs: various effects on the management of adolescent drug dependent patients, by F. Vadasz. SCHWEIZER ARCHIV FUR NEUROLOGIE UND PSYCHIATRIE 141(1):73-87, 1990

Update on street drugs in Mississippi, by D. K. Beebe, et al. JOURNAL OF THE MISSISSIPPI STATE MEDICAL ASSOCIATION 30(12):387-390, December 1989

Complications

Emergency treatments for police dogs used for illicit drug detection, by G. A. Dumonceaux, et al. JOURNAL OF THE AMERICAN VETERINARY MEDICAL ASSOCIATION 197(2):185-187, July 15, 1990

Research

Promising new biological and behavioral correlates of the reinforcing properties of drugs, by J. H. Mendelson, et al. NIDA RESEARCH MONOGRAPH SERIES 92:307-340, 1989

Receptor-transductive mechanisms for drugs of abuse, by L. Abood. NIDA RESEARCH MONOGRAPH SERIES 90:284-294, 1988

Relationship between self-reported drug effects and their reinforcing effects: studies with stimulant drugs, by M. W. Fischman. NIDA RESEARCH MONOGRAPH SERIES (92):211-230, 1989

Research and policy. DRUG AND ALCOHOL DEPENDENCE 25(2):113-250, April 1990

STRYCHNINE

Strychnine poisoning, by B. A. Smith. JOURNAL OF EMERGENCY MEDICINE 8(3): 321-326, 1990

SUICIDE

Clinical value of drug analyses in deliberate self-poisoning, by T. Rygnestad, et al. HUMAN AND EXPERIMENTAL TOXICOLOGY 9(4):221-230, July 1990

Comparative prospective study of self-poisoned patients in Trondheim, Norway between 1978 and 1987: epidemiology and clinical data, by T. Rygnestad. HUMAN TOXICOLOGY 8(6):475-482, November 1989

Drug identification problems in two suicides with neuromuscular blocking agents, by G. Somogyi, et al. FORENSIC SCIENCE INTERNATIONAL 43(3):257-266, December 1989

Effect of controls on sedatives and hypnotics on their use for suicide, by D. Lester, et al. JOURNAL OF TOXICOLOGY: CLINICAL TOXICOLOGY 27(4-5):299-303, 1989

Epidemiologic investigation of potential risk factors for suicide attempts, by K. R. Petronis, et al. SOCIAL PSYCHIATRY AND PSYCHIATRIC EPIDEMIOLOGY 25(4):193-199, 1990

Fatal and non-fatal methomyl intoxication in an attempted double suicide, by T. Miyazaki, et al. FORENSIC SCIENCE INTERNATIONAL 42(3):263-270, August 1989

Health risk behaviors and attempted suicide in adolescents who report prior maltreatment, by S. Riggs, et al. JOURNAL OF PEDIATRICS 116(5):815-821, 1990

Psychiatric study of suicide among urban Swedish women, by U. Asgard. ACTA PSYCHIATRICA SCANDINAVICA 82(2):115-124, 1990

Self-poisoning in Sri Lanka: factors determining the choice of the poisoning agents, by J. Hettiarachchi, et al. HUMAN TOXICOLOGY 8(6):507-510, November 1989

Substance abuse and adolescent suicidal behavior, by F. E. Crumley. JAMA 263(22): 3051-3056, June 13, 1990

Substance abuse and attempts at suicide by burning, by J. R. Swenson, et al. AMERICAN JOURNAL OF PSYCHIATRY 147(6):811, June 1990

SUICIDE

Substance abuse and suicide: the San Diego study, by C. L. Rich, et al. ANNALS OF CLINICAL PSYCHIATRY 1(2):79-85, June 1989

Suicidal indicators in schizophrenics, by A. M. Dassori, et al. ACTA PSYCHIATRICA SCANDINAVICA 81(5):409-413, 1990

Suicide among young men: psychiatric illness, deviant behavior and substance abuse, by P. Allebeck, et al. ACTA PSYCHIATRICA SCANDINAVICA 81(6):565-570, 1990

Suicide and antidepressant overdosage in general practice, by G. Beaumont. BRITISH JOURNAL OF PSYCHIATRY (6):27-31, October 1989

Suicide attempts among adolescent drug users, by A. L. Berman, et al. AMERICAN JOURNAL OF DISEASES OF CHILDREN 144(3):310-314, March 1990

Suicide by nitrous oxide poisoning, by A. Chadly, et al. AMERICAN JOURNAL OF FORENSIC MEDICINE AND PATHOLOGY 10(4):330-331, December 1989

Violent and nonviolent suicide attempts: a controlled Rorschach study, by E. M. Rydin, et al. ACTA PSYCHIATRICA SCANDINAVICA 82(1):30-39, 1990

SURVEYS
see also: Statistics

Adolescent drug use: findings of national and local surveys, by E. R. Oetting, et al. JOURNAL OF CONSULTING AND CLINICAL PSYCHOLOGY 58:385-394, August 1990

Adolescent substance abuse survey: statewide findings for 1988, by R. J. Marshall, Jr. RHODE ISLAND MEDICAL JOURNAL 72(12):464, December 1989

Annual NIDA survey shows continuing declines in drug use by high school seniors. CRIME CONTROL DIGEST 24(8):1+, February 26, 1990; also in JUVENILE JUSTICE DIGEST 18(5):2-3, March 7, 1990

Cocaine-heroin dependence compared: evidence from an epidemiologic field survey, by J. C. Anthony, et al. AMERICAN JOURNAL OF PUBLIC HEALTH 79: 1409-1410, October 1989

Effects of interview mode on self-reported drug use, by W. S. Aquilino, et al. PUBLIC OPINION QUARTERLY 54:362-395, Fall 1990

Latest AMS Foundation survey finds one-third of nation's employers have or are considering drug testing, by J. E. McKendrick, Jr. MANAGEMENT WORLD 19:3-4, March/April 1990

Local drug surveys a first step. JOURNAL OF THE ADDICTION RESEARCH FOUNDATION 19(12):4, December 1, 1990

Mayors discount drug-use polls. CRIME CONTROL DIGEST 24(26):9, July 2, 1990; also in NARCOTICS CONTROL DIGEST 20(14):3, July 4, 1990

Need for improved assessment of adolescent substance involvement, by K. Winters. JOURNAL OF DRUG ISSUES 20:487-502, Summer 1990

SURVEYS

Obtaining report of sensitive behavior: a comparison of substance use reports from telephone and face-to-face interviews, by T. P. Johnson, et al. SOCIAL SCIENCE QUARTERLY 70(1):174-183, March 1989

Patterns of drug use: data from the 1985 National Household Survey, by H. L. Voss. NIDA RESEARCH MONOGRAPH SERIES 91:33-46, 1989

Rangel asserts high school survey understated. JUVENILE JUSTICE DIGEST 18(4): 4, February 21, 1990

Reliability and construct validity of the Needle Sharing Inventory, by M. D. Kipke, et al. INTERNATIONAL JOURNAL OF THE ADDICTIONS 24(6):515-526, June 1989

Reliability and validity of the WHO student drug-use questionnaire among Nigerian students, by M. L. Adelekan, et al. DRUG AND ALCOHOL DEPENDENCE 24(3):245-249, December 1989

Secondary school teachers' knowledge and views about drug abuse in Ogun State, Nigeria: a pilot survey, by M. L. Adelekan, et al. JOURNAL OF DRUG EDUCATION 20(2):163-174, 1990

Student drug use declines: NB survey of grades 7 to 12, by J. Carroll. JOURNAL OF THE ADDICTION RESEARCH FOUNDATION 19(3):4, March 1, 1990

Survey concerning a drugs prevention project: all drugs are bad said the addict and he ought to know, by R. P. De Keijser. ALGEMEEN POLITIEBLAD 138(4):75-77, 1989

Teen drug study indicates rising problem. JUVENILE JUSTICE DIGEST 18(10):8-9, May 16, 1990

This is what you thought: 70% say drugs are a major or the most significant problem in their community— results of survey. GLAMOUR 88:111, February 1990

TEENS

Addiction in adolescents, by M. A. Morrison. WESTERN JOURNAL OF MEDICINE 152(5):543-546, May 1990

Adolescent chemical dependency, by J. A. Farrow. MEDICAL CLINICS OF NORTH AMERICA 74(5):1265-1274, September 1990

Adolescent cocaine abuse: addictive potential, behavioral and psychiatric effects, by T. W. Estroff, et al. CLINICAL PEDIATRICS 28(12):550-555, December 1989

Adolescent drug use and psychological health: a longitudinal inquiry, by J. Shedler, et al. AMERICAN PSYCHOLOGIST 45(5):612-630, May 1990

Adolescent drug use: findings of national and local surveys, by F. Beauvais, et al. JOURNAL OF CONSULTING AND CLINICAL PSYCHOLOGY 58(4):385-394, 1990

Adolescent health status, behaviors, and cardiovascular diseases, by M. Adeyanju. ADOLESCENCE 25:155-169, Spring 1990

TEENS

Adolescent marijuana use: risk factors and implications, by M. Rob, et al. AUS-TRALIAN AND NEW ZEALAND JOURNAL OF PSYCHIATRY 24(1):45-56, March 1990

Adolescent medicine in pediatric practice, by A. Marks, et al. JOURNAL OF ADO-LESCENT HEALTH CARE 11(2):149-153, 1990

Adolescent risk perception: a measure to further our understanding of tobacco and drug use, by H. Stevenson, et al. HYPIE 9(2):27-29, June 1990

Adolescent substance abuse: practice implications, by J. S. Wodarski. ADOLES-CENCE 25(99):667-688, Fall 1990

Adolescent substance abuse survey: statewide findings for 1988, by R. J. Marshall, Jr. RHODE ISLAND MEDICAL JOURNAL 72(12):464, December 1989

Adolescent substance use and perceived family functioning, by L. S. Smart, et al. JOURNAL OF FAMILY ISSUES 11(2):208-227, June 1990

Adolescent substance use and the role of the primary care provider, by S. Riggs, et al. RHODE ISLAND MEDICAL JOURNAL 73(6):253-257, June 1990

Adolescent use of narcotics and toxic substances, by G. Lukacher, et al. SOVIET MEDICINE (6):105-109, 1990

Adolescent values clarification: a positive influence on perceived locus of control, by M. R. James. JOURNAL OF ALCOHOL AND DRUG EDUCATION 35(2):75-80, Winter 1990

Adolescents' first and most recent use situations of smokeless tobacco and ci-garettes: similarities and differences, by G. Hahn, et al. ADDICTIVE BEHAVIORS 15(5):439-448, 1990

Adolescents initiating cannabis use: cultural opposition or poor mental health, by W. Pederson. JOURNAL OF ADOLESCENCE 13(4):327-339, 1990

African-American youth and AIDS high-risk behavior: the social context and barriers to prevention, by B. P. Bowser, et al. YOUTH AND SOCIETY 22:54-66, September 1990

Aftercare services for drug-using institutionalized delinquents, by R. F. Catalano, et al. SOCIAL SERVICE REVIEW 63(4):553-577, December 1989

Age of first use of drugs among rural midwestern youth, by P. D Sarvela, et al. HUMAN SERVICES IN THE RURAL ENVIRONMENT 13(3):9-15, Winter 1990

AIDS and chemical dependency: prevention needs of adolescents, by M. Hoch-hauser. JOURNAL OF PSYCHOACTIVE DRUGS 21(4):381-385, October/December 1989

Alcohol intoxication in teenagers using inhalant stupefacients, by J. W. Tomczak, et al. POLISH JOURNAL OF PHARMACOLOGY AND PHARMACY 41(3):203-206, May/June 1989

Beliefs about AIDS, use of alcohol and drugs, and unprotected sex among Massachusetts adolescents, by R. W. Hingson, et al. AMERICAN JOURNAL OF PUBLIC HEALTH 80(3):295-299, March 1990

Black adolescent crack users in Oakland: no quick fix, by B. G. Silverman. JAMA 264(3):337, July 18, 1990

Characteristics of narcotics and toxic substance abuse by adolescents: clinico-sociological study, by Gla Lukacher, et al. ZHURNAL NEVROPATOLOGII I PSIKHIATRII IMEN S. S. KORSAKOVA 89(8):117-121, 1989

Comorbidity of substance abuse and other psychiatric disorders in adolescents, by M. J. Calache. AMERICAN JOURNAL OF PSYCHIATRY 147(5):681-682, May 1990

Comparison of alcohol, tobacco, and illicit drug use among students and delinquents in the Bahamas, by R. G. Smart, et al. BULLETIN OF THE PAN AMERICAN HEALTH ORGANIZATION 24(1):39-45, 1990

Consequences of marijuana use on intrapersonal and interpersonal functioning in black and white adolescents, by J. S. Brook, et al. GENETIC, SOCIAL, AND GENERAL PSYCHOLOGY MONOGRAPHS 115(3):349-369, August 1989

Correlations of substance abuse and self-image among socially diverse groups of adolescents and clinical implications, by V. M. Uribe, et al. HILLSIDE JOURNAL OF CLINICAL PSYCHIATRY 11(1):25-34, 1989

Declaring the war on drugs: teens fight back, by M. Barbera-Hogan. TEEN 34:56-57+, October 1990

Depression in homicidal adolescents, by C. P. Malmquist. BULLETIN OF THE AMERICAN ACADEMY OF PSYCHIATRY AND THE LAW 18(1):23-36, 1990

Determining the primary cause of substance use disorders among juvenile offenders, by K. Stone, et al. ALCOHOLISM TREATMENT QUARTERLY 7(2):81-95, 1990

Development of psychosocial scales for the assessment of adolescents involved with alcohol and drugs, by G. A. Henly, et al. INTERNATIONAL JOURNAL OF THE ADDICTIONS 24(10):973-1001, October 1989

Development variations in the context of marijuana initiation among adolescents, by S. L. Bailey, et, al. JOURNAL OF HEALTH AND SOCIAL BEHAVIOR 31(1):58-70, March 1990

Developmental variation in the context of marijuana initiation among adolecents, by S. L. Bailey, et al. JOURNAL OF HEALTH AND SOCIAL BEHAVIOR 31(1):58-70, March 1990

Diagnosing attention-deficit hyperactivity disorder and learning disabilities with chemically dependent adolescents, by N. Ralph, et al. JOURNAL OF PSYCHOACTIVE DRUGS 21(2):203-215, April/June 1989

Diagnosis and treatment of adolescent substance abuse, by D. I. Macdonald. CURRENT PROBLEMS IN PEDIATRICS 19(8):389-440, August 1989

Divorce, remarriage, and adolescent substance use: a prospective longitudinal study, by R. H. Needle, et al. JOURNAL OF MARRIAGE AND THE FAMILY 52:157-169, Fall 1990

Drug abuse severity in adolescents is associated with magnitude of deviation in temperant traits, by R. E. Tarter, et al. BRITISH JOURNAL OF ADDICTION 85(11): 1501-1504, 1990

Drug use in British Colombian adolescents, by R. Chamberayne, et al. CANADIAN JOURNAL OF PUBLIC HEALTH 80(6):457-459, November/December 1989

Drugs among youth, by K. Hurrelmann, et al. PADAGOGIK HEUTE 41(12):26-29, December 1989

Early onset of adolescent sexual behavior and drug involvement, by E. Rosenbaum, et al. JOURNAL OF MARRIAGE AND THE FAMILY 52(3):783-798, August 1990

Empirical examination of a mixed boding model of adolescent substance use, by D. T. Mason. DAI A 50(11):3744, May 1990

Ethnicity, communication, and drugs, by F. Korzenny, et al. JOURNAL OF DRUG ISSUES 20(1):87-98, Winter 1990

Evaluation and treatment of adolescent substance abuse: a decision tree method, by R. E. Tarter. AMERICAN JOURNAL OF DRUG AND ALCOHOL ABUSE 16(1-2):1-46, June 1990

Family structure as a predictor of initial substance use and sexual intercourse in early adolescence, by R. L. Flewelling, et al. JOURNAL OF MARRIAGE AND THE FAMILY 52:171-181, February 1990

Family systems and adolescent drug abuse, by R. J. Volk. DAI A 50(11):3764, May 1990

Identification with peers as a strategy to muddle through the troubles of the adolescent years, by M. L. Pombeni, et al. JOURNAL OF ADOLESCENCE 13(3):351-369, 1990

Influence of family and peer group on the use of drugs by adolescents, by J. M. Otero Lopez, et al. INTERNATIONAL JOURNAL OF THE ADDICTIONS 24(11):1065-1082, November 1989

Juvenile addictions, by J. Formoso. POLICIA 49:18-23, 1989

"Latchkey kids" at risk. JUVENILE JUSTICE DIGEST 17(18):3-4, September 20, 1989

Longitudinal study of antisocial behaviors in early adolescence as predictors of late adolescent substance use: gender and ethnic group differences, by M. Windle. JOURNAL OF ABNORMAL PSYCHOLOGY 99(1):86-91, February 1990

Major depression in childhood and adolescence, by D. L. Moreau. PSYCHIATRIC CLINICS OF NORTH AMERICA 13(2):355-368, June 1990

Mental state of marijuana-smoking adolescents, by J. Rabe-Jablonska, et al. PRZEGLAD LEKARSKI 46(12):802-805, 1989

MMPI profiles of adolescent substance abusers in treatment, by S. Walfish, et al. ADOLESCENCE 25(99):567-572, Fall 1990

Model proposing three processes of adolescent marijuana use, by S. L. Bailey. DAI A 50(9):3071, March 1990

No right to party: British youth use drugs at rock music night clubs, by M. Sinker. NEW STATESMAN AND SOCIETY 3:46, April 13, 1990

On drug abuse among teenagers, by A. Y. Grishko. SOTSIOLOGICHESKIE ISSIEDO-VANIYA 17(2):100-102, 1990

Participation exams: how to detect a teenage crisis, by P. Donahue. PHYSICIAN AND SPORTSMEDICINE 18(9):53-56+, 1990

Peer cluster theory and adolescent drug use: a reanalysis, by R. D. Hays, et al. JOURNAL OF DRUG EDUCATION 20(3):191-198, 1990

Perceived effects of drug messages on use patterns in adolescents, by D. M. Mayton, 2nd, et al. JOURNAL OF DRUG EDUCATION 20(4):305-318, 1990

Physical recklessness in adolecence: trait or byproduct of depressive-suicidal states, by D. C. Clark. JOURNAL OF NERVOUS AND MENTAL DISEASE 178(7):423-433, 1990

Progression of chemical dependence and recovery in adolescents, by M. A. Morrison, et al. PSYCHIATRIC ANNALS 19(12):666-671, December 1989

Ratings of behaviour problems in adolescents hospitalized for substance abuse, by C. L. Williams, et al. JOURNAL OF ADOLESCENT CHEMICAL DEPENDENCY 1(1):95-112, 1990

Reasons to avoid drug use among teenagers: associations with actual drug use and implications for prevention among different demographic groups, by M. D. Newcomb, et al. JOURNAL OF ALCOHOL AND DRUG EDUCATION 36:53-81, Fall 1990

Recreational drug use and psychopathology, by D. Lester, et al. PSYCHOLOGICAL REPORTS 62:814, June 1988

Relationship of adolescents' expectations and values to delinquents, hard drug use, and unprotected sexual intercourse, by J. P. Allen, et al. DEVELOPMENT AND PSYCHOPATHOLOGY 2(1):85-98, 1990

Relationship of alcohol, tobacco, marijuana, and other illegal drug use to delinquency among Mexican-American, black and white adolescent males, by W. D. Watts, et al. ADOLESCENCE 25(97):171-181, Spring 1990

School performance, academic aspirations, and drug use among children and adolescents, by M. J. Paulson, et al. JOURNAL OF DRUG EDUCATION 20(4):289-303, 1990

TEENS

Self-reported negative consequences of drug use among rural adolescents, by D. R. Holcomb, et al. HEALTH EDUCATION 21:36-40, July/August 1990

Shyness and sociability: a dangerous combination for illicit substance use in adolescent males, by R. M. Page. ADOLESCENCE 25:803-806, Winter 1990

Significant link found between youth's drug abuse, recidivism. CRIMINAL JUSTICE NEWSLETTER 21(16):6-7, August 15, 1990

Special series: alcohol and drug use among youth, by S. P. Schinke. JOURNAL OF CONSULTING AND CLINICAL PSYCHOLOGY 58(4):383-468, 1990

Street kids: a snapshot of a problem, by J. Hollobon. JOURNAL OF THE ADDICTION RESEARCH FOUNDATION 19(708):5, July/August 1990

Structure of problem behaviors among Irish adolescents, by J. W. Grube, et al. BRITISH JOURNAL OF ADDICTION 8(5):667-676, May 1990

Substance abuse by adolescents, by G. B. Slap. HOSPITAL PRACTICE 25(4):19-20+, April 30, 1990

Teenage substance abuse: life change, personality and family systems parameters, by C. A. Dillon. DAI A 50(11):3753, May 1990

Teenagers blase about steroid use: anabolic steroids. FDA CONSUMER 24:2-3, December 1990

Teenagers' drug use drops. SCIENCE NEWS 137:125, February 24, 1990

Tobacco, alcohol, and marijuana use among black adolescents: a comparison across gender, grade, and school environment, by S. M. Thomas, et al. JOURNAL OF THE LOUISIANA STATE MEDICAL SOCIETY 142(4):37-42, April 1990

Tolerated and forbidden addictive drugs: various effects on the management of adolescent drug dependent patients, by F. Vadasz. SCHWEIZER ARCHIV FUR NEUROLOGIE UND PSYCHIATRIE 141(1):73-87, 1990

Trading sex for crack among juvenile drug users: a research note, by J. A. Inciardi. CONTEMPORARY DRUG PROBLEMS 16(4):689-700, Winter 1989

Use of psychoactive substances among male secondary school pupils in Egypt: a study of a nationwide representative sample, by M. I. Soueif, et al. DRUG AND ALCOHOL DEPENDENCE 26(1):63-80, 1990

Why teenagers put rocks in their ears: hidden drugs and confidentiality, by R. E. Morris. JOURNAL OF ADOLESCENT HEALTH CARE 10(6):548-550, November 1989

TEMAZEPAM

Buprenorphine and temazepam: abuse, by R. Hammersley, et al. BRITISH JOURNAL OF ADDICTION 85(2):301-303, February 1990

TESTING

Acid test, by W. Gallagher. AMERICAN HEALTH 9:60-67, 1990

Acidity and the police. NEW LAW JOURNAL 139(6430):1477, 1989

Adulterants and substitutes, by J. L. Schauben. EMERGENCY MEDICINE CLINICS OF NORTH AMERICA 8(3):595-611, August 1990

Aflatoxins and heroin, by R. G. Hendrickse, et al. BMJ 299(6697):492-493, August 19, 1989

Another look at drug testing, by A. Fraser. JOURNAL OF THE ADDICTION RESEARCH FOUNDATION 19(11):7, November 1, 1990

Comments on the routine profiling of illicit heroin samples, by H. Neumann. FORENSIC SCIENCE INTERNATIONAL 44(1):85-87, January 1990

Computerized classification of drugs for investigation purposes, by J. J. David, et al. INTERNATIONAL CRIMINAL POLICE REVIEW 419:24-25, 1989

Dangers involved in field drug testing. LAW AND ORDER 38(2):5, February 1990

Determination of nornicotine in smokers' urine by gas chromatography following reductive alkylation to N'-propylnornicotine, by Y. Zhang, et al. JOURNAL OF CHROMATOGRAPHY 525(2):349-357, February 23, 1990

Discussion of heroin, morphine, and hydromorphone determination in postmortem material by high performance liquid chromatography, by F. Tagliaro, et al. JOURNAL OF FORENSIC SCIENCES 35(3):520-533, May 1990

Discussion of validity testing of commercial urine cocaine metabolite assays: part I and III, by V. Spiehler, et al. JOURNAL OF FORENSIC SCIENCES 35(2):230-232, March 1990

Does routine screening for benzodiazepines help to diagnose dependence in psychiatric inpatients, by S. Priebe, et al. ACTA PSYCHIATRICA SCANDINAVICA 80(5):514-517, November 1989

Doping control, by M. Ueki, et al. NIPPON RINSHO 48(Suppl):1270-1275, February 1990

Drug abuse will be target of new industry-HHS group Pharmaceutical Manufacturers Association Commission on Medicines for Treatment of Drug Dependence and Abuse. CHEMICAL MARKETING REPORT 238:4, December 3, 1990

Drug and alcohol rehabilitation a win-win solution, by J. P. Kinnan. SAFETY AND HEALTH 142:26-29, December 1990

Drug screening. PEDIATRICS 85(2):231-234, February 1990

Drug testing, by D. Altamirano. FIRE ENGINEERING 143:71-74, February 1990

Drug testing, by P. Lert. AIR PROGRESS 52:39+, February 1990

Drug testing in the private and public sectors, by J. W. Walsh. BULLETIN OF THE NEW YORK ACADEMY OF MEDICINE 65(2):166-172, February 1989

TESTING

Drug testing nightmare: news short. PUBLIC CITIZEN 10(1):8, January 1990

Drug testing treatment, and revocation: a review of program findings, by G. F. Vito, et al. FEDERAL PROBATION 54:37-43, September 1990

Drug testing watchdog or witch-hunt: publishing companies, by W. Berger. FOLIO 19:100-102+, September 1990

Drug tests in pregnant women: abuse of substance or of test, by K. L. Moss. JAMA 262(17):2383-2384, November 3, 1989

Drug use in patients admitted to a university trauma center: results of limited, rather than comprehensive, toxicology screening, by D. N. Bailey. JOURNAL OF ANA-LYTICAL TOXICOLOGY 14(1):22-24, January/February 1990

Drug use testing: the Canadian scene, by A. E. Robinson. JOURNAL OF FORENSIC SCIENCES 34(6):1422-1432, November 1989

Drugs and other issues: Ernst and Young-IMRA 1989-1990 Ounce of Prevention study, by J. Abend. STORES 72:51-53, June 1990

Drugs of abuse in a pediatric outpatient population, by J. M. Hicks, et al. CLINICAL CHEMISTRY 36(6):1256-1257, June 1990

Effects of diphenhydramine on immunoassays of phencyclidine in urine, by B. S. Levine, et al. CLINICAL CHEMISTRY 36(6):1258, June 1990

Foolproofing drug test results, by B. Steinberg. BUSINESS AND HEALTH 8:44-46+, December 1990

Forensic science identification of drugs of abuse, by A. J. McBay, et al. JOURNAL OF FORENSIC SCIENCES 34(6):1471-1476, November 1989

Forensic science implications of site and temporal influences on postmortem blood-drug concentrations, by R. W. Prouty, et al. JOURNAL OF FORENSIC SCI-ENCES 35(2):243-270, March 1990

Free market will prompt drug tests, by K. Selick. CANADIAN LAWYER 14(5):44, June 1990

Human urinary excretion profile after smoking and oral administration of [14C]delta 1-tetrahydrocannabinol, by E. Johansson, et al. JOURNAL OF ANALYTICAL TOXI-COLOGY 14(3):176-180, May/June 1990

Identification of four previously unreported cocaine metabolites in human urine, by J. Y. Zhang, et al. JOURNAL OF ANALYTICAL TOXICOLOGY 14(4):201-205, 1990

Identification of heroin and three structurally related isoheroins, by F. Medina, III. JOURNAL OF FORENSIC SCIENCES 34(3):565-578, 1989

Identifying the acetaminophen overdose, by W. A. Watson. ANNALS OF EMER-GENCY MEDICINE 18(10):1126-1127, October 1989

International news: Canada—coroners testing for cocaine. LAW AND ORDER 38(5): 6, May 1990

Investigation of interference by nonsteroidal anti-flammatory drugs in urine tests for abused drugs, by D. E. Rollins, et al. CLINICAL CHEMISTRY 36(4):602-606, April 1990

Isotopic analog as the internal standard of mass spectra of commonly abused drugs and their deuterated analogs, by Y. S. Ho, et al. JOURNAL OF FORENSIC SCIENCES 35(1):123-132, January 1990

Issues in human drug abuse liabilty testing: overview and prospects for the future, by J. V. Brady. NIDA RESEARCH MONOGRAPH SERIES 92:357-370, 1989

Johns Hopkins breaks controversial new ground in drug testing, by B. McCormick. TRUSTEE 43(7):16-17, July 1990

Limits of linearity and detection for some drugs of abuse, by S. B. Needleman, et al. JOURNAL OF ANALYTICAL TOXICOLOGY 14(1):34-38, January/February 1990

Medical Review Officer, by R. Swotinsky, et al. JOURNAL OF OCCUPATIONAL MEDICINE 32(10):1003-1008, 1990

Methodology, efficacy, and validity of drug testing, by R. E. Willette. BULLETIN OF THE NEW YORK ACADEMY OF MEDICINE 65(2):185-195, February 1989

Morphine and codeine in biological fluids: approaches to source identification, by M. A. Elsohly, et al. FORENSIC SCIENCE REVIEW 1(1):13-22, 1989

Nationwide survey of urinalysis practices of methadone maintenance clinics: utilization of laboratory services, by A. J. Saxon, et al. ARCHIVES OF PATHOLOGY AND LABORATORY MEDICINE 114(1):94-100, January 1990

New Zealand develops THC (tetrahydrocannabinol) tests, by P. McCarthy. JOURNAL OF THE ADDICTION RESEARCH FOUNDATION 19(10):9, October 1, 1990

Ophthalmic use of cocaine and the urine test for benzoylecgonine, by B. B. Brailiar, et al. NEW ENGLAND JOURNAL OF MEDICINE 320:1757-1758, June 29, 1989

Pharmacokinetic and pharmacodynamic drug interactions: implications for abuse liability testing, by E. M. Sellers, et al. NIDA RESEARCH MONOGRAPH SERIES (92): 287-306, 1989

Poly vinyl chloride, matrix membrane electrode for the selective determination of heroin (diamorphine) in illicit powders, by S. S. Hassan, et al. ANALYST 115(5): 623-625, May 1990

Prolonged detection period for cocaine and metabolite, by W. W. Weddington. JOURNAL OF CLINICAL PSYCHIATRY 51(8):347, August 1990

Prolonged presence of metabolite in urine after compulsive cocaine use, by W. M. Burke, et al. JOURNAL OF CLINICAL PSYCHIATRY 51(4):145-148, April 1990

Public sector drug testing: a balancing approach and the search for a new equilibrium, by M. A. Mass. BAYLOR LAW REVIEW 42:231-253, Spring 1990

Rates of drug detection in urine samples from various populations, by P. C. Isaac, et al. CLINICAL AND LABORATORY MEDICINE 10(2):289-299, June 1990

TESTING

Re: drug testing—technical complications of a complex social issue, by G. G. Jamieson, et al. AMERICAN JOURNAL OF INDUSTRIAL MEDICINE 17(3):403-406, 1990

Report: Privacy Commissioner's Report, *Drug Testing and Privacy*, slams drug testing. OCCUPATIONAL HEALTH AND SAFETY CANADA 6(5):13, September/October 1990·

Sampling of multi-unit drug exhibits, by A. B. Clark, et al. JOURNAL OF FORENSIC SCIENCES 35(3):713-719, May 1990

Say "no" to drug testing, by D. J. Greenblatt, et al. JOURNAL OF CLINICAL PSYCHOPHARMACOLOGY 10(3):157-159, June 1990

Screening for drug use among Norwegian drivers suspected of driving under influence of alcohol or drugs, by A. S. Christophersen, et al. FORENSIC SCIENCE INTERNATIONAL 45(1-2):5-14, March 1990

Screening for drugs of abuse: effect of heat-treating urine for safe handling of samples, by K. Wolff, et al. CLINICAL CHEMISTRY 36(6):908-910, June 1990; Erratum 36(8 Pt 1):1530, August 1990

Security wrap-up: drug testing, crime trends. SECURITY 27(4):9, April 1990

Special section: drug testing. PERSONNEL 67:26-36, July 1990

Studies reveal surprising data: health and safety issues, by J. Castelli. SAFETY AND HEALTH 141:42-45, March 1990

Survey of state regulation of testing for drugs of abuse outside of licensed, accredited, clinical laboratories, by D. M. Baer, et al. AMERICAN JOURNAL OF PUBLIC HEALTH 80(6):713-715, June 1990

Synthesis and spectral properties of 2,5-dimethoxy-4-ethoxyamphetamine and its precursors, by A. W. By, et al. JOURNAL OF FORENSIC SCIENCES 35(2):316-335, March 1990

Testing drugs in older people, by J. Folkenberg. FDA CONSUMER 24:24-27, November 1990

Testing-therapeutic drug use conflict [David] Smith, by H. McConnell. JOURNAL OF THE ADDICTION RESEARCH FOUNDATION 19(10):10, October 1, 1990

War on drugs: alternatives to drug testing, by G. M. Lousig-Nont. SECURITY MANAGEMENT 34:48-49+, May 1990

Employment

Airman express this month: civilian drug testing. AIRMAN 34(3):38, March 1990

Alternatives to drug testing, by G. M. Lousig-Nont. SECURITY MANAGEMENT 34(5):48-49+, May 1990

Avoiding the drug-testing rules, by D. Collogan. BUSINESS/COMMERICAL AVIATION 66:96, June 1990

Better approach by management in drug testing, by G. E. Stevens, et al. EMPLOYEE RESPONSIBILITIES AND RIGHTS JOURNAL 2(1):61-71, March 1989

BNA publishes guidebook on employee testing. CRIME CONTROL DIGEST 24(30): 7-8, July 30, 1990

Body invaders: employee drug testing. NATION 250:39-40, January 8-15, 1990

Case studies of drug testing in the workplace, by S. Blume, et al. BULLETIN OF THE NEW YORK ACADEMY OF MEDICINE 65(2):215-242, February 1989

Characteristics of firms with drug testing programs, by H. Axel. NIDA RESEARCH MONOGRAPH SERIES 91:219-226, 1989

Chemical dependency and drug testing in the workplace, by J. D. Osterloh, et al. WESTERN JOURNAL OF MEDICINE 152(5):506-513, May 1990

Chicago hospitals: no drug abusers need apply, by P. Eubanks. HOSPITALS 64(13): 79, July 5, 1990

Cleveland State fires its men's basketball coach after traces of cocaine are found in his system, by D. Lederman. CHRONICLE OF HIGHER EDUCATION 36:27+, July 25, 1990

College students' attitudes toward employee drug testing programs, by K. R. Murphy, et al. PERSONNEL PSYCHOLOGY 43:615-631, Autumn 1990

Corporate testing for drug, alcohol abuse on the increase, by M. S. Reisch. CHEMI-CAL ENGINEERING NEWS 68:17-18, July 16, 1990

Cover your assets: substance abuse plan, by R. Harris. AMERICAN PRINTER 205:48-49, July 1990

Department of Agriculture drug testing: DC. SEARCH AND SEIZURE BULLETIN November 1989, p. 7

Discovery process in drug use testing litigation, by K. L. Long. JOURNAL OF FORENSIC SCIENCES 34(6):1454-1470, November 1989

DOJ lawyers exempt from pre-job testing. NARCOTICS DEMAND REDUCTION DI-GEST 2(6):8-9, June 1990

Drug and alcohol testing in the workplace: objectives, pitfalls, and guidelines, by R. S. Schottenfeld. AMERICAN JOURNAL OF DRUG AND ALCOHOL ABUSE 15(4): 413-427, 1989

Drug monitoring in the workplace: results from the California Commerical Laboratory Drug Testing Project, by M. D. Anglin, et al. NIDA RESEARCH MONOGRAPH SERIES 91:81-96, 1989

Drug screening: surveys show suprisingly few employers use testing, by C. E. Anderson. ABA JOURNAL 75:38+, June 1989

Drug testing: 1990 Hiring and Firing Survey. SUPERVISION 51:6-7, July 1990

Drug testing in police agencies, by G. T. Carper, et al. JOURNAL OF CONTEMPO-RARY CRIMINAL JUSTICE 5(2):89-101, 1989

Drug testing in the police department: Los Angeles. SEARCH AND SEIZURE BUL-LETIN November 1989, p. 7

Drug testing in public agencies: are personnel directors doing things right—survey, by D. E. Klingner, et al. PUBLIC PERSONNEL MANAGEMENT 19:391-397, Winter 1990

Drug testing in the public sector: union member attitudes, by M. H. Le Roy. JOUR-NAL OF COLECTIVE NEGOTIATIONS IN THE PUBLIC SECTOR 19(3):165-173, 1990

Drug testing in the unionized workplace: are there any standards?, by C. D. Dillard. HOUSTON LAW REVIEW 27(3):515-556, May 1990

Drug testing in the workplace: a public sector concern, by G. Bradley. HOWARD LAW JOURNAL 32(1):49-59, 1989

Drug testing in the workplace: return of work issues, by D. V. Baise. BULLETIN OF THE NEW YORK ACADEMY OF MEDICINE 65(2):208-214, February 1989

Drug testing of physicians, by D. Orentlicher. JAMA 264:1039-1040, August 22-29, 1990

Drug testing of public employees: an introduction, by H. Jascourt. JOURNAL OF LAW AND EDUCATION 17(4):699-701, Fall 1988

Drug testing of unionized employees in private, by F. Rossman. TRADESWOMAN 9(3):24, Summer 1990

Drug testing: police and firefighters—during regulated physical, Maryland. POLICE OFFICER GRIEVANCES BULLETIN July 1990, pp. 3-4

Drug testing: police-regulated industry. POLICE OFFICER GRIEVANCES BULLETIN May 1989, pp. 3-4

Drug testing policy hot line. SECURITY MANAGEMENT 33(7):109, July 1989

Drug use down: railroad post-accident testing. TRANSPORTATION AND DISTRIBU-TION 31:10, June 1990

Drug use trends in a nuclear power company: cumulative data from an ongoing test-ing program, by C. E. Osborn, et al. NIDA RESEARCH MONOGRAPH SERIES 91:69-80, 1989

Drugs and booze: how should employers deal with abuse—forest products industry, by T. Blackman. FOREST INDUSTRIES 117:12-13, May 1990

Drugs and transportation safety, by A. J. McBay. JOURNAL OF FORENSIC SCI-ENCES 35(3):523-529, May 1990

Drugs and the workplace: testing without a cause, by R. Schubert. OCCUPATIONAL HEALTH AND SAFETY CANADA 6(3):142+, March/April 1990

Early employment testing for marijuana: demographic and employee retention patterns, by D. L. Blank, et al. NIDA RESEARCH MONOGRAPH SERIES 91:139-150, 1989

Effect of drug testing program characteristics on job applicants' judgments of acceptability of drug testing programs, by C. E. Reilly. DAI A 50(11):3756, May 1990

Empirical evaluation of preemployment drug testing in the United States Postal Service: interim report of findings, by J. Normand, et al. NIDA RESEARCH MONOGRAPH SERIES 91:111-138, 1989

Employee benefit managers assess drug policy: inpatient vs. outpatient drug treatment services, by E. Gilbert. NATIONAL UNDERWRITER. LIFE AND HEALTH/FINANCIAL SERVICES EDITION 94:10-11, December 24, 1990

Employee drug-testing policies in prison systems, by R. Guynes, et al. POLICE STRESS 9(1):21-24+, 1989

Employee testing: making your institution a drug-free zone, by M. Pearlman. CORRECTIONS TODAY 52:52+, August 1990

Employer drug testing programs. BUSINESS AND HEALTH 8(7):8-9, July 1990

Employer poll finds 55% test for drugs, or plan to, by L. Mazzuca. BUSINESS INSURANCE 24:3+, September 17, 1990

Employers crack down: Britain, by P. Ghosh. MANAGEMENT TODAY August 1990, p. 92

Employers' power to fight drug use, by D. Holthaus. TRUSTEE 42(10):20, October 1989

Europeans warned: EAP essential first step before drug testing, by K. Birchard. JOURNAL OF THE ADDICTION RESEARCH EDUCATION 19(9):9, September 1, 1990

Evaluation of drug testing in the workplace, by J. Sheridan, et al. NIDA RESEARCH MONOGRAPH SERIES 91:195-216, 1989

Experimental test of the impact of drug-testing programs on potential job applicants' attitudes and intentions, by J. M. Crant, et al. JOURNAL OF APPLIED PSYCHOLOGY 75:127-131, April 1990

FHWA to develop drug abuse data: truck driver fined for drugs. TRAFFIC WORLD 223:15, September 17, 1990

FRA announces results of pot-accident drug tests. CORPORATE SECURITY DIGEST 4(15):4, April 16, 1990

From the Office of the General Counsel: drug testing of the physicians, by D. Orentlicher. JAMA 264(8):1039-1040, August 22-29, 1990

From the top down, random testing is working on UP: Union Pacific drug testing program, by G. Welty. RAILWAY AGE 191:12, August 1990

Here come the specimen jars. TIME 135:50, January 29, 1990

Industrial employee drug screening: a blind study of laboratory performance using commercially prepared controls, by S. J. Knight, et al. JOURNAL OF OCCUPATIONAL MEDICINE 32(8):715-721, August 1990

Justice Department plans to subject employees to random drug testing limited. CRIMINAL LAW REPORTER: COURT DECISIONS 45(18):2320-2321, August 4, 1989

Latest AMS Foundation survey finds one-third of nation's employers have or are considering drug testing, by J. E. McKendrick, Jr. MANAGEMENT WORLD 19:3-4, March/April 1990

Los Angeles chief orders random drug tests for all commanders, officers. CRIME CONTROL DIGEST 24(16):1+, April 23, 1990

Majority of Ohioans favor drug testing for all employees. CORPORATE SECURITY DIGEST 3(48):2, December 4, 1989

Mechanic's drug testing requirements clarified. BUSINESS/COMMERICAL AVIATION 65:49, October 1989

New technology enhances effort to detect drugs in the workplace, by M. Andrews. OCCUPATIONAL HEALTH AND SAFETY 59:38-40+, October 1990

Officers required to take urinalysis: suspicion of drug use. SEARCH AND SEIZURE BULLETIN September 1989, p. 4

Oregon workers face drug testing, by C. Ashbrook. TRADESWOMAN 9(3):22, Summer 1990

Ottawa surprises employers, unions on drug testing, by A. Toulin. FINANCIAL POST 84(13):3, March 19, 1990

Police drug testing: Massachusetts. POLICE OFFICER GRIEVANCES BULLETIN January 1989, p. 4

Policy does not violate fourth amendment: Mississippi. POLICE OFFICER GRIEVANCES BULLETIN April 1990, p. 4

Preemployment drug screening, by E. D. Wish. JAMA 264:2676-2677, November 28, 1990

Pre-employment drug testing approved. CORPORATE SECURITY DIGEST 4(17):8, April 30, 1990

Pre-employment urinalysis: sanitation employees. SEARCH AND SEIZURE BULLETIN September 1989, p. 5

Preventing employee drug abuse starts with firm policy, awareness, by C. Thieme. OCCUPATIONAL HEALTH AND SAFETY 59:41+, September 1990

Privator sector drug test law. CORPORATE SECURITY March 1990, p. 7

Professional vs. personal factors related to physicians' attitudes toward drug testing, by L. S. Linn, et al. JOURNAL OF DRUG EDUCATION 20(2):95-109, 1990

Public support for mandatory drug-alcohol testing in the workplace, by E. J. Latessa, et al. CRIME AND DELINQUENCY 34(4):379-391, October 1988

"Quality assurance" drug testing, by O. Hatch. CORPORATE SECURITY DIGEST 4(4):8-9, January 29, 1990

Random and post-accident testing of truck drivers. SEARCH AND SEIZURE BULLETIN September 1989, pp. 4-5

Random drug test program for corrections officers upheld. LAW OFFICER'S BULLETIN 14(7):37, October 26, 1989

Random drug testing, by J. Castelli. TRAFFIC SAFETY 90(2):16-17, March/April 1990

Random drug testing: New York. POLICE OFFICER GRIEVANCES BULLETIN June 1990, p. 3

Random drug testing should be tightly restricted, CMA says, by C. Deburggraeve. CMAJ 143(7):652, October 1, 1990

Results of the drug testing program at Southern Pacific Railroad, by R. W. Taggart. NIDA RESEARCH MONOGRAPH SERIES 91:97-108, 1989

Role of physicians as medical review officers in workplace drug testing programs: in pursuit of the last nonogram, by H. W. Clark. WESTERN JOURNAL OF MEDICINE 152(5):514-524, May 1990

Safety survey: most truck drivers support drug tests. PURCHASING 108:41+, June 7, 1990

Search and seizure: random drug testing of probationary corrections officers. CRIMINAL LAW REPORTER: COURT DECISIONS 46(9):1197, November 29, 1989

Students, professors in Georgia angered by drug-test rule, by S. Jaschik. CHRONICLE OF HIGHER EDUCATION 36:1+, July 25, 1990

Substance abuse: the employer's perspective, by R. M. Humphreys. EMPLOYEE RELATIONS TODAY 17:45-52, Spring 1990

Substance abuse: hospital begins drug testing. NURSING 90 20:10, April 1990

Supervisors should look for drug abuse, by M. Schachner. BUSINESS INSURANCE 24:43, May 7, 1990

Survey finds Indiana workers strongly support drug testing. CORPORATE SECURITY DIGEST 4(29):7-8, July 23, 1990

Survey shows Wisconsin citizens back drug tests. CORPORATE SECURITY DIGEST 4(5):10, February 5, 1990

TD drug testing starts at the top, by S. Horvitch. FINANCIAL POST 84(2):3, January 8, 1990

TD to expand drug testing to all new stuff, by G. Scotton. FINANCIAL POST 84(40):4, September 24, 1990

Test negative: a look at the "evidence" justifying illicit-drug tests, by J. Horgan. SCIENTIFIC AMERICAN 262(3):18+, March 1990

Testing fair and square, by A. C. Petersen. SECURITY MANAGEMENT 34(5):40-46, May 1990

Testing, testing: drug, AIDS test upheld. ABA JOURNAL 75:96, February 1989

Transportation drug testing program goes into effect. CORPORATE SECURITY DIGEST 3(51):6-7, December 25, 1989

Two firms curb losses from drug abuse: reducing workplace injuries and improving productivity, by L. Kertesz. BUSINESS INSURANCE 24:16+, June 11, 1990

Union, logistics command sign pact on drug testing. CORPORATE SECURITY DIGEST 4(32):10, August 13, 1990

Unions accept testing plan. ENR 224:4-5, February 8, 1990

Urinalysis: California. SEARCH AND SECURITY DIGEST June 1989, p. 1

Urinalysis required for police officer: held reasonable. POLICE OFFICER GRIEVANCES BULLETIN July 1989, p. 2

USAF plans drug tests for 24,000 civilian workers. CORPORATE SECURITY DIGEST 4(6):5, February 12, 1990

USCF seeks comments on United States random drug testing proposal. CORPORATE SECURITY DIGEST 4(31):9-10, August 6, 1990

"War on drugs" in the workplace: dangerous, by J. True. TRADESWOMAN 9(3):26, Summer 1990

Water sports in the workplace, by L. Niemann. TRADESWOMAN 9(3):20, Summer 1990

Workers back drug testing. ENFORCEMENT JOURNAL 29(1):21, January/March 1990

Workplace drug testing as social control, by S. Hecker, et al. INTERNATIONAL JOURNAL OF HEALTH SERVICES 19(4):693-707, 1989

Workplace issues: survey. TRAINING 27:68-69, October 1990

Yes to drug tests: companies that resist compulsory testing will end up as the employers of last resort, by P. B. Bensinger. BUSINESS MONTH 136:61-62, October 1990

Your analysis is faulty: criticism of J. M. Walsh's statistics supporting the need for employee drug testing, by J. Horgan. NEW REPUBLIC 202:22-24, April 2, 1990

Employment—Laws
Are you ready for a drug test: Ottawa plans to make drug testing mandatory in the transport industry, by A. Morantz. CANADIAN BUSINESS 63(8):19, August 1990

DOT seeks legislation to continue drug testing in mass transit industry. CORPORATE SECURITY DIGEST 4(15):1+, April 16, 1990

DOT to lower passive drug levels, expects go-ahead on random tests, by J. Schulz. TRAFFIC WORLD 224:37+, October 22, 1990

DOT to reimpose drug testing standards, by A. A. Anderson. MASS TRANSIT 17:14-16+, June 1990

Employee drug testing and the duty to bargain: was Johnston-Bateman overruled the day it was decided, by G. S. Folley. EMPLOYEE RELATIONS LAW JOURNAL 16:67-78, Summer 1990

Employee drug testing: significant decisions in labor cases, by C. Hukill. MONTHLY LABOR REVIEW 112:75-77, November 1989

FAA's random drug tests upheld: DOT seeks change in procedures, by J. D. Schulz. TRAFFIC WORLD 223:41-42, July 23, 1990

Federal judge bars drug testing on entire Southern Pacific system, by I. Rosenfeld. TRAFFIC WORLD 222:11, June 18, 1990

Federal judge lifts own order barring SP random drug tests: Southern Pacific Transportation. TRAFFIC WORLD 223:16-17, July 9, 1990

Federal judge orders halt to state drug tests in Georgia. CRIME CONTROL DIGEST 24(30):10, July 30, 1990

Firefighters challenge urinalysis policy: Fourth Amendment privacy rights not violeted—Ohio. SEARCH AND SEIZURE BULLETIN April 1990, p. 5

For love of their children: families of victims in 1987 Amtrak disaster fight for drug testing laws, by T. Armbrister. READER'S DIGEST 137:173-174+, September 1990

Fourth Amendment: the "reasonableness" of suspicionless drug testing of railroad employees—Skinner v. Railway Labor Executives' Association, 109 S. Ct. 1402, 1989, by H. P. Mallory. JOURNAL OF CRIMINAL LAW AND CRIMINOLOGY 80(4): 1052-1085, Winter 1990

Fourth Amendment: suspicionless urinalysis testing—a constitutionally "reasonable" weapon in the nation's war on drugs; National Treasury Employees Union v. Von Raab, 198 S. Ct. K. C. Betts. JOURNAL OF CRIMINAL LAW AND CRIMINOLOGY 80(4):1018-1051, Winter 1990

Legal issues and the drug-free workplace, by C. B. Vogel. SAFETY AND HEALTH 142:30-33, December 1990

Employment—Legal Issues
Boston police trainee drug testing upheld. CRIME CONTROL DIGEST 24(23):6-7, August 20, 1990

CA 7 approves drug testing of corrections officers who come into contact with in-mates. CRIMINAL LAW REPORTER: COURT DECISIONS 46(10):1210-1211, December 6, 1989

California court approves drug testing of private sector job applicants. CORPORATE SECURITY DIGEST 3(48):2-3, December 4, 1989

Court upholds drug testing for transportation workers. CORPORATE SECURITY DIGEST 3(38):8-9, September 25, 1989

Drug screening: AIDS in work place among prominent issues at 1990 AOHC, by M. Tanner. OCCUPATIONAL HEALTH AND SAFETY 59(4):51, April 1990

Drug screening in the workplace: use, abuse and implications, by J. Grabowski, et al. NIDA RESEARCH MONOGRAPH SERIES 95:225-231, 1989

Drug screening urinalysis program upheld: Los Angeles. POLICE OFFICER BULLETIN October 1989, p. 5

Drug test slugfest: 3d cir. upholds random testing, by P. Reidinger. ABA JOURNAL 75:104+, April 1989

Drug testing: dismissal without hearing—due process violation. POLICE OFFICER GRIEVANCES BULLETIN September 1989, pp. 2-3

Drug testing in the workplace: mechanics and legality, by G. W. Klotz. EMPLOYEE ASSISTANCE QUARTERLY 5(4):33-48, 1990

Drug testing in the workplace: an update. HOSPITAL SECURITY AND SAFETY MANAGEMENT 10(6):5-11, October 1989

Drug testing programs: a controversy of rights, by T. Schraeder. PIMA MAGAZINE 72:23, June 1990

Drugs in the workplace: legal developments, by G. P. Scholick. CUPA JOURNAL 40(2):49-59, Summer 1989

Drugs in the workplace: New York State is meeting the challenge, by N. L. Hodes. EMPLOYEE BENEFITS JOURNAL 15(1):21-25+, March 1990

Fired defense workers sue over government's drug policy. CORPORATE SECURITY DIGEST 4(28):8, July 16, 1990

Government seeks to limit court drug testing ruling. CRIME CONTROL DIGEST 24(21):4, May 28, 1990

Judge temporarily bars Georgia from enforcing new drug-testing law, by S. Jaschik. CHRONICLE OF HIGHER EDUCATION 36:17+, August 1, 1990

Labor relations of substance abuse: hospital staff, by M. L. Colosi. HEALTH CARE MANAGEMENT REVIEW 15(3):59-69, Summer 1990

Legal consideration in drug use testing: privacy rights, contracts, and wrongful use of test results, by T. R. Chamberlain. JOURNAL OF FORENSIC SCIENCES 34(6):1477-1481, November 1989

Mandatory urinalysis of police officers without reasonable cause. POLICE OFFICER GRIEVANCES BULLETIN January 1989, pp. 4-5

More employers are utilizing drug-screening programs, by J. Bitter. OCCUPATIONAL HEALTH AND SAFETY 59(4):27-32, April 1990

New York appeals-court upholds drug testing for jail officers. CORRECTIONS DIGEST 20(23):9, November 15, 1989

Plainfield ordered to pay damages for surprise drug test. CRIME CONTROL DIGEST 23(18):6-7, May 7, 1990

Random drug testing: balancing state versus private interest: Illinois. SEARCH AND SEIZURE BULLETIN June 1990, pp. 2-3

Random drug testing of New York City correction officer held permissible. CRIMINAL LAW REPORTER: COURT DECISIONS 46(4):1074-1075, October 25, 1989

Smaller trucking firms cast wary eye as second phase of drug plan nears, by J. D. Schulz. TRAFFIC WORLD 224:12, November 19, 1990

Supreme Court clears family to sue in drug testing case. CRIME VICTIMS DIGEST 7(3):5-6, March 1990

Supreme Court rejects ban on random drug tests sought by United States employees. CORRECTIONS DIGEST 21(4):5-6, February 21, 1990; also in CORPORATE SECURITY DIGEST 4(4):5-6, January 29, 1990 and CRIME CONTROL DIGEST 24(5):2-3, February 5, 1990

Supreme Court upholds random drug testing. CRIME CONTROL DIGEST 24(20):5-6, May 21, 1990; also in NARCOTICS CONTROL DIGEST 20(11):7-8, May 23, 1990

Termination: drug use—grounds for urinalysis, New York. POLICE OFFICER GRIEVANCES BULLETIN March 1990, pp. 3-4

Thin line of workplace drug testing, by M. Kiell. SAFETY AND HEALTH 141:66-69, March 1990

Transport community protests Canadian drug testing proposal, by C. Foster. TRAFFIC WORLD 222:30-31, April 2, 1990

Trends in the law: taking the fourth—apart? ABA JOURNAL 75:80-81, December 1989

United States court upholds surprise drug tests for airline workers. CORPORATE SECURITY DIGET 4(31):6, August 6, 1990

United States Supreme Court declines review of Boston police drug testing policies. CRIME CONTROL DIGEST 23(47):5-6, November 27, 1989

United States to tighten drug tests for pilots in December. CORPORATE SECURITY DIGEST 3(41):10, October 16, 1989

Urinalysis: individual suspicion—reasonableness OK. SEARCH AND SEIZURE BULLETIN March 1990, p. 7

Urinalysis lawsuit: poppy-seed eating job seeker may sue over wrong drug test, by P. Marcotte. ABA JOURNAL 76:29, July 1990

False Positive

Intentional adulteration of urine specimens for drugs of abuse testing to produce false positive results, by C. A. Johnson, et al. JOURNAL OF ANALYTICAL TOXICOLOGY 14(3):195-196, May/June 1990

Poppy seed ingestion and opiate urinalysis: a closer look, by H. N. Elsohly, et al. JOURNAL OF ANALYTICAL TOXICOLOGY 14(5):308-310, 1990

TAC topical anesthesia produces positive urine tests for cocaine, by M. Altieri, et al. ANNALS OF EMERGENCY MEDICINE 19(5):577-579, May 1990

Topical anesthesia using TAC (tetracaine, adrenalin, and cocaine) produces "dirty urine": a word of caution, by R. H. Schwartz, et al. OTOLARYNGOLOGY—HEAD AND NECK SURGERY 102(2):200-201, February 1990

Urinalysis lawsuit: poppy-seed eating job seeker may sue over wrong drug test, by P. Marcotte. ABA JOURNAL 76:29, July 1990

Laboratories

Current list of laboratories which meet minimum standards to engage in urine drug testing for federal agencies: ADAMHA notice. FEDERAL REGISTER 55(172): 36317-36318, September 5, 1990

NIDA (National Institute on Drug Abuse) stops lab's drug tests. JOURNAL OF THE ADDICTION RESEARCH FOUNDATION 19(12):5, December 1, 1990

Steroid testing lab certified. BEIJING REVIEW 33:47, April 23, 1990

Survey of drugs of abuse testing by clinical laboratories in the United Kingdom: Steering Committee for the United Kingdom-External Quality Assessment Scheme for Therapeutic Drug Assays, by D. Burnett, et al. ANNALS OF CLINICAL BIOCHEMISTRY 27(Pt 3):213-222, May 1990

Laws

Death blow for random testing: California Supreme Court decision, by M. A. Veresej. INDUSTRY WEEK 239:47-48, July 2, 1990

DOT preempts state drug law: Vermont, by J. A. Calderwood. TRANSPORTATION AND DISTRIBUTION 31:40+, August 1990

Drug-free Workplace Act given teeth: Federal Acqusition Circular 84-57. OCCUPATIONAL HEALTH AND SAFETY 59:20+, July 1990

Drug-testing service agencies, by R. B. Smith. OCCUPATIONAL HEALTH AND SAFETY 59(4):33, April 1990

Fourth amendment implications of urine testing for evidence of drug use in probation, by C. J. Rosen. BROOKLYN LAW REVIEW 55(4):1159-1253, 1990

Heroin-required identification: scientific or objective tests—Florida. NARCOTICS LAW BULLETIN March 1990, p. 4

Legal Issues

Dole offers testing bill. NARCOTICS DEMAND REDUCTION DIGEST 1(5):8, October 1989

Drug screening is no invasion of privacy, by M. Brosnahan. JOURNAL OF THE ADDICTION RESEARCH FOUNDATION 19(6):3, June 1, 1990

For reasons of state, by J. Hatheway. RFD (61):44, Spring 1990

I'm a liberal, I think: wishy-washy moral relativists have a pretty good record human-rights-wise, by W. Howell. JOURNAL OF THE ADDICTION RESEARCH FOUNDATION 19(7):7-8, July/August 1990

Legal and ethical aspects of drug testing, by P. N. Samuels. BULLETIN OF THE NEW YORK ACADEMY OF MEDICINE 65(2):196-201, February 1989

Legal aspects of urine screening, by E. P. Schroeder. NIDA RESEARCH MONOGRAPH SERIES 95:218-224, 1989

Privacy commissioner's report blasts Canada drug testing program, by C. Foster. TRAFFIC WORLD 222:24, June 18, 1990

Threat to basic freedom: random drug tests are labelled overkill, by J. Hollobon. JOURNAL OF THE ADDICTION RESEARCH FOUNDATION 19(7-8):3, July/August 1990

War on drugs: testing far and square, by A. C. Petersen. SECURITY MANAGEMENT 34:40-46, May 1990

You'd better watch out: avoiding legal hassles—interview with attorney R. Nobile. FOLIO 19:103, September 1990

Methods

Analysis of clinical toxicology urine specimens using the KDI Quick test, by R. M. Kaplan, et al. JOURNAL OF TOXICOLOGY: CLINICAL TOXICOLOGY 27(6):369-373, 1989

Analysis of corticosteroids in urine by HPLC and thermospray LC-MS, by S. J. Park, et al. JOURNAL OF ANALYTICAL TOXICOLOGY 14(2):102-108, March/April 1990

Analysis of currency for cocaine contamination, by J. C. Hudson. CANADIAN SOCIETY OF FORENSIC SCIENCE JOURNAL 22(2):203-218, 1989

Analytical methodology for urine drug testing, by J. Upland. CALIFORNIA PRISONER 18(10):7, June 1990

Antenatal urinary screening for drugs of addiction: usefulness of sideroom testing, by R. G. Condie, et al. BRITISH JOURNAL OF ADDICTION 84(12):1543-1545, December 1989

Application of gas chromatography-mass spectrometry instrument techniques to forensic urine drug testing, by M. Lehrer. CLINICAL AND LABORATORY MEDICINE 10(2):271-288, June 1990

Cocaine and heroin use by methadone maintenance patients, by J. C. Ball, et al. NIDA RESEARCH MONOGRAPH SERIES 95:328, 1989

Cocaine in body fluids: analysis and interpretation of the drug abuse specimens, by H. F. Martin. RHODE ISLAND MEDICAL JOURNAL 73(6):243-248, June 1990

Comments on: "detection of methadone in human hair by gas chromatography-mass spectrometry" and "tetrahydrocannabinols in the hair of hashish smokers," by H. Kaferstein, et al. ZEITSCHRIFT FUR RECHTSMEDIZIN 103(5):393-396, 1990

Comparison of the GC-MS ion trapping technique with GC-FTIR for the identification of stimulants in drug testing, by E. G. de Jong, et al. JOURNAL OF ANALYTICAL TOXICOLOGY 14(2):127-131, March/April 1990

Comparison of various immunologic methods with a CG-MS analysis in cannabinoid detection in urine, by H. Kaferstein, et al. BEITRAGE ZUR GERICHTLICHEN MEDIZIN 47:115-122, 1989

Correlation between "on admission" blood toluene concentrations and the pressure of absence of signs and symptoms in solvent abusers, by T. Miyazaki, et al. FORENSIC SCIENCE INTERNATIONAL 44(2-3):169-177, 1990

Determination of cocaine concentrations in plasma by high-performance liquid chromatography, by P. Jatlow, et al. CLINICAL CHEMISTRY 36(8):1436-1439, 1990

Determination of drugs of abuse in whole blood by means of FPIA and EMIT- immunoassays: a comparative study, by M. Bogusz, et al. FORENSIC SCIENCE INTERNATIONAL 48(1):27-37, 1990

Determination of gestational cocaine exposure by hair analysis, by K. Graham, et al. JAMA 262(23):3328-3330, December 15, 1989

Determination of phenolalkylamines, narcotic analgesics, and beta-blockers by gas chromatography-mass spectrometry, by D. S. Lho, et al. JOURNAL OF ANALYTICAL TOXICOLOGY 14(2):77-83, March/April 1990

Differentiation of morphine abuse from codeine abuse by means of CG-MS examination of blood, by G. Schmitt, et al. ZEITSCHRIFT FUR RECHTSMEDIZIN 103(7):513-522, 1990

Direct automated EMIT d.a.u. analysis of N,N-dimethylformaide-modified serum, plasma, and postmortem blood for amphetamines, barbiturates, methadone, methaqualone, phencyclidine, and propoxyphene, by R. A. Klinger, et al. JOURNAL OF ANALYTICAL TOXICOLOGY 14(5):288-291, 1990

Drug testing in urine, by Y. H. Caplan. JOURNAL OF FORENSIC SCIENCES 34(6):1417-1421, November 1989

Drug-testing methods: what you should know, by E. Berg. SAFETY AND HEALTH 142:52-55, December 1990

Drug testing requires examination of methods, reasons and usefulness, by A. L. Strasser. OCCUPATIONAL HEALTH A ND SAFETY 59(6):52, June 1990

Evaluation of the EZ-SCREEN enzyme immunoassay test for detection of cocaine and marijuana metabolites in urine specimens, by R. H. Schwartz, et al. PEDIATRIC EMERGENCY CARE 6(2):147-149, June 1990

Evaluation of InstaScreen Cannabinoid Drug Screen Test, by R. H. Schwartz, et al. ARCHIVES OF PATHOLOGY AND LABORATORY MEDICINE 113(11):1204, November 1989

Excretion of morphine in urine following the ingestion of poppy seeds, by E. W. Ferguson. MILITARY MEDICINE 155(3):8, March 1990

Federal guidelines for marijuana screening should have lower cutoff levels: a comparison of results from immunoassays and gas chromatography-mass spectrometry, by D. E. Smith, et al. ARCHIVES OF PATHOLOGY AND LABORATORY MEDICINE 113(11):1299-1300, November 1989

Forensic toxicology: an overview and an algorithmic approach, by J. M. Jentzen. AMERICAN JOURNAL OF CLINICAL PATHOLOGY 92(4 Suppl 1):48-55, October 1989

Gas chromatographic-mass spectrometric confirmation of radioimmunoassay results for cannabinoids in blood and urine, by A. J. Clatworthy, et al. FORENSIC SCIENCE INTERNATIONAL 46(3):219-230, 1990

Hair analysis for drug abuse: part II—hair analysis for monitoring of methamphetamine abuse by isotope dilution gas chromatography-mass spectrometry, by Y. Nakahara, et al. FORENSIC SCIENCE INTERNATIONAL 46(3):243-254, July 1990

Hair analysis for drugs of abuse, by C. Brewer. LANCET 335(8695):980, April 21, 1990

Hair analysis for drugs of abuse, by J. Strang, et al. LANCET 335(8691):740, March 24, 1990

Hair analysis for drugs of abuse, by W. A. Baumgartner, et al. JOURNAL OF FORENSIC SCIENCES 34(6):1433-1453, November 1989

Hair analysis in drug screening. JOURNAL OF OCCUPATIONAL MEDICINE 32(8):666+, August 1990

Hair provides telltale drug test. CORPORATE SECURITY DIGEST 3(52):3, December 29, 1989; also in CRIME CONTROL DIGEST 23(52):5-6, December 29, 1989

Hair scare: hair analysis, by J. Newman. AMERICAN HEALTH 9:20, June 1990

Hairy problems for new drug testing method: psychemedics Corporation's use of radioimmunoassay, by C. Holden. SCIENCE 249:1099-1100, September 7, 1990

Identification by GC-MS of 6-monoacetylmorphine as an indicator of heroin abuse, by P. Kintz, et al. EUROPEAN JOURNAL OF CLINICAL PHARMACOLOGY 37(5):531-532, 1989

Identification of two new "designer" amphetamines by NMR techniques, by B. A. Dawson, et al. CANADIAN SOCIETY OF FORENSIC SCIENCE JOURNAL 22(2): 195-202, 1989

Improved thin-layer chromatographic method for the detection and identification of cannabinoids in cannabis, by K. Lavanya, et al. FORENSIC SCIENCE INTERNATIONAL 47(2):165-171, 1990

Mass spectrometric analysis of tobacco-specific nitrosamines hemoglobin adducts in snuff dippers, smokers, and nonsmokers, by S. G. Carmella, et al. CANCER RESEARCH 50(17):5438-5445, September 1, 1990

Meconium prenatal drug-use "Rosetta stone": better than hair-urine tests, by K. Fournis. JOURNAL OF THE ADDICTION RESEARCH FOUNDATION 19(11):3, November 1, 1990

Microcrystalline identification of drugs of abuse: the psychedelic amphetamines, by E. A. Julian. JOURNAL OF FORENSIC SCIENCES 35(4):821-830, July 1990

New drug testing aids. BUSINESS/COMMERCIAL AVIATION 66:49-50, June 1990

Portable drug detector unveiled. CRIME CONTROL DIGEST 24(22):5, June 4, 1990; also in NARCOTICS CONTROL DIGEST 20(12):2-3, June 6, 1990 and CORRECTIONS DIGEST 21(12):4-5, June 13, 1990

Presence of inhibitors to the EMIT test in postmortem urine samples, by J. Taylor. JOURNAL OF FORENSIC SCIENCES 34(5):1055-1056, September 1989

Pretreatment of urine samples for the analysis of 11-nor-delta-9-tetrahyrdocannabinol-9-carboxylic acid using solid-phase extraction, by R. C. Parry, et al. JOURNAL OF ANALYTICAL TOXICOLOGY 14(1):39-44, January/February 1990

Quantitative determination of stanozolol and its metabolite in urine by gas chromatography-mass spectrometry, by H. Y. Choo, et al. JOURNAL OF ANALYTICAL TOXICOLOGY 14(2):109-112, March/April 1990

Quantitative urine levels of abusable drugs for clinical purposes, by F. Tennant. CLINICAL AND LABORATORY MEDICINE 10(2):301-309, June 1990

Quantitative urine screening for the diagnosis and treatment of cocaine abuse, by F. Tennant. NIDA RESEARCH MONOGRAPH SERIES 95:318-319, 1989

Rapid method for the extraction of cocaine and benzoylecgonine from body fluids, by I. R. Tebbett, et al. FORENSIC SCIENCE INTERNATIONAL 39(3):287-291, 1988

Refractometer screening of controlled substances in an operating room satellite pharmacy, by D. L. Gill, Jr., et al. AMERICAN JOURNAL OF HOSPITAL PHARMACY 47(4):817-818, April 1990

Results of comparative determination of morphine in human hair using RIA and CG-MS, by H. Sachs, et al. JOURNAL OF CLINICAL CHEMISTRY AND CLINICAL BIOCHEMISTRY 27(11):873-877, November 1989

Roche diagnostic offers cost-effective, accurate, portable drug testing kit. JUVENILE JUSTICE DIGEST 17(17):9-10, September 6, 1989

Scientist and the sharpies: psychemedics' W. Baumgartner inventor of hair analysis drug test, by F. Meeks. FORBES 146:94-95, August 20, 1990

Screening alcohol and drug use in general practice unit: comparison of computerised and traditional methods, by J. B. Bungey, et al. COMMUNITY HEALTH STUDIES 13(4):471-483, 1989

Screening test of stimulants in human urine utilizing headspace gas chromatography for field test, by H. Tsuchihashi, et al. FORENSIC SCIENCE INTERNATIONAL 45(1-2):181-189, March 1990

Simultaneous identification and quantification of several opiates and derivatives by capillary gas chromatography and nitrogen selective detection, by P. Kintz, et al. ZEITSCHRIFT FUR RECHTSMEDIZIN 103(1):57-62, 1989

Single photon emission computed tomograph in phencyclidine and related drug abuse, by M. Hertzmann, et al. AMERICAN JOURNAL OF PSYCHIATRY 147(2): 255-256, February 1990

Sizing up the hazards of cocaine use: hair analysis—work of Karen Graham and Gideon Koren. SCIENCE NEWS 137:13, January 6, 1990

Specific drug assays: urine drug testing IV, by J. Upland. CALIFORNIA PRISONER 18(13):6, December 1990

Systematic analysis of diuretic doping agents by HPLC screening and GC-MS confirmation, by S. J. Park, et al. JOURNAL OF ANALYTICAL TOXICOLOGY 14(2):84-90, March/April 1990

Systematic analysis of stimulants and narcotic analgesics by gas chromatography with nitrogen specific detection and mass spectrometry, by D. S. Lho, et al. JOURNAL OF ANALYTICAL TOXICOLOGY 14(2):73-61, March/April 1990

Testing human hair for drugs of abuse: I—individual dose and time profiles of morphine and codeine in plasma, saliva, urine, and beard compared to drug-induced effects on pupils and behavior, by E. J. Cone. JOURNAL OF ANALYTICAL TOXICOLOGY 14(1):1-7, January/February 1990

Tetrahydrocannabinols in hair of hashish smokers, by S. Balabanova, et al. ZEITSCHRIFT FUR RECHTSMEDIZIN 102(8):503-508, 1989

THC-carbonic acid determination in serum with fluorescence polarization immunoassay: FPIA, TDA, and GCMS, by H. W. Schutz. BEITRAGE ZUR GERICHTLICHEN MEDIZIN 47:95-96, 1989

Time course of detection of 6-acetylmorphine in urine after heroin administration, by E. J. Cone, et al. NIDA RESEARCH MONOGRAPH SERIES 95:449, 1989

Unreliable urine samples, by S. Brown. BRITISH JOURNAL OF PSYCHIATRY 155: 130, July 1989

Urinalysis update, by T. Shoop. GOVERNMENT EXECUTIVE 22(2):46-47, February 1990

Urinary elimination half-life of delta-1-tetrahydrocannabinol-7-oic acid in heavy marijuana users after smoking, by E. K. Johansson, et al. NIDA RESEARCH MONO-
GRAPH SERIES 95:457-458, 1989

Urinary excretion of furazabol metabolite, by C. Y. Gradeen, et al. JOURNAL OF ANA-
LYTICAL TOXICOLOGY 14(2):120-122, March/April 1990

Urine analysis for benzodiazepines among opiate consumers, by D. Ladewig, et al.
DRUG AND ALCOHOL DEPENDENCE 25(2):145-148, April 1990

Urine drug testing: part I, by J. Upland. CALIFORNIA PRISONER 18(11):7, August
1990

Urine drug testing: part II, by J. Upland. CALIFORNIA PRISONER 18(12):6, October
1990

Urine samples of 1,594 patients from Alcohol and Drug Rehabilitation Service were
analyzed, by E. Rueda-Vasquez, et al. MILITARY MEDICINE 155(5):8, May 1990

Urine screening for abused drugs in new admissions to a VA hospital, by D. E. McMillan, et al. BRITISH JOURNAL OF ADDICTION 84(12):1499-1506, December
1989

Urine screening: what does it mean, by D. E. McMillan. NIDA RESEARCH MONO-
GRAPH SERIES 95:206-210, 1989

Urine testing during treatment of cocaine dependence, by W. M. Burke, et al. NIDA
RESEARCH MONOGRAPH SERIES 95:320-321, 1989

Urine testing of detained juveniles to identify high-risk youth, by R. Demob, et al. JU-
VENILE JUSTICE DIGEST 18(15):1-6, August 1, 1990

Use of cyclic boronates for GC-MS screening and quantitation of beta-adrenergic
blockers and some bronchodilators, by J. Zamecnik. JOURNAL OF ANALYTICAL
TOXICOLOGY 14(2):132-136, March/April 1990

Validity testing of commercial urine cocaine metabolite assays: IV—evaluation of the
EMIR d.a.u. cocaine metabolite assay in quantitiative mode for detection of cocaine metabolite, by E. J. Cone, et al. JOURNAL OF FORENSIC SCIENCES
35(4):786-791, 1990

Value of rapid screening for acetaminophen in all patients with intentional drug overdose, by J. F. Ashbourne, et al. ANNALS OF EMERGENCY MEDICINE 18(10):
1035-1038, October 1989

Voltammetric assay of heroin in illicit dosage forms, by J. R. Rodriguez, et al. ANA-
LYST 115(2):209-212, February 1990

Ways and means of screening: the drug test, by C. R. Carroll. SECURITY MANAGE-
MENT 34:25, July 1990

The Military
Effects of a drug testing program in the Navy, by L. A. Cangianelli. NIDA RESEARCH
MONOGRAPH SERIES 95:211-217, 1989

Judge lifts ban on random drug tests for some in Air Force, by A. Laurent. AIR FORCE TIMES 51(2):7, August 20, 1990

Prisons and Prisoners

Bennett plans for drug testing of arrestees: not a new idea. CRIMINAL JUSTICE NEWSLETTER 20(17):5, September 1, 1989

BJA publishes cost guidelines for pretrial drug testing. CORRECTIONS DIGEST 20(23):10, November 15, 1989; also in JUVENILE JUSTICE DIGEST 18(22):10, January 2, 1990

Does he or doesn't he: new drug test targets hair—criminal suspects, by T. Gest. US NEWS AND WORLD REPORT 108:58, May 28, 1990

Drug testing: know your options—testing offenders, by R. L. DuPont, et al. CORRECTIONS TODAY 52:168-170, August 1990

Drug testing of offenders in all federal courts at issue. CRIMINAL JUSTICE NEWSLETTER 21(6):4, March 15, 1990

Laboratory versus on-site drug testing in criminal justice: an overview, by J. A. Schwartz, et al. JOURNAL OF OFFENDER MONITORING 2(2):1+, 1989

Life inside: urine drug testing—prisoners, by J. Upland. CALIFORNIA PRISONER 18(9):7, April 1990

New DUF report shows up to 82 percent of arrestees test positive for drugs. NARCOTICS CONTROL DIGEST 23(23):6-8, August 21, 1989

Prisons and jails: drug testing of inmates—use of EMIT test results as sole basis for disciplinary action. CRIMINAL LAW REPORTER: COURT DECISIONS 46(6): 1131, November 8, 1989

Urine testing for drug use among male arrestees: United States, 1989. MMWR 38(45):780-783, November 17, 1989

Using drug testing to identify high-risk defendants on release: a study in the District of Columbia, by C. A. Visher. JOURNAL OF CRIMINAL JUSTICE 18(4):321-332, 1990

Schools

Public schools, private vices: proposed introduction of random drug-testing of pupils at public schools, by V. Woods. SPECTATOR May 26,1990, pp. 17-18

Reading, writing and drug tests: two Chicago-area schools enact student drug-testing policies, by P. Marcotte. ABA JOURNAL 75:20-21, December 1989

Students attitudes toward a campus drug-testing program, by D. Thombs, et al. JOURNAL OF COLLEGE STUDENT DEVELOPMENT 31:283-284, May 1990

Who is using what in the public schools: the interrelationship among alcohol, drug and tobacco use by adolescents in New Brunswick classrooms, by C. Grobe, et al. JOURNAL OF ALCOHOL AND DRUG EDUCATION 35(3):1-11, Spring 1990

Legal barriers to student drug testing just got higher: Brooks v. East chambers consolidated independent school district, by B. Sendor. AMERICAN SCHOOL BOARD JOURNAL 177:14+, October 1990

Mandatory urine testing for drugs in public schools and the Fourth Amendment: some thoughts for school officials, by E. A. Lincoln. JOURNAL OF LAW AND EDUCATION 18:181-188, Spring 1989

Sports

Analysis of anabolic steroids using GC-MS with selected ion monitoring, by B. C. Chung, et al. JOURNAL OF ANALYTICAL TOXICOLOGY 14(2):91-95, March/April 1990

Analysis of bumetanide in human urine by high-performance liquid chromatography with fluorescence detection and gas chromatography-mass spectrometry, by C. Y. Gradeen, et al. JOURNAL OF ANALYTICAL TOXICOLOGY 14(2):123-126, March/April 1990

Analysis of corticosteroids in urine by HPLC and thermospray, by S. J. Park, et al. JOURNAL OF ANALYTICAL TOXICOLOGY 14(2):102-108, March/April 1990

Athletes' drug tests emphasize good health: in Ireland, by K. Birchard. JOURNAL OF THE ADDICTION RESEARCH FOUNDATION 19(3):9, March 1, 1990

College coach's "playbook" vs. drug abuse, by G. L. White, et al. SCHOLASTIC COACH 60:56-59, August 1990

Comparison of the GC-MS ion trapping technique with GC-FTIR for the identification of stimulants in drug testing, by E. G. de Jong, et al. JOURNAL OF ANALYTICAL TOXICOLOGY 14(2):127-131, March/April 1990

Deciding whether to test student athletes for drug use: Santa Clara University, California, by C. D. Feinstein. INTERFACES 20:80-87, May/June 1990

Determination of phenolalkylamines, narcotic analgesics, and beta-blockers by gas chromatography-mass spectrometry, by D. S. Lho, et al. JOURNAL OF ANALYTICAL TOXICOLOGY 14(2):77-83, March/April 1990

Drug testing. POSTGRADUATE MEDICINE 66(7):28, November 15, 1989

Drug testing at the 10th Asian Games and 24th Seoul Olympic Games, by J. Park, et al. JOURNAL OF ANALYTICAL TOXICOLOGY 14(2):66-72, March/April 1990

Drug testing in sports. JOURNAL OF ANALYTICAL TOXICOLOGY 14(2):65-136, March/April 1990

Drug tests and amateur athletes, by A. R. Newman. ANALYTICAL CHEMISTRY 62(10):602-603, May 15, 1990

Football league lets white players off drug hook, by B. Day. GUARDIAN 42(15):7, February 7, 1990

Football's racist drug policy, by A. Ola. GUARDIAN 42(21):4, March 21, 1990

NCAA drug program: out of bounds but still in play, by J. M. Evans, et al. JOURNAL OF LAW AND EDUCATION 19(2):161-191, Spring 1990

NCAA tightens drug rules for collegiate gridders. JET 77:48, February 12, 1990

NFL creates tempest in a pee pot, by S. Muwakkil. IN THESE TIMES 14(13):6, February 14, 1990

NFL drug problem faces allegations of racism. JET 77:46+, February 12, 1990

Random testing during training, competition may be only way to combat drugs in sports, by V. S. Cowart. JAMA 260:3556-3557, December 23-30, 1988

Steroids in athletics: one university's experience, by M. Lopez. JOURNAL OF COLLEGE STUDENT DEVELOPMENT 31:523-530, November 1990

Testing your rights: random drug testing—views of NFL players, by W. Ladson. SPORT 81:16, April 1990

Sports—Legal Issues

Appeal court upholds decision barring the NCAA from administering drug-testing plan to Stanford, by D. Lederman. CHRONICLE OF HIGHER EDUCATION 37:43-44, October 3, 1990

Constitutionality of drug testing of college-athletes: a brandeis brief for a narrowly-intrusive approach, by J. T. Ranney. JOURNAL OF COLLEGE AND UNIVERSITY LAW 16:397-424, Winter 1990

Governors of North Carolina system clash with Chapel Hill over drug-testing plan, by D. Lederman. CHRONICLE OF HIGHER EDUCATION 36:27+, July 25, 1990

THEOPHYLLINE
Massive theophylline overdose with atypical metabolic abnormalities, by S. H. Eshleman, et al. CLINICAL CHEMISTRY 36(2):398-399, February 1990

THERAPY
see also:　　Care
　　　　　　　Rehabilitation

12-Step treatment approach for marijuana, cannabis, dependence, by N. S. Miller, et al. JOURNAL OF SUBSTANCE ABUSE TREATMENT 6(4):241-250, 1989

12 steps down the road from recovery, by S. R. Blessing. OFF OUR BACKS 20:19, April 1990

Abstinence and relapse in outpatient cocaine addicts, by A. M. Washton, et al. JOURNAL OF PSYCHOACTIVE DRUGS 22(2):135-147, April/June 1990

Addiction in adolescents, by M. A. Morrison. WESTERN JOURNAL OF MEDICINE 152(5):543-546, May 1990

THERAPY

Addiction medicine: the new specialties: facts or fads, by B. L. Lee. JOURNAL OF THE ADDICTION RESEARCH FOUNDATION 19(3):12, March 1, 1990

Addiction: no way out—detoxification programmes for women drug addicts, by C. Troupp. GUARDIAN May 15, 1990, p. 17

Addiction treatment services in the Russian Federation, by P. I. Sidorov, et al. SOVETSKOE ZDRAVOOKHRONENIE (12):16-21, 1989

Addictions professionals "too soft": only tougher stance will waken legislators, by H. McConnell. JOURNAL OF THE ADDICTION RESEARCH FOUNDATION 19(11): 5, November 1, 1990

Addicts' search: Canadians seek treatment in United States hospitals, by N. Underwood. MACLEAN'S 103(22):51, May 28, 1990

Aftercare services for drug-using institutionalized delinquents, by R. F. Catalano, et al. SOCIAL SERVICE REVIEW 63(4):553-577, December 1989

AIDS prevention and chemical dependence treatment needs of women and their children, by L. D. Karan. JOURNAL OF PSYCHOACTIVE DRUGS 21(4):395-399, October/December 1989

AIDS-related knowledge, attitudes and behaviour in injection drug users attending a Toronto treatment facility, by M. Millson, et al. CANADIAN JOURNAL OF PUBLIC HEALTH 81(1):46-49, January/February 1990

Alameda County Department of Alcohol and Drug Programs Comprehensive Homeless Alcohol Recovery Services: CHARS, by R. W. Bennett, et al. ALCOHOLISM TREATMENT QUARTERLY 7(1):111-128, 1990

Alberta group drops KIDS link. JOURNAL OF THE ADDICTION RESEARCH FOUNDATION 19(10):2, October 1, 1990

Around the nation: Oregon. LAW ENFORCEMENT NEWS 16(313):2, April 30, 1990

ASAM policy on treating the chemically dependent. AMERICAN FAMILY PHYSICIAN 41:341, January 1990

Barriers to community treatment of patients with dual diagnosis, by R. H. Howland. HOSPITAL AND COMMUNITY PSYCHIATRY 41(10):1134-1135, 1990

Behavioral treatment of alcohol and drug abuse: what do we know and where shall we go, by R. K. Hester, et al. RECENT DEVELOPMENTS IN ALCOHOLISM 8:305-327, 1990

Beneficial effects of treatment of nicotine dependence during an inpatient substance abuse treatment program, by A. M. Joseph, et al. JAMA 263(22):3043-3046, June 13, 1990

Benefits outweigh treatment, by H. McConnell. JOURNAL OF THE ADDICTION RESEARCH FOUNDATION 19(11):3, November 1, 1990

Cenaps model of relapse prevention: basic principles and procedures, by T. T. Gorski. JOURNAL OF PSYCHOACTIVE DRUGS 22(2):125-133, April/June 1990

Characteristics of the autonomic nervous system test during group psychotherapy of patients with opioid dependence at the stage of induction of remission, by V. N. Mirtovskaia, et al. ZHURNAL NEVROPATOLOGII IPSIKHIATRII IMENI S. S. KORSAKOVA 89(10):33-35, 1989

Cocaine abuse and its treatment, by R. D. Hicks. HAWAII MEDICAL JOURNAL 48(11): 462+, November 1989

Cocaine abuse and its treatment, by W. C. Hall, et al. PHARMACO10(1):47-65, 1990

Cocaine epidemic: treatment options for cocaine dependence, by N. M. Chychula, et al. NURSE PRACTITIONER 15(8):33-40, August 1990

Cocaine: recognizing, treating the abuser, by P. Coleman. VIRGINIA MEDICINE 117 (6):251-255, June 1990

Combined treatment modalities: the need for innovative approaches, by J. T. Payte. JOURNAL OF PSYCHOACTIVE DRUGS 21(4):431-434, October/December 1989

Combining pharmacological antagonists and behavioural psychotherapy in treating addictions: why it is effective but unpopular, by C. Brewer. BRITISH JOURNAL OF PSYCHIATRY 157:34-40, July 1990

Comprehensive analysis of the data of clinicopsychologic examination of patients with alcoholism to predict early disease relapses, by Y. Tyul'pin, et al. ZHURNAL NEVROPATOLOGII I PSIKHIATRII IMENI S. S. KORSAKOVA 90(2):62-66, 1990

Corrections and revised analyses for psychotherapy in methadone maintenance patients, by G. Woody, et al. ARCHIVES OF GENERAL PSYCHIATRY 47(8):788-789, August 1990

Cost containment through outpatient substance abuse services, by G. D. Lawless. EMPLOYEE BENEFITS JOURNAL 15(1):6-10, March 1990

Crack addiction: treatment and recovery issues, by B. C. Wallace. CONTEMPORARY DRUG PROBLEMS 17:79-119, Spring 1990

Crack: the nation's emergency, by M. A. Horrocks. AMERICAN JOURNAL OF NURSING 90(4):42-43, April 1990

Cranial electrostimulation: (CES) use in the detoxification of opiate-dependent patients, by F. A. Alling, et al. JOURNAL OF SUBSTANCE ABUSE TREATMENT 7(3):173-180, 1990

Culture and social class as intervening variables in relapse prevention with chemically dependent women, by H. D. Weiner, et al. JOURNAL OF PSYCHOACTIVE DRUGS 22(2):239-248, April/June 1990

Current pharmacotherapies for opioid dependence, by T. R. Kosten. PSYCHOLOGICAL BULLETIN 26(1):69-74, 1990

Cut the crack: the policymaker's guide to cocaine treatment, by R. A. Rawson. POLICY REVIEW (51):10-19, Winter 1990

Documenting the effectiveness of adolescent substance abuse treatment using public school archival records, by D. L. Kirk, et al. HIGH SCHOOL JOURNAL 74: 16-21, October/November 1990

Drug abuse treatment "models": Meehl's lament revisited, by W. R. Talbott. INTERNATIONAL JOURNAL OF THE ADDICTIONS 24(11):1083-1089, November 1989

Drug-based therapy may help coke users, but researchers are less sure about crack. LAW ENFORCEMENT NEWS 15(288):5+, March 15, 1989

Drug testing, treatment, and revocation: a review of program findings, by G. F. Vito, et al. FEDERAL PROBATION 54:37-43, September 1990

Effect of pre-bed care on alcoholic patients' behavior during inpatient treatment, by D. J. Conti, et al. INTERNATIONAL JOURNAL OF THE ADDICTIONS 24(7):707-714, July 1989

Ethical and legal dilemmas of Jerusalem treatment model for drug addiction, by N. Fish, et al. INTERNATIONAL JOURNAL OF LAW AND PSYCHIATRY 13(1-2): 155-161, 1990

Evaluation of cognitive skills in ethanol- and cocaine-dependent patients during detoxification using P300 evoked response potentials (ERP's), by L. Amass, et al. NIDA RESEARCH MONOGRAPH SERIES 95:353-354, 1989

Evaluation of treatment of cocaine dependence, by C. P. O'Brien, et al. NIDA RESEARCH MONOGRAPH SERIES 95:78-84, 1989

Expert systems in treating substance abuse, by D. R. Wesson, et al. WESTERN JOURNAL OF MEDICINE 152(5):585-587, May 1990

Extending the system for the treatment of chemical dependencies, by J. F. Guinan. JOURNAL OF STRATEGIC AND SYSTEMATIC THERAPIES 9(1):11-20, Spring 1990

Factors affecting the use of medical, mental health, alcohol, and drug treatment services by homeless adults, by D. Padgett, et al. MEDICAL CARE 28(9):805-821, September 1990

Federal confidentiality regulations for substance abuse treatment facilities: a case in applied ethics, by N. J. Piazza, et al. JOURNAL OF MENTAL HEALTH COUNSELING 12(2):120-128, April 1990

Five paragraphs for better care of mentally disturbed addicts, by M. Berglund, et al. LAKARTIDNINGEN 87(19):1649-1652, May 9, 1990

From theory to practice: the planned treatment of a drug user: interview by Stanley Einstein, by S. B. Coleman. INTERNATIONAL JOURNAL OF THE ADDICTIONS 24(3):247-276, March 1989+ future issues

House OKs expansion of Substance Abuse Monitoring Program for federal offenders. CORRECTIONS DIGEST 20(23):5, November 15, 1989

Improvement of narcotic dependence care and prevention of alcoholism in seamen, by P. I. Sidorov, et al. SOVETSKOE ZDRAVOOKHRONENIE (9):41-45, 1989

Innovations in drug treatment and the therapeutic community, by E. Nebelkopf. INTERNATIONAL JOURNAL OF THERAPEUTIC COMMUNITIES 10(1):39-52, 1989

Inpatient vs. outpatient cocaine abuse treatment, by T. R. Kosten, et al. NIDA RESEARCH MONOGRAPH SERIES 95:312-313, 1989

Integrated treatment model for dual diagnosis of psychosis and addiction, by K. Minkoff. HOSPITAL AND COMMUNITY PSYCHIATRY 40(10):1031-1036, October 1989

Interdisciplinary treatment of drug misuse among older people of color: ethnic considerations for social work practice, by P. R. Raffoul, et al. JOURNAL OF DRUG ISSUES 19(2):297-313, Spring 1989

Kennedy endorses treatment: calls for more spending. NARCOTICS DEMAND REDUCTION DIGEST 1(5):8-9, October 1989

Kirchlindach Therapy Center: a treatment facility for the rehabilitation of alcohol and drug dependent males, by L. S. Liem. THERAPEUTISCHE UMSCHAU 47(5): 418-419, May 1990

Level and extent of rehabilitation needs of black alcohol abuse clients in an outpatient treatment program, by E. R. Smith. DAI A 50(9):3069, 1990

Little fun needed in teens' therapy, by D. Trainor. JOURNAL OF THE ADDICTION RESEARCH FOUNDATION 19(9):4, September 1, 1990

Making treatment decisions, by D. Raistrick. INTERNATIONAL REVIEW OF PSYCHIATRY 1(1-2):173-179, March 1989

Medico-legal aspects of treatment and prophylactic care of narcotic drug addicts, by E. A. Babayan. DRUG AND ALCOHOL DEPENDENCE 25(2):209-212, April 1990

Meharry gets $2.8 million to treat drug-using moms. JET 79:28, November 5, 1990

Methodological issues in the evaluation of treatment of drug dependence, by G. W. Martin, et al. ADVANCES IN BEHAVIOR RESEARCH AND 11(3):133-150, 1989

Model for the treatment of trauma-related syndromes among chemically dependent inpatient women, by K. Bollerud. JOURNAL OF SUBSTANCE ABUSE TREATMENT 7(2):83-87, 1990

More treatment studies needed for Native youth, by R. Woodward. WINDSPEAKER 8(14):10, September 28, 1990

Multiple treatment approach to substance abuse in a resident centre for disturbed people and their follow-up: part II, by L. F. Lowenstein. CRIMINOLOGIST 14(2): 93-105, 1990

Neurobehavioral treatment for cocaine dependency, by R. A. Rawson, et al. JOURNAL OF PSYCHOACTIVE DRUGS 22(2):159-171, April/June 1990

New "est": at AA, OA, CA, NA and PA, you can not only lose an addiction, you can network yourself silly; even find a spouse, by K. Neumeyer. LOS ANGELES 35:130+, March 1990

New York State's shock incarceration programs focus on rehabilitation, by T. A. Coughlin, III. JUVENILE JUSTICE DIGEST 18(9):1-7, May 2, 1990

New York treatment unit criticized by Governor Cuomo. NARCOTICS DEMAND REDUCTION DIGEST 1(5):6-7, October 1989

Nicotine reduction therapy and relapse prevention for heavy smokers: 3-year follow-up, by T. M. Cooper, et al. JOURNAL OF THE AMERICAN DENTAL ASSOCIATION (Suppl):32-36, January 1990

NIDA's Medication Development Program: 1989, by C. R. Schuster, et al. NIDA RESEARCH MONOGRAPH SERIES 95:64-73, 1989

Offers treatment plan for "the most dangerous drug," by C. G. Smith. VIRGINIA MEDICINE 116(11):451, November 1989

Outcomes of cocaine-dependence treatment, by F. Tennant. NIDA RESEARCH MONOGRAPH SERIES 95:314-315, 1989

Outpatient treatment for substance-abusing offenders, by J. D. Hirschel, et al. JOURNAL OF OFFENDER COUNSELING, SERVICES AND REHABILITATION 15(1):111-130, January 1990

Outpatient treatment of adults with coexisting substance use and mental disorders, by M. Hanson, et al. JOURNAL OF SUBSTANCE ABUSE TREATMENT 7(2):109-116, 1990

Outpatient treatment of PCP abusers, by D. A. Gorelick, et al. AMERICAN JOURNAL OF DRUG AND ALCOHOL ABUSE 15(4):367-374, December 1989

Panel recommends more research on programs to treat drug abuse, by C. Raymond. CHRONICLE OF HIGHER EDUCATION 37:12, September 26, 1990

Patterns of inpatient mental health, mental retardation and substance abuse service utilization in California, by C. Stolp, et al. SOCIAL SCIENCE QUARTERLY 70(3):687-707, September 1989

Perceptual changes in addicts as a consequence of reality therapy based group treatment, by A. Honeyman. JOURNAL OF REALITY 9(2):53-59, Spring 1990

Pharmacologic approaches to the treatment of cocaine dependence, by W. A. Taylor, et al. WESTERN JOURNAL OF MEDICINE 152(5):573-577, May 1990

Pharmacologic interventions for the treatment of opioid dependence and withdrawal, by S. K. Guthrie. DICP 24(7-8):721-734, July/August 1990

Preventing relapse in the treatment of nicotine addiction: current issues and future directions, by T. P. Carmody. JOURNAL OF PSYCHOACTIVE DRUGS 22(2):211-238, April/June 1990

PRIDE supporting United States youth treatment. JOURNAL OF THE ADDICTION RESEARCH FOUNDATION 19(10):2, October 1, 1990

Providing cost efficient detoxification services to alcoholic patients, by N. N. Beshai. PUBLIC HEALTH REPORTS 105:475-481, September/October 1990

Psychiatric management of drug addicts in rehabilitation centres, by F. J. Lichtigfeld. SOUTH AFRICAN MEDICAL JOURNAL 77(2):116, January 20, 1990

Psychopharmacologic treatment of cigarette smoking, by N. G. Schneider. JOURNAL OF THE AMERICAN DENTAL ASSOCIATION (Suppl):7-12, January 1990

Psychotherapy for substance abuse, by G. Woody, et al. NIDA RESEARCH MONOGRAPH SERIES 90:162-167, 1988; Erratum, by G. E. Woody, et al. PSYCHIATRIC CLINICS OF NORTH AMERICA 13(1):8, March 1990

Quiet battle in the war on drugs, by R. M. Areissohn, et al. CORRECTIONS DIGEST 52(3):28+, June 1990

Recent trends in the development of alcohol and drug treatment services in Ontario, by B. Rush, et al. JOURNAL OF STUDIES ON ALCOHOL 51:514-522, November 1990

Referral for treatment among adolescent alcohol and drug abusers, by W. R. Downs, et al. JOURNAL OF RESEARCH IN CRIME AND DELINQUENCY 27(2):190-209, May 1990

Refining the BASIC-ISs: a psychospiritual approach to the comprehensive outpatient treatment of drug dependency, by H. P. Brown, et al. ALCOHOLISM TREATMENT QUARTERLY 6(3-4):27-61, 1989

Relapse to substance abuse: empirical findings within a cognitive-social learning approach, by H. M. Annis. JOURNAL OF PSYCHOACTIVE DRUGS 22(2):117-124, April/June 1990

Replay and reproduction of the national socialism past in psychotherapy of adolescent patients, by W. Huck. PRAXIS DER KINDERPSYCHOLOGIE UND KINDERPSYCHIATRIE 39(5):180-184, May/June 1990

Retention and outcome at ACI: a unique therapeutic community, by C. Winick. INTERNATIONAL JOURNAL OF THE ADDICTIONS 25(1):1-26, January 1990

Seafield 911 opens its doors. CRIME CONTROL DIGEST 23(43):10, October 30, 1989

Selecting a substance abuse treatment facility: Council of Better Business Bureaus booklet. SUPERVISORY MANAGEMENT 35:8, February 1990

Selecting substance abusers for long-term treatment, by C. Clemens, et al. INTERNATIONAL JOURNAL OF THE ADDICTIONS 25(1):33-42, January 1990

Self-abuse: until we get to the root of addiction, treatment options will continue to work for some and not others, by N. Sandrin. TODAY'S HEALTH 8(5):28-30+, October 1990

Self-help: from the grassroots up, by E. Hauschildt. JOURNAL OF THE ADDICTION RESEARCH FOUNDATION 19(12):1-2, December 1, 1990

Sentencing: alternative to punishment—disparate treatment of alcoholics and drug addicts. CRIMINAL LAW REPORTER: COURT DECISIONS 46(3):1061-1062, October 18, 1989

Separation of drug markets and the normalization of drug problems in the Netherlands: an example for other nations, by H. J. Van Vliet. JOURNAL OF DRUG ISSUES 20(3):463-471, Summer 1990

Services for alcohol and drug dependent patients with psychiatric comorbidity, by D. Sellman. NEW ZEALAND MEDICAL JOURNAL 102(872):390, July 26, 1989

Serving up *Good Medicine*: music video is part of Canadian Auto Workers campaign to provide support for recovery from alcohol and drug abuse. OUR TIMES 9(3): 11-13, May 1990

Setting up an occupational therapy programme for drug addicts, by J. Busuttil. BRITISH JOURNAL OF OCCUPATIONAL 52(12):476-479, December 1989

Sierra Tuscon treatment center profits from patient's high profile, by J. Nemes. MODERN HEALTHCARE 20(25):49+, June 25, 1990

Smoking cessation using alternative nicotine administration in patients with peripheral arterial occlusive disease: effects on peripheral circulation, hematologic parameters and liproprotein status, by C. Diehm, et al. VASA 29(Suppl):1-53, 1990

Socio-cultural factors affecting drug addiction treatment in Italy: fear of treatment, by I. Maremmani, et al. DRUG AND ALCOHOL DEPENDENCE 25(2):235-239, April 1990

Some personal perspectives on the drug scene, by M. Luger. JOURNAL OF DRUG ISSUES 20:503-507, Summer 1990

Study of various smoking cessation programs based on close to 1000 volunteers recruited from the general population: 1-month results, by F. Clavel, et al. REVUE D'EPIDEMIOLOGIE ET DE SANTE PUBLIQUE 38(2):133-138, 1990

Substance abuse treatment unavailable for most, says latest national survey, by R. H. Feldkamp. NARCOTICS DEMAND REDUCTION DIGEST 2(4):1-2, April 1990

Substance impairment and female victimization therapy, by D. D. Moore, et al. JOURNAL OF SEX EDUCATION AND 15(3):187-199, Fall 1989

Systems issues in serving the mentally ill substance abuser: Virginia's experience, by W. Thacker, et al. HOSPITAL AND COMMUNITY PSYCHIATRY 40(1):1046-1049, October 1989

THERAPY

Taming chemical monsters: cybernetic-systemic therapy with adolescent substance abusers, by M. Selekman. JOURNAL OF STRATEGIC AND SYSTEMATIC THERAPIES 8(2-3):5-9, Summer/Fall 1989

Teen patients: of drug and alcohol addiction—exodus to United States costly, by D. Haynes. JOURNAL OF THE ADDICTION RESEARCH FOUNDATION 19(5):4, May 1, 1990

Tertiary-level interventions for hard-core smokers, by M. Ginne. JOURNAL OF PSYCHOACTIVE DRUGS 21(3):343-353, July/September 1989

Therapeutic community as an interventive milieu, by N. A. Lafferty. INTERNATIONAL JOURNAL OF THERAPEUTIC COMMUNITIES 9(4):263-271, 1988

Therapeutic needs and possibilities of persons in detention assessed immediately after release, by P. Christoffersen. UGESKRIFT FOR LAEGER 152(6):392-394, February 5, 1990

Therapeutic treatment of drug dependence during hospital recovery, by A. Meluzzi, et al. MINERVA MEDICA 81(3):203-221, March 1990

Toxicologic and pharmacologic methods in the control of smoking behavior, by E. Ackermann. ZEITSCHRIFT FUR ERKNANKUNGEN DER ATMUNGSORGANE 173(2):127-133, 1989

Treating drug problems, by D. R. Gerstein, et al. NEW ENGLAND JOURNAL OF MEDICINE 323(12):844-848, September 20, 1990

Treatment needs and services for mothers with a dual diagnosis: substance abuse and mental illness, by S. K. Morris, et al. JOURNAL OF OFFENDER COUNSELING, SERVICES AND REHABILITATION 15(1):65-84, January 1990

Treatment of chronic mentally ill young adults with substance abuse problems: emerging national trends, by M. S. Ridgely, et al. ADOLESCENT PSYCHIATRY 16:288-313, 1989

Treatment of drug addicts: experiences with group therapy. REVUE MEDICALE DE LA SUISSE ROMANDE 109(11):929-938, November 1989

Treatment of drug dependence: what works, by H. D. Kleber. INTERNATIONAL REVIEW OF PSYCHIATRY 1(1-2):81-99, March 1989

Treatment of geriatric alcoholics, by W. A. Canter, et al. CLINICAL GERONTOLOGIST 9(1):67-70, 1989

Treatment of nicotine dependence, by K. O. Fagerstrom. PROGRESS IN BRAIN RESEARCH 79:321-326, 1989

Treatment of patients with psychiatric and psychoactive substance abuse disorders, by F. C. Osher, et al. HOSPITAL AND COMMUNITY PSYCHIATRY 40(10):1025-1030, October 1989

Treatment of perinatal addiction: identification intervention, and advocacy, by M. Jessup. WESTERN JOURNAL OF MEDICINE 152(5):553-558, May 1990

Treatment of phencyclidine-associated psychosis with ECT, by S. H. Dinwiddie, et al. CONVULSIVE 4(3):230-235, 1988

Treatment of young offenders who drink or use drugs: a critique of McMurran and Boyle, by R. Eisenman. PSYCHOLOGICAL REPORTS 67(3):913-914, 1990

Treatment outcome: a neglected area of drug abuse research, by L. E. Holliter. DRUG AND ALCOHOL DEPENDENCE 25(2):175-177, April 1990

Treatment process factors and satisfaction with drug abuse treatment, by G. W. Joe, et al. PSYCHOLOGY OF ADDICTIVE BEHAVIORS 3(2):53-64, 1989

Twelve month follow-up of psychotherapy for opiate dependence and severity of psychiatry symptoms as a predictor of benefits from psychotherapy: the Veterans Administration—Penn Study," by G. E. Woody, et al. AMERICAN JOURNAL OF PSYCHIATRY 146(12):1651, December 1989

Update on behavioral treatments for substance abuse, by A. Childress, et al. NIDA RESEARCH MONOGRAPH SERIES 90:183-192, 1988

Use of mental health services by dually diagnosed patients, by J. S. Lyons, et al. HOSPITAL AND COMMUNITY PSYCHIATRY 40(10):1067-1069, October 1989

Values approach to addiction: drug policy that is moral rather than moralistic, by S. Peele. JOURNAL OF DRUG ISSUES 20:639-646, Fall 1990

Voices of a lost generation: interviews with nine kids undergoing treatment at the Bridge, by C. Saline. PHILADELPHIA MAGAZINE 81:112+, June 1990

What happens to drug misusers: a medium-term follow-up of subjects new to treatment, by E. Oppenheimer, et al. BRITISH JOURNAL OF ADDICTION 85(10): 1255-1260, 1990

Who will treat alcohol and drug abuse patients?, by R. B. Millman, et al. HOSPITAL AND COMMUNITY PSYCHIATRY 40(10):989, October 1989

Work-load for the Danish medical on call system caused by chronic morphine users, by V. M. Schmidt. UGESKRIFT FOR LAEGER 152(35):2482-2485, 1990

Acupuncture
Baltimore tries treating substance abuse with acupuncture. PUBLIC HEALTH REPORTS 105:436, July/August 1990

Drug
Chemical aversion therapy in the treatment of cocaine dependence as part of a multimodal treatment program: treatment outcome, by P. J. Frawley, et al. JOURNAL OF SUBSTANCE ABUSE TREATMENT 7(1):21-29, 1990

Clinical toxicology of drugs used in the treatment of opiate dependence, by A. D. Fraser. CLINICAL AND LABORATORY MEDICINE 10(2):375-386, June 1990

Combination drug therapy complex but promising, by B. L. Lee. JOURNAL OF THE ADDICTION RESEARCH FOUNDATION 19(9):4, September 1, 1990

Comparative effectiveness of alpha-2 adrenergic agonists clonidine-guanfacine, in the hospital detoxification of opiate addicts, by R. Muga, et al. MEDICINA CLINICA 94(5):169-172, February 10, 1990

Comparison of amantadine and desipramine combined with psychotherapy for treatment of cocaine dependence, by W. W. Weddington, et al. NIDA RESEARCH MONOGRAPH SERIES 95:483-484, 1989

Drug treatment of nicotine dependence, by M. Fellhauer. MEDIZINISCHE MONATS-SCHRIFT FUR PHARMAZEUTEN 13(6):184-186, June 1990

From the Alcohol, Drug Abuse, and Mental Health Administration: serious infections other than human immunodeficiency virus among intravenous drug abusers, by H. W. Haverkos, et al. JOURNAL OF INFECTIOUS DISEASES 161(5):894-902, May 1990

Laboratory procedure for evaluation of pharmacotherapy for cocaine dependence, by H. Kranzler, et al. NIDA RESEARCH MONOGRAPH SERIES 95:324-325, 1989

Pharmacological treatment of substance-abusing schizophrenic patients, by S. G. Siris. SCHIZOPHRENIA BULLETIN 16(1):111-122, 1990

Pharmacotherapy of opiate addiction in Marche Region, by V. Moretti, et al. ACTA PHYSIOLOGICA HUNGARICAE 75(Suppl):215-216, 1990

Substitute drug-assisted treatment of drug dependent patients in general practice, by H. Elias. FORTSCHRITTE DER MEDIZIN 108(13):256-268, April 30, 1990

Drug—Bromocriptine

Comparison of bromocriptine and desipramine in cocaine withdrawal, by I. L. Extein, et al. ANNALS OF CLINICAL PSYCHIATRY 1(3):193-197, September 1989

Effects of bromocriptine pretreatment on subjective and physiological responses to IV cocaine, by K. Kumor, et al. PHARMACOLOGY, BIOCHEMISTRY AND BEHAVIOR 33(4):829-837, August 1989

Drug—Buprenorphine

Buprenorphine for treating drug abuse. AMERICAN FAMILY PHYSICIAN 42:241, July 1990

Buprenorphine may be therapeutic alternative for opiate addiction, by F. K. Goodwin. JAMA 263:2725, May 23-30, 1990

Buprenorphine treatment of cocaine abuse, by T. R. Kosten, et al. NIDA RESEARCH MONOGRAPH SERIES 95:461, 1989

Cure: researchers say a nonaddictive painkiller stops cravings for cocaine and heroin: buprenorphine, by K. McAuliffe. OMNI 13(3):20, December 1990

Depressive symptoms during buprenorphine treatment of opioid abusers, by T. R. Kosten, et al. JOURNAL OF SUBSTANCE ABUSE TREATMENT 7(1):51-54, 1990

Opioid antagonist challenges in buprenorphine maintained patients, by T. R. Kosten, et al. DRUG AND ALCOHOL DEPENDENCE 25(1):73-78, February 1990

Outpatient maintenance-detoxification comparison of methadone and buprenorphine, by R. E. Johnson, et al. NIDA RESEARCH MONOGRAPH SERIES 95: 384, 1989

Treatment of cocaine abuse with buprenorphine, by T. R. Kosten, et al. BIOLOGICAL PSYCHIATRY 26(6):637-639, October 1989

Use of buprenorphine in the treatment of opioid addiction: II—physiologic and behavioral effects of daily and and alternate-day administration and abrupt withdrawal, by P. J. Fudala, et al. CLINICAL PHARMACOLOGY AND THERAPEUTICS 47(4): 525-534, April 1990

Drug—Carbamazepine

Carbamazepine treatment of cocaine dependence in methadone maintenance patients dual opiate-cocaine addiction, by K. L. Kuhn, et al. NIDA RESEARCH MONOGRAPH SERIES 95:316-317, 1989

Carbamazepine used in benzo withdrawals, by H. McConnell. JOURNAL OF THE ADDICTION RESEARCH FOUNDATION 19(11):3, January 1, 1990

Dr. James Halikas finds that a pill made for seizures may help cocaine addicts to just say no: carbamazepine (interview), by N. Stesin. PEOPLE WEEKLY 33:81-82, January 22, 1990

Drug—Clonidine

Efficacy of clonidine, guanfacine and methadone in the rapid detoxification of heroin addicts: a controlled clinical trial, by L. San, et al. BRITISH JOURNAL OF ADDICTION 85(1):141-147, January 1990

Evaluation of clonidine suppression of opiate withdrawal reactions: a multidisciplinary approach, by J. D. Cuthill, et al. CANADIAN JOURNAL OF PSYCHIATRY 35(5): 377-382, June 1990

Drug—Desipramine

Comparison of bromocriptine and desipramine in cocaine withdrawal, by I. L. Extein, et al. ANNALS OF CLINICAL PSYCHIATRY 1(3):193-197, September 1989

Desipramine treatment for relapse prevention in cocaine dependence, by S. L. McElroy, et al. NIDA RESEARCH MONOGRAPH SERIES 95:57-63, 1989

Effects of desipramine maintenance on cocaine self-administration by humans, by M. W. Fischman, et al. JOURNAL OF PHARMACOLOGY AND EXPERIMENTAL THERAPEUTICS 253(2):760-770, May 1990

Drug—Dexamphetamine

Dexamphetamine for "speed" addiction, by J. P. Sherman. MEDICAL JOURNAL OF AUSTRALIA 153(5):306, September 3, 1990

Treatment of heroin addicts with dextromethorphan: a double-blind comparison of dextromethorphan with chlorpromazine, by H. Koyuncuoglu, et al. INTERNATIONAL JOURNAL OF CLINICAL PHARMACOLOGY, THERAPY AND TOXICOLOGY 28(4):147-152, April 1990

Drug—Fluphenazine Decanoate
Treatment of patients dependent on tobacco with fluphenazine decanoate, by J. Drtil. ACTIVITAS NERVOSA SUPERIOR 31(2):116-117, June 1989

Drug—Guanfacine
Efficacy of clonidine, guanfacine and methadone in the rapid detoxification of heroin addicts: a controlled clinical trial, by L. San, et al. BRITISH JOURNAL OF ADDICTION 85(1):141-147, January 1990

Drug—Haloperidol
Effect of haloperidol in cocaine and amphetamine intoxication, by R. W. Derlet, et al. JOURNAL OF EMERGENCY MEDICINE 7(6):633-637, November/December 1989

Drug—Heroin
Comparison of oral preparations of heroin and methadone to stabilize opiate misusers as inpatients, by A. H. Ghodse, et al. BMJ 300(6726):719-720, March 17, 1990

Drug—Lithium
Lithium treatment for cocaine abusers with bipolar spectrum disorders, by E. V. Nunes, et al. AMERICAN JOURNAL OF PSYCHIATRY 147(5):655-657, May 1990

Drug—Methadone
Absence of antibody to human immunodeficiency virus in long-term, socially rehabilitated methadone maintenance patients, by D. M. Novick, et al. ARCHIVES OF INTERNAL MEDICINE 150(1):97-99, January 1990

Addict babies better off with mums on methadone, by B. I. Lee. JOURNAL OF THE ADDICTION RESEARCH FOUNDATION 19(2):4, February 1, 1990

Bridging troubled waters, by R. G. Newman. BULLETIN OF THE NEW YORK ACADEMY OF MEDICINE 66(3):266-270, May/June 1990

Challenge of illicit drug addiction for general practice, by J. Cohen, et al. DRUG AND ALCOHOL DEPENDENCE 25(3):315-318, June 1990

Comparison of oral preparations of heroin and methadone to stabilize opiate misusers as inpatients, by A. H. Ghodse, et al. BMJ 300(6726):719-720, March 17, 1990

Corrections and revised analyses for psychotherapy in methadone maintenance patients, by G. Woody, et al. ARCHIVES OF GENERAL PSYCHIATRY 47(8):788-789, August 1990

Deaths of heroin addicts starting on methadone maintenance, by C. H. Wu, et al. LANCET 335(8686):424, February 17, 1990

Deaths of heroin addicts starting on a methadone maintenance programme, by O. H. Drummer, et al. LANCET 335(8681):108, January 13, 1990

Depressive symptoms in opiate addicts on methadone maintenance, by H. Williams, et al. IRISH JOURNAL OF PSYCHOLOGICAL MEDICINE 7(1):45-46, March 1990

Desipramine treatment of cocaine abuse in methadone maintenance patients, by I. Arndt, et al. NIDA RESEARCH MONOGRAPH SERIES 95:322-323, 1989

Edinburgh's community drug problem service: a pilot evaluation of methadone substitution, by J. W. Chalmers. HEALTH BULLETIN 48(2):62-72, March 1990

Efficacy of clonidine, guanfacine and methadone in the rapid detoxification of heroin addicts: a controlled clinical trial, by L. San, et al. BRITISH JOURNAL OF ADDICTION 85(1):141-147, January 1990

Ethnic differences in narcotics addiction: I—characteristics of Chicano and Anglo methadone maintenance clients, by M. D. Anglin, et al. INTERNATIONAL JOURNAL OF THE ADDICTIONS 23(2):125-149, 1988

Examination of drug addicts on methadone treatmen:t HIV antibodies in the county of Frederiksborg, by P. P. Ege. UGESKRIFT FOR LAEGER 151(51):3484-3486, December 18, 1989

Experiences from two HIV prevention projects among drug abusers in Olso: is methadone maintenance treatment useful?, by M. Skogstad. TIDSSKRIFT FOR DEN NORSKE LAEGEFORENING 110(15):1978-1980, June 10, 1990

From the Food and Drug Administration, by S. L. Nightingale. JAMA 263(2):202, January 12, 1990

Heroin addicts in jail: New York tries methadone treatment program, by H. Joseph, et al. CORRECTIONS TODAY 51:124+, August 1989

Heroin users seeking methadone treatment. MEDICAL JOURNAL OF AUSTRALIA 153(2):116, July 16, 1990

Heroin users seeking methadone treatment, by J. Bell, et al. MEDICAL JOURNAL OF AUSTRALIA 152(7):361-364, 1990

Heroin users seeking methadone treatment, by J. R. Caplehorn. MEDICAL JOURNAL OF AUSTRALIA 153(5):305, September 3, 1990

HIV-infected i.v. drug users in methadone treatment: outcome and psychological correlates: a preliminary report, by S. L. Batki, et al. NIDA RESEARCH MONOGRAPH SERIES 95:405-406, 1989

HIV risk behavior: antisocial personality disorders, drug use patterns, and sexual behavior among methadone maintenence admissions, by D. Nolimal, et al. NIDA RESEARCH MONOGRAPH SERIES 95:401-402, 1989

Immune status of unselected methadone maintained former heroin addicts, by M. J. Kreek, et al. PROGRESS IN CLINICAL AND BIOLOGICAL RESEARCH 328:445-448, 1990

Improvement in psychological functioning among drug abusers: inpatient treatment compared to outpatient methadone maintenance, by R. J. Craig, et al. JOURNAL OF SUBSTANCE ABUSE TREATMENT 7(1):11-19, 1990

Increase in desipramine serum levels associated with methadone treatment, by I. Maany, et al. AMERICAN JOURNAL OF PSYCHIATRY 146(12):1611-1613, December 1989

Influence of prolonged stable methadone maintenance treatment on mortality and employment: an 18-year follow-up, by E. Segest, et al. INTERNATIONAL JOURNAL OF THE ADDICTIONS 25(1):53-63, January 1990

Inpatient heroin detoxification: a comment, by C. C. Cook. BRITISH JOURNAL OF ADDICTION 84(11):1369-1371, November 1989

Kallikdrein-kinin system in newborns of the drug addicted, by E. Salvaggio, et al. ADVANCES IN EXPERIMENTAL MEDICINE AND BIOLOGY 247:471-476, 1989

Management of cocaine abuse in methadone maintenance programs, by A. F. Kolar. MARYLAND MEDICAL JOURNAL 38(12):1067-1068, December 1989

Medical and psychosocial effects of methadone substitution in HIV infected substance-dependent patients, by P. Walger, et al. PSYCHOTHERAPIE, PSYCHOSOMATIK, MEDIZINISCHE PSYCHOLOGIE 39(11):381-389, November 1989

"Methadone by bus" project in Amsterdam, by E. C. Buning, et al. BRITISH JOURNAL OF ADDICTION 85(10):1247-1250, 1990

Methadone maintenance: high rate of other substance use disorders and relationship to psychiatric comorbidity, by R. K. Brooner, et al. NIDA RESEARCH MONOGRAPH SERIES 95:442, 1989

Methadone maintenance in the treatment of opioid dependence: a current perspective, by J. E. Zweben, et al. WESTERN JOURNAL OF MEDICINE 152(5):588-599, May 1990

Methadone maintenance programmes and AIDS, by D. Serraino, et al. LANCET 2(8678-8679):1522-1523, December 23-30, 1989

Methadone maintenance programs should be considered in HIV-prevention, by M. Skogstad. TIDSSKRIFT FOR DEN NORSKE LAEGEFORENING 110(15):1978-1980, 1990

Methadone maintenance therapy. MEDICAL JOURNAL OF AUSTRALIA 152(2):105-107, January 15, 1990

Methadone numbers up as guidelines change, by P. Szabo. JOURNAL OF THE ADDICTION RESEARCH FOUNDATION 19(12):5, December 1, 1990

Methadone substitution in HIV-infected drug addicts, by P. Walger, et al. DEUTSCHE MEDIZINSCHE WOCHENSCHRIFT 115(23):919, June 8, 1990

Methadone treatment and acquired immunodeficiency syndrome. JAMA 263(5):658, February 2, 1990

Methadone treatment and acquired immunodeficiency syndrome, by J. R. Cooper. JAMA 262:1664-1668, September 22-29, 1989

Methadone treatment in medical private practice: outcome according to the number of courses followed, by G. Meystre-Agustoni, et al. BRITISH JOURNAL OF ADDICTION 85(4):537-545, April 1990

Miracle weapon against drugs crime: the questionable value of methadone therapy, by P. Loos. KRIMINALISTIK 42(3):120-122, 1988

Mortality in heroin addiction: impact of methadone treatment, by L. Gonbladh, et al. ACTA PSYCHIATRICA SCANDINAVICA 82(3):223-227, 1990

Natural history of parenteral drug addicts treated in a general hospital, by R. Muga, et al. BRITISH JOURNAL OF ADDICTION 85(6):775-778, June 1990

Only two drugs work so far: methadone, nicotine. JOURNAL OF THE ADDICTION RESEARCH FOUNDATION 19(12):5, December 1, 1990

Opiate maintenance and abstinence: attitudes, treatment modalities and outcome, by D. Ladewig. DRUG AND ALCOHOL DEPENDENCE 25(2):245-250, April 1990

Organization and implementation of the Australian methadone program and initial results, by D. Pfersmann, et al. NERVENARZT 61(7):438-443, July 1990

Outpatient maintenance-detoxification comparison of methadone and buprenorphine, by R. E. Johnson, et al. NIDA RESEARCH MONOGRAPH SERIES 95: 384, 1989

Outpatient methadone programme for pregnant heroin using women, by W. Giles, et al. AUSTRALIAN AND NEW ZEALAND JOURNAL OF OBSTETRICS AND GYNAECOLOGY 29(3 Pt 1):225-229, August 1989

Patients successfully maintained with methadone escaped human immunodeficiency virus infection, by A. Barthwell, et al. ARCHIVES OF GENERAL PSYCHIATRY 46(10):957-958, October 1989

Pilot study of a neuro-stimulator device vs. methadone in alleviating opiate withdrawal symptoms, by E. Elmoghazy, et al. NIDA RESEARCH MONOGRAPH SERIES 95:388-389, 1989

Primary care for patients with human immunodeficiency virus (HIV) infection in a methadone maintenance treatment program, by P. A. Selwyn, et al. ANNALS OF INTERNAL MEDICINE 111(9):761-763, November 1, 1989

Prospective clinical audit of methadone maintenance therapy at the Royal Newcastle Hospital, by A. Foy, et al. MEDICAL JOURNAL OF AUSTRALIA 151(6):332-334+, September 18, 1989

Providing HIV counseling and testing services in methadone maintenance programs, by M. L. Cartter, et al. AIDS 4(5):463-465, May 1990

Psychoneuroendocrine effects of methadone maintenance, by M. L. Willenbring, et al. PSYCHONEUROENDOCRINOLOGY 14(5):371-391, 1989

Relationships of SCL-90 profiles to methadone patients' psychosocial characteristics and treatment response, by R. A. Steer, et al. MULTIVARIATE EXPERIMENTAL CLINICAL RESEARCH 9(2):45-54, 1989

Relative abuse liability of benzodiazepines in methadone maintained populations in three cities, by M. Y. Iguchi, et al. NIDA RESEARCH MONOGRAPH SERIES 95:364-365, 1989

Results of empirical studies of methadone treatment, by M. Gmur. SCHWEIZ-ERISCHE MEDIZINISCHE WOCHENSCHRIFT 119(44):1560-1570, November 4, 1989

Schema for evaluating methadone maintenance programs, by J. C. Ball. NIDA RE-SEARCH MONOGRAPH SERIES 95:74-77, 1989

Some reflections on dynamics and dilemmas in a DDU, by D. Summerhill, et al. BRI-TISH JOURNAL OF ADDICTION 85(5):589-592, May 1990

Survey of methadone patients in Canada, by J. M. Ruel, et al. CANADIAN JOURNAL OF PUBLIC HEALTH 81(4):272-274, July/August 1990

Treatment crisis: cocaine use by clients in methadone maintenance programs, by A. F. Kolar, et al. JOURNAL OF SUBSTANCE ABUSE TREATMENT 7(2):101-107, 1990

Validation of MMPI profile subtypes among opioid addicts who are beginning metha-done maintenance treatment, by D. A. Calsyn, et al. JOURNAL OF CLINICAL PSYCHOLOGY 45(6):991-998, November 1989

Drug—Naloxone

Acute opioid physical dependence in humans: effect of naloxone at 6 and 24 hours postmorphine, by S. J. Heishman, et al. PHARMACOLOGY, BIOCHEMISTRY AND BEHAVIOR 36(2):393-399, June 1990

Acute opioid physical dependence in humans: maximum morphine-naloxone interval, by K. C. Kirby, et al. NIDA RESEARCH MONOGRAPH SERIES 95:393-394, 1989

Acute unilateral edema of the lung in a patient with heroin overdose and treated with intravenous naloxone, by A. Navarro Beynes, et al. MEDICINA CLINICA 94(16): 637, April 28, 1990

Effects of sublingually given naloxone in opioid-dependent human volunteers, by K. L. Preston, et al. DRUG AND ALCOHOL DEPENDENCE 25(1):27-34, February 1990

Fractionated opiate withdrawal with tiapride and naloxone: a new treatment approach, by O. Presslich, et al. PSYCHIATRISCHE PRAXIS 16(5):179-181, September 1989

Hyperalgesia during naloxone-precipitated withdrawal from morphine is associated with increased on-cell activity in the rostral ventromedial medulla, by J. B. Bederson, et al. SOMATOSENSORY AND MOTOR RESEARCH 7(2):85-203, 1990

Naloxone challenge as a biological predictor of treatment outcome in opiate addicts, by L. K. Jacobsen, et al. AMERICAN JOURNAL OF DRUG AND ALCOHOL ABUSE 15(4):355-366, December 1989

Rapid opioid detoxification with electrosleep and naloxone, by J. Westermeyer. AMERICAN JOURNAL OF PSYCHIATRY 147(7):952-953, July 1990

Drug—Naltrexone
Naltrexone: an effective aid in the psychosocial rehabilitation process of former opiate dependent, by D. Ladewig. THERAPEUTISCHE UMSCHAU 47(3):247-250, March 1990

Naltrexone for heroin addiction: encouraging results from Italy, by F. Schifano, et al. INTERNATIONAL JOURNAL OF CLINICAL PHARMACOLOGY, THERAPY AND TOXICOLOGY 28(4):144-146, April 1990

Naltrexone in federal probationers, by D. S. Metzger, et al. NIDA RESEARCH MONO-GRAPH SERIES 95:465-466, 1989

Naltrexone: an opioid antagonist to support the drug-free state in previous opioid addicts having stopped the habit, by P. W. Jepsen. UGESKRIFT FOR LAEGER 153(36):2546-2549, September 3, 1990

Drug—Ondansetron
Sites of action of ondansetron to inhibit withdrawal from drugs of abuse, by B. Costall, et al. PHARMACOLOGY, BIOCHEMISTRY AND BEHAVIOR 36(1):97-104, 1990

Drug—Phenobarbital
Detoxication with phenobarbital of alprazolam-dependent polysubstance abusers, by N. V. Ravi, et al. JOURNAL OF SUBSTANCE ABUSE TREATMENT 7(1):55-58, 1990

Drug—Sodium Valproate
Sodium valproate in benzodiazepine withdrawal, by S. Apelt, et al. AMERICAN JOURNAL OF PSYCHIATRY 147(7):950-951, July 1990

Drug—Trazodone
Trazodone for the treatment of anxiety symptoms in substance abusers, by N. R. Liebowitz, et al. JOURNAL OF CLINICAL PSYCHOPHARMACOLOGY 9(6):449-451, December 1989

Economics
Treatment dollars: where are they? NARCOTICS DEMAND REDUCTION DIGEST 1(7):1, December 1989

Comparison of the behavioral effects and abuse liability of ethanol and pentobarbital in recreational sedative abusers, by J. J. Guarino, et al. NIDA RESEARCH MONOGRAPH SERIES 85:453-454, 1989

Corporate America's response to substance abuse: employees addicted to alcohol or drugs, by J. Frieden. BUSINESS AND HEALTH 8(7):32-36+, July 1990

Drug abuse services and EAPs: preliminary report on a national study, by T. E. Backer. NIDA RESEARCH MONOGRAPH SERIES 91:227-244, 1989

Educating educators about alcoholism and drug addiction: the role of employee assistance programmes, by N. Van den Bergh. MEDICINE AND LAW 9(1):713-723, 1990

Employee benefit managers assess drug policy: inpatient vs. outpatient drug treatment services, by E. Gilbert. NATIONAL UNDERWRITER. LIFE AND HEALTH/FINANCIAL SERVICES EDITION 94:10-11, December 24, 1990

Employee utilization of addiction treatment, by A. B. Miller. EMPLOYEE ASSISTANCE QUARTERLY 5(4):13-31, 1990

Europeans warned: EAP essential first step before drug testing, by K. Birchard. JOURNAL OF THE ADDICTION RESEARCH EDUCATION 19(9):9, September 1, 1990

Hospital obligations toward recovering addicted employees, by S. M. Olson, et al. HEALTHSPAN 7(4):3-6, April 1990

Impact of Federal rehabilitation laws on the expanding role of employee assistance programs in business and industry, by G. M. Farkas. AMERICAN PSYCHOLOGIST 44(12):1482-1490, December 1989

Incentives and competition in a worksite smoking cessation intervention, by L. A. Jason, et al. AMERICAN JOURNAL OF PUBLIC HEALTH 80(2):205-206, February 1990

More American firms are using assistance programs. CORPORATE SECURITY DIGEST 3(46):7, November 20, 1989

Perspectives on job-based programs for alcohol and drug problems, by H. M. Trice, et al. JOURNAL OF DRUG ISSUES 19:315-418, Summer 1989

Revisiting the role of the supervisor in Employee Assistance Programs, by B. Googins. NIDA RESEARCH MONOGRAPH SERIES 91:289-304, 1989

Sources and configurations of institutional denial, by P. L. Myers. EMPLOYEE ASSISTANCE QUARTERLY 5(3):43-54, 1990

Start workplace drug policy with help from professionals. SECURITY 27(1):18, January 1990

Substance abuse treatment helps save lives, by J. Richardson. AMERICAN MINING CONGRESS JOURNAL 76:8, August 1990

Treating the cocaine abuser, by M. G. Cooper. EMPLOYEE ASSISTANCE QUARTERLY 4(4):31-47, 1989

Use of EAPs in dealing with drug abuse in the workplace, by P. M. Roman. NIDA RESEARCH MONOGRAPH SERIES (91):271-286, 1989

Family

Children of parents of drug-alcohol programs: are they underserved?, by N. Van den Bergh, et al. ALCOHOLISM TREATMENT QUARTERLY 6(3-4):1-25, 1989

Cognitive marital therapy: a case report, by F. M. Dattilio. JOURNAL OF FAMILY PSYCHOTHERAPY 1(1):15-31, 1990

Contextual therapy: brief treatment of an addict and spouse, by G. Bernal, et al. FAMILY PRACTICE 29(1):59-71, March 1990

Evolution of an integrative family therapy for substance-abusing adolescents: toward the mutual enhancement of research and practice, by F. P. Piercy, et al. JOURNAL OF FAMILY PSYCHOLOGY 3(1):5-25, September 1989

Family-based interventions for helping drug-abusing adolescents, by R. A. Lewis, et al. JOURNAL OF ADOLESCENT RESEARCH 5(1):82-95, January 1990

Family therapy vs. parent groups: effects on adolescent drug abusers, by A. S. Friedman. AMERICAN JOURNAL OF FAMILY THERAPY 17:335-347, Winter 1989

Family therapy with spinal cord injured substance abusers, by M. Perez, et al. SOCIAL WORK IN HEALTH CARE 14(2):15-25, 1989

Family treatment for homeless alcohol/drug-addicted women and their preschool children, by M. Comfort, et al. ALCOHOLISM TREATMENT QUARTERLY 7(1): 129-147, 1990

Mini ethnography of the family therapy of adolescent drug abuse: the ambiguous experience, by N. A. Newfield, et al. ALCOHOLISM TREATMENT QUARTERLY 7(2):57-79, 1990

Overview of marital and family treatments with substance abusing populations, by J. C. Thomas. ALCOHOLISM TREATMENT QUARTERLY 6(3-4):91-102, 1989

Principles of family therapy for adolescent substance abuse, by T. C. Todd, et al. JOURNAL OF PSYCHOTHERAPHY AND THE FAMILY 6(3-4):49-70, 1989

Reflections during a study on family therapy with drug addicts, by S. Reichelt, et al. FAMILY PROCESS 29(3):273-287, 1990

Prisons and Prisoners

Behavioral approach to substance abuse prevention in the correctional setting: a preliminary report, by S. Yen, et al. BEHAVIOURAL RESIDENTIAL TREATMENT 4(1):53-64, January 1989

Congress needs to mandate drug treatment programs for state and local inmates, by R. B. Walton. CORRECTIONS DIGEST 21(18):1-5, September 5, 1990

Heroin addicts in jail: New York tries methadone treatment program, by H. Joseph, et al. CORRECTIONS TODAY 51:124+, August 1989

Long-term therapeutic needs of persons in detention, by P. Christoffersen. UGE-SKRIFT FOR LAEGER 152(6):394-396, February 5, 1990

Outcome evaluation of a prison therapeutic community for substance abuse treatment: Stay'n Out program in New York State, by H. K. Wexler, et al. CRIMINAL JUSTICE AND BEHAVIOR 17(1):71-92, March 1990

Project AIM: a quiet battle in the war on drugs: education and treatment program for county jail inmates in San Diego, by R. M. Ariessohn, et al. CORRECTIONS TODAY 52:28+, June 1990

Rehearsing relapse teaches coping skills: Hillsborough County, Florida, in-jail drug treatment service, by R. H. Peters, et al. CORRECTIONS TODAY 52(2):172+, April 1990

TOLOXATONE
Acute toloxatone poisoning: apropos of 122 cases, by P. Azoyan, et al. THERAPIE 45(2):139-144, March/April 1990

TOLUENE
Anesthetic care of a patient intoxicated with thinner, by J. Aono, et al. MASUI 39(3): 388-390, March 1990

Case of thinner sniffing: part 2—urinary excretion of cresols and methanol after inhalation of toluene and methanol, by S. Kira, et al. INDUSTRIAL HEALTH 27(4): 175-180, 1989

Chronic solvent abuse: 1—cognitive sequelae, by J. Zur, et al. CHILD: CARE, HEALTH AND DEVELOPMENT 16(1):1-20, January/February 1990

Chronic solvent abuse: 2—relationship with depression, by J. Zur, et al. CHILD: CARE, HEALTH AND DEVELOPMENT 16(1):21-34, January/February 1990

Clinical and electrophysiological finding in three patients with toluene dependency, by N. Toyonaga, et al. DOCUMENTO OPHTHALMOLOGICA 73(2):201-207, October 1989

Correlation between "on admission" blood toluene concentrations and the pressure of absence of signs and symptoms in solvent abusers, by T. Miyazaki, et al. FORENSIC SCIENCE INTERNATIONAL 44(2-3):169-177, 1990

Driving under the influence of toluene, by H. Gjerde, et al. FORENSIC SCIENCE INTERNATIONAL 44(1):77-83, January 1990

TOLUENE—Complications

Course of respiration and circulation in "toluene-sniffing," by N. Ikeda, et al. FORENSIC SCIENCE INTERNATIONAL 44(2-3):151-158, February 1990

Toluene dementia, by S. M. Gospe, Jr. NEUROLOGY 40(8):1320-1321, August 1990

White matter dementia in chronic toluene abuse, by C. M. Filley, et al. NEUROLOGY 40(3 Pt 1):532-534, March 1990

Research
Evoked potential changes from 13 weeks of stimulated toluene abuse in rats, by J. L. Mattson, et al. PHARMACOLOGY, BIOCHEMISTRY AND BEHAVIOR 36(3):683-689, July 1990

TRAMADOL
Effects of tramadol in humans: assessment of its abuse potential, by K. L. Preston, et al. NIDA RESEARCH MONOGRAPH SERIES 95:392, 1989

TRANQUILIZERS
Sedative-tranquilizer use and abuse in alcoholics currently in outpatient treatment: incidence, pattern and preference, by B. Wolf, et al. NIDA RESEARCH MONOGRAPH SERIES 95:376-377, 1989

TRIAZOLAM
Zolpidem and triazolam in humans: behavioral effects and abuse liability, by S. M. Evans, et al. NIDA RESEARCH MONOGRAPH SERIES 95:431-432, 1989

UNITED STATES DEPARTMENT OF DEFENSE *see*: DOD

UNITED STATES DEPARTMENT OF JUSTICE *see*: DOJ

UNITED STATES DEPARTMENT OF TRANSPORTATION *see*: DOT

UNITED STATES DRUG ENFORCEMENT AGENCY *see*: DEA

VOLATILE SUBSTANCES
Psychological study in children addicted to inhalation of volatile substances, by L. M. Rojas, et al. REVISTA DE INVESTIGACION CLINICA 41(4):361-365, October/December 1989

Volatile substance of abuse, by C. H. Linden. EMERGENCY MEDICINE CLINICS OF NORTH AMERICA 8(3):559-578, August 1990

VOLATILE SUBSTANCES—Complications

Neurologic complications of drug addiction: general aspects—complications caused by cannabis, designer drugs and volatile substances, by M. Farre Albaladejo. ARCHIVES DE NEUROGIOLOGIA 52(Suppl)1:143-148, 1989

Neurophysiological consequences of volatile substance abuse, by H. Swadi. BMJ 299(6696):458-459, August 12, 1989

Neuropsychological consequences of volatile substance abuse: a population-based study of secondary school pupils, by O. Chadwick, et al. BM J 298:1679-1684, 1989

WHO (WORLD HEALTH ORGANIZATION)

New WHO drug program under way: Sweden's [Hans] Emblad is chief, by A. MacLennan. JOURNAL OF THE ADDICTION RESEARCH FOUNDATION 19(12):2, December 1, 1990

WHO: all-out fight starts against drug epidemic. INTERNATIONAL NURSING REVIEW 37(2):225-226, March/April 1990

WHO Expert Committee on Drug Dependence: twenty-sixth report. WHO TECHNICAL REPORT SERIES 787:1-32, 1989

WHO to intensify campaign against drug epidemic. PUBLIC HEALTH REPORTS 105: 326-327, May/June 1990

WITHDRAWAL

Cocaine attenuates the severity of naloxone-precipitated opioid withdrawal, by T. A. Kosten. LIFE SCIENCES 47(18):1617-1623, 1990

Development of a Short Withdrawal Scale (SOWS), by M. Gossop. ADDICTIVE BEHAVIORS 15(5):487-490, 1990

Ondansetron inhibits a behavioural consequence of withdrawing from drugs of abuse, by B. Costall, et al. PHARMACOLOGY, BIOCHEMISTRY AND BEHAVIOR 36(2):339-344, June 1990

WOMEN

Addiction: no way out—detoxification programmes for women drug addicts, by C. Troupp. GUARDIAN May 15, 1990, p. 17

AIDS, addiction and condom use: sources of sexual risk for heterosexual women, by S. Kane. JOURNAL OF SEX RESEARCH 27:427-444, August 1990

AIDS prevention and chemical dependence treatment needs of women and their children, by L. D. Karan. JOURNAL OF PSYCHOACTIVE DRUGS 21(4):395-399, October/December 1989

Anti-alcohol therapy in the multimodal treatment of patients with primary chronic recurrent pancreatitits and alcoholism, by N. P. Vanchakova, et al. SOVIET NEUROLOGY AND PSYCHIATRY 22(4):96-101, Winter 1989/1990

Back from crack, by J. Nelson. ESSENCE 20:57-58+, January 1990

Characteristics of non-referred cocaine abusing mothers, by I. E. Smith, et al. NIDA RESEARCH MONOGRAPH SERIES 95:330, 1989

Characteristics of women receiving mandated treatment for alcohol and polysubstance dependence in Massachusetts, by B. W. Lex, et al. DRUG AND ALCOHOL DEPENDENCE 25(1):13-20, February 1990

Crack: girls like you on drugs like that, by M. Massing. MADEMOISELLE 96:158-161, May 1990

Dr. Donahue's crack solutions: crack mothers on Phil Donahue show, by P. Yancy. CHRISTIANITY TODAY 34:72, September 24, 1990

Drug-free after 30 years of dependency, by L. Reynolds. AGING (361):26-27, 1990

Health and other characteristics of employed women and homemakers in Tecumseh, 1959-1978: I—demographic characteristics, smoking habits, alcohol consumption, and pregnancy outcomes and conditions, by M. H. Higgins, et al. WOMEN AND HEALTH 16(2):5-21, 1990

Kinin-kininase system in drug addicted woman in pregnancy and puerperium, by A. Virgolino, et al. ADVANCES IN EXPERIMENTAL MEDICINE AND BIOLOGY 247: 463-469, 1989

Marijuana and alcohol effects on mood states in young women, by B. W. Lex, et al. NIDA RESEARCH MONOGRAPH SERIES 95:462, 1989

Marijuana makes a comeback, by J. Malone. MADEMOISELLE 96:184-187, October 1990

Model for the treatment of trauma-related syndromes among chemically dependent inpatient women, by K. Bollerud. JOURNAL OF SUBSTANCE ABUSE TREATMENT 7(2):83-87, 1990

Plasma delta-9-THC levels as a predictive measure of marijuana use by women, by J. H. Mendelson, et al. NIDA RESEARCH MONOGRAPH SERIES 95:152-158, 1989

Psychiatric study of suicide among urban Swedish women, by U. Asgard. ACTA PSYCHIATRICA SCANDINAVICA 82(2):115-124, 1990

Social bonding-drug progression model of amphetamine use among young women, by D. E. Taub, et al. AMERICAN JOURNAL OF DRUG AND ALCOHOL ABUSE 16(1-2):77-95, 1990

Stories of women: project. HEALTH PROMOTION 28(3):22-23, Winter 1989-1990

Substance abuse in women: relationship between chemical dependency of women and past report of physical and-or sexual abuse, by G. B. Ladwig, et al. INTERNATIONAL JOURNAL OF THE ADDICTIONS 24(8):739-754, 1989

Women and crack addiction, by J. Sher. JOURNAL OF THE AMERICAN MEDICAL WOMEN'S ASSOCIATION 44(6):166, November/December 1989

WOMEN

Women and drugs: the untold story, by C. Breslin. LADIES HOME JOURNAL 107:89-91+, January 1990

Women, substance abuse and the law: Project C.O.P.E. HEALTH PROMOTION 28 (3):23, Winter 1989/1990

WORLD HEALTH ORGANIZATION *see:* WHO

ZIPEPROL
Lethal poisoning by zipeprol in drug addicts, by O. Crippa, et al. JOURNAL OF FORENSIC SCIENCES 35(4):992-999, July 1990

ZOLPIDEM
Zolpidem and triazolam in humans: behavioral effects and abuse liability, by S. M. Evans, et al. NIDA RESEARCH MONOGRAPH SERIES 95:431-432, 1989

ZOPICLONE
Zopiclone, by F. Kelly, et al. LANCET 335(8696):1033-1034, April 28, 1990

AUTHOR INDEX

Page numbers are given only for the first subject heading under which an entry appears. The page number is given followed by the number of an entry on any given page (10-1 indicates page 10, entry 1).

Compton, D. R. 210-5
Conde Lopez, V. 55-2
Condie, R. G. 477-16
Cone, E. J. 481-10, 481-13, 482-12
Conlan, M. F. 359-13
Conner, D. L. 269-9
Connors, E. F., III 270-16, 454-4
Connors, G. J. 90-16, 112-3
Connors, S. 237-7
Conroy, M. S. 100-3
Constantine, T. A. 326-13, 360-5
Conti, D. J. 488-5
Convissor, R. B. 182-8
Cook, C. C. 98-2, 499-5
Cook, M. C. 16-6
Cook, R. F. 305-2
Cook, W. L. 96-13
Cooney, N. L. 114-2
Cooper, J. R. 500-2
Cooper, M. G. 504-1
Cooper, M. H. 362-9
Cooper, M. L. 175-1, 189-5
Cooper, R. A. 394-7
Cooper, T. M. 490-5
Coper, H. 441-9
Corberand, J. X. 34-9
Corcoran, K. J. 113-9, 122-8
Cordero, L. 232-12
Cordoba, N. E. 143-10
Corley, F. G. 452-16
Cormack, M. A. 206-14
Corn, D. 419-13
Corner, G. M. 23-4
Corrigall, W. A. 314-12, 315-1, 379-5
Corrigan, B. 446-8
Corrington, J. E. 39-13
Corry, J. W. 302-2
Corssman, R. K. 253-14
Corti, B. 92-1, 196-11
Costa, L. 415-2
Costall, B. 441-3, 502-8, 507-10
Costello, R. M. 65-15
Cottler, L. B. 62-9, 206-5, 258-3
Cotton, P. 415-11
Couglin, T. A., III 490-3
Cousins, P. 305-11
Coustan, D. R. 231-7
Coutinho, R. A. 28-3
Cove, P. 117-13
Cowan, J. M. 152-4
Cowart, V. S. 380-7, 412-6, 485-5
Cowen, R. 153-5, 172-2, 224-9, 241-2
Cowley, G. 97-7
Cox, J. S. 447-18
Cox, K. L. 133-14
Crabb, D. W. 94-3
Crabbe, J. S. 139-2

Craciun, C. 146-1
Craig, J. O. 358-4
Craig, R. B. 273-13
Craig, R. J. 426-17, 436-10
Crandell, J. S. 37-11
Crant, J. M. 469-13
Cratty, B. J. 322-6
Crawford, J. R. 40-8
Crawford, M. G. 182-5
Crawford, R. J. 319-12
Crawford, M. H. 407-13
Crawsford, R. J. 154-6
Creeden, J. E. 168-8
Crespo, M. D. 214-14
Cribb, R. 316-11
Crigger, B. J. 34-15
Crilly, R. G. 53-5
Crippa, O. 509-3
Crisp, T. 335-8
Crofton, J. 249-7
Cross, G. M. 153-4
Crouch, B. G. 74-16
Crouch, D. J. 300-10
Crowe, A. B. 84-5
Crozier, B. 272-17
Cruikshank, D. 416-2
Crumley, F. E. 455-14
Cubric, M. D. 86-2
Cullen, F. T. 448-4
Cummings, K. M. 376-10
Cunningham, C. L. 136-10
Curcione, N. 447-6
Curran, D. A. 32-9
Curriden, M. 227-3
Curry, R. L., Jr. 108-16
Curson, S. 16-2
Curtet, F. 267-2
Curtis, K. 55-12
Cuthill, J. D. 496-9
Cyr, M. G. 73-1
Czajkoski, E. H. 370-3
Czarnecki, D. M. 92-13
D'Agnone, O. A. 430-1
Dackis, C. A. 453-12
Daggett, R. B. 233-17
Dahl, G. 59-11
Dahl, R. E. 221-9
Dai, S. 314-14
Daigle, R. D. 449-6
Dal Cason, T. A. 334-10, 454-2
Dalzell, A. M. 350-8
Dane, A. 359-9
Dani, R. 56-6
Dans, P. E. 388-11
Daoust, M. 142-12
Darke, S. 393-1
Darling, M. R. 210-15

Heather, N. 33-2, 120-9, 159-12
Heatley, M. K. 106-4
Heaton, G. 41-10, 85-10, 103-3
Hebert, J. R. 382-1
Heck, E. J. 73-11
Hecker, R. 52-8
Hecker, S. 472-15
Heckler, J. N. 42-5
Heckmatt, J. 66-2
Hedges, S. J. 248-12, 286-1, 367-12
Heegaard, N. H. 70-9
Heerema, D. L. 292-1
Heffner, J. E. 245-17
Heifer, U. 74-1, 150-14
Heimgard, M. A. 173-1
Heinzl, S. 447-12
Heishman, S. J. 211-7, 342-2, 425-2
Hekmatpanah, C. R. 336-2
Helander, A. 160-5
Helfer, J. 306-6
Hell, D. 126-16
Hellerstedt, W. L. 91-12
Hellman, R. E. 157-11
Helm, S. 281-9
Helmer, W. J. 328-18
Helzer, J. E. 40-2
Henderson, C. E. 389-13
Henderson, M. G. 239-4
Hendrickse, R. G. 463-4
Hendriks, V. M. 245-15
Hengsler, G. A. 331-17
Henly, G. A. 192-4
Henman, A. 274-14
Henman, A. R. 273-14
Hennessy, M. 77-16
Henningfield, J. E. 310-12, 374-11, 375-5, 376-9, 426-14
Henriksson, S. 29-13
Herbeth, B. 33-6
Herd, D. 149-1, 149-5
Herman, R. M. 399-4
Hernandez-Munoz, R. 32-13
Heron, E. 220-15
Herrero, M. E. 439-2
Herrod, J. 388-1
Herschman, Z. 450-9
Hertling, M. P. 255-4
Hertzmann, M. 481-5
Herz, A. 349-7
Herz, L. R. 44-10
Hesse, F. 45-14
Hester, R. K. 153-10
Hettiarachchi, J. 455-13
Hewitt, B. 76-16
Heyser, C. J. 240-13
Hibbard, S. 178-6
Hicks, J. M. 464-8

Hicks, R. D. 223-15, 245-10
Hidalgo, H. A. 199-10
Higgins, M. H. 194-16
Higgins, S. T. 227-5
Higgins-Lee, C. 118-11
High, G. 339-1
Hill, A. D. 246-17
Hill, D. J. 166-12
Hill, R. F. 357-10
Hill, S. Y. 98-11, 176-16
Hill, T. W. 184-1
Hiller, W. 46-14
Hillstrom, R. P. 397-5
Hilton, M. E. 68-11, 114-4
Hindmarch, I. 76-4, 117-16, 380-2
Hindmarsh, H. W. 413-10
Hines, G. 160-10
Hingson, R. W. 18-1
Hinrichsen, J. J. 39-6
Hirayama, T. 185-3
Hirmatsu, M. 335-11
Hirschel, J. D. 490-9
Hirst, M. 80-6
Hiyama, T. 60-3
Hjort, P. 100-7
Ho, A. 135-3
Ho, Y. S. 465-2
Hochhauser, M. 26-13
Hodes, N. L. 474-13
Hodgson, B. T. 151-12
Hodgson, R. J. 333-8
Hoegerman, G. 320-18
Hoek, J. B. 45-16
Hoffman, G. K. 39-14
Hoffman, J. 80-1, 322-12
Hoffman, R. S. 56-11, 228-8
Hofmann, M. A. 212-8
Hogya, P. T. 229-18
Holcomb, D. R. 246-5
Holden, C. 15-6, 264-16, 479-15
Holden, J. 206-6
Holden, M. G. 178-15
Holden, S. C. 451-5
Holder, D. 336-15
Hollander, E. 232-8
Hollandworth, S. 434-9
Hollbon, J. 417-14
Holleran, P. R. 181-9
Hollinger, M. A. 387-4
Hollister, L. E. 171-13, 308-6, 494-3
Hollobon, J. 31-11, 110-7, 143-13, 153-9, 220-5, 440-12, 462-5, 477-9
Holman, J. 157-15
Holmes, R. S. 131-11
Holmes, S. J. 176-15
Holmila, M. 175-12
Holt, S. 71-11, 111-5

Kinnaird, D. W. 35-10
Kinnamon, C. 295-15
Kinnan, J. P. 149-12
Kinsley, M. 403-16
Kintz, P. 479-16
Kipke, M. D. 457-4
Kira, S. 338-3, 384-7
Kirby, K. C. 342-3
Kirhira, Y. 378-3
Kirk, D. L. 488-1
Kirsch, C. M. 395-2
Kirton, M. 114-1
Kiselevski, I. 132-12
Kisling, A. 451-16
Kitfield, J. 339-13
Kiyosawa, K. 396-5
Kjolstad, H. 125-5
Klag, M. J. 48-1
Klages, K. 102-12
Klare, M. T. 339-16
Klatt, E. C. 345-7
Kleber, H. D. 453-15, 493-12
Klee, H. 25-5
Kleiman, M. A. R. 228-9
Klein, H. 40-3, 122-6, 168-10
Klein, J. 381-6
Kleine, T. 277-16
Kleinman, C. C. 449-10
Kleinman, P. H. 428-9
Klemm, B. 31-2
Kletter, R. 320-15, 390-6
Kleven, M. S. 238-13, 240-7
Klimas, N. G. 165-10
Kline, J. N. 234-16
Kline, R. B. 120-14
Kling, W. 150-7
Klinger, R. A. 478-13
Klingner, D. E. 468-3
Klitzner, M. 108-10, 108-11
Klonblauch, D. L. 38-1
Kloppel, A. 54-5
Klotz, G. W. 474-9
Knapman, L. 79-5
Knight, S. J. 470-1
Knop, J. 142-6
Knott, V. J. 378-2
Knowles, E. E. 96-5, 97-2, 119-12
Knox, B. 32-8
Knudsen, G. M. 58-11
Knupfer, G. 149-4
Ko, W. W. 343-4
Koch, E. 201-10
Koepsell, J. 433-12
Kohlenberg-Muller, K. 72-7
Kohli, H. S. 179-5
Kohn, M. 179-1, 312-6
Kokkinos, P. F. 182-14

Kokko, J. P. 228-4
Kolar, A. F. 499-7, 501-8
Kolesnikov, V. 65-4, 65-5
Kollar, K. M. 353-9
Kolotilin, G. F. 155-14
Kolton, R. J. 339-11
Koltringer, P. 62-4
Kondracke, M. M. 326-4
Konovalov, G. N. 187-5
Koob, G. F. 351-4
Kopp, M. 123-13
Koranyi, E. K. 48-3
Korcok, M. 215-15
Koren, G. 229-9
Korf, D. J. 268-7
Kormendy, E. 42-1
Korn, R. R. 201-17, 353-19
Kornet, M. 131-6
Korolenko, C. P. 111-17, 119-9
Koroloff, N. M. 124-7
Korpi, E. R. 137-9
Kortteinen, T. 103-16
Korzenny, F. 460-7
Koshes, R. J. 317-10
Kosten, T. A. 115-4, 237-3
Kosten, T. R. 234-15, 423-16, 487-15, 489-3, 495-12, 496-1, 496-3
Kosten, T. A. 440-3
Kostowski, W. 94-4
Kotlyarov, A. M. 368-8, 368-9
Kottek, S. S. 100-8
Koury, M. J. 235-14
Kovar, K. A. 256-10
Koven, S. G. 370-10
Kovetskii, N. S. 54-11
Kowalski, G. S. 252-9
Koyuncuoglu, H. 342-7, 497-1
Kozak, J. 380-5
Kozel, N. J. 269-3
Kozlovskii, A. V. 61-2
Kozlowski, L. T. 106-1, 376-1, 416-11, 441-14
Kraar, L. 327-14
Krahn, D. D. 291-4
Kramer, L. D. 234-1
Kramer, T. H. 223-7
Krantz, P. 221-4
Kranzler, H. 495-5
Kranzler, H. R. 53-10, 159-1, 159-13
Krarup, G. 148-10
Krasik, E. D. 46-1
Kraska, P. B. 251-8
Kraus, J. F. 151-7
Kreek, M. J. 18-13, 319-9, 499-1
Krendel, D. A. 229-10
Kreutzer, J. S. 156-6
Kril, J. J. 107-5, 132-4, 134-2, 142-7

Mishan, E. J. 371-9
Missak,S. 107-2
Missliwetz, J. 85-12
Mitchell, C. 252-15
Mitchell, J. E. 172-10
Mitchell, W. P. 358-2
Mitic, W. R. 191-6
Mitlohner, M. 170-13
Miyazaki, T. 338-5, 478-7
Mkhize, H. 213-4
Modell, J. G. 32-5, 173-10
Moffatt, K. 90-12
Moffatt, R. J. 451-18
Moffett, L. A. 422-3
Mohr, T. 15-3
Mohs, M. E. 185-4, 245-8
Moiseev, V. S. 51-5
Molamu, L. 39-2, 147-14
Molgaard, H. 58-15
Moll, N. 63-6
Moll van Charante, A. W. 174-8
Monagle, K. 102-6
Moncher, M. S. 341-15
Mondanaro, J. 27-12
Monfardini, S. 18-4
Monteiro, M. G. 99-10, 167-5
Montgomery, N. R., Jr. 166-13
Montgomery, S. A. 197-10
Monti, P. M. 154-1
Montin, M. 43-5
Moody, J. 272-7, 272-14
Mookherjee, H. N. 126-7
Moolten, M. 143-2
Moore, D. D. 492-14
Moore, J. C., Jr. 375-6
Moore, J. T. 277-11
Moore, R. D. 46-8, 186-4
Moore, W. J. 251-4
Moorjani, S. 31-8
Moos, R. H. 112-13
Morales, E. 362-6, 368-3
Moran, J. P., Jr. 370-16
Moran, M. B. 66-1
Morantz, A. 472-19
Moreau, D. L. 460-16
Morelli, S. 58-4
Moretti, V. 495-7
Morgan, H. W. 156-10
Morgan, L. K. 333-7
Morgan, M. Y. 105-16
Morganthau, T. 204-6, 248-14
Mori, H. 198-13
Mori, T. 144-8, 173-3
Moriarty, M. D. 352-3
Morisi, G. 59-16
Morland, B. 45-15
Morlet, A. 22-14

Morley, J. 204-11, 269-6
Morowitz, H. J. 415-4
Morris, R. E. 208-6, 263-19
Morris, S. K. 493-9
Morrison, M. A. 457-11, 461-10
Morrison, S. 446-19, 447-10
Morrison, V. 268-10
Morrow, A. L. 133-6
Morrow, D. 174-2
Morrow, J. 35-3
Morton, J. 265-1
Morvai, V. 58-13
Moskalewicz, J. 42-2
Mosketi, K. V. 120-11
Moss, D. C. 330-14
Moss, H. B. 98-16, 432-3
Moss, K. 407-11
Moss, K. L. 464-4
Motak, E. 121-8
Mothibe, G. 147-15
Motitschke, L. 365-11
Mott, J. 170-17, 253-11
Mourelle, M. 383-8
Moval, V. 55-3
Moya, A. 278-14
Moyer, D. L. 438-6
Moynihan, S. 333-13
Mrvos, R. M. 209-6
Mueller, P. D. 230-1
Mueser, K. T. 306-5
Mufti, S. I. 46-5, 131-7, 136-1
Muga, R. 216-3, 216-8, 495-1
Mulford, H. 154-14
Mullahy, J. 110-6
Mullan, M. 95-13
Mulleady, G. 20-15, 444-15
Mullen, K. 109-14
Muller, A. 150-15
Muller, P. 379-11
Muller, W. E. 206-4
Muller, W. J. 378-12
Mullins, R. M. 373-9
Muntaner, C. 423-12, 429-7
Murata, T. 56-3
Murphy, G. E. 191-3
Murphy, J. M. 143-11
Murphy, K. R. 467-9
Murpphy, S. E. 377-13
Murray, C. A. 293-9, 294-7
Murray, D. M. 298-10
Murray, J. B. 94-2, 160-12, 195-7
Murray, R. J. 234-15
Murray-Lyon, I. 33-3
Murtagh, J. 90-9
Musacchio, A. 421-11
Musacchio de Zan, A. 17-3
Mustafa, M. 395-7

Steele, D. 339-12
Steele, T. D. 336-1
Steensberg, J. 35-18
Steentoft, A. 346-14
Steer, R. A. 430-11, 501-2
Steg, J. A. 89-8
Steger, K. A. 30-12
Stegmayr, B. G. 377-1
Stein, H. F. 426-11
Stein, M. D. 394-4
Steinberg, B. 464-10
Steinberg, J. R. 208-11
Steiner, D. 124-14
Steingrub, J. S. 232-1
Stenbacka, M. 388-9
Stene-Larsen, G. 45-1
Stephan, E. 78-16
Stephen, L. S. 250-6
Stephens, B. 152-6
Sterling, E. E. 325-9
Sternberg, K. 291-9, 291-10, 353-14,
   355-4, 355-5
Sternebring, B. 72-9
Stesin, N. 496-7
Stettler, A. 100-4
Stevens, C. W. 350-14, 351-3
Stevens, G. E. 467-1
Stevenson, H. 411-13
Stevenson, M. 447-7, 447-11
Stewart, D. O. 278-6
Stimson, G. 29-2, 373-11
Stimson, G. V. 20-3, 26-14, 373-8
Stockley, D. 401-13
Stockwell, T. 126-13, 153-15
Stoker, A. 310-6
Stoliarov, A. V. 190-12
Stolp, C. 490-13
Stone, A. J. 28-1
Stone, H. H. 62-11
Stone, K. 459-10
Stone, M. 269-5 , 274-2
Stone, M. H. 387-13
Stone, N. R. 294-8
Stonebridge, P. A. 22-11
Stoudenmire, J. 119-14
Strack, M. F. 126-9
Strang, J. 18-11, 224-5, 225-7, 263-3,
   438-16, 479-10
Strasser, A. L. 479-1
Strauss, A. 235-9
Street, J., Jr. 382-7
Streissguth, A. P. 142-9, 187-9
Stripp, A. M. 258-5
Stumm, E. 114-14
Stutman, R. M. 300-5
Su'a, F. 417-15
Subramanian, M. G. 130-5

Sudo, P. 148-2
Sufian, M. 22-9
Suit, P. F. 72-2
Sulelmanov, Z. M. 57-16
Sullivan, J. L. 98-12
Sullivan, M. E. 269-13
Sullivan. J. T. 163-7
Summerhill, D. 501-6
Sunder, M. T. 79-9
Surkova, L. A. 344-5
Surmak, V. V. 134-1
Suruda, A. J. 346-11
Sussman, S. 296-7
Sutterlin, E. 371-10
Sutton, L. R. 260-1
Suwaki, H. 267-10
Suzuki, K. 178-9
Suzuki, T. 308-5, 343-13, 344-7, 344-12,
   351-5, 351-6
Swadi, H. 193-1, 260-2, 507-2
Swartz, C. M. 438-11
Swayne, L. C. 388-8
Sweeney, D. F. 48-2
Swenson, J. R. 455-15
Swerdlow, B. N. 32-16
Swift, R. M. 34-8, 223-14
Swift, W. 428-5
Swirsky, H. 35-11
Swotinsky, R. 465-6
Sxhwartz, H. 205-3
Sy, W. W. 239-7
Szabo, P. 43-3, 499-15
Szabo, S. 397-1
Szeinbach, S. L. 202-5
Szuster, R. R. 113-8
Szykowny, R. 281-10
Tabaraud, F. 44-7
Tabeeva, D. M. 158-4
Taffaro, C. 435-14
Taggart, R. W. 471-8
Tagliaro, F. 463-10
Takase, S. 32-11
Talamini, R. 65-11
Talbot, K. 297-5
Talbott, W. R. 488-2
Talebzadeh, V. C. 232-14
Taliaferro, E. H. 297-6
Talley, C. R. 437-9
Talley, J. H 207-3
Talonu, N. T. 207-6
Tamkin, A. S. 52-2
Tampier, L. 137-10
Tampke, D. R. 167-2
Tamshen, A. S. 78-6
Tan, E. S. 93-8
Tanaka, T. 60-8
Tanaka, Y. 198-5

SUBJECT INDEX